STRATEGIC TRAINING AND DEVELOPMENT

I dedicate this book to my brother-in-law Rob Berkley, who showed me in his death how to live life fully and with integrity. His love and support gave me the confidence to bring this project to fruition.
—*Robyn A. Berkley*

This book is dedicated to Todd and Drew, who are my daily inspirations.
—*David M. Kaplan*

Sara Miller McCune founded SAGE Publishing in 1965 to support the dissemination of usable knowledge and educate a global community. SAGE publishes more than 1000 journals and over 600 new books each year, spanning a wide range of subject areas. Our growing selection of library products includes archives, data, case studies and video. SAGE remains majority owned by our founder and after her lifetime will become owned by a charitable trust that secures the company's continued independence.

Los Angeles | London | New Delhi | Singapore | Washington DC | Melbourne

STRATEGIC TRAINING AND DEVELOPMENT

Robyn A. Berkley
Southern Illinois University Edwardsville

David M. Kaplan
Saint Louis University

Los Angeles | London | New Delhi
Singapore | Washington DC | Melbourne

FOR INFORMATION:

SAGE Publications, Inc.
2455 Teller Road
Thousand Oaks, California 91320
E-mail: order@sagepub.com

SAGE Publications Ltd.
1 Oliver's Yard
55 City Road
London EC1Y 1SP
United Kingdom

SAGE Publications India Pvt. Ltd.
B 1/I 1 Mohan Cooperative Industrial Area
Mathura Road, New Delhi 110 044
India

SAGE Publications Asia-Pacific Pte. Ltd.
18 Cross Street #10-10/11/12
China Square Central
Singapore 048423

Acquisitions Editor: Maggie Stanley
Content Development Editor: Darcy Scelsi
Editorial Assistant: Janeane Calderon
Production Editor: Bennie Clark Allen
Copy Editor: Melinda Masson
Typesetter: C&M Digitals (P) Ltd.
Proofreader: Susan Schon
Indexer: Jean Casalegno
Cover Designer: Gail Buschman
Marketing Manager: Sarah Panella

Copyright © 2020 by SAGE Publications, Inc.

All rights reserved. Except as permitted by U.S. copyright law, no part of this work may be reproduced or distributed in any form or by any means, or stored in a database or retrieval system, without permission in writing from the publisher.

All third-party trademarks referenced or depicted herein are included solely for the purpose of illustration and are the property of their respective owners. Reference to these trademarks in no way indicates any relationship with, or endorsement by, the trademark owner.

Printed in the United States of America

Library of Congress Cataloging-in-Publication Data

Names: Berkley, Robyn A., author. | Kaplan, David M., author.

Title: Strategic training and development / Robyn Berkley, Southern Illinois University, David Kaplan, Saint Louis University.

Description: Thousand Oaks : SAGE Publications, [2019] | Includes bibliographical references and index.

Identifiers: LCCN 2019011052 | ISBN 9781506344393 (paperback)

Subjects: LCSH: Strategic planning. | Conflict management. | Professional ethics. | Organizational change.

Classification: LCC HD30.28 .B45499 2019 | DDC 658.3/124—dc23
LC record available at https://lccn.loc.gov/2019011052

This book is printed on acid-free paper.

19 20 21 22 23 10 9 8 7 6 5 4 3 2 1

BRIEF CONTENTS

Preface	xv
Acknowledgments	xx
About the Authors	xxii
Introduction to Training and Development	1
CHAPTER 1 • Training and Development Strategy	16
CHAPTER 2 • Legal Issues in Training and Development	45
CHAPTER 3 • Needs Analysis	65
CHAPTER 4 • Learning Theories	93
CHAPTER 5 • Training Evaluation: Reaction and Learning	121
CHAPTER 6 • Training Evaluation: Transfer and Results	157
CHAPTER 7 • Learning Methods	183
CHAPTER 8 • Delivery Options for Face-to-Face Training	205
CHAPTER 9 • Technology-Mediated Training and Development	226
CHAPTER 10 • Careers and Succession	248
CHAPTER 11 • Employee Development	276
CHAPTER 12 • Practical Skills for Training and Development	313
CHAPTER 13 • Training for Differences: Understanding Culture and Diversity	333
Appendix A: Semester-Long Project	366
Appendix B: External Partnerships	370

Appendix C: Managing a Training Session	**380**
Glossary	**388**
Notes	**396**
Index	**418**

DETAILED CONTENTS

Preface	xv
Acknowledgments	xx
About the Authors	xxii
Introduction to Training and Development	**1**
Introduction	2
The Instructional Systems Design Model	3
Analyze	4
Design	4
Develop	5
Implement	5
Evaluate	5
ADDIE Model in Our Textbook	6
Training and Development Career Issues	8
Interest Profile for Trainers	9
Career Outlets for Training and Development	9
Professional Organizations and Certifications	10
Conclusion	13
Key Terms	14
End-of-Chapter Exercises	15
CHAPTER 1 • Training and Development Strategy	**16**
Learning Objectives	16
Internal Environment	18
Tasks	18
People	18
Social	19
Organization	19
Interdependence of the Internal Environment	20
HR Infrastructure	20
Company Strategy	24
Aligning Company and Training Strategies	24
Corporate Strategy Theories	26

External Environment	29
Economic Environment	29
Political-Legal Environment	30
Technological Environment	30
Sociocultural Environment	30
Ethics and Training Strategy	31
Global Issues in Training Strategy	32
Chapter Summary	33
Key Terms	34
End-of-Chapter Questions and Exercises	34

CHAPTER 2 • Legal Issues in Training and Development — 45

Learning Objectives	45
Jurisdiction and Ethics	47
What If a Law Does Not Apply?	48
Equal Employment Opportunity	49
Civil Rights Act	50
Americans With Disabilities Act (ADA)	56
Age Discrimination in Employment Act (ADEA)	58
Affirmative Action	58
Liability and the Provision of Training	59
Safety and Health	59
Affirmative Defense	60
Independent Contractors	61
Chapter Summary	61
Key Terms	62
End-of-Chapter Questions and Exercises	62

CHAPTER 3 • Needs Analysis — 65

Learning Objectives	65
Organization Level	67
Organizational Alignment	68
A Training SWOT	70
Job Level	72
Task-Based or Competency-Based	73
Methods	73
Sources	77
Person Level	79
Conducting a Person-Level Analysis	79
Motivation Theories	81
Results of a Needs Analysis	86
Learning Objectives	87
Why Not to Train	87

Chapter Summary	89
Key Terms	90
End-of-Chapter Questions and Exercises	90

CHAPTER 4 • Learning Theories — 93

Learning Objectives	93
Bloom's Taxonomy: What People Learn	96
Learning Theories	97
Behaviorism	98
Cognitivism	102
Constructivism	103
Humanism	106
Pedagogy, Andragogy, and Heutagogy	107
Pedagogy Versus Andragogy	107
Heutagogy	109
Learning Styles	111
Are There Generational Differences in Learning?	113
Chapter Summary	115
Key Terms	115
End-of-Chapter Questions and Exercises	116

CHAPTER 5 • Training Evaluation: Reaction and Learning — 121

Learning Objectives	121
Training Strategy for Evaluation	123
How Training Strategy Informs Training Evaluation	123
Learning Evaluation Strategy	124
Developing Learning Objectives	125
Planning Objectives	126
Writing Objectives	126
Quantifying Objectives	128
Training Design for Evaluation	129
Nonexperimental Designs	130
Experimental Designs	132
Training Design for Evaluation Summary	133
Reliability and Validity of Training Measures	134
Kirkpatrick's Model for Training Effectiveness	135
Training Evaluation Administration	137
Level 1: Reaction	140
Level 2: Learning	143
Chapter Summary	145
Key Terms	146
End-of-Chapter Questions and Exercises	147

CHAPTER 6 • Training Evaluation: Transfer and Results — 157

- Learning Objectives — 157
- Transferring Learning to Behavior — 159
  - Strategic Focus — 159
  - The Right Kind of Leadership — 160
  - The Ability to Plan For and Manage Change Effectively — 160
  - An Effective Measurement System — 161
  - Success at Levels 1 and 2 — 161
- Kirkpatrick's Model for Training Effectiveness — 162
  - Level 3: Behavior — 162
  - Level 4: Results — 166
- Transfer of Training — 169
  - Near Versus Far Transfer — 170
  - Factors Affecting Transfer — 171
- Training Evaluation Analysis — 175
- Training Budgets — 176
- Chapter Summary — 177
- Key Terms — 178
- End-of-Chapter Questions and Exercises — 178

CHAPTER 7 • Learning Methods — 183

- Learning Objectives — 183
- Traditional Methods — 185
  - Lecture — 185
  - Discussion — 187
- Experiential Methods — 187
  - Debriefs — 187
  - Cases — 189
  - Role Plays — 189
  - In-Basket — 191
  - Games — 191
  - Simulations — 193
- Choosing a Method — 193
- Instructional Aids — 194
  - Overheads and Handouts — 196
  - Blackboards, Whiteboards, and Computers — 196
  - Flipcharts — 196
  - Video and Audio — 197
- Asking Questions — 198
  - Question to Confirm — 198
  - Question to Engage — 198
  - How to Ask Questions — 199

Chapter Summary ... 200
Key Terms ... 200
End-of-Chapter Questions and Exercises ... 201

CHAPTER 8 • Delivery Options for Face-to-Face Training ... 205

Learning Objectives ... 205
Instructional Settings ... 206
   On-Site ... 206
   Off-Site ... 207
   Unspecified ... 207
Factors Influencing Selection of Instructional Settings ... 207
   Control/Standardization ... 208
   Fidelity ... 208
   Costs ... 209
   Social Capital ... 210
   Reward Value ... 211
On-the-Job Training (OJT) ... 212
   Trainer Selection ... 213
   Trainer Support ... 214
   Training Design ... 216
   Training Evaluation ... 217
Workshops, Speakers/Courses, Conferences, and Corporate Universities ... 218
   Features of Classrooms ... 218
   Features of Programs and Providers ... 221
   Corporate University ... 221
Chapter Summary ... 222
Key Terms ... 223
End-of-Chapter Questions and Exercises ... 223

CHAPTER 9 • Technology-Mediated Training and Development ... 226

Learning Objectives ... 226
Technology-Facilitated Learning ... 228
Communicating Virtually ... 229
   Concerns With Virtual Communication ... 229
   Opportunities With Virtual Communication ... 230
Human Resource Information Systems (HRIS) ... 230
   Needs Analysis ... 231
   Succession Planning ... 231
   Training and Development Delivery ... 231
   Training Evaluation ... 234

Online Instruction	**235**
Characteristics of Online Instruction	235
Mobile Instruction	240
Gamification	241
Massive Online Open Courses (MOOCs)	243
e-Mentoring and e-Coaching	244
Chapter Summary	**245**
Key Terms	**245**
End-of-Chapter Questions and Exercises	**246**

CHAPTER 10 • Careers and Succession — **248**

Learning Objectives	**248**
Career Theories	**250**
Career Stages	**252**
Exploration	252
Establishment	253
Maintenance	254
Obsolescence	254
Plateaus	255
Career End or Transition	255
Career Paths	**256**
Mobility Patterns	256
Predictability and Managing Careers	258
Traditional, Protean, and Boundaryless Careers	**258**
Traditional	259
Boundaryless	260
Protean	260
Career Anchors	**261**
Succession Planning	**262**
Approaches to Succession Planning	263
Methods and Tools to Conduct Succession Planning	264
New Careers and Succession Planning	270
Chapter Summary	**271**
Key Terms	**272**
End-of-Chapter Questions and Exercises	**272**

CHAPTER 11 • Employee Development — **276**

Learning Objectives	**276**
Strategic Importance of Development	**278**
Learning Agility	**281**
Employee Development	**281**
Assignments and Enrichment Opportunities	282
Job Design	284

Job Transitions	286
Mentoring and Coaching	287
Leadership Development	306
Chapter Summary	308
Key Terms	309
End-of-Chapter Questions and Exercises	310

CHAPTER 12 • Practical Skills for Training and Development — 313

Learning Objectives	313
Communication Style	315
Nonverbal Communication	317
Improvisational Communication	319
Listening	320
Passive Listening	321
Attentive Listening	321
Active Listening	322
Feedback	323
Conflict Resolution	325
Less Effective Conflict Resolution Styles	326
More Effective Conflict Resolution Styles	327
Self-Awareness	327
Emotional Intelligence	328
Chapter Summary	329
Key Terms	330
End-of-Chapter Questions and Exercises	330

CHAPTER 13 • Training for Differences: Understanding Culture and Diversity — 333

Learning Objectives	333
How People, Organizations, and the Global Context Differ	335
Macro-Level Differences: National Culture and Global Competency	336
National Culture	336
Training Employees for International Assignments	337
Organization-Level Differences: Company Culture	338
Artifacts	339
Espoused Values	339
Basic Underlying Assumptions	339
Onboarding to Train for Organizational Culture	340
Recruitment	341
Orientation	342
General Program Attributes	345

Micro-Level Differences: Individual Differences and Diversity Training	348
Types of Diversity	348
Applying Practical T&D Skills to Diversity Training	355
Ethics and Training Diverse Others	356
Chapter Summary	356
Key Terms	357
End-of-Chapter Questions and Exercises	358

Appendix A: Semester-Long Project	366
Appendix B: External Partnerships	370
Appendix C: Managing a Training Session	380
Glossary	388
Notes	396
Index	418

PREFACE

Welcome to *Strategic Training and Development*. We have written this textbook because we believe that employees represent the most valuable resource that organizations possess. But to fully actualize their potential, organizations need to do more than simply reward them or engage in sophisticated selection techniques. Training and development represent complementary functions for advancing both individual and organizational goals.

This textbook is designed for both advanced undergraduates and graduate students who are interested in learning how to successfully design and implement training and development initiatives. The textbook takes a holistic approach that covers all aspects of training and development while balancing accessibility and practicality. Further, the experiential components of the textbook facilitate those completing courses using this textbook to hit the ground running as training and development professionals after they finish the class.

The accessible and practical design of the textbook also makes it approachable and valuable to corporate trainers and those engaged in continuing professional education. In addition to the professional focus of the textbook, the information it contains is valuable on a more personal level. Specifically, everyone will have a career, and this textbook provides insights for how people can be more personally successful, even as they are learning how to unlock the potential of others.

The inclusion of *strategic* in our title is purposeful because we believe strongly that training and development are most effective when they are part of an overall corporate strategy. Multiple components of this textbook reinforce this point. First, we have developed an organizing framework, shown below, which provides an overview of how all the important elements that impact training and development should be organized to maximize effectiveness. This framework begins with those factors that drive the provision of training and development and ends with evaluation, which both documents the benefits of training and development and facilitates improvement. Second, we include a semester-long project (Appendix A), which allows students to experience all aspects of training and development. Third, the importance of strategy is addressed across multiple chapters.

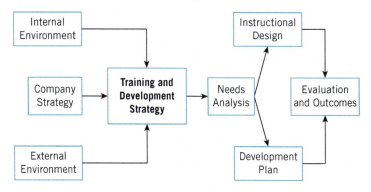

OUR VISION

Our textbook focuses on individual concerns while also recognizing the important role of partnerships in the training and development process. Trainers, as an extension of human resource departments, need to be strategic partners so their initiatives will be successful. Conceptualizing training and development as a partnership also emphasizes the responsibilities that trainers, coaches, and mentors have in the process of individual learning and growth. Further, the text discusses external resources and opportunities available to an organization (e.g., the government) for providing training and development.

Our emphasis on individual concerns manifests itself in multiple ways in the design of the textbook. First, this textbook goes into depth on the individual differences (e.g., learning styles and motivations) that impact learning and the transfer of training. Second, the textbook focuses on interpersonal skills (e.g., feedback) that are critical at the individual level for training to be effective. Third, the textbook places emphasis on the development of employees, which, by its nature, tends to be customized to the individual. Fourth, the textbook includes reflections and lessons for the students/readers to implement as they manage their own careers. Finally, the textbook focuses on training topics such as the delivery of diversity and cross-cultural training, which requires employees to focus on individuals.

WHAT MAKES OUR BOOK UNIQUE

- Focus on organizational strategy and how it should interconnect with training and development, as well as how both strategy and training and development interact with other human resource functions.
- Emphasis on practical skills; moving from theory to implementation. The book includes ample opportunities to practice skills through classroom and homework assignments.
- Information on how to leverage external resources and partnerships.
- Recognition of how technology impacts and creates opportunities for training and development.
- Greater attention to development-related activities and research including career theories and succession planning.
- Extensive discussion of diversity and inclusion, as well as the ethical implications, as key aspects of training and development.

FEATURES

In each chapter, we include the following features to help students reflect upon and become confident in their ability to provide training and development:

- The visual of our strategic framework and where the chapter maps onto it.
- Opening vignettes to get students interested in the material that is covered in the chapter.
- Learning Objectives, Chapter Summaries, and Key Terms to reinforce important points and facilitate student comprehension.
- Ethical scenarios so that students understand the complexity and dynamics of providing training and development.
- Experiential exercises to give students an opportunity to practice what they are learning, including a semester-long project.

CONTENT

Our textbook is divided into 13 chapters, plus an introduction and three appendices:

"Introduction to Training and Development" provides an overview of training and development as both an organizational function and an individual career path. Discussion of the ADDIE instructional design model as it maps to our textbook is also highlighted.

Chapter 1, "Training and Development Strategy," opens up the textbook to reinforce its strategic focus. This chapter defines strategy while also explaining how training and development fits into it along with other human resource functions.

Chapter 2, "Legal Issues in Training and Development," reviews the major pieces of legislation that impact the delivery of training and development. This includes laws focused on providing equal employment opportunities to all employees, as well as those pieces of legislation that mandate or encourage the provision of training.

Chapter 3, "Needs Analysis," focuses on three levels of analysis that organizations need to consider in order to effectively provide employees with training and development. These include the organization level, job level, and person level.

Chapter 4, "Learning Theories," examines the research on how people learn, and how this knowledge can be utilized to make training and development more effective. Among the scholarship that is discussed in this chapter is Bloom's Taxonomy, as well as an important focus on adult learning theories and how they apply to training and development.

Chapter 5, "Training Evaluation: Reaction and Learning," emphasizes the importance of evaluation by focusing on Kirkpatrick's first two levels. The topic of backwards design is introduced to reinforce the importance of determining what needs to be evaluated before the training program is designed and implemented. This is followed with a focus on developing learning objectives that are linked to the training. Lastly, the New World Kirkpatrick Model is introduced, and the first two levels of the model, Reaction and Learning, are addressed in depth.

Chapter 6, "Training Evaluation: Transfer and Results," continues the discussion on training evaluation by addressing Kirkpatrick's remaining two levels, on-the-job behavior through knowledge transfer and organization-level results. This chapter focuses on the tight relationship between company strategy and training and development activities and addresses the importance of assessing key metrics to determine positive training outcomes.

Chapter 7, "Learning Methods," provides options for how training and development can be delivered as well as advice for which option may be best given goals and the situation. These options are divided into those that are traditional (e.g., lecture) and those that are experiential (e.g., role plays).

Chapter 8, "Delivery Options for Face-to-Face Training," covers the various instructional settings that are available for providing training and development. Among these is on-the-job training. The chapter contrasts both formal and informal varieties of training activities.

Chapter 9, "Technology-Mediated Training and Development," offers insights into the way that technology impacts training and development. This includes what are now traditional ways of providing e-learning, as well as how it continues to evolve (e.g., use of mobile devices). Further, it addresses important issues concerning accessibility of training and development.

Chapter 10, "Careers and Succession," explains that while we all have careers, the nature of those careers can be very individualistic. This chapter looks at both how careers evolve over time and how individuals perceive and manage their careers. As well, this chapter focuses on succession planning as an extension of career theories, and discusses how to identify and support high-potential employees.

Chapter 11, "Employee Development," focuses on the vast array of activities an organization can use to develop employees beyond basic training needs. This includes both formal and informal programs, including mentoring and coaching. A more in-depth look at mentoring and coaching activities is addressed. Along with general development activities, the chapter addresses specific leadership development activities to develop the next generation of leaders.

Chapter 12, "Practical Skills for Training and Development," presents interpersonal skills that make trainers and developers more effective when they are proficient at them. The skills covered in this chapter include active listening and providing feedback. The chapter provides opportunities for personal growth in addition to learning about these interpersonal skills.

Chapter 13, "Training for Differences: Understanding Culture and Diversity," discusses how to make organizations more inclusive and individuals more culturally competent. Differences ranging from macro (national culture and organizational culture) to micro (individual) levels of diversity are addressed along with the training programs utilized to train for those differences. Specific attention is given to orientation programs to integrate employees into the company culture, and diversity training initiatives.

Appendix A, "Semester-Long Project," is an opportunity for individuals to put into practice all that they have been learning about in the textbook. The project coincides with the ADDIE model for instructional design and provides a guideline for students to conceptualize, design, and implement their own training program for class.

Appendix B, "External Partnerships," shares information about how external agencies can facilitate the provision of training and development. Attention is given to government agencies, community colleges, and labor unions, and the specific programs and policies they use to support training initiatives.

Appendix C, "Managing a Training Session," provides more practical and granular detail on how to design and implement training and development. Guidelines on how to lead a training session and develop materials are provided.

ONLINE RESOURCES

Log on to: **study.sagepub.com/berkley**

The Instructor Teaching Site is intended to enhance your use of *Strategic Training and Development* by Robyn A. Berkley and David M. Kaplan. The materials on the site are geared toward increasing your effectiveness with this material and maximizing the potential for your students to learn.

- **Microsoft® Word test bank:** This test bank offers a diverse set of test questions and answers for each chapter of the book. Multiple-choice, matching, and short-answer questions for every chapter help instructors assess students' progress and understanding.
- **Microsoft® PowerPoint® slides:** Chapter-specific slide presentations offer assistance with lecture and review preparation by highlighting essential content, features, and artwork from the book.
- **Instructor's manual:** The instructor's manual contains numerous resources for each chapter, including learning objectives, key concepts, suggested teaching strategies, resources, suggested exercises or projects, and answers to end-of-chapter questions/activities. These resources are collated in the instructor's manual files.
- **Multimedia resources:** Videos, articles, and helpful links reinforce and further engage learners.
- **Tables and figures from the book.**

ACKNOWLEDGMENTS

Writing this textbook has been a dream project, and we are grateful to many people for helping us bring this to fruition. We would like to start with thanking our publisher, SAGE. Behind that name is a great team of collaborators. First and foremost, we acknowledge our acquisitions editor, Maggie Stanley, who has patiently helped us through this whole process. Some of the other team members we can thank by name include Bennie Clark Allen, Kerstin Christiansen, Melinda Masson, and Janeane Calderon, but we know there are many others as well.

Along with the SAGE team, we have been fortunate to have a wide network of people who contributed to this textbook. Rob Berkley, Debbie Phillips, Maryann Morgan, Don Sosnowski, and Tammy Carl all graciously offered their time and expertise to share their experiences in training and development with students and future learning professionals. As well, other scholars such as Jack Phillips and Talya Bauer generously shared their materials with us to enhance student learning. We thank them all for their contributions to this textbook.

Roxanne Beard, Jenni Hunt, and Heather McPherson offered their support to provide the ancillary materials for the text, giving their extensive expertise to create the instructor's manual, PowerPoints, and test bank. Heather has piloted using the textbook over several semesters and has provided invaluable feedback allowing us to improve the delivery of materials to the students. Loree Moore provided editorial support early on, helping to fine-tune the voice and focus of the textbook. In addition, we would like to thank Suzanne DeJanasz, Beverly DeMarr, Jerome Katz, and Jeff Mello, who were generous in their advice about writing a textbook.

Lastly, along with all the professional support, we thank our close friends, families, and mentors for the support given to us as we invested our time and energy into writing. Without their love and support, we never would have been able to complete this book.

SAGE would like to thank the following reviewers:

Darlene M. Andert, *Florida Gulf Coast University*

Evelina Atanassova, *Brandman University*

Dennis P. Bozeman, *University of Houston*

C. Darren Brooks, *Florida State University*

William S. Brown, *Marist College*

Joseph Bucci, *Chestnut Hill College*

Renée Cedarberg, *Metropolitan State University*

Christine R. Day, *Eastern Michigan University*

Edward R. Del Gaizo, *Stony Brook University*

Lisa M. Finkelstein, *Northern Illinois University*

C. Allen Gorman, *East Tennessee State University*

Glenda J. Graham-Walton, *South Seattle College*

Gaynell Green, *Texas A&M University, Texarkana*

Judy A. Grotrian, *Peru State College*

Sheri Grotrian-Ryan, *Peru State College*

Eveline R. Higgs, *McKendree University*

Ghadir Ishqaidef, *California State University, Chico*

Uma J. Iyer, *Austin Peay State University*

Millicent J. Kelly, *Barry University*

William R. Kennan, *Radford University*

Michael J. Kirchner, *Purdue University Fort Wayne*

Ashley Prisant Lesko, *Sullivan University*

Shelly Marasi, *Tennessee Tech University*

Jalane Meloun, *Barry University*

Jessica Mesmer-Magnus, *University of North Carolina Wilmington*

Machuma Helen Muyia, *Texas A&M University, College Station*

Vias C. Nicolaides, *George Mason University*

John M. Poirier, *Bryant University*

Kyle C. Ryan, *Peru State College*

Gordon B. Schmidt, *Purdue University Fort Wayne*

J. Adam Shoemaker, *Saint Leo University*

Ali Soylu, *Cameron University*

Edward Ward, *Saint Cloud State University*

Mark Whitmore, *Kent State University*

Otis Williams, *Cincinnati State Technical and Community College*

Thomas A. Zeni, *West Virginia University*

ABOUT THE AUTHORS

Robyn A. Berkley is an associate professor of Management at Southern Illinois University Edwardsville (SIUE). She has been at SIUE since 2006. Before that, she worked at Rensselaer Polytechnic Institute and Pace University. Robyn received her PhD in business from the University of Wisconsin–Madison (2001) where she focused on human resource management, with minors in organization theory and sociology. She received her MBA at Pace University (1993) and her BS in biology from Marquette University (1986). Robyn's area of research focuses on diversity-related topics. More specifically, she has researched in the areas of sexual harassment, concealable stigmas, and business ethics. She has published in *Human Resource Management Review*, *MIS Quarterly Executive*, *Human Resource Management*, *Employee Responsibilities and Rights Journal*, *Journal of Business Ethics*, and the *National Women's Studies Association Journal*. She has been a member of the Academy of Management since 1993 and calls the Gender and Diversity in Organizations Division home. Along with the Academy of Management, she is a member of the Society for Human Resource Management and the Association for Talent Development, and has been certified as a Senior Professional in Human Resources (SPHR) by the Human Resource Certification Institute. At SIUE, Robyn teaches courses in human resource management at both the undergraduate and graduate levels, decision making for graduate students, and ethics at both the undergraduate and graduate levels.

David M. Kaplan is a professor and chair of the Management Department at Saint Louis University. He has developed and taught a variety of undergraduate and graduate courses including Training and Development, Coaching and Mentoring, Talent Management, and Management of Human Resources. His major fields of research are careers and diversity. His research has been published in many respected journals including *Human Resource Management Review*, *Human Relations*, *Journal of Management Education*, and *Career Development International*. He is a member of the Academy of Management, the Management and Organizational Behavior Teaching Society, and the Society for Human Resource Management.

INTRODUCTION TO TRAINING AND DEVELOPMENT

The Association for Talent Development (ATD) is the premier professional organization for talent development, or training and development, practitioners. Whether you perform training and development activities every day, or occasionally support your organization by training peers or subordinates, ATD provides resources to ensure training and development activities are delivered well with a positive impact on the organization's bottom line.

The mission of ATD is to *Empower Professionals to Develop Talent in the Workplace*.[1] ATD believes those leading training and development initiatives in organizations should possess the following skills to ensure success[2]:

- Identify customer expectations.
- Select appropriate strategies, research design, and measures.
- Communicate and gain support for the evaluation plan.
- Manage data collections.
- Analyze and interpret data.
- Apply learning analytics.
- Make recommendations to aid decision making.

Talent development specialists need a mix of skills, but of most importance are business acumen, comfort with data and metrics, and the creativity to conceptualize, design, and deliver effective training and development programs. Our textbook reinforces the important lessons from ATD to ensure students of training and development are well prepared to take on those responsibilities in the workplace.

INTRODUCTION

While organizations use a variety of resources to accomplish their objectives, the most important resource an organization should invest in is its employees. Without the work of employees, a competitive advantage can be neither achieved nor sustained. It is easy to conclude that focusing on the needs of employees is essential for employees to perform at their best and ensure the organization is successful. As you will see throughout this textbook, an employee-centric approach to doing business is instrumental for organizational success, and training and development is an important part of that approach.

Because employees are fundamental to organizational success, they need to possess relevant knowledge, skills, and abilities (KSAs) to be able to compete in the 21st century job market. While the educational system can provide many of those KSAs for employees, the responsibility doesn't rest entirely in secondary and postsecondary education. Employers should ensure their employees have the KSAs needed to do their job today and into the future. As well, employees should take the initiative to ensure that they have the tools they need for the career they desire. Thus, a multipronged approach is required to guarantee that both the organization and its employees have what they need to develop and maintain their competitive advantage.

While many tools are available to employers to manage the KSAs of their employees, the most important tools are **training** and **development.** The **training and development function** is a human resource (HR) management function concerned with developing and improving the performance of individuals and groups in an organizational setting.[3] This function should be utilized to ensure that the performance of employees reflects an effective and efficient use of organizational resources, in direct alignment with the organizational strategy. According to the Association for Talent Development (ATD), the professional association for training and development specialists, training is a process that aims to improve knowledge, skills, attitudes, and/or behaviors in a person to accomplish a specific job, task, or goal.[4] Within an organizational context, this means that employers must take the time to first determine which KSAs are required for employees through job analysis. It is then incumbent upon the employer to invest the time and money to ensure employees have the capabilities to do their job, moving the organization forward.

Alternatively, development focuses upon the activities to which both parties, the employer and employee, may contribute in the future.[5] ATD defines development as learning or other types of activities that prepare a person for additional job responsibilities now and in the future and/or enable him or her to gain knowledge or skills.[6] It is about ensuring employees have the KSAs in advance of future needs, while maintaining alignment with strategic objectives. Development must consider the career paths of the employees, as well as the future direction of the organization. Thus, a training and development strategy ensures the employee is prepared for the organization's short-term and long-term strategic plans. Exhibit I-1 illustrates the difference between training and development based on the focus, emphasis, and goal of the program. Training is primarily focused on the current job an employee performs. When needs analysis identifies a skill gap between what the organization needs the employee to do now and

Exhibit I-1 Difference Between Training and Development

Training	Criteria	Development
Job	**Focus**	Career
Meets Organizational Needs	**Emphasis**	Meets Individual Needs
Current Gaps	**Goal**	Future Capacity

what skills the employee currently has, a training program is developed to support that employee and ensure the organization's objectives are being met. Alternatively, development focuses more on the career trajectory of the employee, not just the job he or she is doing today. The goal of development is to ensure the employee's career needs are being addressed. The future talent capacity of the organization is being enhanced by providing employees with the tools and KSAs they need to successfully navigate a career with the organization.

Training and development work together in a complementary fashion. In both circumstances, the organization, the employee, and the trainer must be clear about what KSAs are needed, as well as the best way for the employee to obtain them, and ensure the information learned is applied effectively on the job. The KSAs acquired today not only help the organization in the present, but also prepare the employees for the organization's future needs and goals. Training and development also require the employees to be willing to learn what is needed for them to be successful now and in the future. In the same manner, the organization is required to facilitate that learning during all stages of the employees' careers, embedding it in the company culture. To do so will lead to training and development becoming an integral piece of the organizational culture.

THE INSTRUCTIONAL SYSTEMS DESIGN MODEL

The **instructional systems design model**—or, as it is popularly known, the **ADDIE** model—guides those involved in training and instruction through the steps needed to effectively design and implement learning opportunities.[7] Initially designed to meet instructional program needs for military in-service training, the ADDIE model has become an important standard by which all training and instructional interventions should abide to develop training or development programs. The acronym ADDIE stands for analyze, design, develop, implement, and evaluate. Originally conceptualized as a linear process, with early phases completed before subsequent phases can be addressed, the model has evolved to be more dynamic and interactive and thus does not necessarily proceed in a linear fashion.[8] Because of this, our book does not proceed with discussing ADDIE in a linear manner, consistent with the dynamic nature of instructional design. We address larger training and development issues and how they map to the ADDIE model.

Analyze

In the analysis phase, the trainer is engaged in gathering data to provide the foundation for the training development, design, and implementation. Concerns may occur at all levels in the organization. At the organization level, there may be problems such as high turnover or low productivity. At the job level, a lot of conflict may be found among team members working on particular tasks regarding what should be done and why. At the person level, a new employee may be experiencing difficulties adjusting to the organizational culture and level of performance expected. Whatever the problem, it is red-flagged, leading the organization to investigate why the issue is occurring and find a solution to the problem. The investigation is handed off to the HR function to determine the source of the problem and recommend how to best address it. If it is determined the problem can be solved with a training intervention, the analysis gets handed off to the training function.

The goal of the analysis phase is to investigate the problem in more depth by analyzing all aspects that could potentially be the cause. We first consider the people in the organization. We need to know the skills and motivation of our employees and how those issues might impact employee performance. Understanding the people who are experiencing the problem is important for getting their perspective on what is or is not working in the organization. Along with looking at the people side of things, we need to look at the way the tasks are set up, and how the jobs and workflow are designed, to see if that is the source of the problem. We may also have to look at the HR systems in place to see if these are the source of the problem. Overall, the purpose of analysis is to gather everything we need to understand the problem, why it is occurring, and how the training intervention will potentially provide a solution.

Design

In the design phase, the information gathered during the analysis phase drives the instructional objectives, serving as the blueprint for the content and design of the training. The analysis results determine what needs to be addressed in the training session. Content must be identified first. What do the trainees need to know? What are the important outcomes from the training, and what metrics will be used to assess training success? After the content is determined, the means by which the material will be delivered and the location of the training are established. Training content can take many forms—computer-based, lecture, video, or textbook, to name a few. As well, training can occur on-site at the company, off-site at a vendor location, or on the internet so the trainees can complete the training at their convenience at home.

Along with designing the content and means of delivery, the training budget should be established before final approval is given for the training intervention. This should include both direct and indirect costs. Direct costs may include the cost of using an external vendor or the money paid to an in-house trainer, the time and effort involved to develop the material, and the costs for implementation, including food, materials, and room rental. Indirect costs may include lost time; while participating in the training intervention, for example, trainees and their managers involved will not be on the job but still get paid. The design and the full budget must be approved before the materials can be developed and tested.

Develop

During the development phase, the blueprints created in the design phase come to life. Lecture notes, instructional plans and guidelines, training manuals, and videos, for example, are written or recorded in preparation for the implementation. All developed materials should be tested to ensure the training flow proceeds as planned, and that the materials are error-free and communicate what was intended during the design phase.

An important consideration during the development phase is to anticipate any potential problems that could interfere with effective training delivery. If you are using technology as a part of your instructional materials, it should be tested to ensure it runs smoothly. Even if everything looks great and tested well, the best-laid plans can fail due to circumstances beyond the trainer's control. This could include a loss of electricity or internet access, misplaced materials, or materials that were sent but never received due to an interruption in mail or package delivery services. Backup plans should be developed to address any potential problems. Lastly, practice makes perfect. Training delivery should be rehearsed so the trainer can identify potential problems before the session begins.

Implement

Now the training is ready to begin. The analysis has been done, the problems have been identified, and the materials have been conceptualized and developed. Training and development programs can take as little as an hour if you are training people on a new software program for data input, or as long as weeks, months, or even years, for example, if you have a coaching or mentoring program for leadership development. During the session, consideration is made to ensure the experience was positive and the trainer was effective. As well, the trainer sets the stage for how the material learned will be assessed to ensure the training itself was effective.

Lastly, guidelines for how to practice the material learned and transfer it to the job should be addressed so the trainee, group, and/or organization will benefit from the training provided. Preparing trainees, as well as their supervisors and coworkers, for how to best integrate and practice the things learned in their training on the job is essential for ensuring training success. Implementation is therefore not just about delivering the training, but also about helping the trainee use the material learned on the job long after the training is completed.

Evaluate

Although evaluation is considered the last phase of the ADDIE model, evaluation should actually be considered, and/or addressed, at all phases of the training system model. During analysis, we have to consider whether or not the data collected were accurate. As well, from those data, we develop our instructional objectives and training blueprint against which our training success will be assessed. During design and development, we have to account for how to best deliver our training to facilitate training evaluation that is reliable and valid. Lastly, we have to conduct parts of the training evaluation during the implementation phase to determine if the session and the trainer were effective, and if the trainee actually learned what he or she was supposed to learn. During the design, development, and implementation phases, attention is paid to formative evaluation (i.e., how to improve training) to ensure the materials being developed and delivered are in alignment with the instructional goals and objectives.

Upon completion of the training or development session, trainers have to facilitate and assess if the information learned is properly transferred to the job and calculate the impact the training had on important organizational outcomes as defined in the instructional objectives. After the training has been delivered, attention is now paid to summative evaluation (e.g., what was learned) to assess if what was ultimately delivered to the trainees accomplished what it was designed to accomplish. Overall, evaluation is a consideration right from the beginning, and what you will evaluate, and how, is addressed at every step of the ADDIE model to ensure training success.

ADDIE Model in Our Textbook

The purpose of our textbook is to step away from traditional thinking about how to teach training and development, to focus more on the essential skills and activities needed to ensure training professionals can hit the ground running in their new job. We consider the strategic context of the organization in our organizing framework and the way we present our content across the chapters. Because current thinking about instructional design is not necessarily linear, we took a step back from designing the textbook around a linear model and focused on a more holistic approach to the material, more akin to how training and development professionals will need to think about the topics and issues. Even though we don't use the ADDIE model as the guide for chapter progression, the importance of the ADDIE model is embedded across each of the chapters.

Training and development strategy is defined as the plan by which an organization ensures its employees have the knowledge, skills, and abilities to meet the organization's objectives. In meeting the organization's objectives, training strategy has to consider (1) the internal organizational environment, including the HR infrastructure and how it can support training and development; (2) the company strategy; and (3) the external environment. Once the plan is in place for how the company will use training and development as part of its larger strategy, the organization will conduct a needs analysis to identify gaps, after which a specific training or development plan will be developed. Ultimately, as Exhibit I-2 demonstrates, the training strategy must be in alignment with the corporate strategy, integrated within the larger HR infrastructure and internal organizational dimensions, and developed into a solid plan that spans from training and development needs assessment to evaluation of outcomes to ensure the plan is a success.

Throughout the textbook, we'll use the Training and Development Strategy Framework to guide the readers. At the beginning of each chapter, the framework will be highlighted in those areas where the chapter content applies. It is important to underscore

Exhibit I-2   Training and Development Strategy Framework

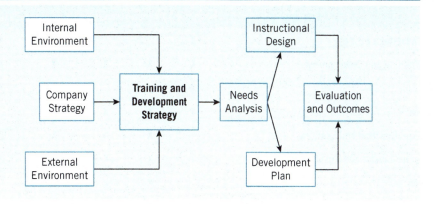

that training and development strategy must work in alignment with company strategy and both the internal and external organizational environment for maximum effectiveness. Chapter 1 goes into more depth on the factors that make up and influence the organization's training and development strategy.

Exhibit I-3 is an important guideline for how ADDIE informs the material in our textbook. This design was intentional because we want readers to recognize that training is not purely a linear process as the ADDIE model implies. By presenting the material in an integrated manner across chapters, it opens up the reader to consider training and development activities in a more interdependent way. For example, under "Analyze," we identify the chapters that have an impact on the analysis phase of ADDIE, covering training strategy, legal issues, needs analysis, learning and career theories, practical skills, and training for differences. The strategy chapter informs what is considered important to the organization, and the issues and concerns in the organization are assessed in reference to the training and company strategies. Analyzing or understanding the legal issues the organization is facing may require greater attention to equal-employment-opportunity-related issues when designing and implementing training.

In terms of the most important impact on each phase of the ADDIE model (represented by the shaded boxes in Exhibit I-3), Chapters 1 and 3 most closely map to how we analyze to determine training needs. Chapters 7, 8, 9, and 11 align with the design, development, and implementation phases as these chapters address the means by which we can design and deliver material to trainees and those engaged in development activities. Chapters 5 and 6 align most closely with the evaluation phase, as these chapters address the ways to ensure proper evaluation of training outcomes has occurred and helps ensure transfer of learning on the job. Overall, the purpose of Exhibit I-3 is to illustrate how content in each chapter directly impacts the ADDIE model. As well, the semester project found in Appendix A follows the ADDIE model format, but we encourage you to consider information in each of the chapters as noted in Exhibit I-3 as you work through the semester project.

Exhibit I-3 ADDIE Model Mapped to the Textbook Chapters

Chapter	Analyze	Design	Develop	Implement	Evaluate
1. Training and Development Strategy	X				X
2. Legal Issues in Training and Development	X	X	X	X	X
3. Needs Analysis	X				X
4. Learning Theories	X	X	X		
5. Training Evaluation: Reaction and Learning		X	X	X	X
6. Training Evaluation: Transfer and Results		X	X	X	X
7. Learning Methods		X	X	X	
8. Delivery Options for Face-to-Face Training		X	X	X	
9. Technology-Mediated Training and Development		X	X	X	
10. Career Theories	X	X	X		
11. Development and High-Potential Employees		X	X	X	
12. Practical Skills for Training and Development	X	X	X	X	
13. Training for Differences: Understanding Culture and Diversity	X	X	X	X	

Note: X indicates information in that chapter is important to the ADDIE phase indicated. Highlighted boxes indicate primary emphasis for that phase in the chapter.

TRAINING AND DEVELOPMENT CAREER ISSUES

Trainers can exist at all levels of an organization. Peers can train others in their department, supervisors and managers can train their subordinates, and HR professionals can lead and design training sessions. As such, it is important for employees at all levels of the organization to be aware of what is needed to be a successful trainer, and the HR department's job is to ensure the trainers have the knowledge, skills, and abilities to deliver a successful training.

If you are interested in a career in training, there are three things you should consider to be prepared. First, are you a good fit for a career in training and development? Second, do you know the different outlets in which you can pursue the training profession? Third, are you aware of the professional organization for trainers and the training certifications it offers? While training opportunities exist in many arenas, the following provide you with guidelines for how to navigate a career in training and development.

Interest Profile for Trainers

An important thing to consider when deciding whether to pursue a career in training and development is the extent to which the profession aligns with your personal interests and aptitudes—in other words, whether there is a good vocational fit. A common framework for determining vocational fit is Holland's **RIASEC** model.[9] There are six main vocational interests: realistic, investigative, artistic, social, enterprising, and conventional. If you take a RIASEC assessment, you will find out your three primary interests, and this will give you a three-letter code. Greater overlap between someone's personal code and the code for his or her profession is predicted to result in higher satisfaction.

To help illustrate this point, let's look at the RIASEC codes for a few different professions. The RIASEC code for training and development specialists is SAC. Therefore, training and development specialists who are social, artistic, and conventional should be the most satisfied. If you consider yourself more enterprising than artistic, then you may prefer a general role in an HR department, as the code for HR specialists is ECS. The commonality between these professions is that they are social and conventional. By comparison, most careers in the sciences are a combination of investigative and realistic and thus require a different set of skills and interests from that of HR professionals.

Career Outlets for Training and Development

Generally, people who are interested in training and development enter the field in one of two ways. First, trainers can work in an HR department as either generalists or specialists. As generalists, they will be responsible for all HR activities, but may be called upon specifically to develop and deliver training and development programs. The skills needed for a generalist are different from those of a specialist. For example, generalists may not have regular expertise in performing training and development activities, but may still need to conduct orientation programs, administer training sessions, or participate in mentoring and coaching for their subordinates or others in the organization. If their training expertise is limited, they may have to call upon external vendors (see below) to provide the training and development activities for the organization. In this situation, their goal is not to design the programs but to work in partnership with the external vendors to ensure the program is successful and meets the organization's strategic needs.

As specialists, people can enter the talent development or training and development areas of the HR function with this as their primary focus. In this case, HR trainers are responsible for conducting needs analysis; designing, developing, and delivering training sessions; and evaluating training outcomes for all training initiatives in the organization. While specialists may have to secure some training with external vendors, typically the bulk of the training and development efforts are done in-house. Regardless of whether the trainer is a generalist or specialist, good talent development ensures the other HR functional areas such as staffing and compensation are integrated with training and development activities. For example, internal applicants should be prepared for advancement opportunities within the organization and should be properly rewarded through "pay for performance" plans for their efforts on the job to develop more KSAs and competencies.

The second way trainers can be involved in training and development is through external organizations that offer training sessions to organizations. These can be consulting firms, universities, or community colleges that specialize in workforce development and executive education. Additional information on how to utilize external resources for training and development will be found in Chapter 8.

Those working in external sources can also be generalists or specialists. Generalists offer a wide array of training and development programs that can be customized for the organization's needs. Typically, organizations that don't have in-house training and development expertise will work with external sources to meet their needs. Alternatively, specialists narrow their offerings and typically focus on one area of expertise. Organizations may choose to use external subject matter experts to fulfill training and development needs if the cost-benefit analysis leans toward "buying" the training expertise they want versus developing the material in-house. Training companies like the Diversity Awareness Partnership (dapinclusive.org) specialize in diversity and inclusion training programs. Other training companies, like Safety Training Resources in Saint Charles, Missouri (www.safetytrainingresources.com), conduct safety training programs. Many governmental organizations also provide training support and attract subject matter experts to conduct training on their behalf. More information on leveraging governmental training resources can be found in Appendix B.

Even if individuals didn't start their career in talent development and HR, they may find themselves leading training initiatives and need to know the basics of how to conduct training and development. As subject matter experts, individuals who are good at their jobs may be asked to engage in training activities to share their KSAs with others. These individuals may be highly skilled employees, supervisors, or managers in the company. They work hand-in-hand with the training and development function to conduct training programs as needed.

There are educational opportunities available to those who want to pursue a career in training post–baccalaureate degree. If you are looking for a more in-depth degree program that covers training and development, there are several graduate programs you can consider. Individuals may choose to pursue a master's degree in HR development or workforce education and development. Typically, such degrees can be obtained through schools offering degrees in education. Alternatively, you could obtain a master's or PhD in industrial/organizational psychology, or a master's, MBA, or PhD in HR management through a school offering degrees in business. If you are not interested in another degree, you may consider a certificate program to provide you with the in-depth knowledge you need for training and development without the advanced degree requirements.

Professional Organizations and Certifications

Several professional organizations, at the global, national, and local levels, support training and development and other HR activities. Often, schools that offer degrees in HR have student chapters for some of the organizations listed below. As well, many local affiliates of national organizations are available in most metropolitan areas, even if they may be listed under different names from their parent organization. Lastly, local organizations not linked to any national group may still support your desire to connect with other HR and/or training and development specialists. It is always a good idea to start your search for local organizations on the national organization website to determine which local organizations are affiliated with your national membership and can provide you with the professional support you desire.

ATD.

The **Association for Talent Development (ATD)** is the premier organization for individuals who are actively engaged in the training and development function, either part-time or full-time. The ATD website (www.td.org) carries a wide variety of resources to assist in the design and implementation of training and development programs. ATD developed a competency-based model, covering 10 areas related to talent development: training delivery, instructional design, learning technologies, evaluating learning impact, managing learning programs, integrated talent management, coaching, knowledge management, change management, and performance improvement. These competencies are supported by foundational knowledge in the following areas: business skills, interpersonal skills, global mindset, personal skills, industry knowledge, and technical literacy. Exhibit I-4 highlights the ATD Competency Model.

ATD offers two certifications, the Associate Professional in Talent Development (APTD) and the Certified Professional in Learning and Performance (CPLP). The APTD is targeted to those who have between three and five years of talent development experience, either full-time or part-time. This certification is especially salient for those who may not have had formal training in talent development through a college degree program but find that they spend at least half their time engaging in training and development activities. The primary focus of the certification is on instructional design. The CPLP is targeted to those who have more than five years of talent development experience, with a more advanced understanding of instructional design, and talent management at a more strategic level.

SHRM.

The **Society for Human Resource Management (SHRM)** is the umbrella organization for HR professionals. While it doesn't have a certification specifically for trainers, the expectation is that, as you advance in your profession from entry-level to senior professional, you know how to design and implement training programs. SHRM offers two exams, the SHRM-CP and the SHRM-SCP. The SHRM-CP is for those in the early stages of their career, requiring anywhere from one to four years of experience, depending on the education and degree program. The SHRM-SCP is for those in a more advanced stage of their career, requiring a minimum of four to seven years of work experience, also depending on the education and degree program. Further information is available at the SHRM website (www.shrm.org).

Exhibit I-4   ATD Competency Model for Talent Development Professionals

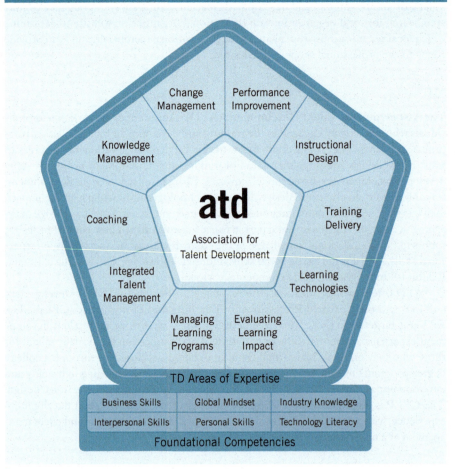

Source: Association for Talent Development (td.org).

HRCI.

The **Human Resource Certification Institute (HRCI)** is the oldest certification program for HR professionals (www.hrci.org). Similar to SHRM, it does not have a specific certification for training and development but offers different levels of certification for HR professionals across their career, with a varied emphasis on training and development depending on the individual's job title in HR. The aPHR is an assurance of learning certification for new college graduates or those who have worked in the HR field without a college degree. The PHR is similar to the SHRM-CP in terms of the years of work experience required, and the SPHR is for those in the advanced stages of their career, similar to the SHRM-SCP.

OD Network.

Related to talent development is the area of organizational development. The **OD Network** (www.odnetwork.org) is targeted to those engaged in consulting for change management. While organizational development involves change at the organizational level, training and development is change management primarily at the individual or group level. Regardless of the level of analysis, many of the practices used by trainers can be applied to OD consultants and vice versa. Often, training and development professionals are brought into the OD department of an organization to facilitate change at the individual and group levels. Although organizational development is not a focus of this textbook, we recognize the tremendous overlap between the two areas. To our knowledge, the OD Network does not provide any certifications, but it does provide resources and networking opportunities for those conducting change management activities in an organization.

ICF.

The **International Coaching Federation (ICF)** is dedicated to coaching professionals, providing both networking and certification opportunities (coachfederation.org). This organization has developed ethical standards for coaching and offers three different levels of credentials. The Associate Certified Coach is for those with a minimum of 100 hours of coaching experience and completion of an ICF Accredited Coach Training Program (ACTP). The Professional Certified Coach must have a minimum of 500 hours of coaching experience, plus ACTP training. Lastly, the Master Certified Coach must have 200 hours of coach-specific training, 10 hours of mentor coaching, and a minimum of 2,500 hours of coaching experience.

CONCLUSION

Training and development activities are an important part of the HR function that contributes to the strategic objectives of a company by ensuring the company's talent has the knowledge, skills, and abilities now and into the future. Training and development must be in alignment with the company's corporate strategy and must consider that in conjunction with the internal and external environment of the organization.

Instructional design should follow a systematic approach to ensure that training is done well and has an impact on relevant outcomes for the organization. Although we don't present our material in a way that directly follows the ADDIE model, the assumptions of ADDIE are embedded in each chapter. Good training and development interventions require systems thinking, not a simple linear perspective, and thus we addressed ADDIE elements in a more integrated way. All of the phases of the ADDIE model have to be considered at every step of the process. When doing analysis, we have to consider feedback from previous training sessions to ensure improvements are made. Design and development cannot be addressed until we understand the outcomes we want to achieve and how we want to evaluate training to ensure we accomplished our goals. Implementation needs to ensure that the issues identified in the needs analysis phase are being addressed when delivering the training. If you only consider ADDIE in a linear way, you'll miss the importance of integrating the ADDIE phases in designing your training and development programs.

There are many ways for individuals to participate in talent development. Whether they work directly for the organization as employees, supervisors, managers, or HR professionals, everyone in the organization may be asked to participate in training and development at some level. Connecting with professional organizations to help get the certifications needed to demonstrate mastery of training and development competencies is essential for career success. Joining professional organizations like SHRM, ATD, ICF, and the OD Network will help budding trainers achieve success.

KEY TERMS

ADDIE. An acronym that outlines the typical steps to instructional system design: analyze, design, develop, implement, and evaluate.

Association for Talent Development (ATD). The premier professional organization for those engaged in talent development, including training and development, activities in organizations. Offers certifications for talent development professionals.

Development. Learning or other types of activities that prepare a person for additional job responsibilities now and in the future and/or enable him or her to gain knowledge or skills.

Human Resource Certification Institute (HRCI). An organization that provides resources, instruction, and certification for HR professionals.

Instructional systems design model. A framework that guides those involved in training and instruction through the steps needed to effectively design and implement learning opportunities.

International Coaching Federation (ICF). An organization that provides resources, instruction, and certifications for coaching professionals.

OD Network. A professional organization for organizational development professionals. Provides resources and networking opportunities for those engaged in OD/change management activities.

RIASEC. A vocational interest model that breaks down the key factors that influence vocational interests and choices: realistic, investigative, artistic, social, enterprising, and conventional.

Society for Human Resource Management (SHRM). The umbrella professional organization for human resource professionals. Provides resources for all HR functions, including talent development. Offers certifications for HR professionals.

Training. A process that aims to improve knowledge, skills, attitudes, and/or behaviors in a person to accomplish a specific job, task, or goal.

Training and development function. A human resource management function concerned with developing and improving the performance of individuals and groups in an organizational setting.

Training and development strategy. The plan by which an organization ensures its employees have the knowledge, skills, and abilities to meet the organization's objectives.

END-OF-CHAPTER EXERCISES

Ethical Scenario

The Case of the Imperfect Match

Mary Jo, a college senior, is hoping to find a job before she graduates. She would like to be a training specialist for a large company but hasn't had any luck finding a position. Alice, her aunt, says that her company, Wholesome Foods, is hiring for a compensation specialist and encourages her to apply. Alice tells her that once she gets hired, she should be able to transfer to the Training Department. Mary Jo is excited until Alice tells her that as part of the hiring process, Wholesome Foods has applicants complete a vocational interest inventory to make sure that someone is right for the position. Mary Jo remembers taking one in her training class and found out she is an SAC, perfect for someone in training, but a bad match for a compensation specialist. Alice reminds her that the test is simple, and she can make herself look like a better fit for the compensation position if she is willing to change a couple of her answers. Mary Jo isn't sure what to do about the test, for now, but decides to apply for the compensation position anyway.

How good and/or ethical is the advice that Mary Jo got from her aunt?

What are the potential outcomes for Mary Jo if she takes the advice?

I.1 Skill Development: What Is My Vocational Interest Score?

In order to determine if a career in training and development is right for you, proceed to the My Next Move website (www.mynextmove.org/explore/ip). Take the interest inventory to determine your vocational fit.

Start the inventory by clicking on "Next" in the bottom right-hand corner of the center graphic titled O*NET Interest Profiler. Follow the prompts to receive your vocational interest score.

If training and development is not a perfect match, which careers does the website recommend as a good match for you? How can you enhance your preparation in college or graduate school to achieve a career that best meets your vocational interests?

CHAPTER ONE

TRAINING AND DEVELOPMENT STRATEGY

Learning Objectives

1. Describe the elements that contribute to training and development strategy.
2. Assess the external environment for training and development opportunities and challenges.
3. Critique internal environment elements for training and development needs and readiness.
4. Illustrate the interrelatedness of training and development activities with other human resource functions.
5. Appraise a company training and development strategy for strategy alignment and contextual relevance.
6. Recall the ethical code for training and development professionals.
7. Recognize the importance of economic conditions for global training and development activities.

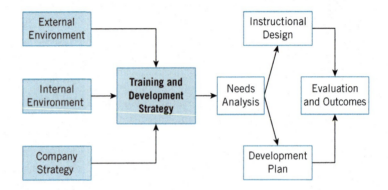

Organizations face increasingly volatile and complex markets. To compete, they need a business strategy that counteracts negative forces and guides individual lines of business toward positive outcomes. The strategy needs to present leaders with guidelines on how to make decisions and allocate resources to accomplish key objectives, as well as define the actions people in the business should take and the factors they need to prioritize to achieve desired goals.

The secret to successful strategy execution involves your employees. As such, a talent and learning strategy will ensure that an organization's workforce has the necessary skills to carry out the actions laid out in the business strategy. With that in mind, it's not hard to make the case that aligning an organization's learning strategy with its business objectives is a worthwhile exercise. However, less than half of companies actually align their learning strategies, according to the ATD Research Report *Aligning for Success*. One-third (33 percent) of leaders in the study say that their strategies are aligned to a high extent, and only 16 percent of companies are aligning learning and business strategies to a very high extent. The report also reveals, however, that organizations that do align learning and talent development with business strategy have better market performance compared with organizations with lower levels of alignment. Among respondents from high-performing organizations, 60 percent said their organization's learning and business goals are aligned to a high or very high extent, contrasted to 49 percent of all organizations in the study.

So, why isn't learning aligned in more organizations with corporate strategy? Research from Bersin by Deloitte done in 2015 finds that not all organizations have an overall talent strategy, which it defines as interlocking decisions related to talent that enable an organization to most effectively execute its business strategy. "The talent strategy should provide leaders with guidance as to the critical investments—as well as some of the tactical decisions—that should be made," explains Stacia Sherman Garr, vice president of talent and HR research for Bersin by Deloitte.

But developing a talent strategy remains a challenge for many organizations. In Bersin by Deloitte's survey of 454 organizations, just 12 percent of organizations have a clear talent strategy with advanced and integrated talent processes in place. The survey also reveals that of those organizations that rate themselves at the highest level of effectiveness on business outcomes, at least half have an established talent strategy with some or many advanced processes in place. "Organizations with a talent strategy are more than four times as likely to be in the top quartile of business outcomes. These business outcomes include innovation, improving processes to maximize business efficiency, and anticipating and responding to business changes efficiently and effectively," says Garr.

Why don't more organizations have a talent strategy? The answer may simply be that one isn't required or expected by top leaders. Talent development expert Edward E. Lawler argues that some business leaders believe their organizations can survive without top talent. No need for talent equates to no need for a talent strategy. Meanwhile, others may acknowledge that talent management is important, but not as important as other business functions such as finance or technology. "Many executives are unable to see the relationship between talent issues and the business strategy of their organization," explains Lawler in a 2016 *Forbes* article. Consequently, chief talent development officers must take it upon themselves to develop a talent and learning strategy and link it to the overall business strategy.

Source: Excerpted and adapted from Ryann Ellis, "All About Alignment," *CTDO Magazine*, Summer 2016. Available from https://www.td.org/magazines/ctdo/all-about-alignment.

The research results discussed in our opening vignette make an important point about the relationship between organizational strategy and organizational success, and the impact employees have on both of these issues. Employees need the tools to be successful and help the organization achieve its objectives. Training and development are essential tools that employees need to have a positive impact on organizational outcomes. To accomplish this, the organization's training and development (or learning) strategy must align with the corporate strategy.

As noted in the introductory chapter, the human resource (HR) department must ensure the company's training and development strategy is in alignment on three factors: the internal environment of the company, the external environment within which the organization functions, and the company strategy. All have to be considered when designing and implementing training and development activities. What follows in this chapter are more in-depth descriptions of each of the key inputs to a training and development strategy.

INTERNAL ENVIRONMENT

The **HR infrastructure** represents the horizontal integration the training and development strategy has across HR functional areas, and across key dimensions in the organization's internal environment. Training and development strategy does not exist in a vacuum, such that the plans made in training and development practices will have an interdependent impact on other aspects of the HR function and all aspects of the internal organizational environment. Training and development programs have to be embedded in a larger system so that HR policies are supported and reinforced across the whole organization. Each department, division, and functional area is so tightly interdependent that, like a Venn diagram, you cannot make a change in part of the organization or HR system without affecting everything to which it is connected. A systematic view of the internal environment indicates four important dimensions to consider: task, people, social, and organization environments.

Tasks

Organizations have to consider the tasks that employees do on a regular basis. These tasks encompass the activities that are essential to the company's business. The **task environment** requires us to understand what employees do, when they do it, and how often they repeat those tasks. This information provides the basis for job analysis and job descriptions. It also requires the organization to know the knowledge, skills, and abilities (KSAs) needed for employees to perform those tasks, which provides the organization with clarity on the job specifications needed for the employees to perform successfully. If an employee is not able to perform the required tasks of the job, this is the opportunity for training to help the employee obtain those skills.

People

The **people environment** includes the demographics of the workforce, including the KSAs, experiences, education levels, and motivations of the employees. The task and people environments of the internal organization directly inform training and development because organizations have to know what tasks are needed for the job, and whether or not employees are ready, willing, and able to perform those tasks. One way the organization understands the people environment is by tracking employee records, including education, certifications, and any competency or skill training employees have undertaken.

Another way to assess the people environment is through surveys to get feedback from employees on their perceptions of the organization and how it is functioning. PepsiCo, for example, regularly assesses employees for feedback on many things, including benefits, working conditions, compensation, career development, and diversity and inclusion initiatives.[1] This information helps PepsiCo understand the people environment and informs how the organization manages its employees strategically.

Social

The **social environment** considers the social systems within which the employees work. Specifically, it includes the ethical and organizational culture, as well as the leadership style and general company climate. When an organization brings in new employees, it must train them on the way people do work, and familiarize them with the key values and ethical considerations that are important to the organization.

The social environment is one of the hardest environments to identify and communicate to new employees. As we discuss in more depth in Chapter 13, while some aspects of culture are visible and easy to identify, such as company logos and important historical events, other aspects are more unconscious and difficult to put into words. Helping employees get up to speed with the company culture is an important part of onboarding and employee development. Orientation programs should include aspects of culture, but it is through mentoring programs, whereby new employees are matched with more experienced employees who can help new employees navigate the company culture, that many of the unconscious aspects of culture are transmitted.

Ethics is also an important aspect of company culture and values. Because of the liability to companies if employees behave unethically, communicating the company's key values is essential if the company wants to avoid a lawsuit. The ethical aspects of the social environment are typically communicated to employees through ethics training and modeling and mentor programs.

Employee development programs can also directly influence leadership style. The company identifies the type of leadership style it values, and develops management and leadership training to meet those needs. Internal coaching can help employees reach their full potential as leaders, and executive training programs, particularly for high-potential employees, will help the company prepare for future leadership needs. We discuss high-potential employees in Chapter 10 and coaching and development in Chapter 11.

Organization

The **organization environment**, through its vertical and horizontal alignment, including the HR infrastructure, as well as the policies and procedures, is also an important consideration for training and development strategy. The company structure, policies, and procedures create the frame within which the training and development strategy functions. Trainers should take into account other HR activities when designing training and development programs to ensure the training is in alignment with HR policies and practices. The structure also informs what should be included in onboarding and orientation programs, as we discuss in more detail in Chapter 13, so employees understand what the company does and how company policies and procedures inform day-to-day activities. If the goal of training employees is to ensure they can perform to their maximum potential, understanding how the company is structured is a key factor that affects their ability to succeed.

Interdependence of the Internal Environment

Exhibit 1-1 illustrates the four major categories of the organization's internal environment and how they are interdependent. As noted, changes in one area have repercussions for the other areas. For example, let's assume the organization wants employees to perform a new manufacturing task, fundamentally changing the process. A new task requires an assessment of whether or not current employees have the skills to perform that task. Investigating the people dimension, 25% of the employees who need to perform the task have previous experience, but the remaining 75% must be trained anew. The new task requires the organization to change the manufacturing process, so this affects the organizational procedures found under the organization dimension. Those new procedures must also be communicated to the employees during a training session. Finally, managers have to take into account the company culture, part of the social dimension, when instituting a change to company procedures to ensure employees buy in to the new process. As you can see, instituting a new change is not simple, and requires a broader organization-level view of how the change affects all parts of the organization, including the training and development function. The field of organizational development (OD) addresses organization-level change management, particularly how to make changes within the context of an organization's corporate culture. OD is at the core of the interdependence of the internal environment, and the training and development function works within OD to support overall organizational changes. As noted in the introduction, although OD is not the focus of this textbook, it is important to recognize how OD and change management work hand in hand with training and development.

Chapter 3 addresses needs analysis, which involves investigating the issues, concerns, and gaps in the internal environment that create a barrier to good performance. While needs analysis doesn't always reveal a need for training, the best way to identify training needs and design an appropriate training intervention is through investigating and understanding the four internal environment dimensions.

HR Infrastructure

Within the organizational environment, how does the HR infrastructure specifically impact the organization's training and development strategy? By exploring how some HR management activities affect training and development, we can see how the HR

Exhibit 1-1 Internal Organizational Environment Interdependence

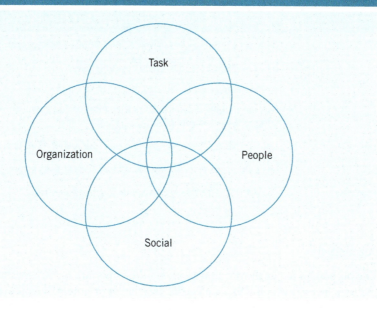

infrastructure informs training strategy. Exhibit 1-2 illustrates the typical training and development concerns relative to other HR activities.

Along with general HR infrastructure concerns, if a company is unionized, this will have a differential impact on the interdependence of HR activities, including training and development goals and activities. The union becomes a partner in the discussion of all HR activities and helps guide the training and development strategy for those employees it represents. Without union voice and buy-in, training programs will likely fail. The collective bargaining agreement should include elements of training and development strategy, along with incentives to encourage union member participation in the training programs.

The goal of the union in collective bargaining is to ensure that employees both personally and professionally benefit from the training interventions. Training should not simply be subterfuge for the organization to generate more profits without sharing those gains with employees. Thus, training and development strategy in a unionized organization should ideally be embedded in a gainsharing program. Gainsharing is a system of management used by a business to increase profitability by motivating employees to improve their performance through involvement and participation.[2] As company financial performance improves, employees retain a share of the savings associated with improved performance. Gainsharing programs provide a clear connection between performance improvement and employee benefits, and give employees ownership of their work output and organizational success.

Exhibit 1-2 HR Activities and Training and Development Concerns

HR Activities	Training and Development Concerns
Job Analysis	• Determine training needs given KSAs identified during job analysis
Staffing	• Develop talent in-house versus acquiring talent • Prepare employees for internal hiring opportunities • Develop training programs for new employees depending on skill set they bring to the organization
Performance Appraisal	• Train employees based on performance gap identified in appraisal process
Compensation	• Design training program with performance incentives embedded
Human Resource Information Systems (HRIS)	• Store KSAs and training development activities on HRIS

Job analysis.

The purpose of job analysis is to understand the important tasks associated with a job and then identify which KSAs are needed by current or potential employees to do the job. Training and development needs start with job analysis because in order to design a training and development program, you first have to understand what is needed of the employees. Thus, training and development programs are born from the results of the job analysis, particularly if employees are found to not have the KSAs needed to do a particular job.

Staffing.

Staffing strategy and training and development strategy are tightly interwoven.[3] Both are directly impacted by corporate strategy and vary depending on the needs of the company. Strategic staffing must consider the staffing levels in the organization, as well as the quality of the employees needed to complete the work of the organization. For example, on the *staffing levels* side, organizations should decide whether they want to acquire talent through the hiring process or develop their talent in-house through the training and development function.[4] Further, they need to decide if they will hire for vacancies from an external or internal pool of employees. When an organization decides to hire from within, care must be taken to ensure its employees are prepared for potential lateral moves or promotions. This entails having a training and development program that addresses the career needs of employees to ensure they are prepared for the organization's internal labor market. Succession planning is also an important aspect of internal hiring and requires close communication between the HR department's staffing and training and development experts.

On the *staffing quality* side, organizations can hire individuals based on either the skills they bring to the job or the person–organization match with the company culture. Southwest Airlines is a great example of a company that hires for the person–organization match and then trains the individuals on the KSAs they need to do their job.[5] Julie Weber, a vice president of people at Southwest Airlines, states the company looks for three characteristics when hiring new employees: a warrior spirit (a desire to excel), a servant's heart (willingness to put others first and proactively serve customers), and a fun-loving attitude (an aversion to taking themselves too seriously).[6] Once hired, employees are sent to Southwest Airlines University to receive the technical, personal, and professional development needed for a career at Southwest.[7]

Other staffing quality issues include whether to hire for specific or general KSAs, both of which have important implications for the kinds of training that employees may receive. Lastly, the decision to have exceptional or acceptable workforce quality impacts hiring decisions, as well as the training and development decisions that follow. Companies like Apple Inc. not only hire high-quality employees, but also ensure employees maintain their high levels of KSAs and competitive advantage through extensive training and development opportunities. Conversely, companies like McDonald's Corporation, when they hire entry-level workers, are more apt to hire for the minimum acceptable quality needed to do a job (e.g., high school education), while training new hires on the specific skills needed (e.g., running the cash register, cooking hamburgers).

Performance appraisal.

The performance appraisal is the first step to identify the gap between actual and desired performance for employees. The appraisal is designed with respect to the tasks and KSAs deemed essential by the job analysis. While managers should provide ongoing performance feedback to employees, the appraisal process is the formal mechanism whereby employees are assessed on their previous period's performance and subsequently develop a plan to improve performance gaps for the upcoming assessment period. Training and development goals are then set based on feedback from the appraisal process.

As well, we know that training managers to do performance appraisals appropriately and effectively can have a direct impact on the quality of employee performance.[8] All too often, organizations invest in sophisticated performance appraisal system design but fail to teach managers how to do performance assessment. Training managers and supervisors how to do performance assessment involves not only documenting employee performance to identify gaps needed for training purposes, but also daily coaching and fostering employee development, both of which are central to the development function, discussed further in Chapter 11.

Compensation.

We know from motivation theories that in order to sustain performance, employees need reinforcement. One way to reinforce employee performance is through a "pay for performance" system. Whether the employees receive merit pay or bonuses as a reward for past performance or are provided an incentive to induce future performance, a pay for performance system must work in conjunction with the training and development strategy to reinforce the KSAs needed to achieve high levels of performance among employees.

Human resource information systems.

An organization's information technology (IT) system should include a human resource information system (HRIS) to keep track of HR activities. More HR activities are being conducted online, including benefits management, recruitment, selection, and training and development. Computer-based training (CBT) is an easy way to track employee progress on training goals and expectations. Along with conducting training online, organizations can keep track of performance data and use the HRIS to manage succession planning and internal hiring and promotions. An HRIS also keeps track of employees' skills through a skill inventory. This database can be searched when trying to identify employees who are qualified for a promotion, and also when determining the types of training individual or groups of employees may need to meet job requirements. Training and development works best when there is an integrated IT system to help employees, managers, and HR professionals keep track of KSAs, as well as the detailed training and development plans for the organization. The role of technology in training and development is discussed further in Chapter 9.

COMPANY STRATEGY

Aligning Company and Training Strategies

Company strategy and training and development strategy must be in alignment in order for training and development to meet organizational needs and be effective. According to the Association for Talent Development (ATD), "If the organization is to successfully act on its strategy and meet its goals, the workforce must possess the necessary skills to carry out the actions described in the strategy. For this to happen, the organization must have a learning strategy that is synchronized and closely aligned with the business strategy."[9] ATD's 2015 report on aligning business strategy and employee performance found that in 2013, almost half of the survey respondents said their training strategy was in alignment with corporate strategy to a high or very high extent.[10] Another third said their training strategy was in moderate alignment with corporate strategy. Only 3% argued there was no alignment. Those organizations that exhibited high or very high alignment between corporate and training strategy also had higher market performance than those with low levels of alignment.

What is probably most disturbing is the difference between what learning professionals felt about the importance of strategy alignment and their perceptions of what business managers thought was the importance of strategy alignment. Ninety-three percent of learning professional respondents thought strategy alignment was highly important or critical, whereas only two-thirds of those surveyed said they thought business managers believed strategy alignment was highly important or critical. This presents a big opportunity for learning professionals to bring managers on board with respect to the importance of aligning training and corporate strategy.

Research by Impact International underscores ATD's findings and argues all levels of management must buy in to the idea that training and corporate strategy have to be in alignment in order for training and development activities to be effective.[11]

This research indicates four key questions that organizations must answer in order to align training and development strategy with corporate strategy.

1. How can you garner support or sponsorship from senior management so that learning and development is regarded as key to driving the business strategy?
2. How do you ensure that the learning and development you are delivering is in alignment with the business strategy?
3. What methodologies can you leverage in your learning and development that will make the company's strategies run through them?
4. How do you involve line managers' pre– and post–learning and development delivery in linking program content to the business strategy?

Impact argues the best way to protect training budgets is to make a clear link between corporate strategy and investment in training and development. By demonstrating value, return on investment, and the real business impact of training initiatives, the use of actual company-specific strategic issues and challenges makes training and development both timely and relevant. Chapters 5 and 6 cover how to evaluate training programs in this way. Impact makes the following suggestions on how to best address these four key issues.

Senior management support.

Without top management support, most corporate initiatives fall flat. Training and development is no different. Impact suggests a good way to get top managers to buy into the company's training and development strategy is to have them experience a portion of the flagship training and development programs for themselves. Once they have actively participated, they will be more likely to play a key role in content and delivery of the programs for other leaders in the company.

Ensuring alignment with corporate strategy.

Because corporate strategy today is much more of a moving target than it was 20 years ago, it is imperative to recruit a strategic steering group that not only understands the importance of training and development but also can identify and respond rapidly to changing training needs as strategy evolves. Just as just-in-time inventory was born from the need to manage inventory strategically, so must just-in-time learning solutions be developed to manage the organization's training and development needs.

Training methodologies to support corporate strategy.

With a rapidly changing environment, evolving strategies require innovative solutions and training methodology. One way to create state-of-the-art training content is to use realistic, live strategy cases and action learning, which are company-specific. This creates transparency, as well as provides trainees with up-to-date information on strategic issues for the company. Impact calls this a "triple hit" approach to training and development—state-of-the-art development techniques (discussed further in Chapters 7 and 8), better understanding and commitment to company strategy, and actual productive solutions to real strategic problems. In fact, recently published research argues that companies that use training and development programs to enhance their corporate strategy are more likely to experience greater productivity among employees and profitability for the organization.[12]

Line managers link training content to corporate strategy.

Line managers are no different from top management when it comes to the importance of buy-in for training investment. Getting them directly involved in aspects of training programs, whether as stakeholders, panelists, or dialogue partners, is key for ensuring training content transfers into action. Another important consideration is to link compensation to training involvement, which helps create a rich culture that values training and development at all levels of the company.

Corporate Strategy Theories

In order to best align corporate strategy to training and development strategy, understanding how corporate theory guides organizational action is important.[13] There are many theories of how corporate strategy helps organizations obtain a competitive edge. In a broad sense, organizations grow, stabilize, or retrench (shrink). Typically, this decision is based on external economic factors (discussed in the next section) and company success, such as profitability and market share. How the company wants to position itself in the market, as compared to competitors, drives its competitive strategy. One researcher, Michael Porter from Harvard Business School, identified generic competitive strategies, describing how an organization responds to competitive pressures to achieve its competitive advantage.[14] Similarly, Raymond Miles and Charles Snow designed their strategy typologies based on the degree to which an organization is aggressive with respect to risk taking and product innovation.[15] Regardless of the strategy undertaken, all organizations can benefit from a well-developed training and development strategy. Training and development activities benefit all companies, and ensuring those activities are in alignment with corporate strategy is the key for an organization's success.

Differentiation and prospector strategy.

Let's start by looking at the strategy typologies of Porter, and Miles and Snow. Exhibit 1-3 illustrates the training and development activities associated with a variety of competitive strategies. Apple computer products are known for being highly innovative and high in quality, with great customer service and state-of-the-art product attributes that are always in high demand. Consider the iPhone; Apple revolutionized the smartphone market, forcing the market leader at the time, BlackBerry, out of market dominance. Apple would be considered to have a **differentiation strategy** under Porter's typology, or a **prospector strategy** under Miles and Snow. Talented employees are a central feature

Exhibit 1-3 Corporate Strategy and Training and Development Activities

Porter	Miles and Snow	Training and Development Activity
Differentiation	Prospector	• Hire and train high-quality employees • Institute development program for employee advancement and high-potential employees
Cost Leadership	Defender	• Train for job-specific skills and cost efficiency • Develop managers in a "cost-conscious" culture
	Analyzer	• Train employees around company core competency • Focus on career development rather than growth opportunities
	Reactor	• Offer outplacement services • Retrain workers when there are reductions in force

of differentiation strategy companies like Apple. Exhibit 1-4 highlights the importance of training and development at Apple Inc. While differentiation strategy companies may be able to hire talented employees right out of the gate, in order for these employees to remain highly innovative and sustain their competitive advantage, they must be trained on the latest technologies and innovations. Further, developing them so they can continue to grow and contribute to the company is essential to retain these highly talented, in-demand employees.[16]

Cost leadership and defender strategy.

Although no one would disagree that companies following a differentiation strategy clearly benefit from a training and development strategy, cost leadership companies

Exhibit 1-4 Training and Development at Apple Inc.

Apple Inc. founded Apple University to initiate employees into the Apple culture and way of doing business. This program, while highly secretive, is a key component of Apple's competitive advantage in the computer, smartphone, and tablet markets. According to a 2014 article in the *New York Times*, the company intranet gives employees the opportunity to sign up for classes that meet their unique needs. Whether they take courses in communication, innovation, or business decision making, all employees are afforded the opportunity to grow and develop with Apple. While the courses are voluntary in nature, according to Brian Chen, Apple has no problem getting employees to enroll.

Source: Brian X. Chen, "Simplifying the Bull: How Picasso Helps to Teach Apple's Style," *New York Times*, August 10, 2014. Available from https://www.nytimes.com/2014/08/11/technology/-inside-apples-internal-training-program-.html.

can also benefit from comprehensive training and development. While this may seem counterintuitive given the costs associated with a plan of this type, consider Walmart's training and development strategy. Walmart competes on price and would be classified as engaging in a **cost leadership strategy** under Porter, or a **defender strategy** under Miles and Snow's typology. Because its focus is on effective cost management in order to compete on low price, one might think the company doesn't engage in training or development for its employees because that represents an extra cost to Walmart. When profit margins are tightly controlled in order to manage profitability, any excess costs are considered detrimental to organizational success. However, in order to ensure employees are cost-conscious, they should be instructed on how to work efficiently. Managers should be trained in how to help employees be cost-efficient as well.[17]

A quick glance at Walmart's website demonstrates that the company takes both training and development activities seriously, for associates as well as for store managers.[18] Of note, Walmart offers mentoring programs, leadership courses, and assistant management training for those interested in a career in retail. Training for associates is very job-specific and includes elements of workplace safety and equipment usage, as well as in-depth knowledge about the products they'll be selling. Training also focuses on how to up-sell products, as well as how to minimize waste. All in all, without clear direction and instruction on how to best meet Walmart's strategic objectives, employees may hinder, not help, the company achieve profitability.

Analyzer strategy.

The **analyzer strategy** is part of the Miles and Snow typology. **Analyzers** fall between prospectors and defenders. They are not first movers, like prospectors, but they like to innovate, usually as second or third to market. Their focus, most often, is on incremental improvements to existing products. Analyzers also find parts of their business may be focused on high-end innovative products, while other parts of their business are focused on cost cutting. As such, they have a balanced portfolio that includes both stable cash generators and cutting-edge innovative products. Training and development strategy for analyzers is the most diverse because it must focus on both innovation and cost management. Workers are trained on the company's core competency, and development activities focus on engaging employees with well-developed succession plans to retain and challenge workers when growth is slow. The evaluation process for analyzers also focuses on redeploying or dismissing unqualified workers and on nurturing core workers.[19]

Procter & Gamble (P&G) is a great example of an analyzer company.[20] P&G has brands that are dependable and profitable, such as Tide detergent and Pampers, but it also has an active research and development program to bring new innovative products to market on a regular basis. P&G prides itself on being a "build from within" company, meaning training, developing, and retaining employees over their entire career is central to P&G's training and development strategy. Leadership training and mentoring programs are also consistent with companies that value incremental improvements to their core competency, as it takes a long-term view of skill development.

Reactor strategy.

Miles and Snow have another strategy category that differs from Porter. The **reactor strategy**, however, is a misnomer. In reality, the reactor strategy company does not have a strategy, but instead reacts to environmental conditions in an inconsistent manner. Companies that are reactors have only two paths: switch their strategy to prospector, defender, or analyzer, or eventually decline and fail. Training and development activities can be directly influenced by a reactor strategy. For example, if a company is laying off employees, it may choose to utilize outplacement training for those being released. Outplacement training helps employees with résumé building, job retraining, career consulting, and career coaching. Organizations may also choose to cross-train employees so those who are retained can also do the jobs of those who are released from the company. The hope is that companies will eventually learn that a reactor strategy is not sustainable and begin to properly invest in and develop the company to compete in the market. Training and development can either help the company right itself to be more strategic or help the company close its doors more efficiently.

EXTERNAL ENVIRONMENT

The organization needs to make decisions based on issues going on in the surrounding environment. The external environment provides the context in which the organization functions. Within the external environment, factors such as the economy, political–legal issues, sociocultural issues, and technology impact the organization. These issues also impact training and development decisions and inform the training and development strategy.

Economic Environment

Given economic conditions, along with variables such as customer demand for the company's products, organizations have to decide how to respond to the market. They may decide to grow to take advantage of market opportunities, shrink and divest themselves of poorly performing divisions with a retrenchment strategy, or focus on how to maintain profitability, without expanding or contracting the business, through a stability strategy. These decisions are driven by economic forecasts. Training needs will differ depending on the direction in which the organizations head. Exhibit 1-5 illustrates how training and development needs may vary given economic conditions.

When a company is growing quickly, employees have tremendous advancement opportunities and must be kept up-to-date in the rapidly changing market. Alternatively, while one might argue that if the company is laying people off, there will be little room in the budget for training and development activities, this is actually the most important time for employees to broaden their skill set so they can learn how to "do more with less." With fewer employees, more will be asked of them, which requires them to have the skills to work more efficiently. Even a stability strategy demands that employees understand how to manage costs if the market is slowing down in order to maintain profitability.

Exhibit 1-5 Strategy Based on Economic Conditions

Strategies Based on Economic Conditions	Impact on Training and Development
Growth	• Keep employees up to speed on skills needed to meet rapid growth needs of company • Provide development and promotion opportunities
Stabilization	• Train employees on efficiency and cost containment • Provide customized career planning to keep employees engaged when growth is slow
Retrenchment	• Cross-train employees for maximum staffing flexibility • Offer organizational development activities to help employees adapt to changes in organization

Political–Legal Environment

The political–legal environment is an important consideration for organizations as well. The law can open or constrain opportunities for businesses. For example, Glass-Steagall legislation from the U.S. Banking Act of 1933 limited commercial bank securities, activities, and affiliations within commercial banks and securities firms.[21] Parts of this legislation were later repealed in 1999 under the Gramm–Leach–Bliley Act,[22] offering an excellent example of the impact government and politics can have on the expansion or contraction of business opportunities. As businesses expand or contract, different types of training and development activities may be utilized to help them adapt to government regulations. Along with the legislation, government programs may create incentives for organizations to invest in certain areas of the economy. Offering grants or low-interest loans and offering training opportunities in certain skill areas are examples of ways the government can support growth and development in different sectors. Appendix B provides information on how companies can outsource their training and development function and build partnerships with government, as well as private agencies.

Technological Environment

Technological advances also offer interesting challenges to businesses, whether a company is in the tech sector or is the beneficiary of technological advances in terms of its ability to offer products or services. Because technology changes so rapidly, employees must be kept abreast of those changes, particularly how the company expects to use the technology now and into the future. This creates a training need for companies if they want to keep pace with these advances. The impact of technology on learning and training delivery is also salient to organizations. These topics are addressed in more detail in Chapter 9.

Sociocultural Environment

Sociocultural issues are also a consideration for organizations. Ethical trends in industry and society have an impact on business decision making. These trends filter down into the organization, putting pressure on it to train employees on the latest in ethical compliance programs. As our workforce becomes more diverse, training employees to work in diverse organizations and manage the inherent conflict that goes along with that diversity is imperative. Working in a global economy also requires high levels of competencies, including adaptability, an openness to new experiences, and a willingness to work with diverse others. Because the organization is considered a microcosm of the sociocultural issues going on in the external environment, and it must respond to the political–legal, economic, and technological challenges ahead, consideration of the external environment is an important input into training and development strategy.

ETHICS AND TRAINING STRATEGY

The training and development industry is held to similar ethical standards as would be expected in any profession or industry. Exhibit 1-6 illustrates the ATD Code of Ethics. While the code does not specifically address issues of corporate and training strategy alignment, as noted in the ATD survey highlighted in the "Company Strategy" section of this chapter, 93% of learning professionals believe alignment of corporate and training strategy is very important or critical. Even if there is strategy alignment, however, this doesn't guarantee that the training and development function will be handled ethically.

Exhibit 1-6   Association for Talent Development Code of Ethics

The Code of Ethics provides guidance to individuals to be self-managed talent development professionals. Clients and employers should expect the highest possible standards of personal integrity, professional competence, sound judgment, and discretion. Developed by the profession for the profession, the Code of Ethics is the public declaration of talent development professionals' obligations to themselves, their profession, and society.

I strive to:

- Recognize the rights and dignities of each individual to develop human potential
- Provide my employer, clients, and learners with the highest level of quality education, training, and development
- Comply with all copyright laws and the laws and regulations governing my position
- Keep informed of pertinent knowledge and competence in the workplace learning and talent development field
- Maintain confidentiality and integrity in the practice of my profession, support my peers, and avoid conduct which impedes their practicing their profession
- Conduct myself in an ethical and honest manner
- Improve the public understanding of workplace learning and talent development
- Fairly and accurately represent my professional credentials, qualifications, experience, and ability
- Contribute to the continuing growth of the profession

Source: Association for Talent Development, "Vision, Mission, Code of Ethics." Available from https://www.td.org/about/vision-mission-code-of-ethics.

The ATD Code of Ethics requires a set of behaviors that minimizes the organization's liability.[23] Only when the company's legal and ethical obligations are being addressed can training and corporate strategy alignment have an impact on company success. Holding training and development specialists to ethical standards is consistent with the need to establish and understand the overall ethical standards highlighted in the social environment (see the "Internal Environment" section).

Another important way training and development professionals can help establish and maintain a company's ethical culture and social environment is to conduct ethics training programs to ensure the organization is in compliance with all legal and ethical standards the company finds important. The relationship between the law and ethics is discussed further in Chapter 2.

GLOBAL ISSUES IN TRAINING STRATEGY

ATD conducted an unprecedented study of 1,373 global talent managers in 2015.[24] The purpose of the study was to develop a benchmark of organizational talent development functions across the globe. "By looking at key metrics by global regions, this research will aid talent development (TD) professionals in benchmarking their practices against those of their peers in their own region. The data will allow TD functions in organizations with global and multinational staff to evaluate learning using statistics and insights from each region, as well as tailor talent development offerings to each region's unique learning environment." The survey addressed four basic questions:

1. What are the influences, challenges, and outlooks that shape the decisions of organizational TD functions?
2. Where does talent development fit within the organizational structure, and what resources and training are organizations offering their talent development teams?
3. How much do organizations budget for talent development activities, to what extent do organizations outsource their talent development activities, and what are some of the challenges in ensuring outsourced activities are effective and efficient?
4. What is the talent development experience like for a typical employee? In other words, how many formal learning hours do employees receive, and what content areas are emphasized? (Formal learning hours refer to learning that occurs, or can occur, as a separate, stand-alone activity, not embedded in work activities.) How is learning content being delivered to employees?

Globally, training and development activities do vary from region to region for a variety of reasons. Government regulation, economic conditions, educational systems, and technology differ depending on where you live and what kind of industry and infrastructure exist to support the growth of business organizations. One point is abundantly clear in the ATD report: Training and development activities anywhere in the world are driven by economic conditions. Where there are more stable economies with industry and job growth, we are more likely to see greater investment in training and development at the organizational level.

ATD's research had several important findings. Because this was the first study of its kind, there is no longitudinal data against which to compare results for the 2015 study. The study, however, came up with four issues of note. First, the number of annual learning hours for employees was relatively stable across regions (no statistically significant difference across regions), averaging 34.4 hours annually. Second, there was agreement between all regions that the most important trend in talent management is ensuring there is a strategic link between learning and employee and organizational performance. Third, respondents in all regions agreed that building a culture that supports learning, training, and development is the most important challenge facing the talent development industry. Lastly, although training content varied across regions depending on regional, local, and organizational needs, managerial and interpersonal skills were seen as important regardless of regional and local needs.

The ATD report underscores the importance of considering the three key inputs in our framework for strategic training and development no matter what region of the world the company is situated. Knowing company strategy, the internal organizational environment, and the external environment within which the organization does business is essential to develop a training and development strategy that meets the organization's need for success. Despite some regional differences, organizations across the globe believe that training and development is a key variable for organizational success, and developing a learning culture is essential to support training and development.

CHAPTER SUMMARY

This chapter introduced the topic of training and development strategy. The organization's internal and external environments—including the employees' skills, motivations, and needs; the company's infrastructure and strategy; and economic, technological, social, and political–legal trends—drive training and development strategy. Taking these issues into account, the organization develops a plan for how to best ensure its employees have the KSAs needed to do the job. Depending on a company's focus, it may design a training program to meet the immediate need for KSAs and/or develop a plan to prepare employees to meet future demands. In all circumstances, a comprehensive needs analysis must be done, and the outcomes from the training and development strategy must be assessed to see if it had the intended impact. Regardless of the company strategy, all companies across the world can benefit from aligning their training and development strategy with their corporate strategy.

KEY TERMS

Analyzer strategy. A company strategy that focuses on incremental innovation, in which the company is typically second or third to market with new products and balances its portfolio with both innovating, high-risk companies and stable cash generators.

Cost leadership strategy. A company strategy based on pricing, specifically setting prices low as compared to competitors.

Defender strategy. A company strategy that protects the company's market share, engages in little new product development, and focuses on improving the efficiency of the company's bottom line.

Differentiation strategy. A company strategy that involves competition based on quality, product attributes, and customer service.

HR infrastructure. The horizontal integration of human resource functional areas, including job analysis, staffing, performance appraisal, compensation, training and development, and human resource information systems.

Organization environment. The way a company is organized, through vertical and horizontal alignment, including policies and procedures.

People environment. The demographics of the workforce, including the knowledge, skills, abilities, experiences, education levels, and motivations of the employees.

Prospector strategy. A company strategy that focuses on product innovation and market opportunity, along with a willingness to take risks.

Reactor strategy. A nonstrategy in which the company reacts to environmental concerns rather than proactively develops a strategy for business success.

Social environment. The social system within which employees work, including the ethical and organizational culture, leadership style, and company climate.

Task environment. What employees do, when they do it, and how often they repeat the tasks of their job.

END-OF-CHAPTER QUESTIONS AND EXERCISES

Discussion Questions

1. What is the importance of developing a training and development strategy that is in alignment with corporate strategy?
2. What are the internal dimensions that impact training and development? How do they interact to have an impact on training? Give an example of a training intervention an organization implements and how it impacts the four internal dimensions of the organization.
3. What type of training and development interventions directly impact the social environment? Do you think training or development has the biggest impact on the social environment, and why?
4. Why is it important to understand the interrelatedness of different HR functions in the company? Illustrate how training activities can influence other HR activities in the company.
5. How do you think unionization will change the way a company does training and development? Why is it important for union buy-in when developing a training and development strategy?
6. Discuss the close relationship between staffing strategy and training and

development strategy. Give an example of how the activities for both functions overlap and support each other.
7. Explain how training and development is an important output from the performance appraisal process. What is learned during performance assessment that informs training and development activities for employees? Why is it important these two functions are closely linked?
8. Training and development strategy should be in alignment with corporate strategy in order to function at its best. Summarize what you think is the reasoning behind Impact International's four major questions that must be addressed.
9. Discuss the reason why cost leadership strategy companies can benefit from training and development. Be specific about the benefits for the organization, for managers or supervisors, and for employees.
10. Analyzer strategy companies face a unique challenge in that areas of their company may compete on product attributes, and other areas may compete on price. Discuss the challenges training specialists may face in designing a training and development strategy. What is the best way to organize the company to meet these unique training and development needs? Outline and describe a training and development strategy in an analyzer company.
11. How can training and development benefit a company if the economy is struggling and the company is in a bad financial position? Describe the benefits of doing training and development in all economic conditions.
12. Discuss the interplay between company culture and ethical training. What is the relationship between training and development strategy and ethical culture? How can training and development have an impact on ethics?
13. Consider an organization that has a global presence. How does training and development strategy differ across different global locations for the company? Is it the same at all locations? If so, why? If not, why not?

Ethical Scenario

The Dilemma of Training People About Ethical Dilemmas

Jane was the director of human resources at Voltage Corporation, having been promoted to the position from her previous role as the training and development manager. Voltage had recently been taken public and now had a whole range of new compliance requirements ordered by the government. Jane had just gotten out of a meeting with the CFO and CEO of the company, and was feeling frustrated.

As the company was ramping up for its initial public offering (IPO), Jane had been developing a comprehensive workplace ethics and corporate compliance training program with the new training and development manager, Tim. Tim had suggested that they make sure employees are trained on compliance laws such as Sarbanes–Oxley[25] as soon as the public offering was completed. Jane agreed and thought it might be beneficial to expand the training to more than just compliance issues. She thought it made sense to also establish the company's ethical norms and help train employees to be aware of ethical dilemmas and reason through common challenges. She and Tim developed the budget and put together the proposal to go to the CFO and CEO for final approval. In the meantime, Tim began developing the materials to be included in the comprehensive training program.

During the meeting, the CEO said the company could *not* afford to do any training right now because it was waiting for the dust to settle financially after the IPO. The CEO said, "Look, we can't train people to be ethical. Why spend the money on something that will give us little return on our investment? We have to be really careful right now because *now* we are beholden to shareholders and their need to maximize profits. Forget training—it's not going to happen. What's next on your list?" Jane responded that at a minimum, they needed to make sure people understood the requirements in Sarbanes–Oxley and some other compliance issues required of publically held companies. The CEO agreed but wanted nothing more than the bare minimum invested in training, so it did not include a comprehensive program that included ethical dilemma training.

Jane knew this was a mistake but needed to find a way to persuade the CEO that dollars for comprehensive ethics training were needed or the company would risk everything it had tried to do by going public in the first place.

You are sitting in a meeting with Jane and Tim. Consider the ATD Code of Ethics; what would you advise them to do? Why is the training essential to help the company be successful and reach its strategic objectives? Compose a detailed argument Jane can use to persuade the CEO to do more than the minimum, but ensure the program includes ethical decision-making training.

1.1 Global Economies and Training Needs

Review the following video on the TED website:

Rainer Strack, "The Workforce Crisis of 2030—and How to Start Solving It Now," TED@BCG, October 2014. Available from www.ted.com/talks/rainer_strack_the_surprising_workforce_crisis_of_2030_and_how_to_start_solving_it_now.

Rainer Strack's TED Talk addresses a number of concepts we discussed in this chapter: global economies, need for skills, technology, people strategy. Given his point of view on the impact of technology on supply and demand for employees and their unique skills, this has huge implications for training and development strategy. Analyze his TED Talk (the transcript is available on the website) and indicate which of the key points in his video will affect training and development strategy for global businesses. Use the textbook main points to describe and support why they will have an impact and make recommendations on how to best address the main points in Strack's talk.

1.2 Strategy Identification and Alignment: Siemens Versus Aldi

A. Siemens

Source: "Training and Development as a Strategy for Growth: A Siemens Case Study." Available from http://businesscasestudies.co.uk/siemens/training-and-development-as-a-strategy-for-growth/introduction.html.

Siemens is a global corporation focusing on electrification, automation, and digitalization. It employs 348,000 employees in over 200 countries. Siemens values training and development and believes its strategy supports training and development.

Answer the following questions about the Siemens corporate strategy, as well as its approach to training and development. Utilize the Siemens website for information, including its financials, as well as other resources available on the internet.

Case

Siemens is a leading technology business and one of the largest electrical and electronics engineering companies in the world. In the UK, it employs over 20,000 people and is in the top three electrical and electronics companies in the world.

It has been a pioneer in innovation since 1843 when Siemens installed the first street light in Godalming, Surrey. In 2006, Siemens UK invested over £74.4 million on research and development.

The company designs and manufactures products and services for both industrial customers and consumers. It operates in three main sectors:

- In industry, Siemens develops systems for transport, for example, London's traffic monitoring for its congestion charge scheme. It is also the second largest provider of trains for major UK rail companies like FirstGroup. Siemens also provides lighting and electrical systems for major construction projects.

- In energy, Siemens' work is wide-ranging. It makes systems for transmitting and distributing power for power companies including building power stations and wind farms. It also provides energy metering services, for example, water meters for businesses and consumers.

- In healthcare, it specialises in equipment to help medical diagnosis, such as MRI scanners and imaging technology. It also provides equipment for testing blood in laboratories.

Siemens's technology appears in every aspect of everyday life, for example:

- the electronic "eye" (Hawk Eye) helps umpires in tennis and cricket matches
- 9 out of 10 cars contain Siemens products
- 20,000 domestic products like toasters are used in homes every day
- systems such as Pelican crossings keep people safe. Car parking systems help guide traffic quickly to free spaces, keeping traffic moving and reducing pollution on the roads

To keep its world-leading position and grow in a competitive environment, Siemens aims to deliver quality products and services. To do this, it needs people with first class levels of skill, knowledge, and capability in engineering, IT, and business.

The size and varied nature of its business means that Siemens requires many different types of people to fill a wide range of roles across the company. These include skilled factory workers, trade apprenticeships, designers, and managers.

This case study explores how Siemens manages its ongoing need for skills through training and development.

Identifying Training Needs

For a business to be competitive, it is important that it has the right number of people with the right skills in the right jobs. Workforce planning enables Siemens to audit its current staff numbers and the skills it has in place as well as identify where it has skills gaps needed to meet its business objectives.

For instance, Siemens is relocating its main plant in Lincoln to a bigger site outside the main city. This will require new skills for the work to be done there. A plan has been constructed to analyse which skills the company has and what training will be needed for staff to use the new technology in the new location.

Siemens needs new skills for many reasons:

- to maintain competitive advantage, in ensuring Siemens has people with the right skills to develop new technologies and innovations
- to ensure Siemens has a pipeline of talent and minimal knowledge gaps, for example, due to retirement
- to fill a gap following the promotion of existing employees

Siemens is a business focused on innovation. This means it needs to anticipate and respond to rapid changes in the external business environment. For example, climate change and the growing emphasis on its carbon footprint has massively increased Siemens's focus on wind turbines and renewable energy sources to address this. Siemens needs to attract employees with the appropriate skills, either by recruiting people into the organisation or by training existing employees to develop more skills.

A recent example of opportunities was the 2012 Olympic Games in London. Siemens helped advise the Olympic bid and has great opportunities in providing security, healthcare provisions, media and communications technology for the Games.

Training

Training involves teaching new skills or extending the skills employees already have. There are two forms of training. As well as induction training, where new employees learn the basic information they need to begin working, Siemens has three main development programmes designed for "Entry Level Talent," i.e. those beginning their career with Siemens after education.

Apprenticeships. Siemens offers a variety of technical apprenticeships, aimed at school leavers who want to "earn as they learn." Apprentices can join a variety of engineering/IT apprenticeships across a variety of locations in the UK, although the majority start their working life from their home town working at their local Siemens site.

Apprenticeship training is a combination of off-the-job college training and on-the-job work experience. Apprentices work to achieve their HND [Higher National Diploma] qualifications in their related field. Entry requirements vary depending on the programme, but fundamentally applicants require good communication skills and the ability to work in a team.

Siemens believes apprenticeships provide a clear route in developing staff for the future growth of the organisation.

Siemens Commercial Academy. The Siemens Commercial Academy was launched in 2005 to further enhance the pipeline of financial and commercial capability within Siemens. The programme lasts four years and is regarded as an alternative to going directly to university.

Aimed at students who have a keen interest in Business and Finance, the programme enables students to rotate around various finance and commercial placements including Accounting, HR, Procurement and Corporate areas.

The trainees who join the programme split their time between studying toward an HND in Business with Finance and working at Siemens. Students study toward the degree at the European College of Business Management, as well as take part in personnel development training such as communication and presentation skills. IT courses and German language training are also available.

Siemens Graduate Programmes. Siemens recruits graduates into three core areas of the business:

- Engineering including electrical/electronic, mechanical/mechatronic systems, broadcast, process, and manufacturing
- IT covering research, development, design, and consultancy
- Business including finance, HR, sales, project, and operational management

All Siemens graduate recruits are treated as individuals. They enter the business with relevant skills, knowledge, and experience and the potential to do many different roles. Each graduate has a discussion with his or her line manager when they start, to decide on their individual training and development plan.

Where appropriate Siemens supports graduates to gain further qualifications. These include gaining chartered engineer status through institutions such as IET [Institution of Engineering and Technology] or IMechE [Institution of Mechanical Engineers]. The typical graduate profile is varied.

Craig Finlayson graduated from the University of Paisley with a degree in Information Technology. He worked on the BBC account in London within the project finance team. He now works in Sales Support and Portfolio on various projects.

Anna Carder, HR Graduate, joined Siemens in 2006 from Aston University with a BSc in Managerial and Administrative Studies. Anna is currently in her third and final placement in the Recruitment & Sourcing team of Global Shared Services. She has previously worked in two other placements in Corporate Personnel where she worked as part of the Talent Management team followed by an HR operational placement within Siemens Traffic Controls in Poole. Siemens is currently supporting Anna in her studies for her CIPD [Chartered Institute of Personnel and Development] qualification through distance learning.

Development

The costs of recruiting staff are high. It is far more cost effective to keep good staff. Siemens need[s] well-trained employees with good key skills and capabilities, especially communication and team working skills.

This gives Siemens a competitive advantage as employees will be more flexible, adaptable to change and be more creative and innovative. They do their jobs better and are able to develop into other roles in the future.

Siemens implemented the Siemens Graduate Development Programme in 2005, as a means of developing graduates with the essential skills set they need in their everyday role and to equip them for a long-term career at Siemens.

Every graduate that joins Siemens, regardless of role or location[,] joins the 2 year programme. This consists of 9 modules including team working, customer focus, project management, communication skills, and business writing. The training is hosted at a number of Siemens sites, so graduates get exposure to different parts of Siemens, learn about the business, and network amongst the graduate population.

By improving the development opportunities, employees feel the company values them.

The motivation theories of Maslow (see Chapter 3) show that staff work better when valued. This delivers long-term commitment and ensures benefits to the company.

Evaluation of Training and Development

Well-trained employees provide a number of benefits that contribute to a business' competitive advantage.

To measure the effectiveness of its training and development, Siemens uses an appraisal system, known as a Performance Management process. Employees and their line managers agree [on] objectives at the beginning of a placement and progress is then monitored formally and informally throughout the placement. This helps to focus everyone on the developing needs of the business.

Annually, the results form the basis of a staff dialogue where the employee's manager reviews the progress toward the objectives that have been set. Feedback is discussed with the employee and any development needs are captured in order to decide appropriate training. Together, new objectives for the following year ahead are set. In some instances, appraisals are linked to pay reviews. In these cases, pay rises depend on employees meeting or exceeding their objectives.

There are several benefits for Siemens in using appraisal. It can:

- ensure that all training is being used well and for the best interests of the company
- keep all staff up-to-date in a fast changing business
- make sure that staff are well motivated
- get feedback from staff on changes
- make sure staff are involved in changes.

Conclusion

Training and development helps the growth of a business.

Siemens has a clear focus on having a well-motivated and trained workforce. The company needs to have motivated and confident staff who have up-to-date skills in order to remain competitive. In addition, well-trained staff are an asset to the business and help to retain customers.

Well-trained staff who remain with the business mean that customers enjoy continuity. This contributes to customer loyalty and leads to repeat business.

Staff who feel valued stay longer in a company. This means that Siemens's costs of recruitment can be reduced, resulting in cost savings across the organisation.

Additional Sources

Siements, "Company: Discover Opportunities." Available from https://new.siemens.com/us/en/company/jobs.html.

Siemens, "Strategy Overview." Available from https://new.siemens.com/global/en/company/about/strategy/overview.html.

Questions

1. Identify the Siemens corporate strategy. Give examples of why you would classify it as such based on the information in the chapter.
2. Analyze Siemens based on our framework for training and development strategy:
   a. What key internal factors does Siemens take into account when developing its training and development strategies?
   b. What external factors has Siemens considered in its training and development strategy?
   c. Discuss the interplay between the internal factors, external factors, and corporate strategy. Perform a SWOT (strengths, weaknesses, opportunities, and threats) analysis with the training and development strategy in mind, and discuss which factors would have the greatest impact.
3. Assess the alignment of the training and development strategy with the internal and external environment, as well as the corporate strategy.
   a. What are the key elements in the Siemens training and development program?
   b. Analyze the training and development program to see if it is in alignment with the key factors. Explain and support your conclusion with material from the chapter as well as the resources provided for you.
   c. What, if anything, do you think Siemens could add to its training and development program?

B. Aldi

Source: "Business and Expansion Through Training and Development: An Aldi Case Study." Available from http://businesscasestudies.co.uk/aldi/business-expansion-through-training-and-development/introduction.html#axzz46JM1Mclm.

Aldi is a grocery store that focuses on low overhead and efficiency in delivering products to consumers. It has 1,500 stores across the United States and in 2014 was the *Store Brands* magazine retailer of the year. Although Aldi differs from Siemens in many ways, it is also a company that values employees and their skill development.

Answer the following questions about Aldi and its training and development strategy. Utilize the company website, including its financials, as well as other sources on the internet.

Case

Aldi is a leading retailer with over 8,000 stores worldwide. It continues to expand in Europe, North America, and Australia. The Aldi brand is associated with value for money. Its stores provide customers with a wide range of products. There is an emphasis on high quality products and providing excellent value for customers.

Aldi's slogan is "*spend a little, live a lot.*" It works hard to keep prices low for its customers. The company buys large quantities of products from carefully selected suppliers. Its buyers are experts who choose the best quality products at the most competitive prices. The savings achieved by sourcing products in this way can be passed on to customers. Aldi keep[s] costs down in other ways. It ensures its operations are as efficient as possible[;] for example, store layouts are kept simple and opening hours focus on the busiest times of the day.

The Importance of Developing People

Aldi places great importance on how it trains and develops its employees. Training is the process of providing employees with the necessary knowledge and skills to perform their tasks and roles competently.

Training not only helps to increase business efficiency, but it can also make staff more motivated by increasing their job satisfaction.

While training is narrowly focused on helping a company become efficient and effective in the short term, development is more about building the long-term capabilities of the workforce. It is about helping individuals to gain knowledge, learn new skills and develop a wide range of attributes. Development makes employees more adaptable and more able to take on a wider range of roles.

This case study will demonstrate how Aldi's training and development programmes help ensure its employees have the skills and competencies that the business requires both now and in the future.

Identifying Training Needs

Workforce planning. Workforce planning is the process of finding out how a business will meet its labour requirements both now and in the future. Aldi, like other businesses, needs to predict its future staffing needs accurately. It needs to plan for both the number of workers it will require and the specific skills that the business will need in the future. The company can then recruit new staff if necessary. It can also ensure that it has training and development programmes in place to meet these needs.

Aldi identifies future training needs through an on-going analysis of company performance in key areas at all levels. For example, the company monitors the availability of its products to the customer within its stores. If the level of availability drops below the targeted level[,] then a programme of training on order accuracy would be undertaken. It also considers future developments within the business and also within the grocery retail sector in order to predict both the total numbers of staff it will need and, more crucially, the skills and competencies that will be required.

Aldi's rapid expansion means that its current workforce cannot meet its future staffing requirements. The company will need to recruit more than 4,000 new members of staff within the next 12 months to meet the requirements of current exceptional sales growth and new store openings. To attract the best candidates, it offers industry-leading salaries at all levels.

To ensure it gets people with the right set of skills, the company produces clear and detailed job descriptions for each post. These show the tasks and responsibilities for that position and in turn, the skills and competencies needed by an individual to succeed in that role.

Interview and assessment. Through a process of interview and assessment, managers identify if candidates have the precise skills and competencies that the job requires. If the selection process shows that they are suitable, then they will be recruited and Aldi can be confident that they will fulfill the challenges of their role.

Although Aldi expects new recruits to make an immediate contribution to the business, it also provides training so that they can develop their careers within the company. Aldi has entry levels for apprentices, store assistants, deputy managers, assistant store managers, trainee store managers and graduate trainee area managers. Aldi organises high-level training for recruits to all levels. For example, in their first year, graduate recruits receive training in all areas of the business. This ranges from training in-store to understand how the retail operation works, to regional office tasks such as logistics, trading, and financial planning.

All new recruits go through a comprehensive structured training plan. New employees learn about the philosophy of Aldi and its expectations of them. This is important in making new employees quickly feel part of the Aldi family. This training will be appropriate to the role, so could be in a store or at an Aldi regional office.

On-the-Job Training

On-the-job training is training that takes place while employees are actually working. It means that skills can be gained while trainees are carrying out their jobs. This benefits both employees and the business. Employees learn in the real work environment and gain experience dealing with the tasks and challenges that they will meet during a normal working day. The business benefits by ensuring that the training is specific to the job. It also does not have to meet the additional costs of providing off-the-job training or losing working time.

There are several methods of providing on-the-job training. Four frequently used methods are briefly described here:

- Coaching—an experienced member of staff will help trainees learn skills and processes through providing instructions or demonstrations (or both).

- Mentoring—each trainee is allocated to an established member of staff who acts as a guide and helper. A mentor usually offers more personal support than a coach, although the terms "mentor" and "coach" are often used interchangeably.

- Job rotation—this is where members of staff rotate roles or tasks so that they gain experience of a full range of jobs.

- "Sitting next to Nellie"—this describes the process of working alongside a colleague to observe and learn the skills needed for a particular process. This can be a faster and more useful way of learning a job role than studying a written manual. The colleague is always on hand to answer any questions or deal with any unexpected problems.

Store managers act as trainers. For most on-the-job training at Aldi stores, the store manager acts as the trainer. A typical format is for the manager to explain a process to the trainee, then to demonstrate it. The trainee then carries out the process, while the manager observes. Once the manager is happy that trainees are competent, they can then carry out the process unaided. This process is used, for example, to teach a store assistant how to operate the till and to instruct a trainee manager how to order stock accurately.

All positions from apprentices through to trainee area managers follow this type of structured "tell, show, do" training. Trainee area managers also undergo job rotation. They have the opportunity to experience all aspects of the business to give them a complete overview of how Aldi operates. They can then see how each department and business operation relates to and links with other parts of the company and other processes.

Off-the-Job Training

As the name suggests, off-the-job training is provided away from the immediate workplace. This might be at a specialist training centre or at a college or at a company's own premises. This type of training can be particularly useful for developing transferable skills that can be used in many different parts of the business. It may be used, for example, to train employees in the use of new equipment and new methods or to bring them up to date with changes in the law. Typical off-the-job training courses offered to employees by Aldi include:

- recruitment, interviewing and selection
- employment law
- influencing skills
- performance reviews (appraisals)
- Aldi Management System (how to develop and performance manage people).

For each aspect of training Aldi decides whether on-the-job or off-the-job training is the better option. Off-the-job training may involve extra costs, such as payments to training organisations. It also means that staff taking training courses are not at work, so their jobs have to be covered by others. This can lead to an increase in payroll costs. However, balanced against these costs are the gains that Aldi makes from off-the-job training. These include the benefits of having more motivated staff, greater staff productivity and employees with better skills and the ability to provide improved customer service.

Aldi's apprenticeship scheme. Aldi provides training opportunities for young people. The Aldi apprentice scheme combines on-the-job and off-the-job training. Apprenticeships are open to 16–18 year olds. Apprentices training as store assistants also study for an NVQ [National Vocational Qualification] in Retail Apprenticeship. They complete store assistant training and gain an NVQ Level 2 in their first year. They then take a store management training programme over two years and work for a Level 3 advanced qualification.

The variety seems to suit apprentices. As Sam, an Aldi apprentice[,] says:

> *"The fast pace of the role is really exciting, with lots of chances to learn new and useful skills. As well as the on-the-job training, there is also studying towards a recognised qualification that I can fit around work."*

Emily, another apprentice, recognises that the programme is a good opportunity:

> *"After attending college I was looking for an opportunity that would allow me to use my customer service skills and the Aldi apprenticeship has given me just that. There is a lot of competition for places, so you really need to want to succeed. I really feel part of the store team. It can be challenging but it is well worth it."*

At the end of their apprenticeships, Sam and Emily will have the knowledge and skills to take on deputy manager or assistant store manager positions. From there each can rise to become a Store Manager in the business. Aldi's current growth means that there are many opportunities for promotion, so Sam and Emily could soon join the many others who have been promoted within the business.

Development

Development is not the same as training. Development focuses as much on personal growth as skills that are directly related to the job. A development programme is designed to make individuals more skilled, more flexible in their approach and better qualified for their chosen careers.

Through a development programme, employees can obtain transferable qualifications that benefit the individuals concerned as well as the business. This can have disadvantages for the business, as it gives workers greater value in the job market. However, Aldi is willing to take this risk as it believes in providing what is best for its staff. Development options for apprentices include working for various qualifications. Aldi has a fast-track approach for graduates. Opportunities for graduate recruits at Aldi include secondments to different international countries to develop all-round expertise.

Aldi retail placement scheme. The Aldi retail placement scheme takes university students on a one-year placement. This allows the chosen individuals to show what they can offer the business and to find out what the business can offer them. Aldi offers an excellent reward package for students on a placement, but in return expects trainees to have enthusiasm, drive, and ambition. Successful students get the opportunity to apply for a place on Aldi's Area Management training programme.

To support their development, managers help employees to set personal goals. These are identified during an appraisal process. This is when a member of staff sits down with their line manager to evaluate past and current performance, to consider what skills are needed going forward and to set targets for the future. This could involve identifying further training or development opportunities.

Conclusion

Aldi seeks to provide its customers with quality products at prices that provide value for money. It wants efficient operations, with its stores staffed by people who are keen and competent. Aldi's success is shown by the fact that it is expanding rapidly. It is opening new stores and experiencing sales growth that requires it to take on more staff. This means that it needs to combine good recruitment policies with robust selection processes.

Staff are recruited from school or college into Aldi's apprenticeship scheme or direct into stores for positions from store assistant up to trainee Store Manager. Those from university with a 2.1 degree or better are able to apply for the Graduate Area Manager programme. All recruits are assured of appropriate on-the-job and off-the-job training, as well as career development opportunities. Promotion is open to all staff, regardless of the route they choose to join Aldi.

Aldi puts great emphasis on developing its people. Over 85% of Aldi directors have been recruited from within the company. This commitment to training and development makes Aldi a business of choice for both ambitious teenagers and top graduates. This is shown by its placing in the Top 5 in The Times Top 100 Graduate Employers and the Graduate Employer of Choice for 2012 for General Management.

Additional Sources

Aldi, "Corporate Responsibility: Our People." Available from https://corporate.aldi.us/en/corporate-responsibility/our-people/.

Aldi, "Our People." https://careers.aldi.us/people.

Aldi, "Store Management & Staff." Available from https://careers.aldi.us/store.

Questions

1. Identify the Aldi corporate strategy. Give examples of why you would classify it as such based on the information in the chapter.
2. Analyze Aldi based on our framework for training and development strategy:
   a. What key internal factors does Aldi take into account when developing its training and development strategies?
   b. What external factors has Aldi considered in its training and development strategy?
   c. Discuss the interplay between the internal factors, external factors, and corporate strategy. Perform a SWOT analysis with the training and development strategy in mind, and discuss which factors would have the greatest impact.
3. Assess the alignment of the training and development strategy with the internal and external environment, as well as the corporate strategy.
   a. What are the key elements in Aldi's training and development program?
   b. Analyze the training and development program to see if it is in alignment with the key factors. Explain and support your conclusion with material from the chapter as well as the resources provided for you.
   c. What, if anything, do you think Aldi could add to its training and development program?

C. Compare and Contrast Siemens to Aldi

1. How does the Siemens corporate strategy differ from the Aldi corporate strategy? List and explain the key differences.
2. Compare and contrast these companies' training and development strategies. How does Siemens compare to Aldi? What is similar, and what is different?
3. Discuss overall how training and development strategy benefits all companies regardless of their corporate strategy. Use examples from the two cases to make a persuasive argument why investing in training dollars benefits companies, no matter their competitive strategy. Include financial considerations, as well as any evidence of corporate reputation, and industry rankings, along with information provided in the case and textbook.

CHAPTER TWO

LEGAL ISSUES IN TRAINING AND DEVELOPMENT

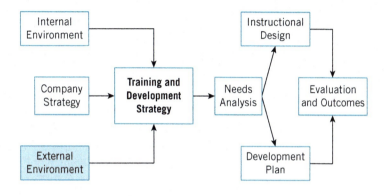

Learning Objectives

1. Identify the key provisions of antidiscrimination legislation.
2. Differentiate between types of discriminatory actions.
3. Assess whether an organization is guilty of discriminating.
4. Discuss how ethics influences behavior.
5. Explain how reasonable accommodation applies to training.
6. Assess whether training has increased or decreased an organization's potential liability.

Shirley Hoffman worked for the Optical Services Department at Caterpillar Inc., and for the majority of her time at Caterpillar, her performance had been rated as average or better. One of the pieces of equipment within her department, but not one that she was required to use, was a high-speed scanner. Furthermore, she was not trained on how to use it. However, many of her coworkers were similarly situated, and only some in the department had been trained to use the high-speed scanner.

What made Shirley's situation different from that of the others who had not been trained to use the high-speed scanner are a few important facts. First, Shirley had requested to be trained on the use of the high-speed scanner. Second, everyone who previous to her had requested to be trained had received the training. Finally, Shirley is disabled, and she felt that fact was the basis for the decision to deny her the training.

Shirley's disability is that she is missing her lower left arm. Under the Americans with Disabilities Act (ADA), Shirley is eligible for reasonable accommodations in her current position. She receives those accommodations and, as stated, has average or better job performance.

Despite those facts, Caterpillar refused to train her on the high-speed scanner. Caterpillar denied her request for a couple of different reasons. One reason was that using the high-speed scanner was not a requirement of her current job, and therefore the company was not obligated to train her to use it. Also, the main issue with using the high-speed scanner was the ability to quickly remove jams from the equipment, which incidentally occurred quite frequently. Based on her current accommodations, Caterpillar did not believe it would be possible for her to operate the equipment at the speed required.

The courts found merits with both sides of the argument. Supporting Caterpillar's position, the court determined that it was not obligated to train Shirley to use the high-speed scanner because it wasn't an essential function of her job.

However, that represented only part of her complaint. In addition, Shirley argued that being trained on the equipment would make her more eligible for other positions within Caterpillar. Therefore, denying her this training was still discriminatory and a violation of the ADA.

Here the courts sided with Shirley because Caterpillar made the decision not to provide training on the assumption that she would not be able to operate the equipment as needed. Under the ADA, making an assumption such as this is problematic. If Caterpillar wanted to deny Shirley training on the basis of her not being able to operate the scanner to the required level, then it should have properly evaluated her physical capabilities.[1]

The law interacts with the provision of training and development in many different ways. Sometimes it is explicitly mentioned in legislation. Similar to other areas of human resource (HR) management practice, employers need to be concerned about the potential discriminatory effects when selecting who will participate in a specific training or development activity. Even if it is not explicitly mentioned in a piece of legislation, the legal environment, which is external to the organization as shown in the framework opening this chapter, impacts the decision of whether an organization should provide employee training.

In most cases, the legal environment encourages organizations to provide their employees with training. The primary way that the law promotes the provision of training is by lowering an organization's potential liability for actions taken by its employees. When an employee injures another person, either a coworker or a customer, or even causes harm to him- or herself, the organization may be held liable for the damages that result. These injuries and damages can take many forms. An employee could literally physically hurt someone by not taking proper safety precautions. The injury could be economic in nature as in the case where a discriminatory employment decision was made (e.g., not hiring someone on the basis on race). Similarly, the injury could be emotional or psychological in the case of harassment. However, if an organization provides its employees with proper training to avoid these negative outcomes, it can point to that training as evidence that it took reasonable steps to limit the possibility that its employees would cause injury. Consequently, the employer would argue that it was not negligent and therefore should not be held liable for any damages incurred.

This chapter explores both the legal requirements and implications of providing employee training. Further, it discusses the ethical implications, particularly in relationship to equal employment opportunities. While much of the law, and this textbook, promotes the provision of training and development, the chapter also discusses the special case of independent contractors, one of the few situations where an employer would not want to provide an individual with training or development opportunities.

JURISDICTION AND ETHICS

Jurisdiction refers to whether or not a specific law applies to your organization. The major focus of this chapter, in terms of both legal coverage and ethical implications, is on laws that protect against discrimination, but it is not limited to these laws. Two important ways that jurisdiction is an issue for organizations in regard to discrimination are geography and size. Depending on how many people your organization employs or where it is located, a particular law may or may not apply to you.

In terms of organization size, most antidiscrimination laws provide for a threshold number of employees. Therefore, if your organization's workforce is under that threshold level, the law does not apply to you. For example, the Civil Rights Act states that it applies to companies with workforces of 15 or more employees. So, from a legal standpoint, if your organization only employs 14 employees, then technically you are not bound by the provisions of the Civil Rights Act. While it is interesting to note the employee threshold for these laws, you should keep in mind that if you work in an HR department, have HR in your job title, or even just have formal responsibilities for HR issues, then you are most likely working in an organization that meets the minimum threshold, and therefore these laws apply to your organization.

Besides size, geography represents the other key jurisdictional concern. For example, federal legislation and Supreme Court decisions apply to workplaces across the United States. For simplicity and applicability, this chapter covers the main components of these laws. However, this does not represent the totality of antidiscrimination legislation, nor does it cover the other laws that impact the provision of training and development. Many states, and even some counties and cities, extend employment protections to additional groups of which you need to be aware. For example, let us compare how protections differ between the states of Illinois and Missouri. This comparison is interesting because these states border one another and yet there are major differences in how they have chosen to extend employment protections. First, in the state of Missouri, as in the majority of states, it is legal for private employers to discriminate against someone on the basis of sexual orientation or gender identity. By comparison, the state of Illinois passed legislation to extend employment protections to those who identify as lesbian,

Exhibit 2-1 Status of Protections for Lesbian, Gay, Bisexual, Transgender, or Queer (LGBTQ) Workers by State

	Exclusively protects LGB workers	Inclusively protects transgender workers	Does not protect any LGBTQ workers
All workers	Wisconsin	California, Colorado, Connecticut, Delaware, District of Columbia, Hawaii, Illinois, Iowa, Maine, Maryland, Massachusetts, Minnesota, Nevada, New Hampshire, New Jersey, New Mexico, New York, Oregon, Rhode Island, Utah, Vermont, Washington	Alabama, Arkansas, Florida, Georgia, Idaho, Kansas, Louisiana, Mississippi, Nebraska, North Dakota, Oklahoma, South Carolina, South Dakota, Tennessee, Texas, West Virginia, Wyoming
Only public sector workers	Alaska, Arizona, Missouri, North Carolina, Ohio	Indiana, Kentucky, Michigan, Montana, Pennsylvania, Virginia	

Source: Human Rights Campaign, "State Maps of Laws and Policies." Available from http://www.hrc.org/state_maps.

gay, bisexual, transgender, or queer (LGBTQ). If you are curious whether your state extends protections to its LGBTQ workers, you can look it up in Exhibit 2-1. You should also be aware that this is an active area of employment law with efforts at both the state and federal levels to further expand these protections.[2]

What If a Law Does Not Apply?

Raising the jurisdictional issue is important because it provides an opportunity to consider the moral reasons that these laws were initially enacted. Specifically, these jurisdictional issues serve to illustrate the difference between legal and ethical behavior. Legally, if a law does not apply to your organization, then you by definition cannot violate it. Therefore, if you live in a state that does not protect a certain category of worker and/or have a company that is small enough that it fails to reach the threshold level of the law, then you cannot be successfully sued for that type of discrimination.

So, if you are safe from lawsuits, why don't you discriminate? One answer is ethics. On a personal and/or societal level, there is a recognition that it is not appropriate to discriminate against another person because he or she belongs to a certain group. Think of a couple of maxims under which many of us were raised. For example, there is "all men are created equal" from the Declaration of Independence. Similarly, there is the Golden Rule, which advises that you "do unto others as you would have them do unto you." Living by such teachings would seem to discourage discrimination. In addition, many professions have standards of practice that include reference to not discriminating. For example, in its Code of Ethics, the Society for Human Resource Management includes guidelines that state that its members should "foster a trusting work environment free of harassment, intimidation, and unlawful discrimination."[3]

But if you can't be sued, how are such ethical standards enforced? If organizations or individuals violate such norms, they may find themselves ostracized. Organizationally, this may be reflected in individuals choosing not to do business with you. Consumer boycotts are one of the most visible responses to organizations that have a reputation for discriminatory behavior. Many organizations and products have been boycotted to varying degrees of success. One of the most successful consumer boycotts was headed by Cesar Chavez and the United Farm Workers, who called for a boycott of nonunion grapes that resulted in improved wages and working conditions for the largely minority farmworkers in California.[4]

However, not all boycotts are equally successful. Two less successful boycotts focused on members of the LGBTQ community. These boycotts are discussed here because they operated in opposite directions. One boycott was called by progressives against Chick-fil-A for its corporate practices and contributions to causes that discriminated against the LGBTQ community.[5] By contrast, there have been boycotts from politically and religiously conservative groups against organizations such as Disney for their support of the LGBTQ community.[6]

In addition to consumer boycotts, which are visible, public, and can directly impact an organization's profitability, other individual and potentially less visible responses to discriminatory behavior can hurt organizational effectiveness. Discriminatory behavior can undermine the cohesiveness and effectiveness of work groups. Individuals who are the target of, or even a bystander to, discriminatory behavior will become demotivated and disengaged. This can lead to an increase in employee turnover, particularly if the organization allows the discriminatory behavior to persist. Such voluntary and arguably preventable turnover represents a real cost to the organization.

Of course, increased turnover presupposes that individuals are already employees. If an organization develops a reputation for discriminatory behavior, then this will result in a smaller applicant pool. Beyond members of the group that is discriminated against being less likely to apply for employment, discriminatory behaviors will also impact the career decisions of their allies and those offended by the general concept of discrimination. Smaller applicant pools generally make it harder for organizations to find the qualified individuals that they need and can result in higher recruitment and selection costs.

EQUAL EMPLOYMENT OPPORTUNITY

When people use the term *equal employment opportunity* (EEO), they are focusing on reducing discrimination. Within the domain of EEO, the main piece of legislation that people think about is the Civil Rights Act. First signed into law in 1964, the act was amended in 1991. When originally passed, the Civil Rights Act protected people on the basis of sex, race, color, national origin, and religion. These are the original **protected classes**. While subsequent pieces of legislation at the federal, state, and local levels have expanded the number of protected classes, they generally follow a similar pattern.

Exhibit 2-2 provides a list of the major pieces of legislation applicable to training and development and the classes of individuals that they protect. In addition to the original year that the legislation was enacted, Exhibit 2-2 provides a column stating when there was a major amendment to a particular piece of legislation. For example, as shown in the exhibit, the Civil Rights Act was originally passed in 1964 and was

Exhibit 2-2 Major Federal Laws Applicable to Training and Development

Act	Enacted	Amended	Summary	Jurisdiction
Equal Opportunity/Nondiscrimination				
Civil Rights Act	1964	1991	Title VII established protected classes/prohibits discrimination based on race, color, religion, sex, and national origin	Employers with 15 or more employees
Age Discrimination in Employment Act	1967	1978 and 1986	Established protected classes/prohibits discrimination based on age, but only for those 40 years old and older	Employers with 20 or more employees
Americans with Disabilities Act	1990	2008	Requires reasonable accommodation and prohibits discrimination for qualified individuals who have a disability, including those who have a history of a disability or are perceived to be disabled	Employers with 15 or more employees
Uniformed Services Employment and Reemployment Rights Act	1994		Prohibits discrimination and provides for reinstatement upon return from active duty	All employers
Pregnancy Discrimination Act	1978		Prohibits discrimination due to pregnancy, childbirth, or related medical conditions	Employers with 15 or more employees
Additional Legislation				
Occupational Safety and Health Act	1970		Employers have a general duty to maintain a safe workplace; depending on the job, there may be additional requirements regarding hazard communication and training	Private employers

amended in 1991. Laws such as the Civil Rights Act are typically amended to clarify or address issues that have been raised because of court challenges. The column showing the year amended is included in the exhibit to remind you that it is important to stay abreast of changes.

Civil Rights Act

Title VII of the Civil Rights Act provides that people be treated equally in compensation, terms, conditions, or privileges of employment. Training and development activities fall within this list, and training is specifically mentioned in the act. It is important to prevent discrimination with training and development not only for its explicit mention and inherent value but also in the more general roles it serves in organizations. From a positive perspective, training represents an opportunity to enhance employees' knowledge, skills, and abilities (KSAs), which will improve career opportunities and increase individuals' value to the organization. For example, individuals who have gone through training become eligible for more desirable work assignments, promotions, and raises. Someone who is denied the right to participate in a specific training program may become ineligible for subsequent organizational rewards and recognitions. Besides the positive perspective, there is the remedial nature of training. Being sent to a remedial training program could be viewed as potentially punitive or harassing, which could also lead to a charge of discrimination.

The potential to discriminate is present in both formal and informal training and development activities. The main area of concern is the selection of employees to participate in a given training or development activity. However, how someone is treated or evaluated within a training and development activity or program could also lead to a charge of discrimination.

Another thing to keep in mind with the Civil Rights Act is that all categorizations within a protected class are equally protected. For example, while women are protected on the basis of sex, so are men. Similarly, someone who is Caucasian is just as covered by the category of race as those who are Asian, African American, multiracial, and so forth. This in no way is meant to diminish the long history of discrimination against women, people of color, and others who were the inspiration of the Civil Rights Act, but is simply a statement of the broad coverage of the legislation.

This section continues with an explanation of the three ways that organizations may be found to be acting in violation of the Civil Rights Act. In each case, the name is descriptive of the type of discrimination that is occurring, and they are treatment, impact, and retaliation. Treatment is the most direct of the three violation types, with a specific decision or behavior having an immediate and/or visible outcome. Impact cases are the results of indirect or inadvertent discrimination, meaning that a decision or policy isn't meant to, visibly, be discriminatory but the outcome still is discriminatory. Finally, retaliation cases represent a negative organizational response to a charge of discrimination.

In addition, the term *adverse* or *disparate* normally precedes *treatment* or *impact*. Basically, adverse treatment and disparate treatment are the same thing, as are adverse impact and disparate impact. Both terms denote that people are treated or impacted differently. The key difference between the terms is that *disparate* is value neutral, simply meaning that two individuals, or groups, are treated or impacted differently. By contrast, *adverse* implies a value difference because *adverse* means something that is preventing success or is harmful. So while both terms are often used interchangeably, it is arguably more accurate to refer to discriminatory behavior as adverse versus disparate.

Adverse treatment.

As its names implies, **adverse treatment** occurs when employers treat their employees differently. Furthermore, this differential treatment is the result of some protected class status and results in a negative outcome for the person making the charge of discrimination. Of the types of discriminatory behavior discussed in this chapter, it is the most immediate, direct, and visible form. Because of its overt nature, adverse treatment is typically considered to be intentional.

Consider the following example and identify which, if any, of the reasons could result in a charge of adverse treatment. Corporate headquarters just sent Michael notice of the annual leadership training program that involves an outdoor/wilderness component, and you have to decide which of your employees to send. The only qualifications for the program are that the employee be a college graduate and have worked for the company at least three years. Based on those criteria, the two people on Michael's staff who qualify are Peter and Sally. In scenario one, Michael decides to send Peter because men make better leaders, so why waste the training on Sally? In scenario two, Michael still decides to send Peter because he is concerned that the outdoor/wilderness nature of the program will be too physically strenuous for a woman to complete. If both scenarios sound discriminatory to you, that is because they both are examples of adverse treatment. In each case, Peter is chosen because he is a man, and because sex is a protected class, Michael is guilty of adverse treatment.

If Michael told Sally that she was not going to receive training for either of those reasons, it would be a relatively simple case for the courts to decide. But even in the absence of a direct statement, it is still possible for Sally to demonstrate that she has been the target of employment discrimination. Sally would be able to show that she has received discriminatory treatment by establishing a *prima facie* case of discrimination through a four-part test.[7]

1. The individual claiming discrimination is the member of a protected class.
2. The organization/employer provides the training for its workers.
3. The individual was eligible for the training.
4. Others who were similarly situated, but not members of the same protected class, were provided with the training.

So let us walk through this four-part test to see how Sally could show that she was the target of discriminatory actions by Michael. First, Sally has to establish that she is the member of a protected class. Keep in mind that we are all members of a protected class; the key issue is which part of Sally's identity is the source of discrimination. Based on the information provided, it can be assumed that she is basing her case on sex, specifically that she is a woman. However, it is not uncommon for plaintiffs to argue that the decision was based on membership in multiple protected classes (e.g., race). Second, given the annual nature of the training program, the case satisfies condition 2 as well. Third, Sally has been with the employer for over three years and has a college degree. If she did not have a college degree or had been with the company for less than three years, then she would be unlikely to have a case. Finally, Peter, a man, was selected over her. Unless he was significantly more qualified because, for example, he had been with the company much longer and/or had advanced degrees, then Sally would have a strong case that she had been the target of discrimination.

Adverse impact.

Adverse impact is discrimination that occurs as a by-product of some seemingly neutral factor or policy. One implication of this is that adverse impact does not require animus or intentionality on the part of the organization. Common reasons that people get sent to training include their performance rating. This can be either positive, in that they qualify for advanced training, or negative, in that they require some level of remedial training. Typical ways of assessing employee performance, and by extension eligibility/need for training, are through regular employee appraisals and aptitude tests.

Ostensibly, the use of appraisals and tests would seem an appropriate and neutral method for determining who should or should not participate in training and development. However, if there is some bias in the appraisal process or an aptitude exam favors one group over another, then members of a particular protected class will be less likely to be selected into a training or development program. If the imbalance is sufficient enough, then the organization may be found guilty of adverse impact, even if it did not intend to discriminate against its employees.

Because there is not necessarily an overt cause of the discrimination, it is difficult to determine adverse impact from a single individual. Determinations of adverse impact rely on statistical analyses. The 4/5ths rule is the general guideline for determining whether or not a specific practice or test is discriminatory. For example, you have 100 men in an organization, and from an aptitude exam, 10 of them are identified as eligible for training. This means that there is a selection rate of 10%. Now if, in that same organization, there are 50 women, how many women will need to be selected in order for there to be no discrimination? Using the 4/5ths rule, the selection rate for women should range between 8% and 12%. Multiply this by the number of women, 50, and you may anticipate that between 4 and 6 women are also eligible for training. If fewer women are achieving the requisite score, this provides evidence that the aptitude exam may be resulting in adverse impact.

Selection issues as so far described represent only one of the ways that organizations can engage in adverse impact. When you are looking at a simple comparison of the selection rates between protected classes, you are focusing on what are known as **flow statistics**. In addition to flow statistics, organizations need to be concerned with *concentration* and *stock* statistics in regard to creating disparate impact. As the name implies, concentration statistics look at where employees are located. While definitely a concern with staffing and deploying employees, it is arguably less of a concern for training, relative to flow and stock statistics.

While people normally focus on flow statistics to determine adverse impact, stock issues may exist even if there are no flow problems. In the case of training and development, stock statistics look at the pool of those eligible to participate relative to those who apply to and/or actually participate. Let's go back to the earlier scenario of Sally not taking part in leadership training, but we'll change the facts some to explain how it could be an adverse impact case. The first change is that someone has to self-nominate or otherwise apply for the training. Michael is no longer the decision maker, so Sally has the same odds of being selected as Peter. For some reason, Sally doesn't apply, so Peter attends the leadership training. If you are thinking that it was Sally's choice so there can't be discrimination, what if we add to the scenario that this pattern is repeated across the company? Now the situation is that there are 20 Peters and 20 Sallys. In 6 departments, both Peter and Sally apply for the program. Half the time, Peter is selected, and the other half of the time, Sally is selected. The selection rates are the same, so there isn't a flow issue. However, in the remaining 14 departments, Sally decides not to apply. As a result, there are 17 Peters and only 3 Sallys in the leadership training program. In other words, 85% of the eligible men are in the program, and only 15% of the eligible women are participating. While this could be just coincidence, the disparity between those participation rates with the stock statistic that is 50-50 does bear closer scrutiny to determine if some common factor could be causing women not to apply and hence be creating an issue of adverse impact.

Impact beyond selection.

While this discussion of adverse impact has focused on selection for and participation in a training or development program, this is not the only time that organizations should be concerned about it. First, organizations should be aware that the method of delivery has the potential to create adverse impact. This is primarily a concern with training or development provided online. Although, as discussed in Chapter 8, one of the strengths of online education is to increase overall access to training and development, it also has the potential to create adverse impact because not everyone has equal access to online resources.[8]

Two other critically important areas include evaluation and transfer of training. While a longer discussion about evaluation takes place in Chapter 5 and 6, note that the method for evaluating learning, just as any neutral test, has the potential for creating adverse impact. Also, after a training or development program has been completed, managers need to be careful about adverse impact during transfer back to the workplace. Transfer involves using newly acquired KSAs and is discussed more fully in Chapter 6. For now, it will suffice to keep in mind that when managers create opportunities to utilize what was learned (i.e., assigning work tasks), they do so in a nondiscriminatory manner.

Retaliation.

Once someone raises a concern about adverse treatment or adverse impact, an organization needs to be careful that it doesn't engage in retaliation. A finding of **retaliation** can occur when the organization punishes or sanctions someone who has made a claim of discrimination. It is important to note that the person making the claim of discrimination is protected regardless of whether that individual is saying that she or he was the target of the discrimination or was simply the observer of someone else who was the target of discrimination. Similarly, individuals are protected from retaliation regardless of whether their initial charge is proved to be true or false.

Examples of retaliatory behavior include, but are not limited to, the following. With regard to development, an organization could be guilty of retaliation for not selecting a person for, or kicking a person out of, a mentoring program who had raised a charge of discrimination. Conversely, someone with a good performance record who is suddenly sent to remedial training after making a charge of discrimination could also be the target of retaliation. As is the case in many scandals, it is not necessarily the initial event but how the organization responds that causes the problem. Therefore, companies should take charges of discrimination seriously and be conscious of how they treat people who bring them.

Religion within the Civil Rights Act.

Religion represents a special case under the Civil Rights Act, which has important implications for organizational training. Specifically, the Civil Rights Act protects individuals on the basis of sincerely held beliefs and holds that they should be provided reasonable accommodations. A **reasonable accommodation** represents a change that makes it possible for a person to do his or her job, or in this case to participate in a training or development activity. What is considered reasonable will depend on the specific circumstances.

A common example of reasonable accommodation involving an employee's religion is scheduling. This often results when training is scheduled on a holiday and/or during a period of time when an employee's religion prevents him or her from engaging in work. Organizations can accommodate these employees by changing the date that the employee is expected to participate in the training. An alternative accommodation could involve changing the delivery format (e.g., from face-to-face to online).

A more complicated request for reasonable accommodation occurs when the employee states that his or her religious beliefs preclude the content of the training itself. While this may seem hypothetical, there have been cases where individuals objected to having to attend diversity training that they felt required them to support LGBTQ coworkers, customers, or patients in a way that was in conflict with their sincerely held religious beliefs. Although courts have determined that supporting diversity can represent a business necessity, organizations still need to be cautious about how and when they discipline their employees.[9]

One implication of referring to an accommodation as reasonable is that some requests for accommodation can be considered unreasonable. Unreasonable accommodations do not need to be provided to an employee because they are considered to represent an undue hardship. There are many reasons that a request for an accommodation could be considered unreasonable, but one example involves safety. Many religions involve requirements for or limitations on the type of clothing that followers must wear. Unfortunately, those requirements or limitations may compromise the ability of the employee to wear necessary safety equipment and/or may represent a hazard depending on the environment or machinery. In these cases, there may not be a way to create a safe training environment while also accommodating an employee's religious beliefs.

A complicating factor for the provision of reasonable accommodations on the basis of religion is that they are based on the individual's sincerely held beliefs. A consequence of this standard is that not all people who belong to the same faith will require the same accommodations. For example, if your organization had several Jews within its workforce and chose to hold a mandatory training program on a Saturday, many would not raise a religious objection and would simply attend. However, an observant Jew would reject on the grounds that Judaism does not allow work (which includes training) to occur on Saturday.

While you might want to say, "Sarah and Ben don't have an objection, so why can't *you* attend?" be careful. Making such a statement and/or disciplining an employee for not attending the training may be interpreted as a violation of the Civil Rights Act. This can be further complicated by the fact that you may have been previously unaware of that employee's religious beliefs and/or that person does not exhibit behaviors you feel are consistent with that level of religious observance. Acting as the judge of what is a legitimate religious belief is problematic under the Civil Rights Act.

Americans With Disabilities Act (ADA)

The Americans with Disabilities Act (ADA) impacts the provision of training and development in two important ways. The law was passed in 1990 and amended in 2008. The ADA prevents discrimination against individuals who are disabled. While the definition of disability may be considered broad, it is not an absolute guarantee that someone will be provided with a specific training and development opportunity. This is because an organization's responsibility to provide someone with training and development opportunities is limited to reasonable accommodation.

Let's begin by defining who is covered by the ADA.

"*In general. Disability* means, with respect to an individual—

(i) A physical or mental impairment that substantially limits one or more of the major life activities of such individual;

(ii) A record of such an impairment; or

(iii) Being regarded as having such an impairment"

It should also be noted that when the ADA was amended in 2008, it was motivated by the need to broaden who was considered disabled (which had been narrowed by court decisions). However, in addition to being disabled, a person needs to be qualified. Someone is considered qualified if she or he has the "requisite skills, experience, [or] education."

Reasonable accommodation.

One of the most important aspects of the ADA is that it provides for reasonable accommodation. Similar to accommodation based on religion, under the ADA, reasonable accommodation involves some alteration of the training to allow the individual with the disability to participate. You may be familiar with some training-related reasonable accommodations that are common on college campuses. First, there are the physical accommodations. For example, is the building or classroom wheelchair accessible? Especially if training is being conducted off-site, do not assume that a facility is wheelchair accessible. Other accommodations are more directly tied to the learning experience itself—for example, the ability to use a note-taker or alterations to the testing environment (i.e., time and/or location).

As the discussion of reasonable accommodation for religious issues shows, this can be a complicated issue. While there are some general concepts and recommendations for applying reasonable accommodation, it is important to keep in mind that each employee and situation is different. Therefore, the best thing for you to do is to keep an open mind and to avoid being judgmental. One of the frustrations that people often have with providing accommodations is not knowing exactly why an accommodation is needed. Regardless of whether the desire to know is motivated by basic curiosity, empathy, or cynicism, the fact is that medical information is private and you don't have a right to that information.

Having said that, it is a good idea to engage with the employee to determine how and which, if there are options, to implement. Although such a conversation is not mandated, it is a gesture of goodwill that can help result in better outcomes, both through determining how to make an accommodation as effective as possible and through employee engagement. Another reason to keep an open mind is that the need for accommodation may not be consistent across contexts. For example, there may be some employees who do not need any accommodation to perform their regular job duties but would need them if they were asked to participate in training. Alternatively, someone who is already receiving accommodations may not require any accommodations in order to successfully complete a training program. Because of this, it is important that someone's accommodation status does not influence training decisions.

While the purpose of the ADA is to see that people with disabilities are not discriminated against when they can be accommodated, there are limitations. Specifically, organizations are only required to provide reasonable accommodations. If an accommodation request is unreasonable and would be considered to create an undue hardship for an organization, then it does not need to be provided. An accommodation request becomes an undue hardship if it creates too great of a burden for an organization. The undue hardship can result from a burden that is excessive in terms of costs or the amount of restructuring that would be required in order to accommodate the employee.

A related consideration with the ADA is that accommodations are simply intended to give someone with a disability an equal opportunity to succeed. This means that if an accommodation is working, then no other performance accommodation is needed. For example, if there is a certification test at the end of a training program, someone who has an accommodation under the ADA does not receive extra points or have a lower passing score. Evidence that a disabled employee is not succeeding, however, may warrant a reconsideration of the accommodation that has been provided.

Another factor to consider with employees with disabilities is the potential impact of stigma. Some disabilities are associated with higher levels of stigma. Examples include, but are not limited to, mental illness and HIV status. This is particularly an issue in development activities because they are more one-on-one, less structured, and/or informal in nature. Stigma can undermine developmental relationships because one party believes that the other is not worthy of the opportunity or is concerned with contagion (physical or social). This is one of the reasons that disability needs to be covered by an organization's diversity training and related initiatives.

Section 508 of the Rehabilitation Act.

While the ADA is the dominant piece of legislation when it comes to providing accommodations for workers, it is not the only one. Section 508 of the Rehabilitation Act requires that technology used in training be accessible to all trainees.[10] Effectively, making technology accessible to employees with disabilities is the same as reasonably accommodating them. For example, closed-captioning video content can be described either as making it accessible to deaf trainees or as reasonably accommodating a deaf employee. While a more complete discussion of making technology accessible takes place in Chapter 9, it is useful to note for now that according to the Web Content Accessibility Guidelines (WCAG), there are multiple times and ways that accessibility is an issue with technology. The closed-captioning of video content focuses on the issue of perceivability. In addition to perceivability, the WCAG has guidelines for making sure that technology is operable, understandable, and robust.[11]

Age Discrimination in Employment Act (ADEA)

Just as employers need to be careful about making assumptions regarding disabled employees, they should also be careful that they do not limit training and development opportunities for older workers. Among the reasons that older workers might face discrimination are false beliefs that they lack the receptivity to be trained and/or represent a bad investment. If older employees are being discriminated against in training and development opportunities, then the ADEA places the burden on the employer to show that there is a "reasonable factor other than age" that explains the situation.

The ADEA was originally passed in 1967 and was amended in 1978 and again in 1986. The ADEA differs from other pieces of antidiscrimination legislation because of how the protected class is defined. Whereas the Civil Rights Act protects both men and women within the category of sex, the ADEA only protects older workers. Specifically, the ADEA only protects those workers who are at least 40. Therefore, individuals who are under 40 are not protected by this piece of legislation.

Affirmative Action

While the main goal of EEO legislation is to prevent discrimination from initially occurring, the law also provides for affirmative action, which is intended to promote the inclusion of systemically and/or historically underrepresented groups. Traditionally, affirmative action has been conceived as a way of addressing the underrepresentation of women and people of color. More recently, affirmative action plans have become more expansive with the inclusion of individuals who are disabled or veterans.[12]

Affirmative action plans are not without controversy. Some claim that they result in the hiring or promotion of underqualified individuals, which causes other groups to be discriminated against. Legally, this is not the case. Any plan that operates in that fashion would likely be deemed illegal.

A few basic tenets should be kept in mind that will help organizations address the need for affirmative action without inadvertently causing harm to another protected class. First, affirmative action plans should address a recognized need. If an organization already has a healthy (i.e., representative) level of diversity and does not have a history of discrimination, then there is not a need for affirmative action. Second, while affirmative action plans need to include goals, quotas are illegal. This means that while organizations need to engage in a good faith effort to hire and promote individuals from underrepresented groups, they should not hire or promote someone just because that person checks specific demographic boxes. Third, organizations need to periodically assess and review their affirmative action plans and progress to determine if any changes are warranted.

Organizational training and development can be either a target or a support for an affirmative action plan. Organizations that systemically and/or historically denied certain groups training and development opportunities need to include those activities in their affirmative action plans. For example, underrepresented groups may be at a disadvantage when it comes to developmental activities like mentoring. Not only is this problematic for the initial selection, but training and development activities are key to organizational advancement. So, when members of underrepresented groups are less likely to be provided with training or mentoring, then they are also less likely to be promoted.

Besides providing previously withheld training and development, there are other ways that training and development can be part of or help support an organization's affirmative action plan. First, there is basic diversity training. While the specifics of diversity training are discussed in Chapter 13, it is important to note here that in more supportive and welcoming organizations, employees will be more inclined to stay engaged, which will help with inclusion and promotion goals. In addition, training, for interviewers and those responsible for performance evaluations, that addresses the importance of standardization and covers rater biases (e.g., similarity bias) will have a beneficial impact on the selection and promotion rates of previously underrepresented groups.

LIABILITY AND THE PROVISION OF TRAINING

The main reasons for providing training should be proactive and positive in nature. This means that you should provide technical training to improve your employees' human capital in order to make them and your organization more efficient, flexible, innovative, and so on. Similarly, you should provide diversity training to promote a more respectful, progressive, and responsive culture. With that said, providing such technical and diversity training serves relatively defensive and protective functions as well. In both cases, the provision of training can reduce an organization's liability by countering claims of either negligence or harassment. However, there is a special case in which the provision could create a situation where an employer becomes liable. This can occur when the training is provided to what an employer considers to be an independent contractor.

Safety and Health

Safety and health represents one of the major categories of employee training. Workplace safety and health is governed by the Occupational Safety and Health Act (OSHA), which is implemented by the Occupational Safety and Health Administration. In order to safeguard worker safety and health, numerous standards have been developed. Some of these standards involve properly training employees. Therefore, if employers do not provide training that is required by an OSHA standard, they can be found in violation of OSHA.

OSHA protects workers against both documented and undocumented hazards. In the case of known hazards, there is the Hazard Communication Standard. As it name states, it requires employers to inform employees if they will be working around a known hazard (e.g., a carcinogen) so that they will be able to properly protect themselves. Even if a hazard is not documented, OSHA includes a **General Duty Clause** as a form of umbrella protection for workers. So even in the absence of a specific standard, if a certain work activity or environment creates a foreseeable threat to employee safety or health, employers are required to take steps to protect their workers. Such protection can take the form of properly training their employees.

Negligent training.

Not meeting the expectations of the General Duty Clause is just one way that an employer can be **negligent** regarding the provision of training. Employers can also be found liable for damages caused by their employees if they did not take the necessary steps to ensure that their employees were properly trained to do a specific task. This can include making sure someone is ready to work without supervision or that an employee has maintained certifications.

Affirmative Defense

While providing training is important to reduce the potential for injury or damages, nothing is absolute. This unfortunately includes the case of employee harassment. Harassment generally falls into one of two categories. First, there is the creation of a hostile environment. Hostile environments are created when an individual or a group of employees says things or takes actions, involving a protected class status (e.g., race or sex), that cause other(s) to feel intimidated or abused in a way that interferes with their ability to properly function within the workplace. Examples of this include racial slurs and sexist comments. Second, there is quid pro quo harassment. This type of sexual harassment involves the exchange of some tangible employment outcome for a sexual favor.

Employers that want to support and promote workplace diversity typically have taken steps to prevent such harassment. These steps typically include providing training to employees so they know how to avoid harassing their coworkers. In addition, these companies have well-defined reporting procedures that employees are also informed (i.e., trained) on how to access and use. Nontraining steps generally include maintaining confidentiality, investigating claims, and appropriately disciplining violators.

Although taking all these steps makes it less likely that someone will be harassed, it doesn't guarantee that harassment won't occur. Unfortunately, some people choose to be harassers regardless of how they are educated and despite the organizational culture in which they work. Assuming that the harasser is not a key manager or officer in the organization, the organization can claim it is not responsible for an individual's rogue action. Citing all the training and related steps it has taken to prevent harassment, the organization makes a case of an **affirmative defense** in order to avoid liability in a harassment case.

Independent Contractors

As this section has discussed, it is generally advantageous for organizations to provide their employees with training and development. But there is one instance when an organization might not want to provide training and development to someone. This is the situation when that someone is considered to be an independent contractor and not an employee. Employers have been increasingly making use of independent contractors compared to traditional employees. One reason for that is because independent contractors are not employees in the legal sense. As such, independent contractors are not owed a variety of benefits, including unemployment insurance and worker's compensation. This makes independent contractors a desirable way for organizations to staff themselves.

When an organization hires someone as an independent contractor, there is often a statement that clearly states the individual's status, and the person may even be required to sign a document stating he or she is aware of his or her status. Despite the existence of such statements and documents, individuals can, and do, challenge their employment status in a court of law. When deciding the appropriate status for that person (i.e., employee or independent contractor), the courts rely upon fact-based tests to make a determination. Although multiple criteria are used to determine whether someone is an employee or an independent contractor, providing someone with training is a factor that would contribute to the finding that the individual is an employee as opposed to an independent contractor.[13] Such a determination would increase an employer's liability. Therefore, organizations should be careful about providing training and development to individuals they consider to be, and would like to keep as, independent contractors.

CHAPTER SUMMARY

This chapter has covered many of the ways that the legal environment impacts the provision of training and development. Some of the impact is positive, meaning that the legal environment encourages the provision of training and development. For example, OSHA has provisions requiring hazard communication. Similarly, organizations may provide training to avoid charges of negligence and liability in the case that an employee's actions cause damages. This is one of the reasons that organizations provide diversity training, because the provision of such training can be used to establish an affirmative defense in case an employee accuses an organization of discrimination. As such, the positive impact of the legal environment on the provision of training and development focuses on the content of training.

Conversely, the negative impact of the legal environment on training and development focuses on the process side. Here, the legal environment is concerned not so much with what is taught but with who receives training and development. For example, organizations typically only train their employees. Because of that, the provision of training can influence a determination of whether someone is actually an employee and not an independent contractor.

In addition, similar to other functional areas in human resources, organizations need to be aware of the potential of, and avoid, discriminatory actions. The main categories of discrimination include adverse treatment and adverse impact. Treatment cases are generally more overt and intentional and tend to occur on an individual basis. Impact cases are the consequence of a seemingly neutral policy or procedure that results in a specific group or protected class being made worse off. Impact cases rely on statistics to provide evidence that a policy or procedure is discriminatory. In addition to these main categories, organizations can violate antidiscrimination laws if they retaliate, or take action against someone, for making a claim that discriminatory actions are occurring. This protection extends to someone regardless of the merits of the initial claim or if he or she is the target or reporter of the discrimination. Although we tend to focus on discrimination in regard to who is selected to participate in training, discriminatory actions can occur at all stages of training. Finally, this chapter has discussed why an organization adheres to the spirit of law (e.g., does not engage in discriminatory actions) even if the organization is not formally covered by the legislation.

KEY TERMS

Adverse impact. A seemingly neutral policy that results in discrimination based on a protected class.

Adverse treatment. Discrimination directed at an individual based on a protected class.

Affirmative defense. A legal argument where an organization provides evidence that it has taken actions to prevent discrimination or harassment to avoid being held liable.

Flow statistic. The primary type of data used to determine if a selection process results in adverse impact.

General Duty Clause. An OSHA requirement that employers reasonably take actions to protect workers against potential hazards.

Jurisdiction. Whether a law applies in a specific location or situation.

Negligent training. If harm results because an organization failed to provide an employee with training, the organization can be held liable for damages.

Protected class. The basis on which a person is covered by a piece of antidiscrimination legislation (e.g., race or sex).

Reasonable accommodation. Action an organization takes to allow an employee to participate on the basis of a disability (e.g., providing closed-captioning for individuals who are hearing impaired) or religion (e.g., scheduling training so it doesn't conflict with a religious observance).

Retaliation. Illegal actions that an organization takes to punish or discourage an employee for/from pursuing a claim of discrimination.

END-OF-CHAPTER QUESTIONS AND EXERCISES

Discussion Questions

1. Who is protected by the Civil Rights Act?
2. What is required to establish a *prima facie* case of adverse treatment?
3. How would your response to alleged discrimination against an LGBTQ employee change, and explain why, if the allegation occurred in Missouri versus Illinois?
4. How is the 4/5ths rule used to determine if discrimination is occurring?
5. What is the difference between flow and stock statistics?
6. If a fellow supervisor told you that she or he was going to discipline an employee for being a troublemaker, because she or he reported that she or he felt a coworker was being

discriminated against, what would you tell that supervisor?

7. What is required for someone to be protected by the Americans with Disabilities Act?

8. If an employee tells you that she or he can't attend a training program because the building where it is held is not ADA compliant, is it okay to just tell her or him to take the online version?

9. If you know someone is going to retire in a year, is it reasonable to turn down a request to attend a training program?

10. How can training and development support an organization's affirmative action plan?

11. What is an affirmative defense, and why is it important?

12. How does the Occupational Safety and Health Act promote employee training?

13. What does it mean for an employer to be negligent in the provision of training?

14. Should an organization provide training to an independent contractor?

Ethical Scenario

Leadership Potential

Samantha is a manager at Managing Expectations (ME), one of the top public relations firms in the city. ME is starting a leadership training program and has asked all department heads, including Samantha, to select an employee with the most potential to be promoted to participate in it. It's not an easy decision for Samantha because she has lots of good employees, so she pulls the most recent round of performance evaluations. Reviewing the evaluations, she eliminates several employees but by the end of the day is having a hard time choosing between Rachel and Simon. Samantha still has time to make the decision, so she decides to sleep on it. That night after dinner, she checks Facebook. Samantha has been careful not to friend anyone who works under her but has a few friends from work. Scrolling down, she sees that Crystal posted congratulations to Rachel. Curious, she clicks and sees that people are talking about Rachel being pregnant, which is news to her. Back at work, Samantha reads through the evaluations one more time and concludes that Simon would be better for the training program.

1. Do you support Samantha selecting Simon for the leadership training?

2. What are your thoughts on mixing social media and work?

2.1 Comparing Protections

How do the workplace protections where you go to school differ from those that are federally mandated? In order to answer this question, go online and visit the web page for the human rights commission (or equivalent body) in your state. You should also see if there is a commission or ordinance at the county or municipal level, which may have further expanded employment protections. Finally, look up the non-discrimination policy for your institution.

2.2 Discrimination Scenarios

The following hypothetical scenarios, similar to the case of Sally in the text, may be examples of discriminatory behavior. Read through each scenario and then discuss either in small groups or as a class the following:

1. What is the possible form of discrimination (e.g., adverse treatment or adverse impact)?

2. Which law(s) apply to the scenario, and why (i.e., which protected class is involved)?

3. Based on the information provided, would you say that there is evidence of discrimination (be sure to explain why or why not)?

4. If you do not feel there is a legal case, are there any ethical concerns?

Chris

Chris has been with the company for over 20 years. His performance reviews have been consistently excellent. In the past, you have sent him to training programs, and he has come back and shared what he has learned with the rest of the department. There is another one of those trainings coming up, but this time you decide to send Alex. Alex is a recent college graduate and is energetic, and besides, you have overhead Chris talking about joining AARP and getting the senior discount at the movie theater.

Jacob

Jacob has been with the company for 10 years and has fulfilled all his promise as a rising star. When you decided to set up a mentoring program for other high-potential employees, you knew that Jacob needed to be one of the mentors in the program. You went through a careful matching process for all the potential mentor–protégé pairs, and based on your assessment, the best match for Jacob was Alice. When you told Alice, she was excited. However, the reaction was not so positive from Jacob. He informed you that he couldn't mentor a woman because the level of intimacy required was inappropriate based on his religious teachings.

Angela

Over the past couple of years, Fortune 2000 has sent 50 of its associates to an advanced coding course. Associates who successfully complete the course usually are promoted within a year. Decisions on who to send to the course are based on an aptitude test that is administered every year. For the third year in a row, Angela felt good when she took the test, but she wasn't invited to participate in the training. After making a complaint, she found out that Fortune 2000 had only sent 10 women compared to 40 men to the advanced coding course. The company countered that only 40 women had taken the test in comparison to 160 applicants who were men.

Miguel

Miguel worked as a loan officer for Big Savings Bank for six years and always got above-average performance. One day soon after the new branch manager started, he had a client come in who started talking with him in Spanish. Seeing the customer was more comfortable with Spanish, he continued speaking to her in it. The next day, the branch manager told Miguel that he was being sent to a customer service training course. When he asked why, the manager said he found it was helpful for all his non-native-speaking employees. Miguel told him that it was both insulting and discriminatory to assume that because he is Latino he isn't a native speaker. He also let the manager know that he was born in Boston and is a native English speaker. The manager apologized and canceled the training. Miguel didn't think anything of it until six months later when the promotion to supervisor that his last manager said would be his went to someone else.

CHAPTER THREE

NEEDS ANALYSIS

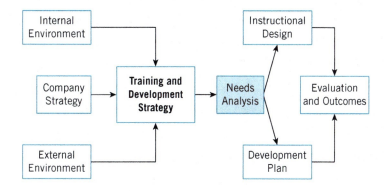

Learning Objectives

1. Explain how a needs assessment promotes effective organizational training.

2. Differentiate between the levels at which a needs analysis can be conducted.

3. Determine if an organization should provide training.

4. Develop a plan to conduct a job-level needs analysis.

5. Provide advice on how to conduct a person-level needs analysis.

6. Differentiate between needs and process theories of motivation.

7. Suggest alternatives to training to address performance issues.

Imagine you are the human resource director of a 200-person manufacturing firm. Overall, you could describe your staff as highly skilled. This reflects the low turnover among most of your employees and the tradition of more senior workers showing new employees what to do. While you remember from your college courses that formal on-the-job training is supposed to be better, you don't have a budget for training and so have decided that if it isn't broken, you're not going to fix it.

Starting a year ago, however, you started to get the impression that something may be broken. New hires had begun to miss the one-year performance numbers upon which you have come to expect and rely. By contrast, senior employees were still doing fine. So far, this hasn't become a major problem, but if the trend continues, it will become one, and you want to be proactive.

You begin your detective work by asking your senior employees what has changed. Are the new hires different? Have the senior employees changed how they are teaching the new hires? Or, has the job changed? The answers to all three questions are basically no, but the senior employees say they have noticed the same issue with the new hires.

Not sure what else to do, you decide to ask your new hires why they aren't learning. But you decide to be a bit more diplomatic in your approach. Your solution is to get them all in the same room so no one feels singled out. It takes some time for the new hires to start talking, but eventually they share a common frustration. The training they received from the senior employees was fine except when it came to a specific machine. That makes sense to you because if they didn't learn how to use that machine properly, it would explain the change in performance you have been seeing.

With this information, you go back to the senior employees. After you press them about what is different with the machine, they remember that two years ago there was a software update. They say it was a pain to adjust, but they all managed. When you ask what is different, they can't explain other than that, from years of experience, they "figured things out." Then you ask about the new hires who don't have years of experience. The senior employees reply that the new hires seem to get it, but they do acknowledge that the new hires make more mistakes and/or take longer to get things done.

Could this be the source of your problem? You count back and realize the lag time is just right to explain the performance problems you are noticing. You decide the answer is to create a more formal way of training the new hires as well as retraining those who have been missing the performance targets.

Conducting a needs analysis is an important step for organizations seeking to effectively implement training and development for their employees. The reason that a needs analysis is so important is that it answers questions about the training and development process. The most basic question it answers is whether a specific training or development program is appropriate for an individual employee. To answer this question, the needs analysis, at least in part, utilizes the information that comes before it in the framework that opens this chapter (i.e., environmental and strategic factors). A thorough analysis will clearly identify training needs and facilitate instructional design, which helps to ensure that the organization is making a good investment of its time and resources.

A needs assessment can be conducted at three different levels of analysis.[1] This chapter will discuss each of these levels in descending order from the most macro to the most micro level. It is also useful to conduct the analyses in this descending order. The most macro level of analysis is the organization level. An organization needs analysis produces information about what type of training or development is required or appropriate for the organization to provide. The middle level of assessment is the job level. A job needs analysis provides information on the type and scope of training or development required for someone to be successful in a specific position. The most micro level is the person level. The person needs analysis focuses on the individual who will be participating in the training or development. This level of analysis lets managers

Exhibit 3-1 Needs Analysis Checklist

Level of Analysis	Reasons or Content	Additional Considerations
Organization	• Strengths/internal drivers (i.e., reinforce existing advantages) • Weaknesses/internal drivers (e.g., customer complaints) • Opportunities/external drivers (e.g., train for growth) • Threats/external drivers (e.g., technological changes)	• Consider consistency with the organization's mission, strategy, and culture • Assess whether policies and procedures facilitate learning and transfer • Determine if the organization has sufficient resources to provide training
Job	• Results from organization-level analysis identify performance issues with a specific job • Job has changed or is expected to change in the near future	• Determine whether a task-based or competency-based focus is appropriate • Pick an appropriate method to conduct the needs analysis • Identify appropriate person(s) to include in the needs analysis
Person	• Employee needs to acquire a specific skill or knowledge for current position or expected transfer • Employee's performance is deficient • Employee needs to enhance knowledge, skills, or competencies for potential promotion	• Determine if employee is trainable • Verify the method selected to conduct the needs analysis is appropriately focused on development

know if a specific employee needs and/or is ready to participate in a specific training or development program.

Because a thorough needs analysis encompasses multiple levels, one can too easily forget a necessary component. To guard against this, and to provide structure to this chapter, Exhibit 3-1 provides a checklist of items that should be considered when conducting a needs analysis. As shown in the columns, two types of information should be collected and considered. First, the needs analysis should identify the reasons for or content of the training or development. Second, at each level, there are additional factors to consider regarding how to conduct the needs analysis and/or the appropriateness or readiness of conducting the training or development.

ORGANIZATION LEVEL

Although individual employees participate in training, that training is either paid for or provided directly by an organization. All organizations want to be sure that they are not wasting time or resources on something inappropriate, so before deciding whether to invest in an individual employee, an organization should engage in an organization-level needs assessment. The organization level of needs analysis is the most strategic of the three levels. As such, it addresses the question of whether training or development should be provided from multiple perspectives. One perspective focuses on the technical. Does or will the organization need employees with specific knowledge or skills to be successful? Another looks at the organization's strategy and culture to determine whether providing training or development is appropriate. This chapter begins with the latter and explores the question of whether training and development align with an organization's strategy and culture before considering technical needs or opportunities.

Organizational Alignment

One part of an organization-level needs assessment is to determine whether it is appropriate to deliver training. This is a question not of content but of whether the training should be provided at all. In fact, three general questions should be asked. First, is the training or development consistent with the organization's mission, strategy, and culture? Second, does the organization have the proper procedures and policies in place to both keep employees accountable and reward them for developing and utilizing the new knowledge or skills? Third, does the organization have sufficient resources to provide the training or development?

Organizational mission, strategy, and culture.

An organization's mission and overall strategic orientation, as shown in our overall framework, provides a starting point for determining whether it is appropriate to provide employees with training.[2] First, let's consider the generic organization strategies discussed in Chapter 1 and their impact on employee training. For example, organizations that adhere to a differentiation strategy are interested in innovation and quality. Not only does this rely upon a high level of training, but in order to promote innovation, it may be appropriate to train employees in areas that do not have immediate or obvious applications. This all-of-the-above approach to training can be contrasted with an organization whose strategy is better described as cost leadership. Cost leaders are concerned with efficiency. Training employees is important to the extent that it promotes efficiency. Therefore, it would only be appropriate to provide training that focuses on clearly applicable job skills. Consequently, knowing which strategy your organization is pursuing will provide a good initial indicator of whether it is appropriate to provide employees with training or development.

As for culture, management's commitment to training and development impacts the efficacy of those activities.[3] For example, are employees encouraged to engage in developmental activities? One indicator could be when training is scheduled. Organizations that require employees to engage in developmental activities during off-hours (i.e., on nights and weekends) may be sending a message that those activities are secondary, especially if that time is not somehow compensated. This can negatively impact employees' motivation to develop their skills, which in turn can impede learning (for more on motivation, see the "Person Level" section of this chapter).

In addition to the initial level of learning, culture can impact the extent that new knowledge and skills will be utilized once the training is completed. While there is an inherent value to gaining new knowledge, skills, and abilities (KSAs), employees must be able to effectively use them at work for organizations to realize a positive return on their investment in training and development. Organizations that do not encourage new ways of doing things and/or do not provide employees with the time or psychological space to practice will limit the use of KSAs gained.

Organizational procedures and policies.

There is also the question of whether the internal organizational environment is supportive of training. Let's begin this discussion by looking at the formal processes for evaluating and rewarding employees. Individuals are more likely to learn and then use new knowledge and skills if they are held accountable. This is especially true when there is not a clear connection, in an employee's mind, between a required training or development program and performance outcomes. For example, it is not uncommon for employees to question the value of attending diversity-related training or development programs. In these situations, research has shown that learning and transfer of behaviors to support diversity improve when employees and managers are made accountable.[4]

There are multiple ways to hold employees accountable. One method is to include the desired behavior in the employee evaluation process. This lets employees know that they will be evaluated on a regular basis as to how effectively they utilize the focal KSAs. When the training or development is provided by an external source (e.g., a university course), it is common for employees to deliver some sort of report or presentation on what they learned. Similarly, many organizations make tuition reimbursement contingent on a student earning a minimum grade in the course.

While holding employees accountable is effective, it is also a good idea to reward employees for acquiring and utilizing new KSAs. By rewarding employees, organizations increase their desire to both learn and subsequently utilize that learning (employee motivation is discussed more thoroughly in the "Person Level" section). One of the most tangible and direct ways of rewarding employees is through a salary or wage increase. However, a reward does not need to be monetary. One simple way to reward an employee is simply to allow him or her to utilize what was learned. That may sound silly or obvious, but all too often, organizations train employees and then do not give them the opportunity to practice what they have learned.

However, take care to ensure that it is possible to properly evaluate and reward an employee. Consider, for example, providing training on how to be a more effective member of a team. The ability to work in teams is one of those interpersonal skills that organizations often state are important. But is the organization properly set up to evaluate and reward team effectiveness? Culturally, the United States is an individualistic, as opposed to collectivistic, society. Consequently, performance tends to be evaluated and rewarded on an individual basis. So, organizations that want to promote truly interdependent teams need to realize that training and developing employees represents only one piece of the puzzle.

Sufficiency of resources.

When determining whether to provide employees with training or development, an organization needs to consider its resource capabilities. For example, what are the financial resources of the organization? In the previous discussion of rewarding employees, providing salary or wage increases is only possible if the organization has the financial resources to do so. When proposing providing employees with training or development, organizational decision makers often want to know the value proposition. This includes both the budget for providing the training or development and the expected outcomes (i.e., return on investment).

While finances are an important component of determining the feasibility of providing training or development, there are other factors to consider. First, does the organization have the capability to provide the training or development itself? This includes possessing both the personnel who would serve as trainers and the physical facilities and/or equipment required. If the organization lacks the internal resources to provide the training or development, it needs to search for a reasonable external provider.

A Training SWOT

While alignment issues are important, as shown in Exhibit 3-1 they represent just part of an organization-level needs analysis. Organizations also must determine what to provide. This involves looking at the content or reasons for providing training or development. One way of conceptualizing this part of the organization-level needs analysis is to consider what pressures the organization is facing. These pressures can originate either internally or externally to the organization, as shown in the framework opening this chapter where the internal and external environments precede the needs analysis. Strategically analyzing these pressures can be achieved through a **SWOT analysis**.

The SWOT analysis looks at four areas of the organization. Typically, this discussion would follow the order of the acronym, but because we are discussing it here as part of a training needs analysis, we will discuss the components according to their impact for determining what training should be provided. First, there are the pressures that generate a need to provide training or development—specifically, the weaknesses (internal pressures) and the threats (external pressures). This part of the SWOT analysis identifies areas of training or development that address organizational deficiencies or vulnerabilities.[5] While weaknesses and threats identify the clearest needs for training and development, strengths and opportunities are also important to know and are discussed later in this section.

Weaknesses.

Weaknesses represent things that an organization does not do well. Some of these deficiencies can be reduced or corrected by providing employees with training or development. Suppose, for example, an organization spends too much on the raw materials it uses as part of the manufacturing process. As a result, the company has a lower profit margin for the goods it produces. So how might this be a weakness that training or

> **Exhibit 3-2 List of Potential Weaknesses Addressable by Training or Development**
>
> Absenteeism
> Citations
> Customer Complaints
> Production/Service Time
> Recalls/Repairs
> Safety Record
> Waste

development could address? The answer is waste. How much waste is produced during the manufacturing process? More importantly, is that level of waste inevitable, or could employees be trained to make fewer errors and/or use materials more efficiently?

Waste is just one of many potential weaknesses that could be reduced or corrected with proper training or development.[6] Exhibit 3-2 provides a list of other potential deficiencies that could be identified as part of an organization-level SWOT analysis. Keep in mind that these factors are meant to be illustrative and not exhaustive. Also, some of the items listed are a matter of framing. Because we are focusing on weaknesses, for example, the table identifies customer complaints; however, that metric could be reframed simply as customer satisfaction. Similarly, the situation described in the opening vignette (i.e., new hires consistently not meeting performance expectations) is an example of a weakness.

Some of the items listed in Exhibit 3-2 may be less obvious and/or interrelated as in the case of absenteeism. Employees may be absent from work because they are recovering from a strain or injury that doesn't rise to the level of, or isn't reported as, a safety violation. Another explanation is that absenteeism is expected to be higher in organizations with inhospitable diversity climates,[7] which is why diversity training (discussed in Chapter 13) is so important. As the example of absenteeism illustrates, these weaknesses represent macro-level factors. So, while these factors may help identify a problem area, additional analysis may be necessary to determine the appropriate training or development program.

The items listed in Exhibit 3-2 can also serve a post-training purpose. Specifically, they can provide benchmarks for evaluating the effectiveness or value of the training or development provided. For example, if training has been prescribed to address a high level of customer complaints, then customer complaints should decrease post-training. Documenting this change in customer complaints is important to establish the effectiveness and value of providing training. More information on how and when to conduct an evaluation is provided in Chapters 5 and 6.

Threats.

Threats represent external challenges or constraints that impact the performance or success of the organization. While many threats will be specific to the industry in which an organization operates, there are some common categories of threats. These include challenges from basic competitive forces, such as technological advancements, as well as regulatory constraints.

These threats can impact how business is regularly conducted and thus necessitate training employees. While the timing of adopting a technological advance may depend on an organization's strategic orientation, learning new technology and competencies eventually will be necessary for most organizations to remain competitive. As for regulatory constraints, organizations need to make sure that their workforces are aware and properly trained to remain in compliance.

Strengths.

Strengths represent what an organization does well. When conducting a training needs analysis, it is easy for an organization to take its strengths for granted. However, organizations need to be aware of their strengths so that they can maintain and/or reinforce them.

Opportunities.

While opportunities may not have the same urgency as threats, organizations should still be on the lookout for them. Opportunities provide organizations with the chance to expand into new areas or exploit a potential competitive advantage. The extent of the need to train or develop employees to take advantage of them will depend on the nature of the opportunities.

JOB LEVEL

The job level of a needs analysis is essentially the application of a job analysis to training and development. With respect to training and development, this level of needs analysis identifies what a person needs to know to succeed within a specific position. As noted in Exhibit 3-1, the need for a specific group of employees to receive training or development may have been identified as part of the organization-level analysis. Regardless, a good starting point for a job-level needs analysis is a review of existing job description(s). Ideally, an organization should already be in possession of up-to-date job descriptions, which will provide the necessary benchmark information to conduct the job-level needs analysis.

The currency of a job description is a relative term. Some jobs are naturally more stable than others. For example, the rate of change in jobs that involve high levels of technology is generally faster than, say, the rate of change in jobs that are more administrative in nature. Therefore, technology-focused jobs (e.g., computers) should be analyzed more frequently. This is one of the reasons it is generally good practice to date job descriptions, as it provides a quick indicator to the trainer whether it will serve as a useful benchmark or if a new job analysis should be conducted.

Regardless of the currency of any existing job descriptions, you eventually will be required to conduct a job-level analysis. Therefore, this chapter reviews the main types and methods of a job analysis that apply to training and development. However, it is important to remember that other purposes for conducting a job analysis (e.g., developing compensation plans or selection criteria) may have additional concerns and issues.

Task-Based or Competency-Based

There are two general approaches to a job analysis as it applies to training and development. The more common approach is a **task-based job analysis**. As its name implies, this approach focuses on the tasks that employees engage in as part of doing their job. Tasks can be both broken down into specific job elements or aggregated into duties or responsibilities. As part of a task-based analysis, the necessary KSAs required to be successful are also identified. Because of this, the task-based approach is a useful method for conducting a job-level needs analysis.

The **competency-based job analysis** approach represents an alternative to the task-based approach that, while used less frequently, may be more appropriate. Instead of focusing on the tasks that a person does, the competency-based approach focuses more on the attributes that enable someone to be successful. Among the more common and generic competencies that an organization may look to develop are leadership and creativity. Competencies such as these easily span jobs, and employers often consider these factors when promoting individual employees. As such, a competency-based approach for conducting a job-level needs analysis is particularly useful when you are focused on employee development, as opposed to training.

Methods

There are numerous options for conducting a job analysis, some of which are highlighted in Exhibit 3-3. These methods are listed alphabetically as opposed to by utility. The utility of a method depends on what type of analysis you are trying to conduct (task versus competency) and what type of information you are currently seeking. The methods described as foundational are best used to start the job analysis process. The explanatory methods provide additional context and/or confirm the information provided by one of the foundational methods.

As this suggests, it is generally a good practice to utilize more than one method. Multiple methods are especially useful when there is not an existing job description or the existing one is significantly out of date. Finally, Exhibit 3-3 provides some advantages and disadvantages of each method. More detailed information for each method is provided in the individual subsections that follow.

Archival

Archival methods are a useful starting point for any job-level needs analysis. Archival sources are records that provide basic job description information that can be easily accessed. There are two main sources of recommended archival information. One source is an organization's existing HR records, such as job descriptions.[8] Similar sources of

Exhibit 3-3 Methods for Conducting a Job-Level Needs Analysis

Method	Type (Task or Competency)	Nature (Foundational or Explanatory)	Advantages	Disadvantages
Archival	Either	Foundational	Accessibility	Nonconfirmatory
Critical Incidents	Competency	Explanatory	Identifies success factors	Difficulty in identifying
Focus Groups	Either	Explanatory	Crowdsourcing	Requires good facilitation and time to analyze
Interview	Either	Explanatory	Depth/quality of information collected	Time to conduct and analyze
Job Log	Task	Foundational	Ease of administration	Sample size and time to analyze
Observation	Either	Foundational	Easy to conduct	Problems with sample size and misinterpretations
Questionnaire	Either	Explanatory	Ability to involve large number of respondents	Limitations of how questionnaire is designed

information include technical manuals and safety specifications.[9] If recent, they may be sufficiently current and useful that they preclude the need for additional analysis. Even if the information is outdated, existing job descriptions can serve as a benchmark or basis for subsequent analysis methods.

A second source of archival information is **O*NET**. O*NET is archival in the sense that it is a preexisting source of readily accessible information. This source is useful if an organization does not have existing job descriptions. O*NET is a service provided by the U.S. Department of Labor and is available online at onetonline.org. In its previous printed form, it was known as the *Dictionary of Occupational Titles*, which provides a better description of the information it contains. O*NET is a searchable database providing information on every job ever identified by the federal government. Basically, this is any job that you can imagine, and if there is not an exact match in the database, O*NET will provide a list of the most likely or similar options.

While O*NET is a good source of information, users should be aware of two things about its content. First, the amount of information it provides, even in the summary mode, is far greater than what is typically found in an organizational job description. Second, much of the information is generic and may not apply to a specific organization. For these reasons, it is important to follow-up an O*NET search with another form of analysis.[10]

Critical incidents.

Instead of examining the day-to-day activities of a job, **critical incidents analysis** focuses on the key moments that differentiate successful from unsuccessful performance.

In determining why someone successfully addressed or completed a critical incident, this form of analysis tends to focus on the characteristics or traits of the individual rather than on specific tasks. As such, the critical incidents method of analysis is more applicable to a competency-based approach and by extension more appropriate for determining developmental rather than training needs.

While the information elicited from a critical incidents approach is valuable for developmental purposes, it is used less often than other analysis methods, mainly because of the ambiguity and rarity of critical incidents. In order to be useful, a job needs to have critical incidents to analyze. Further, the number of incidents must be sufficient to discern which characteristics resulted in the successful outcome. The preferred method for gathering this information is through interviews.

Focus groups.

Focus groups are used to gather information from multiple people at the same time. An advantage of this approach is its crowdsourcing nature. Attendees at a focus group can build on the contributions of others to create a comprehensive description of a job and what training is needed. Another advantage of this approach is that the facilitator can ask follow-up questions. As such, this approach incorporates positive elements from interviews as well as questionnaires (both described later in this section). To improve the efficacy of this approach, it is helpful to organize participants based on the perceived similarity of training needs.[11]

If an organization chooses to use a focus group, there are a few potential disadvantages. First, a focus group is dependent on the quality of the facilitator. If a facilitator allows someone to dominate the discussion and/or does not include everyone, the value of its crowdsourcing potential diminishes. Second, focus groups tend to be more exploratory than the other explanatory methods listed in Exhibit 3-3, which means that it will take time to get quantitative results and may require additional analysis.[12]

Interviews.

Interviews involve asking people who know about the job what is involved. Traditionally, structured interviews are considered the most reliable and valid. Structure means that all interviewees are asked a common set of questions. This facilitates aggregating and analyzing the data. But unstructured interviews can be useful if dealing with a nontraditional or rapidly evolving job.[13] One advantage of interviews is that information is collected directly from a person in real time, which allows the person conducting the interview to ask follow-up questions and/or ask additional questions from those initially identified. The dynamic nature of interviews improves the depth and quality of the information collected.

When organizations decide to use interviews as part of the job-level needs analysis, they need to make several decisions. Assuming a structured interview is being used, they need to identify the questions that will be asked. These questions can be mainly exploratory if the job is evolving or there is no existing description, or confirmatory if there is an existing description.

Separate from the type of interview or questions being asked, it is important to decide who will be interviewed. This decision concerns the number of people to be interviewed as well as the type of person (e.g., job incumbents and/or their supervisors). As discussed in the next section, the source of information can impact both the results and outcomes of the analysis. As for the number of interviews to conduct, interviewing more people, in general, improves the quality and completeness of the results. If a job is noncomplex, then only a few people likely need to be interviewed. As the focal job increases in complexity and/or ambiguity, so too should the number of people interviewed; however, this also increases the time and effort needed to administer and analyze the results, one of the disadvantages of this method.[14]

Job logs.

Once completed, a **job log** provides a list of all the tasks that a person engages in over the course of a day. Whenever someone engages in a task, he or she records this information in the job log. Job logs can show both the variety of tasks (i.e., number of different ones) and their importance (i.e., how often a specific task is completed). As such, a job log can be particularly useful to distinguish between essential and marginal tasks, vital information for determining the need to provide an employee with accommodations. Given the task focus of the job log method, it should be used for determining training needs as opposed to developmental ones.

Both advantages and disadvantages accompany this approach. The main advantage is that it is a foundational method that can stand alone. Because job logs are open-ended by nature, limited research or preparation is needed prior to administration.

All that is needed is to properly instruct people on how to enter the information. If there is a sufficiently large sample, in terms of people and time, it may not be necessary to conduct an additional analysis method.

Unfortunately, representativeness can be a disadvantage of this approach. For example, a task—even an important one that occurs rarely—can easily be missed. Also, the quality of the job log depends on the diligence of the employees completing it. Someone who finds the process intrusive or cumbersome may not complete the job log conscientiously. One way of mitigating this is to employ a large sample of employees to complete job logs. While this should decrease the chance of missing important tasks, it will also increase the amount of time to aggregate and analyze data.

Observation.

Observation basically just involves the person conducting the needs analysis watching employees performing the job in question and then noting what each employee is doing. Although observation has its uses, we do not recommended that it be used as a stand-alone method of needs analysis.

Like the other methods discussed in this chapter, observation has both advantages and disadvantages. The best time to use observation is when there is no existing job description and you are having difficulty making sense of the information provided by other archival methods. Watching people perform their jobs will give the person conducting the needs analysis a sense of what and how people do their jobs. However, many problems come with this approach.[15] Without following up the observation with another method, it is too easy to make wrong assumptions about the job in question. This is particularly an issue if the needs analysis is for developmental purposes and the goal is to identify competencies. The other major problem is the sample. The amount of time that someone can observe a job is limited, so unless the job is very simple and/or repetitive, the observer is likely to miss important attributes of the job.

Questionnaires.

This method involves people responding to numerous questions about what and how they do their jobs. Two main characteristics of questionnaires are simultaneously advantages and disadvantages: the structured nature of questionnaires and the ability to collect information from large numbers of individuals.

Once a survey is developed and distributed, there is generally not an opportunity to make changes without starting over again. This means that questionnaires are highly structured. Normally, structure is a good thing. It means that everyone is asked the same set of questions. This makes it easier to aggregate and analyze the data. However, if the questionnaire has any problems, there isn't an easy way to correct them. Also, these issues may not become apparent until after the data have been collected.

The biggest problems that can occur with questionnaires are that they do not ask the right and/or enough questions.[16] There are two ways of addressing this issue, but both have their own issues. The first approach is to make the questionnaire as comprehensive as possible. This increases the length of the survey, which can negatively impact the response rate and/or diligence of respondents. One way that questionnaire designers hedge against that problem is to add open-ended questions. The downside of this approach is that open-ended questions take away from the standardized nature of the questionnaire. Consequently, the design aspect of this needs analysis method is critical.

Another important characteristic of questionnaires is their ability to gather information from large numbers of people. This is a positive for a couple of reasons. First, the general rule is that as more information is collected, the quality of the data and analysis will increase. Second, the questionnaire process allows more employees to be involved, and this provides them with a voice in the needs analysis, which should make them more satisfied with the results. There isn't an inherent con with the ability to collect information from a large number of people. But the design requirements of questionnaires mean that it is generally not worth the development time unless you have the numbers to justify this approach.

Sources

In addition to deciding how data will be collected, it is important to determine from whom you will collect the information. When deciding whom to include in the analysis, consider both the number and type of individuals. Increasing the number of people generally improves the quality of the analysis. However, the number of people to include in the analysis is in part a factor of the time you have and the method of analysis. More time will allow you to include more people. Also, the method of analysis will either facilitate large numbers (e.g., questionnaires) or encourage fewer sources (e.g., interviews and job logs).

Arguably more important than the number of people to include in the job-level needs analysis is the type of person from whom to collect information. There are three general types of people to consider including in a needs analysis: job incumbents, managers or supervisors, and subject matter experts. The choice of whom to ask can impact both the quality of the information collected and how people respond to the results of the analysis.

This decision relates back to the opening vignette. Depending on a person's role or perspective, she or he will provide information that, while truthful, may conflict with what another person reports. Exhibit 3-4 provides a quick overview of these three sources.

Job incumbents are a good source of information because they are the ones doing the job. Therefore, they can directly report on what they experience. The main concern here is the potential for disconnect between what employees do and what they are supposed to do. This can occur for two reasons. First, members of a work group may informally shift or trade job tasks and responsibilities. The potential impact of this problem increases if you only include one member of the work group in the job-level analysis. One way to minimize this problem is for the person to focus on the job details rather than what she or he does. Another potential problem is an issue called **job inflation**, which occurs when individuals assume and report additional tasks and responsibilities from what they should be doing.

Because of these issues, it is good practice to include either managers and supervisors or subject matter experts. The advantage of including these people in the analysis is that they have a better understanding of what someone in the job should be doing. However, it is still important to include job incumbents in the analysis process. Job incumbents may have problems with a manager- or supervisor-only analysis because of a feeling that managers and supervisors lack an understanding of the day-to-day reality of how things actually get done. There is also the concern that the analysis may be used to either expand or contract the job.

If either managers and supervisors or job incumbents are excluded from the job analysis, there may be a problem with buy-in. **Buy-in** involves the extent that a person agrees with, supports, and/or implements a decision. Generally, buy-in is greater when a person is included in the analysis process. For this reason, it is advisable to include a mix of managers and supervisors as well as job incumbents.

Buy-in is also a reason that subject matter experts should be used prudently. Even though subject matter experts are highly qualified, both job incumbents and managers

Exhibit 3-4 Advantages and Disadvantages of Information Source

Source	Advantage	Disadvantage
Job Incumbent	Knows the day-to-day realities of the job	Potential for job inflation/shifts in responsibilities
Manager/Supervisor	Knows what job should entail	May be perceived as controlling or unaware
Subject Matter Expert	Technical knowledge of the job	Costs

or supervisors may question the validity of their findings. As such, job analyses that rely exclusively on them may undermine employee buy-in. Still, these individuals are likely to have the best technical understanding of the job, and this may necessitate their use. This is particularly the case with new or rapidly changing jobs. Another reason to consider avoiding subject matter experts is the associated costs. However, using multiple sources is a good way to overcome potential problems related to self-serving biases.[17]

PERSON LEVEL

The third level for conducting a training needs analysis is the person level. As the name implies, at this level it is determined whether training or development is appropriate for a specific individual. There are two aspects to a person-level analysis. First is the question of need for training. One reason to provide training or development is to address deficient performance, which may reflect the need to acquire specific skills or knowledge or develop specific competencies. Another reason is to enhance a person's capability in preparation for a transfer or promotion.

Once a need is established, the second aspect of a person-level analysis is a determination of whether the individual is trainable. **Trainability** has two components. One is the issue of ability. Does the employee have the requisite preparation or capability, including self-efficacy (covered in Chapter 4), to successfully complete the training or development opportunity? Another is concerned with motivation. Individuals who lack motivation to participate in training or development are not considered trainable.

Conducting a Person-Level Analysis

Organizations have several options for conducting a person-level needs analysis. Exhibit 3-5 lists the methods discussed in this section that are unique to this level. Besides listing these methods, the exhibit identifies what type of information they provide, and notes how each could be used for an alternative purpose. Some methods from the job level

Exhibit 3-5 Methods for Conducting a Person-Level Needs Analysis

Method	Identifies Need	Assess Trainability		Alternate Use
		Ability/Preparation	Motivation	
Assessment centers	Yes	Yes	Depends	Succession Planning Selection
Placement/technical tests	Yes	Yes	No	Selection
Performance evaluations	Yes	Yes	Yes	Pay Raises Discipline
Skills inventory	Yes	Yes	No	Succession Planning

could also be used to conduct a person-level analysis, but for brevity, we will not repeat their description. The main example is an interview, but it is also possible to use observation or job logs.

Assessment centers.

The information provided by assessment centers is normally extremely comprehensive. The main purpose of assessment centers is to determine the extent of an employee's current abilities and competencies and readiness for promotion. Assessment centers used for developmental purposes, as opposed to selection, tend to focus more on competencies and interpersonal skills.[18] Developmental assessment centers generally produce reports and provide feedback to employees regarding their performance as well as recommendations for development. Assessment centers and reports tend to focus on development as opposed to training needs. While assessment centers can be used to assess employee motivation, either directly in the center or through a debriefing process, this is not always the case. As such, they do not always completely measure trainability.

Assessment centers often occur as part of a larger organizational effort in succession planning. They tend to be reserved for this purpose because, despite being extremely useful, they are also a relatively expensive method of determining an employee's needs. Consequently, assessment centers are typically reserved for executive-level employees and individuals identified as having a high potential for promotion to upper management. A more complete explanation of high-potential employees is provided in Chapter 10 as part of a larger discussion of succession planning.

Placement/technical tests.

One of the more direct ways to determine whether someone needs additional training and/or has the foundational skills necessary to learn and participate in training and development is through placement or technical testing. These tests are specifically designed to test the employee's KSAs. Based on the results, the organization will know to what extent the employee needs and/or is ready for training or development. You may have taken one of these tests when you started at your institution to determine which math, writing, and/or foreign language course you would need to take. As shown in Exhibit 3-5, while these tests measure ability, they do not usually provide information regarding motivation. Also, this type of testing could be used in conjunction with the organization's selection process.

Performance evaluations.

Performance evaluations provide a seemingly excellent opportunity to determine an employee's training and development needs as well as his or her trainability. One of the main reasons that they are an excellent opportunity is that most organizations tend to conduct evaluations on a regular basis. In addition to reviewing past performance, which addresses need and/or preparedness, often performance evaluations involve establishing goals. As part of the conversation to establish goals, supervisors can assess their employees' motivations, which addresses the second component of trainability.

While performance evaluations are potentially an excellent method for conducting a person-level needs analysis, there are a few things to keep in mind. The usefulness of performance evaluations is limited by their design and purpose. Employee development represents only one of the potential uses of performance evaluation data. Another important, and arguably more common, use is to determine merit raises. Unfortunately, it is difficult to frame descriptions of employee performance that would make it useful for developmental purposes but wouldn't also adversely affect a merit raise.

Besides concerns with the organizational intent of performance evaluations, their usefulness is limited by their quality. To determine this, there are several questions to ask about evaluations. First, is employee performance measured in a standardized and usable format? Second, have evaluators received training to minimize the impact of biases (e.g., similarity effects)? Third, does the evaluation process include an opportunity for employees to share their perspectives, interests, and needs? If the answer to all of these questions is yes, as well as having proper intent, then performance evaluations represent an excellent method for conducting a person-level needs analysis.

Skills inventory.

Similar to performance evaluations, personnel files potentially provide another excellent source of information for a person-level needs analysis. When this information is kept in a database as part of a human resource information system (HRIS), it serves as a skill inventory. These systems can keep track of a variety of training and development–related information—for example, what training sessions the employee attended and successfully completed, or information on certifications. In addition, these systems can be programmed to send alerts when employees are due for a refresher course. The main limitations of skills inventory involve the designed functionality and extent to which information is regularly updated. Another factor to remember is that while the information contained is good to assess needs and preparedness, it generally does not address employee motivation.

Motivation Theories

While understanding an employee's current level of ability and need to receive training or development is an important focus of the person level of analysis, the concept of trainability also makes it important to assess an individual's motivation to engage in training and development. Employees who want to learn are generally more successful in a training or development program and subsequently more likely to utilize what they learn. Therefore, it is useful to have a basic understanding of what may be motivating an employee. If employees are not initially motivated, understanding their needs, or what they value, will make it easier to persuade them to more fully participate and engage in training or development.

What motivates people to act is that they are missing something that they need or value. In order to satisfy that need or to attain what they want, they engage in behaviors

Exhibit 3-6 Differentiating Needs and Process Conceptualizations of Motivation

Needs	Process
Pyramid	Expectancy
Existence, Relatedness, and Growth (ERG)	Reasoned Action
Acquired Needs	Equity

that will achieve that purpose. People participate in training or development either because they are interested in learning and self-improvement for its own value, or because they feel that it will enable them to achieve something that they want (e.g., a promotion). Motivation theories are generally sorted into categories based on whether they focus on needs or values. Theories that view motivation through the lens of what people need are categorized as needs theories. Theories that look at what people value or involve calculations are referred to as process theories.[19] Exhibit 3-6 sorts the motivation theories described in this chapter. Related theories are discussed elsewhere in this textbook; for example, Chapter 4 covers reinforcement theory.

Pyramid.

Abraham Maslow developed a theory of motivation that is usually conceptualized as a **pyramid**.[20] Maslow theorized that people are motivated to satisfy one of five types of needs, shown in Exhibit 3-7. As the name implies, these needs can be sorted according to where they should be placed within a pyramid, starting with the basest need and then ascending up the pyramid to higher-level needs.

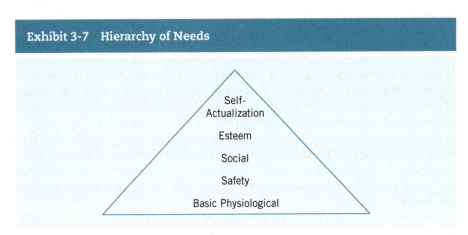

Exhibit 3-7 Hierarchy of Needs

Source: "A Theory of Human Motivation," Abraham Maslow, *Psychological Review*.

As shown in Exhibit 3-7, Maslow classified our basest needs as basic physiological. These needs are essential for survival. They also demonstrate how people tend not to be motivated by a need once it is satisfied. For example, modern plumbing means that many people take having access to drinking water for granted. However, under certain circumstances—for example, the Flint, Michigan, water crisis—these needs increase in priority and consequently focus attention and motivate behavior.

Safety needs expand on our basic physiological needs by moving from immediacy to stability. While still among our baser needs, safety needs start to become relevant in the employment context. Specifically, an employee may be concerned with job or financial security.

Ascending up the pyramid are social needs. These needs relate to the fact that humans are social creatures. As such, being part of a group, connected to other people, is important. This is inclusive of work groups. Training or development that is focused on socialization and/or provides opportunities to develop or deepen interpersonal relationships address this need.

Esteem needs are arguably the most consistent with why most people conceptualize that others are motivated to train. Included among esteem needs are concepts like recognition and status. This explains why many training or development programs provide certifications. Certifications, degrees, and ranks serve to clarify our level of expertise or status within an organization. Also, training and development can facilitate rewards like raises and promotions,[21] which are additional ways to satisfy esteem needs.

The pinnacle of the pyramid is self-actualization. Self-actualization is about individuals fulfilling their potential. Here employees engage in training or development not because of some external reward but because intrinsically there is a desire to learn and/or become a better person.[22]

ERG.

The acronym ERG stands for existence, relatedness, and growth. **ERG theory** reflects an alternative way of categorizing the needs that drive us and was conceptualized by Clayton Alderfer.[23] These needs are not fundamentally different from those listed in the pyramid. One good way of understanding ERG theory is to consider how existence, relatedness, and growth relate to the five needs identified by Maslow.

Mapping the pyramid's five needs onto the three identified by Alderfer is a fairly straightforward process. First, existence basically encompasses both basic physiological and safety needs. Next, relatedness is roughly the equivalent of social needs. Finally, growth clearly relates to self-actualization. As for esteem needs, those that are more externally focused should be categorized with relatedness, whereas those that are internally focused are consistent with growth.

Acquired needs.

According to **acquired needs theory**, people's needs are developed over time, shaped by lived experience, and not inherent. Among these are the need for affiliation, achievement, and power.[24] This theory was developed by David McClelland, and while still a needs theory, it is less consistent with ERG or the pyramid.

In describing the theory, it is useful to identify how it differs from the other needs theories discussed in this chapter. First, there is no equivalent to the existence, basic physiological, or safety needs found in the other theories. Instead, the third clear need identified is the need for power. In this context, power focuses on a person's ability to control others. There is no clear equivalent to this need in either of the other theories.

The remaining needs, affiliation and achievement, do parallel the other theories. Affiliation focuses on our need to establish and maintain relationships and has the strongest connection with the other theories. Specifically, this need corresponds to relatedness, and by extension love and belonging. As for achievement, here the focus is on our need to accomplish tasks and be successful. There is some connection to growth and esteem needs, but the link is not as clear as with the need for affiliation.

Expectancy theory.

The first of the process theories discussed in this chapter is **expectancy theory**. This theory was developed by Victor Vroom and has three components: expectancy, instrumentality, and valence.[25] The theory is named after the expectancy component. According to the theory, motivation represents the force or effort individuals are willing to expend on a specific behavior or action. Individuals determine or predict how much force can or will be exerted using the calculation presented in Exhibit 3-8, which involves all three components.

To explain how expectancy theory functions, it is useful to consider an example with which you are likely familiar: the decision you make as to how hard to study for a specific exam. According to the equation, F stands for force, essentially the level of motivation. In the context of studying for your exam, think of it as the amount of time and/or intensity that you choose to study.

To determine force or motivation, the first thing to consider is E (expectancy) of studying. Expectancy is the perceived relationship between your actions and your performance. In the context of the exam, will studying more or harder raise your grade? The more you believe that studying will improve your grade on the exam, the more motivated you will be to study.

The next thing to consider is the I (instrumentality) of studying. Instrumentality is the relationship between your performance and an outcome. How will your grade

Exhibit 3-8 Equation to Determine Motivation

$$F = E \sum(I * V)$$

Source: Vroom, V.H. (1964).

on this exam affect your overall class grade? For example, imagine you are on the cusp of getting an A in the course, assuming you do well on the exam. In this scenario, your performance matters, which means you are more motivated to study. Conversely, if you can do enough extra credit work that your grade on the exam doesn't matter, you will be less motivated to study for the exam.

The last letter of the equation is *V* (valence), focused on the value of the outcome. In this example, the last question you need to ask yourself is whether you care how you do in the class. Let's assume you plan to apply to law school after graduation, in which case having a high GPA is important. In this scenario, because you care about your grade, you are motivated to study. Alternatively, you have caught a case of *senioritis*, and all you want to do is graduate. In that case, if you are confident you will pass (based on the other components of expectancy theory), you will be less motivated to study.

Before completing this discussion of expectancy theory, we present two important caveats. First, although the example used is extrinsically focused, that is not a requirement of the theory. As long as an outcome is valued (valence), it doesn't matter if the outcome is something extrinsic and measurable or intrinsic and intangible. Second, the equation contains a Σ, sigma. This means that an individual's level of motivation may be influenced by more than one valued outcome. Some of these additional outcomes will be complementary and increase motivation. In the current example, eligibility for a scholarship would be complementary and result in studying harder. Conversely, the outcome could be competitive and decrease motivation. For example, you need to work at your internship where you hope to receive an offer of employment after graduation.

Reasoned action.

A process theory of motivation that is similar to expectancy theory is **reasoned action theory**, developed by Martin Fishbein and Icek Ajzen.[26] The motivational force in this theory, referred to as behavioral intention, is influenced by two factors. First are the person's attitudes toward the behavior. Positive attitudes are similar to the calculations made in expectancy theory and are associated with greater behavioral intentions. Second are subjective norms, or communal and cultural forces that influence how we behave. Similar to attitudes, positive subjective norms are associated with greater behavioral intentions.

Of course, these two factors do not always work in concert with one another. It is possible for attitudes to be positive and subjective norms to be negative, and vice versa. Weighing your personal assessments against external influences results in how strong your behavioral intentions will be. This explains why it is important for an organization to have a strong positive and supportive culture for training and development. In such an organization, even if an employee does not personally see the benefit of engaging in training or development, he or she may participate because social forces so strongly encourage it.

Equity.

The final process theory discussed in this chapter is **equity theory**, developed by John Stacey Adams.[27] Equity theory helps to explain both motivation and satisfaction. According to the theory, people want to exist in an equitable relationship and are motivated to work toward achieving that. If a person is in a position of positive inequity, also known as overpayment, then he or she will increase his or her contributions in order to reestablish balance. However, if the person experiences negative inequity, also known as underpayment, then theoretically he or she will decrease his or her contributions in order to reestablish balance. Negative inequity decreases satisfaction and helped to spur theories of organizational justice.

So how do people determine which equity state (equitable, positive, or negative) they are currently experiencing? First, they weigh their inputs and outputs. Inputs are the contributions that a person brings to a relationship. In an employment context, inputs include the employee's education, certifications, experience, and effort expended. Conversely, outputs include pay, position, and work opportunities. Individuals then compare the ratio of these inputs to outputs to a referent other to determine whether they are being treated equitably or being undercompensated or overcompensated.

The impact of equity theory on employee motivation to engage in training or development is more cautionary than explanatory. Keep in mind that training and development serve to increase an employee's perceived inputs. Consequently, the employee will expect a commensurate increase in outputs (e.g., salary). If not, then he or she will likely experience negative inequity, which will result in dissatisfaction and/or reduction in contributions that he or she controls (e.g., work effort). Even if the employee was in a state of positive inequity (i.e., overpayment), he or she might still reduce contributions because the addition of training or development would mean that he or she wouldn't have to work as hard to reduce the inequity. Alternatively, the person might pick a different referent other, which would result in no increase in effort. Finally, if an employee is asked to participate in training or development seen as remedial in any way, while perceived similar employees are not, this will likely result in negative outcomes such as reduced satisfaction or increased counterproductive workplace behaviors.[28]

RESULTS OF A NEEDS ANALYSIS

Besides determining whether a specific training or development program is appropriate for an individual employee, as stated in the introduction to this chapter, there are two key outcomes from a training needs analysis. First, it allows for the creation of learning objectives, which serves to facilitate the provision of training and development. The second outcome is an understanding of why training is not appropriate, which may also identify alternative actions to address performance issues.

Learning Objectives

While correctly diagnosing a need to provide training or development is important, organizations also want to be sure that their employees are learning and then utilizing the right content. This involves taking the information collected as part of the needs analysis to create learning objectives. Learning objectives represent the specific instructional goals that address the more general content areas identified during the needs analysis. While this discussion focuses on the purpose of learning objectives, a more detailed explanation on how to craft them is provided in Chapter 4.

For example, the needs analysis may have determined that a person requires training because of customer complaints. While the needs analysis will likely have determined if the employee needs technical training (e.g., lacks sufficient knowledge of the organization's product or service) or interpersonal skills training (e.g., customers do not feel the employee addresses their needs), both issues are still fairly general. Interpersonal skills can be further subdivided into content areas like active listening and conflict resolution (as discussed in Chapter 12). Trainers will want to ensure that they cover all the relevant points of the specific topic. These relevant points become the basis for learning objectives. Staying with active listening, these would likely include the ability to distinguish between different types of listening, explain what steps to take to ensure you are actively listening, articulate why active listening is important, and successfully engage in active listening.

Once learning objectives are identified, they facilitate the successful provision of training in multiple ways. First, they ensure that the content of the training covers all the necessary material. Second, evaluation materials (discussed in Chapters 5 and 6). can be developed to ensure that trainees are learning the material as well as successfully utilizing what they have learned back at work. As such, learning objectives improve the effectiveness of training and development.

Why Not to Train

This final section addresses that the result of the needs analysis could be that training or development may not be the most appropriate answer to the situation.[29] Although this may seem odd for a training and development textbook to state, it is important to recognize that providing training or development may not always be the right thing to do. Understanding why a training or development program may not be appropriate will help to differentiate the multiple levels at which a needs analysis can and should be conducted.

There are three general reasons why an organization should not provide a specific training or development program.[30] First, it is not right for the organization. Second, it is not right for the job. Third, it is not right for the employee. These three general reasons correspond to the three levels at which a needs assessment can and should be conducted.

Organization level.

So, what does it mean for a training or development program to not be right for an organization? As discussed in Chapter 1, organizations have different strategic orientations.

The implication of some of the orientations, such as cost leadership, means that the organization may be less inclined to provide its employees with certain types of training or development opportunities. So, unless the training or development is somehow required, focused on reducing liability, and/or not available outside the organization (e.g., involves organization-specific knowledge), the organization is more likely to determine that it should not be provided. Aside from a generic strategy, each organization should have its own mission and vision statements. These statements should drive many organizational decisions. For example, if an organization's strategy is focused on a specific market (e.g., college students), providing employees with training focused on another market (e.g., baby boomers) is less likely to be productive. Further, the organization may not have a supportive culture or policies in place to encourage employees to participate in training or development. Additionally, the organization may lack the resources to provide the training.

Job level.

Even if the training or development program is appropriate for the organization, based on its strategy, it may not be appropriate at the job level. There are two reasons why this may be the case. First, there may be alternatives that would be more effective or efficient. For example, instead of training employees on how to maintain an outdated piece of machinery, a better option might be to replace it with a newer piece of equipment.[31] The new machinery would pay for itself because it would require less maintenance and/or employees would not require additional training to maintain it.

At the job level, it is also important to determine if the training or development is appropriate for specific job(s) or group(s) of employees. Within an organization, people perform various jobs with differing responsibilities and tasks. What may be appropriate for employees in one job may not be necessary for others, or what employees need to know may differ by their job or function. For example, an organization that has decided to implement a new performance management system needs to train its supervisors on how to conduct employee appraisals, but it would probably be unnecessary to provide that same training to nonsupervisory employees. Often, this answer will be technical and obvious, as new techniques, rules, or technology relate only to specific jobs within an organization.

Person level.

Even if a training or development program is appropriate for an organization and a job, it may still be inappropriate for a specific employee.[32] As the expression goes, you need to learn to walk before you can run. If an employee is missing the foundational skills or prerequisite training, then providing more advanced training is likely to be inefficient and ineffective. This isn't necessarily an indictment of the employee. Many employees, especially those who are new to a position, generally need more basic training before they are ready for advanced opportunities. Therefore, the training or development program would be inappropriate, but just for now. As that employee builds experience and/or masters more basic knowledge and skills, she or he will be ready. However, sometimes the results of the person level of the needs analysis process are an indictment of the employee. In these cases, the problem is that the employee lacks the ability or willingness to perform at a given level. In these unfortunate cases, the answer is not training or development, but something more serious. If the issue is just technical, and the employee is otherwise a good one, then the organization may consider a transfer. Otherwise, the appropriate decision may be discipline or even discharge.

CHAPTER SUMMARY

This chapter looked at the process of determining the need and appropriateness of providing an employee with a specific training or development program. The chapter also discussed reasons why it might not be appropriate to provide an employee with training or development. To make this determination, you should consider multiple levels of information. First, is the training or development appropriate for, or needed by, the organization? Next, what does the job itself require? Finally, does the specific employee need the training or development? Further, is the employee trainable, which looks at both preparation and motivation? Going through all these steps will help ensure that the organization is making the best uses of its training and development resources.

When considering the appropriateness from an organizational perspective, there are a couple of factors to consider. First, does providing the training or development to the employee align with the organization's strategy and culture? Next, does it address a specific need? To determine need, the chapter suggested that organizations conduct a training and development–focused SWOT analysis. For example, are there any known weaknesses (e.g., poor safety record) that providing training or development could correct or mitigate?

When conducting a job-level analysis, several decisions need to be made. First, are you conducting a needs analysis focused on tasks or competencies? Your choice of focus will help determine the appropriateness of the method (e.g., interviews or job logs) you use to conduct the needs analysis. The final important decision to be made at the job level is whom to include. Some combination of job incumbents, supervisors or managers, and subject matter experts will be used. Using multiple sources serves to increase the quality and reliability of the analysis as well as the buy-in and acceptance of the results by the employees, who will be asked to participate in the training or development, and their supervisors or managers, who will be asked to support them.

The final important level of needs analysis is the person level. Having determined that the training or development is needed and appropriate for the organization and job, you need to make sure that it will be effective and useful for the specific employee. The person-level analysis has multiple components. In addition to determining whether the training or development is needed, you must assess the employee's trainability. Trainability considers both the employee's technical readiness and his or her motivation to participate in the training or development. These final steps will help ensure that the training or development program will be effective and a good use of organizational resources.

KEY TERMS

Acquired needs theory. The theory that people are motivated by one of three needs (affiliation, achievement, or power).

Buy-in. The extent to which employees agree with the findings of an organizational decision, such as the results of a needs analysis.

Competency-based job analysis. An approach to job-level needs analysis that focuses on the abilities and traits (e.g., creativity) employees need to be successful in their jobs.

Critical incidents analysis. A method for conducting a job-level needs analysis where the focus is on key events and interactions rather than all tasks that are performed.

Equity theory. The theory that people are motivated by maintaining equilibrium between their contributions and organizational rewards.

ERG theory. The theory that people are motivated by one of three needs (existence, relatedness, or growth).

Expectancy theory. The theory that people are motivated by assessing the connection between their behavior and desired outcomes.

Job incumbent. A person who is currently performing a specific job.

Job inflation. Occurs when job incumbents report that they engage in higher-level or additional tasks than they should be.

Job log. A method for conducting a job-level needs analysis where employees record each task that they perform as it is completed.

O*NET. A repository of basic information produced by the U.S. Department of Labor for all types of jobs.

Pyramid. The conceptualization that people are motivated by a hierarchy of five needs (basic physiological, safety, social, esteem, and self-actualization).

Reasoned action theory. A theory of motivation related to expectancy theory that adds the contribution of subjective norms to the equation.

SWOT analysis. A strategic planning method that is useful for conducting an organization-level needs analysis of strengths, weaknesses, opportunities, and threats.

Task-based job analysis. An approach to job-level needs analysis that focuses on the actions (e.g., writing a report) that employees perform in order to complete their jobs.

Trainability. A measure of an employee's readiness to participate in training that encompasses both ability and motivation.

END-OF-CHAPTER QUESTIONS AND EXERCISES

Discussion Questions

1. How can a SWOT analysis be used to determine an organization's training and development needs?
2. Explain how an organization's culture can influence the decision of whether to provide training or development.
3. What is the difference between task-based and competency-based analyses?
4. When and how can O*NET be used as part of job-level analysis?
5. Compare and contrast foundational and explanatory methods of needs analysis.

6. When conducting a job-level needs analysis, is it better to use focus groups or questionnaires?

7. Why is it a good idea to include job incumbents in a job-level needs analysis but a bad idea to only use them as a source of information?

8. What needs motivate someone to participate in training or development?

9. How does acquired needs theory differ from other needs theories?

10. How would expectancy theory help you to determine how much effort you would put toward learning new knowledge or skills?

11. Explain why it is or is not a good idea to overcompensate for attending a training or development program.

12. Discuss the pros and cons of using performance evaluations for a person-level needs analysis.

13. Discuss the relationship between learning objectives, needs analysis, and the success of a training or development program.

14. At the job level, what alternatives do organizations have to providing employees with training?

Ethical Scenario

The Focus of a Focus Group

Paul decided to use focus groups to conduct a job-level needs analysis for the customer service representatives at Cache 22 Security Systems. Paul felt it was more efficient than individual interviews, and he didn't know enough about what the representatives do to construct a questionnaire. At the start of the focus group, Paul asked the participants to be as honest as possible as this would ensure that any training they did receive would help them be more successful and not waste their time. He also let them know that he would be taking notes but didn't say that he was writing down the names of who said what.

One thing he found interesting was that some of the representatives updated their customer files right away while others waited until the end of the week or when things were slow. He mentioned this to Frank, one of the customer service supervisors, because he wondered how important it was to do that task. Frank was obviously bothered and said not updating the system was one of the major issues generating customer complaints and that Paul should tell him which employees weren't updating their files right away so they could be disciplined.

1. Should Paul have recorded who said what during the focus group?

2. Should Paul share this information with Frank?

3. Besides training, how else could the company address this issue?

3.1 Organizational Alignment

Assume that the provost of your institution has come to your class to help determine what training or development opportunities should be provided to your faculty. From the following list of potential training and development topics, identify and explain which option is the most important to provide and which is the worst fit for your institution. Base your decision and explanation on what you know about your institution's mission, culture, history, and other characteristics.

Topics:

1. Becoming more entrepreneurial
2. Conflict resolution
3. Writing successful research grants
4. Addressing the needs of international students

5. Developing an effective online course
6. Implementing innovative face-to-face teaching methods

3.2 Conducting a Job-Level Analysis

Using a job assigned to you by your instructor, or one of your choice (if so directed), conduct a job-level analysis using any two of the methods discussed in this chapter. Then:

1. Discuss the person(s) from whom you collected information and explain why you chose them.
2. Summarize the information from each method.
3. Discuss the differences you collected and experienced from the multiple methods.
4. Combine the information from the multiple methods and sources to produce a job description.

3.3 What Motivates You?

Review the six motivation theories discussed in this chapter. Which one best describes your personal motivation most of the time, and why?

CHAPTER FOUR

LEARNING THEORIES

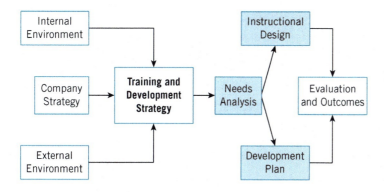

Learning Objectives

1. List the domains and subdomains of Bloom's Taxonomy and organize them from lowest to highest level.

2. Identify which level of Bloom's Taxonomy is applied to learning objectives.

3. Describe the different learning theories.

4. Identify learning theories used in different training and development interventions.

5. Compare and contrast the differences between pedagogy, andragogy, and heutagogy.

6. Design a training program taking into account adult learning assumptions.

7. Summarize the differing learning theories and recommend the best approach to address different learning styles.

8. Assess the unique needs of each generation in the workplace and recommend training and development interventions consistent with those needs.

While the chief learning officer (CLO) is a common fixture in top management teams today, organizations have not always valued having the human resource function in the C-suite. It took the foresight of General Electric (GE) to make the decision to appoint the first CLO in a major corporation. Steve Kerr was on faculty at the University of Southern California when he was tapped to first consult with, and eventually work full-time for, GE as its CLO. Kerr led what is considered to be the most prestigious corporate management training program, ranked first in 2014 by the "Aon Hewitt Top Companies for Leaders." Kerr is quoted as saying, "It was my 15 minutes of fame. Then I had to figure it out. My job became to identify the barriers. What is it about the way we organize work and build rewards? What is it that keeps people from wanting to communicate, and what adjustments in rewards, and norms, and so on would create more motivation?"

According to Bersin by Deloitte, the CLO must hold a full complement of skills including business analytics, technology, learning theory, performance consulting, and scientific inquiry.

Further, the firm argues, today's CLO must play five distinct roles: chief capability officer, chief leadership officer, chief change officer, people technology and measurement officer, and chief talent officer.

- Chief capability officer—must focus on understanding the detailed capability requirements of critical positions in the company. Companies that focus on capability outperform those that focus solely on skills-based training.
- Chief leadership officer—must understand, drive, and/or own the company's leadership development, integrating functional training with leadership training.
- Chief change officer—must play a critical role in creating and driving change at all levels of the organization.
- People technology and measurement officer—must be comfortable with technology and data, and utilize them to deliver learning and measure outcomes.
- Chief talent officer—must understand the role training and development play with other talent management functions, such as recruiting, performance management, employee engagement, coaching, succession planning, and compensation.

CLOs must be able to use every tool in their toolbox to help employees learn what is essential and impact the organization's bottom line. Learning techniques they use include coaching, engagement, mentoring, and management training. The bottom line is that learning isn't just about obtaining skills. It is about assessing the type of learning that is strategically important to the organization and developing an integrated system to engage employees to be psychologically invested in the learning process and reinforce their ability to utilize those skills and capabilities across the organization. Learning is considered a strategic business imperative, and organizations need to ensure their human resource systems are prepared to address learning at all levels of the company.

Source: Adapted from Curtis J. Morley, "How the Chief Learning Officer Got Its Name," *eLearning Industry*, December 31, 2014, http://elearningindustry.com/chief-learning-officer-clo-got-name; and Bersin by Deloitte, "Solutions: Learning and Employee Development," https://www2.deloitte.com/us/en/pages/human-capital/solutions/bersin-employee-development-methods-for-hr.html.

The concept of learning elicits images of students, sitting in rows, listening to their teacher lecture on the topic of the day. It is a term closely linked to educational systems across the globe. **Learning** is defined as the acquisition of knowledge or skills through experience, study, or being taught. Learning is at the core of training and development; it facilitates individuals taking in information and using new knowledge or skills to better do their jobs now and in the future. As our opening vignette shows, learning isn't just something you can force upon employees. You can place them in training programs, but a willingness to learn is what enables them to be successful. Therefore, no matter how much we understand learning theories, it is important that employees are willing and motivated to learn.

Individuals may learn a particular skill to do their job today, but increasingly, training and development professionals think of learning as more broad-based, and much more related to long-term career development.[1] The rise of the chief learning officer as a C-suite position informs the industry that learning, both short- and long-term, has value for organizations and is the strategic focal point for competitive advantage.[2]

Given the variety of things employees must learn to do their jobs effectively, there isn't a one-size-fits-all approach to instruction and learning. Some things are best learned through firsthand experience. Others are best learned through reading, memorizing, and reciting the information. In developing training and development programs, care must be given to consider the best way to deliver new information such that it maximizes the ability of the person to learn and utilize the information provided. We discuss how to deliver different kinds of information in Chapters 7 and 8; however, this chapter is dedicated to *how* people actually learn.

Learning and learning style theories address the manner in which people absorb, process, and retain information. They are important to training and development because employees who need to develop new knowledge, skills, and abilities (KSAs) to do their job don't always learn the same way. As well, things that employees need to learn must be taught in a certain way to maximize the employees' ability to understand and apply the material.

For example, you may run a local grocery store in your community. The people you hire to cut, trim, and package meat need to learn through hands-on experiential exercises, whereas the cashiers would better benefit from verbal instruction on how to use the cash register and scanner. A lecture format would not give the meat cutters ample time to develop their skills, as meat cutting is a specialized skill that requires a lot of manual practice. Your assistant store manager will learn how to navigate store problems and customer concerns through social learning and observing the store manager. In short, each skill that employees use in the workplace must be imparted in a different and unique way so it is optimally learned. While there is still some debate as to whether individuals do, indeed, have preferred learning styles that should be considered when developing training and development programs, it is important to ensure individuals have retained the information and are able to use it. Knowing the different ways people learn can help trainers develop appropriate programs.

Our chapter framework highlights the needs analysis, instructional design, and development plan boxes. Learning theories inform how training programs are designed or development plans are made by taking into account information learned during the needs analysis phase. Once we identify what employees need to learn, the next step is to determine the best way to help trainees learn the material. The material being learned, the means of learning employed, and the learning outcomes expected must be aligned. Learning theories help us ensure the material learned achieves the desired outcomes.

BLOOM'S TAXONOMY: WHAT PEOPLE LEARN

Before we can address how people learn, it is important to establish exactly what people learn. In essence, as people engage in the learning process, what are typical objectives or outcomes of learning? Benjamin Bloom, along with colleagues, developed a taxonomy of learning objectives that is used in education but also applies to training and development.[3]

As shown in Exhibit 4-1, **Bloom's Taxonomy** has three main learning domains: cognitive, affective, and psychomotor. The **cognitive domain** involves knowledge and

Exhibit 4-1 Bloom's Taxonomy of Learning Outcomes

Domain	Subdomains (Highest to Lowest Order)
Cognitive	• **Evaluation**—present and defend opinions by making judgments about information • **Synthesis**—build a structure or pattern from diverse elements • **Analysis**—examine and break information into parts by identifying motives and causes • **Application**—use acquired knowledge to solve problems in new situations • **Comprehension**—organize, compare, translate, and interpret learned material • **Knowledge (Remembering)**—exhibit memory of learned materials
Affective	• **Characterizing**—build abstract knowledge about attitudes, emotions, and feelings • **Organizing**—put together different values, information, and ideas to accommodate them within one's own schema • **Valuing**—attach value to an object, phenomenon, or piece of information • **Responding**—actively participate in the learning process • **Receiving**—passively pay attention
Psychomotor	• **Origination**—create new movement patterns to fit a situation or problem • **Adaptation**—modify movement patterns to fit special requirements • **Complex Overt Response**—perform motor acts that involve complex movement patterns • **Mechanism**—learned responses have become habitual • **Guided Response**—learn a complex skill that includes imitation and trial and error • **Set**—be mentally, physically, and emotionally ready to act • **Perception**—use sensory cues to guide motor activity

Source: Adapted from Lorin W. Anderson and David R. Krathwohl, eds., *A Taxonomy for Learning, Teaching, and Assessing: A Revision of Bloom's Taxonomy of Educational Objectives* (Boston: Allyn and Bacon, 2001).

comprehension of facts and concepts. The subdomains include (from lowest to highest) knowledge, comprehension, application, analysis, synthesis, and evaluation. At the lowest level, this involves information that is memorized. As the cognitive domain increases, learners must understand, apply, and extrapolate to other situations.

The **affective domain** involves how individuals relate emotionally to knowledge—specifically, how they gain feelings, values, and attitudes about the given topic. The affective domain includes (from lowest to highest) receiving, responding, valuing, organizing, and characterizing. When learners are able to affectively and emotionally engage with the material they are learning, the likelihood that they will learn and utilize the information increases.

The **psychomotor domain** depicts the ability to physically utilize an object, such as a tool. The subdomains include (from lowest to highest) perception, set, guided response, mechanism, complex overt response, adaptation, and origination. Similar to the cognitive domain, the psychomotor domain moves the learner from basic sensory cues for how to use a new tool, to adapting and extrapolating use of a tool in a new context.

While the original focus of Bloom's Taxonomy was directed toward primary and secondary education, understanding the taxonomy has applications for workplace training as well.[4] It isn't enough to just memorize new information to perform a job. Employees are expected to both understand and apply to workplace situations the KSAs they learn. All three domains should be used where appropriate to maximize learning outcomes for employees. Effective training and development programs ensure trainees are provided with the knowledge they need to do the job, but also the skills needed to apply that knowledge to achieve high levels of performance. How to accomplish that transfer is addressed in greater detail in Chapter 6. Bloom's Taxonomy, however, provides trainers with a good checklist of domains to consider when designing training programs, as illustrated in Chapters 7 and 8. Setting learning objectives is addressed in Chapter 5, but it is important to note here that trainees don't necessarily need to see them. Bloom's Taxonomy was developed for teachers and trainers, not for trainees, so it provides a guideline for creating the learning objectives to design the training. Trainees need to know what they will be learning, but not necessarily in the form of a structured training objective.

LEARNING THEORIES

While there are many theories of how people learn, a subset of those theories is relevant to training and development in organizations. **Behaviorism** focuses on the observable behavior as evidence of learning. **Cognitivism** posits the learner should be viewed as an information processor, like a computer. **Constructivism** argues learning is an active, constructive process. Lastly, **humanism** sees learning as a personal act that is instrumental in fulfilling one's potential. While each theory in and of itself does not fully explain the learning process for individuals in organizations, understanding how each theory contributes to the way people learn can provide us with guidance for how to best develop training programs for employees.

Behaviorism

Behaviorist theories of learning are probably the most familiar theories related to learning, training, and development. Generally speaking, behaviorists believe that people are passive and learn from stimulus–response and social modeling. Within the behaviorist theories of learning, we find three relevant theories: classical conditioning, operant conditioning, and social learning theories.

Classical conditioning.

The most famous researchers associated with **classical conditioning** are Pavlov[5] and Watson.[6] Classical conditioning, considered a building block for how people learn, is based on so-called associative learning. Pavlov's dogs are a prime example of classical conditioning. The dogs were given an unconditioned stimulus, meat powder, and exhibited an unconditioned response, salivation. After a while, the dogs began to associate events with introduction of the meat powder. Eventually, all Pavlov had to do was sound a bell (conditioned stimulus), and the dogs would start to salivate, even if the meat powder was not provided (conditioned response), because they believed that the meat powder would follow the sound of the bell. Watson performed similar tests with a human baby, inducing fear in the baby by associating a loud noise with the presence of a rat. While experiments like Watson's would likely be considered unethical by today's standards, his work, as well as Pavlov's, provides insight into the stimulus–response approach to learning, or learning at its most basic level. Although it may be difficult to see how classical conditioning directly impacts training and development, it's more important to understand how classical conditioning influenced other behaviorist theories of learning.

Operant conditioning.

B. F. Skinner took classical conditioning a step further and introduced rewards and punishment as a way to reinforce the behaviors one wanted an individual to learn.[7] **Operant conditioning** is the basis for reinforcement theories of motivation, and helps individuals make the association between a particular behavior and a consequence. For example, once a desired behavior is observed, a reward is introduced so the behavior continues and becomes "learned"; and, conversely, after the observation of an undesired behavior, a punishment is introduced so the behavior is discouraged and becomes "unlearned." The individual learns that rewards come from exhibiting desired behaviors, and punishment comes from exhibiting undesired behaviors.

Reinforcement theories explain the way managers and employers ensure newly learned desirable behaviors introduced in training programs, such as a new work process or a new computer program, are rewarded. Rewards can be monetary, such as a pay increase or a bonus, or they can be nonmonetary, such as verbal praise and thanks for a job well done. The reinforcement theory of motivation requires two factors to impact behavior: consequences for the behaviors, and the schedule for which the consequences are meted out.[8]

There are four basic approaches to applying consequences: positive reinforcement, negative reinforcement, positive punishment, and negative punishment. Reinforcement increases a behavior, and punishment decreases the behavior. With positive reinforcement, a stimulus or reward is given when an individual exhibits the correct behavior. When employees learn a new skill, they may receive a pay increase for performing well. Negative reinforcement involves an undesired stimulus that is either removed or avoided in order to increase the desired behaviors. For example, to avoid getting yelled at by your boss, you make sure to submit your report on time in exactly the format the boss likes.

Positive punishment adds an undesired stimulus after an individual exhibits an undesired behavior. For example, the first time an employee is late, a note goes in his personnel file indicating he has violated company policy. Negative punishment involves removing a desired reward or privilege as punishment for exhibiting a behavior. If an employee takes advantage of a company's unlimited sick day policy, her pay may be docked for the time she was absent after a certain allotment of days.

After the type of consequence to deliver to either increase or decrease behaviors, the next consideration is the time schedule for communicating the reinforcements. While constant reinforcement may have some appeal, we know from research on perception that after a while, individuals will ignore a constant stimulus because it no longer grabs their attention. As such, a constant reward or punishment will make the learners indifferent to the consequences because it will eventually stop gaining their attention.

In lieu of a constant stimulus, reinforcements can be delivered on either a ratio or interval schedule. A fixed interval means after a certain amount of time goes by, a reward may be delivered. For example, receiving a semimonthly paycheck means employees know that they will get paid twice a month, without fail, for the work they perform. A variable interval means the time between reinforcements may vary. Random drug testing works effectively using a variable interval, as employees never know when they may be tested.

A fixed ratio means after a certain number of behaviors are exhibited, the learner receives a reward. Sales commissions work as a fixed ratio. Salespeople know for every number of items they sell, they will receive a certain reward. A real estate agent makes a 7% commission on the sale of a house, so if the sale price for the house is $100,000, the guaranteed commission to be received is $7,000. A variable ratio means the rate at which the stimulus is received after exhibiting behaviors will vary. A slot machine in a casino is an example of a variable ratio. Machines are programmed to pay out after a varying number of pulls on the lever. In one instance, it may take 100 pulls to get a reward, while the next time a reward may be provided after only 25 pulls. Because the reward is unexpected, it reinforces the learner to keep pulling the lever because the reward may come at any time.

Reinforcement is one important way to get employees to engage in desired behaviors. Whether employees are following company policies or learning new skills on the job, consequences and reward systems must be in place to ensure the behaviors are not just learned, but internalized and made habitual. As discussed in Chapter 6, in order for KSAs learned in training sessions to be continually reinforced and utilized on the job, trainers should reward the behaviors with desirable incentives.

A 2018 article in *TD* magazine highlighted a form of behavioral learning conceptualized by educational psychologist Edward Thorndike.[9] In this article, the author discussed applying behavioral learning to personality assessment training—an area of training often neglected when it comes to the application of learning theories. The article highlights why personality assessment training must follow the same learning theories and offers three important "laws" of learning: first, the readiness (law of readiness) such that trainees learn best when they are both prepared and engaged; second, the time to practice (law of exercise), as trainees learn best when they have time to repeat what they are learning multiple times; and, third, a positive environment established for learning (law of effect). Not only should the learning environment be positive, but the third law also posits that positive application of material will increase the likelihood of learning, whereas negative application of material and unpleasant ideas will decrease the likelihood of learning and retaining the material.

Social learning theory.

Social learning theory posits that people learn from each other via observation, imitation, and modeling.[10] According to Albert Bandura, who developed this theory, four conditions are necessary for effective social learning and modeling: attention, retention, reproduction, and motivation. Attentional factors increase or decrease the amount of attention paid to the modeled event. Retentional factors help the individual remember what was observed. Reproductive factors increase the likelihood the individual can reproduce what was observed. Lastly, motivational factors are an individual's reasons for imitating what was observed. Exhibit 4-2 illustrates the steps for social learning.

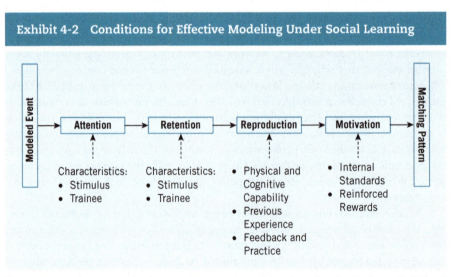

Exhibit 4-2 Conditions for Effective Modeling Under Social Learning

Source: Adapted from Albert Bandura, *Social Foundations of Thought and Action* (Englewood Cliffs, NJ: Prentice Hall, 1986).

Bandura moved beyond the basic stimulus–response point of view of Pavlov and argued that learning involves a cognitive process, can occur by observing both behavior and the consequences of behavior vicariously, and can occur without an observable change in behavior. Reinforcement can impact learning, but not at all times. Lastly, reciprocal determinism plays a role such that cognition, the environment, and the learner's behavior all mutually influence each other so the learner is not simply a passive recipient of information.[11] Typical stimuli for learning include live modeling, verbal instruction, and symbolic modeling (such as characters in the media or in literature).

The skills needed to successfully model behavior parallel some of the domains of Bloom's Taxonomy highlighted in Exhibit 4-1. The characteristics of the stimulus (modeled behavior), as well as the trainee's characteristics, affect which aspects of the modeled behavior will get the trainee's attention, similar to the way the perceptual process works. The learner needs to develop awareness about which KSAs are important to model, and must have the capacity to perceive and understand the modeling. Once the modeling has gotten the trainee's attention, he or she must figure out how to organize the information in order to retain it. The ability to organize and retain the information is again influenced by the stimulus and trainee characteristics.

After organizing and retaining the information, the trainee must reproduce the modeled behaviors. His or her cognitive and physical abilities, previous experience with similar training, and ability to learn from feedback impact the extent to which the modeled behavior can be reproduced. Lastly, one must consider the motivations for modeling the behavior, including the presence of reinforcements like rewards and incentives, as well as the trainee's own internal standards of performance. Trainees are far more likely to adopt a modeled behavior when there is a positive outcome and positive reinforcement for the behavior, than when there is a negative outcome and negative reinforcement.

Social learning theory plays an important part in training and development programs. Employees involved in mentoring programs can model the behavior of their mentors. Employees who are apprentices getting on-the-job training in certain trades are also learning through live modeling, as well as verbal instruction. Trainees using computer-based training to learn new KSAs are using symbolic modeling if they are expected to model behavior they see in an online training program. When the conditions are favorable, as shown in Exhibit 4-2, trainees are better able to learn and demonstrate the KSAs obtained through modeling.

In terms of trainee characteristics, Bandura argues that the single most important factor to consider is the trainee's **self-efficacy**, or the belief in one's ability to succeed in specific situations or accomplish a task.[12] In order to succeed at modeling another's behavior, the extent to which trainees believe they can actually learn the KSAs must be high.

Self-efficacy is an important predictor of a trainee's readiness to learn and, as discussed in Chapter 3, an important consideration during needs analysis. A trainee's self-efficacy is influenced by how much others encourage the trainee to succeed, the similarity of the new KSA to past KSAs learned and mastered, how confident and successful peers are who are modeling the desired behaviors, and how successful the trainee was in previous training situations.[13] High self-efficacy is likely to lead to individuals working hard, even if the training is difficult or poses obstacles. Those with low self-efficacy are more likely to give up, or simply withdraw if they face difficulties or obstacles. Self-efficacy is important not just for learning but also for transferring what is learned in training sessions to the job. This is discussed further in Chapter 6.

We can make a few conclusions from the discussion on self-efficacy and learning. First, high self-efficacy can help ensure the trainee is successful, both within the training program and in transferring the material to the job. High self-efficacy enables the employee to work hard to achieve the training goals and also transfer the training and learning success to daily practice (see Chapter 6). Second, it is important to note that self-efficacy isn't a fixed trait. Employees can develop higher self-efficacy with the support of their supervisors, managers, and organizational leaders. By focusing on helping employees with low self-efficacy to believe more in their ability to accomplish a task or succeed in a training program, the organization helps build overall confidence within its employees and increases the likelihood that training programs will, in fact, be successful.

Cognitivism

Cognitivism differs from behaviorism because it posits people are more than just programmed to respond to stimuli.[14] People must be active participants in their learning process, and observable behaviors are a representation of the cognition going on inside the human mind. As noted in Bloom's Taxonomy, higher-level cognition involves problem solving and developing mental constructions of what trainees are experiencing and trying to learn. Learning happens when the mental constructions adapt or change based on the new information obtained. Like a computer, information enters the trainee, it is processed in the brain, and certain outcomes occur based on the information and the way it is processed. Two examples of cognitivism are cognitive load theory and information processing theory.

Cognitive load theory.

Cognitive load is the total amount of mental effort being used in working memory.[15] John Sweller argues that when designing instructional programs (in our case, training programs), cognitive load must be reduced to maximize learning. Cognitive load has three components: *intrinsic*, *extraneous*, and *germane*. Intrinsic load is the effort associated with a specific topic, for example the difficulty of learning algebra versus advanced calculus. There is an inherent difficulty in all instructional topics that is immutable, or unchanging. Extraneous load is associated with the means the trainer uses to present information to the learner. The more complex the means used to present information, the higher the extraneous load. The germane load is the cognitive load used to process, construct, and automate the information. Because cognitive load is additive and intrinsic load is considered immutable, trainers can have the greatest impact on managing cognitive load by using instructional design methods that minimize cognitive load so more cognition can be focused on processing, constructing, and automating the new information. If trainers can manage extraneous load to simplify the way material is presented

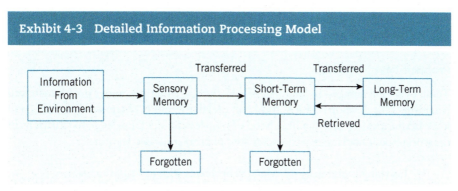

Source: Adapted from "Information Processing Theory," *Learning-Theories.com*. Available from http://www.learning-theories.com/information-processing-theory.html.

and ensure it matches the learning going on, then more cognition can be focused on managing the germane load.

Information processing theory.

Learning occurs through the process of memory encoding and retrieval, according to **information processing theory**. Richard C. Atkinson and Richard M. Shiffrin originally developed this idea, called *stage theory*.[16] It has been adapted over time to include David C. Rumelhart and James L. McClelland's *connectionist model* that argues information is stored simultaneously all over the brain, connected as a neural network.[17] Information processing is generally thought to have three major components: sensory memory, short-term memory, and long-term memory. This basic model is reflected in Exhibit 4-3.

Both sensory memory and short-term memory have limited capacity; however, long-term memory has no known limits. Information is gathered, processed, and sorted through the senses and through short-term memory. If information is deemed relevant and necessary, it is encoded into long-term memory and organized to facilitate retrieval when necessary. If it is deemed unnecessary or irrelevant, both sensory memory and short-term memory will "forget" the information and not encode it for future retrieval. In designing training programs, the trainer's goal is to help move information from the senses and short-term memory to long-term memory to be encoded and used.

Constructivism

According to constructivism, learning is a constructive process that is active, not passive. Higher-order cognitive processes, such as those addressed under Bloom's Taxonomy (see Exhibit 4-1), are utilized to develop interpretations and construct knowledge in the learning process. There isn't, however, one objective body of knowledge the trainee is learning. Instead, the trainee's experiences, as well as contextual factors, create a mental representation that is subjective and unique to the trainee. Three constructivist theories of note are problem-based learning, active learning, and organizational learning/communities of practice.

Problem-based learning.

Trainees are encouraged to apply knowledge to new situations under **problem-based learning**. This develops critical thinking, creativity, and problem-solving skills, and increases motivation and the likelihood of transferring the knowledge to situations in the workplace. There are five characteristics of problem-based learning[18]:

1. Learning is driven by open-ended problems with no "right" answer.
2. Cases are context specific.
3. Trainees are self-directed and work in small groups.
4. Problem solving is done by consensus, and the solution must be agreed upon and implemented.
5. The trainer is a facilitator, not an instructor providing memorizable facts to the trainees.

While not all training would benefit from this approach, this might be applicable, for example, when training employees about ethical decision making. Because ethics is a challenging concept to teach due to not having one "right" answer, problem-based learning allows trainees to reason through a number of different solutions to the ethical dilemmas. Ethics cases are presented to the trainees, who work through, and compare and contrast, potential solutions. This approach also encourages trainees to think of solutions from multiple perspectives, helping them avoid typical decision-making biases, such as a confirmation bias (searching only for information that supports one's position). Because a lot of decision making in organizations is done with incomplete, or ambiguous, information, it is essential that employees develop the skills to see potential solutions through many different perspectives. Thus, problem-based learning would also be an important consideration when designing development programs.

Active learning.

Active learning theory has two major components.[19] First, learners, or trainees, control their own learning. The trainee assumes primary responsibility for learning decisions, and thus there is an internal regulation of learning. The second component presumes active learning promotes an inductive learning process, whereby individuals explore and experiment with new material to arrive at new solutions, and thereby engage in the learning process. Hence, the learner constructs knowledge internally, rather than internalizes existing knowledge that is external to the learner.

A growing trend in training and development is self-managed or self-determined learning (see the "Heutagogy" section later in this chapter), of which active learning is an important part. Research in this area is still relatively new and untapped. A study by Bradford S. Bell and Steve W. J. Kozlowski found that strategies to help trainees control their emotions resulted in lower stress for trainees.[20] Further, these researchers found that self-evaluation activities, central to active learning, had a positive impact on strategic knowledge (how to apply and use knowledge). Lastly, when trainees had a mastery orientation with respect to learning new material, they experienced higher levels of intrinsic motivation, self-efficacy, and metacognition when using active learning. Overall, active learning appears to be an important theoretical consideration when designing training and development programs.

Organizational learning.

Organizational learning theory takes two distinct approaches to learning. One aspect argues that the firm as a whole learns cognitively, likening the organization to one big brain made up of the individual members of the organization. The other aspect argues that organization members construct their own knowledge through a community of practice in the organization.

Organizational cognition. In explaining the first aspect of organizational learning, Chris Argyris and Donald A. Schön argue organization members hold maps in their head to explain how they plan, implement, and review their actions.[21] There is a difference, however, between their stated behaviors (espoused theories) and their actual behaviors (theory-in-use). This disconnect between espoused behaviors and actual practice, Argyris and Schön argue, is an opportunity for learning.

Single-loop learning changes the tactic one uses to achieve the desired behaviors, assuming a different approach will result in the outcome one wants. Double-loop learning changes the overall goal or assumptions instead of the tactic. When individuals reconsider their assumptions, there is a greater opportunity for learning. Single-loop learning occurs when there is a need for high control over the environment, resulting in more defensiveness and less freedom of choice over outcomes. Double-loop learning occurs when there is greater participation and shared control. This gives those involved the opportunity to challenge assumptions and change the way they think about a situation. It is easy to see that single- and double-loop learning parallels Bloom's Taxonomy. For example, single-loop learning focuses on lower-order cognition, and double-loop learning allows trainees to learn material more deeply and adapt the way they think based on what they learn. Organizational learning occurs as the members examine the disconnect between espoused and actual behaviors and collectively resolve the mismatch, another form of higher-order cognition.

Community of practice. John Lave and Etienne Wenger argue a community of practice occurs when individuals share a domain of interest, interact with each other within a defined community, and have a shared repertoire, or practice, of stories or experiences.[22]

Learning occurs as individuals interact and share information, both intentionally and unintentionally. Specifically, Lave and Wenger argue that learning is driven by individuals' motivation to become a central part of the community by modeling the skills of those they admire (similar to Bandura's social learning theory). In short, learning occurs through the social learning process when individuals share common interests and collaborate over a period of time. The learning, however, is socially constructed by the community.

Humanism

The last category of learning theories we address is the humanism approach. Humanism posits learning occurs as a personal act to fulfill one's potential. It closely matches Maslow's hierarchy of needs (see Exhibit 3-7, page 82), such that the goal of human development is self-actualization. Two theories of note in the humanism school are experiential learning and adult learning. Malcolm Knowles developed the theory of teaching adults (andragogy), addressed in more detail in the next section, which compares and contrasts pedagogy, andragogy (adult learning), and a new concept called heutagogy.

Experiential learning.

David A. Kolb developed **experiential learning theory**, which argues learning is a process done through experience and reflection on doing.[23] Given experiential learning requires self-initiative, it fits in perfectly with the humanistic approach. In order to maximize learning through this method, four conditions must be met:

1. The learner must be willing to be actively involved in the experience.
2. The learner must be able to reflect on the experience.
3. The learner must possess and use analytical skills to conceptualize the experience.
4. The learner must possess decision-making and problem-solving skills in order to use the new ideas gained from the experience.

Experiential learning also maps to Bloom's higher-order cognitive domain (see Exhibit 4-1) such that learners must be able to analyze, synthesize, and evaluate the material they experience in order to create knowledge. Kolb's experiential learning model, shown in Exhibit 4-4, has four stages: concrete experience, reflective observation, abstract conceptualization, and active experimentation. Let's use the example of an employee learning how to use a new piece of equipment on the job. In stage one (concrete experience), the employee starts working on the piece of equipment to perform a task. After the initial experience using the equipment, the employee can engage in stage two (reflective observation) to determine what worked and what failed in that first attempt. Stage three (abstract conceptualization) entails brainstorming on ways to improve the next attempt at using the new equipment, and stage four

Exhibit 4-4 Kolb's Experiential Learning Cycle

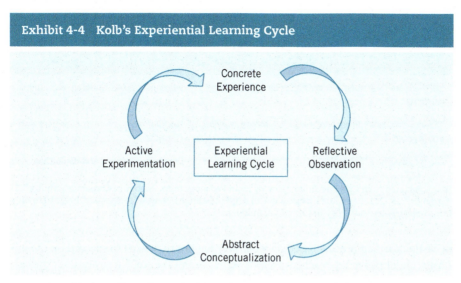

Source: Adapted from David A. Kolb, *Experiential Learning: Experience as the Source of Learning and Development* (Englewood Cliffs, NJ: Prentice Hall, 1984).

(active experimentation) is the trial and error pattern of repeating stages one through three until the equipment is mastered.

In the workplace, when an employee is ready, willing, and able to learn something new, experiential learning is an appropriate tool that empowers employees to learn new material in a fun and engaging way. The end result is more efficient learning than that facilitated by more passive instructional tools, and a greater likelihood of trainees internalizing and mastering the new material, with greater intrinsic rewards.

PEDAGOGY, ANDRAGOGY, AND HEUTAGOGY

Pedagogy Versus Andragogy

A great deal of attention is paid to **pedagogy**, or the study of education and how to best teach.[24] We see this in debates over No Child Left Behind, for example, or the Common Core State Standards for primary and secondary education. While some theories of pedagogy may spill over into training and development, of greater importance to organizations and training and development professionals is **andragogy**, or the theory and practice of educating adults.[25] Exhibit 4-5 compares the principles of pedagogy and andragogy.

While pedagogy argues learners depend on the instructor for directing them on what to learn, andragogy posits that adults are self-directed but guided by instructors. In pedagogy, teachers take full responsibility for determining what students should learn and how they should learn it. Adult learners are instrumental in their own learning process. They are more proactive in doing the work needed to facilitate learning, and they

Exhibit 4-5 Pedagogy Versus Andragogy

Pedagogy	Andragogy
Learners are dependent on instructor for direction and learning	Learners are self-directed, facilitated by instructor
Teacher assumes full responsibility for what is taught and learned	Learners are responsible for their own learning
Teacher assesses learning	Learners engage in self-evaluation

Source: Adapted from Kyle Freedman, "Moving From Pedagogy to Andragogy in Corporate Training," TD, November 15, 2012. Available from www.td.org/Publications/Newsletters/Links/2012/11/Moving-from-Pedagogy-to-Andragogy-in-Corporate-Training.

drive the learning process based on what they believe they need to succeed on the job. Lastly, under pedagogy, teachers assess whether or not the students learn what they are expected to. Adult learners engage in self-evaluation, committing to work continuously until they master what they need to learn.

The workplace includes employees who range in age from 16 to upwards of 70 years. As such, adult learning must be at the center of training and development activities because adults, not children, are being employed to do the work of the organization. As they gain more knowledge and experience, adults approach learning in a different way than do children. Therefore, outdated models of teacher-centric approaches to learning will not be as successful when engaging in training and development activities. Adult learners are driven by intrinsic motivators to achieve autonomy, mastery, and purpose, and are more likely to be active participants, rather than passive participants, in learning.

Malcolm Knowles popularized the term *andragogy* and has attempted to build a comprehensive theory of adult learning. According to Knowles, there are six basic assumptions regarding the ways adults learn[26]:

1. Adults need to know the reason for learning something.
2. Experience provides the basis for learning activities.
3. Adults need to be responsible for their decisions on education and be involved in the planning and evaluation of their instruction.
4. Adults are most interested in learning subjects having immediate relevance to their work and/or personal lives.
5. Adult learning is problem-centered rather than content-centered.
6. Adults respond better to internal than external motivators.

Although there is some debate as to whether Knowles has created a theory of adult learning or simply a guideline for practice,[27] Knowles argues that his model of assumptions created a baseline for further research on how adults learn.[28] In fact, Knowles acknowledges that perhaps there isn't a fundamental difference between child and adult learning, and that all learning occurs on a continuum,[29] dependent on the individual differences of the learners and the context within which they are learning.[30] While adults are more likely to have the maturity, experience, and self-awareness to engage in self-directed learning, this does not preclude some children from having the same predilection to take responsibility for their own learning.[31] Overall, a general rule of thumb is that there is a pull strategy to get students in primary and secondary education to learn. The teacher and the educational systems make demands, and the students must respond. Adult learners, on the other hand, adhere more to a push strategy, pushing corporate trainers to design training programs that meet their needs to improve workplace performance.

Paying attention to how adults learn can also help employees get more from their online computer-based training. If computer-based training is modeled after the teacher-centric approach, adult trainees will struggle far more than necessary to learn new material. Researcher Barry Chametsky argues that paying attention to adult learning when developing online classes and computer-based training can improve the learning experience, as well as the learning outcomes.[32]

In summary, adults come to the table with a vast amount of experience that frames how they understand information presented to them. The perceptual process continues to influence how adults learn and make sense of their environment. As individuals mature, it becomes less about "telling" them new facts and information for the sake of knowing, and more about "engaging" them to internalize what they learn and apply it readily on the job and in their personal lives. Knowles's ideals are important to consider, regardless of the audience, so they remain relevant as trainers design training programs for adult employees.

Heutagogy

A relatively new term has evolved regarding a subset of adult learning practices. **Heutagogy** is the study of self-determined learning whereby learners drive their own learning, rather than learning being conceptualized as teacher- or curriculum-centric. Where heutagogy goes beyond andragogy is the assumption that learning will encompass development of both learner competency (ability to acquire knowledge) and learner capability (confidence in one's competency). Knowing how to learn is a fundamental issue given 21st century innovation and the changing structure of communities and workplaces.[33] Technological advances have created opportunities for different ways of learning that are self-determined by the learner to understand, create, and apply knowledge and skills. In short, teaching people how to be lifelong learners, rather than limiting learning needs to the teacher or organization's perspective, is the goal of heutagogy.

Central to heutagogy is the concept of double-loop learning and self-reflection.[34] Learning entails not only addressing how to solve an existing problem, but also adapting one's beliefs and actions given the learning experience. Self-reflection enables the learner to apply competencies to solve both familiar and unfamiliar problems.

Self-determined and self-directed learning is not limited to exempt employees and those who exhibit high potential for advancement and promotion to upper-level positions in the company. Alan Clardy did research and found that nonexempt workers also may be driven to engage in self-directed learning.[35] Their reasons may differ from those of exempt workers, but their needs must also be addressed by the organizations that employ them. Clardy found some nonexempt workers may be entirely self-motivated to learn more because of the joy of learning in and of itself. Other nonexempt workers are driven by job- or career-related changes. Still others are motivated by new contextual conditions in the organization that induce the employees to seek out training opportunities on their own. In the end, it is beneficial to both employees and their employer if all employees, regardless of their position and rank in the organization, take on the mantle of lifelong learning.

How does self-directed learning, versus employer-directed learning, impact how the training and development department functions? Exhibit 4-6 outlines a subset of the competencies needed for training and development professionals who want to promote more self-directed learning in their organization (more information on practical skills for trainers is provided in Chapter 12). Trainees must develop a learning plan or learning contract, including objectives, resources, and assessment tools, to ensure learning has occurred, but it also requires a savvy trainer who can facilitate the learning in this way. This means that the trainer may have to give up some autonomy in directing trainees, and allow them to develop their own plan. Further, not all companies are ready for self-directed learning, nor are all employees good candidates for self-directed learning. In order for self-directed learning to take hold and flourish, the organization must be open to change and create a lifelong learning culture.

Exhibit 4-6 Facilitator Competencies for Self-Directed Learning

Facilitators must know:

- How adults acquire and use skills, knowledge, and attitudes
- How to apply different learning styles
- How to help people establish personal and work-related goals
- How to offer feedback on a timely basis
- How to observe groups unobtrusively and gain information and insight
- How to influence people to accomplish tasks and learn continuously
- How social systems at work influence productivity and quality
- How to communicate often and effectively in visual, oral, and written formats, using verbal and nonverbal communication
- How to use quantitative and qualitative methods to analyze skill and learning needs

- How to gain others' short- and long-term commitment to learning
- How to build cohesive, viable work teams and self-directed groups
- How to apply workplace-learning and performance-improvement theories
- How to accept uncertainty and get others to accept uncertainty
- How to show concern and empathy for diverse learners and workers
- How to coach individuals and groups
- How to give appropriate verbal and behavioral responses in stressful work situations
- How to help reduce learners' stress in different work settings

Source: Adapted from Timothy G. Hatcher, "The Ins and Outs of Self-Directed Learning," *Training and Development* 51, no. 2 (1997): 35–39.

Recent case research indicates that blending formal, nonformal, and informal learning is important for organizations of all sizes, but particularly for smaller organizations where resources are slim.[36] Small poultry enterprises in Kenya were studied to understand how lifelong learning played a role in helping enterprise members become more engaged. The researchers argued that pedagogy, andragogy, and heutagogy, together, are important for learning in small enterprises.

LEARNING STYLES

There is a lot of talk in the training and development industry about the importance of considering individual **learning styles** when designing training programs. A vast list of theories have tried to explain how learning styles affect learning outcomes. Given this flurry of attention, many training specialists find it imperative to identify trainees' learning styles to best match the training method to the trainee. A 2004 study by Frank Coffield and his colleagues investigated 13 different models of learning styles to assess their differences and accuracy.[37] Some were found to have poor reliability and validity; others had relatively strong psychometric properties. Only one model, Christopher Allinson and John Hayes's Cognitive Style Index (CSI),[38] met all four criteria in their review (internal consistency, test–retest reliability, construct validity, and predictive validity). The CSI is a single bipolar measure with intuition on one extreme and analysis on the other. It was designed with adults in the workplace in mind, which makes it most relevant for training and development consideration. Both the Myers-Briggs Type Indicator (MBTI) and the Kolb Learning Style Inventory (LSI), used heavily in training and development, fell short of the standards set in the Coffield et al. review.

Given much of the evidence that measures of learning styles, or research methods using those measures, are flawed, what should trainers conclude about the need to consider learning styles? One conclusion is that even though researchers haven't found a

Exhibit 4-7 Sample of Learning Style Dimensions

Convergers vs. Divergers
Verbalizers vs. Imagers
Deep vs. Surface Learning
Activists vs. Reflectors
Noncommitters vs. Plungers
Random vs. Sequential Learners
Initiators vs. Reasoners
Concrete vs. Abstract Learners
Intuitionists vs. Analysts
Extroverts vs. Introverts
Sensing vs. Intuition
Thinking vs. Feeling
Judging vs. Perceiving
Left Brain vs. Right Brain

Source: Adapted from Frank Coffield, David Moseley, Elaine Hall, and Kathryn Ecclestone, *Learning Styles and Pedagogy in Post-16 Learning: A Systematic and Critical Review* (London: Learning and Skills Research Centre, 2004).

definitive measure of learning styles, the way people take in information and learn is still an important training design consideration. To give you an idea of the disparity in learning style theories, Exhibit 4-7 lists some of the more commonly researched learning style dimensions. What current researchers on the topic recommend is a balanced approach to instructional design.[39]

Richard M. Felder makes a strong argument that in order to succeed in professional life, people have to use many different learning style categories.[40] When designing training programs, rather than assessing individuals' learning styles and customizing delivery to them, it is more important to present information in several ways so that the information is mutually reinforced through different approaches[41]—for example, lecturing on the material while also providing visual guides (PowerPoint slides) and finishing with an experiential exercise to apply the information learned. This would appeal to several different learning styles.

Another conclusion is that the match between content and the instructional method used to effectively teach that content may be more important than learning styles.

Taking into account Bloom's Taxonomy and acknowledging, for example, the difference between new information, which must simply be memorized, and teaching people how to reason through an ethical dilemma ensures that we minimize cognitive load and utilize a delivery method that best meets the requirements of the material. While simultaneously reinforcing a lesson through multiple ways of delivering the information, as noted by Felder, training design can maximize learning for trainees.

ARE THERE GENERATIONAL DIFFERENCES IN LEARNING?

Although we are in a unique place in history where multiple generations actively participate in the working population, it is still under debate whether there are meaningful differences in the way each generation learns. While it is agreed upon that Millennials are more familiar with learning online because of their longtime exposure to computer technology, older generations are not necessarily uncomfortable with technology. Nor does it mean that older generations learn differently, or better, than Millennials, also known as Generation Z. What may be construed as different ways of learning, or preferred learning styles, may simply be a reflection of the historical context of each generation.[42]

As current research indicates, there is little evidence that generations learn differently or have a preferred learning style.[43] And given the existing controversy over learning styles, this undermines even more the notion that generations learn differently. What we do know, factually, is that each generation's values and experiences are shaped by the events that occur during their lifetime. For example, Traditionalists (born 1922–1945) were greatly shaped by the Great Depression (1929–1939), Baby Boomers (born 1946–1962) were changed by the civil rights movement and the Vietnam War, the values of Generation X (born 1963–1981) were influenced by Watergate and the *Challenger* disaster, and Millennials (born 1982–1997) describe their defining moment as the September 11, 2001, attacks on the World Trade Center towers. These events had an impact not only on the lenses individuals use to make sense of their world, but also on their views about work, career goals, and learning. Exhibit 4-8 highlights a few important ways that generations differ in terms of beliefs that may impact learning and, by extension, training and development.

It is important to note that despite some key differences between generations, not every person in a certain generation shares the same values. Think of these generational values as an average; on average, Millennials share current experiences and values. It is important to be careful about stereotypes. For example, don't assume all Millennials think and learn the same way, or that all Boomers think and learn similarly.

The key takeaway when considering different generations is that the individual differences between these generations, based on their experiences and historical context, as well as where they are in their career, will impact how they approach learning and training and development.[44] We discuss career path characteristics and issues in Chapter 10. Regardless of employees' career stage, research has found that each generation values

Exhibit 4-8 Key Generational Differences

Views Toward:	Boomers	Generation X	Millennials
Levels of Trust	Confident of self, not authority	Low toward authority	High toward authority
Loyalty to Institutions	Cynical	Considered naive	Committed
Career Goals	Build a stellar career	Build a portable career	Build parallel careers
Rewards	Title and corner office	Freedom not to do	Meaningful work
Evaluation	Once a year with documentation	"Sorry, but how am I doing?"	Feedback whenever I want it
Education	Freedom of expression	Pragmatic	Structure of accountability

Source: Adapted from Michael D. Coomes and Robert DeBard, *Serving the Millennial Generation: New Directions for Student Services* (San Francisco: Jossey-Bass, 2004).

careers and learning in different ways, consistent across their career life span. Boomers are more driven to have careers that grow within a company, while Gen Xers and Millennials are more driven to have careers with maximum flexibility and portability. Gen Xers are more pragmatic in their approach to training and education, and Millennials want more structure and accountability. Different groups value feedback and evaluation in different ways. Lastly, while Boomers and Gen Xers are less likely to give their loyalty to a single organization, Millennials, perhaps because of their high trust of authority figures, are much more committed to their organizations.

Consultants from Vertex Solutions recommend the following to address a multigenerational workforce's training needs.[45] Overall, organizations need to take a blended approach to training and development. They should accept and embrace generational differences in learning and communication preferences, invest in the right teaching technology for their target audience, utilize experienced employees as master trainers, and customize communication to the target audience about organizational changes and training and development plans. Knowing the fundamental differences between the generations enables training and development professionals to consider how to frame and present training and development opportunities depending on the generation, and where employees are in their careers. We address diversity and individual differences much more in Chapter 13. We also discuss career paths and career-related issues in Chapter 10.

CHAPTER SUMMARY

Bloom's Taxonomy guides the learning outcomes expected from training and development programs. How individuals learn and take in information varies. Behaviorism, cognitivism, constructivism, and humanism are just a few learning theories relevant to corporate trainers. Understanding that adults are more cognitively adept than children is important as it informs how trainees in the workplace will, as a rule, approach learning. As the theory of andragogy argues, adult learners, in our case workplace trainees, are self-directed but require the help of the instructor to facilitate their learning. Trainees must take responsibility for their learning, and they are more likely to self-assess their progress against the standards provided by the organization. Helping employees to become active, self-directed learners should be an important goal in training and development; therefore, empowering trainees to embrace learning is key.

There is a lot of debate over learning styles and generational differences in learning. By and large, because there isn't one definitive learning style that explains how people take in information and learn, a balanced, multifaceted approach to learning should be a high priority when designing training programs. Using a multimodal approach introduces trainees to a wide variety of learning styles, necessary for success in the 21st century workplace. It also helps reinforce learning when multiple approaches are used to reinforce what the trainees must learn.

KEY TERMS

Active learning theory. A constructivist theory by which learners have control over their learning, with learning occurring as an inductive process.

Affective domain. How individuals relate emotionally to knowledge, such as how they gain feelings, values, and attitudes about a given topic; one of three main learning domains of Bloom's Taxonomy.

Andragogy. The theory and practice of educating adults.

Behaviorism. The theory that observable behaviors show evidence of learning.

Bloom's Taxonomy. A taxonomy of learning outcomes used in education and training and development; includes cognitive, affective, and psychomotor domains.

Classical conditioning. Also known as Pavlovian or respondent conditioning, refers to a learning procedure in which a biologically potent stimulus (e.g., food) is paired with a previously neutral stimulus (e.g., a bell). It also refers to the learning process that results from this pairing, through which the neutral stimulus comes to elicit a response (e.g., salivation) that is usually similar to the one elicited by the potent stimulus.

Cognitive domain. Knowledge and comprehension of facts and concepts; one of three main learning domains of Bloom's Taxonomy.

Cognitive load theory. An example of cognitivism concerned with the total amount of mental effort being used in working memory; when designing instructional programs, cognitive load must be reduced to maximize learning.

Cognitivism. A learning theory that views the learner as an information processor.

Constructivism. The theory that learning is an active, constructive process.

Experiential learning theory. The humanist theory that learning is a process done through experience and reflection on doing.

Heutagogy. The study of self-determined learning whereby learners drive their own learning, rather than learning being conceptualized as teacher-centric.

Humanism. The theory that learning is a personal act that is instrumental in fulfilling one's potential.

Information processing theory. A theory of how learning is encoded in one's memory and then retrieved when needed.

Learning. The acquisition of knowledge or skills through experience, study, or being taught.

Learning styles. The way in which people learn; according to a range of theories, learners can be classified accordingly.

Operant conditioning. Rewards and punishment are used as a way to reinforce the behaviors one wants an individual to learn.

Organizational learning theory. A constructivist theory comprising two perspectives: (1) The organization learns as one big brain made up of its individual members, and (2) organization members construct their own knowledge through a community of practice in the organization.

Pedagogy. The study of K–12 education and how to best teach.

Problem-based learning. A constructivist theory by which trainees are encouraged to apply knowledge to new situations; there are no right answers, problems/cases are context specific, trainees are self-directed and work in small groups, problem solving is done by consensus, and the trainer is a facilitator.

Psychomotor domain. The ability to physically utilize an object; one of three main learning domains of Bloom's Taxonomy.

Self-efficacy. Belief in one's ability to succeed in specific situations or to accomplish a task.

Social learning theory. The theory that people learn from each other via observation, imitation, and modeling.

END-OF-CHAPTER QUESTIONS AND EXERCISES

Discussion Questions

1. What is Bloom's Taxonomy, and why do trainers need to pay attention to learning outcomes?

2. How does operant conditioning affect training and development? How can you use this model to get employees to perform at the highest level?

3. How does social learning theory affect employee development? Describe the process using this model.

4. Describe the process by which trainers can minimize cognitive load. Apply Bloom's Taxonomy in describing the process of managing cognitive load.

5. Describe problem-based learning and discuss the benefits of using this kind of learning for management and leadership training.

6. Compare social learning theory to communities of practice. How are they similar? Give examples of how you think they can work together in the context of training and development.

7. Describe the experiential learning process and give examples of how it can be used in training and development.

8. Compare and contrast pedagogy and andragogy. Why is it relevant to differentiate adult learning from child learning? What implications does this have for training and development?

9. How does heutagogy impact the role of the trainer and the training and development function? In what ways does self-directed learning affect the training and development process?

10. Given the wide variety of learning styles, discuss the arguments around considering different learning styles when developing training and development programs. Are there some learning styles that seem more relevant than others? What value is there for using a multitude of learning styles in training and development programs? How does this impact organizational performance and maximize the value of training and development?

11. What is the value of considering generational differences when developing training and development programs?

Ethical Scenario

Adults or Children: Who Are We Training?

Tessa Silverman recently graduated with her master's in human resources and began working at Essic Total Parts and Manufacturing. Essic was growing quickly due to a new product it developed that caught on like wildfire. Every manufacturer in the region wanted to include this new innovation in its design decisions, so Essic was hiring people at a rapid pace to fill all areas in the company. Tessa was brought in as the third person in the HR Department after the director of HR, Hal Rooker, and an administrative assistant, Brenda Button, who handles all secretarial and administrative issues. Hal had been there 30 years, and while he knew a lot about HR laws and the basics of managing the HR function, the CEO had confided in Tessa when she was hired that the company was excited to have her on board because she would be able to help Hal get up to speed on cutting-edge HR issues. Tessa's current job is primarily to coordinate all of the training and development activities that need to happen given Essic's rapid growth. With growth comes lots of internal promotions and new hires, and with that the need to train people to make sure they are prepared for their new job responsibilities.

Tessa was finishing up the design plans for those working on the line in the manufacturing plant. She was carefully following the ADDIE model (see the introductory chapter) and remembered to consider learning theories when designing the training programs. Tessa brought her plan in to Hal, who had to sign off on her ideas before she could develop the materials. Since this was her first solo project, she was a bit nervous. Tessa walked Hal through the program and discussed her reasons for designing the program to focus on intrinsic motivators, providing good reasons for the employees to understand what they were doing and why, and teaching the employees to be empowered to solve problems independently. The program was going to be experiential in nature, with lots of hands-on instruction and practice. After her presentation, Hal smiled, then started to laugh. He said, "Tessa, all this newfangled learning stuff will be lost on these good old boys on the line. Most of them barely graduated high school, and they hate learning new things. Just toss them the manual and let them figure it out on their own. Maybe take an hour to tell them what to do, but otherwise you are wasting too much time trying to make this *relevant* [said with sarcasm and an eye roll] to them."

Tessa left the meeting shocked and disappointed. She now faced a dilemma. Should she do what Hal, her boss, said, or should she find a way to convince him that her new plan was a good idea, given what she learned in her studies about the importance of making training for adults relevant, practical, and experiential? Hal's idea sounded like the worst of high school—read this, take a test, no relevance, no explanation. Was Hal right that the guys on the line would prefer being tossed the new process manual so they could learn it themselves, or would Tessa's plan be the better approach? How would you recommend Tessa proceed?

4.1 Bring on the Learning Revolution

Review the following video on the TED website:

Sir Ken Robinson, "Bring on the Learning Revolution!," TED2010. Available from https://www.ted.com/talks/sir_ken_robinson_bring_on_the_revolution/transcript?language=en.

Sir Ken Robinson humorously addresses the human resource climate crisis facing organizations. His argument is that our current educational system is based on conformity—putting out massive amounts of the same thing, like a fast-food restaurant. Alternatively, it should be more like a fine restaurant where the food is customized to the needs and abilities of the customer.

List the key concepts in Sir Robinson's talk and compare them to the learning theories and learning outcomes addressed in this chapter. Which theories and concepts apply to his argument? What are the implications for training and development strategy in an organization? What considerations should be made for improving learning for organizations of the future?

4.2 Using Bloom's Taxonomy

As the trainer, you need to develop learning objectives using Bloom's Taxonomy. Below is a list of different learning objectives associated with a variety of training programs. Identify the cognitive domain and subdomain of Bloom's Taxonomy being utilized, and explain why you would assign that domain.

After the training session, trainees should be able to:

1. Modify the operating room for surgery in the right order, depending on the type of surgery scheduled (e.g., move the operating table, disinfect all countertops).
2. Critique financial statements to give advice to investors.
3. Demonstrate ability to program Excel to perform a macro calculation.
4. Design a training strategy to be in alignment with corporate strategy.
5. Diagnose problems with the computer numerical control (CNC) machine when it does not function.
6. Label the appropriate stages of hiring an employee.
7. Summarize statistical results into narrative descriptions of the research outcomes.
8. Formulate a compensation plan that rewards employees fairly.
9. Appraise employees using a behavioral anchored rating scale.
10. Name the steps for developing an advertising plan.
11. Contrast a differentiation strategy with a cost leadership strategy.
12. List the types of medications that can be prescribed for restless legs syndrome.
13. Estimate restaurant supplies needed to make 100 gallons of soup.
14. Translate words from Spanish to English for the exam.
15. Calculate inventory levels for weekly report.

4.3 What Kind of Training Is That?

Read the following descriptions of training and development programs at various companies, and identify which learning theories they used to design their respective programs.

Case 1

Elemental Corporation is a manufacturing company that specializes in equipment and processes to be used in environmentally conscious mining and fracking. The company has an active research and development (R&D) department, and believes in continuous, lifelong learning for its employees. Elemental is especially proud of its research innovation development program. Once a quarter, employees in the R&D department gather for two days. They review recent activities, discuss successes and failures, and work together to bring to the R&D group issues, opportunities, and problems they face in their jobs at the present moment. The group then collectively works through different scenarios, and works to empower younger, less experienced workers to be creative and explore a wide range of possible solutions. On a monthly basis, the workers meet on their own to work through immediate issues that can't wait for the quarterly meeting.

Case 2

Brennan's Sporting Goods is a small organization that employs approximately 30 people. The company wanted to help employees, particularly new ones, learn its policies. Managers were finding that some employees weren't reading the company manual and were violating policies central to Brennan's core values as an organization. After presenting employees with the manual and testing them on its contents, Brennan's implemented a progressive discipline program. The first time an employee violates a policy, he or she gets a verbal warning. The employee's supervisor discusses the behavior and the policy, and reinforces to the employee the importance of the policy and why it exists. If the employee's behavior changes, the employee is praised, and there is no need for continual meetings and discussions. If the behavior is repeated, the supervisor escalates the punishment to level 2 with a written warning, and retraining on the company policies the employee is violating. If the behavior still does not change, punishment escalates to a suspension without pay, and then the employee is fired after the fourth violation. Brennan's found, after six months, that policy violations decreased by 75%.

Case 3

Acme and Smith Insurance Company (ASIC) has a coveted management development program. Each year, 200 people apply for 10 management trainee positions. Newly graduated MBA students are hired into the program and rotate among four positions over two years, spending six months at each position. They learn from existing department managers by actively observing the managers as well as working at their side, learning on the job. At the end of the two-year program, they collaborate with the department managers and human resources to determine which program is the best match for them to continue to work at ASIC. Once a determination is made, they receive an offer and transition to their permanent position in the department best matched to their interests and skill set.

Case 4

George was responsible for setting up annual ethics training for his organization. The ethics training included compliance issues that all employees needed to know (e.g., Foreign Corrupt Practices Act, Sarbanes–Oxley), as well as scenarios to help them learn how to reason through potential ethical dilemmas. In the training, he placed the employees in small groups and presented them with several scenarios common for their job. The groups then worked through the scenarios together and presented info to the larger group about the facts of the case, where the challenges were, and what they believed was or was not an ethical way to address each scenario. George understood there were no right or wrong answers, but he wanted to have the employees work together to practice reasoning through ethical scenarios and build consensus on each case. (Note: The U.S. Congress passed the Sarbanes–Oxley Act of 2002 to help protect investors from fraudulent financial reporting by corporations. Also known as the Corporate Responsibility Act of 2002, it mandated strict reforms to existing securities regulations and imposed tough new penalties on lawbreakers. See https://www.investopedia.com/terms/s/sarbanesoxleyact.asp.)

Case 5

Jim worked for an electrical company. He was a master electrician with over 20 years of experience.

This week, he was beginning a project and was assigned a new employee who was hired only two weeks ago. While the new employee had taken all sorts of course work at the local community college to understand the basics of electrical contracting, she had not yet worked in the field; this was her first job. Jim's company had an apprenticeship program where newly trained people interested in becoming a licensed electrician could work to fulfill the prerequisite number of hours on the job for application to the license with the state. The apprentices worked their way up in terms of skill building side by side with the senior electrician until they were able to work independently, typically midway during their fourth year of working as an apprentice. At the end of their fourth year, assuming they had worked the requisite number of hours during their apprenticeship period, they would be able to apply for the license. Jim's new apprentice was eager to begin. During the first day, Jim discussed what he was doing each step of the way and asked her to repeat back what he said, then actually perform the task as she had explained it. Jim made corrections where appropriate.

CHAPTER FIVE

TRAINING EVALUATION
Reaction and Learning

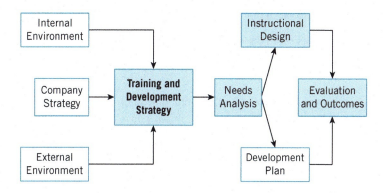

Learning Objectives

1. Select a training evaluation strategy in alignment with the company and training strategy.

2. Construct learning objectives using Bloom's Taxonomy.

3. Design training programs with training evaluation in mind.

4. Explain the difference between experimental and nonexperimental designs for training evaluation.

5. Explain the difference between reliability and validity of training evaluation measures.

6. Categorize training evaluation questions based on the first two levels of the New World Kirkpatrick Model for training evaluation.

Invista Performance Solutions (IPS) was approached by Amazon to develop a formal training program for the maintenance staff at the Amazon World Wide Research and Development Center. There wasn't an existing training program for these employees, and it was imperative they had the proper safety and equipment training before they used the equipment on-site. Some of the equipment on which Amazon wanted them to be trained included a vertical band saw, a miter saw, a drill press, a right-angle grinder, and a hydraulic press. As well, employees needed to demonstrate mastery of how to use personal protective equipment so they could keep themselves and others safe while operating the equipment.

IPS first conducted a needs analysis to determine what knowledge, skills, and abilities (**KSAs**) the maintenance staff needed to do their jobs. After that, IPS conducted small group (no more than four employees) training cohorts over the course of eight months to ensure the employees got the attention they needed and accurate training on all necessary equipment. Each employee fulfilled 40 hours of training and received a certificate of completion noting he or she had accomplished successfully a written test, as well as a hands-on test demonstrating proper techniques with the equipment.

IPS's responsibility didn't end with the close of the classes. IPS performed training evaluations on the trainees to ensure the training was received well, the trainees met the learning objectives by passing the written and hands-on tests, and the trainees successfully used the material on the job. IPS went back to the KSAs assessed in the needs analysis and developed evaluations to ensure the trainees learned the intended skills at the level expected to be successful on the job. IPS received the following feedback on its training sessions:

- 100% of the participants will use what they learned on the job.
- 95% of the participants rated the instructors as excellent.
- 98% of the participants rated the course as excellent.
- 100% of the participants rated the course materials as excellent.

IPS understood that trainee satisfaction with the training session was not enough to convince Amazon to continue using its services. The company developed an evaluation plan to ensure, at a minimum, that employees could and would use the material learned on the job. In the end, the Amazon training was a successful partnership for all involved, with the promise for future collaboration on the horizon.

Source: Adapted from Amazon, "Client Profile: Amazon R&D Center." Available from http://www.invistaperforms.org/wp-content/uploads/2018/11/Client-Profile-Amazon-Case-Study-1.pdf.

A 2005 column in the magazine *Fast Company* presented a blistering critique of the human resource management function in an article titled "Why We Hate HR."[1] Keith Hammonds provided four main points for why the HR function was failing business organizations. Of particular relevance to the field of training and development was the concern that HR professionals were not measuring the impact of HR activities, specifically the impact of training dollars on key organizational outcomes. Hammonds argued many HR professionals would report how many people received training, but neglected to look at the strategic impact of that training. Clearly, counting training hours is not as relevant as understanding how training improves the organization's bottom line. Hammonds's article was a clarion call for HR professionals to focus on outcomes relevant to businesses, including company strategy, customers, and competitors, as well as the impact of HR practices on company financials and employee performance.

Fast-forward to a decade later, and you will find a plethora of articles, websites, and blogs addressing the importance of metrics and key performance indicators. Although Donald Kirkpatrick developed his model of training effectiveness in 1954, at no time more than the present has measuring outcomes from training programs had such strategic importance for organizations. Kirkpatrick acknowledged over 60 years ago that the best way to ensure effective training was to measure its impact on the organization. Although his model has been modified and updated to keep up with changes in the business environment, the fundamental principles of measuring training effectiveness still represent the gold standard against which all training programs are evaluated.

In Chapter 4, we provided a broad overview of how people learn and the implications for designing training and development programs for employees. Further, we addressed the different levels of learning objectives with Bloom's Taxonomy to illustrate that learning can range from awareness of a concept to applying the concept and creating something new given the original information learned. Chapters 5 and 6 are dedicated to understanding training evaluation and important metrics that assess the value of training dollars invested in employees. In this chapter, we provide an overview of the importance of understanding training strategy when evaluating training outcomes, provide guidelines for developing learning objectives, and reinforce the importance of keeping evaluation in mind when you develop your training design. This chapter also introduces the New World Kirkpatrick Model for training evaluation and goes into depth on the first two levels of evaluation to ensure the training accomplished what it set out to do. The chapter that follows maintains the focus on strategic metrics addressing the next two levels of evaluation. For example, did employees use the new material on the job, and did the training have a positive impact on organizational strategic outcomes? As well, it addresses the key mechanisms needed to ensure proper transfer of training knowledge from the classroom/training module to the workplace.

Training evaluation is informed by the ways people learn and the level of learning expected from the training program. Establishing learning objectives, given the training and development strategy of the company, up front is necessary to assess training effectiveness. As our chapter framework illustrates, training evaluation must be considered concurrent with training and development strategy, and learning goals, to ensure the evaluation measures outcomes of value to the organization. Before you design a training program, it is essential to understand what outcome the organization desires and how that outcome should and will be measured. Kirkpatrick's model for training effectiveness guides our discussion as we consider the different levels of training effectiveness and the key metrics of value to organizations.

TRAINING STRATEGY FOR EVALUATION

How Training Strategy Informs Training Evaluation

In Chapter 1, we discussed the importance of aligning training and development strategy with corporate strategy. If training is not done in the service of the corporate strategy, the training dollars will be largely wasted. While step one in designing a training and development program involves conducting a needs analysis, step two involves having a clear understanding of the outcomes the organization wants to achieve with the training program. Both the needs analysis and the outcomes should be tightly linked to corporate strategy.

Backwards design is a term used in K–12 education that argues in order to design curriculum, you must first understand what goals you want students to accomplish, then build the curriculum to meet those goals.[2] Although not a new concept in manufacturing processes in business organizations, it was applied to curriculum development around 1998, and by extension, many training professionals have adopted this approach to training design. Backwards design requires three important steps: (1) identify the desired results from the training, (2) determine the acceptable evidence that the training goals were accomplished, and (3) design the learning experiences and instruction to achieve the desired results.[3] This applies to our recommended approach to corporate training because we argue you cannot design a training program until you establish what is important and what needs to be assessed.

As the training and development strategy evolves and learning objectives are developed for a training program, the training design should take into consideration the outcomes of value to the organization. This involves understanding what outcomes will be measured, as well as how they will be measured. The "what" question addresses issues related to the corporate strategy and informs the learning evaluation strategy. These key issues include understanding the organization's key strategic imperatives and how the training program will affect those imperatives. Whether the imperative is customer satisfaction or an improved internal manufacturing process, training design should ensure the outcomes from the training have the greatest impact on the company's strategy.

The "how" question has implications for designing the training program. Sometimes the things we want and need to measure are not easily measurable. In fact, the link between training programs and return on investment is oftentimes not easy to quantify because of the time lag between training and its long-term impact.[4] As well, we need to consider whether to do the training in one or multiple locations to assess effectiveness. Is it sufficient to train one group of employees and assess their knowledge after the training to ensure they learned the material and the training changed their behavior? Or is it more beneficial to run a controlled experiment to offer strong evidence of training effectiveness before the program is rolled out to the entire organization?

Learning Evaluation Strategy

A 2012 article in *TD* magazine argues that organizations should have a clear **learning evaluation strategy** to guide the design and implementation of learning evaluation.[5] Research indicates 70% of learning is obtained from assignments and on-the-job experiences, 20% comes from relationships and networks, and the remaining 10% occurs in formal training processes.[6] Although formal training represents a small percentage of the learning involved for employees, in order for that formal training to be successful, it must be embedded in a larger context that takes into account barriers and supports for learning. Kirkpatrick's model addresses this by ensuring (1) a skilled trainer or facilitator guides the learning process, (2) material is presented in such a way that trainees can effectively learn the material, (3) the context facilitates using the newly acquired information on the job, and, most importantly, (4) the training will have a strategic impact on the organization's bottom line. The assignments, on-the-job experiences, and networking play a key role in ensuring the 10% learned in the classroom is effectively utilized in the workplace. Thus, the remaining 90% of learning depends on the company culture, policies, and management team to help training knowledge become effectively used in the workplace, thus impacting organizational outcomes.

Five basic principles drive a learning evaluation strategy[7]:

1. Focus on high-priority learning areas.
2. Address evaluation requirements of multiple stakeholders.
3. Foster shared responsibility for performance improvement.
4. Collect data and use resources efficiently.
5. Conduct action planning.

High-priority learning areas involve strategic imperatives that are key to organizational success and provide the most "bang for the buck." Taking into account the needs of key stakeholders will ensure the training aligns with strategic needs and outcomes are measured based on the metrics stakeholders believe are important for long-term success. Because only 10% of learning occurs in the training classroom, the organization must take responsibility for ensuring the training is reinforced and utilized in the larger organizational context. This means supervisors, managers, and coworkers, in alignment with corporate policies, need to facilitate learning transfer after classroom training occurs.

In these times of limited resources, organizations must pay attention to both effectiveness and efficiency. With little resources to spare, training must be focused on what will have the greatest impact on organizational outcomes. It follows that the data collected to assess training effectiveness must be focused on those key organizational outcomes as well. Lastly, action plans must ensure that training delivers what it promised to deliver. If learning objectives are linked to business challenges important to strategy, then the action plan takes information learned in the evaluation stages to guide future actions. This could include beginning one kind of training while ending another, reapportioning funding to address new challenges unearthed, or putting greater funds into ensuring training activities are properly reinforced and supported. Training needs will change as business needs change, and the training strategy along with what will be evaluated will change as well.

DEVELOPING LEARNING OBJECTIVES

In Chapter 4, we discussed Bloom's Taxonomy and its importance in guiding learning goals for training programs. Once an organization determines the level of cognitive, affective, and psychomotor skills it wants to accomplish in its training, it must establish **learning objectives** to guide the trainer in designing the training session. Before the trainer can design the training, however, both learning objectives and training outcomes must be established up front. Training strategy drives both to ensure objectives are consistent with the overall strategic goals of the company, and we are subsequently evaluating those outcomes of value.

Training goals are determined during the needs analysis stage, and the learning objectives naturally flow from those goals. The Association for Talent Development (ATD) defines a learning objective as the knowledge or skill that the trainee must obtain and exhibit in the training session to achieve the training goals.[8] ATD argues learning objectives explain in specific and measurable terms what trainees will do to learn the defined knowledge or skills and demonstrate this learning. The process of writing learning objectives can be broken down into three parts: planning objectives, writing objectives, and quantifying objectives.[9]

Planning Objectives

In planning the objectives, you must first understand and determine the overall purpose of the training. Ideally, this has been addressed during the needs analysis process and is expressed in the training goals. The expectation is that a gap exists between the skills employees have now and what they need to accurately perform their jobs; training is intended to bridge that gap to ensure employees receive the appropriate training.

The planning process includes consideration of four aspects: the intended audience of the training, the actions or behaviors expected, the conditions or context in which the training will occur, and the standards against which the trainees' behaviors will be assessed. First, the training goals make clear the intended audience for the training (typically assumed to be the trainees or employees). Be explicit regarding which employees will undergo the training.

Second, the trainer must identify the expected performance of the trainees in the form of an action or behavior. Once the trainer gets to the writing phase, the objective must contain an action verb that can be observed and measured. If the objective is ambiguous or too subjective in tone, it will be difficult to determine if the learning objective has been successfully met.

Third, the trainer must be able to identify the context or conditions in which the training will occur. Typical contexts or conditions include what must happen before the tasks can be completed, what tools and support might facilitate task completion, and what environmental conditions to address.

Finally, the trainer must determine a set of clear standards for the trainees that meet the minimum acceptable expectations of success. Typically, these standards are expressed in terms of percentage of tasks completed correctly, by a certain deadline, and of a particular magnitude. At this point in the training program, do not expect mastery or excellence. Ideally, the standards directly relate to what is necessary to indicate a trainee has adequately learned the material. Mastery of the training skills comes later, as we'll see in our discussion of Kirkpatrick's levels of training evaluation.

Writing Objectives

In order to write the objectives once they are conceptualized, trainers must use clear, direct language that is easily identifiable and actionable. For example, there is a substantive difference between training with "understanding" as a learning objective and training with "demonstrate" as the objective. It is ambiguous at best to measure understanding.

Demonstrate is an action verb and lends itself to assessment. Exhibit 5-1 ties in the levels of Bloom's Taxonomy (see Exhibit 4-1, page 96) with examples of key verbs you can use to design learning objectives.

Exhibit 5-1 Sample Action Verbs for Learning Objectives on the Cognitive Domain

Bloom's Taxonomy Subdomain	Action Verbs for Learning Objectives	
Knowledge	Draw	Select
	Identify	Outline
	Locate	Recite
	Label	Record
	Name	Repeat
Comprehension	Explain	Convert
	Relate	Match
	Describe	Discuss
	Paraphrase	Estimate
	Confirm	Predict
Application	Apply	Solve
	Modify	Report
	Build	Sketch
	Construct	Produce
Analysis	Analyze	Compare
	Sort	Debate
	Categorize	Differentiate
	Investigate	Examine
Synthesis	Combine	Generate
	Design	Plan
	Invent	Formulate
	Originate	Devise
	Compose	Revise
Evaluation	Solve	Assess
	Critique	Conclude
	Criticize	Justify
	Appraise	Judge

Source: Adapted from "How to Write Learning Objectives: Verb Wheel Based on Bloom's Taxonomy." Available from www.instructables.com/id/How-to-write-learning-objectives/.

> **Exhibit 5-2 Sample Learning Objective**
>
> Given specifications for a PV [photovoltaic] system, a site survey, and a series of 20 questions about a PV installation (*conditions*), each trainee (*audience*) will make correct installation decisions (*action/behavior*) by answering 19 out of 20 questions correctly (*degree or standard*).

Source: Interstate Renewable Energy Council, "The ADDIE Model: Sample Learning Objective." Available from www.irecusa.org/workforce-education/training-resources/best-practices-the-series/best-practices-3-developing-a quality-course/the-addie-model/.

When possible, it is advantageous to frame the objective in terms of realistic or applied events. These can be linked to customer, vendor, supplier, or employee needs specifically, and related to the organization's goals. The objective should also be framed around a very specific level of performance expected of the trainee upon successful completion of the training.

Lastly, keep the objectives concise, typically expressed in one sentence. The longer the objective, the more difficult it will be for the trainee to understand it, and the more challenging it will be to assess training success around the objective. Exhibit 5-2 illustrates an example of a learning objective used by the Interstate Renewable Energy Council. This learning objective contains the four key elements for designing a learning objective.

Quantifying Objectives

In quantifying objectives, as noted, standards need to be specific. As well, standards should follow the guidelines of SMART goals or objectives: specific, measurable, attainable, relevant, and time bound. Without following SMART guidelines, it will be difficult to focus training on specific outcomes, and there will be no way to accurately measure if objectives were met. For example, it is not enough to say that a trainee must be "aware" of how to do something; the trainee must "demonstrate" how to do something at a sufficient quantity and quality to ensure achievement of the learning objectives. Exhibit 5-3 highlights important tips for creating learning objectives.

Exhibit 5-3 Tips for Creating Learning Objectives

- Learning objectives identify what the learners will do to learn and to demonstrate their learning during the training session.
- Learning objectives must be specific, observable, and measurable.
- Learning objectives should begin with an active verb.
- Learning objectives should follow a logical sequence of activity.

- There should be sufficient learning objectives to accomplish each stated goal.
- Objectives are best when kept simple.
- The sequence of learning objectives will usually move through the stages of learning, from knowledge to comprehension to application, and beyond, if applicable.
- For most technical training, the first learning objective will relate to the definition of any technical terminology.
- Include a learning objective that expresses the reason why the training is important from the learner's perspective. This is usually one of the first learning objectives.
- If safety is a consideration, there should *always* be a learning objective that checks for comprehension *prior* to a learning objective that provides for application.

Source: Deborah Spring Laurel, "Jump Start Your Learning Objectives," *InfoLine* 25, no. 0804 (April 2008): 13.

TRAINING DESIGN FOR EVALUATION

When designing a training program, organizations must take into account up front the plan for evaluation. How the evaluation program is designed informs the extent to which we have confidence in the results of the training program. When we can control the influence of factors external to the training itself that may affect the outcomes we measure, our confidence the training was effective increases. While the ideal would be to create an experimental design, complete with experimental and control group conditions, this is not always feasible in an organizational setting. It is particularly challenging in smaller organizations where only a small handful of employees will get training at any point in time. In the next section, we discuss the most common nonexperimental and experimental designs, which trainers may consider when designing their training programs. If you are interested in learning more about different types of designs not included here, refer to Campbell and Stanley (1963) noted in the Exhibit 5-4 source. Exhibit 5-4 summarizes some of the designs one can use when developing training programs.

Exhibit 5-4   Training Design for Evaluation Examples

Nonexperimental Designs			
One-Shot Case Study		X	O
One-Shot Pretest–Posttest Design	O	X	O
Static-Group Comparison		X	O_1
			O_2

(Continued)

Exhibit 5-4 (Continued)

Experimental Designs				
Pretest–Posttest Control Group Design	R	O	X	O_1
	R	O		O_2
Posttest-Only Control Group Design	R		X	O_1
	R			O_2
Solomon Four-Group Design	R	O	X	O_1
	R	O		O_2
	R		X	O_3
	R			O_4

O = Measurement (done before and after training)
X = Training activity
Subscript # = Group number
R = Random assignment of trainees to group

Source: Adapted from Donald T. Campbell and Julian C. Stanley, *Experimental and Quasi-Experimental Designs for Research* (Boston: Houghton Mifflin, 1963).

Nonexperimental Designs

When resources are limited and/or the number of employees going through training is small, it isn't feasible to design a full-blown experiment, complete with control and experimental groups. Many times, trainers have to settle for assessing outcomes based on the small convenience sample of employees participating in the training program. Many different kinds of biases can influence how to interpret training results. Some nonexperimental designs are more successful than others at controlling for these biases, but none of the nonexperimental designs control for all anticipated biases. We highlight three designs in this category.

One-shot case study.

Typical for most organizations, with limited resources and too few employees to run a formal experiment, the **one-shot case study** is most common. In a design of this nature, employees are provided a training program and then tested to see if the training program was effective. While this is a convenient design, particularly when resources are limited and the organization is small, a lot of problems can occur with the types of conclusions you can draw.

First, we don't know if something other than the training program had an impact on the training outcomes during the same time as the training. For example, if new resources were made available to the group simultaneous to or after the training, but before measurement of the outcomes, it would be unclear if the training or the new resources affected the training outcomes. This is called a *history* effect. Another concern has to do with a *maturation* effect. This means that even without the training, the trainees could have simply gotten better at their task due to repetition over an extended period of time. The training may have had no impact at all and was simply an artifact of doing the same thing long enough that they finally mastered how to do it properly.

Another concern may be the characteristics of the group we chose to train, or a *selection* effect. The group chosen for the training may not be representative of all employees, such that they were collectively much better or much worse than other employees. This is an artifact of using a "convenient" group of employees on which to conduct training. The behavior expressed in the post-training measure may have had less to do with the training program and more to do with the baseline skill set of the employees selected for the program.

It is important to note that even though it may be difficult to draw conclusions about the training effectiveness, this may be the only option available to organizations. That does not mean the training program isn't effective at some level, particularly if it is offered from a vendor that can demonstrate validation of the training in multiple settings. It simply means that you cannot definitively say the training had the impact on the outcomes you desire. If your organization requires documentation of training effectiveness at a higher, more strategic level, it may be difficult to associate the training with the outcomes of interest.

One-shot pretest–posttest design.

An improvement on the case study design involves a **one-shot pretest–posttest design**. Again, this design may be the only option for those with limited resources or volume of trainees with which to perform a proper experiment. With this design, we can effectively eliminate any bias associated with the *selection* effect. We have a pre-training measure and a post-training measure that indicates at some time between the two measurements the group influenced a change in training outcomes, regardless of who was selected for the training group.

Unfortunately, this design does not eliminate problems associated with the *maturation* of the trainees, or with the potential for another factor, such as the resources noted above, to have influenced the training outcomes (*history* effect). This design also adds another complication. Perhaps the subjects were influenced by the pre-training measurement and, when they were measured post-training, they remembered the measurement questions and answered correctly the second time around. This *testing* effect gives the impression of improvement in training outcomes where none really exist.

Static-group comparison.

The last nonexperimental design compares two groups, one that received the training and one that did not. While this **static-group comparison** may present problems with drawing conclusions about the training because of characteristics of the group(s) chosen, similar to the case study design, it effectively manages the impact of something extraneous to the training on the training outcomes. The control group would likely experience the same extraneous effects; thus, the difference between the control group and the experimental group would more accurately reflect the impact of the training. As well, this design controls for how much employees may have learned just from simple maturity.

By only post-testing, you remove the likelihood of a problem called *regression to the mean*. Regression to the mean simply means that with opportunities for pre- and posttest measures, we are likely to see extremes in scores for no other reason than random luck—or, more accurately, random error. Scoring high the first time one takes a test may be associated with those who were "lucky" and guessed at responses. These subjects are more likely to score lower the next time they take the test because of random error. Low scores are also associated with "luck," albeit bad luck, and respondents with low pretest scores are more likely to improve in scores the second time they take the test. This natural variation has nothing to do with training, and everything to do with random error that occurs in any kind of measurement. Lastly, because there is no pretest, there is no concern about subjects learning how to answer the questions from the pretest having an impact on the posttest measurements.

Experimental Designs

We highlight three experimental designs that trainers can use to assess training outcomes. The common factor associated with experimental designs, as compared to nonexperimental designs, is the random assignment of subjects to training conditions. As we know from our discussion of nonexperimental designs, many external factors can influence training outcomes. While some nonexperimental designs are better at managing some factors than others, none of the nonexperimental designs can control for all external factors. One department, or training class, may have characteristics that another group doesn't have, which ultimately affects the interpretation of training outcomes.

Random assignment is a way to make the groups statistically equivalent. Each participant has an equal chance of being assigned to a different condition. The result is that any systematic bias is equally distributed over the conditions, effectively controlling for those biases. Random assignment is not feasible in small organizations where training classes are typically smaller in size; however, larger organizations may benefit from using experimental designs because they have a sizeable number of employees, making random assignment feasible.

Pretest–posttest control group design.

The **pretest–posttest control group design** is the experimental design most trainers are familiar with from a basic science class. A control group gets no training but experiences similar conditions to the group getting the training—the experimental group. Subjects are randomly assigned to both conditions, and both pre- and posttest measures are taken. Because subjects are randomly assigned, systematic error is controlled. Further, the pre- and posttest measures ensure that other external factors that may occur concurrent with the training, such as a history or testing effect, are managed as well. This type of design leaves the trainer with a high level of confidence that the training outcomes are a direct result of the training itself.

Posttest-only control group design.

The **posttest-only control group design** is comparable to the static-group comparison noted in the "Nonexperimental Designs" section. The only difference between the posttest-only design and the static-group comparison is the use of random assignment for the trainees. Otherwise, once subjects are randomly assigned to either training condition, the training occurs, and then post-training measurements are taken to see if the training was effective.

Solomon four-group design.

The **Solomon four-group design** is a combination of the pretest–posttest design and the posttest-only control group design. Training subjects are randomly assigned to one of four conditions. In condition one, trainees encounter a pretest measure, undergo training, and then are measured for effectiveness in a posttest. In condition two, trainees encounter a pre- and posttest measure but do not experience training. In condition three, trainees are measured not before training, only after. In the last condition, trainees are only measured after the other groups experience training; however, this group is not pretested and does not undergo the training. While this design is more complex and requires more subjects, it is the most effective at adding additional assurance that all potential bias has been controlled.

Training Design for Evaluation Summary

Trainers need to consider the outcomes they want to evaluate, as well as the factors they need to control for, as they design their training programs. It is too late after the training takes place to consider whether they successfully controlled for selection or history bias, or whether they need a control group to ensure there was an adequate comparison between the trained and untrained groups. Knowing in advance if other factors may influence training outcome measures will inform how the trainer designs the training program. Planning for the outcomes you want before the training occurs is the only way to ensure you have a training program designed to maximize training effectiveness.

When random assignment is not feasible because too few employees are involved in training, or only one group or department is eligible for the training, it is important to pick a training design that controls for those factors of greatest concern to the trainer. When random assignment is feasible, the simplest, most cost-effective design is the posttest-only design. Regardless of the design the trainer uses, it is important to know the outcomes of strategic value to the organization before designing and implementing the training program.

RELIABILITY AND VALIDITY OF TRAINING MEASURES

Before we begin the discussion of the different levels of training evaluation that organizations use, it is important to provide a brief reminder about the importance of ensuring your measures of training effectiveness are reliable and valid. Any metric used by organizations must meet these criteria to be useful. Consistent with the measures we use to assess job candidates under consideration for hiring, a measure is only useful if it is predictable and measures what it is intended to measure.

A reliable measure must be consistent and measure the same thing over time, across different evaluators or internally in an instrument. This applies to training because we want to be sure each time we assess a specific training outcome—satisfaction with the trainer, for example, or assessing learning post-training—it gives us consistent results. In the context of needs analysis, if we want to assess trainees' skills and knowledge in a pretest measure, we also need to be sure the measure is consistent. The responses from each trainee must be consistently assessed so the summary of their results accurately reflects their skill and knowledge level. Exhibit 5-5 illustrates the different types of reliability to consider when writing training measures.

A valid training measure must assess what it purports to assess. For example, if I argue a training measure assesses learning (training outcomes), I need to ensure that it actually measures learning, not some other aspect associated with the training process. In selection assessment, a valid measure assesses the ability of the measure

Exhibit 5-5 Types of Reliability

- **Test–retest reliability** indicates the repeatability of test scores over time.
- **Alternate or parallel forms reliability** indicates how consistent test scores are likely to be if a person takes different forms of a test assessing the same thing.
- **Interrater reliability** indicates how consistent test scores are likely to be among two or more raters who score the test.
- **Internal consistency reliability** indicates the extent to which items on a test measure the same thing.

> **Exhibit 5-6 Training Measure Validation Methods**
>
> - **Content Validity**—the extent to which the instrument represents the training program's content.
>   - *Low Content Validity*—the instrument doesn't represent a true summation of the program content.
>   - *High Content Validity*—the instrument represents a good balance of all the program content.
> - **Construct Validity**—the degree to which an instrument represents the construct it is supposed to measure.
>   - The abstract variable, such as skill or ability, is the construct.
>   - Can be defended through expert opinion, correlations, logical deductions, and criterion group studies.
> - **Concurrent Validity**—the extent to which an instrument agrees with the results of other instruments.
> - **Criterion Validity**—the extent to which the assessment can predict or agree with external constructs.
> - **Predictive Validity**—the extent to which an instrument can predict future behaviors or results.
>
> *Source:* Adapted from ASTD Learning System: "Measuring and Evaluating," p 6.

to accurately predict job performance. Similarly, a valid training measure assesses the ability of the measure to accurately reflect training outcomes. Validity can typically be assessed through content validity (the assessment instrument represents the training content) or construct validity (the extent to which the training measure accurately represents the construct it is supposed to measure). Exhibit 5-6 illustrates the range of validity methods trainers can use to ensure their metrics are valid.

Ultimately, the same care we give to selection assessment measures we must give to training measures. Measures must be both reliable and valid. Accurate measurement is essential if we want to have confidence in all our training metrics and the conclusions drawn from the needs analysis and training evaluation.

KIRKPATRICK'S MODEL FOR TRAINING EFFECTIVENESS

Donald Kirkpatrick's doctoral dissertation outlined the criteria for assessing the effectiveness of training.[10] Training effectiveness is not one-dimensional. Just as we utilize multidimensional measures of performance to assess performance effectiveness for employees, training effectiveness requires attention to several key aspects of training. While Kirkpatrick's work was initially done in the 1950s, the integrity of the model has withstood the test of time and evolved to what is now called the **New World Kirkpatrick Model**. In fact, a 2009 survey from the Institute for Corporate Productivity surveyed 704 business, human resource, and learning professionals, and found that Kirkpatrick's model is the most commonly used tool for assessing training effectiveness.[11] Exhibit 5-7 highlights what the New World Kirkpatrick Model adds to the original Kirkpatrick model.

Exhibit 5-7 New World Kirkpatrick Model of Training Effectiveness

Dimension Level	Original Kirkpatrick Model	New World Kirkpatrick Model Additions
1. Reaction	**Customer Satisfaction**—the degree to which the participant is satisfied with the training	**Engagement**—the degree to which participants are actively involved in and contributing to the learning experience **Relevance**—the degree to which training participants will have the opportunity to use or apply what they learned in training on the job
2. Learning	**Knowledge and Skills**—the degree to which the participants acquire the intended knowledge and skills, based on their participation in the training **Attitude**—the degree to which the trainees have a positive attitude toward training opportunities	**Confidence**—the degree to which the participants believe they can use the new KSAs on the job **Commitment**—the degree to which the participants intend to use the new KSAs on the job
3. Behavior	**Knowledge Transfer**—the degree to which participants apply what they learned during training when they are back on the job	**Organizational Processes and Systems**—reinforce, encourage, and reward performance of critical behaviors on the job
4. Results	**Outcomes**—the degree to which targeted outcomes occur as a result of the training and the support and accountability package	**Leading Indicators**—short-term observations and measurements suggesting that critical behaviors are on track to create a positive impact on desired results

Source: Adapted from Kirkpatrick Partners, "The New World Kirkpatrick Model." Available from https://www.kirkpatrickpartners.com/Our-Philosophy/The-New-World-Kirkpatrick-Model.

While scholars and practitioners argue these are different levels of evaluation, Kirkpatrick did not refer to the four criteria for evaluation as levels. "I was just trying to determine if my programs for managers and supervisors were successful in helping them to perform better on the job."[12] In actuality, these four criteria simply represent different aspects of training effectiveness, internal to the organization. As Jim and Wendy Kirkpatrick argue, levels 1 and 2 are focused on effective training (i.e., measure the quality of the training program and the degree to which it resulted in knowledge and skills that can be applied on the job), while levels 3 and 4 focus on training effectiveness (i.e., measure on-the-job performance and subsequent business results that occur, in part, because of training and reinforcement).[13] There is no implied level of importance of one criterion over another, although some researchers argue that the fourth level is indeed the most important as it is linked to strategic goals, and should be considered first in assessing training effectiveness.[14] Each criterion has its own importance and impact on training effectiveness. It does follow, however, that training programs that can establish training effectiveness using all four criteria would be considered most successful.

The remaining part of this chapter is dedicated first to guidelines for administering training evaluation assessment, and second to what the Kirkpatricks call training effectiveness. The focus is on outlining and describing the elements included in both level 1 and level 2 evaluation to ensure the training program was adequate in quality and content and trainees learned what was expected in the learning objectives. The next chapter focuses on the value of training for job behaviors, as well as on key organizational strategic outcomes. It will address level 3 and level 4 evaluation, analysis of training evaluation data, and the elements needed to facilitate learning transfer from training programs to the job.

Training Evaluation Administration

Training evaluation occurs during the training program, as well as afterward while trainees work on the job, to evaluate all of Kirkpatrick's levels. There are many considerations for how to administer the evaluations, including how to write appropriate evaluation questions, when to collect the data, and how to choose the most effective method of data collection for the type of questions you are asking. Level 1 evaluation for customer satisfaction, for example, should be assessed at the end of the training session to capture participants' reactions to the training session itself. Depending on training design, you may need to collect information before the training and then after the training to be more confident that trainees learned the material. As well, online surveys may be the only way to determine reactions from trainees engaging in computer-based training.

Exhibit 5-8 Guidelines for Administering Training Evaluation

Level	Information Assessed	When to Assess	Method to Assess
1. Reaction	Customer Satisfaction	• Immediately after training	• Online or paper-and-pencil survey
	Engagement	• During session • Immediately after training	• Observation • Online or paper-and-pencil survey
	Relevance	• Immediately after training	• Online or paper-and-pencil survey
2. Learning	Knowledge and Skills	• Before training/pretest (if possible) • Immediately after training	• Online or paper-and-pencil survey for knowledge • Performance test for skills
	Attitude	• Immediately after training	• Online or paper-and-pencil survey
	Confidence	• Immediately after training • A period of time after training to assess sustained confidence toward using new skills	• Online or paper-and-pencil survey
	Commitment	• Immediately after training • A period of time after training to assess sustained commitment to using new skills	• Online or paper-and-pencil survey

(Continued)

Exhibit 5-8 (Continued)

Level	Information Assessed	When to Assess	Method to Assess
3. Behavior	Knowledge Transfer	• Before training/pretest • A period of time after training to assess knowledge retention and use on the job	• Observation • Online or paper-and-pencil survey
	Organizational Processes and Systems	• Following training when trainees return to the job	• Observation
4. Results	Outcomes	• Before training/pretest • A period of time after training to assess key metrics	• Online or paper-and-pencil survey
	Leading Indicators	• Before training/pretest • At intervals after training to determine if critical behaviors are on track after training	• Observation • Online or paper-and-pencil survey

Source: Adapted from Donald Kirkpatrick and James D. Kirkpatrick, *Transferring Learning to Behavior: Using the Four Levels to Improve Performance* (San Francisco: Berrett-Koehler, 2005).

Exhibit 5-8 outlines the type of information assessed for training evaluation, the ideal time to collect the data, and the type(s) of methods that can be used to collect the data.

Paper-and-pencil and online surveys are generally the most common ways to collect training evaluation data. The advantage is that both protect respondent anonymity as names do not need to be collected. A downside of using paper-and-pencil surveys, however, is that they are typically administered by the trainer at the end of the training session, which may lead to some trainees not providing honest responses to the questions for fear of repercussions, undue pressure from the trainer to receive high evaluation marks, or possible loss of anonymity. One way to combat this concern is to ask a trainee to collect the surveys while the trainer steps out of the room. While online surveys avoid the problem of undue pressure from trainers to receive high evaluations, the return rate may suffer if the trainees must find a computer at the end of their training session. Many trainees may simply choose not to respond or may forget to respond to requests for the evaluation. One way to resolve this issue is to limit online surveys to those doing online or technology-mediated training sessions and require trainees to fill out the survey before they leave the training interface and receive certification that they successfully completed the training program.

In addition to surveys, many items can be observed, including on-the-job behaviors as assessed by trainers, peers, subordinates, or superiors to the trainee. We also broadly use the term *observation* to indicate the way to collect data from existing information available in the organization (e.g., profitability, sales, customer satisfaction) or identifying existing human resource programs and systems to support successful training transfer. In short, the trainer can easily find this information without directly surveying trainees to assess some types of training evaluation.

The last issue to address in training evaluation administration is how to properly write survey questions. While this may seem easy, writing questions that are easily measurable and can provide confidence in the results has some important guidelines to follow. First, it is important to be aware of the different types of questions you can ask during training evaluation (see Exhibit 5-9). Subjective questions are best for assessing a person's perceptions about the training session itself, or something the individual learned during the training. Objective questions are best for gathering metrics to assess outcomes or results. Open-ended or essay questions are ideal when we want people to elaborate on information. These are typically associated with subjective questions, although not all subjective questions will be in an open-ended format. Closed-ended questions are used when there is no interest in having trainees elaborate on their observations or perceptions. Both true/false and multiple-choice questions are best for testing trainees on job knowledge to ensure learning occurred. Lastly, Likert-like scale questions may be used to provide some structure and measurability to subjective questions, rather than an open-ended response that elaborates using written narrative.

Exhibit 5-9 Types of Survey Questions

Question Type	Description
Subjective	Opinion based on perceptions using feelings, emotions, and aesthetics • How comfortable was the room in which you received your training?
Objective	Quantifiable, fact-based answer that is measurable • How long have you worked for the company?
Open-Ended/Essay	Requires unrestricted response to a question or statement using subject's knowledge, observations, or feelings • Describe the advantages of using this new process over our existing process to manufacture eyeglass frames.
Closed-Ended	Question that requires a short answer or a simple yes/no response • Were the course materials clear and easy to understand? Yes or No
True/False	Question that requires an understanding of the accuracy of the statement • The oven temperature must be 350°F when baking chocolate chip cookies. True or False
Multiple-Choice	Question that provides a prompt and requires respondents to choose among several options to find the correct answer • Which employment law states we cannot discriminate based on disability? (a) Title VII (b) ADEA (c) ADA (d) FMLA
Likert-Like Scale	Question that provides an odd number of anchors to a question; similar to a multiple-choice question but the response is on a continuum and typically assesses a subject's subjective experience from highest to lowest value • How comfortable was the room in which you received your training? (a) very comfortable (b) comfortable (c) neither comfortable nor uncomfortable (d) uncomfortable (e) very uncomfortable

Second, when writing questions, we have to make sure they are easy to understand and facilitate good measurement and interpretation of results. First, questions should use simple, direct language.[15] People, on average, read at an eighth-grade level, so it is important not to use complex words or words with more than one meaning. The motto here is to keep it simple and straightforward. Second, questions should be specific.[16] For example, don't ask, "Do you exercise regularly?"—a closed-ended question that provides you with no real data to meaningfully analyze. Instead, ask, "How many days a week do you exercise?"

Third, break down big ideas into multiple questions.[17] For example, customer satisfaction is a complex concept. Instead of asking, "How satisfied were you with the training session?," focus on the different aspects of customer satisfaction. Ask questions such as (1) "Did you enjoy participating in this training session?" (2) "Will this training session help you do your job better?" and (3) "Would you participate in a training session with this instructor again?"

Fourth, avoid leading questions.[18] We have all read surveys that pose questions in such a way as to bias how the researchers want us to respond to the question, leading us by the nose to provide the answer they are looking for to justify their ideas. For example, don't ask a question such as "Do you think we should shorten this training session to save money?" You will get a very different answer to that question than if you asked, "What do you consider to be the ideal length of time to spend in this training session?"

Lastly, don't ask more than one thing in a question, also known as a double-barreled question.[19] It is difficult to analyze this type of question because you don't know if participants agreed or disagreed with both issues in the question or agreed with one item more strongly than the other and felt compelled to answer higher than they would have if the two issues were asked separately. For example, don't ask, "Did your company prepare you for your first day, and was your supervisor available and responsive?" It is possible the company prepared you for the first day, but your supervisor wasn't very responsive or available. Break it down into two (or more) separate questions, just as you would break down a complex concept like customer service into its more specific components.

Overall, the goal is to keep the questions simple, straightforward, and explicit in what they are asking. If you can ask for information to assess something with more than a simple yes or no, this is important for truly understanding the value of the training session. Seek to obtain answers that can provide you with the rich information you need to improve your training delivery and training effectiveness.

Level 1: Reaction

As noted previously, 10% of learning occurs in the classroom, or during training programs specifically. Chapter 4, on learning theories, discussed the importance of designing programs and delivering material in a way that maximizes learning. Whether we are decreasing cognitive load through managing the delivery of material, or ensuring delivery of material in a way that maximizes retention and recall by using a multimodal approach, the key is the trainer and the training context.

While Kirkpatrick's original model laid the burden of training **reaction** on the trainer, the New World Model argues that the effectiveness of the trainer and the context are only one aspect of a positive training experience. Trainees must be engaged with the material in order to react positively to the training. Further, they need to perceive the training as relevant, or the chances of their applying the training on the job are slim.

The 2009 study by the Institute for Corporate Productivity found that 92% of respondents used level 1 to assess effective training.[20] Unfortunately, for many organizations, that is the only training assessment tool used. While the information gathered from level 1 training assessment is of great interest to trainers, this information is of lesser interest to organization leaders with its negligible direct impact on organizational outcomes.[21] Think back to our discussion at the top of this chapter of the *Fast Company* article. If we simply argue that 95% of our employees enjoyed the training session, that does not tell the senior executives whether or not the money was well spent, or whether the training will have an impact on the organization's bottom line. It is easy to conclude that level 1 training evaluation, while important to the trainer, is not sufficient to affect strategic training goals. Trainers should be careful to consider the cost-benefit analysis of assessing level 1 reactions over more strategic levels such as behaviors or results. Less effort and cost should be invested in assessing reactions, and greater attention should be paid to training outcomes of strategic value to the organization.[22]

Because level 1 and 2 training evaluation is oftentimes the primary focus of post-training assessment, sometimes level 1 and 2 assessment is done at the risk of having a low response rate from participants, thus leaving no benefit to the organization. Streamlining and rethinking what to assess at levels 1 and 2 not only gets a greater response rate, but also provides for more personal and meaningful responses from trainees, which can benefit trainers in designing future training programs. The New World Model recommends shifting level 1 and 2 evaluation from a trainer-focused perspective to a learner-focused perspective.[23] This makes sense given adult learning is, by definition, learner-focused. Exhibit 5-10 provides a few examples of how to adapt evaluation questions to provide more meaningful data for trainers, for maximum impact with minimal effort and cost.

Exhibit 5-10 Learner-Focused Questions

With the learner-focused questions below, use the following prompt to ask questions of the participants.

Please indicate the extent to which you agree with the following statements:

(a) strongly agree (b) agree (c) neither agree nor disagree (d) disagree (e) strongly disagree

Trainer-Focused Questions	Learner-Focused Questions
The course materials were well organized.	I found the course materials easy to follow.
The facilitator demonstrated a good understanding of the content.	My learning was enhanced by the knowledge of the facilitator.
The material was relevant to my needs.	I will be able to apply what I learned immediately.

Source: Adapted from Jim Kirkpatrick and Wendy Kirkpatrick, "The Four Levels of Evaluation: An Update," *TD at Work* (February 2015): 8.

Customer satisfaction.

This dimension is from Kirkpatrick's original model. The focus is on customer (trainee) reactions and satisfaction with the trainer, the program, and the training context. This dimension is typically associated with the "smiley face" reaction sheet commonly used after training sessions. Am I satisfied with the training experience? Was the room comfortable? Do I like the trainer?

Assessing this dimension is key to understanding how well the trainer managed the session and the requisite materials used for instruction. This dimension plays a key role in evaluating the trainer as effective, thereby ensuring his or her continued employment (if an in-house trainer) or continued contract (if an external trainer). As noted in Chapter 4, the trainer needs to be knowledgeable about the subject matter and able to present the information in a way that minimizes cognitive load and maximizes learning potential for the trainees. Given that the foundation for learning on the job happens in the classroom, the curriculum and the context need to have maximum impact to increase the likelihood of employees using the training content on the job.

Engagement.

As also discussed in Chapter 4, learners must be engaged with the material to best learn the content. Bloom's Taxonomy requires increased engagement as training programs approach higher-order learning. Engagement speaks to the trainees' motivation to immerse themselves into the training program.

As previously discussed, adult learners as a rule are self-directed with respect to their learning if they are motivated to engage in the training in the first place. Circumstances may occur where trainees are indifferent to a training program, particularly if past experience tells them the training will be wasted and not used because of systemic problems in the company. As well, if the trainees are not motivated to learn the training content, the training investment will be wasted on them. Engagement activities, however, increase the likelihood that trainees will stay motivated and actively participate in the training. Like motivation, engagement is the responsibility of the trainee. It is the responsibility of the trainer, however, to offer a training program that actively invites the trainee to participate throughout. As well, trainee engagement may be low because the organization has dropped the ball in the past in helping the trainees use the skills learned (training transfer), or the organization simply made poor hires in the first place, which resulted in a poor person–job match. Regardless of why individuals are not engaged, trainee engagement is a necessary condition for successful training initiatives.

Relevance.

The usefulness of the training program—specifically, whether or not it is useful on the job for trainees—is another important dimension to assess for level 1 reactions. Training must be relevant and usable immediately in the service of their jobs, or trainees will not be motivated to engage in the training, nor will they be satisfied with the training program.

As well, given the importance of strategic training as discussed in Chapter 1, why would the company spend money on training if it was not important and relevant to the organization's bottom line? This would result in a waste of resources, with nothing to show for the investment.

Level 2: Learning

Level 2 addresses the issues around **learning** and the factors that contribute to learning the training materials. First, each training program offers specific knowledge and skills the trainees are supposed to learn. The goal of the program is to ensure each trainee internalizes the new knowledge and skills and uses them on the job. When employees subsequently fail to perform, the first assumption is that they didn't learn the knowledge and skills needed and therefore need to be retrained on the basics. Just as it is easy to neglect non-performance-related factors when engaged in the performance evaluation process of employees, it is just as easy to neglect those same factors when addressing performance, post-training.

Performance depends on three basic factors: trainee ability, trainee motivation, and a supportive context (including both role clarity and a positive work environment).[24] *Ability* is addressed through the knowledge and skills taught in the training program, as well as through hiring those with the skills and/or a motivation to learn new skills. Ability can be assessed at level 2 (KSAs). *Motivation* to perform is addressed through engagement, as discussed in level 1; trainee attitude, confidence, and commitment, as addressed in level 2; and the consistency with which the organization reinforces training transfer through organizational policies, as addressed in level 3 (discussed in more detail in the next chapter). The *context* is addressed across several levels. First, context is considered through customer service–related issues in level 1. As well, it is addressed in level 2 with organizational policies. It is an oversimplification to assume that an employee who does not perform well after training simply needs more training. The motivation to perform, as well as the training context, will have a huge impact on post-training performance, and these factors cannot be ignored when doing training evaluation.[25]

Just as we need to consider the cost-benefit analysis associated with level 1 training evaluation, the same can be said for level 2. Learning is important, but just because employees *can* learn does not mean they *will* learn, nor does it mean they will use the newly learned knowledge and skills on the job. For example, an employee could perform lousy on a knowledge-based assessment post-training, but might work hard to practice the new skills on the job later on. Likewise, a trainee could score well on the post-training assessment but not have the motivation or support to transfer the skills to the job. While it is important to assess that trainees have learned the training content to make sure it is effective training, it is also important to ensure that the information can be used on the job and will have a strategic impact for the organization, resulting in training effectiveness. Thus, the New World Kirkpatrick Model argues that learning must go beyond assessment of the knowledge and skills, and must address trainee attitudes, confidence in using the new material, and a commitment to using it on the job after completing training.

KSAs.

KSAs refer to the knowledge, skills, and abilities obtained during a training program. Training is considered necessary when a skill or knowledge is needed for the employees to perform their jobs. Knowledge addresses the information the trainees comprehend, and skill is focused on the trainees' ability to do something or perform a task right now. Level 2 evaluation requires us to determine what, if anything, the trainees retained during the training session.

Attitude.

Along with knowledge and skills, trainees must have the proper attitude to make training worthwhile. If a trainee believes the training will not have any benefit, it will be difficult to overcome that attitude and experience an effective training program. Thus, trainers must make a good argument to the trainee for why the training is worthwhile and beneficial. Just like motivation and engagement, attitude comes from within trainees, and the decision to have a good attitude about the training program rests primarily in their hands once the organization properly communicates what will occur in the training, and why it is important to the employees and the organization. A discussion of how to deal with problem trainees is provided in Appendix C, "Managing a Training Session."

Confidence.

The New World Kirkpatrick Model added confidence to level 2 evaluation. Trainees need to believe they can perform the task on the job effectively after the training and feel confident in their abilities.[26] Another way to consider this is to think about self-efficacy, or the belief in one's own ability to complete tasks and reach goals.[27] While the Kirkpatricks use the term *confidence*, in reality, they likely mean the construct, self-efficacy. As Albert Bandura argues,

> the construct of self-efficacy differs from the colloquial term "confidence." Confidence is a nonspecific term that refers to strength of belief but does not necessarily specify what the certainty is about. I can be supremely confident that I will fail at an endeavor. Perceived self-efficacy refers to belief in one's agentive capabilities, that one can produce given levels of attainment. A self-efficacy belief, therefore, includes both an affirmation of a capability level and the strength of that belief. Confidence is a catchword rather than a construct embedded in a theoretical system.[28]

As we think about motivation and its impact on performance, expectancy theory, as discussed in Chapter 3, is a great way to consider the impact of confidence (or self-efficacy). In order for trainees to be motivated, they must believe if they put forth the effort, they can perform the task at hand. Without confidence and belief in their ability to utilize their new skills and knowledge, trainees are unlikely to be motivated to learn. Therefore, whether we call it self-efficacy or confidence, the trainees must believe in themselves for the training to be effective.

When we consider which outcomes to measure for level 2 evaluation, it is important to use variables and terminology that can be effectively measured. It is fine to measure confidence, as opposed to self-efficacy, as long as we are very specific about the issue on which we are assessing the trainee's confidence. Specifically, "How confident do you feel about using this new information on the job correctly?" is a better question than "How confident do you feel after this training session?" The former question gets at how confident trainees feel performing a specific task or skill, while the latter gets at general confidence. The latter question is not very useful when assessing training effectiveness because it doesn't address what the trainee is confident about. Perhaps, as Bandura notes, the trainee is completely confident she or he will *not* be able to perform the task on the job. Thus, when assessing confidence, specify which dimension of the training trainees feel confident in, such that you are assessing how their ability to perform on the job improved.

Commitment.

Along with feeling confident they can perform their new skills or use their new knowledge on the job, trainees need to commit to actually using their newfound knowledge and skills on the job. Just because individuals can master a new skill and feel confident in their ability to use it doesn't mean they will actually use it. Therefore, the extent to which trainees are committed to using the skills and knowledge is an important part of level 2 assessment, and gets at the importance of trainee motivation to use the new knowledge and skills.

Of course, employees may be initially committed to using their new skills and knowledge on the job, but that doesn't necessarily translate into actual use and transfer of those skills to the job on a consistent, daily basis. A wide variety of factors influence whether or not material learned in a training session will translate into actual changes in behavior on the job. The process of actually using the training information on the job is discussed in the next chapter on level 3 and 4 assessment, and in a separate, more detailed section on knowledge transfer later in Chapter 6.

CHAPTER SUMMARY

Before we design our training programs, it is important to ensure we understand the strategic goals for the training and consider the important outcomes in advance. Knowing what we want to measure for outcomes enables us to design the training program so we are confident in the results and can accurately draw conclusions. There are many threats to the conclusions drawn from training programs. Did the applicants have different experiences in the training session? Did they really learn, or was it an artifact of the way they measured outcomes? Understanding what you can and cannot conclude about your training outcomes, based on how you designed the training program, is essential for making the case for the impact on important strategic outcomes for the organization.

Along with understanding how to design the training programs, ensuring the learning objectives for the training are accurately reflected is key for training success. Learning objectives must include the context within which the training will occur, the intended audience of the training, the actions or behaviors the trainees are expected to demonstrate, and the standards against which the trainees will be assessed. The trainees then have full information on what they need to do, where they need to do it, and how they need to do it to be successful.

Once the learning objectives and training design considerations have been determined, the different levels of evaluation must be delineated. The New World Kirkpatrick Model of training effectiveness outlines four basic levels of evaluation trainers must consider. Level 1 assesses how trainees reacted to the training itself, including satisfaction with aspects of the training, engagement of the trainees in the training sessions, and relevance of the training for the trainees' jobs. Level 2 assesses what trainees learned during the training sessions, including the KSAs needed for the job, as well as the attitude, confidence, and commitment by trainees to utilize the newly acquired KSAs on the job. Both level 1 and level 2 are necessary, but not sufficient, to achieve the higher levels of training evaluation that will have a strategic impact for the organization. Level 1 and level 2 assess if the training was effective, but that doesn't always mean it will have the intended impact on the organization's bottom line. Trainers pay close attention to level 1 and 2 outcomes to ensure they deliver good training and that the trainees learned what they set out to teach them.

KEY TERMS

Backwards design. A concept applied to curriculum design by Wiggins and McTighe that argues for understanding the outcomes you want to accomplish before designing the training curriculum, including the following steps: (1) identify the desired results from the training, (2) determine the acceptable evidence that the training goals were accomplished, and (3) design the learning experiences and instruction to achieve the desired results.

Learning. Kirkpatrick level 2 evaluation that assesses knowledge, skills, and abilities learned, and trainee attitudes, confidence, and commitment to use new skills learned in the training.

Learning evaluation strategy. A guide for organizations to use to design and implement their learning evaluation that should naturally evolve from their corporate and training and development strategies, including five principles: (1) focus on high-priority learning areas, (2) address evaluation requirements of multiple stakeholders, (3) foster shared responsibility for performance improvement, (4) collect data and use resources efficiently, and (5) conduct action planning.

Learning objectives. The knowledge or skills that trainees will have to obtain and exhibit in the training session to achieve the training goals.

New World Kirkpatrick Model. The accepted standard for evaluating training at the reaction, learning, behavior, and results levels for the organization; based on Donald Kirkpatrick's doctoral dissertation, and adapted in 2010 to include 21st century considerations based on years of research.

One-shot case study. A nonexperimental design in which a group of employees are provided a training program and then tested to see if the training program was effective.

One-shot pretest–posttest design. A nonexperimental design similar to the one-shot case study, but that also includes a pretest as well as a posttest to assess learning effectiveness.

Posttest-only control group design. An experimental design similar to the static-group comparison nonexperimental design in which trainees are randomly assigned to training conditions, and pre- and posttest assessments are done to determine learning effectiveness.

Pretest–posttest control group design. An experimental design with two groups in which trainees are randomly assigned to training conditions, the experimental group gets the training, and pre- and posttest measures are compared to determine learning effectiveness.

Reaction. Kirkpatrick level 1 evaluation that assesses trainee satisfaction, trainee engagement, and relevance of training to participants.

Solomon four-group design. An experimental design combining the pretest–posttest control group design and the posttest-only control group design in which trainees are randomly assigned to training conditions, and pre- and posttest measures are compared to determine learning effectiveness.

Static-group comparison. A nonexperimental design similar to the one-shot case study, but that involves two groups—one that receives the training and another that does not—and posttest measures are compared to assess learning effectiveness.

END-OF-CHAPTER QUESTIONS AND EXERCISES

Discussion Questions

1. Define the five elements of a learning evaluation strategy. Give an example of a training program you could develop for a company, and apply the learning evaluation strategy to the training program. Who would be the stakeholders? What would be the high-priority learning area? Who should share responsibility for performance improvement?

2. What four items should be included in learning objectives? Why are all four of these items essential to training programs and learning objectives? What would happen if a trainer did not use a learning objective?

3. When designing a training evaluation program, which designs, experimental or nonexperimental, are the easiest to use for corporate training? Discuss the importance of thinking about evaluation before you decide on the content in your training program.

4. What are the four levels of Kirkpatrick's model of training effectiveness? How do the additions to the New World Model change or enhance training effectiveness?

5. What is the value of using backwards design when developing a training program? Explain how this helps when deciding what and how to evaluate training metrics.

Ethical Scenario

P Is for Perfection (and Pizza)

Shawn recently completed his master's degree and took a new job with Integrity Systems as its first dedicated trainer. His first task was to bring in-house all training for the company's sales force. Although he wasn't told that he had to conduct an evaluation, he felt that doing so would show initiative and a good evaluation would demonstrate that Integrity Systems had made a good decision to hire him. Shawn felt confident about his ability to develop a training program that sales staff would enjoy, so he knew he would conduct a level 1 evaluation. Being new to the company, however, he wasn't sure of the culture and the degree to which he could trust that the sales staff would choose to utilize the training once completed, so he was unsure about conducting a higher-level evaluation. He knew his professors would tell him to do a thorough evaluation, but then they didn't have to worry about keeping his job. Fortunately, his boss was happy with just doing a level 1 evaluation.

When it came time to deliver the training, Shawn decided to use some of his budget to provide pizza and beer to the sales staff at the end of the training. After people had started drinking, Shawn remembered that he hadn't distributed the evaluation form. So, he passed the evaluations out and asked everyone to complete them. As he did that, he joked that "no one gets a second beer until you all give me 5s," which was the top score on the evaluation form.

1. What do you think about Shawn's evaluation strategy (i.e., doing just a level 1 evaluation)?
2. What do you think about how Shawn administered the evaluation?
3. What suggestions do you have for improving the evaluation process for the sales training?

4.1 Developing Learning Objectives

Write one possible learning objective for each of the following hypothetical training programs. Research will need to be conducted on potential training content and what would be considered successful completion of training.

a. Diversity training for middle-level managers
b. New data input software training for accounting staff
c. Safety training on blood-borne pathogens for all employees
d. Training for cashier at McDonald's
e. Training for new hostess at a local restaurant
f. Training on how to use a floor polisher for a school janitor

4.2 Identify Level of Analysis

For each of the evaluation statements listed below (to be answered on a Likert-like scale from *strongly disagree* to *strongly agree*), identify which level of evaluation (level 1 or level 2) is being assessed.

a. The meeting room was comfortable.
b. I learned information I can use on the job.
c. Indicate the extent to which you expect to use the skills learned today on the job.
d. I am confident in my ability to perform these new skills correctly.
e. I found the materials easy to understand.
f. The training was relevant to my job.
g. The time allotted for the training was sufficient.
h. The trainer was well prepared.
i. The trainer answered all my questions.
j. I was actively engaged with the material during the session.
k. How do you hope to change how you do your job based on the training?
l. What aspects of the training could be improved?
m. I am excited to practice these new skills on the job.
n. I am motivated to learn all that I can.

4.3 Training Design to Assess ROI

Source: Adapted and used with permission from the ROI Institute. Jack J. Phillips and Patti P. Phillips, "Nations Hotel: Measuring ROI in Business Coaching," in *ROI at Work: Best Practice Case Studies from the Real World* (Alexandria, VA: American Society for Training and Development, 2014).

Background

Nations Hotel Corporation (NHC) is a large U.S.-based hotel firm with operations in 15 countries.

The firm has maintained steady growth to include more than 300 hotels in cities all over the world. NHC enjoys one of the most recognized names in the global lodging industry, with 98% brand awareness worldwide and 72% overall guest satisfaction.

The hospitality industry is very competitive, cyclical, and subject to swings with the economy. Room rentals are price sensitive, and customer satisfaction is extremely important for NHC. Profits are squeezed if operating costs get out of hand. NHC top executives constantly seek ways to improve operational efficiency, customer satisfaction, revenue growth, and retention of high-performing employees. Executives—particularly those in charge of individual properties—are under constant pressure to show improvement in these key measures.

The learning and development function, the Nations Hotel Learning Organization (NHLO), conducted a brief survey of executives to identify learning needs to help them meet some of their particular goals. NHLO was interested in developing customized learning processes including the possibility of individual coaching sessions. Most of the executives surveyed indicated that they would like to work with a qualified coach to assist them through a variety of challenges and issues. The executives believed that this would be an efficient way to learn, apply, and achieve results. Consequently, NHLO developed a formal, structured coaching program—Coaching for Business Impact (CBI)—and offered it to the executives at the vice president level and above.

As the project was conceived, the senior executives became interested in showing the value of the coaching project. Although they supported coaching as a method to improve executive performance, they wanted to see the actual return on investment (ROI). The goal was to evaluate 25 executives, randomly selected (if possible) from the participants in CBI.

The Program

The following communicates the steps in the new coaching program from the beginning to the ultimate outcomes. This program involves 14 discrete elements and processes.

1. *Voluntary Participation*—Executives had to volunteer to be part of this project. Voluntary commitment translates into a willing participant who is not only open to changing, improving, and applying what is being learned, but also willing to provide the necessary data for evaluating the coaching process. The voluntary nature of the coaching program, however, meant that not all executives who needed coaching would be involved. When compared to mandatory involvement, however, the volunteer effort appeared to be an important ingredient for success. It was envisioned that as improvements were realized and executives reflected on the positive perceptions of coaching, other executives would follow suit.

2. *The Need for Coaching*—An important part of the process was a dialog with the executive to determine if coaching was actually needed. In this step, NHLO staff used a checklist to review the issues, needs, and concerns about the coaching agreement. Along with establishing a need, the checklist revealed key areas where coaching could help. This step ensured that the assistance desired by the executives could actually be provided by the coach.

3. *Self-Assessment*—As part of the process, a self-assessment was taken from the individual being coached, his or her immediate manager, and direct reports. This was a typical 360-degree assessment instrument that focused on areas of feedback, communication, openness, trust, and other competencies necessary for success in the competitive hospitality environment.

4. *Commitment for Data*—As a precondition, executives had to agree to provide data during coaching and at appropriate times following the engagement. This up-front commitment

ensured that data of sufficient quality and quantity could be obtained. The data made evaluation easier and helped executives see their progress and realize the value of coaching.

5. *Roles and Responsibilities*—For both the coach and the executive, roles and responsibilities were clearly defined. It was important for the executive to understand that the coach was there to listen, provide feedback, and evaluate. The coach was not there to make decisions for the executive. This clear distinction was important for productive coaching sessions.

6. *The Match*—Coaches were provided from a reputable business coaching firm where NHLO had developed a productive relationship. Coach profiles were presented to executives, and a tentative selection was made on a priority listing. The respective coach was provided background information on the executive, and a match was made. After this match, the coaching process began.

7. *Orientation Session*—The executive and coach formally met during an orientation session. Here, the NHLO staff explained the process, requirements, timetable, and other administrative issues. This was a very brief session typically conducted in a group; however, it could also be conducted individually.

8. *The Engagement*—One of the most important aspects of the process involved making sure that the engagement was connected to a business need. Typical coaching engagements focused on behavioral issues (e.g., an executive's inability to listen to employees). To connect to the business impact, the behavior change must link to a business consequence. In the initial engagement, the coach uncovered the business need by asking a series of questions to examine the consequences of behavior change. This process involved asking "So what?" and "What if?" as the desired behavior changes were described.

As the business needs were identified, the measures must be in the categories of productivity, sales, efficiency, direct cost savings, employee retention, and customer satisfaction. The engagement should be connected to corresponding changes in at least three of those measures. Without elevating the engagement to a business need, it would have been difficult to evaluate coaching with this level of analysis.

9. *Coaching Sessions*—Individual sessions were conducted at least once a month (usually more often) lasting a minimum of one hour (sometimes more), depending on the need and issues at hand. The coach and executive met face to face, if possible. If not, coaching was conducted in a telephone conversation. Routine meetings were necessary to keep the process on track.

10. *Goal Setting*—Although individuals could set goals in any area needing improvements, the senior executives chose five priority areas for targeting: sales growth, productivity/operational efficiency, direct cost reduction, retention of key staff members, and customer satisfaction. The executives selected one measure in at least three of these areas. Essentially, they would have three specific goals that would require three action plans, described next.

11. *Action Planning*—To drive the desired improvement, the action planning process was utilized. Common in coaching engagements, this process provided an opportunity for the executive to detail specific action steps planned with the team. These steps were designed to drive a particular consequence that was a business impact measure. Figure 5-1 shows a typical action planning document used in this process. The executive was to complete the action plan during the first two to three coaching sessions, detailing step-by-step what he or she would accomplish to drive a particular improvement. Under the analysis

section, Parts A, B, and C are completed in the initial development of the plan. The coaches distributed action plan packages that included instructions, blank forms, and completed examples. The coach explained the process in the second coaching session. The action plans could be revised as needed. At least three improvement measures were required out of the five areas targeted with the program. Consequently, at least three action plans had to be developed and implemented.

12. *Active Learning*—After the executive developed the specific measures in question and the action plans, several development strategies were discussed and implemented with the help of the coach. The coach actually facilitated the efforts, utilizing any number of typical learning processes, such as reading assignments, self-assessment tools, skill practices, video feedback, journaling, and other techniques. Coaching is considered to be an active learning process where the executive experiments, applies, and reflects on the experience. The coach provides input, reaction, assessment, and evaluation.

13. *Progress Review*—At monthly sessions, the coach and executive reviewed progress and revised the action plan, if necessary. The important issue was to continue to make adjustments to sustain the process.

14. *Reporting*—After six months in the coaching engagement, the executive reported improvement by completing other parts of the action plan. This includes Parts D, E, F, and G, and intangible benefits and comments. If the development efforts were quite involved and the measures driven were unlikely to change in the interim, a longer period of time was utilized. For most executives, six months was appropriate.

These elements reflected a results-based project appropriately called Coaching for Business Impact.

Figure 5-1   ROI Action Plan

Action Plan: Coaching for Business Impact

Name: _____   Coach: _____   Date: _____

Impact Objective: _____   Evaluation Period: _____ to _____

Improvement Measure: _____ :   Current Performance: _____   Target Performance: _____

Action Step	Analysis
1. _____	A. What is the unit of measure? _____
2. _____	B. What is the value (cost) of one unit? $ _____
3. _____	C. How did you arrive at this value? _____ _____ _____

(Continued)

Figure 5-1 (Continued)

Action Step	Analysis
4. _____	D. How much did the measure change during the evaluation period? (monthly value) _____
5. _____	E. What other factors could have contributed to this improvement? _____
6. _____	F. What percent of this change was actually caused by this program? _____%
7. _____	G. What level of confidence do you place on the above information? (100% = Certainty and 0% = No Confidence) _____
8. _____	
Intangible Benefits:	

Comments: _____
_____
_____

Objectives

An effective ROI study flows from the objectives of the particular project being evaluated. For coaching, it is important to clearly indicate the objectives at different levels. Figure 5-2 shows the detailed objectives associated with this project. The objectives reflect the four classic levels of evaluation plus a fifth level for ROI. Some of the levels, however, have been adjusted for the coaching environment. With these objectives in mind, it becomes a relatively easy task to measure progress on these objectives.

Figure 5-2 Objectives of Business Impact Coaching

Level 1. Reaction Objectives

After participating in this coaching program, the executive will:

1. Perceive coaching to be relevant to the job
2. Perceive coaching to be important to job performance at the present time
3. Perceive coaching to be value added in terms of time and funds invested

Level 3. Application Objectives (continued)

3. Show improvements on the following items:
   a. Uncovering individual strengths and weaknesses
   b. Translating feedback into action plans
   c. Involving team members in projects and goals

4. Rate the coach as effective
5. Recommend this program to other executives

Level 2. Learning Objectives

After completing this coaching program, the executives should improve their understanding of skills for each of the following:

1. Uncovering individual strengths and weaknesses
2. Translating feedback into action plans
3. Involving team members in projects and goals
4. Communicating effectively
5. Collaborating with colleagues
6. Improving personal effectiveness
7. Enhancing leadership skills

Level 3. Application Objectives

Six months after completing this coaching program, executives should

1. Complete the action plan
2. Adjust the plan accordingly as needed for changes in the environment

   d. Communicating effectively
   e. Collaborating with colleagues
   f. Improving personal effectiveness
   g. Enhancing leadership

4. Identify barriers and enablers

Level 4. Impact Objectives

After completing this coaching program, executives should improve at least three specific measures in the following areas:

1. Sales growth
2. Productivity/operational efficiency
3. Direct cost reduction
4. Retention of key staff members
5. Customer satisfaction

Level 5. ROI Objective

The ROI value should be 25%.

Planning for Evaluation

Figure 5-3 shows the completed data collection plan for this project. The plan captures the following techniques and strategies used to collect data for this project:

1. *Objectives*—The objectives are listed as defined in Figure 5-2 and are repeated only in general terms.
2. *Measures/Data*—Additional definition is sometimes needed beyond the specific objectives. The measures used to gauge progress on the objective are defined.
3. *Data Collection Method*—This column in Figure 5-4 indicates the specific method used for collecting data at different levels. In this case, action plans and questionnaires are the primary methods.
4. *Data Sources*—For each data group, sources are identified. For coaches, sources are usually limited to the executive, coach, manager of the executive, and individual/team reporting to the executive. Although the actual data provided by executives will usually come from the records of the organization, the executive will include the data in the action plan document.
5. *Timing*—The timing refers to the time for collecting specific data items from the beginning of the coaching engagement.
6. *Responsibilities*—The responsibilities refer to the individual(s) who will actually collect the data.

Figure 5-3   Data Integration Plan

Data Category	Executive Questionnaire	Senior Executive Questionnaire	Action Plan	Company Records
Reaction	X			
Learning	X	X		
Application	X	X	X	
Impact			X	X
Costs				X

The data collection plan shows how the various types of data are collected and integrated to provide an overall evaluation of the program. A sample plan is located in Figure 5-4.

Figure 5-5 shows the completed plan for data analysis. This document addresses the key issues needed for a credible analysis of the data and includes the following:

1. *Data Items*—The plan shows when business measures will be collected from one of the five priority areas.

2. *Methods for Isolating the Effects of Coaching*—The method of isolating the effects of coaching on the data is estimation, where the executives actually allocate the proportion of the improvement to the coaching process (more on the consequences of this later). Although there are more credible methods, such as control groups and trend analysis, they are not appropriate for this situation. Although the estimates are subjective, they are developed by those individuals who should know them best (the executives), and the results are adjusted for the error of the estimate.

3. *Methods of Converting Data to Monetary Values*—Data are converted using a variety of methods. For most data items, standard values are available. When standard values are not available, the input of an in-house expert is pursued. This expert is typically an individual who collects, assimilates, and reports the data. If neither of these approaches is feasible, the executive estimates the value.

4. *Cost Categories*—The standard cost categories included are the typical costs for a coaching assignment.

5. *Communication Targets*—Several audiences are included for coaching results, representing the key stakeholder groups: the executive, the executive's immediate manager, the sponsor of the program, and the NHLO staff. Other influences and issues are also detailed in this plan.

Questions

1. How did the decision to conduct an ROI study influence the design of the coaching program?

2. Critique the evaluation design and method of data collection.

3. Discuss the importance of getting participants committed to provide quality data.

4. What other strategies for isolating the impact of the coaching program could have been employed here?

5. Discuss the importance of credibility of data in an ROI study.

Figure 5-4. Sample Data Collection Plan

Program: Coaching for Business Impact **Responsibility:** Jack Phillips

Date: _____

Level	Objective	Measures/Data	Data Collection Method	Data Sources	Timing	Responsibilities
1	**Reaction/Satisfaction** • Relevance to job • Importance to job success • Value add • Coach's effectiveness • Recommendation to others	• 4 out of 5 on a 1-to-5 rating scale	• Questionnaire	• Executives	• 6 months after engagement	• NHLO Staff
2	**Learning** • Uncovering strengths/weaknesses • Translating feedback into action • Involving *team* members • Communicating effectively • Collaborating with colleagues • Improving personal effectiveness • Enhancing leadership skills	• 4 out of 5 on a 1-to-5 rating scale	• Questionnaire	• Executives • Coach	• 6 months after engagement	• NHLO Staff
3	**Application/Implementation** • Complete and adjust action plan • Identify barriers and enablers • Show improvements in skills	• Checklist for action plan • 4 out of 5 on a 1-to-5 rating scale	• Action Plan • Questionnaire	• Executive • Coach	• 6 months after engagement	• NHLO Staff
4	**Business Impact (3 of 5)** 1. Sales growth 2. Productivity/efficiency 3. Direct cost reduction 4. Retention of key staff members 5. Customer satisfaction	1. Monthly revenue 2. Varies with location 3. Direct monetary savings 4. Voluntary turnover 5. Customer satisfaction index	• Action Plan	• Executive	• 6 months after engagement	• NHLO Staff
5	**ROI** • 25%					

Comments: *Executives are committed to providing data. They fully understand all the data collection issues prior to engaging in the coaching assignment.*

Figure 5-5   ROI Analysis Plan

Data Items (Usually Level 4)	Methods for Isolating the Effects of the Program	Methods of Converting Data to Monetary Values	Cost Categories	Intangible Benefits	Communication Targets for Final Report	Other Influences/ Issues During Application	Comments
• Sales growth • Productivity/ operational efficiency • Direct cost reduction • Retention of key staff members • Customer satisfaction	Estimates for executive (Method is the same for all data items)	• Standard Value • Expert input • Executive estimate (Method is the same for all data items)	• Needs assessment • Coaching fees • Travel costs • Executive time • Administrative support • Administrative • Communication expenses • Facilities • Evaluation	• Increased commitment • Reduced stress • Increased job satisfaction • Improved customer service • Enhanced recruiting Image • Improved teamwork • Improved communication	• Executives • Senior executives • Sponsors • NHLO staff • Learning and Development Council • Participants for CBI	A variety of other initiatives will influence the impact measure including our Six Sigma process, our service excellence program, and our efforts to become a great place to work.	It is extremely important to secure commitment from executives to provide accurate data in a timely manner.

CHAPTER SIX

TRAINING EVALUATION
Transfer and Results

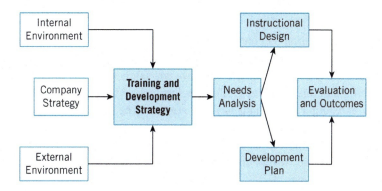

Learning Objectives

1. Describe the five foundations for transferring learning to behavior, and explain how they can be used to support level 3 and 4 training transfer.

2. Explain the relationship between level 1 and 2 evaluation (effective training) and level 3 and 4 evaluation (training effectiveness).

3. Describe the importance of strategy when designing level 3 and 4 evaluation.

4. Quantify and analyze training budgets.

5. Formulate training metrics to assess level 4 outcomes of training evaluation.

6. Compare near transfer and far transfer and their impact on training evaluation.

7. Describe the five factors that facilitate the likelihood of training transfer.

It is unsurprising that Procter & Gamble (P&G), a leader in consumer products design and development, would also be on the cutting edge of logistics and employee training. Maryann Morgan was the operations support manager at DB Schenker, a global logistics service company that manages P&G's warehouse in Edwardsville, Illinois. She was tasked with the need to reduce the 70% turnover rate P&G was experiencing with new hires. Through a needs analysis, Maryann recognized room for improvements in the training program for new hires. This involved changes not only in the training content itself, but also in how the employees implemented the learning once they left the classroom for the warehouse floor.

Maryann started by revamping P&G's new employee training program to ensure workers understood what they needed to do and when, safely and reliably over time. Using a classroom-style setup to maximize adult learning opportunities, trainees spend upwards of a week with their training coordinator, understanding work flows and the tasks they must complete to be successful on the job.

Training, however, does not end there. The next step was to ensure things learned transferred to the job in a seamless way.

Upon completion of the classroom portion of the training, trainees are assigned a training mentor to help them make the transition from the classroom to the warehouse floor. During the trainee's next two weeks on the job, the mentor conducts on-the-job training with the new employee, so the knowledge and skills learned in the classroom transfer to the daily tasks performed. In side-by-side fashion, the trainee is able to practice working on equipment, and demonstrate competence, with guidance from the mentor. Once the side-by-side training is completed, the new trainee is then integrated into production, with approval from the training mentor and the trainee's supervisor. Maryann knew that if you want employees to truly internalize and practice what they learn in the classroom, a good system must be in place to reinforce what the employees learned.

The mentor training program is competitive, and only the best employees are chosen to serve as mentors for new trainees. Because they represent the company, to even be considered for the position, they must not have any safety or quality issues in their own work records. Mentors are responsible for actively tracking and working with the new employees, and during the training period, there should be 100% accuracy and no incidents in each new trainee's work performance. As new employees are assessed at 30, 60, and 90 days, the training coordinators evaluate how well the new employees are doing. Along with assessing the new employees, they also assess the impact of the mentor on the trainee's performance. Every two years, the mentors' performance must be assessed, and their contract renewed.

The mentors understand that P&G and DB Schenker are not successful unless new trainees are successful. Three years into this program, the turnover rate was cut in half, falling from 70% to 35% turnover. Low turnover means a more stable workforce for the company, and greater profits overall. In the end, Maryann Morgan and her company knew that investing in training up front with the training mentor program meant profitability and success in the long run for all involved.

Our opening vignette highlights how an organization can facilitate the transfer of knowledge learned in a training program to be used on the job successfully. While the previous chapter addressed the evaluation concerns to produce a successful training session that helps trainees learn key knowledge and skills, this chapter focuses on how organizations can increase the likelihood that successful training programs will result in changes in behavior in the workplace and successful outcomes organizations desire. The mentor training program at DB Schenker illustrates the extent to which organizations can and should go to improve performance and other training outcomes. Our focus now moves from effective training (making sure the training session is successful) to training effectiveness (making sure the training impacts workplace behaviors and organizational outcomes).

> **Exhibit 6-1 Kirkpatrick and Kirkpatrick's Five Foundations for Transferring Learning to Behavior**
>
> Strategic Focus
>
> The Right Kind of Leadership
>
> The Ability to Plan for and Manage Change Effectively
>
> An Effective Measurement System
>
> Success With Levels 1 and 2

Source: Kirkpatrick, D. & Kirkpatrick, J. Transferring Learning to Behavior: Using the Four Levels to Improve Performance. San Francisco: Berrett-Koehler Publishers, Inc.

TRANSFERRING LEARNING TO BEHAVIOR

In their 2005 book *Transferring Learning to Behavior*, Donald and James Kirkpatrick noted a big challenge to level 3 and 4 evaluation: "This challenge, of course, is huge, since we lose much of our influence as trainees return to their jobs. In other words, Levels 1 and 2 are within our control [as trainers]; Levels 3 and 4 are only within our influence."[1] They go on to offer five necessary conditions for **knowledge transfer** to the job. Some of these require great influence on the part of the trainer; others require important work to create the infrastructure and context within which level 3 and 4 evaluation occurs.

First, Kirkpatrick and Kirkpatrick argue the organization must have a strategic focus such that its strategy drives all activities, including training and development. Second, they believe the right kind of leadership is essential for training transfer. Third, the organization at all levels must be able to plan for and manage change effectively. Fourth, there must be an effective measurement system. Finally, training transfer can only occur when there is success at levels 1 and 2 (see Exhibit 6-1).

Strategic Focus

Kirkpatrick and Kirkpatrick make clear that in order to do proper evaluation at all four levels, you must first consider level 4 and proceed backwards from there, designing and implementing the training evaluation program.[2] This is consistent with our discussion in Chapter 5 of backwards design. We start by asking what outcomes are strategically important to the organization (level 4). Then we ask what the organization needs for support to ensure training transfer occurs and outcomes are successfully reached (level 3). We follow this by addressing what knowledge, skills, and abilities (KSAs) we need to see mastered to ensure learning occurred (level 2), and finally address how to design the training program to ensure the environment is conducive to learning.

In order for good level 4 evaluation to occur, the company needs a systematic strategic focus and plan. As well, transparency and clear communication on the company's strategic vision is essential so everyone is on board. Kirkpatrick and Kirkpatrick call this a cascading strategy; strategy is everyone's job, and therefore everyone needs to be on the same page about what that means.[3] The key to training transfer is based here because without a clear strategy, it is difficult to align training to strategy, and difficult then to support the transfer of learning to the job.

Following from this discussion of strategy alignment, another consideration for training evaluation is the **Anderson Model for Learning Evaluation**.[4] Similar to Kirkpatrick, the Anderson Model assumes alignment of the learning function with the organization's strategic priorities. The Anderson Model differs slightly from Kirkpatrick's model in that it focuses on learning evaluation at the organizational level, whereas Kirkpatrick's model focuses primarily on the impact of specific learning interventions. It is easy to see, however, that these two approaches are complementary. The Anderson Model assesses the learning function as a whole relative to the strategic priorities, which extends training evaluation beyond the specific impact of learning interventions as noted in Kirkpatrick's model. The Anderson Model is important for strategic focus because it ensures the entire learning function supports the strategic vision of the company.

The Right Kind of Leadership

Successful training transfer comes from the top. It requires a strategic vision, and a leadership team that supports the learning process. In order to ensure training transfer occurs, leaders must be on board and ready to help facilitate learning that will have an impact at the strategic level. It is essential to first ensure that the company has a vision for what it wants from its leaders. One example comes from James Kouzes and Barry Posner, authors of *The Leadership Challenge*.[5] They argue leaders need to challenge the process, inspire a shared vision, enable others to act by fostering collaboration, model good behavior, and encourage and celebrate accomplishments.[6] This list of attributes is just one example of many to consider when developing your leaders to best support training effectiveness. Whichever model of leadership you choose, make sure the attributes you focus on will help the organization achieve its strategic goals.

Kirkpatrick and Kirkpatrick argue that a balanced leadership approach is necessary to facilitate training transfer.[7] There needs to be a balance between leadership that provides support and encouragement and leadership that demands accountability. Both extremes can be detrimental to effective training transfer. Support without accountability may not push people to do what is necessary; accountability without support may result in burnout and turnover. Setting expectations while also providing support to get the work done is an important balance any leader should master.

The Ability to Plan For and Manage Change Effectively

Training transfer is, at its core, change management. In order for trainees to change their old behaviors by participating in training and embracing new behaviors, a system that facilitates change management must be put in place. First, the case for change needs to be made. If top managers are on board with these changes, they are more likely to help facilitate the training transfer process. Once the plan is in place to support training transfer, they must communicate what is expected from the trainees and those with whom they work to facilitate training transfer with a clear timetable and expectations. If we don't consider training transfer within the confines of a change management process, the roadblocks and barriers common to change management efforts will inhibit transferring the skills learned to the job.

An Effective Measurement System

Consistent with the company's strategic vision, a measurement system needs to be in place to facilitate assessment. Training evaluation at levels 3 and 4 naturally follows from the means organizations use to measure whether or not their strategy was successful. As you will see in the next section, one way to clearly define strategy and develop a structure within which to measure effectiveness is to use a process like the **balanced scorecard (BSC)**.

Once the organization chooses a measurement system, a training evaluation plan is developed accordingly. For example, the BSC approach represents core strategic drivers such as financial/production, customers, internal systems, and learning and growth.[8] For financial/production, the organization can look at employee retention as a key measure. How do training and development activities impact employee retention? Alternatively, we may look at another BSC category, learning and growth. Learning and growth can be evaluated at levels 1, 2, and 3. First, have managers learned how to support and coach employees (level 2) so the employees are better able to practice skills learned in training on the job (level 3)? Assessing how trainees react to their training session (level 1) helps support strategic goals as well.

Success at Levels 1 and 2

You cannot measure level 3 and 4 training evaluation unless you have attended to effective training (levels 1 and 2). In other words, how can we worry about whether or not learning transferred to the job if we are not clear that trainees learned what they needed to in the first place? Therefore, the information discussed in Chapter 5 is essential to master before you can consider whether or not the training will have a strategic impact.

We can do many things before, during, and after a training session to increase the likelihood level 2 learning occurs. Much of our discussion in previous chapters, as well as in future chapters, reinforces this list, but it pays to repeat the interdependent nature of training and development activities. Exhibit 6-2 lists the suggestions for enhancing level 2 learning. An important theme through the list is to ensure clear communication and clear expectations are set up with respect to what trainees will learn, why they will learn it, and how the learning will take place and be used on the job. Incorporating many of the learning techniques taught in Chapter 4 will increase the likelihood that level 2 learning will occur, paving the way for level 3 transfer of learning.

> **Exhibit 6-2 Tools to Enhance Level 2 Learning**
>
> 1. Discuss pre- and post-training expectations with trainee bosses to set expectations for learning and post-training implementation.
> 2. Use trainee supervisors and executives as trainers.
> 3. Have front-line employees present their best practices.
> 4. Inform trainees what to expect in terms of end-of-class KSA assessment.
> 5. Inform trainees they will report learning and application to their teams post-training.
> 6. Have trainees demonstrate new behaviors, either live or via videotape.
> 7. Include role playing where relevant.
> 8. Use visuals, anecdotes, stories, and illustrations during the training session for engagement (see Appendix C).
> 9. Use e-Learning effectively (see Chapter 9).
>
> *Source:* Adapted from Donald Kirkpatrick and John D. Kirkpatrick, *Transferring Learning to Behavior: Using the Four Levels to Improve Performance*, digital book location 763 (San Francisco: Berrett-Koehler, 2005).

KIRKPATRICK'S MODEL FOR TRAINING EFFECTIVENESS

The previous section addressed the context needed to facilitate training transfer and level 3 and 4 evaluation. We continue the discussion by understanding the specific factors to assess when evaluating at levels 3 and 4. Exhibit 6-3 outlines the New World Kirkpatrick Model, previously discussed in Chapter 5.

Level 3: Behavior

In advancing to level 3, our concern shifts from effective training (whether the training accomplished what it set out to accomplish) to training effectiveness (whether the training had an impact on the job and on organizational outcomes). Level 3 evaluation has a strategic importance to the organization because changes in **behavior** are the ultimate goal of training interventions. If the training does not impact on-the-job behavior, the money invested has been wasted, and organizational goals will not be accomplished.

As we learned in Chapter 4 about how people learn, consistent across most theories is the need for trainees to practice newly learned skills in the appropriate context to master what they learned. Whether we are talking about social learning theory[9] and the importance of reproducing the modeled behaviors, organizational cognition[10] and the need to bridge the gap between stated and actual behaviors (where the opportunity for learning takes place), or experiential learning[11] and active experimentation with new knowledge and skills, trainees must practice what they learned and have a supportive context in which

Exhibit 6-3 New World Kirkpatrick Model of Training Effectiveness

Dimension Level	Original Kirkpatrick Model	New World Kirkpatrick Model Additions
1. Reaction	**Customer Satisfaction**—the degree to which the participant is satisfied with the training	**Engagement**—the degree to which participants are actively involved in and contributing to the learning experience **Relevance**—the degree to which training participants will have the opportunity to use or apply what they learned in training on the job
2. Learning	**Knowledge and Skills**—the degree to which the participants acquire the intended knowledge and skills, based on their participation in the training **Attitude**—the degree to which the trainees have a positive attitude toward training opportunities	**Confidence**—the degree to which the participants believe they can use the new KSAs on the job **Commitment**—the degree to which the participants intend to use the new KSAs on the job
3. Behavior	**Knowledge Transfer**—the degree to which participants apply what they learned during training when they are back on the job	**Organizational Processes and Systems**—reinforce, encourage, and reward performance of critical behaviors on the job
4. Results	**Outcomes**—the degree to which targeted outcomes occur as a result of the training and the support and accountability from leaders	**Leading Indicators**—short-term observations and measurements suggesting that critical behaviors are on track to create a positive impact on desired results

Source: Adapted from Kirkpatrick Partners, "The New World Kirkpatrick Model." Available from https://www.kirkpatrickpartners.com/Our-Philosophy/The-New-World-Kirkpatrick-Model.

to use the knowledge and skills consistently. Given 90% of learning occurs outside of the training classroom, it is essential to give trainees ample opportunity to practice on the job what they learned in the classroom.

One of the biggest contributors to poor training outcomes is a context that does not support practicing and utilizing the training information obtained.[12] We cannot assume poor performance post-training means that the trainee just needs more training sessions. Translating lessons learned in the classroom into meaningful on-the-job behaviors is essential and requires a multipronged approach. As consultant Ann Latham argues, the organization must encourage the desired behaviors it wants to see employees use post-training.[13] For training to be successful, the trainee must have clear expectations, the right skills, and a willingness to do well, and the organization must be sure to surround the trainee with forces encouraging the right behaviors and discouraging the wrong behaviors. Reward systems, ample resources, and time to practice new material learned are necessary for classroom lessons to transfer to on-the-job behaviors. The importance of ensuring a context conducive for transfer of training to the job cannot be overestimated. Therefore, while we address level 3 assessment in overview in this section, a more in-depth discussion of the factors that influence successful transfer of training will follow.

Knowledge transfer.

In the initial Kirkpatrick model, level 3 is the extent to which participants apply what they learned during training when they return to the job. Simply put, how often does the trainee use the training on the job? The training, and the evaluation that follows, needs to focus primarily on the critical behaviors regarded as most important for organizational success. If employees fail to exhibit the critical behaviors, several things may have occurred. First, the training may not have focused on the most important aspects of the job—a failure of needs analysis and training design. Second, the trainees may not have properly learned what was offered in the training program—a failure of the instructional design process. Lastly, the trainees may have learned the proper knowledge and skills, but did not receive the contextual support to practice and internalize the new information while on the job.

Organizations can accomplish level 3 evaluation in several ways. Transfer can be assessed through basic observation of the employee on the job. More specifically, observers should assess trainees through critical incidents to ensure they are utilizing and consistently repeating important behaviors. The three basic categories of measures of training transfer include measures of learning, self-reported measures of change, and rated measures of performance.[14] Through a combination of observation and trainee self-report data, the trainer can begin to better understand the extent to which learning can be transferred from the training to the actual job.

When the stakes are high and the risks are numerous, organizations can assess transfer through simulations. Imagine, if you will, an airline pilot learning takeoff and landing procedures. The pilot will study in the classroom and demonstrate she learned the material through some sort of paper-and-pencil test. It may not be reasonable, however, to immediately put the pilot in the cockpit of a Boeing 747 to practice takeoffs and landings because of the catastrophic risk of failure. Therefore, an airplane simulator would be the next logical step to ensure the pilot understands the procedures and can demonstrate mastery before she takes the next, higher-risk step, with an airplane in the air. Once the pilot can demonstrate she understands how to physically take off and land an airplane in the simulator, in various simulated circumstances, she can then take to the air in the 747.

After determining that employees are not exhibiting the critical behaviors, organizations must determine the cause for the poor transfer. It is important to assess whether or not the training program appropriately identified the knowledge and skill gap and designed the training program accordingly. If not, then the training program needs to be updated to avoid future problems. If the training program has, however, addressed the knowledge and skill gap appropriately, then the next step is to assess the motivation and trainability of the trainee, as well as the transfer context, to uncover any barriers to utilizing the training on the job.

Organizational processes and systems.

In order for trainees to use their training on the job, integrated **organizational processes and systems** must be designed by the HR department to make the training come alive. The Kirkpatricks call these the "required drivers."[15] Managers, coworkers,

HR, top management, and all support staff must work in concert to encourage, reinforce, monitor, and reward new knowledge and skills on a regular basis. Without such a system in place, transferring training to the workplace will face challenges. Researchers argue that with a proper system in place to facilitate transfer of learning to the workplace, organizations can expect up to an 85% success rate of transfer. Without such a system, the best you can expect is about a 15% success rate of transfer from training intervention to the job.[16]

Encourage.

Trainees need encouragement from their peers and supervisors to facilitate transfer of knowledge on the job. Two of the most common ways to accomplish this are via coaching and mentoring. While they are discussed in more detail in Chapter 11, it is important to note here that both coaching and mentoring are important for training transfer, as well as employee development.

Reinforce.

On-the-job training is one important way to reinforce transfer of knowledge and skills from training programs to jobs. Moving from the classroom to workplace practice requires the assistance of experienced peers and supervisors who ensure that the trainees practice what they learned on the job. Other ways for the organization to reinforce training transfer include checklists, follow-up sessions, reminders, and executive modeling. Checklists ensure trainees follow the proper procedures in an orderly fashion. Follow-up sessions provide gentle reminders to trainees who may need additional lessons to deal with any potential gaps in training transfer. Executive modeling uses social learning to help employees practice what they see their supervisors and leaders doing to embrace new KSAs. Reinforcement methods require a concerted effort from all members of the organization, at all levels of the organization. Our opening vignette highlights a successful reinforcement program for new hire training at Procter & Gamble.

Monitor.

Once trainees return to their job after training, they should be regularly monitored to ensure they are using the knowledge and skills as expected. The simplest way to monitor trainees on the job is through observation. The supervisor, HR department, a peer training mentor, or coworkers can participate in monitoring and regularly reporting on the behaviors that the trainees exhibit. As well, the trainees can self-evaluate. Along with observing trainees, organizations can use surveys, meetings, and interviews to monitor what the trainees are using, how they are using it, and the extent to which they exhibit mastery. When trainees are clearly not using their new knowledge and skills, organizations can make course corrections as appropriate. They can establish key performance indicators (KPIs) for each employee unique to his or her job, and to which employees will be held accountable during their performance evaluations. Our opening vignette also highlights how training mentors can help with monitoring post-training behaviors.

Reward.

As we discussed in Chapter 1, training and development must be embedded in the context of other HR activities to support and reinforce training outcomes. A company's compensation system can support training and development efforts by ensuring a reward system is in place for training transfer to occur. The reward system does not have to be monetarily based. In fact, it is important that the reward system combine financial and nonfinancial rewards to reinforce a wide variety of behaviors.

Research done by four Massachusetts Institute of Technology economists investigated how onetime incentives impact performance.[17] For example, if we create an incentive for performing a certain function on the job after a training program, what kind of incentives work best and under what conditions? The researchers found that when the job required higher-order cognitive skills, larger financial incentives resulted in lower performance. The implication for this is that if we pay people an incentive to perform a newly learned skill on the job, the incentive may backfire, and we may see lower, not higher, performance.

That is not to say that financial incentives don't work in some circumstances. Evidence supports that basic mechanical skills that require no higher-order cognition benefit from applying incentives to get people to perform the tasks. However, as the requirements for cognition and creativity increase, financial rewards decrease in their viability for improving performance. Instead of financial rewards for training transfer, intrinsic rewards such as autonomy, mastery, and purpose are more likely to encourage training transfer and higher levels of on-the-job performance when the job is more cognitively complex.[18] The important takeaway is to use financial incentives judiciously when trying to encourage training transfer.

Moving beyond onetime incentives, an appropriate reward system with a long-term impact might include pay increases after trainees have mastered and demonstrated use of a skill consistently. A promotion may also serve as a reward as it represents the next step in a career ladder for the employee who has successfully learned and transferred his or her KSAs to the job. Pecuniary rewards that occur after trainees master a skill and transfer it to the job differ from onetime incentives to push people to use a skill post-training. This is the equivalent of paying kids for every chore they are expected to do. Incentives are not in the control of the person or entity offering the incentive; the control rests in the hands of the individual asked to perform the task. Eventually, kids may choose not to do chores because the incentive no longer matters to them ("I don't care about the money"), or the incentive is no longer enough to motivate them to perform ("I need more money"). Similarly, if the only thing encouraging employees to perform a task is a onetime incentive, there is no guarantee they will continue to perform on the job over the long haul. Focus on rewards that encourage people to perform the newly learned KSAs consistently over time on the job.

Level 4: Results

Level 4 evaluation, based on the strategic impact of training outcomes, is the single most important aspect to measure, yet tends to be the least utilized and understood.[19] While organizational departments and divisions can assess how training interventions impact their own goals, ultimately, the most important outcome is the impact of training on the entire organization's mission and goals. The question to ask is "Did the training have a positive impact on what the organization exists to do, deliver, or contribute?" As in any kind of strategic planning, if the departments and divisions focus more on their own needs and less on how their goals align with the overall corporate goals, the company has a greater likelihood of suffering from ineffectiveness and misalignment within its boundaries. Therefore, assessing division and departmental outcomes is important only in the context of how they impact and support organization-wide goals. Depending on whether you are assessing short-term or long-term goals, it is important to design your assessment to properly differentiate between the two. Long-term goals are not easily assessed because it may take months and years before the company feels an impact; therefore, organizations need to measure short-term proxies in lieu of long-term goals.

According to the Kirkpatricks, level 4 evaluation is the simplest and least resource-intensive of all the levels: "If something is a true Level 4 result, it is important enough that someone in the organization is already measuring and monitoring it, and it is simply a matter of obtaining the data."[20] The challenge comes when trying to draw a link between the training, the on-the-job behaviors, and organizational **results**. If organizations neglect level 3 evaluation, level 4 evaluation becomes a challenge because it is impossible to link the training intervention with the organizational outcome, and unclear if the training improved on-the-job behaviors. As well, only 18% of respondents in a study by the Institute for Corporate Productivity measured **return on investment (ROI)**,[21] yet 75% of respondents believe that level 4 evaluation has high or very high value to organizations.[22] The study also found that organizations who performed level 4 evaluations, and did so effectively, performed better in their markets than those who did not evaluate at level 4. Some trainers consider ROI level 5.[23] For the purpose of simplicity, however, we include ROI as a part of level 4 evaluation, consistent with the Kirkpatricks' model. Whether you consider it level 4 or level 5, as does Jack Phillips, it is an essential measure to ensure training has an important impact on the organization's bottom line and strategic focus.

For internal trainers, obtaining performance data should be easy. External trainers, however, may not have access to that information, as companies are reluctant to provide private corporate data to a third-party vendor. In fact, external trainers may only be able to perform level 1 and 2 evaluations, unless the company is willing to share short- and long-term performance data. Thus, external trainers may only be able to assess effective training for their clients, leaving the question of training effectiveness unknown to them. It is incumbent upon the HR department, then, to collect those data to ensure the training has strategic value to the organization.

Outcomes.

A wide range of organizational **outcomes** are relevant to level 4 evaluation. The most prevalent is return on investment. ROI is represented by the following formula: (Benefit − Cost) ÷ Cost = ROI. Expressed as a percentage, ROI assesses the benefit of training to the organization, as related to the cost of the training. Thus, if a company invests

$100,000 in training and sees a $200,000 increase in revenue directly related to the training, the ROI is (200,000 − 100,000) ÷ 100,000 = 100% return on investment.

Another way to consider outcomes of value to organizations is the balanced scorecard.[24] Robert Kaplan and David Norton designed this strategy performance management tool with three critical characteristics. First, the BSC must focus on the organization's strategic goals. Second, the BSC must monitor key data items relevant to the strategic goals. Lastly, the data items must be a mix of financial and nonfinancial items of strategic importance to the organization. Within the BSC are four perspectives from which the key data must be assessed: financial/production, customer, internal business processes, and learning and growth. The BSC informs the outcomes of interest for level 4 evaluation by guiding training evaluation to align with company strategy.[25]

Exhibit 6-4 highlights corporate trainer Bryant Nielson's "Top 10 List of Training Metrics."[26] As you can see from the exhibit, 8 of the 10 items on Bryant's list address level 4 evaluation. The remaining two focus on level 1 evaluation. While this may seem contrary to previous discussions on the value of level 1 evaluation, it is important to note that as a corporate trainer himself, Nielson should put emphasis on level 1. Trainers emphasize levels 1 and 2 because that helps them ensure their material is delivered as appropriate to meet customer demands. From a strategic perspective, level 1 evaluation is key to Nielson's work. One might argue that by evaluating and emphasizing level 1 for his clients, he is actually doing level 4 evaluation for his own corporate training company.

Regardless of the perspective, this list reinforces the importance of level 4 evaluation, whether you are the trainer delivering the intervention or the client receiving the

Exhibit 6-4 Top 10 List of Training Metrics

Training Metric	Level of Evaluation
Increased Retention	Results
Increased Sales	Results
Increased Operational Efficiency	Results
Customer Service Results	Results
Company-Defined Scorecards	Results
Cost of Training	Results
Return on Investment	Results
Revenue Generation	Results
Instructor Performance	Reaction
End User Satisfaction	Reaction

Source: Adapted from Bryant Nielson, "Top 10 Training Metrics," *Your Training Edge*, May 9, 2018. Available from http://www.yourtrainingedge.com/top-10-training-metrics/.

training. Note, however, that level 3 evaluation appears not to have made the list. As noted earlier, level 3 evaluation is a necessary input to determine the strategic impact of training, and thus no level 4 evaluation should be considered until level 3 evaluation has been addressed. It should also be noted that this list of training metrics is not exhaustive of those an organization can use to evaluate level 4. Strategy has to drive the level 4 results you want to assess. This list does, however, provide a starting point to determine what is essential to the organization.

Leading indicators.

Because training may not have an impact for a few years, organizations can't just focus on immediate results for training evaluation. They must investigate **leading indicators** to ensure the organization is trending in the direction of the long-term goals. For all intents and purposes, the leading indicators work as proxies for the longer-term strategic goals of organizations, and help bridge the gap between the department/divisional goals and the overall organizational mission and goals.

Common leading indicators include customer satisfaction, employee engagement, sales volume, cost containment, quality, and market share.[27] Each of these, on its own, is important at the department and division levels, but organizations must take care to ensure these are proper indicators of future success and will impact overall organizational success. Each of these indicators, in essence, is necessary, but not sufficient, to achieve organizational success. For example, an organization may focus on developing high-quality products, but if customers are not satisfied and market share is low, success on one indicator does not translate to overall organizational success. Further, a company may excel at cost containment, but do so at the risk of producing poor-quality products consumers don't desire because too many shortcuts are taken during design and manufacturing. The indicators must all be considered in alignment and not work at the detriment of other, equally important goals.

In choosing leading indicators to assess, it is necessary to ensure the indicator has an impact, short- or long-term, on the bottom-line results important to the organization. In short, will this indicator affect the reason why the organization exists; will it affect the organization's mission and overall goals? If so, then it should be assessed regularly to monitor short- and long-term training success.

TRANSFER OF TRAINING

Because of the high importance placed on level 3 evaluation of work behaviors, we include a more detailed discussion of the factors to consider in ensuring transfer of training occurs as desired. Alan Clardy, from Towson University and an expert in human resource development, argues that with training investments exceeding $50 billion annually in the United States as of 2000, the money wasted if training doesn't transfer will be staggering.[28] This section goes into more detail addressing how to best ensure transfer of training occurs.

Near Versus Far Transfer

Transfer of training can be broken down into two basic categories: near transfer and far transfer. **Near transfer** assumes that the job conditions to which the transfer is occurring are similar to the training conditions.[29] For example, shadowing somebody when you start a new job to see how the work is done is a great example of near transfer. **Far transfer** assumes that the training must generalize learned skills from the training session to different settings, people, or situations, as well as assumes maintenance of the learned skills over time.[30] For example, far transfer involves transferring skills learned in the military to civilian jobs upon retirement from active duty. Far transfer requires much more of Bloom's higher-order cognitive skills, such as application, analysis, and synthesis, whereas near transfer may be satisfied with lower-order cognitive skills, such as knowledge and comprehension.

It makes sense that the most ideal circumstance for a training to result in perfect, or close to perfect, transfer would be those conditions identical to the training session itself. As you will see with on-the-job training programs in Chapter 7, this approaches near-ideal conditions for training transfer, as the learning actually occurs on the job where the training conditions are identical to the work conditions. This does not work for all training programs. As realistic training conditions begin to erode due to financial or logistical concerns, the risk to training transfer increases. Whenever possible, training conditions should emulate actual working conditions as closely as feasible.

According to Clardy, Otto Jelsma and Jeroen van Merriënboer[31] identified two schools of thought in the 1990s that considered this idea of near versus far transfer.[32] While some argued that transfer would only occur when the tasks practiced in a training situation were identical to those actually performed on the job,[33] the Gestalt school posited a theory that modeled the assumptions behind Bloom's Taxonomy. This argument stated transfer occurred when a learned procedure was so fully understood it could be applied to other situations (similar to Bloom's higher-order cognition). The former argument, called the Associationist school, appears to be the foundation for the concept of near transfer, whereas the Gestalt school attempts to explain the mechanism by which far transfer can occur. It is easy to conclude that the factors influencing transfer are not a one-size-fits-all approach, and include such varied factors as training motivation, training design, and workplace conditions.

Knowledge transfer from military service.

With respect to far transfer, among the growing trends in workplace practice is the concern with how to translate skills learned by veterans during their military service to civilian jobs. A variety of websites such as military.com, www.careeronestop.org/Toolkit/ACINet.aspx, and realwarriors.net are designed to help veterans transfer military experiences and skills into language that can be translated into civilian-focused résumés. The Department of Labor has a Transition Assistance Program (TAP), accessible for all veterans from all branches of the military. Exhibit 6-5 highlights this program and the law, put into effect in 2011, supporting it. The goal of TAP is to ease the transition of military personnel to civilian life and work—far transfer validity at its best, assisting those who proudly served the United States.

> **Exhibit 6-5 U.S. Department of Defense Transition Assistance Program**

In 2011, Congress passed, and President Obama signed into law, the VOW (Veterans Opportunity to Work) to Hire Heroes Act of 2011. The VOW Act requires, among other things, that separating service members must attend TAP. The VOW Act also required the Department of Labor to redesign its employment workshop, the largest component of the TAP curriculum, to better apply to the realities of today's job market. The Veterans' Employment and Training Service (VETS) fulfills this requirement for the Department of Labor and manages the implementation of the employment workshop at hundreds of military installations worldwide for thousands of separating service members.

In 2013, the Department of Defense launched a TAP virtual curriculum through its Joint Knowledge Online (JKO) learning management system. This TAP virtual curriculum is designed to provide service members who are unable to attend the TAP in person due to military exigencies with the ability to fulfill their TAP obligations. The Departments of Defense, Veterans Affairs, and Labor were informed that providing the TAP curriculum to veterans and spouses of service members might be helpful to them, too, so the JKO system now provides the full TAP curriculum to anyone who might benefit. Access the TAP virtual curriculum at www.dodtap.mil/virtual_curriculum.html.

Source: U.S. Department of Labor, Veterans' Employment and Training Service, "Transition Assistance Program (TAP) Information." Available from https://www.dol.gov/vets/programs/tap.htm.

Factors Affecting Transfer

Many models out there have attempted to predict the specific factors that influence training transfer. Timothy Baldwin and Kevin Ford established their model for training transfer to include trainee characteristics, training design, and the work environment.[34] Broadly speaking, their model addresses the most important considerations when designing and implementing a training program to ensure training transfer has the greatest likelihood to succeed. A broader view of the literature identified a range of factors that expand on Baldwin and Ford's model[35]:

1. Trainee characteristics
2. Trainee experiences prior to attending a program
3. Workplace climate
4. Characteristics of training design and delivery
5. Post-training experiences

Among the many ways to identify and measure if learning transfer has occurred, a measure exists to help researchers and training practitioners alike measure the extent to which an organization has a system in place to facilitate learning transfer. The Learning Transfer System Inventory (LTSI) comprises 16 factors necessary for training transfer,[36] as shown in Exhibit 6-6.

Exhibit 6-6 Learning Transfer System Inventory

Learner readiness
Motivation to transfer
Positive personal outcomes
Negative personal outcomes
Personal capacity for transfer
Peer support
Supervisor support
Supervisor sanctions
Perceived content validity
Transfer design
Opportunity to use
Transfer effort and performance expectations
Performance outcomes expectations
Resistance or openness to change
Performance self-efficacy
Performance coaching

Source: Elwood F. Holten III, Reid A. Bates, and Wendy E. A. Ruoa, "Development of a Generalized Learning Transfer System Inventory," *Human Resource Development Quarterly* 11, no. 4 (2000): 333–360.

The authors of the LTSI state that training practitioners can use the measure in the following ways[37]:

1. To assess potential transfer factor problems before conducting major learning interventions
2. As part of follow-up evaluations of existing training programs
3. As a diagnostic tool for investigating known transfer of training problems
4. To target interventions designed to enhance transfer
5. To incorporate evaluation of transfer of learning systems as part of regular employee assessments
6. To conduct needs assessment for training programs to provide skills to supervisors and trainers that will aid transfer

Using a validated measure to assess learning transfer can aid training professionals in assessing level 3 training evaluation. What follows is a more detailed discussion of the different factors that influence training transfer.

Trainee characteristics.

Personality is a big predictor of training transfer success, and the Big 5 personality traits play an equally big role in training transfer. Conscientiousness, agreeableness, and extroversion have a positive impact on motivation to improvement work through learning.[38] As well, conscientiousness, emotional stability, and openness to experience directly and indirectly affect training transfer for pilot trainees.[39] Another study investigated the role of proactivity on training transfer and found that a proactive personality is related to the motivation to learn (level 2), which increased the motivation to transfer training to the job and ultimately impacted actual transfer to the job (level 3).[40]

Trainability is also a key characteristic for trainees, considered a function of trainee ability, trainee motivation, and trainee perceptions of the work environment.[41] Trainees' motivation, and hence their trainability, is dependent on belief in their direct responsibility for results (internal locus of control), belief that training will lead to desired personal results, willingness to manage their own career, and openness and responsiveness to feedback.

Self-efficacy is also an important variable to consider in trainees. Research indicates that trainees' self-efficacy as they enter training programs, as well as their self-efficacy upon exit, can have a positive impact on both learning in the training program and training transfer.[42] High levels of self-efficacy can also help new hires transfer information learned about company culture from orientation programs to the job.[43] Overall, it is important to consider trainee characteristics when designing training programs to increase the likelihood of training transfer.

Pre-training experiences associated with training.

A variety of pre-training conditions and experiences affect learning transfer.[44] The first important consideration is the attendance requirement for the program. When attendance is voluntary, trainee entry motivation and learning improve. Thus, if training is mandatory as it often is in organizations, it may be more challenging for training transfer to occur.

How the program is advertised, or positioned, to the trainees also has an impact. When realistic training information is provided, trainees have more positive attitudes toward the training and are more eager to learn. As well, the reputation of the training program influences trainee motivation if there is perceived utility of the training for job performance.

Finally, the role of the trainees' supervisor should not be underestimated. When supervisors are apprised of how to best support the training process, transfer is more likely to occur. Clardy's summary of these pre-training efforts underscores the importance of not only designing an appropriate training program, but also communicating and preparing employees and their supervisors for the training program that lies ahead.[45]

Workplace climate.

The more the organization's climate or culture supports training transfer in word and action, the greater the likelihood that training will transfer to the job.[46] In fact, one study found that supervisor and peer support, opportunity to use the training, supervisory sanctions if the training is not used, and resistance to using skills if they violated workplace norms all were climate issues that contributed to the success or failure of training transfer.[47] We know culture and climate can make or break any workplace change, and training transfer is no different. If we want employees to take the changes seriously, and implement the changes taught in the training program, the organization has to demonstrate its willingness to ensure training is supported by creating mechanisms to encourage both supervisor and peer support during training.

Training program design and delivery.

Although training transfer does not automatically occur post-training, the likelihood of transfer is enhanced when the training program results in the necessary learning expected of trainees. Hence, when level 2 evaluation indicates greater amounts of learning, it is a necessary condition for level 3 transfer to occur. Higher-order cognition contributes to training transfer; therefore, trainers need to incorporate ways for higher-order learning to occur, according to Bloom's Taxonomy. Relapse prevention is also important to help trainees anticipate the ways in which training transfer may encounter roadblocks and work to prevent relapse from occurring.[48] When higher-order learning and relapse prevention are used in conjunction with proper goal-setting frameworks, training transfer is more likely to occur.

Along with focusing on higher-order learning, we also need to pay attention to cognitive load. When we space out cognitive training, this increases the likelihood of training transfer.[49] This means that when training people on a new skill, particularly one that takes a lot of cognitive effort, following up the initial training with regular-interval refreshers to help trainees learn more complex concepts and tasks eases the cognitive load and facilitates learning and transfer.

Post-training experiences at the worksite.

The biggest contributor to effective training transfer is almost self-evident. If trainees do not have an opportunity to utilize their new skills and knowledge on the job, training transfer is almost certain not to occur. Even with the best of intentions, without support from the supervisor giving them the opportunity to practice their new skills, or support from coworkers, there is no chance for training to be integrated into their on-the-job behaviors. Clardy also argues that group support is essential for training to become learned and practiced on a daily basis.[50] Providing support groups and follow-up check-in meetings for trainees may increase their comfort with the training material, and allow them an opportunity to discuss problems they may be having and brainstorm ways to overcome their challenges and better practice their new skills.

TRAINING EVALUATION ANALYSIS

Once the organization has finished training and gathered all the data, the process of interpreting the evaluation data begins. As discussed in Chapter 5, some information is received immediately after training, providing initial evaluations of levels 1 and 2, while other data may take longer to assess, as expected with some key strategic metrics. Once data are received, there is no benefit to sit on it and wait until all the data come in to analyze and make changes. By gathering and analyzing in a continuous fashion, the trainers can quickly assess and make changes based on the data.

One example of how to assess and quickly adapt based on data or feedback is trainer assessment of trainee engagement during the training sessions. An experienced trainer can sense very quickly when the trainees are not engaged with the training session. Should trainers wait until the end of training evaluations to see what they could do differently? The answer is a resounding no. If trainers sense participants are not engaged with the material, they should learn how to assess and switch gears in the moment to diagnose the problem. This requires good self-awareness by trainers and a quick wit to adapt their approach if it is not resonating with the trainees.

When assessing level 2 learning, end-of-session knowledge and skill assessment will indicate the extent to which trainees learned the necessary level of skill to demonstrate mastery. If trainees did not learn as expected based on the learning objectives, the instructional design team must diagnose and make changes immediately while the feedback is fresh, rather than wait until implementation of the next training session.

Regardless of the level of evaluation you are conducting, the Kirkpatricks recommend three basic questions to ask once the analysis is done and you have the results in front of you[51]:

- Does this result meet our expectations?
- If not, why not?
- If so, why?

Understanding the expectations and examining your results relative to those expectation standards is the central part of training evaluation. It is important to ask yourself not only why the results don't meet the standards, but also why and how they do meet the standards. Understanding why a training program was successful enables trainers to continue to duplicate those results, assuming a similar training context. Understanding why it was not successful enables trainers to learn from mistakes and/or failures to overhaul and improve training programs.

There is no one-size-fits-all approach to training evaluation standards. What is acceptable to one company or industry may not be acceptable to another. Each standard set by the organization should consider factors such as (but not limited to) industry norms, company strategy, and stage of intervention (early intervention vs. maintenance of standards). Once an organization considers a variety of contextual factors that impact the expectations, internal benchmarks should be established with an eye toward continuous improvement.

Lastly, after analyzing data and drawing conclusions, the next question is who needs to know this information.[52] The best advice is always to know your audience. Provide information that offers value to each stakeholder. Typically, level 1 and 2 analysis targets instructional designers and trainers to improve program development and delivery. Level 3 transfer of learning metrics targets two groups. Training leaders need level 3 metrics to improve on follow-up and reinforcement to increase training transfer. Trainee supervisors and managers need level 3 metrics to improve training choices for their direct reports, provide better support and accountability for trainees on the job, and improve overall trainee performance.

Level 4 metrics are needed for training leaders, trainee supervisors and managers, and business executives. Training leaders can use this information to ensure training aligns with strategy and reduce costs by removing training programs that don't align properly. Supervisors and managers use level 4 metrics to improve upon department/division KPIs. Executives use level 4 metrics to communicate the company strategy to focus training and reinforcement efforts, as well as model the behaviors needed to facilitate training, improve performance, and properly execute the business strategy.

TRAINING BUDGETS

When determining measures such as ROI and other financial metrics, it is important to consider the totality of training costs. The following are typical costs for training programs:

- Preparation time for trainers
- Administrative support for training development and delivery
- Rental/leasing costs for space and any equipment needed
- Food provided during sessions
- Trainee wages
- Instructor salaries
- Materials for training, including handouts and equipment needed for training session
- Trainee awards/certificates for recognizing achievement

If the training occurs off-site and/or is managed by a third-party vendor and requires some degree of travel, the following costs should be considered in addition to the costs listed above:

- Travel costs for trainees, including meals, lodging, and travel expenses
- Registration fees for training session

Along with identifying training costs, organizations should consider potential revenue streams and/or productivity improvements. If outsiders are allowed to attend the training, fees can be charged to external participants. With respect to other ways of generating revenue, if equipment purchased is no longer needed, the company may be able to recoup costs by reselling the used equipment. Lastly, the organization should consider the range of productivity improvements targeted by the training program. Sales and productivity changes, accident rates and loss of associated productivity, and wear and tear on equipment are among the factors to be considered in calculating program benefits or returns.

CHAPTER SUMMARY

Level 3 and 4 evaluation focuses more on training effectiveness—or, in other words, the impact of the training on the company's strategy. While trainers focus more on levels 1 and 2, top management teams care much more about levels 3 and 4 so they can justify the money spent on training initiatives. Level 3 is assessing employee behaviors after the training sessions. In other words, did the information learned in the training session transfer to the job, and are the organizational systems in place to support effective transfer of the training knowledge? Level 4 is assessing the outcomes, and leading indicators if outcomes are expected over the long term. If one level of evaluation is essential for training success, it is level 3. Without proper transfer of the knowledge learned in training to the job, all the other levels of evaluation don't matter.

Proper transfer requires trainees who are conscientious and motivated to bring KSAs learned to the job. They must also believe that efforts put into training will result in rewards, both intrinsic and extrinsic, on the job. Transfer of knowledge is also enhanced when employees' pre-training experiences are positive. These include making the training voluntary when possible, helping the trainees see the strategic importance of the training, and getting buy-in and support from the trainees' supervisors to ensure a system is in place for successful transfer of the knowledge learned. A supportive workplace climate benefits the training transfer as well. Lastly, keeping the training system and delivery as similar to the actual on-the-job experience (near transfer) as possible greatly enhances transfer of knowledge. The further the training system is from how and where the training will be used on the job (far transfer), the more challenging it will be to ensure effective transfer of the training to the job. While near transfer is not always feasible given organizational constraints, understanding those constraints will enable the trainees, their peers, and their supervisors to develop better systems to overcome the limitations of transfer when far transfer is the only option.

Understanding and managing your training budget is important. Because ROI is an important consideration with respect to training outcomes, understanding what you spend money on, and why, is important for any training and development department. Assessing important metrics across the board ensures successful training across all levels, including calculating ROI.

KEY TERMS

Anderson Model for Learning Evaluation. Extends Kirkpatrick's model for evaluation by also assessing the impact of the company's learning evaluation program on strategic priorities.

Balanced scorecard (BSC). A measure developed by Kaplan and Norton that provides organizations with a strategic focus and key metrics on which to focus for training evaluation; includes financial/production considerations, customer focus, internal systems, and learning/growth.

Behavior. Kirkpatrick level 3 evaluation that assesses knowledge transfer to the job and the organizational processes and systems in place to encourage the transfer of skills from the training session to the job.

Far transfer. The training must generalize learned skills from the training session to different settings, people, or situations, and the learned skills must be maintained over time.

Knowledge transfer. The degree to which participants apply what they learned during training when they are back on the job.

Leading indicators. Short-term observations and measurements suggesting that critical behaviors are on track to create a positive impact on desired results; includes customer satisfaction, employee engagement, sales volume, cost containment, quality, and market share.

Near transfer. The job conditions to which the transfer is occurring are similar to the training conditions.

Organizational processes and systems. Required drivers needed to reinforce, encourage, and reward performance of critical behaviors on the job.

Outcomes. The degree to which targeted outcomes occur as a result of the training and the support and accountability from leaders.

Results. Kirkpatrick level 4 evaluation that assesses training outcomes and the leading indicators needed to create a positive impact on the desired training results.

Return on investment (ROI). Expressed as a percentage, ROI assesses the benefits of training to the organization, as related to the cost of the training.

END-OF-CHAPTER QUESTIONS AND EXERCISES

Discussion Questions

1. What is the difference between "effective training" and "training effectiveness"? Which level of evaluation is more important to trainers, and which level is more important to the organization? Explain why.

2. What types of KSAs are needed for leaders to help facilitate training transfer? What role should leaders play in helping new trainees use their skills on the job?

3. How does level 1 and 2 training evaluation impact level 3 and 4 training evaluation? Can level 3 evaluation occur if level 1 and 2 evaluation was done poorly? How and why?

4. Explain how training transfer is an example of change management. If people are resistant to change, what chance do we have to ensure successful training transfer? How do you recommend trainers overcome resistance to change?

5. How does the Anderson Model for Learning Evaluation complement Kirkpatrick's model? What does Anderson do differently

from Kirkpatrick? What value do you think Anderson's model has for organizations trying to assess level 4 training evaluation?

6. What is the difference between near and far transfer of training? Give an example of near transfer and an example of far transfer. How does Bloom's Taxonomy impact the concept of far transfer of training?

7. What trainee characteristics are ideal to increase the likelihood of training transfer? Since organizations may not be able to control for those personality traits, how can they help employees who may not have the traits to be successful on the job, post-training?

8. What is the value of providing post-training support groups for new trainees? How does this impact training transfer?

Ethical Scenario

And She Did It His Way

Jackie had just completed a corporate-provided training on how to install the new receivers for Community Cable. She knows her supervisor, John, had sent her because she was the newest member of her team and, as he said, "women need all the help they can get with this stuff." So, she was feeling pretty good about the fact that she was the only person in her cohort to get a perfect score. John said that was nice, but with a tone and body language that made her think he wasn't being truthful. Over the next few weeks, whenever John would come to an installation site for a spot check (a normal company procedure), he would tell Jackie that she was doing it wrong. Jackie explained each time that she was doing it the way they trained her, but John insisted she do it the old way. After a few more times, she got tired of being criticized and went back to "John's" way of installing the equipment. Despite no more complaints from John, when she got her performance evaluation, she was rated as "Needs Improvement" with the comment that she has problems following directions.

1. Assess how John handled the situation and say what he should have done to facilitate transfer.

2. Assess how Jackie handled the situation and say what you would suggest she do.

3. Explain why Community Cable should be concerned with this situation and how the company should handle it.

6.1 You've Been Transferred

Review the following YouTube video about the importance of developing transferrable skills: https://youtu.be/6AQCLM5senE. According to Business-Dictionary (www.businessdictionary.com/definition/transferable-skills.html), transferrable skills are any aptitude and/or knowledge acquired through personal experience, such as schooling, jobs, classes, hobbies, and sports. The assumption is transferrable skills are any talent a person develops that can be used in future employment.

Central to training and development is the ability to transfer skills from one context to another. Once you review the video, answer the following questions:

1. Apply Bloom's Taxonomy to the concept of transferrable skills. Why should trainers consider the importance of helping employees develop transferrable skills? Which level of Bloom's Taxonomy is relevant to transferrable skills?

2. Why are the skills discussed in the video important for all workers, but especially for entry-level workers? What role can trainers play in helping entry-level workers be successful on the job?

3. In what ways are transferrable skills important to consider for employee development programs?

6.2 How Much Did That Cost?

Healthful United, a national insurance company with over 10,000 employees, sends managers with growth potential to a leadership development program at

National Training Industries. Employees who successfully complete the assessment center are given the fast track to advanced leadership positions at Healthful United. The remaining employees are provided development opportunities, but are not fast tracked to advanced positions. National Training Industries charges $2,500 per employee for a weeklong program. Due to the competitive nature of the program, only 25% of those who complete the program are flagged as high-potential managers.

Once the high-potential employees are identified, they are provided external coaches from a local consulting company. The high-potential managers are expected to spend one hour per week with their external coach. The high-potential managers make an average of $92,000 per year. The executive coaching firm charges a $5,000 rate annually to cover the administrative costs of coordinating the coaching plans for the high-potential managers at Healthful United, and then an additional $125 for each billable hour for the coaches.

Healthful United has found that individual high-potential managers who are coached on average bring a $15,000 benefit to the bottom line of the company.

1. How much does it cost to identify 20 high-potential managers?
2. Assume the company has identified those 20 high-potential managers and now implements the coaching program. Calculate the cost for one year of the coaching program. Assume 40 hours a week, 52 weeks per year, and two weeks per year of paid vacation (no coaching required) for the managers.
3. Calculate the ROI for the high-potential employees for the coaching program.

6.3 The Difference Between Learning and Using

Wendy just finished delivering a training program and wanted to determine the readiness of her organization and its employees to transfer the information learned in the training to the job. She decided to utilize the Learning Transfer System Inventory to assess the transfer context. After distributing the inventory and collecting responses, she had the following results reflecting the average responses from trainees. Each question was assessed on a 5-point Likert-like scale with the following anchors:

1 = Strongly Disagree

2 = Disagree

3 = Neither Agree nor Disagree

4 = Agree

5 = Strongly Agree

Factor	Definition	Average Factor Score (5-point scale)
Leader Readiness	The extent to which individuals are prepared to enter and participate in training *e.g., Before the training, I had a good understanding of how it would fit my job-related development*	3.93
Motivation to Transfer	The direction, intensity, and persistence of effort toward utilizing in a work setting skills and knowledge learned *e.g., I get excited when I think about trying to use my new learning on my job*	4.03

Factor	Definition	Average Factor Score (5-point scale)
Positive Personal Outcomes	The degree to which applying training on the job leads to outcomes that are positive for the individual e.g., Employees in this organization receive various "perks" when they utilize newly learned skills on the job	3.27
Negative Personal Outcomes	The extent to which individuals believe that not applying skills and knowledge learned in training will lead to outcomes that are negative e.g., If I do not utilize my training, I will be cautioned about it	3.01
Personal Capacity for Transfer	The extent to which individuals have the time, energy, and mental space in their work lives to make changes required to transfer learning to the job e.g., My workload allows me time to try the new things I have learned	3.85
Peer Support	The extent to which peers reinforce and support use of learning on the job e.g., My colleagues encourage me to use the skills I have learned in training	3.74
Supervisor Support	The extent to which supervisors/managers support and reinforce use of training on the job e.g., My supervisor sets goals for me that encourage me to apply my training on the job	2.98
Supervisor Sanctions	The extent to which individuals perceive negative responses from supervisors/managers when applying skills learned in training (high score means no support) e.g., My supervisor opposed the use of the techniques I learned in training	4.13
Perceived Content Validity	The extent to which trainees judge training content to reflect job requirements accurately e.g., What is taught in training closely matches my job requirements	4.74
Transfer Design	The degree to which (1) training has been designed and delivered to give trainees the ability to transfer learning to the job, and (2) training instructions match job requirements e.g., The activities and exercises the trainers used helped me know how to apply my learning on the job	4.82
Opportunity to Use	The extent to which trainees are provided with or obtain resources and tasks on the job enabling them to use training on the job e.g., The resources I need to use what I learned will be available to me after training	2.97
Transfer Effort and Performance Expectations	The expectation that effort devoted to transferring learning will lead to change in job performance e.g., My job performance improves when I use new things that I have learned	3.67
Performance Outcomes Expectations	The expectation that changes in job performance will lead to valued outcomes e.g., When I do things to improve my performance, good things happen to me	3.58

(Continued)

(Continued)

Factor	Definition	Average Factor Score (5-point scale)
Resistance or Openness to Change	The extent to which prevailing group norms are perceived by individuals to resist or discourage the use of skills and knowledge acquired in training e.g., People in my group are open to changing the way they do things	3.75
Performance Self-Efficacy	Individuals' general belief that they are able to change their performance when they want to e.g., I am confident in my ability to use newly learned skills on the job	3.87
Performance Coaching	Formal and informal indicators from an organization about an individual's job performance e.g., After training, I get feedback from people about how well I am applying what I learned	2.45

1. Analyze the results from the LTSI administered. What patterns do you see in the data?

2. What recommendations would you make to Wendy on how to improve her training transfer context?

CHAPTER SEVEN

LEARNING METHODS

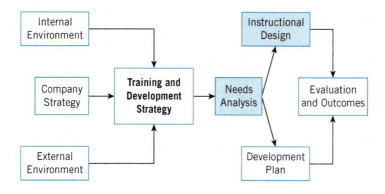

Learning Objectives

1. Distinguish between traditional and experiential learning methods.
2. Choose an appropriate method for providing instruction.
3. Discuss the effective use of debriefs.
4. Select effectively an instructional aid to support learning.
5. Explain which method is preferred for asking questions.

Imagine that you are the captain of a military vessel. You are on a normal reconnaissance mission when you receive a distress call. The call is garbled, and you can't verify it. The facts of the situation as you understand it are as follows: (1) You are the only vessel within range that can come to the aid of the distressed ship; (2) if you don't come to the ship's assistance, it will sink with a loss of life of everyone on board; (3) the distress call originates from the other side of a no-go zone; and (4) you have been ordered not to cross into the no-go zone, and if you go after the ship and are discovered, there is a high likelihood that your vessel will be fired upon, a war will start, and/or you will be disciplined when you get back to base. It is possible that the message is fake and/or the ship is not in the no-go zone. If you ask your communications officer to make contact with the ship or authenticate the message, she will tell you that it is not possible. If you tell your helmsperson to enter into the no-go zone, he will remind you of the danger to your ship and crew as well as to the current cease-fire. So, what do you do?

This opening scenario represents three different things that are discussed in this chapter, all different methods or teaching aids for use in training employees. First, as written, this scenario represents a short case. As discussed in this chapter, short cases are good to generate discussion. Second, the scenario described paraphrases the situation in the simulation of the Kobayashi Maru, which is named after the ship that made the distress call. Simulations are good because they allow you to experience the implications of your decisions. If you are wondering if you would have made the right decision in the Kobayashi Maru simulation, the answer is no. Don't feel bad—the simulation was designed to be a no-win situation. If you went to save the ship, then you would find out that it was a trick and your vessel would be attacked and destroyed. If you did not go to the aid of the ship, then the Kobayashi Maru would be lost with all hands. If you feel that isn't fair, that is okay. The purpose of this simulation, unlike others, is not to see what decision you would make but rather to see how you would respond to a no-win situation.[1]

If something about the Kobayashi Maru sounds familiar, then you are likely a fan of science fiction. The Kobayashi Maru is a training simulation that cadets at Starfleet Academy go through. It is shown in two separate Star Trek movies, *Star Trek II: The Wrath of Khan*[2] and *Star Trek*[3] (the 2009 reboot of the movie franchise). Though based in fiction, this simulation provides a template on which to develop real-world leadership training.[4] The fact that this simulation comes from a movie represents a third item that is discussed in this chapter, namely the use of movies or videos as an instructional aid. Movies are often used in training to provide examples of a concept and/or generate discussion. Using a clip of the Kobayashi Maru in a training session allows trainees to see an example of a simulation without having to engage in one. Further, it allows the trainer to talk about the attributes of a simulation. Finally, the clip also raises important ethical issues (it involves cheating), which can be either an alternative purpose for showing the clip or a secondary discussion.

Once an organization has decided what topics to include in a training program and determined who will participate, its next focus is how to provide that training. This chapter addresses this question by focusing on the nuts and bolts of implementation. In terms of the organizing framework, it is time to move from the needs analysis to the instructional design. This chapter covers many of the training options available to designers, several of which trainees may take for granted. Although trainers can take advantage of many of these options either online or in-person, this chapter focuses on the face-to-face implementation of these methods.

As the opening vignette illustrates, trainers have multiple options for teaching the same topic. Why do trainers choose one method over another? Their explanation for choosing a particular method or aid reflects some combination of technical and personal factors. Technically, some methods and aids are more effective or appropriate than others, and this depends on both the content and the context. The personal level refers to both the trainees and the trainers. As discussed in Chapter 4, trainees have different preferences regarding how they learn. Using different and/or multiple methods of instruction increases the likelihood of addressing an individual's preferred learning style, thereby improving the opportunity to learn. Also, just as trainees have learning preferences, so do trainers. Trainers may choose teaching methods and aids that reflect their personal strengths and preferences.

TRADITIONAL METHODS

In organizing the presentation of learning methods available to trainers, this chapter focuses on the nature and usage of the method. Broadly speaking, the options available to trainers can be sorted into two categories: traditional methods, including lectures and discussions, and experiential methods, where trainees learn through doing.

Lecture

Lectures represent one of the most widely used and traditional teaching methods.[5] It is based on the assumption that the person giving the lecture is an expert and the listeners are there to record and absorb what the lecturer says. As such, lectures are a relatively formal, albeit passive, method of instruction. They are considered more effective when the content of instruction is largely declarative, meaning they emphasize basic knowledge acquisition as opposed to higher-order outcomes like problem solving.

In their purest form, lectures represent one-way communication with the lecturer speaking to those being trained.[6] That said, individuals do not typically experience a pure lecture without any other instruction method or aid being employed—at a minimum, generally some combination of blackboard or computer visuals, handouts, and questioning. As for length, there is no set duration for what constitutes a lecture. While they can be the sole method of instruction taking up the entire length of a class or training session, lectures can also be a shorter method of communication to introduce a topic before some other training method is utilized.[7] Such a combination is particularly important if the focus is skill development.

Trainers choose to use lectures as their method of instruction for many reasons. First, lectures represent an efficient way to disseminate a large amount of information. As for the speed of transmitting the information, this depends upon how fast the lecturer speaks and/or how often she or he repeats or reviews a concept. Learning the appropriate pace for a lecture is important. Trainers need to go slow enough that trainees can keep up with note-taking but not so slow that trainees feel impatient or mentally wander.

Another advantage of lectures is the ability to scale up the number of trainees receiving instruction at any one time. Although many trainees enjoy and value smaller classes, if the trainer relies solely on lectures as the method of instruction, the size of the class does not matter. While there is no rule against using lectures as the sole method of instruction even in an independent study, generally the larger the class, the more the trainer will rely upon lectures. So what is the upper limit on the number of people who can be instructed via a lecture? Assuming a room with good acoustics, the number of people who can receive such instruction is limited only by space. One of the authors can testify to enrolling in a college course with nearly 2,000 students, which represented the maximum number of people allowed in the auditorium by the fire department. While that may seem like a lot, it is just a fraction of the number of people who can listen to or watch a lecture once it has been uploaded to the internet.

This brings us to two additional advantages of lectures, costs and consistency or control. An implication of lectures being so scalable is that while there is a fixed cost for the lecturer, the variable cost of adding trainees can be close to zero. This contributes to an argument that one large lecture is better than multiple smaller sections. Another advantage of lectures is the high degree of consistency or control regarding the content of instruction. The more a trainer relies on lecturing, the greater the consistency in content taught and control over what trainees learn. Consider the example of a lecture that has been uploaded to the internet. The first person and the 500th person viewing that lecture will hear and see the same information. While other forms of instruction involve more interaction, that interaction also introduces greater variability.

Of course, that very lack of interaction is the source of the disadvantages experienced with lectures. Given the nature of lectures, communication is mostly one-way. This limits the opportunities for trainees to clarify information, which in turn limits understanding and learning. Similarly, lectures that lack variation can be demotivating and contribute to trainees losing focus, which also impairs their ability to learn.

Asking questions, which is important to help clarify what the lecturer is saying, isn't always easy, for several reasons. Some trainers, for example, discourage the audience from asking questions. Sometimes this is intentional, with the trainer knowingly not providing opportunities to ask questions or not calling upon trainees who raise their hands. Other times, lecturers just get caught up in their lectures and/or don't see trainees trying to ask questions. Trainees can also get so caught up in trying to take notes that they miss opportunities to ask a question. Note also that the trend of using a computer to take notes, in the belief that you record more information, has been found to result in a lower level of learning.[8] Additionally, even one of the strengths of lectures can impair the ability to ask questions, namely the ability to teach large numbers. As classes grow in size, it becomes increasingly harder to ask questions, especially if someone is not sitting near the front of the lecture. Returning to the example of the 2,000-person class, imagine sitting in the balcony and either getting the trainer's attention or calling out a question.

Another problem with some lectures is that they lack dynamism. As the length of the lecture increases, it becomes harder to follow the trainer's point. This is particularly true for older trainees.[9] It can also be exacerbated by another strength of lectures, specifically their ability to convey large amounts of information. At some point, the law of diminishing returns takes over, and the more information a trainer tries to cram into a lecture, the less the trainees learn. Along with a loss of focus comes a loss of energy and motivation. Even if you have stayed awake through every lecture you have attended, in all likelihood you have seen a classmate fall asleep. Every time a trainee loses interest, focus, or consciousness, that individual learns less. Therefore, while lectures can be very effective, it is beneficial for trainers to supplement them with instructional aids and/or other methods.

Discussion

Although they can stand alone as a method of instruction, discussions are frequently used to supplement lectures. Discussions, or focused conversations on a specific topic, are a good way to involve trainees in the learning process. While it is easy to have a discussion, it can be difficult to have a good one. Trainers can take several measures to increase the richness of discussions and the ability for trainees to learn from them.

Among the first things that trainers should think about is whether the topic is appropriate, and the trainees are prepared, to engage in a discussion. Discussions are good when trainers want to explore the nuances in a topic and/or want their trainees to engage in critical thinking. However, this requires that trainees have adequate preparation to fully engage—one reason that discussions are often used to supplement lectures. Even if a lecture precedes a discussion, the richness of a discussion often depends on the level of trainee preparedness.

Trainers can do several things to improve the quality of the learning from discussions. First, they must remember that a discussion is not a substitute for preparation. Trainers need to identify the main learning concepts and objectives and be prepared to ask the questions that will guide the discussion in the proper direction. If not, learning can be sacrificed to a tangent. Second, trainers should strive to make discussions egalitarian. If a discussion is dominated by a couple of trainees, the group fails to benefit from the potential collective wisdom of everyone present. Also, if trainees are not participating in a discussion, it becomes easy for them to disengage and cease to benefit. Finally, trainers should conclude by summarizing the main concepts and learning objectives to clarify and confirm to trainees what to take away from the discussion.

EXPERIENTIAL METHODS

While traditional methods are common and represent useful ways to provide instruction, there is increasing interest in teaching individuals in more engaging ways.

Instruction that is fully **experiential** comprises four stages: concrete experience, reflective observation, abstract conceptualization, and active experimentation.[10] Types of experiential instruction discussed in this chapter are cases, role plays, in-baskets, games, and simulations.

Debriefs

One good reason to present the experiential learning methods together is that they rely heavily on an effective debrief. **Debriefs** are a special type of discussion, addressed here separately because of when to use them as part of training and development activities. Debriefing participants after completing an experiential exercise serves to confirm and/or complete the learning that took place in the activity.[11] Debriefs also provide an opportunity for participants to reflect upon what they have just experienced, which serves to deepen their understanding.

Across the different types of experiential activities, the process of debriefing is relatively consistent. While experiential learning opportunities are generally designed around a specific concept or point, learning can be idiosyncratic, so it is important that trainers plan debriefing[12] in order to ensure that trainees gain an understanding of the intended purpose of the exercise. When planning to debrief an activity, it is useful to consider the four stages of experiential learning. Exhibit 7-1 provides a guideline and sample questions around which to organize a debriefing.[13]

As presented in Exhibit 7-1, one stage logically progresses to another. The questions in the exhibit are by necessity generic and should be tailored or supplemented to meet the needs of the specific training or development activity. While there is no set length for a debriefing, a thorough and complete discussion involves each of the stages. Asking questions about what participants experienced, both what they felt personally and what they observed in others, addresses the first two stages and creates a foundation for the latter stages. Building on these, trainers should guide the debrief so trainees understand how their experiences relate to or illustrate key concepts and learning objectives. While the first three stages may be enough for learning to occur, for the activity to be truly successful it should change workplace behavior. This is the role of the final set of questions. By focusing on applications and continued growth, trainers will facilitate the utilization of the knowledge and skills that trainees have gained when back at work.

Exhibit 7-1 Suggestions for Debriefing Experiential Exercises

Stage	Purpose	Sample questions
Concrete Experience	Trainees share what they experienced.	• What outcomes did you achieve? • How did you feel?
Reflective Observation	Present trainees with additional perspectives.	• What assumptions did you make? • What did you observe in others?
Abstract Conceptualization	Connect the trainees' experiences to course objectives, concepts, and theories.	• What do you feel explains your experiences in the activity? • What commonalities can you draw from the other participants?
Active Participation	Consider future applications/"what if" scenarios based on what was learned in the activity.	• What changes could you make that would improve your outcomes? • How could you apply what you learned back at work?

Source: Adapted from Robert F. Dennehy, Ronald R. Sims, and Heather E. Collins, "Debriefing Experiential Learning Exercises: A Theoretical and Practical Guide for Success," *Journal of Management Education* 22, no. 1 (1998): 9–25.

Cases

Cases represent a common method of instruction. In fact, some collegiate courses and even some graduate programs teach exclusively using the case method. Cases involve trainees reading and analyzing a situation. The trainees then engage in developing alternative solutions to the problem or situation presented. In some cases, this involves outside research. During the discussion or debrief that follows, the trainer points out the key concepts to be learned and/or considerations to keep in mind when analyzing and acting upon similar scenarios. This process may also involve the presentation of more formal models and guidelines.

While cases share many common elements, they can vary drastically in scope. For example, the first paragraph of the opening vignette could serve as a case. It is rich enough to generate a discussion of the ethics of helping the crew of the Kobayashi Maru as well as the laws and treaties that apply in the situation. Cases can also be much longer and provide more detailed information and background. For example, it is not unheard of for a case to be equivalent in length to the typical textbook chapter notwithstanding appendices and tables with reference information.

There are, of course, tradeoffs with cases that depend on their length. Shorter cases (e.g., those ranging from one to just a few pages long) represent a good way to supplement lectures because they can be handed out, read, analyzed, discussed, and debriefed, often in a single class session. The downside is that they are, by definition, short. It is not unusual for trainees to get frustrated with not having more information available to make a decision—a problem that is alleviated with longer cases, which allow for provision of more contextual information. As such, longer cases also make it easier to see and explore the complexity of real-life situations. The potential downside of longer cases is that they require participants to prepare in advance. Just imagine trying to read a chapter-long case in a class, not even counting the time to understand and analyze it, much less to discuss and debrief it.

Role Plays

The simplest explanation for **role plays** is that they involve trainees acting out a scenario to better understand a concept or how to handle a situation. Particularly good to help trainees learn about and practice interpersonal skills, role plays are an example of experiential learning. Trainers who choose to utilize role plays need to make two key choices: first, whether to use scripted or unscripted role plays, and second, whether participation should be modeled or participatory. As shown in Exhibit 7-2, the combination of these decisions results in four types of role plays.

In scripted role plays, participants receive dialogue to read. Basically, trainers give them a scene from a play. Among the advantages of scripted role plays are that the trainers know exactly what will be said and that the dialogue will address specific points that they want the trainees to know and understand, with the added benefit of alleviating trainee reticence or discomfort with role play.[14] Another advantage of providing participants with a script is that they can easily annotate it to review later. However, a limitation of a predefined script is the lack of spontaneity and ability of participants to drive the role play.

Exhibit 7-2 Options for Structuring Role Plays

	Scripted	Unscripted
Modeled	Starring	Developmental
Participatory	Case	Exploratory

Although control is a strength of scripted role plays, it would be improper to say that there is no control in an unscripted role play. In unscripted role plays, trainees still receive some background information, about both the situation and their individual role as well as the issue or problem to be addressed. On their own, trainees usually touch on the points that the trainer wants made, even if not in the way the trainer expects. Both the advantages and disadvantages with unscripted role plays involve the level of trainee involvement. On the positive side, trainees can become more engaged with unscripted role plays, which allows them to internalize the material better. However, some trainees don't take unscripted role plays seriously and/or focus on the background information that they don't have, which inhibits their ability to both participate in and learn from the activity.

The other important decision for trainers regarding role plays is whether to invite a couple of participants to act out the role play in front of the whole group, or have the participants team up and individually work through the script or scenario. When a trainer decides to have a pair, or group in larger role plays, act out the role play in front of the entire group, the participants are modeling the scenario for everyone. The advantage of this approach is that all trainees observe the same scenario. The disadvantage is that those not modeling the role play do not individually experience the scenario. Conversely, when the role plays are participatory and everyone is doing them, each participant experiences the scenario for him- or herself. One disadvantage of this approach is the potential confusion from conducting multiple role plays simultaneously if the room does not provide adequate space.

In deciding among the alternatives highlighted in Exhibit 7-2, a trainer needs to consider how much focus or control is desired versus how important it is for individuals to experience the scenario and develop a more personal understanding. If a trainer wants to ensure a common understanding, the combination that provides for the greatest degree of control involves role plays both scripted and modeled. Here we refer to this as *starring* because it is easiest for the trainer to highlight specific points being acted out by a couple of participants. By contrast, the least amount of control but the greatest potential for personal experience and understanding occurs with *exploratory* role plays because their unscripted and participatory nature maximizes the potential engagement of trainees.

The level of engagement and control is mixed for both *case* and *developmental* role plays. *Case* role plays are so called because, while written in dialogue as opposed to prose, they function similar to other cases that trainers would utilize. This type of role play favors control because the trainer knows exactly what is occurring, but the level of trainee engagement with the material is not as rich. *Developmental* role plays are good if you want participants to learn what to do or not to do. Because there is no script, the trainer gives up some control, but that is compensated by the fact that all participants observe the same role play. As for engagement, although most individuals in the training do not personally engage in the role play, assessment and coaching with developmental role play tend to be more engaging than with scripted role play.

In-Basket

In-basket activities, a form of situational judgment test, combine elements of both cases and role plays. While they are commonly accepted for organizational selection, research has also shown situational judgment tests to be effective for training purposes.[15] In some ways, in-baskets are like mini-cases, but after analyzing the situation, individuals need to take some action. This need to take action, after being presented with an initial scenario, is what makes them similar to role plays. However, in-baskets are not full role plays because there is not another person to interact with and/or there is not a full script.

Although they do not involve a two-way interaction with another person, in-baskets can still be useful in developing interpersonal skills. In the typical in-basket task, a trainee receives information about an organization and his or her role in it. Then the individual is presented with a series of emails that need to be answered. While each email may be on a completely different topic, a strength of this method is that the emails can vary just enough to illustrate the nuances of a particular issue. Further, the responses can provide a lot of information about someone's communication, conflict resolution, and/or decision-making styles. As such, in-baskets can also be incorporated into a needs assessment, and some organizations even use them in the selection process. As with other experiential exercises, the learning component with in-baskets comes during the debriefing of the activity.

The term *in-basket* harkens back to the pre-computer days when office desks often had two baskets or trays on them. One of these was the in-basket in which employees placed new work assignments. Workers would take the communication or work request out of the in-basket, complete it, and then place it in the second basket or tray, referred to as the out-basket. This is one of just many examples where technology has advanced but the fundamental instructional method remains the same.

Games

Although not used as often as some other experiential learning methods, games can be a good way to engage trainees. Many different types of games are available from which a trainer can choose. This chapter sorts games into two categories. The first category, very specific in nature, comprises solely what are known as business games. The second category is more general, serving as more of an umbrella term for a variety of activities. To illustrate the contrast, we refer to this second type as nonbusiness games. While both categories can be referred to as instructional games, they differ significantly in terms of logistics.

Business games are specialized activities developed to provide participants with practice and insight into making business decisions. One place where you may personally experience a business game is as part of a capstone course at your university. In a college environment, a single game is often stretched over multiple class sessions. This is not a necessity because, despite their complexity, these games normally rely upon computers to calculate the impact of decisions. Some business games will approximate simulations (discussed in the next section). Because of their complexity and reliance on programming, many business games are developed by outside vendors. So while they may be good to use, they can be costly and may be limited because of their programming.

Nonbusiness games are usually shorter in duration and intended primarily to engage trainees and/or demonstrate a limited set of concepts. In many instances, trainers use games as **icebreakers**, short activities used at the beginning of a training session to help get everyone engaged. An example used by one of the authors involves crossword puzzles (although it could be revised to use sudoku or some similar activity; see Exhibit 7-3). Unless there is a ringer in the room—something that can be determined ahead of time or be part of the debriefing—the activity is good for demonstrating the concept of synergy and explaining different ways of organizing work.

Other nonbusiness games are exactly that, mass-marketed games used to demonstrate or practice a concept or skill. For example, in an increasing number of mass-marketed games, winning is achieved through cooperation rather than competition. These cooperative games provide an opportunity to teach about or practice team-focused interpersonal skills. Team-building and related skills, such as leadership and conflict resolution, represent areas where other activities that fall under the broader umbrella term of *games* is useful. Some fun activities that have been used for these purposes include rope courses, scavenger hunts, and LEGO bricks.[16]

Exhibit 7-3 Experiencing Crossword Puzzles

The class is divided into a minimum of four groups. Each person is given the same crossword puzzle to solve. One group is allowed to work together, while the other three must work individually.

After a period of time, the rules for two of the groups are changed. One group of independent workers is told to trade their crossword puzzle with someone else's in their group. Another group is now told they can work together. A few more minutes are given to solve the puzzles, and then results are shared.

If all goes as planned, the group that worked together from the beginning should have completed the puzzle first or at least completed the most. This is the interdependent group, and it helps demonstrate the concept of synergy. The group that should have done the worst was the one where everyone worked individually all the time, the independent group. Improving on the independent is the sequential group (the one that had to trade puzzles) followed by the pooled group (the one that could eventually work together). Students in the pooled group tend not to do as well as those in the interdependent group because of the time to coordinate once they are allowed to work together.

Games are also a place where trainers can take advantage of some creativity. If you are curious about just how creative you can get, a good place to look is with the Management and Organizational Behavior Teaching Society, or **MOBTS**. Among the resources available through MOBTS is an archive of the activities presented at the organization's conferences. If you go to mobts.org, you can search through those archives and either be inspired or find an activity that you can use to teach an organizational behavior, human resource, or interpersonal concept or skill.

Simulations

While the opening vignette of this chapter described a fictitious simulation, simulations represent one of the best options for training and development individuals. Simulations are designed to replicate real-world situations and be interactive. The goal is for the person in the simulation to experience the real-time impact of decisions and actions. Because of their complexity, simulations can be difficult and expensive to both create and use.[17] Therefore, simulations are not used frequently; however, they may be the best way to train and develop individuals when the needed skill or ability is critical to success and/or survival.

Survival may seem like a big word to use when talking about training and development, but one of the more common industries that use simulations is the transportation industry. While you may have used, or still use, a flight simulator on your game system, flight simulators represent an important element of pilot training because the cost of failure is very high. If you do the wrong maneuver while simulating a flight in your living room, you can simply press the reset button. Unfortunately, that feature is unavailable on modern aircraft.

Simulations are also useful as part of leadership development.[18] While an interpersonal scenario may not have the life-or-death consequence of flying an airplane, having the right leaders is critical to organizational success. Simulations are desirable in this situation because other forms of development activities may lack either the intensity or the level of control that the organization desires. Another interesting aspect of using simulations in the development of interpersonal skills is that they work both as the method of instruction and as part of the needs assessment process. In these cases, organizations often include simulations as part of a larger assessment center.

CHOOSING A METHOD

When deciding which method to use, several factors facilitate that decision. Exhibit 7-4 provides an overview of all the instructional methods presented in this chapter, as well as reminders on when to use each method and its relative advantages and disadvantages. For example, Exhibit 7-4 reminds you that lectures are beneficial when the instructional goal is largely to inform, and they have the advantage of providing breadth of material as well as accommodating large numbers of trainees. However, the exhibit also includes the reminder that a disadvantage of lectures is passive learning, which can impact motivation and focus.

Exhibit 7-4 Choosing an Instructional Method

Method	When to Use	Advantages	Disadvantages
Lecture	Learning goal is informational	Breadth of material Can accommodate a large number of trainees	Trainees are passive Concern with focus and motivation
Discussions	Want to encourage participation and problem solving	Engages trainees	Unequal participation Trainees may get sidetracked
Cases	Focus on problem identification and diagnosis	Draws on knowledge and experience of trainees	Potential lack of fidelity Trainees may get sidetracked
Role Plays	Want to develop interpersonal skills	Provides opportunity for practice and feedback	Trainees may not take seriously Lack of sufficient information
In-Basket	Focus on communication style and problem resolution	Can cover multiple issues or focus on nuances	Lacks two-way interaction Depends on debrief
Games/Business Games	Want to engage trainees	Fun (nonbusiness) Shows impact of decisions (business)	Ratio of time spent to knowledge or skill gained (nonbusiness) Costs (business)
Simulations	Need to learn how to handle a complex and/or high-risk situation	Provides real-life experiences without risk	Potential lack of fidelity Cost of development/use

Source: Adapted from Bridget N. O'Connor, Michael Bronner, and Chester Delaney, *Training for Organizations*, 2nd ed. (Cincinnati, OH: South-Western, 2002).

Of course, the instructional methods listed in Exhibit 7-4 and presented in this chapter do not constitute all the options available for trainers to use. For example, options discussed separately in this textbook are on-the-job training (Chapter 8) and a variety of methods covered under the heading of e-learning (Chapter 9). For now, this chapter continues with instructional aids and includes a section on asking questions.

INSTRUCTIONAL AIDS

In addition to the methods so far discussed, it is helpful to supplement them with **instructional aids** to support learning. There are two main reasons to encourage the use of instructional aids. First, communicating information in different ways helps to summarize and/or reinforce the main instructional method. Second, as discussed in Chapter 4, individuals have different preferences for learning, not all of which are necessarily addressed by the learning methods presented in this chapter. For example, traditional methods of instruction (e.g., lectures and discussions) primarily benefit auditory learners. As for kinesthetic learners, the active nature of experiential learning methods applies to them. However, without supplementary instruction, neither method addresses the interest of visual learners.

Exhibit 7-5 provides a list of instructional aids that can be used to support learning. This chapter discusses the general use of these instructional aids. For more comprehensive advice on content and design, refer to Appendix C. Following the columns of Exhibit 7-5, the advantages and disadvantages of each of the instructional aids presented are discussed along with which **learning modality** it addresses. The learning modalities presented in Exhibit 7-5 are consistent with physiologically based learning styles,[19] commonly referred to as auditory (listening), kinesthetic (tactile), read/write, and visual. For example, handouts are helpful for conveying visual information whereas videos can provide an additional way to meet the needs of kinesthetic learners.

Exhibit 7-5 Choosing an Instructional Aid

Aid	Learning Modality	Advantages	Disadvantages
Audio	Auditory	• Adds variety	• Need to focus
Blackboards/whiteboards	Visual and Read/Write	• Can be created spontaneously	• Not permanent • Variable quality
Computer (presentation)	Visual and Read/Write	• Easy and/or appealing to read • Easy to review	• Can lack spontaneity
Flipcharts	Visual and Read/Write	• Facilitates debrief of small group activities	• Can be cumbersome
Handouts	Visual and Read/Write	• Easy to refer to for future reference • Can assist with note-taking	• May be distracting • Trainees can jump ahead
Overheads	Visual and Read/Write	• Adds variety	• Can disrupt flow
Video (popular)	Auditory, Visual, and Kinesthetic	• Entertaining/engaging	• Connection to topic may be weak or not obvious
Video (specialized)	Auditory, Visual, and Kinesthetic	• Focused on topic	• Production values may detract
Videoconferencing	Auditory	• Facilitates guests • Adds variety	• Video quality and interactivity

Source: Adapted from W. Wayne Turmel, "Technology in the Classroom: Velcro for the Mind," pp. 97–106 in *The ASTD Handbook of Training Design and Delivery: A Comprehensive Guide to Creating and Delivering Training Programs: Trainer-Led, Computer-Based, or Self-Directed*, ed. G. M. Piskurich, P. Beckshi, and B. Hall (New York: McGraw-Hill, 2000).

Overheads and Handouts

When discussing in-basket activities, we mentioned that while technology has changed, the fundamental instructional method remains the same. This statement is also true when it comes to instructional aids. For example, depending on the technology available in the classroom, overheads can be projected onto a screen using transparencies (which are the most archaic), document cameras, or a computer to show a scanned file or access information from a website. Overheads are also often used in conjunction with handouts. Handouts can either mirror the information on an overhead or else intentionally contain less information to encourage and structure participant note-taking. Overheads are a good visual aid and can help mix things up in a training, but if used sporadically, turning on or off a projector can disrupt the flow of the training.

Blackboards, Whiteboards, and Computers

Another example of how technology has changed the training experience involves blackboards. Although blackboards and chalk remain popular with some trainers, they have been replaced in many cases with either whiteboards and markers or computers. Today, many people have grown accustomed to the PowerPoint presentation as the primary instructional aid. The reason that the exhibit refers to computers and not PowerPoint is that PowerPoint is simply a software package that can be replaced. For example, Prezi is a more recent software package that is growing in popularity.

Further, trainers can use computers for many functions beyond simply projecting a PowerPoint presentation. Some other basic uses include accessing and projecting audio and video clips. Trainers with poor penmanship and/or who want to capture trainee responses can record and project these via a computer rather than a black- or whiteboard. In addition, trainers can use computers to help demonstrate instructional points by accessing websites and or projecting software packages (e.g., databases, spreadsheets, and statistical packages) onto a screen. Similarly, computers allow for videoconferencing, which allows additional presenters or trainees, not physically co-located to where the training is occurring, to participate.

Flipcharts

Flipcharts have been a popular option among trainers, but as technology continues to develop, this may cease to be the case. Flipcharts were particularly useful when a trainer was unsure of whether the room that would be used contained a blackboard, whiteboard, or computer. In the absence of those tools, flipcharts provided an easily transported item that could be utilized to write down the main points. However, as laptops and portable projectors have become increasingly accessible, this need for flipcharts has decreased.

The other main use of flipcharts has been in conjunction with learning exercises that involved breaking up training participants into smaller groups. Flipcharts allowed these groups to easily write down their ideas and/or results in a manner that would be easy to share with the others in the training. While this remains a popular use, the proliferation of computers may be making this type of instructional aid redundant.

Video and Audio

Video and audio provide a distinct change of pace and are usually very popular with trainees. Of the two, video is generally preferred in comparison to audio mainly because audio, for many people, is less engaging than video. Without a picture to help focus attention, it may be difficult to keep participants engaged, especially if the audio is not of high quality or the recording is long.

Trainers utilize videos as an instructional aid for two main reasons. First, there is the case approach. Videos can be used to present some or all of the information needed for the case method of instruction. This is a good alternative to the more common text method because a video can provide richer information (i.e., more context) and may be able to do so in less time than it would take someone to read.[20] In this way, videos address trainees who prefer auditory and visual learning. Second, videos can be utilized for behavioral modeling. When used for this purpose, a video can help trainees develop interpersonal skills (e.g., conflict resolution or customer interactions)[21] and is consistent with a kinesthetic approach to learning. Here, a video presents a situation and shows how individuals either should, or should not, approach that situation. Another way of thinking about behavioral modeling with videos is that it can substitute for the starring method of role plays.

While video is often a favorite of participants, not all videos are created equally. For this reason, Exhibit 7-5 distinguishes between popular and specialized videos. Here the term *popular* refers to mass-produced or wide-released videos whereas *specialized* refers to videos designed to accompany a specific training program.

Popular videos.

The category of popular videos largely encompasses movies and television shows and even commercials. Participants often like these types of videos because they have high production values and may come from a show that they already enjoy watching.[22] The main downside is that popular videos were not made with the primary purpose of use in a training setting. As such, the trainer may need to provide some additional context and/or corrections so that the video supports the learning objective being covered. Another issue to consider is that the scene(s) a trainer wants to use may contain content that is not appropriate for a corporate or educational setting (e.g., violence, sex, or drug use) or accessible to the trainees (e.g., cultural and/or language barriers).[23]

There is also the issue of logistics. The ability to use a video clip is limited by both technology and availability. For example, as DVDs took over for VHS tapes, many trainers had to convert, reinvest in, or substitute videos that they had been using. Eventually, DVDs will also likely be replaced by another format. Because of this, streaming has become increasingly popular. However, many trainers have found out too late that videos they assumed were available had been taken down from streaming sites. This is often related to copyright issues, so trainers should verify that a desired video is fair use. Even if a video is available online, an inadequate internet connection may cause buffering issues that mar the presentation of the video.

Specialized video.

Specialized videos are good to use because they have been either selected or produced to support a learning objective. As such, access and copyright issues are not a concern. Another advantage is that they usually more clearly relate to the topic being trained. Unfortunately, these videos sometimes suffer from poor production values, which may cause trainees to become distracted or disengaged. If you need a video, a source of relatively high-quality videos, which tends to balance access and relatedness, is TED.com.

ASKING QUESTIONS

Asking questions is vital for learning. There are lots of ways, and reasons, to ask questions.[24] The questions discussed in this section occur during the delivery of training. This is meant to distinguish between questions that are part of the instructional process and those that come at the end of training and are focused more on assessment and evaluation. When it comes to asking questions during a training session, a trainer has several options. We begin this discussion by considering why trainers ask questions and follow that up with their options for asking questions.

Question to Confirm

In regard to confirming understanding, asking questions works in both directions. It is also why there are no stupid questions. Participants need to ask questions in order to make sure they understand and learn the material. As a trainee, you may have been reluctant to ask a question because you were concerned that the answer would be too obvious or show you weren't paying attention. Keep in mind that if you have a question, at least one other person in the room likely has the same one, and they will be thankful that you asked it.

Trainers also appreciate when participants ask questions because it provides ongoing feedback. Depending on the nature of the question asked, trainers will know how well they are communicating a concept. If the question is basic, then they know that the trainees are struggling with understanding, which means that trainers need to reinforce a concept through either repetition or an alternative means of conveying the information. If the question is more advanced, it confirms that the trainees understand the core concept.

Question to Engage

Questions encourage engagement in two ways. First, the act of asking a question involves trainees in the process of learning. Answering questions shifts trainees from being passive to more active learners. Second, questions are meant to get trainees more interested in or involved with a concept. So even if trainees are not physically answering a question, the goal is to get them to answer mentally. This is one of the reasons that trainers ask how trainees feel about a topic.

A special version of an engagement question is known as a hook. **Hooks** are usually asked at the beginning of a session or when a new topic is introduced. These questions are meant to be interesting and may not have an obvious connection to the topic being covered. The goal of a hook is to get trainees thinking and wanting to know more about the training topic.

How to Ask Questions

When it comes to the mechanics of asking questions, trainers must make two key decisions. One decision is whether to ask a closed or open-ended question. When a question is closed, the trainer is looking for a specific answer. When a question is open-ended, there is no specific right answer. A second consideration is whether to target or lob it. Trainers who target ask the question of a particular trainee. **Lobbed** questions are presented to the class as a whole, and anyone is free to answer. When these decisions are combined, they result in four types of questions, presented in Exhibit 7-6. While there are reasons to ask each type of question, trainer preference is a major determinant of which will be utilized.

One important difference among these types of questions is how trainees respond to them. Of the four types of questions identified in Exhibit 7-6, trainees tend to dislike those characterized as *quizzing*, which are closed and targeted. This combination means the trainer calls on a specific participant and has a specific answer in mind. These types of questions can make a trainee feel pressured. Trainers who simply want to verify understanding without pressuring trainees have the option of asking *confirming* questions. Here, trainers are still looking for a specific answer, because the question is still closed, but instead of picking out a specific trainee, the trainer lobs the question. This lessens the potential for trainees to feel pressured because no individual is responsible for the answer.

There is also generally less pressure to answer an open-ended question because it does not have a set answer. One reason that trainers like to ask open-ended questions is that they are a good way to engage trainees. We call open-ended and lobbed questions *provoking* here because they encourage trainees to think further on the topic. Where *provoking* questions help get trainees to think, *involving* questions are designed to get trainees to participate. One reason that trainees use *involving* questions is to engage trainees who otherwise say little. While this could also be achieved with a *quizzing* question, it is better to ask an *involving* one because it is less likely to make trainees anxious, which may also be the reason for their reluctance to speak or answer a lobbed question.

Exhibit 7-6 Types of Questions

	Closed	Open-ended
Targeted	Quizzing	Involving
Lobbed	Confirming	Provoking

CHAPTER SUMMARY

This chapter covered the basics of how to implement training once the content and participants have been identified. It began its coverage with the most common and traditional methods of instructions, lectures and discussions. The chapter continued with an explanation of experiential methods, which included cases, role plays, in-baskets, games, and simulations. While many of the methods in this chapter could be implemented in either a face-to-face or online format, the discussion assumed that the trainer and participants would be co-located.

The options trainers choose to utilize depend on both the nature of the training to be provided and personal preferences. For example, the reasons that lectures are so common include the lecturer's ability to convey a large amount of information, and many trainers find the control over the material to be comfortable. Conversely, role plays can introduce a lot of ambiguity, which makes some trainers reluctant to use them despite the fact that they are an excellent way to provide training for interpersonal skills. Among the methods utilized the least are games and simulations. The reasons for this include the amount of time, thought, creativity (particularly with games), and/or costs (particularly with simulations) needed to develop and implement them.

Regardless of personal preferences or the nature of the training, a couple of recommendations generally apply. First, it is a good idea to mix up training with more than one method. Although we discussed instructional aids (e.g., handouts and videos) separately from the teaching methods, they represent a good way to mix up training, particularly if the primary or sole method of instruction is a lecture.

Related to this is another recommendation, that in some form training should make use of discussion. This does not mean that training must utilize the traditional method of discussion, as presented in this chapter; it takes a more expansive meaning of the term. Keep in mind that the "Experiential Methods" section started with an explanation of debriefs, a type of discussion intended to ensure that trainees understand the connection between an experiential exercise and the specific learning objective(s). Similarly, while questions alone may not constitute what is normally perceived of as a discussion, they are important because they provide a means for two-way communication (which is lacking with lectures), and depending on how the question is asked, it can engage trainees and/or provide feedback.

Trainers should also keep an open mind when it comes to designing and implementing training. While a trainer may prefer or feel comfortable with certain methods or specific instructional aids, things change. For example, an amazing video eventually becomes outdated, grows stale, or ceases to be available. Updating content and materials is both necessary and enriching. The same applies to learning methods. First-time trainers are often most comfortable with lectures, but as they gain experience with both the process and the content, the inclusion of new or experiential methods may improve the training experience for all involved. Finally, keep in mind that this chapter did not cover all forms of training and development activities. Important options discussed later in this textbook include e-learning and on-the-job training.

KEY TERMS

Debrief. Discussion at the end of an experiential exercise to reinforce learning objectives.

Experiential method. An umbrella term to describe instructional options (e.g., role play) that actively engage trainees.

Hook. A question at the start of training meant to generate interest in the topic.

Icebreaker. A short activity at the beginning of a training session to help get everyone engaged.

In-basket. A type of experiential exercise where trainees are given multiple short scenarios to which they need to respond.

Instructional aid. A device (e.g., computer) or supplement (e.g., handout) to facilitate and/or enhance learning.

Learning modality. A sensory approach to learning (e.g., auditory or visual).

Lecture. A traditional method of providing training where the trainee passively receives information from a trainer.

Lobbed. A question that is asked of the entire group rather than a specific trainee.

MOBTS. The Management and Organizational Behavior Training Society provides lots of information on how to make instruction more engaging and effective.

Role play. An experiential instructional method where trainees act out a scenario to better understand a concept or how to handle a situation.

END-OF-CHAPTER QUESTIONS AND EXERCISES

Discussion Questions

1. What are the advantages and disadvantages of lectures?
2. Are experiential instructional methods better than traditional ones? Why or why not?
3. How and why would you debrief an experiential instructional method?
4. Describe and explain which type of role play you would be most likely to utilize.
5. When would you want to use a simulation, and when would you not?
6. What are your thoughts about using games as an instructional method?
7. Which experiential methods do you think should be used more frequently? Explain why.
8. When would you want to use flipcharts?
9. What kind of videos do you think are most effective? Provide an example that demonstrates this.
10. Why do trainers ask questions? How do you think trainers should ask questions? Explain why.

Ethical Scenario

Participation Pointers

Logistics firm Moving Targets recently instituted a monthly lunch and learn seminar series covering a combination of current topics and customer relations issues. The sole instructional methods are lecture and discussion. Monica leads the customer relations seminars. Toward the end of her first session, she quizzed people who hadn't asked questions or participated in the discussion. When she started her second session, she acknowledged that she had received feedback that some people didn't like being quizzed, but she told everyone that "you need to get used to participating because you can't choose to not participate with our customers." The only person who didn't participate this time was Mark, who everyone liked but also knew was a major introvert. Just as the seminar was about to end, Monica seemed to realize this and said, "Mark, you're the only one here who hasn't spoken up yet. So please answer this question: What is the correct way to handle the customer complaint I just explained?" It was clear from the look on Mark's face that he wanted to be anywhere else than there. All he managed to say was "Umm." After what felt like an hour, but was just a few seconds, Monica answered her own question and let everyone leave.

1. Should Monica have quizzed Mark?
2. What other methods could Monica have used to encourage participation?

7.1 Creating Handouts

Pick a topic covered in this class and create two handouts that you could use to supplement a lecture. Design one version of the handout to be consistent with a read/write learning modality. Design the second version of the handout to convey the same information, but presented in a format that addresses the needs of visual learners.

7.2 Pick a Video

Identify a scene from a popular (e.g., mass-produced and wide-released) movie or television show that you could use to help teach a concept or interpersonal skill covered in this or a previous course. Your write-up of the scene should include the following information:

a. Identify the concept or interpersonal skill covered by the video.
b. Identify the movie/television show.
c. Provide a short description of the scene.
d. Explain why this scene is a good instructional aid for the concept/interpersonal skill.

7.3 Practice With Instructional Methods

Here are examples of a short case, in-basket exercise, and unscripted role play.

Each of these examples focuses on the concept of mentoring, particularly problems that can arise between mentors and their protégés. This approach is used for two purposes. First, mentoring is a development concept that we cover in Chapter 11; however, you will be able to complete each of these exercises without reading that chapter. Second, keeping the content consistent helps to show the potential of these three methods, both individually and in concert.

While you should complete the exercises as you would in any other course, you should then reflect upon the role of each case and how you might use short cases, in-baskets, and role plays in the future.

7.3a Short Case

When the company decided to implement a formal mentoring program, both Pat and Chris were interested and among the first people to sign up.

Pat has been with the company for 30 years. She started in an entry-level position directly out of undergrad and slowly rose through the ranks, eventually becoming an area vice president (AVP). She managed to do that despite never getting an MBA—a point of both pride and frustration for Pat. As the only AVP without an MBA or similar degree, she is proud. However, she is also frustrated, as her lack of a higher degree means that it took her longer than the other AVPs to be promoted to that level. Pat has also been told that without an advanced degree, she will probably not receive any further promotions. Despite that, Pat is highly committed to the company and continues to work long hours. Over the years, Pat has seen other AVPs informally mentor younger associates, but has never personally attracted a protégé. Pat is highly motivated to mentor someone as a means of personal enrichment as well as giving back to the company.

Chris has been with the company for just two years. He interned with the company as an MBA trainee, and that internship turned into a full-time position upon graduation. In the two years since, Chris has already been promoted once and feels like he is on the fast track. Chris's goal is to be the youngest AVP the company has promoted. Chris feels that all he needs is the right mentor to show him the ropes and get him noticed by the right people. Despite Chris's goal and motivation, he has been indecisive on whom to ask. When human resources sent around the memo that the company was starting a formal mentoring program, Chris felt sure this was a sign and would ensure he got the right mentor.

Because both Pat and Chris were the first to formally apply, they were paired together.

They met for the first time at a kick-off reception for everyone participating in the mentoring program. They were from different departments and so had not previously met. They also did not have any information about each other because human resources thought a big reveal would add to the excitement. At the reception, they got along quite well. As an icebreaker, Pat asked Chris about the past weekend. It turns out that they both had attended the same concert of a popular 1980s band. They spent the whole time talking about their favorite songs and other groups they liked, and before they knew it, the reception was over.

On their way out, human resources handed them each an information sheet. A few bullet points listed the major functions of mentoring (e.g., networking), a suggestion that they should meet sometime in the next couple of weeks, and contact information.

It took a month for them to meet again. Both Chris and Pat were busy, and their schedules didn't allow them to meet earlier. At this meeting, they finally shared some background information. Chris was surprised to hear about Pat's lack of MBA and slow rise within the company. Similarly, Pat was dismayed that the person she liked at the reception turned out to be one of these MBA hotshots who seemed to get all the promotions.

They left with an agreement to see each other soon but did not set an exact day or time. Walking out, Chris was unsure about Pat, but thought human resources wouldn't have paired them if there wasn't a good reason and so was willing to give this some more time. As for Pat, while acknowledging that Chris had good taste in music, she wasn't sure how much she wanted to help another hotshot MBA.

After that meeting, Chris called and emailed multiple times, but Pat never responded. After two months and becoming thoroughly annoyed, Chris decided to show up unannounced at Pat's office when Pat's secretary said she would be there.

7.3b In-Basket

Please read through all of the email messages in this section before responding to any of them. For this task, you are Alex, the human resource associate responsible for the mentoring program discussed in the previous case. The first thing to do is assign a priority to each email and then write all the replies that you think are required following that order. One additional note—your supervisor directly reports to Morgan, vice president of human resources, and the mentoring program is the first task that she has directly assigned you since you started.

To: Alex, HR Associate

From: Jamie, Junior Associate

Subject: Mentor Assignment

At the orientation for new employees that you led last month, you mentioned the mentor program. I was wondering when mine would be assigned.

To: Alex, HR Associate

From: Pat, Associate Vice President

Subject: Pushy Protégé

The mentoring program seemed like a good idea when your office first asked for volunteers, but it appears my protégé has unrealistic expectations about how often we can/should be meeting. My protégé, Chris, seems totally unaware and unconcerned with how busy is my schedule. As you know, annual performance evaluations need to be completed for all of my direct reports, and I won't have time for any extras, like the mentor meetings, until they are completed. Given the number of emails that he has sent, I thought it best to ask you for suggestions before replying to Chris.

To: Alex, HR Associate

From: Jesse, Event Coordinator

Subject: Mentor Luncheon

Waiting on the final numbers and menu for the luncheon you wanted to hold in two weeks. Remember that my office requires a week's notice, or we may not be able to accommodate you.

To: Alex, HR Associate

From: Micah, Junior Associate

Subject: Thanks

Just wanted to say thank you for setting up the mentor program. My mentor and I have met several times and have been receiving some great advice.

To: Alex, HR Associate

From: Chris, Senior Associate

Subject: Mismatch?

When I met my mentor, Pat, at the reception, we seemed to have a lot in common. But that feeling has gone away. Although we share common interests, I am unsure how much she can help me. After meeting once, it has been almost two months since I have heard from Pat. So I have decided to skip lunch tomorrow so that I can go to Pat's office and figure out this mentoring thing.

To: Alex, HR Associate

From: Jules, Associate Vice President

Subject: Mentor Selection

I've been informally mentoring our younger employees for years, and looking at the positions they now hold in our company, I believe I have been a good mentor to them. So you may understand my surprise when I heard that the company had started a formal mentoring program and I wasn't asked to participate.

To: Alex, HR Associate

From: Morgan, Vice President of Human Resources

Subject: Mentor Status

How is the mentoring program going?

7.3c Role Play

Use the case above as the background for this role play. The situation is the unannounced meeting between Chris and Pat. Follow your trainer's directions on how to use this role play (i.e., modeled/developmental or participatory/exploratory) and who will play each part. In addition to the information provided in the case, you should also read and consider the email you (i.e., Chris or Pat) sent to Alex as part of the in-basket exercise. However, you would not have knowledge of any of the other emails (as well as any responses from Alex), so try and disregard any information contained in them as you prepare for and participate in the role play.

CHAPTER EIGHT

DELIVERY OPTIONS FOR FACE-TO-FACE TRAINING

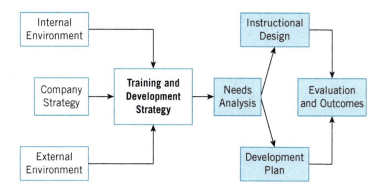

Learning Objectives

1. Describe and categorize the training setting options that organizations have.

2. Select the setting that is appropriate for a specific training or development need.

3. Assess the formality of on-the-job training.

4. Discuss how a room's layout can impact instruction and learning.

5. Explain what differentiates corporate universities from other instructional environments.

Hamburger University (HU) was founded in 1961 by McDonald's Corporation. On its main campus in Oak Brook, Illinois, there is a full-time faculty of 19 professors. In addition to the staff, the Oak Brook campus has 13 teaching rooms, a 300-seat auditorium, 12 interactive education team rooms, and 3 kitchen labs, as well as service training labs. Aside from the main campus, there are 22 regional training centers and online courses.

The curriculum at HU includes courses on shift and systems management and offers learning paths for midlevel managers as well as executive development. Employees also learn to spot and solve everyday problems that might occur in a restaurant.[1]

For example: "Two boxes of french fries stacked on the kitchen floor, rather than stored in a freezer. An empty salt shaker at the fry station. A dry, unseasoned cheeseburger served on a hardened bun."[2]

HU started with an initial class of 15 students, and today over 7,500 attend each year. Despite its name, it is no joke. Students can make the dean's list and graduate with a diploma. In addition, they can earn college credit, and not just anyone can enroll. When HU opened up its campus in Shanghai (one of seven global campuses) in 2010, 1,000 potential students applied. In the end, 8 students were selected, making HU mathematically more selective than Harvard.[3]

As for alumni, HU has over 275 graduates who account for approximately 40% of McDonald's global leaders. It is also one of the reasons that McDonald's has been cited as a great place to work. This is important because it helps attract and retain employees. Further, HU is considered one of the reasons that McDonald's employees are so productive, which gives the restaurant chain a competitive advantage.[4] McDonald's, however, is not alone in creating a corporate university to give itself a competitive edge. Some other popular companies with corporate universities include Apple, Disney, and Southwest Airlines.

Learning can occur anywhere, but deciding where training will occur and how to provide it should be purposeful. Training should take place in an environment that maximizes the potential for an individual to learn and promotes subsequent transfer. Akin to training delivery methods, some environments are more conducive to learning than others. One reason for this involves trainee preferences. Some trainees both prefer and learn better in face-to-face environments, the options discussed in this chapter. In addition, the content or purpose of the training may dictate the most appropriate setting. This chapter focuses on options for where and how to provide training and what implications that may have on the learning process and training outcomes.

INSTRUCTIONAL SETTINGS

Among the most common questions concerning training and development is where it will occur. Generally, training and development take place either on-site or off-site. These general categories can be subdivided into more settings. When sorting settings by on-site and off-site, however, some training and development settings don't neatly fit into either category. For purposes of categorization, we refer to these settings as unspecified.

On-Site

Training provided on-site is usually organization-centric. One aspect of being organization-centric is that the training occurs within the organization. Often, this training is designed and/or delivered by a coworker, a supervisor or manager, or a member of the human resource department. Even when it is provided by an outside vendor, the training occurs on the organization's property and often is customized to address specific organizational needs.

Not all organizational settings are the same, and there are important differences among those that can be categorized as on-site. For example, on-site training can be hyper-local in that the instruction occurs on the job itself. In this situation, the trainees learn in the environment where they normally perform the same functions. However, on-site training can also refer to using a conference or training room within the facility where the trainees work. Therefore, this chapter discusses on-the-job instruction separately from what we refer to as on-site workshop training and development.

Off-Site

Training and development provided off-site tends to be less organization-centric. This results from the fact that the organization takes advantage of a training or development opportunity offered by another entity. As such, the content is less likely to be specifically developed or tailored for the organization. However, customization is merely a comment on content, not quality.

Off-site training also encompasses a range of options. Locally, organizations can take advantage of training opportunities within the communities where they reside. These training programs can also range in duration from one-shot opportunities (e.g., presentations by local associations) to traditional courses offered by nearby schools. For the discussion here, the duration is less important than the setting. So, we discuss these options together under the heading of speaker/course. Looking at nonlocal off-site options, organizations can send employees to conferences in another city or state.

Unspecified

While seemingly the categories of on-site and off-site should encompass all settings, the corporate university is a notable option for providing training and development that encompasses characteristics of both on-site and off-site instruction. Corporate universities often have their own campuses, or at the very least buildings, with dedicated trainers and faculty and established curricula. As such, corporate universities are relatively centralized, so unless trainees are taking an online course, or by chance are located nearby, they will need to travel to the corporate university. This supports the argument that a corporate university should be classified as an example of off-site training. However, on-site training and development is often synonymous with being provided by the organization. Because the corporate university is a part of the same organization and, therefore, focused on the organization's needs, one could also argue that, at least in spirit, the corporate university is an example of on-site training and development.

FACTORS INFLUENCING SELECTION OF INSTRUCTIONAL SETTINGS

When deciding on an instructional setting, organizations should consider several factors, including control/standardization, fidelity, investment/costs, social capital, and reward value. These factors are presented in Exhibit 8-1, which also shows how the various instructional settings rate on each of these. Further, the settings are organized in terms of being on-site, off-site, or unspecified.

Exhibit 8-1 Comparing Instructional Settings

Location Type	Specific Setting	Control/Standardization	Fidelity	Costs	Social Capital	Reward Value
On-site	On-the-job	Depends	High	Depends	Low	Low
	Workshop	High	Low	Mixed	Internal/Low	Low
Off-site	Speaker/Course	Low	Low	Mixed	External/Mixed	Mixed
	Conference	Low	Low	Mixed	External/High	High
Unspecified	Corporate University	High	Depends	High	Internal/High	Mixed

Control/Standardization

Exhibit 8-1 shows how control/standardization can differ among the various instructional settings. While control and standardization are separate concepts, they often work in concert when it comes to designing and delivering training. First, **control** involves how much influence an organization has over the content and process of training. Generally, organizations have the most control over training design and delivery when it is provided on-site. This explains the high designation for both on-site workshops and corporate universities. Not only do off-site settings normally lack this control over design, but there is no guarantee about the delivery, which is why these settings are relatively low on this dimension. An exception to this occurs when the on-site training is decentralized or the organization enters into a partnership with an external provider. Having control facilitates **standardization** (i.e., different groups of trainees experience the same training).

The biggest question when it comes to control/standardization involves on-site setting of on-the-job training. While focus should always be good with on-the-job training, control and standardization are other matters. This is because, as discussed in the "On-the-Job Training" section, on-the-job training covers a wide spectrum of instructional formality. When on-the-job training is more formal, it involves more planning and hence control and standardization. However, much of on-the-job training is informal, which results in less certainty about what is taught and learned. So, depending on the formality, the on-the-job setting can be either high or low in terms of control and standardization.

Fidelity

Fidelity is the degree to which the environment for training mirrors the environment where the trainees will use what they learned. Fidelity can be described in terms of both physical and psychological similarity,[5] and one does not guarantee the other. Higher levels of fidelity are generally better, but not always possible. Consider, for example, the case of CPR training. Training people to provide CPR is important, but unfortunately, there are limits on how realistic such training can be. First, it is not possible to practice CPR on a living person. Second, CPR involves a life-or-death situation—something not easily facilitated in the multipurpose rooms where CPR training is often conducted.

Fidelity increases the effectiveness of training through two different mechanisms. First, it increases employee motivation and aligns with andragogy (i.e., adult learning theory).[6] This occurs because trainees more easily recognize the relevance of the training when the content and delivery is more realistic. As a result, trainees should learn more when the fidelity of training is high relative to low-fidelity training. Second, fidelity promotes the transferability of training.[7] In general, the more realistic the setting, the more likely trainees will be able to utilize what they have learned after completing the training. One reason is that trainees are more likely to recognize that the training applies to a specific situation. Further, they will not have to spend time figuring out how to adapt what they learned to the situation. Conversely, the more the learning environment differs from the work environment, the greater the chance of some barrier to learning transfer. For example, an airplane flight attendant role playing how to deal with an irate passenger in an otherwise quiet workshop is very different from dealing with one while experiencing turbulence at 20,000 feet.

As listed in Exhibit 8-1, on-the-job training consistently has the highest level of fidelity among the instructional settings. This should not come as a surprise because on-the-job training is by definition on the job. As such, fidelity is strong both physically and psychologically, one of the reasons that on-the-job training is a popular option for organizations.

By comparison, fidelity tends to be low for on-site workshops and off-site settings. This is true for both physical and psychological fidelity. In terms of psychological fidelity, the pressures of work (e.g., time and emotions) can be difficult to reproduce. Further, the goals or needs of the training, especially for the off-site settings, may not be conducive to a high level of fidelity. In addition, the layout and other constraints of the space in which the training is being provided may prevent a high level of physical fidelity.

As for the fidelity of training that occurs within corporate universities, that depends on the design decisions. At one end of the fidelity spectrum, courses at corporate universities resemble courses at noncorporate universities. While the relevance and realism of the examples may be better, if the training occurs in a basic classroom and the instructional method is primarily lecture, then the overall fidelity will be low. However, one factor that distinguishes corporate universities from other instructional settings is the amount of resources dedicated to training and development. As such, corporate universities can create specialized classrooms that provide for a higher degree of physical fidelity. Similarly, course designers can dedicate the time and resources to develop instructional methods (e.g., simulations and role plays) that are high in terms of fidelity. Therefore, the fidelity of training in corporate universities can be high, but there is no guarantee of that.

Costs

When providing training, another factor to consider is how much it costs to provide and the level of investment it represents. This is one reason that organizations often provide low-fidelity training even if it is less effective than high-fidelity training. When thinking about the financial aspects of training and development, keep in mind that not all costs are the same. For example, this discussion of costs focuses on direct costs (e.g., amount spent to develop the training) versus indirect costs (e.g., the value of lost productivity when a trainer is engaged in on-the-job training).

When discussing the direct costs of training, it is useful to separate fixed costs from variable costs. **Variable costs** increase with the number of people being trained. This is easiest to see when discussing off-site settings. For example, if attending a conference costs $500 per person, then the total cost of training can simply be determined by multiplying the number of employees being sent by the cost of the conference.

Fixed costs present a larger concern when the training is developed and/or delivered on-site. Many fixed costs can also be considered sunk costs. For example, if an organization develops its own training program, then it must pay for that development regardless of whether it ever delivers that training. The same goes for a piece of equipment purchased for the sole purpose of delivering training. Other costs—for example, the cost of hiring a trainer—are relatively fixed. If trainers can train 20 people per program, they generally charge the same whether there are 18, 19, or 20 trainees. Only when there is a 21st trainee, and therefore a need for a second training cohort, does the trainer cost increase. However, while the cost of the trainer may be fixed, other training costs (e.g., supplies needed by each trainee) will remain variable.

As shown in Exhibit 8-1, costs differ by setting. Starting with off-site settings, the costs are mixed. Fixed costs tend to be low for off-site settings. An exception to this is any membership costs that are required to be paid to the host organization before anyone can register for the training. That said, the variable costs (i.e., registration price per trainee) can be relatively high, particularly for conferences or longer-term speakers and courses.

Depending on how an organization handles its internal accounting, the direct costs of on-site training tend to be low. Among the considerations for on-site settings is the opportunity cost of training or development. Specifically, what else could the designers, instructors, and/or learners do with the time devoted to training or development? Even if the organization tracks the internal expenses of providing instruction, it will not have the additional expenses of registration or tuition found with off-site settings. As such, variable costs tend to be less of a concern than fixed costs.

Corporate universities are listed as high for a couple of different reasons. First, the sunk costs cannot be ignored. While an organization may choose not to calculate the time and expenses associated with a salaried member of the human resource department developing and providing individual instances of training or development, this cannot be done with a corporate university. Corporate universities have dedicated staff and facilities, which are clearly and easily identified on a budget. Similarly, travel costs for employees attending corporate universities need to be accounted for.

Social Capital

When managers think about training or development, their initial focus is on increasing their employees' human capital. *Human capital*, an economic term, focuses on the value of the knowledge, skills, and abilities (KSAs) possessed by employees. Related to human capital is employees' **social capital**, or the value of an individual's relationships. Social capital increases with the strength and scope of a person's network, or people one knows. These relationships have value because they improve performance and outcomes.[8]

Relationships improve performance and outcomes for several reasons. At the most transactional level, having social capital means that individuals know people whom they can ask for assistance. Social capital can also be an indicator of interpersonal trust, in that social capital that is internal to an organization can improve teamwork. People with strong internal organizational networks are also more embedded in the organization, which makes them less likely to engage in turnover. As for external networks, these can help the organization when a job or task relies on outside relationships.

While valuable, social capital is not normally the primary focus of training or an immediate outcome of development. Regarding development, the focus is usually on skills and competencies that, when properly exercised, increase social capital. For example, teaching individuals how to improve their personal network increases their human capital. Only when they successfully exercise their new skills and competencies can they increase their social capital. However, social capital can be an indirect outcome of attending training or development. Through participating in training or development, for example, employees meet people, or get to know them better, which allows them to develop new or improve existing relationships.[9]

This indirect benefit of attending training or development varies with the setting. On-site settings have a relatively low potential for increasing social capital, mainly because on-site training or development provides fewer opportunities to meet new people. This is especially true for on-the-job training. Also, on-site settings are internal to the organization. Even though the people involved may already know each other, however, there is still the opportunity to improve and strengthen these relationships.

The potential for speakers and courses to develop individuals' social capital is mixed. While they provide a good setting to meet people outside of one's organization, hence the external designation in Exhibit 8-1, there is not always the opportunity to network. Interestingly, longer-term courses may provide more face-to-face time, but less structured opportunity to engage in networking. By comparison, speakers often include dedicated time for networking as an inducement for people to register and attend.

The best opportunities to develop social capital are expected with conferences (off-site) and corporate universities (unspecified). Conferences tend to be longer than speakers and generally include multiple scheduled opportunities for networking. In addition, many conferences recur annually, which provides opportunities for attendees to renew and strengthen relationships with people they don't regularly see. While corporate universities are internal to organizations, they provide an opportunity to meet new people with whom employees may work on projects in the future. In addition, attending a corporate university may be an important step in socializing and/or being recognized as a high-potential employee.

Reward Value

Social capital is not the only side benefit of providing training; some employees also view training as a reward.[10] The **reward value** of training can come from one of several sources. First, extrinsically motivated employees may value the opportunity to engage in training and development because it will allow them to earn more money or be eligible for more desirable positions.[11] Alternatively, intrinsically motivated employees may simply value the opportunity to learn[12] and the ability to engage in self-actualization.[13] Each of these sources could be considered desirable, and organizations should consider them when designing, delivering, and supporting the transfer of training.

As for the remaining reasons to view training as a reward, they are to differing degrees problematic. In both cases, they represent a poor use of training dollars. First, for those employees who lack goals for self-advancement or self-improvement, the time spent in training and development may be worthwhile simply because they are not doing their regular jobs and may be grateful just for the change in routine. As described, these employees lack the proper motivation to train and therefore are not considered trainable, as discussed in Chapter 3. Trainees not being motivated or open to train can undermine the effectiveness of the training. Second, management could be complicit and use a desirable training opportunity as a way of rewarding an employee. However, we recommend that organizations separate tangible rewards from training and development opportunities.

So, even if rewarding employees with training should not be encouraged, the reward value differences among the instructional settings should be acknowledged. First, the setting with the greatest reward value is conferences. Aside from the opportunity to learn and expand social networks, conferences tend to require concentrated periods of time away from work and involve travel. Sometimes they are offered in a desirable location (e.g., Las Vegas or Florida), which allows trainees, when not participating in sessions, time to enjoy themselves. At the opposite end of the reward spectrum is on-the-job training, with no change of pace from one's normal work routine. On-site courses are slightly better, but the change of pace is short lived, and again the employee does not leave the organization.

The reward value of speakers/courses and corporate universities is mixed. Corporate universities often involve some travel, but not necessarily desirable travel. However, employees may find some value in their perceived status for being selected. As for speakers/courses, they represent a change of pace and a chance to get outside of the organization. They may even include meals or receptions, although these tend to be limited to speakers. However, these breaks are shorter than conferences and generally don't involve travel. So, the reward value of these settings is relatively small.

ON-THE-JOB TRAINING (OJT)

One of most common forms of training provided to individuals is on-the-job training, or **OJT**. OJT has many benefits, which explains why it is so often utilized. Key advantages of OJT, as shown in Exhibit 8-1, include the fidelity of the training and a low level of investment/costs. One potential disadvantage concerns the level of control/standardization—a problem because it can impact the OJT's eventual effectiveness.

When choosing on-the-job as the training setting, managers need to remember that it is still training. Therefore, they should apply to it the same level of thought, preparation, and evaluation as to any other form of training. However, in reality, the provision

Exhibit 8-2 Differentiating Informal and Formal On-the-Job Training

	Informal	Formal
Trainer Selection	By default	Based on criteria
Trainer Support	Limited	Inclusive
Training Design	Ad hoc	Systematic
Training Evaluation	Doesn't occur	Multiple levels

of OJT falls along a wide spectrum of formality. Generally, formalized OJT produces better outcomes than more informal versions.[14] Unfortunately, traditional OJT is relatively informal.[15] Exhibit 8-2 highlights some characteristics that differentiate informal and formal OJT. The more attributes that an OJT program shares with the right-hand column, the more formal it will be considered.

While it is interesting to note the differences between formal and informal OJT, it is also important to do so because of the impact on learning. Generally, individuals learn more when provided with formal compared to informal OJT. By extension, organizations benefit more when they utilize formal OJT. An underlying reason that ties selection, support, design, and evaluation together is that with formal OJT comes greater intentionality.

Trainer Selection

One of the first differences that someone will notice between informal and formal OJT is who provides the training. The choice of trainer matters because the ability and quality of the person providing the training has an impact on the experience and subsequent learning of the trainee. While it is possible to have a competent trainer regardless of the selection method, the odds are improved when the selection process is intentional. This occurs because the organization utilizes objective criteria to identify a competent trainer as opposed to relying upon luck. As shown in Exhibit 8-2, the use of criteria to select a trainer is consistent with a formal approach to OJT.

Selecting trainers in informal OJT.

While the process for selecting trainers with informal OJT is less systematic than formal OJT, there is still a range of options that differ in terms of intentionality. Informally, a trainer can be selected to provide OJT in one of three easy ways. These default options for identifying who should provide training include the person available, the best worker, and/or the employee's supervisor.

The most simplistic choice of trainer is the person who, at the moment, has the time to provide the training. Two notable problems are associated with this. First, the organization puts no thought into the quality of the trainer. Just because people have free time does not mean that they are good workers, much less that they would make good trainers. Also, free time is both relative and finite. Just because people are free now does not mean that they will remain so long enough to properly train someone else. This method relies on the greatest level of luck that the trainer is competent.

While choosing the best worker within the group or department is more intentional, and therefore an improvement, there are still concerns with this approach. For example, what constitutes best? The best person is often determined to be the individual with the highest performance rating or the greatest experience or seniority within the work group. Although this method has the benefit of using some criteria for the decision (i.e., quality versus just availability), the best worker is not necessarily the best trainer. The best worker may lack the necessary insight, patience, or interpersonal qualities that characterize a good trainer.

Another possibility is that the responsibility for training defaults to the employee's supervisor. Organizations sometimes assume that because this individual is a supervisor, she or he is also in the best position to provide training and/or it falls within the job's responsibilities. While this option makes sense, the supervisor may still not be the best person to provide the training, with a few key explanations. First, supervisors may no longer regularly perform the tasks for which training is required. As such, they would lack the familiarity and understanding necessary to provide the training. Second, supervisors may have other responsibilities and not have sufficient focus or time to properly provide the training. Third, even if supervisors have the competence and time, they may still not be the best people to provide training, for reasons similar to the best worker (i.e., the skills or temperament to be a trainer).

Selecting trainers in formal OJT.

In order to improve the provision of OJT, organizations should follow some process for selecting a trainer. While it is relevant to consider the technical aptitude of a potential trainer, it should not be the only criteria used to make the decision. Organizations should select trainers based on their communication and interpersonal skills. For example, how well can an individual explain how to do a specific task? We discuss several of the specific skills and abilities that management would want to select for in a trainer in Chapter 12. In addition, it is desirable to select trainers who have a willingness to share, are respected, and have demonstrated commitment to the organization.[16]

Trainer Support

While having a process in place to select a prospective trainer is an important step in making OJT more formal and effective, it is not the only one. Another difference between formal OJT and informal OJT occurs in the type and amount of support provided to the trainers. Just as using objective criteria to select a trainer has a positive impact on its effectiveness, providing the trainer with support is similarly important. Among the ways that management can support OJT are to provide adequate time for training, to train trainers, and to reward them.

Providing time.

Arguably the least formal way that organizations can support OJT is to provide adequate time for training. Both trainers and trainees need time for instruction and learning to occur. Trainers can feel rushed if not given the proper time to train, which can result in either the breadth or the depth of instruction being compromised.[17] Similarly, if trainers are not properly released from other job duties, they may resent being assigned the responsibility of OJT. In addition, trainees need time to learn. Cutting short the training period or not reducing onerous workloads decreases trainees' time for practice and to reflect upon what they are being taught. This may increase trainees' level of anxiety and decrease the amount or quality of learning.[18]

Providing training.

Of course, time is not the only resource that management can provide to improve OJT. In addition to allowing trainers the time to provide OJT, organizations should consider improving the skill sets of those they ask to train others.[19] Training the trainer is an important function that can improve the effectiveness of OJT. As just stated, one of the problems with informal OJT is the potential for using a trainer who doesn't have the proper skills and abilities to provide training. However, while someone may have the innate ability or transferable skills to teach others, that may not be enough to ensure an effective training. "Train the trainer" programs serve to empower potential trainers by giving them instruction and confidence in their ability to teach others, which allows them to be more effective trainers. We discuss some of the interpersonal skills that can make someone a better trainer and should be included in a "train the trainer" program in Chapter 12.

Providing rewards.

While motivation is an essential component of trainability for employees, it is also an important factor for those asked to do the training. Regardless of the method for selecting the OJT trainer, this person will have other duties, many of which the trainer may prefer to be performing. Therefore, management needs to be mindful to address or satisfy factors that will motivate a person to conscientiously be an OJT trainer.

Just as different factors motivate trainees, there are numerous ways to motivate someone to be a conscientious trainer. First, external rewards can be an effective method for motivating trainers. Organizations can choose financial rewards and/or status enhancements as ways to motivate someone to serve as a trainer. Some common financial rewards for trainers include providing them with a wage premium (i.e., paying them more for the time they spend as a trainer) or a bonus. As implied by the need to train the trainer, training involves a greater investment in and use of human capital, and therefore paying someone more for serving as a trainer is appropriate.

As for motivating people to become trainers through enhancing their status, this normally involves giving them an official designation. If an organization goes this route, management usually selects one or two people from a work group or department to serve as the trainer(s). As such, this method of rewarding OJT trainers already requires a certain level of formality (i.e., the trainer is preselected). The exact title or designation given to the trainer is less important than awareness by people within the organization of who serves as the official trainers. Some may think of being designated the official trainer as a sort of promotion. At the very least, the designation is validating because it sends a signal from management about the value and ability of the individual selected. For nontrainers, it may even create a career goal (i.e., becoming trainers) for them to pursue. Finally, it represents a tangible way for management to demonstrate its commitment to training.

Training Design

While training design could be considered a form of support, the idea merits a separate discussion. In reference to this discussion of OJT, design encompasses a range of activities. At a minimum, design could just mean developing a checklist of what a trainer is supposed to teach someone. Increasing in depth, design may involve identifying a set of learning objectives. Separately, design can involve gathering or developing instructional aids to be used during the training. These activities both support the trainer and promote the effectiveness of training.[20]

Checklists and objectives.

So how does a checklist provide support to a trainer or promote the effectiveness of training? Regarding the trainer, a checklist reduces ambiguity. Keep in mind that one of the problems with informal OJT is that the trainer doesn't know what to do. Part of that is skill or ability related in that the trainer doesn't know how to teach. Another part is content related, meaning that the trainer either doesn't know what to teach or doesn't think to teach everything that should be taught.

Before dismissing this as a silly idea, consider the example of lending or borrowing a car, especially on a sunny day. How much training is typically provided? Let us take as a given that you or the other person knows how to drive, but what else do you take for granted? How often have you been in a new car when it turns dark and you can't find the lights? Ever fumbled looking for the wipers? What about pulling into a gas station and having to figure out where the gas tank is located and/or how to open it? With a borrowed car, these issues usually resolve themselves pretty quickly, because even though cars are laid out differently, there are a few general locations for these features, and what we know about other cars is transferable. However, in the workplace, especially if skills are not as clearly transferable, such lapses in instruction can lead to problems. Having a checklist to make sure everything is covered can limit those lapses from occurring.

Of course, a checklist is not a panacea, but it is still better to have one than to not. For example, what if there isn't enough time to complete every item on the checklist? At the very least, it can show what an employee doesn't know. Without a checklist, it is easier to assume that someone has been completely trained, which makes it more likely for employees to be placed in situations, or expected to complete tasks, for which they are not prepared. When that occurs, mistakes can happen, and they can be costly.

Another way a checklist helps promote training effectiveness is that it facilitates the development of learning objectives. Once an organization has determined the content of the training, it is easier to think about the level of proficiency needed and/or how to focus the instruction. As discussed in Chapter 4, providing individuals with objectives helps them to learn, which increases the effectiveness of the training.

Training manuals.

Training manuals are a type of instructional aid that organizations can provide to facilitate and improve the delivery of training. While sharing many of the characteristics of a checklist, training manuals provide greater depth of information and thereby support. Further, training manuals represent a valuable resource for both trainers and trainees.

Providing trainers with training manuals is useful for multiple reasons. One is focus, in that training manuals serve to clarify what someone is supposed to teach. Training manuals also are good reference documents for trainers. As a reference source, they encourage standardization of instruction. Such standardization also minimizes both ambiguity and the need for trainers to determine how to deliver training, which can reduce anxiety and save resources (e.g., time).

Training manuals are likewise a useful instructional aid for trainees. The use of instructional materials also helps trainees to learn. As discussed in Chapter 4, individuals have different preferences regarding how to learn. OJT relies heavily on kinesthetic learning. While an appropriate method for instruction, training manuals provide an opportunity to convey information in different ways, which may help people by allowing them to learn according to their personal preferences and/or reinforcing the instruction by simply using a different method. Further, when organizations allow trainees to keep their training manuals, they can refer to them after conclusion of the face-to-face instruction. This will help to reinforce what was taught and by extension facilitate the use of the new skill or knowledge once the training has been completed.

Training Evaluation

As often mentioned in this textbook, it is important to evaluate training, and OJT is no exception.[21] Training, regardless of type, becomes more formal when it is evaluated. Organizations should evaluate OJT for several reasons. First, it documents what someone has learned. If people are experiencing problems with learning the material, trainers can also use evaluations to improve the training itself, which should improve learning for subsequent trainees. These statements imply that evaluation can occur for both the trainee and the trainer, and both types of evaluations can improve the effectiveness of OJT.

Evaluating what a trainee learns makes OJT more formal and can improve the learning experience. The process of creating an evaluation helps to identify the goals and objectives of the training. In turn, this clarifies to the trainers what they need to teach. It also creates a rubric for the trainers, which makes it easier for them to ensure that they have fully and adequately trained someone. As a result, OJT that utilizes evaluation should result in fewer gaps in the knowledge of trainees, leading to more effective training.

In addition to evaluating the trainee, it is useful to evaluate the trainer. Not only does it provide feedback that allows the design to be revised and/or the trainer to improve his or her performance, but evaluating the trainer also increases accountability. Trainers who are held accountable are expected to work harder to make sure that their trainees master the content of the training. That said, we recommend that if management holds a trainer accountable for the outcomes of training, it should also provide compensation or incentives (as mentioned in the "Trainer Support" section) for serving as the trainer.

WORKSHOPS, SPEAKERS/COURSES, CONFERENCES, AND CORPORATE UNIVERSITIES

While OJT is distinct from the other settings because of the dyadic (i.e., one-to-one) nature of the instruction, there is greater consistency among the settings of workshops, speakers/courses, conferences, and corporate universities, so these are discussed together. Essentially, instruction in each of these settings generally takes place in something resembling a classroom environment. A classroom here is broadly defined as a space with at least one teacher providing instruction to a group of individuals.

One important caveat with this definition is that it does not require a classroom or a dedicated space. Of the settings discussed here, only corporate universities are expected to have dedicated classrooms, and this is one reason we refer to this setting as a university (more about the nature of corporate universities is discussed later in this chapter). As for speakers/courses, the presence of a dedicated space depends on the nature of the training or development program. Like corporate universities, multisession courses are expected to take place in something resembling a dedicated classroom. Speakers, which tend toward more onetime events, do not need and are less likely to occur in a physical classroom. As for workshops, it depends on the organization. Some organizations have a dedicated training space on their premises, but others make use of a conference or meeting room for instruction.

Even if the instruction takes place outside of a dedicated classroom, the layout of the space should share some common features. Larger spaces—be it a hotel ballroom, conference center, or meeting hall—are generally set up with the trainer(s) at the front of the room and the chairs laid out in rows for participants. This is reminiscent of a lecture hall even without stadium seating or a desk/tabletop on which to take notes. Smaller spaces, such as a conference room, are difficult to visually distinguish from the more traditional seminar rooms found in most institutions of higher learning.

Features of Classrooms

A useful, but often overlooked, consideration in training design and implementation is the configuration of the physical space.[22] One obvious difference between spaces concerns the number of trainees or participants who can receive instruction at any one time. However, other differences (e.g., available technology and room layout) can impact the choice and/or effectiveness of a specific training method. Broadly speaking, while traditional methods (e.g., lectures) and some experiential methods (e.g., case studies) are possible in most spaces, the effectiveness of other methods (e.g., role plays) can be impacted greatly by the configuration and constraints of a specific classroom. Therefore, when possible, trainers should be thoughtful in choosing where to conduct training and/or how to arrange the space.

Technological and physical constraints.

The reason that we refer to the physical and technological attributes of a classroom as constraints reflects the fact that an organization is unlikely to refurbish a room to accommodate an individual training or development program. However, corporate universities and larger organizations may have multiple spaces available, allowing a trainer to avoid a particular constraint and/or take advantage of a specific technology. One warning that most veteran trainers will share is to prepare for the unexpected (i.e., never assume that the space will be fully functional).

This discussion of technological constraints is expansive and includes not just computers but also basic equipment (e.g., blackboards). In terms of equipment and the caveat of "don't assume," we'll start with something that many take for granted. Just because a room has a blackboard or whiteboard, don't assume that chalk or markers and/or erasers will be available. While more and more dedicated classrooms have computers, they are not universal and are less likely to be present if a nondedicated space is used. Even if a computer and projector are available, trainers need to ensure that they can access the internet, access their files, and/or connect peripherals. Again, most veteran trainers will share stories where they didn't have the right connecting cable or a long enough extension cord, and/or the technology failed somehow. Of course, this discussion is meant to be illustrative and not exhaustive of potential technological and equipment issues.

Besides these technological and equipment issues, organizations should consider other physical attributes of a potential instructional space. One attribute that we have already discussed is size. Another set of attributes can be referred to as potential distractors, some of which come from unlikely sources. For example, while computers and projectors are normally perceived as instructional aids, if the technology is unused but visible, it can negatively impact learning because of unfulfilled trainee expectations.[23] However, distractors are usually things that a trainer cannot use and/or has limited ability to change, but that still may impact his or her effectiveness.

Many distractors involve concerns with sound. Specifically, can trainees adequately hear the trainer? While sometimes this is an issue of size and/or acoustics, it can also be an issue with competing noises. For example, one of the authors taught classes in a room next to the main building entrance as well as in the room next to the building's air-conditioning system. In both scenarios, it was difficult for trainees to remain engaged. Besides sound, another issue is visual. Do the sight lines and/or lighting make it difficult for trainees to see what is put on the board?

Layout of a classroom.

While the layout of a classroom can be a constraint if tables and chairs can't be moved, often a trainer will be able to exert some influence over the layout. Therefore, a trainer

Exhibit 8-3 Options for Arranging a Classroom

| Rows | Circle | Horseshoe | Pods |

Note: ** is the trainer

should give some careful thought into the setup of the tables and chairs in a room. Four common ways to set up a room, as shown in Exhibit 8-3, are rows, circles, horseshoes, and pods.

The most traditional of these is rows, which are good for keeping the focus of the room toward the board, screen, and/or professor. This setup is particularly beneficial when lecture is the primary method of instruction. It also serves to reinforce the power dynamic of the trainer being the most important individual in the room. However, if the trainer would prefer a more egalitarian classroom culture and/or would like to encourage discussion, setting the classroom up in rows will impede these interests.

The reverse situation occurs with a room set up in a circle. For an example/explanation, consider the case of King Arthur and his round table. First, why was the table round? The most common explanation is that no one knight would be the "center" of attention and that all would be considered equal. As such, it is a physical reminder/reinforcement of an egalitarian culture. Sitting in a circle makes it easier to hold a discussion because everyone can see each other. The main downside comes when those sitting with their backs to the board or screen need to move or contort themselves to read what the trainer is presenting.

The **horseshoe** represents a compromise between rows and circles. While the room is still oriented around the trainer, trainees can now see each other as well. This balances the needs of the trainer to utilize the board or screen with facilitating classroom discussions. In terms of power relations, while the trainer still stands front and center, there is less physical distance and a more egalitarian layout.

Setting up a classroom in **pods** is the most progressive of the four options. The strength and emphasis of this setup is on group work. Learning occurs more experientially with trainees working on projects or cases with one another. In the best of these classrooms, not only are trainees situated in small groups, but there are boards or screens on each wall to facilitate collaboration and lessen strain for those not facing the single board or screen in the classroom.

Features of Programs and Providers

Although the settings of speakers/courses and conferences do not generally involve design (unless there is a partnership, discussed in Appendix B), managers still have decisions to make. Speakers/courses and conferences normally have upfront registration and/or tuition costs. These represent direct payments to external vendors, unlike some of the costs associated with on-site settings, which can be hidden, so managers need to doubly be sure to make good choices in terms of how they allocate their training and development budgets.

Aside from costs, managers should consider a few key factors when deciding to send an employee to an off-site training or development option. One factor to consider is the content. Even though managers may not be able to influence the content of an off-site training or development session, they should make sure that there is a large degree of overlap between the content offered and the content identified as part of the needs analysis.

If the organization's needs and the proposed content are not strongly in alignment, then an employee should not be sent to the speaker/course or conference unless one of the following is true: The cost is low; the KSA is sufficiently critical; and/or it is difficult to find instruction in the KSA. Another reason an organization may still send an employee is social capital. Sometimes it isn't about what an employee learns as much as it is about who that employee meets.

The remaining factors that managers should consider focus on the quality of the provider. If it is sending an employee to a training or development program, the organization wants some assurance that the employee will receive quality instruction. Quality instruction will increase the likelihood that the employee will learn and then use the new KSA back at work. Although a manager may not know the specific trainer ahead of time, the manager will hopefully have some experience with the organization or know of its reputation.

Corporate University

Although many similarities occur in the instructional environments of the settings discussed in this section, there are important structural/organizational differences with corporate universities. These reflect the size, complexity, and institutional nature of corporate universities. Corporate universities primarily or exclusively educate the employees within the organization that created them and should not be confused with for-profit institutions of higher education. While some corporate universities have fun names, such as Hamburger University (described in the opening vignette), others are eponymous (e.g., employees at Motorola attend Motorola University).

Corporate universities come in many shapes and sizes. At one end of the spectrum, corporate universities resemble traditional institutions of higher education, meaning that they have a campus/building(s), have a set curriculum, may offer academic credit and/or degrees (although often in partnership with a traditional institution), and may even enroll students who are not employees of the organization.[24] At the other end of the spectrum, they look more like a robust training department, distinguishable mainly in orientation and branding.

Despite these differences, corporate universities and the organizations that form them generally share several characteristics. While most of these differences relate to the orientation and conceptual makeup of the universities, note that because of resource needs, corporate universities are not typically found in small organizations. Also, because of the resources required, a greater emphasis is placed on the strategic function of employee training and development. As such, corporate universities tend to be more proactive in their delivery of training and development than traditional training departments. Further, maintaining a corporate university signals to employees that the organization values and encourages employee learning and development.

While the extent of the curriculum within corporate universities varies, there are some commonalities. As first noted in Exhibit 8-1, the level of control and standardization in the delivery of training and development is greater in corporate universities than in many of the other instructional settings. It has also been noted that the curriculum generally encompasses the three *C*s: corporate citizenship, contextual framework, and core workplace competencies.[25] Corporate citizenship involves teaching employees about the organization's values, culture, history, and traditions. Contextual framework educates employees about how the organization interacts with its environment (i.e., the organization's strategy and industry trends). Finally, core workplace competencies focus on the KSAs that will make employees more productive.

CHAPTER SUMMARY

This chapter focused on the location and environment for training. Specifically, where training occurs can impact its effectiveness. The chapter also discussed many of the factors that managers should consider when choosing a setting for training. For example, how important is it for the organization to exert control over what is taught? Will the setting improve the fidelity of training, and at what cost? In addition, is the training or development all about a specific knowledge, skill, or competency, or should the organization also consider the ability of employees to expand their social capital? Similarly, to what extent is the goal to reward an employee in addition to providing instruction?

Specific settings for training were organized into three different settings. First, there were the fully on-site settings, including OJT and workshops. Second, organizations can take advantage of speakers/courses as well as conferences, all examples of off-site settings. Finally, the setting of corporate universities was categorized as unspecified. Even though corporate universities are self-contained within organizations, favoring a designation of on-site, they also share characteristics with off-site instruction (e.g., involves travel).

In addition, this chapter discussed environmental issues within the space where training occurs that are often overlooked but still impact training effectiveness. For example, the layout of the classroom (i.e., seating) can foster or hinder discussion and interaction among trainees. Further, trainers need to be aware of how a training space is outfitted in terms of technology and other equipment, which may facilitate training, as well as potential distractors (e.g., noise) that can make effective training more difficult.

KEY TERMS

Control. The degree to which design and delivery of training are centralized within the organization.

Fidelity. The degree to which the environment for training mirrors the environment where trainees will use what they learned.

Fixed costs. Costs that an organization must bear to provide training regardless of how many employees are trained.

Horseshoe. A classroom layout, where trainees are situated in a semicircle around the trainer, that promotes group discussion.

OJT. On-the-job training; can be formal or informal and is provided in the trainee's work environment.

Pods. A classroom layout, where there is no central focus and trainees sit in groups, that facilitates group interactions.

Reward value. The extent to which training is perceived as a reward provided by the organization.

Social capital. The value of an individual's relationships.

Standardization. The degree to which training is delivered in a consistent manner.

Training manual. An instructional aid whose use is consistent with formal on-the-job training.

Variable costs. Costs of training that increase with the number of employees trained.

END-OF-CHAPTER QUESTIONS AND EXERCISES

Discussion Questions

1. Is it always important for an organization to have control or standardization over training?
2. Discuss why organizations should consider social capital when choosing a setting for training.
3. Is it beneficial or problematic to have employees think of training as a reward?
4. Which costs of training should organizations be most concerned about containing?
5. Which instructional setting do you prefer, and why?
6. Discuss the advantages and limitations of OJT.
7. What factors contribute to making OJT formal or informal?
8. Is it better for a classroom to be arranged in pods or rows?
9. How would you assess or choose an off-site provider of training or development?
10. What makes corporate universities different from other instructional settings?

Ethical Scenario

Making Connections

Simon has worked for the Bridger Organization for eight years, but it has been three years since he received a promotion or was given any meaningful new job responsibilities or assignments. Simon was beginning to believe that his career was stalled and that perhaps it was time to find a new employer. A friend from the local professional organization suggested that he become active again and start attending the weekly speaker series. He told Simon that the speakers are both interesting and a great way to network; in fact, that was how he had found his current job. Simon decided that this was a great idea and talked to his boss about getting the time off (the speakers were scheduled for Friday afternoons) and paying for him to attend. He told his boss that the speakers covered topics that would help him do his job better and showed her the upcoming schedule.

1. What do you think about how Simon asked his employer to pay for the speaker series?
2. Is it okay to use an employer-funded training opportunity as part of a job search strategy?
3. What do you think the organization should have done in this situation?

8.1 A Tale of Two Rooms

Take a moment and reflect upon two classrooms where you have been a student. One should be a classroom that you liked, and the other a classroom that you disliked. Remember the initial focus is on the room and not the course itself.

What were the features and layout of the room you liked? How were they appropriate for the course you were taking? In what way(s) did the physical space support learning?

What were the features and layout of the room you disliked? In what way(s) did the physical space make it harder for you to learn? How could the physical space have been changed to improve your educational experience?

8.2 What Went Wrong?

Tom, the owner's grandson, was home from college for the summer. His grandfather thought it would be a good exercise for him to learn the business from the bottom up. So he told Phil, one of his foremen, to put Tom to work on the production floor. Phil told the owner, "Great idea," but inwardly groaned and thought about where Tom would do the least damage.

Feeling confident that Tom would ask his grandpa for a transfer, no matter what, Phil decided he wouldn't waste his time training him (although he usually did for his crew). Looking around, he saw that Carl, the most senior guy on his crew, wasn't busy. So he introduced Tom to Carl, told Carl to "show him the ropes," and walked away.

Carl told Tom to "watch me." Tom tried to ask a few questions, but every time, he was told, "Just watch." After 20 minutes, Carl completed his task and then told Tom to "give it a try." Over the next hour, Tom repeated the task with some corrections from Carl. When Tom finished the task, Carl thought that he did a good enough job and set him to work at the empty station at the other end of the room. Along the way, Carl introduced him to the other five members of the crew.

Tom went to work and was able to finish the task again in an hour. Over the course of the afternoon, the other members of the crew came over at some point to look at what he was doing and offer some advice on how to do things faster. Surprisingly, some of the advice contradicted what Carl had told him. Tom thanked them but didn't feel comfortable trying something different. Although he might be slow, he thought at least he was getting it done. The next day, the other people on the crew were friendly, but Tom wasn't offered any additional advice. By the end of the day, Tom was able to finish the task in 50 minutes, so he felt he was getting the hang of things. Each day for the rest of the week, he got a little faster. People remained friendly, and he got to know the other people on the crew.

A week later, Phil stopped the crew and said that he was getting complaints about a quality problem. He looked over to see what everyone was doing and stopped when he saw Tom's finish pile. He was not happy, and asked out loud, "Who told you to do it this way?" The person at the station next to him said, "I told him not to do that," and went back to work. When Phil confronted Carl, Carl said, "I wouldn't have told him to do that. I showed him the right way, and while he was slow, he seemed to get it." Exasperated, Phil walked away, but not before saying, "Show him again."

1. How would you categorize the training described in this scenario?
2. How could you improve the training provided to Tom?

8.3 Which Training to Pick?

You are a manager, and you want one of your employees to receive training. Anna is one of your best workers, and you believe that one day she will have your job on her way to the C-suite. You know money is tight right now, and if you don't use your training budget (you currently have $2,000) by the end of the quarter, the company will take it back. Also, you have heard rumors that the raise pool will be low this year. With this in mind, you have two developmental options for Anna (the days conflict, so you can only send her to one of them).

Decide which of the following options you would choose for Anna, and explain why.

Option 1

A local professional organization is bringing in a national speaker you have always respected. The topic is how to become a more transformational leader. Currently, Anna does not supervise anyone, but you think she will benefit from attending. You plan on attending yourself, and you have heard that a couple of your organization's vice presidents will be in attendance as well. There is minimal cost, and Anna would only have to miss half a day of work.

Option 2

There is a two-day (Thursday–Friday) conference in San Francisco. Your industry's trade association is hosting the conference, and the topic sounds like something Anna could use now. In addition, you know the meals and receptions are a good chance to meet people from other companies and learn about what they are doing. Looking at costs, you realize that it will pretty much use up what is left in the training budget. One personal thing you remember is that Anna has family in the area that she hasn't seen in a long time.

CHAPTER NINE

TECHNOLOGY-MEDIATED TRAINING AND DEVELOPMENT

Learning Objectives

1. Explain how an HRIS can be used to facilitate training and development.
2. Describe the features of an LMS.
3. Explain how technology changes the way people learn.
4. Discuss the pros and cons of virtual communication.
5. Identify the challenges to learning that technology creates.
6. Assess the advantages and disadvantages of online training and development.
7. Explain how technology allows training and development to go mobile.
8. Discuss how webinars are provided.
9. Provide advice for how to maximize learning from MOOCs.
10. Discuss how e-mentoring differs from traditional mentoring.

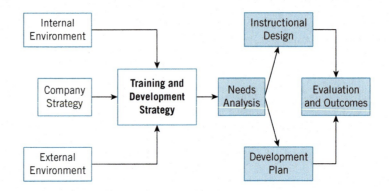

A new generation of virtual reality is bringing immersion to new levels. According to Anders Gronstedt, an expert on bringing new technologies to the learning experience, virtual reality simulators are a good option for any task "that's too dangerous, expensive, or inconvenient to practice in real life." Flight simulators for pilots and virtual training for soldiers or medical practitioners are great applications of virtual reality in the workplace today.

Vinay Narayan, HTC Vive's executive director, agrees. He says that VR offers two distinct value propositions. One is immersion, or the degree of the user's mental engagement. "The higher the immersion, the better the training and learning environment," says Narayan. The other is access: "VR gives you access to environments that are imagined, difficult to create or re-create, and those that are inaccessible."

It should come as no surprise that UPS has incorporated VR technology into its driver training. Narayan explains that VR technology is an extremely useful training tool, especially in applications such as defensive driving. "When trying to develop such corrective behavior, you can reinforce habits effectively because the experience feels real and mimics real-life situations."

Joe Finamore is vice president of global leadership and talent development for UPS. In *UPS: Driving Results Through Virtual Reality and Simulation-Based Training*, he describes how UPS uses a blended approach to teach driver candidates how to safely and confidently perform three vital tasks: handle their vehicles, employ a delivery information acquisition device, and pick up and deliver packages.

For the VR portion of this training, the "drivers" are safely seated behind a desk at a UPS training facility, with their hands gripping a simulated steering wheel. The virtual reality headset presents a 360-degree panorama of an urban streetscape, complete with assorted safety hazards. During the exercise, learners are expected to correctly identify each safety hazard before proceeding on a tightly routed journey through a neighborhood.

Already a success at UPS, an ATD Research report notes the company is interested in seeing how the fast-growing VR field will add eye-tracking technology that will measure where the eyes of a learner wearing a VR headset is looking. Laura Collings, a UPS learning manager, says that she eagerly awaits this advance, adding that it has "direct application to the hazard awareness learning module."

No doubt, VR training has drawn enthusiastic support from the employees and talent development staff. But the company's new chief information and engineering officer, Juan Perez, as well as its president of U.S. operations, Myron Gray, are also on board, in large part because "employing new technologies wherever they might improve performance" is an integral part of UPS's mission to maximize service to its customers.

Perez states, "Virtual reality offers a big technological leap in the realm of driver safety training, [and] creates a hyper-realistic streetscape that will dazzle even the youngest of our drivers whose previous exposure to the technology was through video games."

Technology has the opportunity to advance and enhance training, particularly in situations where safety is important but the risk of failure in a realistic context is high. A high-fidelity, virtual reality experience can teach trainees what they need to learn and allow them to practice their skills in a safe environment.

Source: Adapted from Ryann Ellis, "Get in the Driver's Seat: UPS Explores VR Training," *Association for Talent Development*, February 21, 2018. Available from https://www.td.org/insights/get-in-the-drivers-seat-ups-explores-vr-training.

As technology has advanced, so has the administration and provision of training and development. Technology provides for a wide array of design and implementation options in excess of what has been previously discussed in this textbook. While online instruction represents a major category of these options, the impact of technology is far greater. Starting with a needs analysis, technological advances touch upon all aspects of training and development, through evaluation. While many of these advances are positive, in that they offer either new efficiencies or opportunities, there are also some potential downsides as not everyone benefits equally from the transition from traditional learning to e-learning. Following the systems approach that underpins this book, this chapter discusses many of the ways that technology impacts the training and development function.

TECHNOLOGY-FACILITATED LEARNING

A 2012 article in the *New York Times* argued that technology is changing how students learn.[1] There appears to be some evidence that the use of technology is affecting the behavior of individuals because of the heavy stimulation and shifts in attention that occur while using computers and the internet. The Common Sense Media group conducted research and found that 71% of teachers felt technology was hurting attention span "somewhat" or "a lot," and 60% felt it hindered critical thinking and communication skills. Although the evidence is mixed that use of technology results in shorter attention spans, many argue that perhaps it is the way we teach people that needs to be adjusted.[2] If people learn differently, particularly given exposure to technology, education and training systems should adjust accordingly.

Technology is here to stay and becoming an important part of training and development systems in the workplace. What types of adjustments do organizations need to make given the different way learning takes place with technology? SHIFT eLearning argues technology changes the way people learn in four main ways[3]:

1. Learning shifts from individual to collaborative learning.
2. Learning shifts from passive to active or brain-based learning.
3. Focus shifts to differentiated instruction from a one-size-fits-all approach.
4. More multitasking means less effective absorption and processing of information.

The first and second points on this list map consistently to many of the learning theories discussed in Chapter 4. Technology enables people to engage in lifelong collaborative learning that uses higher-order cognitive functions to create new knowledge. The downside, however, is that, perhaps in the rush to build new knowledge, individuals are attempting to multitask and don't give enough time and attention to each item learned to engage with the material at the depth needed to fully internalize it. While trainees may think they can do more than one thing at a time, because technology makes it seem easy to do so, the end result is that multitasking only works when the tasks attempted are simple and don't compete for the same mental resources. Lastly, given the discussion in Chapter 4 about learning styles, reinforcing the need for a balanced approach to delivering information to trainees is key. This is particularly important because technology provides enormous opportunities for presenting information in engaging ways to maximize learning.

The lesson for future trainers is that technology can be an important tool to present information in a variety of ways to facilitate deeper-level learning. The challenge is to guard against the tendency to multitask while using technology. When trainees multitask, this has a negative impact on learning. Technology is an important tool but can be a lousy master if the challenges posed are not managed through proper instructional design and training procedures.

COMMUNICATING VIRTUALLY

Although some e-learning may take advantage of technologies like video chat, which allows instructors to see their trainees when they ask questions or during a discussion, the majority of communication will not be face-to-face, and this has several implications. Like most things, some are beneficial, and others detrimental, to learning. Further, some are inherent in the technology while others result from how e-learning intersects with individual diversity.

Concerns With Virtual Communication

Text-based communication, especially when mediated through a computer, is significantly less rich than when communication occurs face-to-face. This reflects the fact that someone reading text on a computer screen from a colleague or trainer is missing a lot of nonverbal information, some visual (e.g., facial expressions and body language) and other auditory (e.g., tone). This lack of additional information makes it much easier for miscommunications to occur[4]—particularly when communicating internationally and/or with non-native speakers because they may not be familiar with a specific interpretation of a word that might be more obvious with verbal inflections or visual cues. Further, the sender is less likely to correct the miscommunication because he or she also lacks the visual or auditory hints that would imply the need to provide more explanation.[5]

Virtual communications may also create psychological distance. This can be particularly bad because individuals who feel disconnected from a group are more likely to engage in aggressive behavior,[6] and it is potentially exacerbated when the sense of disconnection also manifests in a perception of anonymity. Surprisingly, the psychological distance created by virtual communication may also provide a benefit. Specifically, this distance may create a sense of security for non-native and international speakers to communicate.[7]

Diversity may also negatively impact virtual communication because of individual access to and comfort with virtual communication. It is easy to assume that everyone has reliable access to the internet; however, the socioeconomic reality is that this is not the case. Many people do not have such access, which makes it more difficult for them to communicate, and hence train, online. As for comfort, there appear to be some clear generational differences in how people respond to technology,[8] with younger workers (i.e., Millennials and Generation Z) being more literate. Discomfort with virtual communication should not be discounted because it reflects a greater lack of computer confidence, which in turn plays an important role in successful transfer of training on the job.[9]

Opportunities With Virtual Communication

Of course, there are several positives with organizations utilizing virtual communication, including the costs and capabilities of communicating virtually as well as other benefits based on employee diversity. Starting with cost and capabilities, virtual communications can increase and improve trainee and protégé interactions with peers, trainers, mentors, and coaches. The prevalence of video chat and conferencing software and apps facilitates richer communication among people who cannot meet face-to-face—particularly important for mentoring relationships. Further, this technology enables geographically dispersed employees to participate in a common training program. Besides improving quality and access, this technology has a significant cost, and time, advantage over having employees travel for face-to-face trainings or meetings.

Utilizing virtual communications, especially as part of training and development, can also be part of an organization's diversity and inclusion strategy. An important caveat is that these benefits generally occur with **lean communication** (e.g., email and text) versus **rich communication** (e.g., video). One reason for this is that without video or audio, the diversity characteristics of the people in the communication become less salient. Because people forget or don't realize they are conversing with a member of a minority group and/or woman, these groups tend to have better outcomes when communicating virtually.[10] Other aspects of learner communication methods that make them more inclusive is that they tend to be text based and are more likely to be asynchronous (i.e., there is a delay or lag between messages). These characteristics allow time for non-native speakers to both rehearse and reprocess the messages being sent and received, which improves their ability and comfort with communicating with native speakers.[11]

HUMAN RESOURCE INFORMATION SYSTEMS (HRIS)

Increasingly, organizations are making use of human resource information systems (HRIS). An **HRIS** is typically software that manages employee data across all human resource functions (e.g., recruitment and selection, compensation and benefits, and training and development). In addition to HRIS, there are three related acronyms: HRMS (human resource management system) is basically synonymous with HRIS. Alternatively, a company may choose to use an HCM (human capital management) system. Finally, an organization may have a specialized LMS (or learning management system, discussed later in this chapter) that is focused on training and development and may be either a stand-alone system or integrated within a larger HRIS. One of the better-known examples of an HRIS/HRMS is PeopleSoft.

HRIS provides organizations with access to large amounts of data to facilitate and promote employee training and development. While an organization can customize an HRIS to meet its needs, some basic data fields are typically included. At the most general level, an HRIS should include all employee qualifications (e.g., formal degrees and certifications). In addition, the HRIS should contain a list of all training and development activities. Ideally, these entries should include dates of attendance and/or successful completion. Even more specifically, an HRIS could list the individual skills and competencies that an employee possesses.[12] Further, these systems contain a range of potentially useful information, from basic biographical data (e.g., employee age, race, and sex), to attendance records, to performance evaluations.

Needs Analysis

Starting with just the historical information, an HRIS can be useful for identifying and tracking employees. Information on completed training and development activities provides a handy checklist on who still needs to participate. Further, information on when such activities and/or certifications were completed can be important to make sure that an employee remains up-to-date and in compliance. This information can also be used to make sure that an employee has the necessary background to successfully participate in a more advanced training or development activity.

In addition to such historical data, an HRIS contains other information that can be useful for selecting individuals for training and development. For example, organizations can make use of both the performance and biographical data as part of the needs analysis and selection stages for assigning employees to training and development. Regarding performance data, employees can be sorted easily in terms of their performance, with those at the lower level of the spectrum being targeted for remedial training, while higher performers are scouted for further development. As for biographical data, it can be used to determine whether training and development assignments are being made in an equitable manner or if there is any potential discrimination based on an employee's protected class (e.g., age, race, and sex). As such, equal employment opportunity/affirmative action compliance can be coordinated easily through an HRIS.

Succession Planning

Aligning with the scouting function, an HRIS can also be used to manage employee careers.[13] The succession planning and management processes discussed in Chapter 10 can easily be automated in an HRIS. First, organizations can utilize the performance data contained in an HRIS to identify high-potential employees. Once identified, the system can be used to chart out learning and development paths for individual employees including both content and timing of activities. This can also allow human resources to monitor progress to ensure that the employee is on track to take on new roles and leadership within the organization.

Training and Development Delivery

A learning management system, or **LMS**, is a subspecialty of an HRIS that enables trainers to provide information to their trainees in one online location. While an LMS can be a stand-alone system, it is discussed here because it can also be embedded as part of a

Exhibit 9-1 Common Learning Management Systems

LMS Company	Website
Blackboard (Higher Ed)	www.blackboard.com
Moodle	www.moodle.org
Canvas by Instructure (Higher Ed)	www.canvaslms.com
Absorb LMS	www.absorblms.com
Bridge by Instructure	www.getbridge.com
SmarterU LMS	www.smarteru.com

Source: Adapted from Capterra, "LMS Software." Available from https://www.capterra.com/learning-management-system-software/.

larger HRIS. As students, you are probably already familiar with one of the many online learning interfaces such as Canvas, Edmodo, or Blackboard. Teachers provide readings, videos, exercises, discussion boards, and exams all online to facilitate learning at the student's convenience. Organizations provide the same learning interfaces for those who utilize the training and development function. The LMS may be customized based on time, date, and content, for example, so people can enter and readily find the material they need for their training or development session. Mentors and coaches can also use an LMS to set up a schedule of activities they will engage in with the coaching or mentoring partner. Exhibit 9-1 contains the names and websites of a few of the most common learning management systems.

Typically, computer-based training modules can be uploaded into the LMS. This enables the instructional designer to set up videos, readings, lecture content, downloadable content, and interactive exercises to help people learn the material. Quizzes can be embedded in each module and automatically scored. Content can be created in an external source, such as Adobe Captivate, Prezi, or PowerPoint, and then uploaded into the LMS. If an LMS is SCORM (Sharable Content Object Reference Model) compliant, this means that the LMS meets the standards and specifications for web-based electronic education technology (i.e., e-learning). If a learning module is created, for example, it can be saved as a specific zip file (package interchange format) and uploaded into any SCORM-compliant LMS. Almost anything that can be done in a live classroom can be done online through an LMS. Exhibit 9-2 is an example of a course **dashboard** trainers might see when developing it for their LMS.

An LMS should ideally be integrated into your HRIS. This will allow you to view in one integrated database the LMS dashboard that tracks usage metrics of participants. It will also allow for skill and credential tracking to enable the training function to track employees' progress with development of knowledge, skills, and abilities (KSAs) and the staffing function to identify potential internal candidates for positions within the company, and would facilitate that the organization is in compliance with industry standards and regulations.[14] Exhibit 9-3 illustrates a typical dashboard interface illustrating usage metrics of participants.

Exhibit 9-2 Sample Trainer Course Dashboard

Source: FinancesOnline, "Comparison of Bridge LMS Competitors: Litmos, Mindflash and Firmwater." Available from https://financesonline.com/comparison-bridge-lms-competitors-litmos-mindflash-firmwater/.

Exhibit 9-3 Docebo Trainer Dashboard for Usage Metrics

Source: www.docebo.com, Reprinted with permission.

CHAPTER 9 • TECHNOLOGY-MEDIATED TRAINING AND DEVELOPMENT   233

Training Evaluation

Evaluation of training and development typically follows Kirkpatrick's four levels of training evaluation (i.e., reactions, learning, behavior, and results), discussed in Chapters 5 and 6. An LMS can easily address the first two levels, and a robust HRIS can potentially facilitate conducting all four levels of evaluation. It is a simple matter for the data collection and assessment needed for the first two levels of training evaluation to be automated in an LMS or HRIS. Having feedback data available in one location enables trainers to see trends in concerns from participants and adjust training delivery as they plan future training sessions. Although it is important to keep trainee reactions anonymous, data on employee learning can be made part of each trainee's file and then used to conduct the higher levels of evaluation. Examples of the variety of evaluation data that can be collected and then presented in a training dashboard as part of an HRIS are presented in Exhibit 9-4.

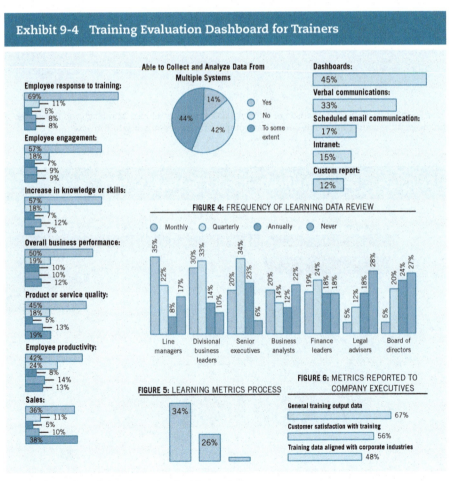

Exhibit 9-4 Training Evaluation Dashboard for Trainers

Source: Mike Prokopeak (2018). Reprinted with permission.

As demonstrated by the types of data presented in Exhibit 9-4, trainers can also use an HRIS to conduct the third and fourth levels of evaluation. If information on an employee's completion and/or level of learning from a training or development program is properly integrated into the HRIS, trainers can combine it with other available data to conduct the higher levels of evaluation. For example, when the HRIS includes job performance and/or appraisal data, an organization can begin to assess the level of behavioral changes or learning transfer that has occurred. Additionally, trainers can combine these data with more macro organizational data to determine the overall impact of providing the training or development. Of course, organizations must take care when designing an HRIS and dashboards to ensure that the appropriate metrics are being captured and presented in an appropriate format to facilitate decision making. This will enable the organization to focus training dollars on areas that provide value.

ONLINE INSTRUCTION

Keep in mind that online instruction continues to evolve as technology advances. There was a time when online instruction was no more than a glorified correspondence course (where materials were mailed back-and-forth through the postal service). The first advancements generally involved the addition of discussion boards. Today, trainers of online courses can engage in real-time chats and stream lectures.

When it comes to online instruction, organizations have numerous options and factors to consider. First, this section discusses the characteristics of online instruction that organizations should consider before adoption of this method. In addition, we discuss mobile instruction, gamification, webinars, massive online open courses (MOOCs), and e-mentoring, all specific applications of online training and development.

Characteristics of Online Instruction

Exhibit 9-5 lists some of the defining characteristics of online instruction. Depending on your perspective, these represent either an advantage or a disadvantage. So, along with the defining traits (listed alphabetically in the center column), Exhibit 9-5 provides an overview of how each characteristic, discussed in full in the following subsections, can be an advantage or a disadvantage.

One factor not listed in Exhibit 9-5 is participant anxiety. Historically, managers have been concerned about the potential for employees to become anxious by the medium or technology, and that this anxiety would undermine the employees' ability to learn. The concern with participant anxiety during online instruction originated when computers were less pervasive, and reflected the fact that older employees were less familiar and comfortable with computers. But the workforce has seen a major generation shift since then, with the increasing number of retirements among Baby Boomers and the emergence of Millennials, typically noted for their comfort and competence with technology.[15] Further, older employees have largely had sufficient time to acclimate and become comfortable with the tools of online instruction. So, while undoubtedly a segment of the workforce will continue to be anxious about online instruction, this more likely reflects individual learning preferences or personal barriers to effectively utilize technology.

Exhibit 9-5 Characteristics of Online Instruction

Advantages	Characteristic	Disadvantages
convenience ability to participate	**Access**	verification disparate impact
fidelity	**Computer Based**	fidelity
variable	**Cost**	fixed
ability to participate ability to respond	**Asynchronous**	ability to question
convenience appropriate challenge	**Self-Paced**	time management dropping out

Access.

Providing greater access to training and development is one of the main reasons that organizations choose to utilize online instruction. As long as individuals have a reliable internet connection, they can participate in online instruction. For some, this merely represents a convenience, but for others, it is a vital characteristic. Without the flexibility, someone who works and/or lives in a remote location may not be able to participate in training or development because of the logistics involved in traveling to where face-to-face instruction is being conducted. Even organizations that are not located in remote areas may lack the resources or numbers (of employees needing the training or development) to provide their employees with a local face-to-face option.

While this positive aspect of providing access to training and development normally outweighs the negatives, there are potential disadvantages to consider.[16] First, similar to concerns about telework, managers are often concerned with engagement of employees if they are not being monitored. For example, will the location individual employees choose allow them to sufficiently concentrate on the material? In addition, is there a way to make sure that the employees don't fast-forward through the material and/or cheat on any tests?[17]

The other potential disadvantage with online instruction involves the requirement for reliable internet access. While it is easy to assume that most employees have personal computers and internet access, this is not the reality for many. Lower-level employees with less income, for example, are less likely to have the personal computer equipment and internet service necessary to equally participate in online training and development. Researchers and policy professionals refer to this as the digital divide.[18] If organizations are unaware or do not provide alternatives, this can negatively impact the ability of these employees to participate in, and successfully complete, online training or development. Besides the obvious problem with this, organizations should be aware that this could also result in disparate impact, depending on the demographic makeup of these employees.

Exhibit 9-6 Ways to Make Technology Accessible

Perceivable	Operable
Closed-captioning	Simplify navigation
Present content in different ways	All features accessible via a keyboard
Understandable	**Robust**
Content appears in predictable ways	Compatibility with multiple platforms
Designed to avoid mistakes	

Source: Adapted from Kevin Gumienny, "E-learning FOR ALL," *Talent Development* 71, no. 8 (2017): 38–43.

In addition, there is an access issue in terms of disabilities. As originally mentioned in Chapter 2, Section 508 of the Rehabilitation Act requires that technology is made accessible for trainees.[19] For example, trainees with visual impairments may require screen readers whereas trainees with hearing impairments may benefit from closed-captioning. The Web Content Accessibility Guidelines (WCAG) 2.0 identify four areas to consider when making sure that technology is accessible.[20] Exhibit 9-6 lists these categories and provides sample guidelines. As shown in the exhibit, WCAG 2.0 identifies closed-captioning as one method to make training content perceivable. Designers can address the need for operability by simplifying how to navigate training technology and content. As for making content understandable, WCAG 2.0 recommends that it appear in predictable ways. Finally, a robust design is compatible across multiple platforms.

Computer based.

For the characteristic of computer based, Exhibit 9-5 lists fidelity as both an advantage and a disadvantage. Whether online instruction is high or low in fidelity depends largely on its content. While this may appear tautological, it is not. If trainees are engaged in online instruction, it requires them to use a computer. However, the topic does not have to be computer related, and this explains difference in fidelity.

If the KSA is computer related, then by virtue of using a computer for instructional purposes there is the potential for a good level of fidelity. In these cases, online instruction could be considered as a form of experiential learning. The final level of fidelity then depends on the match of computer systems, environment, and/or examples used instructionally compared to what the employee will use and experience when back at work.

If, however, online instruction is merely the method of content delivery, and this is divorced from the content, then fidelity would be expected to be lower.[21] Let's revisit the flight attendant example presented in Chapter 8 where the topic was how to handle an irate passenger. We discussed that even if the instruction were enriched with videos of such altercations, a level of detachment would still be created by watching the video on a computer, which detracts from its overall level of fidelity. For these kinds of skills and competencies, the need to use a computer results in a lack of fidelity, a disadvantage of online instruction.

Virtual reality (VR) enables trainees to truly immerse themselves in a high-fidelity simulation, using technological advances. As our opening vignette highlights, technology-enhanced training like VR allows trainees to approach full realism in experience, in a safe environment. VR helps UPS drivers handle their trucks in a safe space, for example, while experiencing a full range of problems they could expect while driving their routes. This ability to cover numerous critical but dangerous and/or real scenarios is a major advantage of this technology.[22] While the current applications of VR technology are exciting, we are still in the beginning stages of untapping its potential to enhance the training and development experience for trainees.

Cost.

The cost involved in providing online instruction is often discussed as one of the disadvantages of this instructional setting.[23] While this is sometimes still the case, it is not always true—in large part because technology has evolved. Today, computers are faster, cheaper, and more portable than ever. In our Wi-Fi-enhanced world where phones can function as hotspots, it may be hard to imagine a time when computers didn't all come with modems, and those that did were dependent on wired dial-up service. Similarly, special, and expensive, equipment is no longer required to either create or view video. At the same time, the KSAs required to produce online instructional content have become more commonplace. Of course, costs are still associated with the development and delivery of online instruction, and to the extent that these are fixed, they represent a disadvantage of online instruction.

When discussing training and development, it is important to differentiate between variable and fixed costs.[24] Specifically, how much extra will it cost to include an additional person? When it comes to online instruction, the variable costs can be negligible. This statement is even truer if the administrative functions are also automated and therefore fixed and/or individuals participate in the training or development using their own computers. In part, this relates back to the level of access provided by online instruction. For example, there aren't any concerns about running out of space or the ability of a trainer to handle additional trainees (unless physical grading or administration is required). Combined, these factors make online instruction easily and highly scalable.[25] Therefore, variable costs represent an advantage of online instruction.

Asynchronous.

Synchronicity refers to the timing of instruction. Traditional face-to-face instruction is synchronous, meaning that the trainer is providing the training at the same time the trainee is learning. One of the strengths of online instruction is that it seldom requires that someone participate at a specific time. Because the trainee can choose when to engage in training, this makes the training **asynchronous**. Even if an online training involves testing, there is often a window of time for taking exams or quizzes, which provides trainees with sufficient flexibility.

As such, online instruction enables people to participate in training and development they would otherwise not be able to experience because of their schedules (e.g., working third shift). In this regard, the asynchronous nature of instruction results in a temporal advantage for online instruction, similar to the advantage discussed in the "Access" section. Also, online instruction enables trainees to work when it is convenient to them, at different points in time, which differentiates it from the face-to-face or synchronous learning that occurs in more traditional training and development settings.

Another major impact of the asynchronous nature of online instruction occurs with trainee questions and discussions. Unlike face-to-face instruction, which occurs in real time, there is a delay between when a question is asked and when it is answered. For many, this can be frustrating. To the extent that the question or answer is ambiguous, and requires clarification, this problem or frustration is compounded. This can discourage questions and undermine learning, which is why the asynchronous nature of online instruction can be a disadvantage.

There are instances, however, where the asynchronous nature of online instruction can improve the question-and-answer process. Individuals who are reluctant to ask, or respond to, questions in a face-to-face environment may feel more comfortable doing so in an online context. The additional time to compose a question or answer can be helpful for people who otherwise would be less likely to participate because of cultural, linguistic (i.e., non-native speakers), or personality (e.g., introverts) factors.[26] Especially for these people, the asynchronous nature of online instruction represents an important advantage of this locale.

Self-paced.

Online instruction is often self-paced. This means the participants determine for themselves how quickly to go through the material—something that is not possible in face-to-face locales where instruction is constrained by the schedule or trainer availability. Besides the ability to simply participate in the training and development, as just discussed as an advantage of its asynchronous nature, the self-paced nature represents a more general convenience factor enjoyed by many trainees.

Besides convenience, appropriate challenge is another potential advantage of the self-paced characteristics of online instruction. In face-to-face instruction, the trainer normally dictates the pace of learning. But the pace that the trainer chooses for instruction may be too fast, resulting in participants getting lost, or too slow, resulting in boredom. Each of these scenarios can undermine learning, but this is not a problem with self-paced instruction. Participants can choose to go faster if they find the material easy, or slow down or repeat the material when it is difficult. This can improve both satisfaction and learning and explains why the self-paced nature of online instruction is an advantage.

Unfortunately, the self-paced nature of online instruction may be too much of a good thing. If participants are not good at time management, they may procrastinate or try to rush through the material. Rushing the material can undermine learning. Additionally, procrastination can easily turn into dropping out. High attrition rates for online instruction are a common problem.[27] For these reasons, being self-paced represents a potential disadvantage of online instruction.

Mobile Instruction

An important and growing subset of e-learning is **m-learning**, with the *m* referring to mobile (i.e., training or development on a mobile device). A wide range of devices and apps qualify as mobile, and the technology in this area is constantly changing. Today, m-learning focuses on smartphones and tablets. However, less than 10 years ago (as of the writing of this textbook), people were advocating developing materials on a variety of technologies that have since become redundant or even obsolete (e.g., MP3 players and BlackBerrys).[28] Further, it is only a matter of time before widespread m-learning is designed for wearable tech (e.g., Fitbits and Apple Watches).

While there are many advantages to m-learning, the technology comes with its own concerns that organizations need to address in order to create effective training or development. It is prudent to address the concerns first because some of the advantages cannot be realized if the training or development is poorly executed. Exhibit 9-7 identifies three guidelines to keep in mind for creating effective m-learning opportunities.

A central theme to the guidelines listed in Exhibit 9-7 is that size matters.[29] The first two guidelines, limit scrolling and consider need and ability to respond, refer to the size of the mobile devices. A common complaint among people who use their smartphones to access websites that do not have mobile versions is the difficulty of navigating them. Therefore, design features that limit the need to scroll, like pop-up windows, make it easier for users to find information. In addition to smaller screens, mobile devices have smaller keyboards (whether physical or virtual) than traditional computers. This makes it more cumbersome for someone engaged in m-learning to provide long text responses. Consequently, organizations should consider reducing the need to respond and/or finding alternatives to typing when designing m-learning.

The last guideline in Exhibit 9-7 concerns how and when people use the technology rather than its physical limitations. For example, people often access their mobile devices when they have small periods of free time and/or are in distracting environs (e.g., commuting on public transportation). In these situations, people do not have the time or ability to focus on large or complex lessons. Alternatively, some people may be interested in a quick refresher, and having the information organized in smaller discrete modules will make accessing the desired information easier. A secondary benefit of creating discrete modules is that the training or development is friendlier to the size of a mobile device.

This brings us to the advantages of mobile devices. First, technology increases the convenience and accessibility of training, already one of the advantages of e-learning. Second, m-learning can increase the amount of learning and transfer. Because effective m-learning is divided into smaller modules, people are better able to focus on, and retain,

---

Exhibit 9-7   Guidelines for Creating Effective m-Learning

Limit Scrolling

Consider Need and Ability to Respond

Focus on Discrete Modules

the information. Similarly, m-learning facilitates looking up past lessons, which increases trainees' ease and confidence in utilizing what they learned.[30]

Gamification

While we initially discussed using games in providing training in Chapter 7, the use of technology and gamification is an emerging concept. Basically, **gamification** seeks to shift games from entertainment to the basis of employee training. The principle of gamification in training is simple: The typical elements of game playing (rules of play, point scoring, competition with others) are applied to other areas of activity, specifically to engage users in problem solving.[31] While gamification was originally used in marketing, there are many applications for employee training.

Gamification allows for friendly competition between trainees to encourage engagement in a format already familiar to them.[32] Digital badges, like the merit badges from scouting, allow people to share achievements in a public forum. Trainees can compete to accomplish tasks in the training modules and can score points to advance through succeeding levels of the training, just as they would do in digital games. Exhibit 9-8 outlines the steps to implement gamification in a training program and the typical activities associated with it.

Exhibit 9-8   Steps for Implementing Gamification

Step	Description	Examples
1	Understanding the Target Audience and Context	• Who are the trainees, and what is the context within which they will learn the new material?
2	Defining Learning Objectives	• What does the trainer want the trainees to learn in the session by using gamification (e.g., greater engagement)?
3	Structuring the Experience	• What are the stages and milestones that lend themselves to gamification, and what are the learning obstacles that interfere with learning progression?
4	Identifying Resources	• Can a tracking mechanism be applied to this specific stage? • What would be the currency (points, dollars, etc.), and what determines the accomplishment of a level? • Are there clear rules that can be implemented? • Does the overall system give the student and/or instructor feedback?
5	Applying Gamification Elements	Apply gamification elements: • **Self-elements** can be points, achievement badges, levels, or simply time restrictions. These elements get trainees to focus on competing with themselves and recognizing self-achievement. • **Social elements** provide interactive competition or cooperation, for example leaderboards. These elements put the trainees in a community with other trainees, and their progress and achievements are made public.

Source: Adapted from Wendy H.-Y. Huan and Dilip Soman, *A Practitioner's Guide to Gamification of Education*, Research Report Series: Behavioural Economics in Action (Toronto: Rotman School of Management, 2013).

It is important to note that while gamification directly affects motivation and engagement, it only indirectly affects acquiring knowledge and skills.[33] Referring back to our discussion of training evaluation, level 1 evaluation assesses the extent to which trainees are engaged with the material. Engagement increases the likelihood that a trainee will learn the material because increased engagement means more opportunities to practice and master the material. Organizations must take care, however, to not make gamification the purpose for the training. Gamification is a tool to increase engagement and impact learning outcomes, but should not be the end, in and of itself. Nor should gamification replace designing appropriate learning modules and learning outcomes in a comprehensive training program.

Webinars.

While the technology behind a **webinar** may not be cutting-edge, it does represent a ubiquitous form of e-learning. Webinars typically provide instruction on stand-alone topics and are not overly long (generally about an hour).[34] One explanation for the common duration of webinars is that they have become a popular option for individuals who need to maintain professional credentials or certifications, such as lawyers, accountants, and even training and human resource professionals (as discussed in the introductory chapter). Further, the bodies that certify the continuing education (CE) credits typically assign them in hour increments and have time minimums for a webinar, or any training or development opportunity, to qualify.

The provision of webinars.

There are many ways to utilize webinars as part of an organization's portfolio of training and development options. First, an organization can produce its own webinars. Further, these can be created and accessed in an LMS. Organizations that want to create their own webinars can choose among a variety of popular programs. Some of the most common programs currently in use include Zoom, Skype for Business, Join.Me, Adobe Connect, and Google Hangouts. These programs typically enable participants to synchronously screen share and view live demonstrations, slide shows, and voice-over instruction on the topic of interest. Webinars can also be recorded using the recording options available in the webinar software or using tools such as Screencast-O-Matic or Capto that capture and record what goes on during a webinar in a digital movie format.

While individuals can view webinars produced by their employing organization, they typically will register for ones hosted by a third party. Examples of third-party providers of webinars include professional, industry, and trade organizations. Another common source is educational institutions. While any source of webinar could grant CE credit if approved by the accrediting body, additional sources of CE-providing webinars include major firms in the field and even the accrediting body itself.

Dynamism and interactivity.

Webinars can vary dramatically in terms of **dynamism** and interactivity. The first webinars were extremely static and one-directional in nature—essentially, just a series of slides with a voice-over or an individual talking into a camera—and were usually not more exciting than this description, aka "death by PowerPoint."[35] Fortunately, creators of webinars today can now provide information in a more stimulating way (e.g., using animation and videos), which positively impacts learning.[36] However, this doesn't address the issue of interactivity.

Concerns about interactivity can be addressed easily when webinars are live (i.e., synchronous). Live webinars allow individuals to message questions to the presenter. Concerns about receiving too many or inappropriate questions can be addressed by employing someone to screen and moderate them. Alternatively, trainers can set up a discussion board function for participants to ask questions and/or even engage in group-related activities.[37] While the potential for interactivity is greatly curtailed when a person is viewing an archived (i.e., asynchronous) webinar, it is still possible to provide an accompanying discussion board or comments section.

Massive Online Open Courses (MOOCs)

An important subset of online education is the massive online open course, more popularly known as a **MOOC**. As the name implies, anyone with internet access can register for a MOOC. Because the goal of MOOCs is to expand access to education, they are offered at no charge to students. This aspect makes them an inviting option for organizations that want to increase their employees' knowledge and skills, but do not have the money or desire to invest in training and development. In addition, the perceived quality of MOOCs is relatively high as they are often sponsored by major universities (e.g., Harvard, MIT, and Stanford) and then hosted by third-party providers.[38]

While MOOCs are popular, they are not without drawbacks. For example, the free version of a MOOC seldom comes with any certification that someone has learned the material. When a MOOC does provide certification, there is often a cost, which lessens the economic appeal. While an employer may be willing to live with this drawback, the lack of certification decreases the value of the training for employees, especially for those looking to change employers. This can decrease employee motivation and may partially explain why MOOCs are known to have low completion rates, arguably their most important drawback. A third drawback to keep in mind with MOOCs is that because they are aimed at being "massive," they tend to be better at providing instruction in broad and/or generic areas of knowledge rather than addressing the specific applications and/or niche needs of an organization.[39] Also, searching through the vast array of available MOOCs can take significant time and energy.

Organizations that want to include MOOCs in their portfolio of training and development options should follow the advice highlighted in Exhibit 9-9 to increase their efficacy. First, a MOOC should not be a stand-alone activity. To support successful completion of a course, employees should be engaged in activities that reinforce learning. Discussion groups, whether online or in-person, are one good example. Second, order and cluster MOOCs in a logical progression, which creates learning paths for employees. Third, even employees who have already been trained should be encouraged to register for a MOOC in an area where they could benefit from a refresher.[40] Fourth, organizations should choose MOOCs with a certification option, even if it comes with a cost, as a means of increasing employee motivation and course completion.[41]

> **Exhibit 9-9 How to Maximize MOOCs**
>
> 1. Incorporate MOOCs with other activities to support learning.
> 2. Order and cluster MOOCs to create learning paths.
> 3. Encourage employees to utilize MOOCs as a refresher.
> 4. Opt for certification.

e-Mentoring and e-Coaching

Is it possible to have a mentor program when the potential mentors and protégés are geographically dispersed? Mentor programs can work well whether interactions take place face-to-face or virtually, but organizations must take care to ensure the challenges of distance do not overwhelm and negatively impact the value of the mentoring program. The Australian Women in Resources Alliance (AWRA) faced just such a dilemma.[42] Many of the women worked in remote locations but still desired a mentoring experience. AWRA established a virtual mentoring program and after only three years had successfully matched and managed 300 participants. The organization uses resources such as Skype, telephones, emails, and text messaging, which offers the benefit of faster, more immediate responses to mentoring interactions. As well, the virtual atmosphere mitigates the challenges associated with mixed-gender and mixed-ethnicity mentoring pairs. Lastly, broad geographic boundaries enable companies to have a larger pool of mentors and protégés than would be expected, leading to better matches for participants.

Women appear to greatly benefit from e-mentoring, as do those who work in multinational or global businesses. The asynchronous communication that is central to virtual, or e-, mentoring benefits those who juggle multiple responsibilities, such as working mothers or women with elder-care responsibilities.[43] Although men can certainly benefit from e-mentoring, women in the United States are still more likely than are men to take the primary responsibility for child and elder care in families. Asynchronous communication can also benefit those who work at remote locations across the world. For example, a mentor can live and work in the United States, while a protégé can work in the Middle East. Mentoring across cultural boundaries also needs to consider factors such as concern for cultural differences based on Hofstede's dimensions (see Chapter 13), or differing norms based on religion (e.g., a male mentoring a female employee from Saudi Arabia). When organizations give care and consideration to ensuring mentoring matches take into account national culture and interpersonal and religious norms, the mentoring relationship has the potential to thrive.

There are a few considerations when planning for an e-mentoring program. First, the margin for error is much tighter for e-mentoring programs as compared to traditional programs.[44] It is important for companies to plan for the greater amount of administrative time needed to manage the mentoring program and the mentoring partners. As such, using a mentoring administrative platform will help manage e-mentoring programs. Second, all training materials and resources must be made available online.

This includes readings, articles, exercises, and video and audio recordings that not just report what to do but demonstrate how to do certain aspects of the program. Lastly, the match needs to consider the challenges that may arise from communicating virtually, so organizations must take care during mentoring training to build an open, trusting relationship among mentoring partners.

Compared to e-mentoring, e-coaching is more likely to embrace technology as a means to facilitate the coaching relationship. While there are benefits to meeting face-to-face, a lot of work with external coaches occurs via telephone or videoconferencing with Zoom or Skype for Business. Although external coaching lends itself to the use of technology, as you will see in Chapter 11, organizations must take care to use rich communication media like videoconferencing to minimize communication problems and facilitate a strong relationship between coach and client.

CHAPTER SUMMARY

This chapter covered the many ways that technology impacts training and development. Technology influences and/or can be used in all facets of training and development from the initial stages of the needs analysis to its design and delivery and subsequently to evaluation. In terms of administering training and development, organizations can utilize an LMS and/or an HRIS. Specifically, they can use these systems to facilitate several processes, including needs analysis, succession planning, and evaluation.

As for the provision of training and development, technology provides both opportunities and challenges. Some opportunities include the ability to expand the access and increase flexibility to participate for individuals. At the same time, not everyone has the same ability to benefit from online training and development because of either resources or learning styles. This is true of basic training topics as well as some popular trends (e.g., MOOCs and e-mentoring). Keeping up with technology will continue to be an important task for training professionals because change is the only constant that one can expect when it comes to technology.

KEY TERMS

Asynchronous. A typical characteristic of online instruction and communication where training/communication does not occur in real time.

Dashboard. The visual output of HRIS data.

Dynamism. How static and one-directional information is provided online; the more static, the less dynamic.

Gamification. Application of design principles from games applied to employee training.

HRIS. Human resource information system; a software package that an organization can utilize to manage and monitor all aspects of employee training and development.

Lean communication. Communication that lacks contextual information (e.g., tone and nonverbals), such as texting and email.

LMS. Learning management system; a software package that an organization can use to manage the delivery of training.

m-learning. Training that takes place via an app or mobile device.

MOOC. Massive online open course; a format of training that is often free and in which anyone can participate.

Rich communication. Communication that contains contextual information (e.g., tone and nonverbals); face-to-face communication is the richest type.

Webinar. A seminar that is presented in an online format.

END-OF-CHAPTER QUESTIONS AND EXERCISES

Discussion Questions

1. What types of information should be included in an HRIS, and how does this facilitate training and development? Are companies that use an HRIS at an advantage over companies that do not?
2. Discuss how you can use an LMS to improve training and development outcomes.
3. Discuss how technology changes the way people learn. Give an example of a training program that moves from no technology to using technology. How would it differ, and how would it have an impact on the learners?
4. What does it mean for communication to be lean, and is that a good or bad thing? Under what conditions do you think lean communication would be fine?
5. Identify the key characteristics of online instruction.
6. Argue whether fidelity is an advantage or a disadvantage of online instruction.
7. Discuss how individual diversity intersects with technology. How can an organization use technology to be more inclusive?
8. Explain how technology enables training and development to go mobile. Describe a training program that you could transition from a traditional training method to a mobile app.
9. What is gamification, and is it a good thing for training?
10. Provide advice on how to best utilize webinars for a training and development program.
11. What factors should organizations consider before deciding to utilize MOOCs?
12. Explain how e-mentoring changes employee development.

Ethical Scenario

See No, Hear No, Speak No Training

Doug poked his head into Sean's office and asked him if he had completed the new compulsory online sexual harassment training course. Sean answered that he had and that it was okay once he realized that he could turn off the sound and run it in the background. Doug thanked him for the tip, but then asked about the quiz at the end of video. Sean told him that it was the same stupid questions that they always asked. "Great, so I really don't need to watch it," Doug responded.

1. On a personal level, what do you think about Doug's plan to play the sexual harassment training in the background without sound?
2. On an organizational level,
   a. Should you be concerned that employees are not really watching the sexual harassment training?
   b. What could be done to make sure that people like Doug would be more likely to watch the training?

8.1 MOOC It Up

Develop a personal learning path for yourself using MOOCs. Go online and identify three MOOCs that you could take. Explain how they are connected and will provide you with the knowledge or skill development that you need. Be sure to identify the order that you believe they should be completed in and state why.

8.2 Caught in the Webinar

Find and participate in a webinar. Assess its level of dynamism and interactivity and then write a reflection on your reactions to participating in it.

8.3 All I Need Is an e-Mentor

Identify someone you would want to be a mentor, but would not be able to meet with face-to-face. Once you have identified this person,

1. Explain why you have chosen this person, including:
    a. Why do you think this person would be a good match for you?
    b. Which career and/or personal goals will this person be able to help you with?
2. Write an introductory email.

CHAPTER TEN

CAREERS AND SUCCESSION

Learning Objectives

1. Discuss the relationship between jobs and careers.
2. Determine which career stage an employee is experiencing.
3. Discuss the goals and challenges experienced at each career stage.
4. Differentiate between the directional paths that a career can follow.
5. Compare and contrast traditional, boundaryless, and protean careers.
6. Describe and categorize career anchors.
7. Assess the appropriateness of providing training or development based on an employee's career stage or type of career.
8. Explain the importance of succession planning and differentiate between the different approaches.
9. Explain how an assessment center works.
10. Discuss the interaction between employee potential and performance.
11. Complete and interpret an organizational depth chart.
12. Understand the impact of career theories on succession planning.

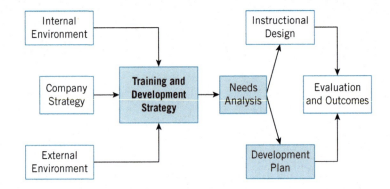

Ursula Burns is formerly the chairperson and CEO of Xerox Corporation and in that role regularly appeared on lists of the most powerful women in business. Her assuming the helm of Xerox marked a couple of important corporate milestones. For one, she became the first African American woman to lead a Fortune 500 company as CEO. Further, she assumed control of Xerox from Anne Mulcahy, which represented the first time that one woman succeeded another as the CEO of a Fortune 500 firm.

Given those firsts, you might think that this is the lead-in to discuss the virtues of diversity. Certainly, the story of an African American woman, raised by a single mother in the projects, who becomes CEO of one of the country's biggest corporations would be appropriate for that. But this is the chapter on careers and instead is looking at what we can learn from an intern who became CEO.

Ursula Burns is what is sometimes referred to as a lifer, meaning that she has spent her professional life essentially within a single organization. Learning that she had spent nearly 30 years with Xerox before becoming CEO, it is easy to envision a picture of a mechanical engineering intern working her way sequentially up a corporate ladder. Even so, that isn't how her career unfolded.

The turning point in her career occurred when she attended a quality of work life meeting. At that meeting, someone questioned if the organization was lowering standards in pursuit of diversity. While the person leading the meeting stated that wasn't the case, that wasn't good enough for Ursula Burns. She spoke up and explained that she was surprised that it was necessary to even answer such a question.

Although she didn't know Wayland Hicks, the person who answered the question, was the president of marketing, that was soon to change. He called her into his office and, instead of the reprimand that she expected, offered her a job. Not only was the offer unexpected, but so too was the job—to be his assistant. Remember the imagery of a corporate ladder? This was not the next rung for someone with a master's degree in mechanical engineering who had been with the company for the better part of a decade.

So why did she become his assistant? One piece of advice that probably helped her to make that decision was some wisdom passed down from her mother who taught her that "where you are is not who you are."[1] Related to that is a work attitude where she was open to possibilities. As she stated, "So they said how about this and I say so okay and we'll go and do that."[2] The position was also more than its name might imply. It gave her opportunities to learn about and help with decisions both from and with an important corporate leader.[3] Eventually, she would move into leadership positions with more obvious job titles, which would prepare her to become the chairperson and CEO of Xerox.

The story of Ursula Burns's career provides an opportunity to highlight some of the key issues covered in this chapter. While Burns may have been a lifer at Xerox, her career did not follow a traditional pattern. Rather, in managing her career, she took advantage of opportunities for growth even if they did not follow an orderly upward progression. As such, she represents an emerging tension that individuals and organizations face in today's world—namely, that the nature of careers has changed and that individuals, even if they stay with a single organization, need to be aware of and manage the direction of their own careers. At the same time, organizations still need to engage in succession planning to make sure that they have the employees they need to step up into leadership to ensure continued success.

With all this talk about careers, it is useful to differentiate between jobs and careers. One thing to consider is whether the difference is simply a function of status, meaning that some people have jobs and others have careers. For example, managers and professionals (e.g., doctors and lawyers) have careers, whereas secretaries and factory workers have jobs. The answer to that question is no. Everyone who works has both a job and a career.

So how can you distinguish between jobs and careers? One way to conceptualize them is to say that a job is what a person is doing now in order to make money, but a career relates to the overall picture of a person's working life and how one derives meaning from it.[4] An implication of this is that jobs are very task-oriented. As such, training is generally associated with a specific job. By comparison, careers are more than just a person's current employment, so growth and improvement are more often achieved with development activities.

Another aspect of careers is their more personal nature. For example, two people may work in the same office and do the same tasks or jobs yet have very different careers.[5] One explanation is that some people pursue careers that align with and accommodate their nonwork lives while others seek to keep their jobs separate. People also hold different career attitudes and pursue individual goals. Some want a career composed of a series of identifiable and stable job opportunities while others prefer the challenge of an unpredictable environment and life. These statements will make more sense when reviewing the various theories that have been developed to explain careers. This chapter covers four different theories of careers.

These theories provide alternative ways for explaining career differences, both in nature and in status, found within an organization's workforce. The main purpose of exploring these theories is to better understand the career needs, motivations, and goals of individual employees. Understanding how individuals perceive and experience their careers is helpful to provide them with the appropriate support and development opportunities, as well as for engaging in successful succession planning.

CAREER THEORIES

The first theory presented in this chapter is **career stage** theory.[6] As the name suggests, careers are composed of various stages. This theory focuses on the status of an employee's career rather than its nature. Regardless of how an employee identifies with his or her career, careers generally follow a life cycle. At the very least, all careers have a beginning, and what employees experience and need at the beginning of their careers is very similar. This allows career stage theory to be relatively prescriptive in terms of the support and development activities for employees.

The remaining career theories focus more on how employees identify with and manage their careers. Here differences emerge between employees. So even seemingly similar employees, in terms of job title and career stage, may describe their career motivations and goals very differently. Protean[7] and boundaryless[8] theories discuss these differences by contrasting how individuals perceive and manage their careers along various dimensions. Although these are separate theories with distinct dimensions, they are often intermingled,[9] in part because both contrast with what are commonly referred to as more traditional careers, and are therefore presented together in this chapter. These theories are particularly interesting because they discuss how managing careers has changed in response to societal changes.

The final theory presented in this chapter is career anchors.[10] While career anchors theory also deals with issues of how employees identify with their careers, it focuses more on a person's needs and motivations. Career anchors theory also differs from protean and boundaryless theories because it doesn't draw a contrast to what can be described as a traditional career. Instead, it proposes that a person's career corresponds to one of eight different anchors. As such, this theory allows for the most differentiation among people in regard to their careers.

Another way to conceptualize the differences between these career theories is in the type of questions they answer and the guidance they provide organizations regarding how they should or should not develop the careers of their employees. Individuals and organizations have lots of questions about careers and career management. Some of the most common include the following:

When should career management assistance/support be provided?

What type of career management assistance/support is needed or appropriate?

Who is responsible for providing career management assistance/support?

Why is someone making a specific career management decision?

Exhibit 10-1 shows which career theories address each of these questions. Career stage theory is the most temporal of the four theories, and as such, it makes sense that it addresses the question of *when*. Career stage theory also discusses how the needs and goals of people change as a function of which stage they are currently experiencing. This allows career stage theory to be prescriptive to a degree. As a result, career stage theory also addresses the question of *what*.

By comparison, the question of *who* is not really addressed by career stage theory. However, the question of *who* is a major focus of both protean and boundaryless career theories, which discuss how careers have changed over time. *Who*, for example, is responsible for guiding and providing career development? These theories discuss how there has been a general shift from the employer provision of career guidance and development to the individual. However, they also acknowledge how some employees continue to rely upon their employers.

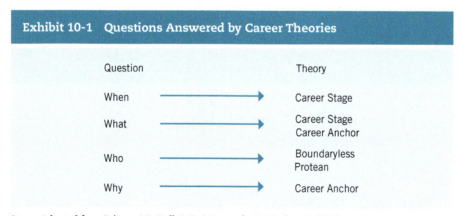

Exhibit 10-1 Questions Answered by Career Theories

Question	Theory
When	Career Stage
What	Career Stage / Career Anchor
Who	Boundaryless / Protean
Why	Career Anchor

Source: Adapted from Briscoe, J. P., Hall, D. T., & Frautschy DeMuth, R.,L. (2006).

The final question of *why* is addressed by the theory of career anchors. This theory also in part addresses the question of *what*. Of the four theories discussed in this chapter, career anchors most directly answers questions of identity. As such, it can explain *why* people in otherwise similar circumstances may make different career choices. Career anchors theory also stresses the congruence between someone's anchor or identity and work situation. Because of this, career anchors can partially answer the question of *what*. However, there is greater emphasis on *what* is appropriate as opposed to *what* is needed.

CAREER STAGES

Career stage theory is the oldest of the theories discussed in this chapter, and as such, it reflects a more traditional view of individual careers. For example, the sequential nature of the theory is more consistent with stable career ladders[11] within organizations than more modern conceptualizations of careers. Still, all careers have a beginning and generally follow a life cycle even if it is experienced in multiple environments.

Career stage theory views a career as composed of four sequential steps, as outlined in Exhibit 10-2. Careers start in an exploration phase and end in a disengagement stage. In between, careers progress through establishment and maintenance stages. Originally, these stages were conceptually connected to a person's chronological age. While there was a certain logic to this approach (e.g., most people begin their careers after high school or college), careers are idiosyncratic and do not always correspond to a timetable.[12] So, while people may experience career stages at different times, they generally progress through them. Therefore, understanding each career stage and the associated recommendations for what to consider while in a particular one is valuable for an individual's career development.

Exploration

Career theory may not be rocket science, but a rocket analogy is useful for understanding each of the four stages. Despite its name, in this analogy the exploration stage is equivalent to the countdown, and the employee is the astronaut. She or he is in the

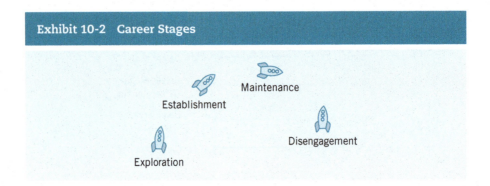

Exhibit 10-2 Career Stages

rocket, and a career has started, but it hasn't taken off yet. The employee has had basic training (e.g., high school or college) and is ready to get started but so far has limited experience. The employee still has a lot to learn at this career stage, and you can envision the astronaut checking off a list of items to make sure she or he is ready for the rocket to blast off. Of course, if something is wrong (i.e., the person realizes she or he is on the wrong path), there is still time to abort.

All careers begin with a period of exploration. The exploration stage occurs when employees learn what is expected. It is also a time for employees to gain personal insight and make sure that they have chosen the correct career. At this stage, many people still rely on external guidance. Think of a person's first supervisor and/or mentor as mission control helping to get a career off the ground. Alternatively, if individuals determine that they have chosen the wrong job or profession, this is one of the easiest times to abort and pick a new career.

This is also the time in a person's career where the individual both needs and should be looking for career guidance. The amount of technical training needed at this career stage depends on the individual's academic or technical preparation and the extent that an organization utilizes specific knowledge, skills, and abilities (KSAs). However, organizations can easily address this by a needs analysis. Individuals in the exploration stage are likely to need socialization. They need to learn what it means to be a member of a particular occupation and/or organization, and only through gaining this information and insight can they properly assess whether they are pursuing the correct career.

Establishment

Once individuals have committed to a specific career and learned what they need to be successful, they enter the establishment career stage. Continuing the rocket analogy, this is the person's career blasting off. Mission control (i.e., the employee's supervisor and/or mentor) takes a step back as the employee shifts from primarily learning to primarily contributing. In this stage, individuals clarify their worth both personally and organizationally as they begin to make individual contributions to the organization. In many ways, the establishment stage occurs when employees reach their highest point in terms of being an individual contributor. This is because they are no longer exploring learners but also not yet expected to pick up responsibilities for developing others. In terms of talent management and succession planning, this is when individuals confirm, or potentially have their last opportunity to show, whether they are high-potential employees.

The development needs at this stage are less technical and more personal. Having just gone through the exploration stage, individuals should be fully socialized into the organization or profession. At the same time, they should be new enough to not yet need major updating of technical skills. What they do need at this stage is to lay the foundation for those interpersonal skills required when the individual contributor of the establishment stage matures into the manager or leader of the later career stages. Another potential need at this stage is for help in establishing a healthy work–life balance. While people go through each of the career stages at their own pace, it is not uncommon for individuals in the establishment stage to be starting families.

Maintenance

The maintenance stage is a period of uncertainty. Using the rocket analogy, the initial fuel that launched the rocket is running low, which in career terms means that the initial KSAs and motivation that employees started their careers with has started to diminish. Just like a rocket, employees' careers can take one of three basic trajectories. Most managers hope that their employees will reach space or a high orbit, meaning that the employees continue to be successful and valuable contributors to achieving the organization's strategic goals. But just as a rocket requires a booster to break the inevitable pull of gravity, an individual's career needs to be reinvigorated to maintain this positive trajectory. Depending on the employee, this requires either career counseling, for motivation, or training, to maintain competency. One way for organizations to keep this from becoming an acute need is to develop a culture that fosters lifelong learning.

As that initial description suggests, the maintenance stage is filled with both opportunities and threats to a person's career. In terms of opportunities, people who have engaged in ongoing development of their technical and professional skills will find all that time and investment paying off. Having been noticed in the establishment stage, these individuals now find themselves assuming positions of greater status and authority. In addition to formal organizational roles, individuals in the maintenance stage, especially those continuing to advance, will find themselves becoming mentors to less experienced workers. So while technical training may still be relevant, there is also a need to develop and exercise managerial and interpersonal skills.

A culture of lifelong learning could help prevent either of the remaining options from occurring. One alternative to continued success occurs when an employee's career has lost momentum. This isn't necessarily a catastrophe. In the rocket analogy, the ship has reached a low but stable orbit. Although individual employees may be stuck in that orbit, they can still contribute to the organization. A problem emerges when the employees lack the basic drive or ability to maintain their KSAs. In this situation, there is no momentum for the employees' performance to meet organizational needs and expectations. If the career were a rocket, it would only be a matter of time before the pull of gravity dragged the ship back to Earth.

Unfortunately, the maintenance stage can be a hard time for many people. If someone is not being sought out by less experienced workers as a mentor, he or she may see those workers with their drive and up-to-date technical skills as threats. The extent of those threats, and the accompanying need for technical training, depends on whether the individual is experiencing a career plateau or career obsolescence.

Obsolescence

Between obsolescence and plateaus, obsolescence is the greater worry. **Obsolescence** is the process of becoming obsolete. In the rocket analogy, this is a person's career falling back to Earth—an especially strong concern for people in fields with rapidly advancing technology. For example, who wants a computer programmer who can only program in a language that is no longer used?

So, what should an organization do to prevent or handle obsolescence? The best prevention is ongoing performance evaluations and a culture of lifelong learning that encourages and supports employees to maintain their KSAs and motivation. If neither of these is present in an organization, then employee obsolescence may not become evident until the problem is acute. In these situations, the organization should still provide training and/or career counseling with the goal of alleviating the obsolescence. Unfortunately, some employees may not be trainable, either because they lack the motivation or because their existing knowledge and skill base is too outdated. In this situation, if the organization is not able or willing to internally transfer such employees, they will be at risk of being fired.

Plateaus

While people currently on a **career plateau** may be better off than those experiencing obsolescence, that doesn't mean that is a good place to be. Basically, in a plateaued career, there is no longer an expectation of upward progression, which can lead to considerable stress for the plateaued employee.[13] One reason for this is that a plateau may only be tenable while the work environment remains stable. Once things begin to change, it may be too late for someone to adapt and can easily result in obsolescence or redundancy, either of which could result in the person being fired.

Career End or Transition

All good things must come to an end, and careers are no different. In this chapter, we focus on planned ends and transitions. Ideally for employers, management knows when an employee has decided on leaving and can plan and prepare for the event. Employers also know ahead of time when they decide to downsize or otherwise fire an employee, but planning and preparation should already have gone into that decision. While this obviously creates a crisis for the employee, it is outside the scope of our discussion here. When employees decide to end their current career, they can engage in either disengagement or recycling.

The proper final stage of a career is disengagement. Retirement is often associated with this stage.[14] Organizationally, having employees who are involved in disengagement represents a potential threat for management. Some of the threats are known (e.g., needing to reassign specific duties or customers) and relatively easy to handle, but organizations need to prepare for what they do not know. Most longtime employees will have some combination of tacit knowledge and institutional memory. Unless efforts are made ahead of time to capture and transfer this knowledge, the loss will likely not become known until after the employee leaves. Therefore, organizations should have a process in place to address this threat. One factor that should help organizations to safeguard this knowledge is that having a legacy is often an interest of employees at the end of their careers. Therefore, the training and development efforts at this stage are not necessarily focused on the individual as the recipient but involve what knowledge that person can imbue others with before leaving.

Some scholars have suggested a fifth career stage.[15] Referred to as recycling, this stage involves a person starting over. While an encore career, when someone has disengaged, is one example, recycling can also occur during either the establishment or maintenance stages. In this regard, recycling is a person's response to a career plateau or obsolescence.[16] While people who recycle their careers don't lose their vast knowledge and experience, they nonetheless start over in a new career. One thing for organizations to consider is that an employee who chooses to engage in recycling does not need to leave. For employees who seek to recycle within their current organization, the organization should provide training and development opportunities that facilitate this transition.

CAREER PATHS

Often when people talk about how careers unfold, they discuss career progression over time. Typically, the word *progress* suggests forward and/or upward movement. While many careers move in an upward direction, not all do. Even those that move upward do not always do so linearly. Protean and boundaryless career theories can help explain why careers may not adhere to the classical metaphor of a career **ladder**, meaning that a career follows a linear upward progression generally prescribed by an organization or profession.

Mobility Patterns

Before discussing the various career theories that focus on career paths, we begin with generic patterns of career mobility.[17] These are presented in Exhibit 10-3 and as shown can be broadly categorized into traditional and nontraditional patterns. The traditional patterns are similar in that they focus on upward mobility. Individuals whose careers follow one of these patterns move to jobs with increasing levels of responsibility, authority, and/or status. By comparison, career moves within the nontraditional patterns can be in any direction.[18]

The two traditional career patterns are the "ladder" and the "fork." The "ladder" is the most basic pattern, and those who pursue it start at the bottom rung or position within an organization. These individuals then get promoted, moving up the "ladder" within that company throughout their career. The "fork" follows the same basic pattern, but with a key decision point of divergence. Careers that follow the "fork" pattern are often scientific or technical in nature. Individuals begin these careers with lots of advanced training, but once they start working, they are eventually faced with a reality check. Specifically, the currency of technical knowledge and skills erodes over time. This leads to the question of whether to update their knowledge and skills or move on to something else. Individuals who choose to update their knowledge and skills will continue following a linear pattern along a technical sequence of jobs. The main alternative to this technical sequence is a more administrative and managerial one. However, the progression along the managerial alternative is still basically linear. Further, people tend to make that choice only once because the cost of switching becomes higher as time passes. That is why this career path is considered to "fork." However, other than the decision point, the "fork" and the "ladder" are largely the same. Historically, the emergence of the MBA reflects this type of career progression because it was intended largely for individuals in technical or scientific professions who chose to become managers.

Exhibit 10-3 Mobility Patterns

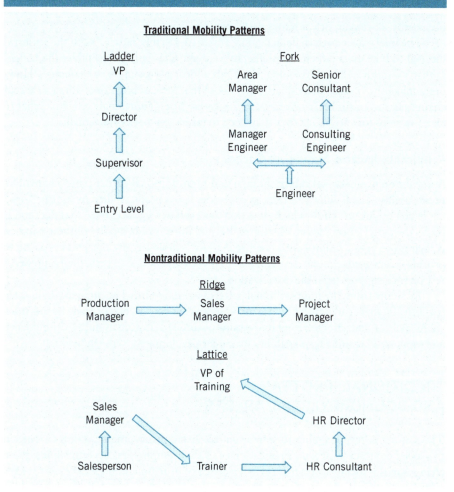

Source: Adapted from Herbert G. Heneman III, Timothy A. Judge, and John D. Kammeyer-Mueller, *Staffing Organizations*, 7th ed. (New York: McGraw-Hill Irwin, 2012).

By contrast, we classify the remaining career patterns in Exhibit 10-3 as nontraditional. These are what we refer to here as the "ridge" and "lattice" paths. The key difference between the "ridge" and traditional career patterns is that the "ridge" focuses on horizontal career movement. Individuals choose a career that follows the "ridge" pattern because they desire the opportunity to develop new KSAs and/or experience new challenges more than acquiring more responsibility, authority, or status that one gets with a "ladder" career. The choice of the word *ridge* to describe this pattern is also purposeful. One could conceivably describe this pattern as a plateau, but given the choices and movement reflected in this pattern, it is very different from the issue of career plateaus discussed as a threat to a person's career. Also, like a mountain ridge, these careers are not perfectly level, whereas a career that has plateaued, at best, stays at the same level without necessarily movement or conscious decisions.

The final career pattern depicted in Exhibit 10-3 is the "lattice," both the least traditional and the most difficult to predict movement. The "lattice" resembles the "ridge" in that it is motivated by developing new KSAs and/or addressing new challenges. However, unlike the "ridge," individuals who choose the "lattice" are more willing to accept changes in responsibility, authority, and/or status. These individuals recognize that to take two steps forward or up, they may need to take a step back or diagonally.

Predictability and Managing Careers

A key difference between the traditional and nontraditional career patterns involves predictability. The hallmark of the career "ladder" is its predictability. As for the "fork," while you might not know which direction a person will choose, once that decision is made, the pattern becomes much clearer. Related to the predictability of these patterns is their more organization-centric nature. As such, employers are in a good position to provide career guidance and development to their workers, and in turn, their employees rely on such support from the organization.

By comparison, the nontraditional patterns are inherently less predictable, in large part because these career patterns are more dependent on the choices made by individuals. As such, organizations are not in the same position to provide useful career guidance and support. This shifts responsibility for career development to the individual.

TRADITIONAL, PROTEAN, AND BOUNDARYLESS CAREERS

The shifting in responsibility for career guidance and management reflects changes in the social contract between organizations and their employees. Accompanying these changes in the social contract is the emergence of protean and boundaryless careers. A key characteristic of both of these theories is that individuals take a more active role in managing their own careers. Another commonality is that both theories position themselves as alternatives to a traditional career, and both theories conceptualize traditional careers in a similar fashion. In addition, five other factors that contrast traditional from protean and boundaryless careers are presented in Exhibit 10-4.

Although there are important differences between protean and boundaryless theories, discussed later in this section, according to the factors listed in Exhibit 10-4, they are largely similar and therefore for simplicity presented as a single contrast to traditional careers. First to follow up on the commonality already mentioned between protean and boundaryless careers is responsibility for career management. While those pursuing a protean and/or boundaryless career take responsibility for career management, individuals with traditional careers continue to rely on their employing organization for

Exhibit 10-4 Contrasting Traditional Careers to Protean and Boundaryless Careers

Career Aspect	Traditional	Protean and Boundaryless
Responsibility for Management	Organization	Individual
Social Contract	Security for Loyalty	Employability for Flexibility
Common Mobility Patterns	Ladder and Fork	Ridge and Lattice
Training and Development	Greater Reliance on Formal Training	Greater Reliance on Job Experiences and Relationships
Expertise	Know How	Learn How
Assessing Success	Promotions and Raises	Psychological Success

career management. In part, this reflects differences in the social contract between organizations and their employees. Protean and boundaryless employees work under the assumption that their employers will continue to provide opportunities as long as they continue to remain marketable. By comparison, traditional workers generally expect that their employers will reward their loyalty with job security. These factors help to explain expected career patterns, with traditional employees generally adhering to the "ladder" and "fork" patterns whereas the alternative patterns of the "ridge" and "lattice" are more common among protean and boundaryless workers.

The three remaining factors presented in Exhibit 10-4 all relate back to one of the first three. For example, it should not surprise you that traditional workers who look to their employers for career management also rely more on formal training. A similar situation exists regarding how to describe career-related expertise. First, *learn how* focuses on someone's ability to adapt, an important characteristic for protean and boundaryless workers who work under a social contract of employability for flexibility. Second, *know how* focuses on someone's current expertise and is more consistent with the security for loyalty exchange under which traditional workers operate. Finally, it makes sense that traditional workers who follow "ladder" and "fork" career patterns also measure their success through promotions and raises. By contrast, the rewards of the "ridge" and "lattice" patterns are less measurable, which increases the importance of psychological success, consistent with protean and boundaryless careers.

Traditional

The traditional career is an organizational one. The foundation of traditional careers is built on the pillars of loyalty and security. Traditional employees remain loyal to their employers and in return are rewarded with continued job security. Other characteristics of traditional careers include a sense of predictability and an emphasis on hierarchical growth. The metaphor of a career ladder where a person moves up within an organization in a linear progression, step by step, epitomizes the traditional career. A by-product of this is that individuals do not need to manage their own career development. The organization knows what it needs and makes sure that the employees slated for promotion get the training and development required.

While the traditional career model may have competition, many employees still continue to desire and pursue it,[19] but this can be problematic. Today, organizations often lack the ability and/or desire to support such traditional careers. Organizations often require more from their employees than just loyalty and, in more competitive and turbulent environments, cannot offer the same level of job security as they did in the past. Organizations want to be more flexible than what is required by static career ladders and may no longer be as confident in directing the training and development of their employees. However, they still need to be cognizant of the fact that not every talented worker will be protean or boundaryless, and therefore should accommodate the career needs of all employees.

Boundaryless

A **boundaryless** career is not necessarily limited or focused on a single organization. This is in contrast to the traditional career, largely defined or bounded by a single employer. A career can be considered boundaryless in one of two ways: physical or psychological. While many people are both physically and psychologically boundaryless in how they pursue their careers, it is possible to be one and not the other.[20]

The most visible aspect of a boundaryless career is the physical dimension. Someone who pursues a physically boundaryless career engages in a higher level of mobility than someone in a traditional career. Two important aspects of this mobility are that it is voluntary and purposeful. Physically boundaryless workers use their job mobility as a method for achieving growth and personal goals, as opposed to wayward individuals who have many jobs because they lack the ability to maintain one.

However, individuals are not required to change employers in order to pursue a boundaryless career. A good example of this is Ursula Burns, introduced in the opening vignette. Although she spent her entire career at Xerox, when she talks about her career, it sounds very boundaryless. In addition to physical boundarylessness, a career can be psychologically boundaryless. Individuals such as Burns who are psychologically boundaryless maintain an orientation or openness to change and growth. So even if they choose to stay with the same employer, they pursue their own path as opposed to just climbing the next rung of an organizational career ladder. This seems like a fitting description for a mechanical engineer who became an assistant to an executive on the way to becoming the CEO of a Fortune 500 firm.

Protean

Another way of envisioning your career is with **protean** career theory. This theory provides an additional contrast to the traditional organizational career. That said, protean careers are distinct from boundaryless ones. While many people's careers are both protean and boundaryless, it is possible for a career to be consistent with one but not the other.[21] Besides the contrast with traditional careers, another similarity to boundaryless theory is that someone can be protean along one of two distinct dimensions: self-directed or value-driven.[22]

Self-direction is one of the defining dimensions of nontraditional careers. This means that individuals proactively manage their careers—a response both to personal desires for greater control and to recognition of the reality that employers are less likely to serve that function. Similar to the psychological dimension of boundaryless careers, individuals can be protean without having to change employers.

The other dimension of protean careers is that they are value-driven. In a value-driven career, a person intentionally makes career decisions such that employment opportunities align with personal values. Given this focus, it is not surprising that individuals who pursue protean careers are more focused on growth and personal fulfillment and are less concerned with more traditional status-oriented measures of success.

CAREER ANCHORS

While it is important to have a sense of an employee's career path, it is also valuable to be aware of the underlying motivation driving career decisions. This aspect of individual careers can be explained through Schein's theory of **career anchors**.[23] Career anchors refer to how people understand themselves relative to their career, and comprise perceptions regarding talents, abilities, values, and motives. Career anchors develop as a function of an individual's early career and life experiences. Once formed, they remain relatively stable for the rest of one's working life.

Despite the name, career anchors should not be thought of as a drag on a career. Most of the time, people do not think about their career anchors and may not even be aware that they have one. Career anchors become tangible when people reach a critical juncture in their careers, and they help to shape what direction to go or decision to make. While individuals may make career choices that are not congruent with their career anchors, the theory postulates that people experience greater satisfaction and more positive outcomes to the extent that there is congruence.

Currently, eight career anchors are commonly accepted: autonomy and independence, security and stability, lifestyle, technical and functional competence, managerial competence, entrepreneurship and creativity, service and dedication, and pure challenge.[24] Generally, individuals are considered to manifest just one of the eight anchors. One way of understanding the differences between the anchors, as shown in Exhibit 10-5, is to sort them into three categories: talent-based, needs-based, and value-based anchors.[25]

Exhibit 10-5 Categories of Career Anchors

Talent-Based	Needs-Based	Value-Based
Technical/Functional Competence	Autonomy and Independence	Service and Dedication to a Cause
Managerial Competence	Security and Stability	Pure Challenge
Entrepreneurial Creativity	Lifestyle	

The first category identified in Exhibit 10-5 is talent-based career anchors, including technical/functional competence, managerial competence, and entrepreneurial creativity. A primary focus on one's type of work is a common element of these anchors. The most purely work-focused anchor is technical/functional competence. The content of the work itself matters the most to people with this anchor. By contrast, individuals who manifest the managerial competence anchor are more excited when given the opportunity to solve problems and/or build a team to achieve a goal. While those with an entrepreneurial creativity anchor could also be considered problem solvers, they are more focused on the act of creation than on managing an existing project.

Autonomy and independence, security and stability, and lifestyle are all examples of needs-based anchors. A common thread among these three anchors is that work should accommodate individuals' personal lives and desires. Individuals who manifest the autonomy and independence anchor desire careers free of organizational constraints in which they can control when, where, and how they work. If given the choice, these people would choose employment situations that provided more freedom than opportunities for promotion. By contrast, individuals with security and stability anchors seek to become embedded within their organizations. They prefer the loyalty for security, a social contract consistent with traditional careers (as discussed in the previous section). The last of the needs-based anchors is lifestyle, and individuals with this anchor are primarily motivated to find employment situations that maximize work–life balance.

The remaining career anchors, service and dedication to a cause and pure challenge, comprise the value-based category. These anchors differ somewhat from the others in that they focus on how individuals identify with their careers. Individuals who develop a service and dedication to a cause anchor want more than anything else to be in a situation where they feel they are making a difference in the world even if it means that they are not making the best use of their skills. By contrast, what drives those with a pure challenge anchor is arguably less noble albeit more personal. These people are driven to overcome obstacles and to see problems purely as things to be solved, without the focus on bringing people together (managerial competence) or creation (entrepreneurial creativity).

SUCCESSION PLANNING

While all organizations hire people who they feel match their needs and have the potential to be successful, not all employees are equal. Even for organizations with the reputation, resources, and procedures to recruit and select the best prospects, some employees will be better than others. The best of the best, those who exceed expectations in their current positions and show promise for leadership and advancement, are known as high-potential employees. Identifying and cultivating these employees, sometimes referred to as being on the fast track, is a critical function for organizations to ensure their continued success. In addition to training and development, this includes building loyalty and commitment to the organization.

The process of identifying and cultivating these employees is the goal of **succession planning**. Through effective succession planning, management will ensure its ability to internally source replacements for leaders who retire or otherwise leave the organization. This makes effective succession planning an important strategic activity. One factor that makes it so critical is that not all talent is interchangeable. Rather, what constitutes talent for an organization depends on the demands of an industry, and the specific needs and culture of an organization.[26] Therefore, if the succession planning process is effectively managed, then the organization's talent will be rare, valuable, imitable, and non-substitutable. This combination of factors means that effective succession planning can lead to a sustained competitive advantage for the organization.

Consequently, organizations that engage in succession planning need to do so thoughtfully. For example, it is too easy to assume that the person who should be selected for a promotion is the one who performs best in his or her current position. But just as is the case with selecting the trainer for on-the-job training, this could be a mistake. The decision to simply promote these employees can result in the realization of the **Peter principle**. According to the Peter principle, good employees continue to be promoted until they rise to a position where they lack the needed ability and as a result fail in their new job. Essentially, they are promoted into incompetence[27]—a problem both for the otherwise successful employee and for the organization that now has an incompetent leader.

Approaches to Succession Planning

So how do organizations engage in effective succession planning to ensure they have the next generation of leaders that they need? To begin, there are two approaches to succession planning: the heir model and the pool model. These approaches are not mutually exclusive, and organizations can pursue both at the same time.

Heir model.

By its name, the **heir model** creates a royal image to this approach to succession planning. This approach can also be described as replacement planning.[28] While this approach doesn't necessarily target a specific organizational "ruler," it tends to limit succession planning to key leadership positions within an organization. Consistent with this metaphor, there exists an heir apparent or a "crowned prince" to take over when the current "monarch" or leader passes or retires. These heirs are groomed for their eventual promotions, and their identities may be known. While it is prudent for organizations to identify and groom backups or spares, this does not always occur. Also, depending on the organization, this can be a rather informal process. For example, in an entrepreneurial firm or family business, the succession plan may literally be the heir (i.e., a child or close relation to the founder or owner).[29]

Pool model.

As its names implies, the **pool model** takes a deeper approach to succession planning. Where the heir model focuses on specific positions, the pool model instead is concerned with the overall robustness of the workforce.[30] While individuals may still be identified as likely to receive a promotion, it deemphasizes the importance of any one person to the process. Rather, it serves to ensure that when an opening occurs, someone will be in place who is ready to be promoted. Given the wider scope of this approach, it needs, and tends, to be more formal than the heir model.

Methods and Tools to Conduct Succession Planning

Those taking a formal approach to succession planning should start by defining what constitutes a talented and/or a high-potential employee. If organizations fail to have a working definition, then it will be difficult to effectively identify and develop employees to become the next generation of leaders. Therefore, conducting a needs analysis in order to define talent should be considered a best practice for succession planning.[31] Given the leadership focus of succession planning, organizations should look to develop a competency model[32] for organizational leaders.

The remainder of this section focuses on useful tools and methods for the succession planning process. Regardless of the tool or method selected, each will benefit from conducting a needs analysis. The tools and methods discussed in this chapter include assessment centers, promotability ratings, and depth charts. Assessment centers, discussed first, represent a more formal approach to the heir model, although they are not limited to this model. By comparison, promotability ratings are useful for those utilizing the pool model. Finally, depth charts reflect a more integrative approach.

Assessment centers.

One of the most effective ways to determine the potential of employees is to put them through an **assessment center**. Although assessment centers are effective for identifying employee potential, organizations tend to limit the extent to which they use them. This has to do with their complexity. It takes considerable resources, both time and money, to develop and then conduct assessment centers. For example, a person can spend multiple days participating in a single assessment center, and this generates significant amounts of data to be analyzed. For this reason, assessment centers are often limited to more critical functions (i.e., succession planning vs. more general employee selection) and key positions for an organization.

While ideally they are tailored to the organization, assessment centers share some common characteristics. First, they involve multiple methods for assessing individual ability. Common methods include simulations, in-basket exercises, group discussion, and case analyses. Although these methods also apply to training and development (see Chapter 7 for an explanation of each), the goal here is to determine an individual's potential, as opposed to increasing his or her human capital in the assessment center. Other commonly used methods include interviews, tests, and inventories.[33] While organizations also typically use these methods for applicant selection, this makes sense given that succession planning eventually leads to promotion decisions. Second, multiple assessors rate the individuals who take part in an assessment center. These assessors then provide a report detailing the strengths, weaknesses, and potential of the individual. Finally, while assessment centers should be tailored to the needs of an organization, the process itself is standardized.

Exhibit 10-6 Examples of Commonly Measured Attributes in Assessment Centers

Attribute	Explanation
Behavioral Flexibility	Ability to modify behavior and achieve a goal when confronted by an opposing attitude, behavior, belief, or opinion
Interpersonal Sensitivity	Evidence in behavior of consideration for the needs and feelings of others
Judgment	Ability to make decisions and develop courses of action
Organizational Sensitivity	Understanding of how actions and decisions will impact the organization
Perseverance	Ability to maintain efforts until desired goal is achieved
Tolerance for Stress	Stability of performance under pressure

Source: Adapted from Robert M. Guion and Scott Highhouse, *Essentials of Personnel Assessment and Selection* (Mahwah, NJ: Erlbaum, 2006).

Besides employing similar methods, assessment centers generally share the common goal of identifying and providing information to help develop the next generation of organizational leaders. While organizations may take advantage of assessment centers to rate technical knowledge and skills, their main value for succession planning is to evaluate less tangible attributes that contribute to someone being an effective leader within the organization. Again, while organizations may define successful leaders differently, some attributes are commonly measured in an assessment center. Examples and definitions of these are presented in Exhibit 10-6.

According to the International Taskforce on Assessment Center Guidelines,[34] a proper assessment center requires 10 essential elements, listed in Exhibit 10-7. Further, it is reasonable to categorize these elements into three components: designing, evaluating, and executing. We start with executing because it involves only one element, and this element should apply to all other parts of the assessment center. Specifically, assessment centers should be standardized. This means that all individuals who participate in an assessment center are provided with the same opportunity to display their potential and have it evaluated.

Designing an assessment center involves multiple steps: conduct a needs analysis (systematic analysis to determine job-relevant behavioral constructs), classify this information (behavioral classification), and then operationalize it (linkages between behavioral constructs and assessment center components). This last step basically means to plan or identify how the behavioral constructs will be assessed. Regarding components, as mentioned, assessment centers should have multiple methods, and one of these should be a simulation.

The evaluating component can be divided into two parts. The first part deals with the people who will do the evaluating. Basically, multiple people should do the evaluation, and they should be properly trained.[35] The second part focuses on the evaluation itself. This involves a systematic procedure to initially record and score individual behaviors

Exhibit 10-7 10 Essential Elements of an Assessment Center

Designing
1. Systematic Analysis to Determine Job-Relevant Behavioral Constructs
2. Behavioral Classification
3. Linkages Between Behavioral Constructs and Assessment Center Components
4. Simulation Exercises
5. Multiple Assessment Center Components

Evaluating
6. Assessors
7. Assessor Training
8. Recording and Scoring Behavior
9. Data Integration

Executing
10. Standardization

and employee potential, and then a process for integrating the responses from the individual assessors in order to generate a report.

In addition to these elements, organizations need to keep some ethical guidelines in mind when deciding to use an assessment center.[36] First, participation in an assessment center should be informed, which means individuals will know that they are participating in one, why they are participating, and what rights they have. Included among these rights is receiving a copy of the results and/or report from the assessment center, and surety that the data, once collected, are properly protected.

Promotability ratings.

Although not as intensive as an assessment center, promotability ratings also provide managers with valuable information for determining how individual employees fit into an organization's overall succession plan. While promotability ratings may be determined during the performance evaluation process, they are distinct. Because performance evaluations focus on an individual's current performance, using them for succession decisions makes them vulnerable to the Peter principle (i.e., promoting people who lack the ability to succeed). Therefore, organizations should limit the use of performance evaluations as part of succession planning.

Instead, organizations should utilize promotability ratings. As the name implies, these ratings focus on the perceived ability or potential of individuals if they were to be promoted. While people's current level of performance may factor into their readiness to be promoted, the promotability rating encompasses an overall assessment of one's potential (e.g., inclusive of interpersonal skills and political savvy).[37] There are multiple ways to rate someone's promotability—for example, single numerical listings (e.g., 0 = *not at all promotable* to 5 = *highly promotable*) or categorizations (e.g., *ready* or *needs development*).

Within the general concept of promotability ratings is the **nine-box matrix**, an example of which is presented in Exhibit 10-8. As the name implies, employees are sorted into one of nine boxes or categories ordered along two dimensions. One dimension is the employee's current level of performance, and the second dimension is the employee's assessed potential (i.e., readiness for promotion).[38] Each dimension has three levels: poor, average, and high. This creates a 3 × 3 matrix, which gives the nine-box matrix its name. In addition to providing information about an individual employee, the nine-box matrix provides an overview of the robustness of a workforce. Among the goals of this process is to get an honest assessment of the workforce. Therefore, employees should be sorted naturally and not according to a forced distribution.

While the boxes of the matrix are fairly standard, the names used in this chapter for each box are intended to help you understand the type of employee it represents. Understanding the type of employee represented by each box of the matrix will help ensure that organizations make good succession decisions. The four corner boxes represent the employees who tend to be of greatest interest or concern to organizations: resident experts, high potentials, diamonds in the rough, and mulligans. Employees who fall along the inner axis are to some degree average but still important contributors to an organization's productivity.

In discussing the four corners of the nine-box matrix, we begin with the top left and work clockwise. *Resident expert* is the name given to those with high performance but poor potential. These are employees you want to keep, but you want to keep them where they are. Promoting a resident expert risks invoking the Peter principle (i.e., promoting someone into incompetence). The top-right box is the home of the high-potential employee, those with both high performance and high potential. These are the coveted employees in the succession planning process, and the ones you want to cultivate (i.e., focus on their development and commitment). The bottom right is the home of the diamonds in the rough, employees with high potential but low performance.

Exhibit 10-8 Nine-Box Matrix

	High	Resident Experts	Technically Ready	High Potentials
	Average	Technically Sufficient	Medians	Culturally Ready
Performance	Poor	Mulligans	Culturally Sufficient	Diamonds in the Rough
		Poor	Average	High
			Potential	

If you remember the childhood story, the ugly duckling (aka diamond in the rough) turns out to be a beautiful swan, but unfortunately is the wrong place. Theoretically, these employees will prosper if transferred or promoted; however, it is hard for people to see the sparkling diamond (i.e., potential) if they are focused on the uncut rock (i.e., performance). The final corner is where the mulligans reside. *Mulligan*, a term from golf, refers to a do-over because of a mistake. Lacking both potential and performance, it is arguably better to replace (i.e., do over) than develop these employees.

While the corners may be the focus of interest, it is important not to forget the inner cross. Within the cross, the technical skills refer to ability. The idea suggests that the technically ready are likely to be promoted based on their ability rather than their organizational fit. While the technically sufficient may not be promoted, they maintain their employment based on their ability rather than their organizational fit. The converse is true with the culturally sufficient, who are poor performers but may retain their positions based on being an otherwise good fit with the organization. By comparison, the culturally ready may be promoted based on the belief that they have the right organizational fit, and that what they are missing to be a true high potential can be addressed in training. Finally, the medians represent the middle ground. They do not stand out in any respect but are nevertheless good employees.

Depth charts.

The final tool discussed in this chapter that organizations can use as part of the succession planning process is the **depth chart**. The depth chart integrates the heir and pool approaches to succession planning. Consistent with the heir approach, it designates all the positions of the succession planning process. For each position included in the succession planning process, the depth chart identifies the heir(s). In addition to identifying the heir(s), the depth chart provides information on promotability, which reflects the contribution of the pool approach.

An example of a depth chart is presented in Exhibit 10-9. As can be inferred from the exhibit, there is an emphasis on identifying multiple people as potential successors for any given position. The number of potential successors is referred to as the organization's bench strength. Terms like *depth chart* and *bench strength* conjure an image of a sports team, a useful analogy. The goal of the depth chart is to ensure that an organization has people ready to take over when a player or leader leaves the field, court, or organization. Ideally, organizations will have deep and strong benches so that they can effectively manage potential instability caused by turnover within the leadership team. This is an important goal for organizations, even those with a good history and culture for employee development, to ensure the ability to meet future challenges.[39]

Looking at the information displayed in Exhibit 10-9, what inferences can we make about this organization's ability to effectively manage succession? First, a goal of the organization appears to be identifying three people as potential successors for each position. Designating multiple people as potential successors is important because it gives the organization options, particularly if one of the employees identified leaves or otherwise does not wish to be promoted. There is no magic number of people who should

Exhibit 10-9 Example of an Organizational Depth Chart

CEO
Current: Bruce Springsteen
Successors:
1. Tyler Smith (R)
2. Fred Gold (ND)
3. Chris Wallace (ND)

CFO
Current: Fred Gold
Successors:
1. Julie Silver (R)
2. Adam Cruz (ND)
3. _____

COO
Current: Tyler Smith
Successors:
1. Regina Cooper (ND)
2. Chris Wallace (ND)
3. Max Hill (ND)

VP Finance	VP Accounting	VP Production	VP HR
Current: Adam Cruz	Current: Julie Silver	Current: Regina Cooper	Current Chris Wallace
Successors:	Successors:	Successors:	Successors:
1. Peter Fox (ND)	1. Chris Petty (ND)	1. Max Hill (R)	1. Dana Pryde (R)
2. Sam Coates (NSD)	2. _____	2. Frank Stamp (R)	2. Jonah Meeks (ND)
3. _____	3. _____	3. Alex Quick (NSD)	3. Megan Clark (ND)

Notations: R = Ready; ND = Needs Development; NSD = Needs Significant Development

be on a depth chart. As the example shows, just because you have slots on a depth chart, you don't necessarily have people identified. Further, just because individuals are on the depth chart, they aren't necessarily ready to be promoted.

Now let us look more specifically at the positions and people. The place with the greatest bench strength is with the vice president (VP) of production where more than one potential successor is deemed ready for promotion. By comparison, there appears to be a severe lack of bench strength for the COO track (including the vice presidents of finance and accounting). No matter who is chosen to be the next COO, at least one position will be backfilled with someone who needs development. Besides showing which employee needs development, depth charts can also distinguish how much, and/or what types, of development employees need. This example simply distinguishes between those needing development and those needing significant development, but other organizations may prefer to have more specific information.

New Careers and Succession Planning

An implicit characteristic of succession planning, particularly with the need to identify and cultivate high-potential employees, is consistency with a more traditional career perspective. Unfortunately, this creates a dilemma for organizations.[40] On the one hand, organizations seek to develop their high potentials and depend on them to remain with the organization. On the other hand, employees now have a propensity to pursue protean and boundaryless careers that undermines their cultivation. Therefore, organizations that wish to have effective succession planning need to understand and manage this dilemma.

As discussed earlier, traditional careers are organizationally focused. This means that much of the guidance and responsibility for career management and development comes from the organization. This is both consistent with and critical for succession planning as organizational definitions and needs for leadership are relatively idiosyncratic. This is not a problem for people pursuing a traditional career because the social contract is one where the organization ensures job security in exchange for their loyalty.

Unfortunately, the cultivation of high-potential employees is not entirely consistent with new conceptualizations of careers (i.e., protean or boundaryless). Individuals pursuing protean or boundaryless careers are more self-directed in their career development and place less emphasis on continued organizational tenure. These aspects of protean and boundaryless careers would seem to undermine the goals and effectiveness of succession planning. One could further argue that employees identified as high potential, because of their very potential, have a greater ability and opportunity to pursue a protean or boundaryless career, which exacerbates this dilemma.

While this dilemma does exist, there are ways for organizations to minimize or mitigate it. The first methods involve the selection process. There are ways to assess the degree to which applicants are protean or boundaryless in their career orientations. This allows organizations to screen for career orientation in the selection process. Alternatively, while succession planning emphasizes the utilization of internal labor markets, organizations should remain open to bringing in external talent even at higher levels in the organization.

A third option is to overtly segment the workforce.[41] This means taking the classification from an exercise like the nine-box matrix to the next level. Employees designated as part of the talent pool, consisting of high potentials (but possibly including members of the adjacent boxes in the nine-box matrix), will be treated differently than those who do not make the cut. The preferential development of these employees would reduce turnover because it is rewarding and validating, signals future organizational rewards, and/or develops a reciprocal relationship. However, organizations should consider the ethical and practical implications of segmenting the workforce for employees not designated as members of the talent pool.[42] This could lead to resentment, turnover, and charges of discrimination if not handled carefully and thoughtfully.

CHAPTER SUMMARY

This chapter presented multiple ways for understanding how careers take shape from both theoretical and succession planning perspectives. It is important to say *take shape* rather than *evolve* because a career changes over time as the result of decisions, whether initiated by an individual or an organization. Regardless of where a career is lived, there is a general life cycle as outlined by career stage theory. All careers start in a period of exploration. Assuming that they are not brought to a premature end (e.g., termination), a career will mature and move through the establishment and maintenance stages before ending either through disengagement or recycling. Each stage has its own training and development needs and challenges. For example, workers in the exploration stage benefit from training and development activities that focus on orientation and socialization. Then when people's careers mature into the maintenance stage, they need more technical training to avoid plateaus and obsolescence.

Training and development activities for individuals with protean and/or boundaryless careers are less obvious, mainly because these theories focus on how workers perceive and manage their careers. These workers take responsibility for their training and development and are more interested in opportunities and psychological success than formal promotions. In both cases, these careers contrast with more traditional ones where employees continue to look to their employers for career guidance. Knowing the career orientation of your employees is useful when engaging in succession planning, discussed in the next chapter.

Career anchors theory provides a little more guidance as it offers insight into people's career motivation. Career anchors serve to ground one's career identity and decisions. Although there are eight distinct anchors, they are organized into three categories: talent-based anchors (technical/functional competence, managerial, or entrepreneurial creativity), needs-based anchors (autonomy and independence, security and stability, or lifestyle), and value-based anchors (service and dedication to a cause or pure challenge). Employees will be most motivated to participate in training and development activities that align with or further their career anchor.

Shifting from theory to practice, succession planning and the identification of high-potential employees is an important development function for organizations concerned with making sure that they have the right and adequate number of leaders. When approaching the succession planning process, organizations can take an heir perspective, which focuses on a few key positions and individuals, or a pool perspective, which takes a wider view of the workforce. Both perspectives are useful and not mutually exclusive. This becomes apparent when looking at a depth chart as a way of organizing the succession management process.

Other methods and tools that are useful to consider include the assessment center and promotability ratings. Assessment centers are used to determine the ability and potential of employees being considered as future leaders. While a good way to determine employee potential, assessment centers are complex and require significant resources, which tends to limit their use. More generally, organizations can utilize promotability ratings, in addition to traditional performance evaluations. Focusing on promotability as a separate issue from performance is important because employees who are good in their current position may lack the competencies to succeed in a higher-level position. This is why a nine-box matrix, with separate axes for performance and potential, is a useful tool. Further, the Peter principle reminds us of the danger of promoting someone into incompetence and the importance of effective succession planning.

KEY TERMS

Assessment center. A process for identifying talent and developmental needs of employees as part of succession planning.

Boundaryless. A type of career where a person engages in a high level of mobility (physically boundaryless) and/or openness to opportunities (psychologically boundaryless).

Career anchor. A person's underlying motivation that drives career decisions.

Career plateau. Occurs when a person's career ceases to advance.

Career stage. A career theory with a temporal orientation that divides careers into four phases.

Depth chart. A method of identifying and organizing an organization's talent as part of succession planning.

Heir model. An approach to succession planning that focuses on key individuals and positions.

Ladder. The most traditional career pattern where the career follows a predictable path of upward progression typically within a single organization.

Nine-box matrix. A tool for succession planning where employees are categorized based on both performance and potential.

Obsolescence. Occurs when a person's key knowledge, skills, and abilities have become obsolete.

Peter principle. The idea that successful people are promoted into positions of incompetence.

Pool model. An approach to succession planning that looks to develop a robust workforce ready to assume leadership positions.

Protean. A type of career that is self-directed and/or value-driven.

Succession planning. The process an organization engages in to make sure that it has the internal talent ready to become the next generation of leaders it needs.

END-OF-CHAPTER QUESTIONS AND EXERCISES

Discussion Questions

1. When you graduate, will you be starting a job or a career?
2. Which is a bigger threat to a person's career, a plateau or obsolescence?
3. Identify and discuss the career paths or directions that you are both most and least likely to take.
4. Discuss which type of career you would prefer (i.e., traditional, boundaryless, or protean).
5. What role or obligation does an organization have to provide employees with career guidance and development?
6. Discuss how careers are anchored and whether this is good or bad.
7. Why do organizations engage in succession planning?
8. Why should organizations be concerned with the Peter principle, and how should they respond to its potential?
9. Is it better to organize succession planning using an heir or pool approach?
10. How would you construct and use an assessment center?
11. How does a nine-box matrix facilitate succession planning?

12. Why do protean and boundaryless careers create a dilemma for succession planning?

Ethical Scenario

Welcome Back, Lana?

Since graduating college 12 years ago, Sara had worked for Dynasty Communications. Over the years, she consistently received developmental opportunities and a series of promotions. Although the company didn't have a formal succession plan, she was clearly moving up the corporate ladder. Recently, she had a meeting where Leo Luthans, the company's founder and CEO, asked her to take a developmental assignment so she would be ready for an expected opening at the VP level. Sara believed that all her loyalty was paying off and felt justified for turning down offers from other companies that had tried to hire her away. So, a few months later when Lana Luthans, a niece of Leo's who had left the company years ago to open her own business, which had recently failed, was named VP, Sara felt betrayed.

1. How would you describe Sara's career based on the career theories discussed in this chapter?
2. What do you think about the decision to hire Lana rather than promote Sara?
3. What advice would you provide for managing succession at Dynasty Communications?

10.1 Are You Traditional, Protean, and/or Boundaryless?

The following 27 questions will help you understand to what extent your personal attitudes are consistent with a traditional, protean, and/or boundaryless career.[43] There are no right answers, so respond as honestly as possible. Instructions for how to score the survey are provided at the end.

Using the following scale, write the number in the space after the statement that most accurately states how true it is for you.

1. To a little or no extent
2. To a limited extent
3. To some extent
4. To a considerable extent
5. To a great extent

1. When development opportunities have not been offered by my company, I've sought them out on my own. ____
2. I am responsible for my success or failure in my career. ____
3. Overall, I have a very independent, self-directed career. ____
4. Freedom to choose my own career path is one of my most important values. ____
5. I am in charge of my own career. ____
6. Ultimately, I depend upon myself to move my career forward. ____
7. Where my career is concerned, I am very much "my own person." ____
8. In the past, I have relied more on myself than others to find a new job when necessary. ____
9. I navigate my own career, based on my personal priorities, as opposed to my employer's priorities. ____
10. It doesn't matter much to me how other people evaluate the choices I make in my career. ____
11. What's most important to me is how I feel about my career success, not how other people feel about it. ____
12. I'll follow my own conscience if my company asks me to do something that goes against my values. ____
13. What I think about what is right in my career is more important to me than what my company thinks. ____

14. In the past, I have sided with my own values when the company has asked me to do something I don't agree with. _____

15. I seek job assignments that allow me to learn something new. _____

16. I would enjoy working on projects with people across many organizations.

17. I enjoy job assignments that require me to work outside of the organization. _____

18. I like tasks at work that require me to work beyond my own department. _____

19. I enjoy working with people outside of my organization. _____

20. I enjoy jobs that require me to interact with people in many different organizations. _____

21. I have sought opportunities in the past that allow me to work outside the organization. _____

22. I am energized in new experiences and situations. _____

23. I like the predictability that comes with working continuously for the same organization. _____

24. I would feel very lost if I couldn't work for my current organization. _____

25. I prefer to stay in a company I am familiar with rather than look for employment elsewhere. _____

26. If my organization provided lifetime employment, I would never desire to seek work in other organizations. _____

27. In my ideal career, I would work for only one organization. _____

Scoring: For each of the following dimensions, a higher number denotes a more protean or boundaryless attitude. Lower numbers are associated with more traditional career attitudes.

Sum questions 1–8. This is how protean you are on the self-directed career management dimension.

Sum questions 9–14. This is how protean you are on the values-driven dimension.

Sum questions 15–22. This is how boundaryless you are on the boundaryless mindset dimension.

Sum questions 23–27. This is how boundaryless you are on the organizational mobility preference dimension.

10.2 What's Your Anchor?

You have two options to gain insight into your personal career anchor.

Option 1: You can take the official assessment. This will provide you with the best information; however, there is a fee that you will need to pay in order to take it. If you are interested in this option, visit www.careeranchorsonline.com/SCA/about.do?open=prod.

Option 2: You can take the career orientations inventory, available from https://www.ucc.ie/en/media/support/disabilitysupportservice/careers/CareerOrientationsExercise.pdf. It is not as scientific but will provide some insight into your career.

10.3 Your Next Move

Although the first career stage is labeled exploration, you are engaging in many exploratory activities now as a student. There are many development tools out there to help you determine if you are in the right major and/or focused on the careers that best match your interests. Here is a link to one such tool: www.mynextmove.org.

My Next Move is connected to Onetonline.org (discussed in Chapter 3 as a way to conduct a job-level needs analysis). After completing the survey, it will direct you to those careers that most closely match your vocational interests. Some questions to consider:

a. How similar is your three-letter code to those of others in the class?
b. How well does this confirm your plans?
c. What was the most surprising career option listed?

10.4 In Her Words

Hear more of Ursula Burns's story at www.makers.com/blog/how-ursula-burns-worked-her-way-ceo-fortune-500-company.

While there, search through and listen to the career stories of other women. Then reflect upon:

a. How do their stories increase your understanding of the career theories discussed in this chapter?
b. How do their stories provide personal insight on the potential and future of your career?

10.5 Nine-Box Exercise

Assess your current teammates or a team you have experienced in the recent past. How would you classify your team members using the nine-box matrix? Provide a constructive explanation for why you would place someone in a particular box, and make recommendations on how each person can improve for the future.

CHAPTER ELEVEN

EMPLOYEE DEVELOPMENT

Learning Objectives

1. Identify what it takes to have learning agility.

2. Identify the steps to improve employee development programs.

3. Compare and contrast the different methods of employee development.

4. Differentiate between mentoring and coaching.

5. Design an effective mentoring program.

6. Compare and contrast the value of internal versus external coaching.

7. Describe the steps to identify what employees need for leadership development.

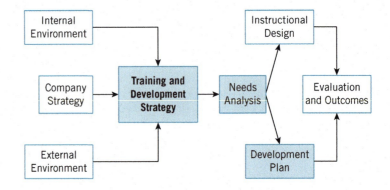

Few people understand the coaching industry better than Debbie Phillips. Debbie has been a coaching professional since the 1990s during the nascent years of the industry. Before becoming a coach, Debbie worked in journalism, and in public administration as the deputy press secretary for John Glenn during his run for the Democratic nomination for president, and as the press secretary for former Ohio governor Richard Celeste. One thing she observed is the low number of female role models at the executive level and in public administration. Even within small networks of women, she encountered women who were not willing to share their strategic insights, reminiscent of the "Queen Bee" phenomenon. She recognized women needed strategic support that went beyond knowledge and skills learned in school. So, informally, she began her own network of female friends who met regularly to share insights, offer support, and guide each other in areas where women were few and far between. She found, after a while, that both men and women were looking for a more personal touch to help them develop their own private strategies for career management and navigation. While organizational development initiatives addressed some of these issues at the organizational level, people were really looking for more personal support and guidance. Debbie began working in an investment banking firm, providing this type of personal strategic support for the leaders in that organization.

In 1996, a *Newsweek* article highlighted the work of Thomas Leonard, a CPA who had applied the term *coach* in a business context, started a training organization called Coach University, and founded the International Coach Federation. When Debbie read about this, she finally realized that the work she had so adeptly recognized as necessary now had a name—coaching. Debbie immediately reached out to Thomas and began her education as one of the first trained coaches in the world. After that, she left her work as an internal coach, and began working as one of the most sought-after executive coaches in the country.

After working in the coaching industry for a number of years, Debbie was again reminded of the importance of building a network to support women. The glass ceiling was, and is still, a barrier to the advancement of women in organizations, and she wanted to find a way to help women feel less isolated and more supported by their peers. She found upwards of 80% of her clients at that time were women, and she knew there was a niche that needed to be filled. Thus, in 2003, Debbie founded the organization Women on Fire, whose mission is to offer women a powerful community that provides support as they achieve their greatest ambitions and navigate their toughest transitions. Now over 100,000 women strong, WOF supports women regionally, nationally, and internationally to achieve success, no matter their profession, age, or stage in life.

Debbie believes that personal connection and strategic support are necessary for anyone to achieve success and reach his or her dreams. Connecting with one's core values is key, and coaches are poised to help people reach their full potential. It is Debbie's mission to ensure that we don't stand on the shoulders of others once we achieve our own success, but reach down to help everyone reach their full potential. It is the role of the coach—whether a manager, supervisor, or external coach—to provide support, guidance, and inspiration to others, and Debbie embodies this in her own life as she seeks to inspire other women to greatness. For more information about Debbie Phillips and WOF, go to www.womenonfire.com.

The textbook, up until this point, has largely addressed the training side of training and development. Specifically, in addressing the needs analysis and instructional design process, most attention has been placed on the need to assess current gaps between desired and actual performance of employees. Development, however, goes hand in hand with training, as noted in the introductory chapter, as it looks beyond current needs and focuses on the career path of employees and the knowledge, skills, and abilities (KSAs) organizations identify as necessary for the future.

Because of the tight link between training and development activities, development is naturally addressed alongside many of the training topics discussed in this textbook. It is important to note that training and development strategy, legal issues, needs analysis, learning theories, and training evaluation are equally important to both training and development activities. Strategy must drive development activities to ensure the KSAs focused on are important to the organization. Organizations must also comply with the law when designing development programs and choosing who will participate. Learning theories apply to development programs, just as they do to training activities, and must be considered when designing and developing these programs. Needs analysis is key to determine what is needed for development and why. Lastly, just as we would evaluate training programs, the same must be done for development activities to ensure the development program accomplished what it set out to accomplish, participants learn what is expected and utilize what they learned on the job, and development activities have a strategic impact on the organization's bottom line.

While training and development activities work in concert, what differentiates training from development is the time horizon of the program. Training programs focus on the KSAs needed immediately, whereas development programs focus on the KSAs needed now and into the future. Both the organization and its employees must ask a clear question to address employees' current KSAs: What skills do employees have now, and how can they best prepare for potential organizational needs and a long future career with the company? One way to think about this is to consider that training employees to do their job now is an essential first step to prepare them for the organization's future needs. We start in the present moment to develop employees for their work now and into the future.

In the chapter on careers and succession (Chapter 10), we began a more in-depth discussion on development, and the impact of how employees think about their careers and how organizations develop career paths for them. Comparing the career paths in the organization to the career desires of employees is important for building a development plan in the organization. As well, succession planning addresses the depth and breadth of expertise in the company to prepare employees for advancing careers within the organization. It is important to anticipate employee needs so the organization is ready for changes in personnel and is building a pipeline of talent ready to step in where needed. Identifying good internal talent, known as high-potential employees, and helping them achieve their potential through the pipeline is another key strategic aspect of employee development.

STRATEGIC IMPORTANCE OF DEVELOPMENT

The strategic importance of employee development cannot be overstated. As an organization develops short-term and long-term plans to accomplish its mission and objectives, a ready workforce is essential for success. If the organization has an eye to the future about where it wants to be, the employees have to be prepared to help the organization achieve that objective. This requires the organization to be clear about where it wants to go and the KSAs employees need to get there. It also requires planning to, first, understand how

> **Exhibit 11-1 Seven Ways to Improve Employee Development Programs**
>
> 1. Ignite managers' passion to coach their employees.
> 2. Deal with the short shelf life of learning and development needs.
> 3. Teach employees to own their career development.
> 4. Provide flexible learning options.
> 5. Serve the learning needs of virtual teams.
> 6. Build trust in organizational leadership.
> 7. Utilize different learning options to reinforce learning across all learning styles.
>
> Source: Adapted from Keith Ferrazzi, "7 Ways to Improve Employee Development Programs," *Harvard Business Review*, July 31, 2015. Available from https://hbr.org/2015/07/7-ways-to-improve-employee-development-programs.

ready the workforce is to meet those goals and, second, be ready to develop employees in anticipation, and advance, of those needs where necessary.

HBR.org highlights a discussion about development that states organizations spend upwards of $164 billion on learning and development, yet the executives who run those programs are at a loss on how to improve and enhance the programs they have.[1] The strategic importance of development programs makes it imperative organizations ensure they are as effective as possible. Exhibit 11-1 lists the seven challenges organizations must address to create development programs with a meaningful impact on the strategic objectives of the organization, and to deliver what organizations need to be ready for future opportunities and challenges.

As discussed in Chapter 6, managers play an important role in ensuring material employees learned in training and development programs transfer to on-the-job performance. Coaching is one way that managers can fulfill that role. Even if there isn't a formal learning opportunity for employees where coaching can have an impact on direct transfer, the manager or coach is responsible for helping the employee deal with unanticipated workplace or job-related issues. We discuss this in the context of internal coaching.

Inertia can also present a problem for organizations when it comes to learning and development. Many managers assume that the development program they delivered in the past is still relevant today. As we noted in Chapter 1 on training and development strategy, with a rapidly changing environment, the organization must be ready to adapt the KSAs employees need to succeed on the job. Add in the challenge of trying to predict what they will need in three to five years, and organizations face even greater hurdles to stay current, let alone forecast the future. Development is an ongoing process, and development plans need to be updated as often as strategic plans and objectives.

Development must take into consideration the organization's needs, as well as the employees' career development needs. However, the organization can only advocate for what it wants and needs from employees. This is because the organization's needs may conflict with what employees need for their careers. In circumstances where the employees have aspirations, but the organization lacks resources or the strategic impetus to develop the employees as they might like, the onus is on the employees to take control of their development. This may include volunteering for or requesting development opportunities, actively participating in development opportunities when offered, or looking outside the organization to develop and enhance their own skill set. In Chapter 12, "Practical Skills for Training and Development," we discuss a range of skills employees may seek to obtain, whether organization- or employee-directed. We also emphasize the importance of employees owning their own career development.

As discussed in Chapters 4 and 6, utilizing a wide variety of training approaches can be very advantageous to improve learning and, ultimately, transfer of learning to the job. First, a multimodal approach to development provides ample opportunity to reinforce KSAs employees need to master to be ready for future job opportunities. Second, as we expect more from employees with fewer available resources, time is limited for them to engage in training and development programs outside of the job. Therefore, to manage the dearth of free time employees have to participate in development programs, greater flexibility in development delivery is needed. Technology is just one way that development can be made readily available for employees. As well, greater flexibility means employees who work remotely via telecommuting or in global locations can access development opportunities previously offered only to those employees who work on-site.

Because global or telecommuting employees are oftentimes "out of sight and out of mind," they face two major obstacles to development. First, because they work at a distance, their development needs may not be readily identified. Second, even if those needs are identified, because the employees are not working proximate to their senior managers, they may be overlooked when development opportunities are available. This "face time" challenge can be managed when the organization makes the effort to ensure managers are properly trained in how to manage telecommuting and other distance employees. Also, by using more technology-based training and development programs, these programs facilitate greater opportunities for all employees, especially for those working at a distance. More details on the impact of technology on training and development are provided in Chapter 9, "Technology-Mediated Training and Development."

Lastly, and most importantly, organizations need to build a culture of trust between leaders and employees. Transparency is needed with respect to who gets chosen for developmental opportunities and why. As well, if organizations want managers to lead by example, what managers are doing for their own development should be visible for all to see. As noted in social learning theory (see Chapter 4), as employees observe what others are doing for development, they model that behavior. If managers are self-starters and take control of their own development opportunities, employees do the same. If upper management models active engagement in all development opportunities, employees follow suit. It is important employees trust that the opportunities made available to those above them in the corporate hierarchy will be made available to them when the time comes. Be consistent in how you handle development opportunities for all employees to build trust and avoid lawsuits.

LEARNING AGILITY

An underlying assumption of employee development is that employees are eager and able to learn continuously and adapt to changes and mistakes where necessary. **Learning agility** is defined as the mindset and corresponding collection of practices that allow leaders to continually develop, grow, and utilize new strategies that will equip them for the increasingly complex problems they face in their organizations.[2] Leaders have to remain open to new ways of thinking and to continuously learn new skills. The research done by the Center for Creative Leadership shows us that leaders who refuse to let go of entrenched patterns of behavior tend to derail, whereas successful leaders continue to develop on the job. We now know that these successful leaders are learning agile, meaning they show the willingness and ability to learn throughout their careers.

Learning agility is a necessary characteristic for employees who want to grow and develop. We can see this in two ways. First, employees with high learning agility are willing to take ownership of their own career development. As well, organizations recognize those employees who are learning agile, and are therefore more willing to provide development opportunities for them. Whether the development is self- or organization-directed, learning agility is important for success.

Employees who are learning agile typically exhibit the following characteristics.[3] First, they are willing to be innovative and question the status quo. Second, they perform well by staying calm when faced with difficulty. Third, they reflect on their experiences to learn from them. Fourth, they are willing to take risks and volunteer for learning opportunities even if there is a chance of failure. Lastly, employees who are learning agile are open to learning and resist the temptation to become defensive in the face of adversity. They seek feedback, process it, and adapt, and are highly self-motivated to learn and grow. When employees exhibit learning agility, they find themselves on the path to leadership and leadership development opportunities within the organization. In the next section, we outline the different types of employee development opportunities. Regardless of the approach organizations take for development, learning agility is necessary for employees to succeed.

EMPLOYEE DEVELOPMENT

Chapter 10 addressed the variety of theories that explain the career decisions and paths of individuals. Whether we are addressing the different career stages in which an employee is ensconced, or the career anchors that indicate the driving forces behind the employee's career plan, the challenge in developing and designing a development plan is to balance the needs of the organization with the career aspirations and development plans of the individual employee. Further, while training is more focused on groups of employees who may need training in broad areas, development tends to be much more customized to the individual employee's needs, as defined in the employee's career objectives and during annual evaluations of performance.

Performance appraisal is directly related to employee development and has two broad purposes. First, and most common, appraisals function as evaluation tools, and are inputs for determining appropriate rewards or punishments given the employee's performance over the previous review period. Promotions, for example, are considered a reward for good performance, which directly impacts the career path of the employee. Second, and less common, the appraisal serves as the framework for employee development plans. The gap between current KSAs and desired KSAs given the employee's career aspirations and the organization's needs informs the development plan provided for the employee. The focus is less on the reward or punishment or evaluative aspect of the appraisal, and more on the goals for improvement and growth of the employee over the next review period.

Employee development focuses on two areas: how individuals manage their careers within and between organizations, and how organizations structure the career progress of employees in alignment with organizational goals. Development has both formal and informal components. While the most common tools for consideration in development are coaching and mentoring, the scope of activities that can be included in employee development is much broader. Exhibit 11-2 illustrates a variety of development tools available to organizations.[4]

Assignments and Enrichment Opportunities

Not all development opportunities are embedded in a formal, structured program. Development can just as easily occur within the boundaries of normal work activities and

Exhibit 11-2 Approaches for Employee Development

Development Activity	Definitions
Stretch Assignments and Projects	Special project assignments outside of the scope of the employee's normal job
Job Enrichment	Knowledge and skill development within the scope of the employee's normal job
Extra-Role Enrichment	Volunteer activities that benefit the employee's current role
Job Shadowing	Employees follow others in different positions for exposure to other job opportunities
Job Rotation	Employees rotate through different job opportunities over a period of time
Lateral Move	Movement to a position at a similar level of responsibility and pay, but with different skills to develop
Promotion	Movement to a position at a level above one's current position to reward performance and develop new skills
Mentoring	A formal or informal program in partnership with a senior employee for long-term career growth
Coaching	A formal or informal program with a direct supervisor or external coach for performance improvement or resolution of work issues

Source: Adapted from Jerome Ternynck, "7 High-Impact Approaches for Employee Development," *Inc.*, February 2, 2015. Available from http://www.inc.com/jerome-ternynck/7-high-impact-approaches-for-employee-development.html.

assignments, as it can within a formally planned and designed development intervention. Even if the organization does not have the resources to engage in intensive development programs, managers, and the human resource (HR) professionals who support them, can direct employees to programs, assignments, and opportunities as they become available in the organization and as the employees grow in KSAs.

These **assignments and enrichment opportunities**, however, should not be meted out haphazardly. Whether a formal needs analysis has been done or the developmental goals evolved out of the performance appraisal process, the assignments should align with the developmental needs of employees.

Stretch assignments and special projects.

Stretch assignments and projects are typically outside of the scope of the employee's day-to-day work activities but still within the boundaries of direct job-related projects. These opportunities, however, represent unique learning and development opportunities for employees. Because they are special assignments, they provide the visibility needed for an employee's efforts to be noticed in a public way. As well, these special projects and assignments represent occasions for skill development employees wouldn't typically get in the normal scope of their job. These special assignments and projects may not come up often, so it is imperative that the employees chosen are ready for the opportunity and will directly benefit from the experience in their development plan. An example of a special project is the need for an ad hoc committee to address new technology or new processes the organization is considering adopting. The committee would have a central role in researching and recommending what would best meet the organization's needs. The employees chosen for this committee would have a visible role in advancing the needs of the company and would be able to showcase skills that might not be apparent in their current job.

A major consideration in utilizing special assignments and projects is to ensure you are fully considering all the employees who may benefit from these assignments, not just those the manager likes or with whom the manager has the closest relationship. The HR professional may recommend to managers which employees would most benefit from the special assignment. If special assignments are the only development tools available in the organization, this could represent a liability issue if the company isn't mindful about spreading out the opportunities among a wide variety of employees. Before leaping into assigning a favored employee to the special project, take the time to assess the readiness, motivation, and development goals of all employees who are eligible for the assignment and ensure the reasons for the assignment are not biased or discriminatory in any way.

Job enrichment.

While *job enrichment* is a term typically associated with job design activities (e.g., Hackman and Oldham job characteristics theory),[5] enrichment activities in this context include opportunities in the course of job-related activities that benefit employees and can be added to their job assignment on a permanent basis. As employees develop greater mastery in certain areas of their job, additional opportunities can be provided for them to broaden the range of skills they possess. This type of growth is usually on a predictable trajectory, building on existing KSAs as the foundation for the next level of development. An employee might move from a team member to a team leader, entering the rotation of leaders who take turns leading projects. Or the employee may move from behind-the-scenes preparation of projects to becoming a key member of the presenting team. As employees grow in experience, they are given increasingly more difficult, and broader, opportunities to develop.

Job enrichment activities are typically part of a formalized development plan, but may not necessarily be formalized as such. This plan could be explicitly outlined in a development plan, but could also just be a normal progression of job training as identified in the job description (an example of the overlap between training and development programs). The most important consideration is to ensure employees are developing at a reasonable pace, as they prepare to advance to the next level. If an employee's progress is ignored and/or delayed for no good documented reason, this could erode trust in organization leadership, further eroding the effectiveness of employee development programs.

Extra-role enrichment.

While special projects and job enrichment function within the boundaries of job-related projects, extra-role enrichment activities go beyond projects directly related to the job. If the company develops extra-work committees, such as a diversity committee or a volunteerism committee (e.g., coordinating a United Way or blood drive campaign), these committees provide enrichment opportunities outside of the direct work of the organization. The employees can then develop and showcase KSAs during a visible company-wide campaign or activity. This not only develops and demonstrates good competencies that apply to job-related activities, but can also benefit the organization and its employees by modeling ethical and socially responsible activities.

Job Design

Motivation considerations are important for training and development as noted in the needs analysis (Chapter 3), training evaluation (Chapters 5 and 6), and training transfer (Chapter 8) discussions. Motivation has both extrinsic and intrinsic components. One key aspect of intrinsic motivation is how jobs are designed, not only to meet the job demands, but also to address issues of intrinsic motivation among employees. Two easy areas in which development can be aligned with **job design** are job shadowing and job rotation.

Job shadowing.

Job shadowing is the process by which employees follow around, or "shadow," coworkers to get exposure to other job opportunities. They walk with and observe the daily workings of other employees doing jobs the shadow employees are interested in pursuing. While it may not be a direct development activity, shadowing is important to the early exploration stage of career planning and development. It enables employees to understand what career opportunities may be available for them as they consider their future in the organization. The decision to job shadow could be employee driven or organization driven. In either circumstance, job shadowing serves as a realistic introduction to career opportunities so employees are aware of what it takes to do a certain job, the KSAs needed to advance to that position, or the KSAs one would develop by taking that position.

Job shadowing is an important aspect of apprenticeship programs. Apprentices learn on the job while shadowing an employee with greater skill and experience. More discussion about apprenticeship programs is given in Appendix B, "External Partnerships."

Job rotation.

In job shadowing, employees get to observe job opportunities on a one-on-one basis with employees in those jobs. Job rotation is similar, but instead of simply observing as they would do under shadowing, employees get a taste for particular jobs by working in those positions for a period of time. The time frame can vary depending on the intentions of the organization and the objectives of the rotation program, as well as the organization's size and access to key resources. For example, if the rotation program is used to help employees exhibit mastery of a skill, the time frame of the rotation will be much longer than if the purpose of the program is to simply introduce the employees to a wider variety of skill and job opportunities.

Some organizations bring in high-potential management trainees and expose them to a variety of career options over the first year of their employment. The management trainees are hired for their broad knowledge and competencies, as well as for person–organization match, not for job-specific KSAs. The intention is to rotate trainees through different jobs on a quarterly basis, giving them enough time to learn about the job and begin skill development needed for career advancement. For example, a new management trainee could rotate through positions in operations, HR management, customer relations, and new product development. Not only is this a great opportunity for the management trainee to learn about the company and different career advancement options, but the organization uses this opportunity to assess management potential and determine which career track would be best for the trainee. This option is ideal for larger organizations with greater flexibility and resources to absorb the low productivity of trainees for their first year as they rotate through the varying positions.

Another way to use job rotation is to shorten the rotation periods and have employees continually rotate through a variety of jobs. This serves two purposes. First, as we know from the job design literature, job rotation breaks up boredom and monotony. Second, rotation expands opportunities for employees to develop skills, preparing them for possible future job prospects. Rotation can be as short as a week (most common) or as long as a few months. Typically, these rotations occur within a team-based environment. As employees become more adept across a broad range of KSAs, this increases job opportunities for the employees and also serves to expose them to a variety of career options. Typically, this type of rotation is common with lower-level, nonmanagerial employees, as there is no guarantee an employee will advance from the rotating jobs. This type of rotation may also be the only type a smaller organization can use to develop employees, due to insufficient resources and employee depth to carry redundant employees while moving them through temporary positions for job exposure, as noted in the first rotation example.

Job Transitions

Transitions enable the company to reward employees for good performance, as expected with the evaluative function of the performance appraisal, but also to use these transitions as a step in the career progression of the employee. Thus, transitions serve as both a development opportunity and a reward for good performance. Any type of career progression provides employees with opportunities to learn new skills. When an organization only hires outside of the company and does not provide growth and development opportunities for existing employees, employees are more likely to leave, or decrease their overall productivity and performance. **Job transitions** are an important tool, not just from the perspective of development but also for increasing employee retention and motivation. This demonstrates how tightly integrated HR activities are, and how important it is to keep a consistent, employee-centered approach.

Lateral move.

As discussed in Chapter 10, an employee can take a variety of career paths. Nontraditional methods, or lateral moves, include both "ridge" and "lattice" approaches to career paths. A lateral move doesn't assume that the employee moves ahead along a narrow, predictive path, from lower to upper levels of the company. Lateral moves are much more focused on providing broader skill development that may ultimately result in upward movement along career ladders as in the "ridge" approach, or in a wide variety of directions as in the "lattice" approach. Lateral moves, in essence, give employees a broad set of options for career paths and development.

The "fork" approach is an example of a traditional career ladder that uses development opportunities to help employees make lateral moves from one fork to another. For example, if a research scientist wants to move from the science side of the career fork to the management side, organizations will engage in management development training to facilitate that transition. Both internal and external coaching are the tools most commonly used to help employees move from one path along the career ladder to the other. We discuss this process in more detail under "Coaching."

Promotion.

Traditional career ladders presume upward progression of the employee's career from lower to upper levels of the company. Each upward move the employee makes not only serves as a reward for the past, but also presents an opportunity to grow and learn new KSAs. This is not the only advantage to using promotions for the purpose of development. Just as we want to ensure employees have the support they need as they complete training and try to transfer information learned to the job, those promoted into new positions must also get the support they need to succeed. **Mentors** help employees make the transition to a new position at any level in the organization. This works for lower-level employees as well as upper-level executives. Coaching, both internal and external, also helps ensure employees can problem solve and adjust to new work situations and problems. We discuss more on the impact of mentoring and coaching in the next section.

Mentoring and Coaching

The two most commonly discussed and used methods of employee development are mentoring and coaching. While these are the most common, as indicated, they are not the only tools available for employee development. Ideally, coaching and mentoring should be integrated within a wide scope of development activities as highlighted in Exhibit 11-2.

Even though coaching and mentoring are mentioned in the same breath, they are very distinct and provide development support for employees in differing ways. Both coaching and mentoring can be formal or informal. Coaching can be done internally with the employee's direct supervisor, the company's HR professional, or a designated internal coach, or in a more formal relationship with an external coach. Mentoring typically does not involve the employee's direct supervisor, but matches the employee with a more senior employee not in his or her chain of command. Internal coaching is often done within the scope of the supervisor–employee relationship, in the course of managing employees on a daily basis. Mentoring, however, is not a typical job expectation, and requires assent (formal or informal) between the mentor and the protégé as they develop a working relationship. Exhibit 11-3 highlights an informal mentoring program developed at McCarthy Building Companies to help women in the construction field develop leadership skills to support career advancement.

The more purposeful the relationship between mentor or coach and employee, the more the employee and the organization benefit from this type of development. While informal programs are certainly beneficial, the more structured and formal the relationship, the easier it is to see clear benefits for the organization. Despite the costs associated with formal coaching and mentoring programs, the benefits far outweigh the costs, as employees are better prepared for future career opportunities.

Exhibit 11-3 Mentoring at McCarthy Building Companies

McCarthy Building Companies, like others in the construction industry, faced the challenge of finding skilled workers to replace those who were retiring. As well, McCarthy encountered additional concerns with attracting and retaining women, further compounding the companies' talent management problems. Through a grassroots effort, women at McCarthy approached their leadership asking for career support. The women argued they needed a network to better support them in the field, and they wanted to have more developed career paths. Given the forecast for a skills shortage in the industry, and

(Continued)

> **Exhibit 11-3 (Continued)**
>
> as the 15th largest domestic general contractor, McCarthy understood this was a situation it could not ignore.
>
> After a lot of research and brainstorming, and with an eye toward developing resources that could have a quick and meaningful impact, the companies implemented three new programs directed toward attracting, retaining, and developing women. First, McCarthy developed training and awareness programs for women at the companies to address their specific issues and concerns. Second, the companies ensured there was not only diversity in their hiring pool, but also diversity in the recruitment and selection staff so more women were involved in the hiring process itself. Lastly, given these programs, the companies redesigned their marketing materials to illustrate the diversity at McCarthy as well as the programs available to support women at the company.
>
> The development program originally started as an employee resource group, but as the company embraced the program nationally, the name changed to the McCarthy Partnership for Women (MPW), which recently graduated its first class of women through its development program and has begun training its second class. The program addresses issues such as strategic thinking and communication, emotional intelligence, and working within a company culture. Although MPW has provided these opportunities for women, and continues to support them, it also empowers the women to drive their own careers. As such, the women have created mentoring and networking committees so they can build on the momentum gained through the first training class and pass that energy and commitment on to the women who will follow them through the program. MPW is already seeing the fruits of its labor as several women in the partnership have been elected to the leadership of the Women in Construction Operations (WiOPS). Although MPW doesn't have a formal mentoring program, the women of the partnership are taking it upon themselves to mentor and support women across McCarthy sites. With foresight and openness to new ideas, MPW has successfully addressed two major talent management issues: an industry skills shortage, and continuing glass ceiling issues for women in construction.

Mentoring

Mentoring is defined as "an intense work relationship between senior (mentor) and junior (protégé) organizational members. The mentor has experience and power in the organization and personally advises, counsels, coaches, and promotes the career development of the **protégé**. Promotion of the protégé's career may occur directly through actual promotion decisions made by the mentor, or indirectly through the mentor's influence and power over other organizational members."[6] You may also hear the protégé referred to as the mentee or mentoree.

Mentoring support is broken down into two general categories: career development support and psychosocial support.[7] Exhibit 11-4 lists the subfunctions associated with each. While Kathy Kram lists coaching under career development support, to avoid confusion with our use of the term *coaching*, we changed it to career coaching. Mentors typically are not involved in the daily activities of their protégés; therefore, coaching refers to those activities attributed to direct supervisors while daily managing

Exhibit 11-4 Mentoring Support

Career Development Support	Psychosocial Support
• Sponsorship	• Role Modeling
• Exposure	• Acceptance
• Visibility	• Confirmation
• Career Coaching	• Counseling
• Protection	• Friendship
• Challenging Assignments	

Source: Adapted from Kathy E. Kram, *Mentoring at Work: Developmental Relationships in Organizational Life* (Glenview, IL: Foresman, 1985).

their employees, whereas career coaching refers to the career advice that mentors may provide for their protégés.

The distinction between these two types of support mechanisms is important. Career development support focuses on the direct support or advice given related to the protégé's career. For example, the mentor may advocate for the protégé to be considered for a high-visibility assignment in the organization. Mentors may also advise protégés directly on career advancement issues such as potential positions to consider when they are looking for a promotion. Alternatively, psychosocial support is the provision of psychological and social resources believed necessary to help protégés cope with problems they may be facing. These resources aren't directly applicable to the job but are more indirect as they increase the likelihood protégés will succeed when they engage in the career development activities. Given the importance of building a relationship between mentor and protégé, both types of support are important and should be present to maximize the benefits associated with the mentoring relationship.

Informally, junior and senior employees may meet and choose to develop a professional friendship such that the more senior employee provides advice and support to the junior employee. More often, an organization has a formal mentoring program that matches junior and senior employees together in a structured program with clear guidelines for how the program is supposed to progress. More details on the differences between formal and informal programs follow.

Benefits of mentoring for the organization. The Society for Human Resource Management argues there are many benefits for organizations that utilize mentoring programs as part of their development plan.[8] Mentoring increases retention and morale through mutual loyalty between the employees and the employer. Mentoring also helps new employees and expatriates acclimate to their new job and learn the company culture much quicker. We discuss this point in great detail in Chapter 13, as we address orientation programs and how to help employees learn company culture. Mentoring also helps employees feel more engaged with the organization, resulting in greater productivity and ultimately improved organizational performance. Lastly, mentoring promotes diversity, which leads to an innovative and creative work environment where employees are exposed to new ideas and opportunities. Overall, the organization should gain a workforce that is more cooperative, productive, and focused on delivery of good service to internal and external customers.

A corporate-level mentoring strategy is an integral part of a well-constructed mentoring program. If the company does not place strategic value on mentoring, making it an integral part of the organization's culture, the benefits that can be gained from a mentoring program will not be maximized. The formal mentoring program should be in alignment with the organization's strategic position in order to achieve maximum effectiveness.[9]

Characteristics of a good mentoring relationship. Not all mentoring relationships are created equal. When there is a mismatch between mentor and protégé, this results in an unproductive, and perhaps detrimental, working relationship. In order for mentoring to work, certain issues must be taken into consideration.[10] Exhibit 11-5 highlights the characteristics of a good mentoring relationship.

First, there should be genuine interest and motivation to participate from both the mentor and the protégé. From the perspective of the mentor, if the protégé is not coachable or approaching the relationship with a learning orientation, this mentoring relationship will be a waste of time for the mentor. From the perspective of the protégé, if the mentor is not interested in being a mentor, he or she will not provide adequate support for the protégé, leaving the protégé disillusioned and pondering job opportunities elsewhere within or outside of the organization. Regardless of the perspective, this is one of the primary reasons why mentoring programs should be voluntary, not mandatory. If one or both parties are not interested in the mentoring relationship, it is a waste of time and money for all involved.

Exhibit 11-5 Characteristics of a Good Mentoring Relationship

Interest and Motivation to Participate From Both Mentor and Protégé

Time and Commitment to Participate

Confidentiality

Clear, Open, Two-Way Communication

Active Listening

Clear Goals

Second, there should be time to participate in the mentoring program, and commitment from both parties to make the mentoring relationship work. Even with the best of intentions, if neither mentor nor protégé can commit the time to developing the relationship, the program will not meet the organization's strategic needs and goals. If neither is committed to make the time, even if each has the stated desire to be involved in the mentoring relationship, the mentoring program will likely fail.

Third, confidentiality is essential. The mentor may hear things that are extremely personal. One goal of the mentoring relationship is to help protégés learn about the culture and build their own self-awareness as they grow as employees. As protégés explore these things within the boundary of the mentoring relationship, they may reveal personal details that should not be for professional consideration in the workplace. For example, protégés may share that they have a hidden disability, or that they are in a same-sex relationship. While the mentor may not have issues with either piece of information, it is not the mentor's responsibility to share that information with others. This violates trust and will destroy the budding relationship between the two. If the protégé does not feel safe to confide in and share information with the mentor, this creates a barrier between them, eroding the benefits of a mentoring relationship.

Fourth, communication is the lynchpin of a good mentoring relationship. This involves clear, open, two-way communication, and good listening skills for both parties. The importance of good communication, along with ways to develop better communication skills, is addressed further in Chapter 12, "Practical Skills for Training and Development."

Lastly, a good mentoring relationship must establish clear goals. The goals must be in alignment with the strategic needs of the organization, and also benefit both mentor and protégé. Each person enters the mentoring relationship with personal and professional goals in mind. Those goals should be discussed explicitly in the beginning phase of the relationship so the mentor and protégé know what to expect from each other and the outcomes they'd like to see at the close of the formal mentoring relationship. Some organizations use a formal contract that explicitly addresses the expectations for goals and outcomes. An example of a mentoring contract is found in Exhibit 11-6, from the Institute of Physics. A contract can be developed according to the organization's strategic needs, as well as the needs of both mentor and protégé.

Stages of the Mentoring Relationship. There are four stages in the mentoring relationship: initiation, cultivation, separation, and redefinition (see Exhibit 11-7).[11] In the initiation stage, which lasts six months to a year, the relationship is in its beginning stages, and the mentor is admired as a role model and for his or her ability to provide support and guidance to the protégé. The relationship parameters are established, and trust is being developed. In the cultivation stage, which lasts two to five years, both career development and psychosocial support are maximized. The relationship has developed a strong emotional bond, and both protégé and mentor benefit from the relationship. At this stage, they may meet more frequently to build greater synergies.

Exhibit 11-6 Sample Mentoring Contract

Mentoring Agreement Form

We are both voluntarily entering into this partnership. We wish this to be a rewarding experience, spending most of our time discussing developmental activities. We agree that . . .

1. The mentoring relationship will last for _____ months. This period will be evaluated every three to six months and will end by amicable agreement once we have achieved as much as possible.

2. We will meet at least once every _____ weeks. Meeting times, once agreed, should not be canceled unless this is unavoidable. At the end of each meeting, we will agree on a date for the next meeting.

3. Each meeting will last a minimum of _____ minutes and a maximum of _____ minutes.

4. In between meetings, we will contact each other by telephone/email no more than once every _____ weeks/days.

5. The aim of the partnership is to discuss and resolve the following issues:

    a.

    b.

    c.

6. We agree that the role of the mentor is to:

    _____
    _____
    _____

7. We agree that the role of the mentee is to:

    _____
    _____
    _____

8. We agree to keep the content of these meetings confidential.

9. The mentor agrees to be honest and provide constructive feedback to the mentee. The mentee agrees to be open to the feedback.

Date: _____

Mentor's signature: _____

Mentee's signature: _____

Date for Review: _____

Source: Institute of Physics, "How the Partnership Works." Available from https://www.iop.org/membership/prof-dev/tools/mentoring/partnership/page_38867.html.

Exhibit 11-7 Stages of the Mentoring Relationship

The separation stage is the transition point for the protégé who is likely to desire more autonomy in the relationship. Work commitments may have shifted for both mentor and protégé, or the usefulness or instrumentality of the mentoring relationship may have decreased. Either way, at this point in time the protégé and mentor begin to spend less time together, and the dependency of the protégé on the mentor fades. There may be frustration or disappointment at unattained goals, or sadness that the relationship is in a formal transition.

In the redefinition stage, the mentor–protégé relationship shifts to become a relationship of equals, or peers. The emphasis at this stage is on friendship, rather than on role modeling and learning. It may feel awkward in the beginning as the protégé transitions from a subordinate role in the relationship. How this awkwardness is managed determines whether the relationship continues in a redefined way, or fades away entirely. Addressing the redefinition stage in training mentors and protégés is important for successful mentoring outcomes.

Antecedents for mentoring support. A wide variety of studies have tried to investigate the factors that lead to greater mentoring support, as defined in Exhibit 11-4. Rajashi Ghosh compiled the research in this area and conducted an analysis that revealed which factors appear to have the greatest impact on mentoring support[12]—for example, the individual characteristics of the protégé and mentor, relationship factors describing the mentoring relationship, and structural or organizational factors. He also differentiated between the two types of mentoring support, career development and psychosocial support. Exhibit 11-8 outlines the results of his study.

To summarize Ghosh's findings, protégés who were proactive had a high internal locus of control (believed they had control over the outcomes of their life), and those who had a high learning goal orientation were more likely to get career development support. The same can be said for psychosocial support except locus of control, which did not have an impact on psychosocial support. Mentors who exhibited transformational leader behaviors and had a high learning goal orientation were also more likely to provide career development and psychosocial mentoring support.

Gender-similar dyads (male and male, or female and female) were more likely to have both career development and psychosocial support than mixed-gender dyads, as were those dyads where mentor and protégé perceived greater similarities between them. Ethnically similar dyads were more likely to have psychosocial support, but not career development support. Trust, informal mentoring, and perceived organizational support for mentoring programs all contributed to both career development

Exhibit 11-8 Antecedents of Mentoring Support

Career Development	Psychosocial
Proactive Protégé	Proactive Protégé
Internal Locus of Control of Protégé	High Protégé Learning Goal Orientation
High Protégé Learning Goal Orientation	High Mentor Learning Goal Orientation
High Mentor Learning Goal Orientation	Mentor Is Transformational Leader
Mentor Is Transformational Leader	Gender-Similar Dyad
Gender-Similar Dyad	Ethnically Similar Dyad
Perceived Similarity	Perceived Similarity
Cognition- and Affect-Based Trust	Cognition- and Affect-Based Trust
Informal Mentoring	Informal Mentoring
Supervisory Mentoring	Organizational Support for Mentoring
Organizational Support for Mentoring	
Early Mentoring Stages Over Late Stages	
Undifferentiated Between Career and Psychosocial Mentoring Support	
Protégé Emotional Intelligence	
Protégé High Self-Monitoring	
High Self-Disclosure Between Protégé and Mentor	

Source: Adapted from Rajashi Ghosh, "Antecedents of Mentoring Support: A Meta-analysis of Individual, Relational, and Structural or Organizational Factors." *Journal of Vocational Behavior* 84, no. 3 (2014): 367–384.

and psychosocial support. However, supervisors who engaged in mentoring were more likely to provide career development support. As well, career development was more likely to be seen during early phases of the mentoring relationship rather than later phases.

Lastly, some results did not differentiate between career and psychosocial mentoring support. For example, high protégé emotional intelligence (ability to read and manage one's own emotions and to be aware of others' emotions) and self-monitoring (how much people monitor their self-presentation, expressive behavior, and nonverbal affective displays) result in greater overall mentoring support. As well, when both mentor and protégé engage in a high level of self-disclosure (sharing personal information about oneself), there is much greater overall mentoring support.

These findings have a direct impact on how training professionals choose and prepare both protégés and mentors for mentoring programs. As well, demographic characteristics such as gender or ethnicity, or the extent to which the protégé and mentor perceive they are similar in outlook, perspective, values, and work habits, are relevant to successful matches. It is important to note that age differences do not have a meaningful impact on the likelihood for mentoring support. As well, if the emphasis is on psychosocial support over career support, ethnicity similarity matters and is more likely to result in greater psychosocial support. If the emphasis is on greater career support, the direct supervisor may be better prepared to provide that support, over a mentor in a different area from the protégé.

Mentor and protégé training. Both mentors and protégés should be trained in how to best prepare for the mentoring relationship. Once the organization has determined the expectations around the mentoring program, potential mentors and protégés should trained on what to expect if they participate in the program. Exhibit 11-9 is an example of a model mentoring training program, highlighting the goals of the program.

Exhibit 11-9   Model Mentoring Training Program Goals

Program Goal

The program will help develop identified candidates who have shown potential for growth and interest in leadership. The role of the mentoring program is to build relationships, share organizational knowledge, and develop leadership skills. Leadership candidates will meet regularly with current leaders (mentors) who have volunteered to share their contacts, knowledge, skills, and expertise.

As a mentor, you will be expected to support the mentoring initiative, and your protégé. The following are characteristics of successful mentors. Consider these as you make the decision to participate in the mentoring program.

- Desires to mentor another employee and is committed to the protégé's growth and development
- Understands the importance of emotional intelligence and is sensitive to the emotions and feelings of the protégé
- Knows the organization's vision, goals, and values, and aligns mentoring activities accordingly
- Can actively engage in productive relationships between departments and individual contributors
- Knows the culture of the organization and can apply cultural knowledge to leadership
- Demonstrates integrity in all actions
- Is willing to help develop a protégé through guidance and coaching
- Embraces stewardship in the organization

Mentor–Protégé Relationship

Before you are matched with a potential protégé candidate, you will complete a questionnaire indicating your strengths and what you are willing to offer your match. Candidates will also have input into the process by requesting a certain skill set in their possible mentors.

Source: Adapted from Annette M. Cremo and Tom Bux, "Developing a Leadership Pipeline," *TD at Work* 34 (October 2017): 8.

Exhibit 11-10 Sample Mentor and Protégé Training

Preparation for Mentors	Preparation for Protégé Candidates
• The importance of mentoring	• Defining mentoring
• The role of the mentor	• The importance of the mentoring relationship
• The process of mentoring	• Responsibilities of the protégé
• The match	• Matching the protégé to the mentor
• Preparing for success	• Working relationships with the mentor
• Setting expectations with the protégé	• Developing expectations
• Confidentiality	• Confidentiality
• The agreement	• Boundaries
• Goals of the relationship	• The mentoring agreement
• Setting objectives	• Accountability
• Possible learning methods: journaling, role playing, shadowing	• Welcoming feedback
• Meeting times/frequency	• Evaluating your success
• Coaching overview	
• Evaluating success	

Source: Adapted from Annette M. Cremo and Tom Bux, "Developing a Leadership Pipeline," *TD at Work* 34 (October 2017): 8.

Making a good match between protégé and mentor is important to minimize challenges and maximally benefit the organization. This match depends on proper training for both mentor and protégé. Good mentors should be trained to know what is expected of them, and to provide their protégés with the competencies to make the mentoring relationship work. As well, protégés should be informed why the mentoring program is important to the organization; how the protégé, mentor, and organization benefit from the program; and what is expected of the protégé to make the program and the mentoring relationship a success. Exhibit 11-10 highlights the types of things that should be included in mentor and protégé training.

Formal versus informal mentoring. As noted previously, mentoring programs can be formal or informal. While informal mentoring relationships may cover the same ground as formal relationships, it is done without the structure and support of the organization. Despite the lack of formal structure, HR and training professionals can encourage and advise their employees in how to best navigate a mentoring relationship, even if the organization does not formally support a mentoring program. Exhibit 11-11 outlines the differences between formal and informal mentoring.

Exhibit 11-11 Formal Versus Informal Mentoring

Formal Mentoring	Informal Mentoring
• Connection to a strategic business objective of the organization	• Unspecified goals
• Established goals	• Unknown outcomes
• Measurable outcomes	• Limited access to the program
• Open access for all who qualify	• Self-selection of mentors and protégés
• Strategic pairing of mentors and protégés	• Long-term mentoring
• Mentoring engagements lasting 9–12 months	• No expert training or support
• Expert training and support	• Indirect organizational benefits
• Direct organizational benefits	

Source: Adapted from "Business Marketing Matters: What Is the Difference Between Informal and Formal Mentoring?," Management Mentors. Available from http://www.management-mentors.com/about/corporate-mentoring-matters-blog/bid/90851/what-is-the-difference-between-informal-and-formal-mentoring.

One of the most important differences between formal and informal programs is the missing connection to strategic business objectives found in informal mentoring programs. This doesn't mean that informal mentoring cannot benefit the organization's bottom line in the long run. However, without clear guidelines, there are no guarantees that the parameters of an informal mentoring relationship will directly benefit the organization.

Another important consideration is the self-selection of mentors and protégés versus open access for all who qualify. Self-selection can make the organization vulnerable to charges of discrimination if mentors are left to their own devices in selecting and working with protégés. We know that people prefer to work with others who look and think like them. If managers only choose their favorite employees to mentor, entire classes of employees may miss out on the benefits of a mentoring relationship. Women and minorities in particular, because they exist in such small numbers at the top of many organizations, may not find a mentor who looks like them. This perpetuates issues such as the glass ceiling, inhibiting advancement in the organization.

Overall, with guidance from the HR department, even an informal mentoring program can benefit the mentors and protégés as long as care is given to provide some simple guidelines for the mentors and protégés to follow as they build their mentoring relationship. Reminding mentors about the dangers of discrimination when selecting protégés can help mitigate any legal concerns. As well, helping the mentoring dyads develop goals and expectations for their mentoring relationship ensures even informal programs have an achievable outcome.

Threats to mentoring programs. Even in the best-designed mentoring programs, unexpected problems may arise. For example, jealousy can arise between the mentor and protégé if the protégé's career begins to skyrocket beyond that of the mentor, or if the protégé is expanding her or his network beyond the mentor's scope of influence. The mentor may get controlling and choose not to let the protégé move on from the mentoring relationship, or may undermine the protégé in a public setting. Addressing issues of jealousy should be integrated into mentor–protégé training so that both parties know how to identify when a mentoring relationship has become toxic and dysfunctional.

As well, in the later stages of mentoring, the relationship changes from one where the protégé depends on the mentor to one where they are equals or the protégé surpasses the mentor in position and influence. The mentor needs to recognize the changing nature of this relationship and let it evolve to one of mutual respect and collegiality, rather than expect the protégé to remain in a subordinate position to the mentor. In the end, the mentors must recognize that they have done their job well if the protégés have grown and developed into successful organizational leaders.

The final consideration that may threaten mentoring relationships and programs is diversity-related. While gender- and ethnically similar dyads may result in greater mentoring support, these types of dyads may not be available for women and minorities in organizations. Thus, if the majority of mentors are white males, then white male protégés will benefit the most from a mentoring program. Emphasis should be placed on finding generalized similarities between the mentor and protégé rather than on demographic characteristics. In other words, dyads should be matched based on similar values, outlooks, and personality characteristics, rather than basic demographics.

As well, additional problems may occur with gender-dissimilar dyads. For example, a male mentor may be uncomfortable building a relationship with a female junior employee. This may be a result of religious beliefs associated with more conservative faiths such as Hasidic Judaism or conservative Islam or Christianity, where opposite-sex relationships outside of marriage, even if just professional relationships, are discouraged. Legal issues around sexual harassment may occur in gender dissimilar dyads as well. While it is more common to see a male sexually harass a female subordinate, there is precedent for females sexually harassing male subordinates, or even same-sex harassment as seen in many court cases. Don't assume that female mentors do not need training on the legal issues surrounding sexual harassment.

Coaching

While mentoring involves addressing larger, developmental issues for an employee's career path, **coaching** is more focused on helping employees achieve better daily performance to enhance their careers.[13] The International Coach Federation (ICF) defines coaching as partnering with clients in a thought-provoking and creative process that inspires them to maximize their personal and professional potential. While ICF's primary focus is external coaching, the definition can be inclusive of those who primarily identify as internal coaches if the organization considers direct reports as internal clients or partners.

Given that coaches can be both internal and external, it is important to compare and contrast these two roles in the context of administrating employee development programs. The 2016 ICF Global Coaching Study found that coaches identify their role somewhere along a coaching continuum.[14] On one extreme is the manager or leader who uses coaching skills with direct reports. The next level is the HR professional or talent manager who uses coaching skills at the organizational level. From there, the shift moves toward the coaching professional. Along the continuum, some coaching professionals can have a foot in both roles; they may have an internal focus—for example, as an HR professional—but also have a side career as an external coach across different organizations and industries. At the next-highest level is the fully **internal coach** who is tasked with acting as an executive coach across many employees in the organization. Internal coaches may be part of the talent management team, and their job title may reflect their role internally in coaching select higher-level executives in the company.

Lastly, we have the **external coach**. These individuals work outside of the organization's boundaries and have their own pool of clientele across organizations. In essence, the external coach functions like a consultant, outside of the domain of the organization, and works individually with executives as needed across different organizations.

The majority of coaches function more as coaching professionals, and represent approximately 80% of those who self-identify as coaches. Women represent approximately 67% of those who identify as coaching professionals, and 66% of those who identify as manager or leader coaches.[15] This may be unsurprising as coaching tends to have a strong communal and interpersonal focus, an attribution more likely associated with women than men in the workplace. Lastly, approximately 99% of coaching professionals have coaching training, with the vast majority (89%) getting their coaching training from accredited or approved programs.[16] Similarly, managers and leaders who identify as coaches have similar training; of the 93% who received training, the majority (73%) came from accredited or approved programs. The ICF has three levels of coaching accreditation: Associated Certified Coach, Professional Certified Coach, and Master Certified Coach. All require varying numbers of study hours and minimum requirements for certification.[17]

Internal versus external coaching. The most common internal coach is the employee's direct supervisor or manager. These coaches are responsible for helping employees grow within the confines of their jobs and preparing them for future job opportunities. Referring back to Exhibit 11-2, the supervisor may use assignment and enrichment activities to ensure the employee progresses along a desired career trajectory. As well, the supervisor may be instrumental in helping with issues such as job design and job rotation. Lastly, supervisors must regularly assess employees as they do their jobs through the performance appraisal process. The information gathered in the performance assessment may be a key factor in lateral moves or promotion decisions for individual employees. It is easy to see how the supervisor or manager is the most important coach an employee has in an organization.

Talent management departments in organizations may also employ an internal coach, or the HR professional in the company may take on that role directly. An internal coach is a talent management professional whose role is to work with those employees who need or desire coaching to help their careers. Although in some instances the internal coach may be reserved for a certain level of employee (e.g., higher-level executives), the internal coach may also be asked to work with supervisors and managers to ensure they have some basic coaching training to help all levels of employees in the organization achieve their development goals.

One common way an internal coach works with employees is to help them navigate the transition between the two tines of the career fork. For example, a senior engineer may want to be more involved in strategic business management, and less involved with direct participation in and supervision of engineering projects. The coach will work with the senior engineer to help change his or her management mindset from one within the scope of science and engineering, to one that considers a broader scope of business-related issues and concerns. Career forks have been a common component in technology and manufacturing firms' organizational structure. These companies would greatly benefit from a dedicated internal coach to help with the unique career developmental needs of those in the science, technology, engineering, and mathematics (STEM) fields.

The external coaching professional typically works as an independent consultant, identifying and serving clients across a whole range of expertise. Coaches can range from spiritual or life coaches, to specialized executive coaches. Each coach has a unique skill set she or he can offer clients, and it is important, when looking for a coach, that you find one who matches your values and needs. Common to business organizations are business or executive coaches. An important difference between internal and external coaching is that the internal coach, while helping the employee, works for the organization, whereas the external coach works for the employee or client. External coaches have greater expertise in broad categories such as industry or functional expertise. Alternatively, internal coaches have greater expertise on the organization's environment, and are aware of where the landmines and challenges exist within the organization.

Balancing the pros and cons of internal and external coaches is important when committing to building a coaching relationship. The Society for Industrial and Organizational Psychology has published guidelines on when to use internal versus external coaches.[18] External coaches are more appropriate when you are looking for coaches for employees at the highest levels of the organization, when there is a culture of low trust, and/or when coaching is considered a last-ditch effort to improve performance of an employee. In short, it is important to use an external coach when political neutrality, maximum objectivity, and the highest level of confidentiality are needed in the coaching relationship.

Alternatively, internal coaches may be preferred for a variety of reasons. First, organizations should use internal coaches when they value reliability and consistency in approach. This is because coaching education among external coaches is currently unregulated and curriculums vary across coaching training programs (voluntary accreditation only exists through ICF). Because the coaching industry is not regulated in the same way, for example, CPA credentials are regulated, a coach acquired for one executive may differ in approach and outcomes from a coach acquired for another executive. Therefore, if consistency of approach is important, organizations should consider internal coaches.

Second, internal coaches may be preferred when financial constraints exist. The cost for external coaches is expensive. Even though the investment may yield a good return, if the company is experiencing financial difficulties, internal coaches are a more cost-effective solution. Lastly, internal coaches may be preferred when quicker, more efficient integration and system-level interventions are needed. As company insiders, internal coaches can more effectively coach employees to success because they are familiar with the organization's political and cultural environment, as well as the structure, policies, and procedures in place.

In terms of who pays for external coaches, coaches may be secured for employees by the organization if it does not have a formal internal coaching program. As well, employees may choose to contract and pay for their coaches directly, without the explicit support of the organization. If the organization pays, the external coach has to walk a line between meeting the contractual needs of the organization and serving the coaching client. The organization's and the client's needs may not always be in alignment, so negotiating the role of the coach and understanding the coach's philosophy in advance is important.

The cost and time commitment associated with using an external coach should not be underestimated, but the value such coaches can bring to individuals is extensive. Research on coaching effectiveness has faced challenges to draw conclusions because it is difficult to design research to measure properly the specific impact of coaching. Research done by Anna Blackman, Gianna Moscardo, and David Gray concluded there are practical challenges to measuring the impact of coaching on business outcomes because of the inability to assign subjects randomly to different coaching conditions.[19] However, just because there are research challenges doesn't mean we should dismiss the impact of coaching on employees and the organizations where they work. In their review of a cross section of 111 studies, Blackman and colleagues identified a number of benefits to employees and their organizations when coaches and coaching practices are utilized. Exhibit 11-12 summarizes the benefits found in their research.

Exhibit 11-12   Benefits of Coaching

Benefit to the Employee	Benefit to the Organization
• Better Work–Life Balance	• Increased Productivity
• Improving Psychological and Social Competencies	• Support Mechanism for Other Training Programs
• Improving Career Development	• Improvements to Communication
• Improving Self-Awareness and Assertiveness	• Effectiveness of Organization and Teams
• Increasing Confidence	
• Developing Relationship, Network, and Interpersonal Skills	
• Adapting to Change More Effectively	
• Helping to Set and Achieve Goals	
• Role Clarity	
• Behavior Changes	

(Continued)

Exhibit 11-12 (Continued)

Benefits to Employee and Organization

- Improvements in Interpersonal Dynamics and Teamwork
- High Levels of Motivation
- Increased Job Satisfaction, Job Retention, and Company Loyalty
- Increased Skill Levels
- Ability to Deal With Stressful Situations
- Improved Leadership and Management

Source: Adapted from Anna Blackman, Gianna Moscardo, and David E. Gray, "Challenges for the Theory and Practice of Business Coaching: A Systematic Review of Empirical Evidence," *Human Resource Development Review* 15, no. 4 (2016): 459–486.

Coaching phases. The coaching process tends to move across four phases.[20] First, clients focus on what to address. With the help of the coach, the employee is able to identify and focus on the issues that need to be addressed through coaching. Second, clients focus on the relationships they have and/or need to develop. Particularly as employees advance to higher levels in the organization, understanding the value of key players in the organization and the importance of building networks or coalitions of coworkers is important for success. Exhibit 11-13 highlights a blog post from Master Executive Coach Rob Berkley on the importance of leaders providing support to those they actively coach on the job. We include this here as it addresses the importance of building supportive relationships between employees and their coaches.

Third, clients create alignment between intentions and actions. Where they find their values are not in alignment with their actions, they can work to ensure intentions and actions are consistent. Fourth, clients make change in their organizations. Effective change cannot occur unless and until employees have a good sense of their strengths and weaknesses, are building positive and supportive relationships across the organization, and are ensuring their values align with their actions. The coach's job is to ask the right questions and help employees find the answers to these questions in each phase of the coaching process.[21]

MetrixGlobal conducted research to determine where the greatest return on investment occurs when organizations use business coaching to aid their employees to grow and develop,[22] and found three things. First, the monetary impact of executive coaching on the business increases as the coaching relationship progresses through the four phases. In fact, MetrixGlobal found 8 in 10 clients whose coaching made it to the second phase had a positive impact on business outcomes. Those who made it to the fourth phase had an even greater impact. Second, less than half of coaching relationships make it beyond the second phase. It is easy to conclude that coaching is underutilized with respect to its return on investment if it doesn't progress to helping employees make lasting change. Lastly, MetrixGlobal found that approximately 70%

Exhibit 11-13 Giving Support

Many leaders I work with initially complain their teams and certain individuals are not able to function independently without their direct input. When we discuss the situation, it often becomes clear the leader has not allowed the team or people to fully develop their skills without the leader stepping in to "speed things up," "fix things," or "show them how to do it." If you want independent teams and individuals, two leadership skills are essential.

The first is the ability to develop others. The second is the ability to support people. These two skills go hand in hand. This discussion focuses on supporting others.

When associates and teams are learning something difficult, suffering from loss, wrestling with an issue, striving to change, or engaged in conflict, they need support from you. They do not need you to step in and "fix it" unless there is danger or they are really stuck.

Support is the skill of connecting emotionally with people, acknowledging their struggle, empathizing with them, and making your care and concern evident to them as they go through something powerful and important.

It is not giving unasked-for advice, doing it for them, or intervening in such a way that they do not resolve the situation themselves. Being proficient at supporting others means:

1. Being emotionally available.
2. Having the patience to stay with them as they wrestle with an issue. Learning, growth, and change take time.
3. Understanding and acknowledging the difficulty of the task or process. After they have mastered it, people often forget how hard it was to do something.
4. Seeing when someone is truly stuck and needs help to move forward.
5. Understanding when a situation requires support.
6. Knowing how to deliver important messages in a clear, direct, and compassionate way.
7. Having the ability to really listen to others, hear what they are going through, and respond directly to it.

Struggling with issues, learning, and change allows your associates to develop the "muscles" to do their jobs better, to be more resilient, and to function independently. Giving support is the extra ingredient that bolsters them to hang tough when the going gets tough.

Without that ability developed over time at each level of their career or life, many people fold at the slightest challenge, and you will find yourself forever having to do their jobs—and yours.

Rob Berkley was the co-founder, with his wife, Debbie Phillips, of the executive coaching firm GroupMV. Rob was a Master Certified Coach from the International Coach Federation. Before opening his consulting practice, he served as a CEO, CIO, and board director for several well-known private and public companies in the technology, banking, and publishing industries, including Banker's Trust, Simon & Schuster, and Pearson. Until his death in 2018, Rob maintained a blog about leadership and coaching.

Source: Giving Support, Rob Berkley, http://www.robberkley.com/giving-support/.

of the monetary value of coaching comes from those coaching relationships that have evolved into phase three or four.

Keys to successful coaching. There are several factors to consider when designing and implementing an effective coaching program. Just as we consider the characteristics of the mentor and protégé, the same has to happen for the coach and client. Certain characteristics are essential to find in a coach. Similarly, coaching is most effective when the coachee, or client, exhibits certain characteristics. Care must be taken in building a trust between the two over the course of the coaching relationship. As well, just like any training program, the context, or coaching culture, must be amenable to ensure that the lessons learned in the coaching relationship can be transferred to the job to benefit the company. Lastly, the coaching process itself works best with key elements as part of the coaching relationship. Exhibit 11-14 highlights the factors needed for an effective coaching relationship.

Exhibit 11-14 Factors Leading to Successful Coaching

Coach	• Experience with coaching
	• Experience with relevant sector
	• Likable
	• Self-confident
	• Empathetic
	• Warm
	• Organized
	• Creative
	• Calm
	• Communicates clearly
	• Honest
	• Maintains confidentiality
Coachee/Client	• Self-efficacy
	• Motivation
	• Internal locus of control
	• Confident
	• Committed
	• Involved
	• Willingness to put forth effort
	• Ability/competence

Relationship	• Match between coach and client
	• One-on-one interaction
	• Trust
	• Authenticity
	• Challenge
	• Commitment by both parties
Organizational Context	• Support
	• Goal alignment
Coaching Process	• Encourage appropriate action
	• Use priorities and timelines
	• Relate personal to organizational goals
	• Identify blind spots
	• Constructive view of difficult issues

Source: Adapted from Anna Blackman, Gianna Moscardo, and David E. Gray, "Challenges for the Theory and Practice of Business Coaching: A Systematic Review of Empirical Evidence," *Human Resource Development Review* 15, no. 4 (2016): 459–486.

The match between coach and client is central to the coaching relationship because of the close personal work that must occur for coaching success. As represented by Debbie Phillips in the opening vignette, coaching is more than training or organizational development. It's about developing a deep personal relationship based on trust and authenticity. Coaches get to know their clients deeply so they can ask the right questions and challenge the clients to work toward their goals. Ensuring perceived similarities between coach and client based on outlook, perspective, values, and work habits helps to secure a successful match.

Coaches require a unique skill set to maximize effectiveness. Not all managers or supervisors are naturally effective coaches, so providing training in these areas will be helpful. Regardless of whether an individual is an internal or external coach, the following skills are generally agreed upon as essential for coaches. First, coaches should ensure alignment of intention and meaning when they speak to their clients.[23] Consider a simple example of agreeing where to meet when engaged in coaching. Although most coaching occurs over the phone so that the coach can focus on the client's words to hear what is being unsaid, oftentimes the coach and client may agree to meet face-to-face. Because coaching is about having a supportive, permissive relationship where the coach seeks permission to make suggestions if the client agrees, it is always better to err on the side of asking for and securing permission, rather than telling clients what to do. Instead of saying, "We will meet in a coffee shop during our next session because I think that is best," it is better to explain and then secure permission: "It is good every once in a while for us to meet face-to-face; are you OK if we meet in a coffee shop for our next session?" Directness is key, but not so direct you do not give the coaching clients the right to express their needs and desires. Coaches should consider how someone may interpret their words, not just assume their intent comes across clearly. We address more on communication in Chapter 12.

Along with clear communication regarding intent, coaches typically have high emotional intelligence,[24] enabling them to read and understand their own and others' emotions. Because of the deep personal relationship built between coaches and clients, managing the emotional context is important. Coaches should also be able to show empathy, know how to build rapport, engage in active listening, know how to ask questions first instead of providing solutions, and provide feedback with tact and diplomacy.[25] Again, we provide more details on these skills in Chapter 12.

Lastly, as will be discussed in Chapter 13 on training for differences, understanding cross-cultural issues and concerns is essential when dealing with a global workforce. Coaching isn't just limited to those who live and work in the same country. Coaching relationships can extend across global boundaries and work very well in a virtual context. The most important thing to remember is that coaches in one country cannot assume that their norms and values apply to an employee from another country.[26]

LEADERSHIP DEVELOPMENT

An important area in development activities involves **leadership development**. In fact, we can argue that the main goal of development in and of itself is to develop employees so they can become leaders in the organization. Even without that implied assumption, a central part of organizational development activities includes developing leaders to create a good basis for the organization's succession plan. While we could write an entire book on the importance of leadership development, we narrow our focus here to include the essential skills for leaders in the 21st century and the important steps for developing leaders.

A 2017 article in the *Harvard Business Review* states organizations are failing at an important metric for success—leadership development.[27] The authors highlighted research done by the Corporate Executive Board that found 66% of executives surveyed engaged in leadership development activities but only 24% of them believed their programs were successful. The raw talent is there, but not translating into action in organizations. The article shares eight leadership competencies on which organizations should focus: results orientation, strategic orientation, collaboration and influence, team leadership, developing organizational capabilities, change leadership, market understanding, and inclusiveness. Exhibit 11-15 defines these areas further. Performance on each competency may range from the lowest level, "baseline performance," to the highest level, "extraordinary performance."

In order to ensure your leadership development process not only finds leadership potential but also produces good leaders, the following steps should occur. First, organizations need to determine the most important competencies for leadership roles in their organization. Then, they must assess employee potential. There are five key predictors of leadership success: motivation, curiosity, insight, engagement, and determination.

Exhibit 11-15   Eight Essential Leadership Competencies

Competency	Predictors	Baseline Performance	Extraordinary Performance
Results Orientation	• Curiosity • Determination	Completes Assignments	Transforms Business Model
Strategic Orientation	• Curiosity • Insight	Understands Immediate Issues	Develops Breakthrough Corporate Strategy
Collaboration and Influence	• Curiosity • Determination • Engagement	Responds to Requests	Forges Transformational Partnerships
Team Leadership	• Curiosity • Engagement	Directs Work	Builds High-Performance Culture
Develop Organizational Capabilities	• Curiosity • Engagement • Insight	Supports Development Efforts	Instills Culture Focused on Talent Management
Change Leadership	• Curiosity • Determination • Engagement • Insight	Accepts Change	Embeds Culture of Change
Market Understanding	• Curiosity • Insight	Knows Immediate Context	Sees How to Transform Industry
Inclusiveness	• Curiosity • Engagement • Insight	Accepts Different Views	Creates Inclusive Culture

Source: Adapted from Claudio Fernández-Aráoz, Andrew Roscoe, and Kentaro Aramaki, "Turning Potential Into Success," *Harvard Business Review*, November–December 2017.

Upon assessing how leaders score on these five predictors, it is important to map leadership potential to the competencies required on the job, and assess the extent to which the employee exhibits those competencies. For example, referring to Exhibit 11-15, if inclusiveness is an important competency to the organization, potential is determined by the level of curiosity, engagement, and insight of the employees. Where a gap exists between the competency needed and what the employee exhibits, emerging leaders should be provided with development opportunities (see Exhibit 11-2), coaching, and the support they need to strengthen their critical competencies.

Leadership development is essential for organizations to be successful now and in the future. Good leadership development helps define the organization's succession plan and creates the infrastructure that allows all employees to succeed on the job. Just as we discussed the nine-box matrix in Chapter 10 to assess the development needs of all employees, leadership development helps us lay the groundwork for all members of the organization to be successful.

CHAPTER SUMMARY

Employee development is strategically important to organizations. When planning for the organization's future, it is important to ensure that employees are prepared for whatever is ahead to meet the organization's strategic needs. Development works closely with many HR functions and activities, and must be planned and assessed like any other training program.

Hand in hand with the strategic importance of development is the importance of employees being able to demonstrate learning agility. Learning agility assumes employees are willing to learn from mistakes and continue to grow and develop over the course of their career. Learning agility is essential for employees to reach their highest potential in the organization.

Development activities cover a wide variety of areas. First, managers can help employees to develop by ensuring they have the right kinds of assignments and enrichment opportunities. Some of those projects may be in the scope of the employee's job, but some can also be outside of that scope through volunteer roles such as participating in diversity committees and leading philanthropic activities. Second, jobs can be designed in such a way to help employees benefit over the course of their time on the job. Activities such as job shadowing and job rotation can expose employees to different opportunities and skill sets. When ready, they can expand on those skills and move toward different job opportunities both within and outside of the organization. Third, both traditional and nontraditional career paths can help employees map out a clear plan for their development. Knowing what opportunities lay ahead in their path can give them focus when seeking job opportunities. Even in nontraditional paths, or lateral moves, exposure to a broad range of skills and experiences is a huge benefit for employees to consider as they plan their careers.

Mentoring and coaching are also important tools that organizations can use to support employee development. Mentoring programs help ensure employees are supported as they traverse the organizational landscape. Care must be taken to ensure the mentoring program is tightly connected to the strategic goals of the organization. As well, the mentoring relationship must be planned for, and developed with care, so that both mentor and protégé can benefit from the program. Selecting and training mentors and protégés is imperative to ensure successful mentoring programs. Even if the mentoring program is informal, employees and their organizations can benefit from programs of this type. Overall, mentoring can result in greater employee retention and morale, help employees adapt to new cultures, and result in greater productivity and organizational performance.

While mentoring occurs within the boundaries of organizational relationships, coaches can be internal and/or external. There are pros and cons to both types of coaching, and organizations should be clear about what they want to accomplish before they make a commitment to either approach. While coaching can offer benefits to organizations even if the coaching relationship doesn't evolve much past identifying programs and developing relationships, it is important for coaches and clients to commit to achieving the desired outcomes.

Lastly, leadership development requires organizations to determine the key leadership competencies they want to see in their employees. Then, they can assess their employees to see how well they exhibit those areas needed for their jobs and their careers. Leadership development programs follow from these assessments so that custom programs are provided to employees as needed. Good leadership development is an important precursor to overall employee development and organizational capabilities. Good leaders ensure all employees have the capabilities to be the best they can be.

KEY TERMS

Assignments and enrichment opportunities. Development opportunities that are embedded in normal work activities and assignments, as well as special projects outside of the normal scope of work.

Coaching. A development activity focused on helping employees achieve better daily performance to enhance their careers.

External coach. Typically an independent consultant who contracts with the employee to provide career and performance advice. Expertise can range from spiritual and life coaching, to specialized executive coaching.

Internal coach. Typically a supervisor or manager, in-house human resource professional, or dedicated internal coaching professional who provides career and performance advice to the employee.

Job design development opportunities. Development opportunities that are embedded in the design of the jobs and work employees do, including job shadowing (following an experienced coworker around to learn the job) and job rotation (rotating through different job assignments to learn new skills).

Job transition development opportunities. Development opportunities that include typical vertical promotions as well as horizontal lateral moves in job progression and career ladders.

Leadership development. A specialized type of employee development with the purpose of identifying and developing future leaders in the organization; works hand in hand with succession planning.

Learning agility. The mindset and corresponding collection of practices that allow leaders to continually develop, grow, and utilize new strategies that will equip them for the increasingly complex problems they face in their organizations.

Mentor. A senior employee who advises, counsels, coaches, and promotes the career development of a junior employee.

Mentoring. A development opportunity that involves an intense work relationship between senior and junior organizational members; and involves advising, counseling, career coaching, and promoting the career development of the junior employee.

Protégé. A junior employee who builds a relationship with a more senior employee for the purpose of career development.

END-OF-CHAPTER QUESTIONS AND EXERCISES

Discussion Questions

1. Describe the strategic importance of development. Why should companies balance their focus on both training and development?

2. Discuss the role the HR department can play in improving employee development programs. What should HR do to ensure the organization is prepared for implementing and valuing employee development?

3. What challenges do multinational or global companies have when developing their employees? What HR activities can help overcome these barriers?

4. How do stretch assignments and job enrichment differ from extra-role enrichment?

5. What is the best way for HR managers and supervisors to determine who should get access to special assignments and project opportunities when they are available?

6. How do job shadowing and job rotation benefit small businesses over larger businesses as a form of employee development?

7. Discuss the role of performance appraisal in employee development. How can the outcomes from appraisals help with basic employee development?

8. Describe the two types of support that occurs in mentoring relationships. How do they differ? Why are both types important when building mentoring relationships?

9. What types of benefits are associated with mentoring programs?

10. Describe the characteristics of a good mentoring relationship. Explain why each characteristic is important.

11. List the four stages of the mentoring relationship. What occurs at each stage, and how can we best prepare mentors and protégés for these four stages?

12. What impact does gender and ethnicity have on the mentoring relationship? What kinds of outcomes can we expect, and how can technology (e-mentoring) help mitigate some of the problems?

13. What characteristics are important for a good protégé? What can one do to get the most from a mentoring relationship?

14. What are some of the advantages and disadvantages of using formal versus informal mentoring?

15. Explain the continuum of coaching roles, and describe the difference between internal and external coaching.

16. Explain the pros and cons of internal versus external coaches and under what circumstances each may be beneficial.

17. What benefits can one expect from coaching for employees and their organization?

18. What are the four phases of coaching? What kind of benefits can be expected as coaching relationships move through the four phases?

19. Describe the factors needed in the coaching client and the coaching relationship for a successful coaching experience. Can you draw parallels between the characteristics needed for success in mentoring and success in coaching?

20. Can coaching work well across global boundaries and in a virtual context? Explain how and why.

Ethical Scenario

Bill finished looking over the leadership potential assessments he collected from the employees in his organization. Bill knew that not everyone had the potential to be a leader in the company, but he believed that all employees needed to develop their skills to reach their full potential. One of the reasons why he loved working for his company is that management always put money behind development efforts. By combining the nine-box matrix with the leadership potential assessments, he fine-tuned his list of employees and the types of development he believed every employee needed to grow in the company. He presented his ideas to his new boss, Barb, who was the talent management director. Barb reviewed Bill's list but immediately told him he had listed too many employees: "I've never seen such an extensive plan for development. This is not reasonable. We should only focus our attention on high-potential employees to get the biggest bang for the buck." Bill argued with Barb, but she said her word was final.

Bill knew that Barb's boss, the chief HR director, believed in development for all. However, given Barb's statements, Bill was unclear if this meant there was a change in policy for the organization, or if Barb was just not aware of how important and extensive the employee development plan has been historically. Bill didn't know if he should simply comply with Barb's directive, or if he should go over her head to the chief HR director. Barb's actions are not illegal as they don't systematically discriminate against protected classes of employees, but somehow it doesn't feel right, or fair, to Bill.

a. What would you advise Bill to do in this scenario?

b. If he goes over Barb's head, what are the implications for Bill in terms of his relationship with Barb?

c. If he complies with Barb's directive, what are the implications for Bill within the organization, and in the eyes of the chief HR director?

11.1 Video Case: The Pecking Order

Review the TED Talk by Margaret Heffernan called "Forget the Pecking Order at Work," available from www.ted.com/talks/margaret_heffernan_why_it_s_time_to_forget_the_pecking_order_at_work?referrer=playlist-how_to_be_a_good_mentor#t-935533. Consider the discussion in Chapter 10 about managing high-potential employees and developing succession plans to enhance careers as you answer the questions below.

a. Summarize the message of the video about the dangers of only developing the highest potential employees.

b. What value is there in ensuring all employees get developed, not just your high-potential employees? How does it impact the whole organization when we ensure all employees have the skills to do their job and have opportunities to grow throughout their careers?

11.2 Video Case: "How NOT 2" Perform Coaching

Watch the following video by Michael Brown on what not to do when coaching an employee: https://youtu.be/pUYzoJWw44. Answer the questions below.

a. Identify the mistakes the coach makes in this coaching session.

b. Make recommendations for how the coach could improve on each mistake.

11.3 Mentee Readiness Assessment
Mentee Characteristics Survey

Complete this survey to assess your readiness to be a mentee. Assess each characteristic by putting an X in the appropriate box using the scale below as a guide. Look at your score on effective versus ineffective characteristics. Are you ready to be a mentee (protégé)? What areas do you need to develop to prepare for a mentoring relationship?

	Always	Frequently	Sometimes	Rarely	Never
Effective Characteristics	1	2	3	4	5
1. Am I Goal-Oriented?					
2. Do I Seek Challenges?					
3. Do I Take Initiative?					
4. Do I Show Eagerness to Learn?					
5. Do I Accept Personal Responsibility?					
6. Am I Proactive When Facing Challenges?					
7. Do I Change Depending on How I Want Others to Perceive Me?					
Ineffective Characteristics	1	2	3	4	5
1. Am I Too Self-Promoting?					
2. Am I Too Busy?					
3. Do I Lack Focus?					
4. Am I Overly Dependent?					
5. Do I Panic When Faced With a Crisis?					
6. Am I Unable to Manage Emotions Well?					
7. Do I Have a Hard Time Taking Feedback?					

Source: Adapted from University of Wisconsin–Madison, "Mentoring Resources." Available from https://acstaff.wisc.edu/professional-development/mentoring-resources.

CHAPTER TWELVE

PRACTICAL SKILLS FOR TRAINING AND DEVELOPMENT

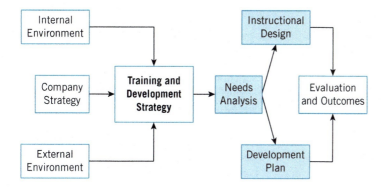

Learning Objectives

1. Explain how each of the different types of skills needed for training and development is important for trainers and trainees alike.

2. Select the appropriate conflict resolution style for a specific situation.

3. Explain how and why you should engage in assertive and supportive communication.

4. Discuss how to provide effective feedback.

5. Differentiate between levels of listening.

6. Provide advice on how to become a more effective listener.

7. Explain how people communicate nonverbally.

8. Recognize the importance of self-awareness and emotional intelligence for trainers and trainees.

Larry David teaches us about the "Chat and Cut" in Season 8, Episode 5, of *Curb Your Enthusiasm*.[1] You have likely witnessed this move and may have even been the perpetrator of it at some point, without even realizing it. In the scene, Larry is in the buffet line at a party when a woman walks up to a man in front of him and engages the man in conversation. Larry nudges his friend and explains that she is engaged in a "Chat and Cut" and will soon be picking up a plate and thus cutting in line. When she does that, Larry confronts the woman, and after a short discussion, she agrees to get out of line. However, she continues the conversation and uses that as an opportunity to cut in line behind Larry instead of in front of him. Larry applauds her skills, and the scene ends as the remainder of the people in line, who have been cut in front of, mutely stand there.

Most people would agree to a couple of things about this scene. One is that cutting into a buffet line is not polite. However, in the grand scheme of things, most people would also say that it is not that big of a deal. So, with those things in mind, here are a couple of questions about the situation. First, which person in the scenario are you (i.e., Larry, the woman, the man she talks to, or someone at the back of the line)? Second, did Larry handle the conflict appropriately?

While this scene highlights different ways of resolving a conflict, which are discussed in this chapter, it doesn't represent an employee performance issue. So, let's alter the scenario and see how that changes your answers to the previous questions. Instead of a buffet line at a party, the woman works in a retail store and is impolite to a customer. Further, Larry is now one of the store's managers. Does this change your estimation of Larry's behavior, and if so, how? Understanding how you would naturally respond to a conflict, as well as knowing the appropriate way to resolve it, represents an important interpersonal skill that an instructor, coach, or mentor should have.

Management guru Peter Drucker wisely understood that a manager's most important skill is the skill of learning new skills.[2] In other words, you must be willing to learn and adapt to new information and develop skills over a lifetime. Not just managers benefit from skill building. Training and development are all about building knowledge, skills, and abilities (KSAs). Thus, not only do managers benefit from building new skills, but so do employees and trainers. Whether you are leading the training or development session or participating as a trainee, it is important to develop basic skills to get the most out of the training session. This chapter is dedicated to essential skills we believe employees, their managers, and organization trainers need, at a minimum, to successfully navigate training and development activities.

We believe anyone engaging in training and development, as trainer or trainee, should possess five essential skills, as defined in Exhibit 12-1. First, one's communication style as a trainer or trainee is important to ensure what is being communicated is understood, and is an appropriate style given the context. Important areas of communication style include nonverbal communication and improvisational communication.

Hand in hand with communication style is listening skills. Both trainers and trainees need to be able to listen intently to understand what the other is communicating to facilitate learning the training material. We focus on differentiating the different levels of listening with an emphasis on developing better active listening skills.

Feedback skills naturally extend from communication style and listening skills. Trainers, managers, and trainees need to learn how to give effective feedback to enable the trainees to improve performance and apply learning on the job. We offer guidelines for providing effective feedback in this section.

Next is conflict resolution. In any interpersonal situation, miscommunication and differences of opinion and values will arise. While there is great value in having differences of opinions, mechanisms need to be in place to help organizations manage when conflicts over those differences arise.

Exhibit 12-1 Essential Skills for Training and Development

Skill	Definition
Communication Style	• The way in which we interact and share information with others
Listening	• The ability to accurately receive and interpret messages during the communication process
Feedback	• The ability to provide knowledge to others about the results of their behavior
Conflict Resolution	• The skills needed to resolve disagreements in values, motivations, ideas, or desires
Self-Awareness	• Knowing your motivations, preferences, and personality and understanding how these factors influence your judgment, decisions, and interactions with other people

Source: Adapted from Suzanne C. de Janasz, Karen Dowd, & Beth Schneider, McGraw Hill: NY, (2001).

The final skill is **self-awareness**, more specifically the impact of emotional intelligence on one's ability to be more self-aware. In order to engage in all these essential skills, self-awareness is needed to communicate as others need you to communicate, listen with the intent to understand, and manage conflicts judiciously as they arise. Self-awareness and emotional intelligence are needed to bring all of these skills together to become an effective trainer or a successful trainee.

Our goal is to present these skills to students of training and development so you can start your career with the essential basics to be an effective trainer. Each skill set is presented from the mindset that regardless of whether you are a peer, supervisor, manager, or corporate trainer, these essential skills will give you a solid foundation to participate in training and development activities as a trainer or trainee.

Unless you are designing computer-based or technology-enhanced training, when you present material to a room full of participants, you must exercise high levels of interpersonal competence to manage how you deliver the content as well as issues and concerns that arise. Appendix C addresses how to manage a training session, especially how to deal with disruptive trainees. In order to manage your training classroom, particularly through disruptions, you must know how to best communicate the training content, how to actively listen to understand the participants, how to communicate proper feedback, how to manage conflict as it may arise, and how to manage the emotional environment of the training session through self-awareness and emotional intelligence.

COMMUNICATION STYLE

How someone communicates has the power to help build or undermine relationships. This explains why it is important for trainers to recognize the communication style that they employ when communicating with trainees. Although there are different ways of describing communication styles,[3] this section focuses on three. Styles that promote interpersonal relationships, and by extension facilitate training and development, include assertive and supportive communication. Although there are differences between assertive and supportive communication, for the purposes of skill development they are sufficiently similar that we discuss them together as a single style. In turn, we contrast them with aggressive communication, which tends to make people defensive and thereby undermines instructor effectiveness. It is also important to note the difference between style and content. There will be times when you have to engage in difficult conversations and share information that a person may not want to hear or that would otherwise be considered negative. Although few people like being on the receiving end of negative information, they tend to be much more receptive to it when it is delivered in either an assertive[4] or supportive style.[5] Exhibit 12-2 highlights a blog post from master coach Rob Berkley about the value of **assertive/supportive communication**.

Among the clearest ways to discern whether someone is engaging in aggressive or assertive and supportive communication is the extent that someone says "you" as

---

Exhibit 12-2 It's Your Choice: Assertiveness or Aggressiveness

In a recent planning session I facilitated, I had the honor of watching a CEO demonstrate beautifully the skill of assertiveness.

During the intense two-day meeting, he proposed his ideas clearly and directly. He explored the inevitable resistance to change and new goals without anger, impatience, or frustration.

He was poised, calm, engaged, and comfortable inhabiting his role as the team took in his proposal and pushed back as high-functioning teams do. And he was comfortable standing firm on several points while changing his position as he gathered and incorporated the wisdom of his team.

Even though there were plenty of opportunities to do so during the meeting, the CEO never became aggressive. There was no acting out toward anyone, no bullying, no one-upmanship, no expressed anger, eye-rolling or frustrated facial expressions designed to intimidate and cow the others in the meeting.

As a leader of your own teams, what do you notice about your own stance, emotions, and tendencies when it comes to assertiveness?

The team left more tightly connected, even though everyone did not get his or her way. Good decisions were made, and there was agreement on focused action.

The strongest, most effective leaders are assertive. They have strong opinions. They have a strong inner foundation that allows them to hold their position calmly. And they do not need to resort to aggression to get things done.

I hope this has you thinking strongly about mastering the skill of assertiveness, which is listening, responding directly, affirming, embracing others' ideas, and reflecting.

Truly, it is one essential skill well worth developing as a leader.

Rob Berkley was the co-founder, with his wife, Debbie Phillips, of the executive coaching firm GroupMV. Rob was a Master Certified Coach from the International Coach Federation. Before opening his consulting practice, he served as a CEO, CIO, and board director for several well-known private and public companies in the technology, banking, and publishing industries, including Banker's Trust, Simon & Schuster, and Pearson. Up until his death in 2018, Rob maintained a blog about leadership and coaching.

Source: It's Your Choice: Assertiveness or Aggression, Rob Berkley, http://www.robberkley.com/its-your-choice-assertiveness-or-aggression/.

opposed to "I." People who communicate aggressively tend to use "you" more often. One implication of saying "you" is that it distances the speaker. Think about some common usages of "you": *You need to do that*, for example, and *Why did you do that?* The tone of the former is more of an order or demand than a request. Similarly, the explanation required from the latter makes it seem like a person did something wrong. At best, this style of communication is transactional, but even when viewed that way, it fails to recognize or build relationships.

Conversely, people with a more assertive or supportive style tend to use "I" with greater frequency.[6] When people use "I," they are often taking responsibility and/or providing an explanation. As such, there is less blame and more cooperation with assertive and supportive communication. Other characteristics of assertive and supportive communication include being more honest and direct but also fair and tactful.[7] From a training and development perspective, assertive and supportive communication creates an environment more conducive to learning.

In thinking about ways to improve your communication, especially in terms of training and development, Exhibit 12-3 provides advice on how to focus conversations. Items listed under the "Do" heading are consistent with assertive and supportive communication, whereas items listed under the "Don't" heading are consistent with more aggressive communication. In addition, we can think of assertive and supportive communication as a foundational skill for feedback, the topic of the next section.

Nonverbal Communication

When communicating with other people, it is not sufficient to focus on just what people are explicitly stating. People also communicate nonverbally, and it is important to both read those nonverbal messages and consider what messages you are sending through your nonverbal communication. This discussion of nonverbal communication is grounded in a U.S. context. People from differing cultures may interpret the same behavior or gesture quite differently. For example, how should the hand gesture, presented in Exhibit 12-4, be interpreted? The answer depends upon the cultural origins of the person viewing the gesture. People in the United States see OK; someone in Japan sees money; in France, it is the zero sign; and in Brazil, Germany, or Russia, you may offensively be referring to a body part.[8]

Exhibit 12-3 Ways to Improve Communication for Training and Development

Do (being more supportive/assertive)	Don't (being more aggressive)
Use "I"	Emphasize "you"
Describe	Evaluate
Focus on problem	Get personal
Offer solutions	Make judgments

Exhibit 12-4 Interpreting a Hand Gesture

When someone is making this gesture, she or he is communicating which of the following:
A. Something is OK
B. Money
C. Zero
D. Offensively referring to a body part

The behaviors used in the explanation of Exhibit 12-4 represent only some of the many ways that people communicate nonverbally. Although this textbook does not have the space to provide an exhaustive list of all nonverbal behaviors and their accepted interpretations, it is useful to think about the ways, or categories of behaviors that people can engage in, to communicate nonverbally. A listing of these is presented in Exhibit 12-5.

Kinesics are basically what people refer to as body language. Most of the time, when people think about nonverbal communication, they are thinking of a kinesic behavior, encompassing messages communicated with gestures and posture. In terms of posture, leaning in during a conversation is generally positive and sends the message that someone is more actively listening. As for gestures, tapping fingers during a conversation sends a negative message (e.g., boredom, disinterest, or impatience).

As the example of tapping fingers demonstrates, a potential problem with nonverbal communication is its lack of explicitness, which can result in multiple interpretations. In employment situations, this problem is particularly acute with **haptics**, or communication through touch. Receiving a "pat on the back" for a job well done is a classic example of a haptic. Haptics are also useful for demonstrating empathy. Unfortunately, the physical nature of haptics can be off-putting to some people and may be interpreted as sexually harassing; therefore, you should be cautious when engaging in this form of communication.

A third category of nonverbal communication is **proxemics**. Proxemics involves messages communicated through the use of physical space. Although not explicitly labeled as proxemics, this type of nonverbal communication has already been discussed (see Chapter 8 and the discussion of classroom arrangement). Similarly, anyone who has participated in planning a big event (e.g., a wedding) knows the politics involved in who

Exhibit 12-5 Types of Nonverbal Communication

Type	Basis	Example	Explanation of Example
Kinesics	Gestures/postures	Thumbs down	Disapproval
Haptics	Physical contact	Pat on the back	Job well done
Proxemics	Physical space	Sitting in a circle	Equality of status
Chronemics	Time	Spending extra time with someone	Person/relationship is important

sits where. Another important element with proxemics is personal space, but keep in mind that the appropriate amount of space between people varies by culture.[9]

The final type of nonverbal communication listed in Exhibit 12-5, **chronemics**, involves the use of time and can help denote how important someone views a relationship. Providing people with more time communicates to them that they, and/or the topic of discussion, is important. Similarly, if someone is frequently made to wait and/or wait a long time, that can communicate that he or she is not particularly important. As such, people in developmental relationships should keep chronemics in mind. For example, mentors need to provide their protégés with sufficient time to feel important.

Improvisational Communication

Organizations are paying closer attention to the benefits of improvisational training for improved communication, creativity, conflict management, and negotiation outcomes. Television shows such as *Saturday Night Live* and *Whose Line Is It Anyway?* and theater groups such as Second City in Chicago focus on the entertainment side of **improvisation**. Jazz music is another example of improvisation as entertainment. Improvisation goes beyond entertainment, however, and directly benefits communication, collaboration, and decision making in organizations.

More companies are bringing in improvisational trainers, through groups such as the Applied Improvisation Network, to help their employees apply the concept of "Yes, and . . ." to their daily work. "Yes, and . . ." is the concept whereby we accept what our negotiating or communication partner gives us and build on that to create synergy and greater collaboration. When we accept another's opinion as valid and work from that perspective, "Yes, and . . ." helps us to listen more effectively and be open to different opinions with the end goal of achieving mutual gains for all. Exhibit 12-6 shares an interview with improvisational actor and consultant Ed Reggi about how improvisation benefits organizations. Improv training can help trainers learn how to deal with conflict and effectively lead a training program.

Exhibit 12-6 Importance of Improvisation With Ed Reggi

Ask Ed Reggi to talk about improv, and he becomes laser focused. Not only is Ed an accomplished actor in his own right, trained at Second City with an Emmy Award for his work in TV; he is also a passionate advocate for the use of applied improvisation to help businesses be more successful. Improvisation had its roots during the Works Progress Administration (WPA) era in Chicago at Hull House. It was developed by Viola Spolin, and began as what we'd today call "drama therapy." Many residents at Hull House were immigrants and did not share a common language, nor were they very educated. According to Ed, "Viola had to figure out ways to remove both physical and language barriers to help residents work together." By developing what she called "theater games," she helped the residents to be more present, and facilitated a mind–body connection for them. The goal was for participants to be not in their body or in their head, but in the space "in between" to create something collectively—not what "I" want, not what "you" want, but what "we" want together.

(Continued)

Exhibit 12-6 (Continued)

From these theater games, Viola developed the concept of "Yes, and . . . ," which in essence means the agreement to act within a set of rules, whether individuals are playing basketball on the court or performing on stage. When we approach each interaction with the mindset of "Yes, let's play . . . let's work together!," we are working more toward building the relationship among the players involved, rather than forcing our will on another. This applies naturally to negotiation and business decision making. Ed believes improv moved to business organizations as employers brought in improvisational acting troupes like Second City to entertain employees at corporate events. Because the work on stage seemed so effortless, some savvy business executives asked how they could bring the magic of improv to their organizations. From this, the Applied Improvisation Network was born in the mid-1990s. Ed has been doing applied improvisation for about 15 years himself as a consultant with businesses all across the country.

When asked what he believed was the value of improvisation for businesses with respect to managing diverse others, Ed argued that the one thing he hopes clients take away from sessions with him is the nature of agreement. "'Yes, and . . .' has greater value for businesses than 'No, but . . .' because when they use 'No, but,' the lights go out in the room and all creativity and desire for agreement disappears. When execs realize they are getting in their own way and they realize they need to improve how they fundamentally listen, that's when you know the light bulb has gone on and they can make changes."

Ed argues "give and take" is the second thing he'd like clients to take away from his work with them. "Give and take" isn't just "I'm done with my part, so here you go—you take it now." "Give and take" is synergistic because it isn't my part and your part, but our work together. Team members take responsibility for each other. Sometimes we need support from our team when we are struggling, and sometimes we step up to the plate and take the lead, even when we might not be ready to or it wasn't part of the original plan. People have to be in the moment, and they have to adapt, because plans change quickly, particularly when organizations are continuously working more in areas of uncertainty or ambiguity. Scripts are good when things are programmed or easily predictable, but in the space of the unknown, improv helps people get out of their heads and into the situation so they can adapt to what is in front of them, not what they want things to be.

Ed concludes that when applying improv to training, it's important to recognize that we all have different points of view and different ways of experiencing the world. Just as improv helps people find the space between—not my idea, or your idea, but our idea—improv helps diverse people find common ground and ways to work together. "By staying in the world of agreement, you might find you were wrong, or the other person was wrong, and you might learn something new about yourself and the situation you are facing. And there is a lot of power in that."

Ed Reggi is the director of Paper Slip Theatre in St. Louis, Missouri, and works as an applied improvisation coach and consultant. He can be reached at edreggi@gmail.com.

LISTENING

"Can you hear me now?" was the basis of a Verizon marketing campaign. While hearing is great, what most people really mean when asking that question is whether someone is listening. Hearing is basically just an awareness of or response to a stimulus. Unlike listening, hearing does not necessarily involve conscious thought or effort. For training and development to be effective, both trainee and trainer need to listen to each other. Trainees need to listen so that they fully understand what is being taught. However, trainers need to listen as well. Those who don't listen are more likely to misdiagnose problems and less likely to successfully adapt their instruction—particularly important for mentors and coaches who focus on individual development.[10]

Exhibit 12-7	Levels of Listening	
Level	**Activity**	**Description**
Passive	Sensing	Just hearing or waiting to speak
Attentive	Processing	Reacting to what is said or jumping to conclusions
Active	Responding	Building understanding or relationships

Before providing tips to become a better listener, it is important to clarify and differentiate between hearing and listening. It is useful to think of listening as encompassing a continuum of behaviors that can be separated into three different levels.[11] At the lowest level, people are simply sensing, but as they become more effective listeners, they also engage in processing and responding.[12] These levels will be formally referred to as passive, attentive, and active listening. Exhibit 12-7 presents these types of listening in terms of listener activity at each level.

Passive Listening

When people listen passively, they may hear what the other person is saying, but they are unlikely to fully comprehend what is being said. One reason for this is that the passive listener is not applying any filter or looking for any key words to provide context and/or structure. This can happen even if a person thinks that he or she is listening more intently as in the case of taking notes. For example, think about a time that you worked furiously in a class to write down everything the instructor said, and when you looked over your notes, they didn't make any sense. The notes prove that you heard what the instructor said, but the lack of comprehension shows the need for a higher level of listening.

It is also possible to start at a higher level of listening, but then descend into passivity. This frequently occurs when people really want to say or ask something. In these situations, a person may have been actively listening but begins to rehearse a question and/or holds on to a thought so strongly that he or she ceases to follow the conversation, discussion, or lecture. You may notice this in class when a fellow student says something that the instructor has just addressed and/or is no longer relevant.

Attentive Listening

Attentive listening is an improvement over passive listening. Here listeners understand more of what is being said, but are still not fully engaged. Again, there are multiple symptoms of attentive listening, one of which is typified by the following example. Think about a conversation where you are discussing taking a vacation and mention the location, and the other person immediately asks where you are going.

Another issue with attentive listening occurs when someone makes assumptions. Think about a game show where contestants want to beat their opponent and ring in before the question or clue is completed. Sometimes the contestant gets lucky, but often jumping to conclusions means not hearing that necessary information, which results in an incorrect answer. A similar situation occurs with training when the trainee doesn't wait until the end of instructions before starting on an exercise or project. As a result, the trainee may have trouble finishing a task and/or make mistakes. In these situations, the attentive listener has paid enough attention to know basically what is said but fails to listen for the relevant details. While better than passive listening, this can still undermine learning.

Active Listening

The highest level of listening is **active listening**. Individuals who listen actively are fully engaged in a discussion or training. While active listening incorporates the activities of the levels of listening below it, it can also change their nature. For example, proponents of active empathetic listening explain how sensing grows from just a response to auditory stimuli to an awareness of nonverbals, which provides greater nuance and understanding.[13] The benefits of active listening include increased understanding and improved relationships, because active listening is more confirmatory and validating. Exhibit 12-8 provides a list of seven attributes associated with active listening,[14] and organizes them to help explain how they improve understanding and build relationships.

One of the first things that active listeners do is to make efforts to hear what a speaker is saying. While hearing may not be sufficient for understanding, it is a necessary condition. Active listeners also remove distractions (e.g., turning off the TV or music and putting away cell phones). This makes it easier for the listener to focus on the speaker. In addition, the listener doesn't interrupt, but rather waits until the speaker finishes what she or he is saying before speaking in return.

Active listeners also consider the whole message. While hearing is necessary for listening, words represent only part of the message, for a couple of reasons. First, listeners should keep in mind the context of the conversation and speaker. This reflects the fact that the meaning of a word or phrase can vary culturally. This is one important reason not to use idioms when having a conversation with a non-native speaker. Also, it is possible to communicate without using words. A person can use nonverbal communication to emphasize a point, but people who are not careful can contradict what they are trying to say. Demonstrating each of these points is eye contact. In the United States, maintaining eye contact allows the listener to let the speaker know that she or he is listening actively. Conversely, failing to maintain eye contact can convey to the speaker that the listener is not paying attention to what is being communicated. However, in some cultures, it is not appropriate, especially if the speaker is of a higher social status, to look another person in the eye.[15] We provide more on this in the following subsection.

Exhibit 12-8 Attributes of Active Listening

Improve Hearing	Consider the Whole Message	Confirm the Message
Remove distractions	Recognize context	Clarifying questions
Focus on speaker	Aware of nonverbals	Paraphrasing/summarizing
Don't interrupt		

Finally, active listeners don't assume that they got the message correct the first time around. Confirming the message both improves understanding and validates the importance of the message and messenger. One way of doing this is to simply ask clarifying questions. If a listener does not understand something, he or she should follow up with the speaker. Even if you feel the listener understood everything, he or she should still paraphrase or summarize what was said as this allows the original speaker to correct any misunderstandings.

FEEDBACK

Employees need feedback, but many people avoid providing it.[16] There are numerous reasons for this, but they generally fall into one of the following broad categories. Some people simply don't think feedback is necessary or effective. This can reflect an external locus of control where the belief is that people can't sufficiently control outcomes. It is also common for individuals to be performing well but it doesn't occur to their trainer or supervisor to provide feedback. Other trainers and supervisors may simply find themselves too busy, and while they may feel feedback is important, they don't have or make the time to provide it. Discomfort is another reason people avoid providing feedback and contributes to the so-called mum effect[17]—particularly if someone is not doing a good job and the instructor or supervisor either doesn't want to be mean or is concerned with how the employee will react.

Despite these reasons for not providing feedback, the benefits that employees and organizations gain explain why it is a skill worth developing. These benefits depend on whether they are associated with positive or constructive feedback. Positive feedback is provided when someone is doing a good job. People both like and need this type of feedback. Positive feedback recognizes good performance, and this can be both validating and rewarding to someone who has been working hard. Positive feedback also clarifies and reinforces behavior and lets individuals know how they are progressing toward a goal.[18] There are two dangers if someone doesn't receive positive feedback. One danger is that the person can become demotivated. Alternatively, people may change their behavior because it wasn't made clear to them what they should be doing, which could impair their performance.

In comparison to positive feedback, **constructive feedback** is provided to an employee when his or her performance does not meet expectations or requirements. Constructive feedback identifies what the employee is doing wrong and what steps he or she needs to take to correct the performance issue. The goal of constructive feedback is that by helping employees change their behavior, performance improves. Without constructive feedback, performance issues tend to persist and/or become more acute[19] because employees are unlikely to change their behavior. Note also that constructive feedback is not the same as negative feedback. Although negative feedback also informs employees that they are doing something wrong, it usually fails to do so in a way that facilitates behavioral change. Another way to think about the difference between constructive and negative feedback is how the information is delivered. Constructive feedback tends toward a more assertive or supportive style of delivery whereas negative feedback is delivered more aggressively.

Expanding on the advice from communication style, Exhibit 12-9 lists guidelines that facilitate the effective provision of feedback. Generally, you should follow these guidelines whether you are providing positive or constructive feedback. The guidelines are organized into three categories. The first area to consider is the currency of feedback.[20] Currency here refers to the temporal nature, rather than any monetary aspects, of feedback. First, feedback should be timely. The sooner feedback is given, the fresher the behaviors will be in the mind of the individual. As time passes, the rewarding and validating value of positive feedback fades. When not positive, individuals are more likely to become defensive to delayed feedback. Increasing the frequency of feedback helps to both normalize it and help it to be delivered in a more timely fashion.

While knowing when to provide feedback is important, trainers should not lose sight of the actual content of the feedback.[21] The first thing to remember is that feedback should be specific. Specific feedback helps to focus the conversation and clarifies which behaviors should be reinforced or corrected. Vague feedback is not particularly useful. Another aspect of being specific is that the trainer should limit the number of behaviors discussed. Feedback, especially when it is meant to be constructive, should be verifiable. Verifiability means that examples and evidence are provided. Besides providing clarification, examples and evidence increase the legitimacy of the feedback and decrease the chances that someone will react defensively. In addition, a person should be able to exert some level of control over his or her behaviors and/or the situation.[22] If people can't control things, how will they be able to either repeat or change their behavior?

The last aspect of providing feedback to keep in mind is how to deliver it.[23] The delivery of feedback is particularly important when it is not positive. Even if the currency and content of the feedback is good, you can undermine its effectiveness if you deliver it improperly. First, the feedback should be objective. Objectivity means that you are not getting personal and are treating the other person in a professional manner. For example, if the feedback contains anything resembling "What kind of idiot does that?," the other person is likely to get defensive and/or not listen to you. Also, it is generally a good idea to avoid, or at least limit, including your personal opinions. The final guideline is to keep feedback balanced.[24] When possible, when you are telling someone that she or he needs to change or correct a behavior, it is also good to provide some positive feedback. This tends to increase the perceived fairness of the feedback and makes a person more receptive to it.

One caveat for Exhibit 12-9 is its focus on providing feedback within a U.S. context. People from other cultures may respond differently to the same feedback. For example, in some cultures, a balanced delivery is not as effective. In these cultures, the balanced delivery softens the criticism, which lessens the perceived need to change behavior.[25]

Exhibit 12-9 Guidelines for Effective Feedback

Currency	Content	Delivery
Timely	Specific	Objective
Frequent	Verifiable	Balanced
	Controllable	

CONFLICT RESOLUTION

In a perfect world, the people being trained, coached, or mentored will fully engage in the process. Unfortunately, this is not a perfect world, and at times, trainers, coaches, and mentors experience pushback from the person with whom they work. Such pushback is just one example of conflict that individuals will experience at work and in life. As such, the ability to effectively manage conflict should be one of the interpersonal skills in which a trainer, mentor, or coach is adept.[26]

The first step in resolving a conflict successfully is to correctly diagnose it. Exhibit 12-10 shows the two important elements of conflict[27] that need to be identified in order to choose the appropriate resolution style. The first element, represented by the x-axis, is the importance of the outcome. The second element, represented by the y-axis, is the importance of the relationship. In addition, most of us have a preferred conflict resolution style (you will have the opportunity to explore yours in the end-of-chapter exercises); however, it may not be appropriate when you are engaged in training, coaching, or mentoring. Recognizing the appropriateness of your preferred conflict resolution style can make you a better trainer, coach, or mentor.

To help you understand the different conflict resolution styles represented in Exhibit 12-10, let's examine the opening vignette. Remember this is an example of a "Chat and Cut" where a woman engages a man in conversation with the purpose of cutting into a buffet line. The woman is engaged in competition. Cutting into line is her goal, and she doesn't seem to care about the people behind her. Larry David is also competing because he only seems concerned about policing the line and not letting her get in front of them. Although they eventually reach a compromise, because neither fully wins, that is not the conflict resolution style employed because neither of them initially intends or expects to reach a middle position. Similarly, the man she talks to is engaged in accommodation because after they talk he initially is willing to allow her to cut in line behind

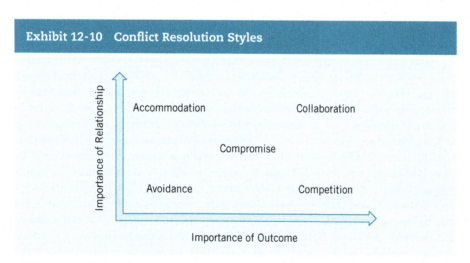

Exhibit 12-10   Conflict Resolution Styles

Source: Adapted from Kenneth W. Thomas, "Conflict and Conflict Management," in *The Handbook of Industrial and Organizational Psychology*, ed. M. Dunnette (Chicago: Rand McNally, 1976).

him. As for the people at the back of the line, they are engaged in avoidance because they do not get involved at all. Finally, collaboration is not represented in the scene.

So, which person(s) acted appropriately in the scenario? That really depends on how much value is attached to one's place in the buffet. If there is agreement that maintaining the order in the buffet line is an important outcome, and because there is not a relationship between Larry and the woman, then their competing would be appropriate. However, if there is consensus that cutting into a buffet line is not an important outcome, then they did not act appropriately. In this case, the man who accommodates could be considered to act appropriately because the woman tries to establish a relationship. Similarly, the people at the back of the line who engage in avoidance are acting appropriately because they do not care about a relationship or the outcome in this situation.

When thinking about conflict resolution in the context of training or development, it is possible to be somewhat prescriptive as to which styles should or should not be used. This is because the importance of both the relationship and the outcome can be anticipated. The five conflict resolution styles can be sorted into those that are either less likely or more likely to be effective when engaged in training or development. Specifically, avoidance, accommodation, and competition are likely to be less effective. Conversely, compromise and collaboration are expected to be more effective. Knowing which styles to engage in, as well as which not to use, allows for those participating in training or development to have more successful outcomes regarding employee learning and growth in addition to the actual conflict.

Less Effective Conflict Resolution Styles

In a training or development context, it is unlikely that avoidance will ever be the most appropriate method. While the depth or expected length of the relationship between people and their trainers, coaches, or mentors may differ, a relationship does exist between the parties. Similarly, while the criticality of the KSA that you are trying to impart will vary, there is some level of importance to the outcome of training or development. Therefore, trainers, coaches, and mentors should generally pick a conflict resolution style other than avoidance, unless they have some strategic reason for doing otherwise.[28]

Although instances may occur where accommodation or competition is appropriate, these conflict resolution styles are generally less effective in a training or development context. This is because each of these styles takes a relatively extreme position. Starting with accommodation, people who choose this option are basically making the decision that the relationship is more important than what the other person is, or is not, doing. While a limited application of this may be appropriate in a training or development context, this is untenable in the long term. The reason people engage in training or development is to learn, grow, and/or change. If trainers, coaches, or mentors allow the people they are working with to persist in their behavior, then they are not doing their job.

At the other end of the spectrum from accommodation is competition. Again, there may be instances where this is the appropriate response to a situation, but this is seldom the case with training or development. When individuals choose to resolve a conflict through competition, they are basically saying that the only thing that matters is the outcome. Ignoring the relationship, especially when engaged in development, can be counterproductive as it is unlikely to result in a positive reaction from the other individual (for more, see the discussion of negative feedback earlier in this chapter). Arguably, using competition to correct performance issues is more consistent with a disciplinary approach than a developmental one.

More Effective Conflict Resolution Styles

The remaining two conflict resolution styles, compromise and collaboration, are more in keeping with the ethos of training and development and should therefore lead to better results.[29] Each of these styles balances the needs of the relationship as well as the outcome. One of the main things that distinguishes these two styles is a person's mindset. A person can have a **distributive** mindset where conflict is conceived as a zero-sum game or an **integrative** mindset where a win-win scenario is possible.[30]

Of the remaining conflict resolution styles, compromise is most consistent with a distributive mindset. One way to see this is to, using Exhibit 12-10, draw a straight line from accommodation to competition. Falling at the midpoint of this line is compromise. This line reflects a distributive mindset where the two parties in the conflict are working with a fixed value and simply divide it between them. So, while compromise shows a general willingness to work with another person, the outcome is somewhat limited. This results in a more standard and predictable outcome. While the results should be good, they are not likely to maximize an individual's potential.

By comparison, collaboration is more likely to maximize the potential of the opportunity and to fully meet the needs of those involved. One reason for this is that the person sees both the outcome and the relationship as more important and therefore puts forth more effort. Because collaboration takes advantage of a more integrative mindset, there is a greater willingness to engage in problem solving and to be more creative. While the results of collaboration can be superior to those of compromise, it does take more effort. If someone is interested in being more collaborative, several of the skills discussed in this chapter will help to achieve that (e.g., active listening and emotional intelligence). However, the process can be more involved, and the value of the potential outcome and/or relationship may not warrant its use.

SELF-AWARENESS

Ben Franklin has been attributed with the saying "There are three things extremely hard: steel, a diamond, and to know one's self." *Self-awareness* is defined as knowing your motivations, preferences, and personality and understanding how these factors influence your judgment, decisions, and interactions with other people.[31] There will be moments when you are leading or participating in a training or development session when you are faced with an issue that stretches your abilities or triggers you to have a negative reaction. Understanding why a situation is challenging is important to help you manage and avoid the problem in the future. Self-awareness can also help you communicate more clearly, manage training sessions more effectively, and navigate potential conflicts. Finally, as you finish leading a training session and are debriefing to adjust for the future, it is important to understand how your own strengths and weaknesses contributed to

> **Exhibit 12-11 Report Like an Astronaut**
>
> The coaching and mentoring you receive will be more effective if you learn to report about your inner world like an astronaut does when on a mission. Astronauts and other explorers are trained and have the ability to describe the new worlds they are exploring. Their words can paint a picture so vivid others can share their experiences without being there.
>
> As your coaching progresses and your self-awareness grows, work on sharing in exquisite detail your experiences, your thoughts, your feelings, and your discoveries about yourself so your coach can participate with you in your growth and development.
>
> The practice of self-observation, reflection, and reporting back strengthens the coaching partnership and speeds your progress.
>
> By doing so, you will develop a lifelong skill that will allow you to make personal changes effectively and increase your effectiveness as a leader and developer of others.
>
> How are you at taking others along on your journey of self-discovery? Without this skill, you're a bit like an astronaut on the moon without a two-way radio.
>
> *Rob Berkley was the co-founder, with his wife, Debbie Phillips, of the executive coaching firm GroupMV. Rob was a Master Certified Coach from the International Coach Federation. Before opening his consulting practice, he served as a CEO, CIO, and board director for several well-known private and public companies in the technology, banking, and publishing industries, including Banker's Trust, Simon & Schuster, and Pearson. Up until his death in 2018, Rob maintained a blog about leadership and coaching.*
>
> Source: Rob Berkley, Report Like an Astronaut http://www.robberkley.com/report-like-an-astronaut/.

the success of the training. Being willing to get feedback that may be less than positive is enhanced by being self-aware and clear about your strengths and weaknesses.

We develop our self-concept by examining our behaviors, personality, attitudes, and perceptions, along with understanding the perceptions others have of us. We also explore and learn about ourselves when we encounter diverse experiences. For every new experience, we gain new information about who we are and what we like or dislike. All of these factors influence our self-concept and help us to be a better trainer or trainee. Exhibit 12-11 highlights a blog post from master coach Rob Berkley on the importance of self-awareness during the coaching or mentoring process.

Emotional Intelligence

One method we can use to be more self-aware is to develop our emotional intelligence. **Emotional intelligence** is the ability to perceive, understand, regulate, and use emotions well in oneself and in others.[32] Although the concept was popularized around 1996 when Daniel Goleman's book[33] made the *New York Times* Best Seller list, the importance of emotional intelligence was established long before his book was published. A lot of measures in the public domain assess aspects of emotional intelligence, including the Emotional Quotient Inventory (EQ-i),[34] the Emotional Competence Inventory (ECI),[35] the Schutte Self-Report Inventory (SSRI),[36] the Trait Emotional Intelligence Questionnaire (TEIque),[37] and the Mayer-Salovey-Caruso Emotional Intelligence Test

(MSCEIT).[38] Whether you believe emotional intelligence is a trait or an ability dictates which measure you would use to assess it. The most commonly used measure among researchers is the MSCEIT, considered an ability measure. If it is an ability, this means that people can develop their emotional intelligence over time and with training. For the purpose of training and development, we believe that emotional intelligence is an ability, and we encourage all employees, whether trainers or trainees, to find ways to develop their ability to understand and manage their emotions.

According to the MSCEIT, emotional intelligence is hierarchical, meaning ability grows as you master each level of emotional intelligence. At the base is *perceiving/identifying emotions*. In order to be emotionally intelligent, you must be able to identify an emotion and recognize it in yourself and others. The next level is *using emotions*, followed by *understanding emotions* and, lastly, *managing emotions*. We all experience emotions, but the ability to strategically use emotions and control their use is important for any manager, trainer, or employee in general.

Imagine you are leading a training session and one of the participants is being aggressive and acting upset that she has to attend the session. She speaks out of turn, and constantly interrupts you as you are trying to explain the information. It would be easy to let emotions escalate and end up in a verbal or, worse yet, physical confrontation with her if you were not in tune with your emotions and how to best handle the situation. But by being emotionally intelligent, you recognize that she is angry, remain calm while you try to defuse the situation, and ultimately find a way to calm the participant and have her engage in a more productive manner. Being emotionally intelligent enables you to manage conflict more effectively and manage your training sessions with greater success. You can adapt to the various emotions in the room and adjust your emotions to keep the session calm, engaging, and interesting. Even as a trainee, having high emotional intelligence enables you to have patience when you feel frustrated with a training session that may not be managed in the best way to facilitate your ability to learn.

CHAPTER SUMMARY

Trainers need some fundamental skills, regardless of whether they are peer trainers, managers, or professional trainers. First, those leading training sessions need to be able to present well and manage the classroom environment. An essential part of level 1 training evaluation is to ensure the training environment is conducive to learning, and the trainer is effective. Thus, the trainer has to know how to facilitate the training session and present the material effectively.

Because training is essentially an interpersonal experience, trainers need to communicate well, listen to their trainees, provide feedback, and manage conflicts as they arise. Trainees also need to have strong interpersonal skills to make the most out of the training session and be able to communicate their training needs more clearly. Even mentoring or coaching pairs need to build a good rapport based on strong communication and a willingness to give and receive feedback. Regardless of the level of the employees, good interpersonal skills extend beyond training and development, enhancing individual, group, and organizational performance.

Lastly, self-awareness, specifically emotional intelligence, makes all of the above possible. Self-awareness enables trainers, mentors, and coaches to support those they are trying to help by knowing their own strengths, weaknesses, motivations, and values. One of the best tools to become more self-aware is to develop your emotional intelligence. Once individuals can recognize and manage their own emotions, they can more effectively manage a training session and exhibit greater interpersonal competence. Self-awareness also opens the door for trainees to recognize where they need to improve, and how to best learn the material given to them from a trainer, coach, or mentor.

KEY TERMS

Active listening. The highest level of listening; occurs when the listener is fully engaged in the conversation (e.g., aware of context in addition to content).

Assertive/supportive communication. A style denoted by honesty and tact that builds relationships and makes difficult conversations easier.

Chronemics. A category of nonverbal behavior involving the use of time.

Constructive feedback. Communication given to change a person's behavior that is done in an objective manner and provides information to help correct the behavior.

Distributive. An approach to conflict resolution where the outcome is perceived as zero-sum (i.e., winners and losers).

Emotional intelligence. The ability to perceive, understand, regulate, and use emotions well in oneself and in others.

Haptics. A category of nonverbal behavior involving physical contact (e.g., pat on the back).

Improvisation. The concept of accepting what a person is given by a communication or negotiation partner with the goal of building upon it to create synergy and greater collaboration.

Integrative. An approach to conflict resolution where there is a belief that a win-win outcome is possible.

Kinesics. The most commonly thought of category of nonverbal behavior, which involves gestures and posture.

Proxemics. A category of nonverbal behavior involving the use of space.

Self-awareness. How well a person knows his or her motivations, preferences, and personality and understands how these influence personal judgments, decisions, and interactions.

END-OF-CHAPTER QUESTIONS AND EXERCISES

Discussion Questions

1. Identify and explain which conflict resolution styles instructors, coaches, and mentors should avoid.
2. Discuss what you can do to become a more assertive and supportive communicator.
3. Why is it important to provide feedback?
4. What factors make feedback more effective?
5. Explain how there are different ways of listening.
6. What should you do to be a more active listener?
7. Provide an example and explanation for each category of nonverbal behavior.
8. Recommend some ways that we can be more self-aware and learn about ourselves and our strengths and weaknesses. How can we create ongoing attention to the need to learn and grow to be a better manager, employee, or trainer?

Ethical Scenario

Missed Connection

Stan was doing a presentation on emotional intelligence for the employees at his organization. He was explaining the concepts, but also wanted to connect with his audience more deeply. Because people always told him he was funny, Stan thought that tossing some light-hearted humor into the presentation would be helpful. As he started talking about emotions management, he said, "We know it is important to manage our emotions, even when it is difficult. We don't want to get overly emotional like women get, right?" He noticed some people laughed, but some people bristled at the joke. It seemed it didn't create the connection he had expected because the energy in the room plummeted and people stopped participating voluntarily.

1. Discuss the ethics of Stan's joke choice. While he did nothing illegal, how did this gender stereotyping hurt his presentation? What impact did his joke have on the training session and the trainees? What could he have done differently to accomplish his goal?

2. Now, replace the name *Stan* with the name *Sarah*. Sarah was leading the discussion and made the same statement: "We don't want to get overly emotional like women get, right?" Would your reaction be different if Sarah made the comment, not Stan? Why or why not? Was it a form of self-deprecating humor, or still a form of gender norm stereotyping when Sarah said it? How would you provide appropriate feedback to your trainer if you heard either a male or female use that statement?

Skill-Building Exercises

12.1 Managing a Conflict With an Employee

You have been a supervisor with Creative Marketing for five years, and you feel that the group you direct works well together. Eight months ago, you hired Alex, and overall you have been impressed with how quickly Alex has learned the job and is currently performing. However, you have noticed that other people in the group are still submitting Alex's financials. While this is typical for the first month or two, by now Alex should have started submitting those personally. When you solicited feedback for Alex's six-month review, everyone just had positive things to say, and no one mentioned an issue with submitting the financials for Alex.

Based on this information, rank the following options from best (1) to worst (5).

A. ____ Confront Alex and explain that submitting the financials is his responsibility and, if he hasn't figured out how to do them, he better learn quickly.

B. ____ Assign Christine, the senior person in the group, to work with Alex so that he learns how to submit the financials on his own.

C. ____ Do nothing; no one is complaining, so the group members must have worked something out.

D. ____ Thank the other employees in your group and reassure them that you are sure Alex will pick up on how to do the financials soon.

E. ____ Have a conversation with Alex to find out why he isn't submitting the financials himself and then work on a plan so that he will be able to start submitting them on his own.

Categorizing responses by conflict resolution style:

A = Competition

B = Compromise

C = Avoidance

D = Accommodation

E = Collaboration

12.2 Active Empathetic Listening

The following adapted scale[39] provides you with an opportunity to assess the extent that you engage in active empathetic listening. Using the scale provided, record how often each of the following statements is true when you are having a conversation with another person.

1	2	3	4	5	6	7
Never or Almost Never True	Usually Not True	Sometimes but Infrequently True	Occasionally True	Often True	Usually True	Always or Almost Always True

1. ____ I am sensitive to what the other person is not saying.

2. ____ I am aware of what the other person implies but does not say.

3. ____ I understand how the other person feels.

4. ____ I listen for more than just spoken words.

5. ____ I assure the other person that I will remember what she or he says by taking notes when appropriate.

6. ____ I summarize points of agreement and disagreement when appropriate.

7. ____ I keep track of the points the other person makes.

8. ____ I assure the other person that I am listening by using verbal acknowledgments.

9. ____ I assure the other person that I am receptive to his or her ideas.

10. ____ I ask questions that show my understanding of the other person's positions.

11. ____ I show the other person I am listening by my body language (e.g., head nods).

Sum the entire scale for your overall level of active empathetic listening. To understand how you listen in terms of the individual dimensions of active empathetic listening, sum the responses for each of the following sets of questions.

Questions 1–4 = Sensing

Questions 5–7 = Processing

Questions 8–11 = Responding

12.3 Emotional Intelligence

Go to the following link and take the emotional intelligence questionnaire: www.ihhp.com/free-eq-quiz.

First, answer the following questions:

a. How did you score on the emotional intelligence test? Was your score lower or higher than you expected?

b. What areas does your score reveal you could improve on?

Next, review the following video about ways to improve emotional intelligence: Ramona Hacker, "6 Steps to Improve Your Emotional Intelligence," *TEDxTUM*, available from https://youtu.be/D6_J7FfgWVc.

c. Based on what you reviewed in the video, develop an action plan for how you will develop your emotional intelligence.

CHAPTER THIRTEEN

TRAINING FOR DIFFERENCES: UNDERSTANDING CULTURE AND DIVERSITY

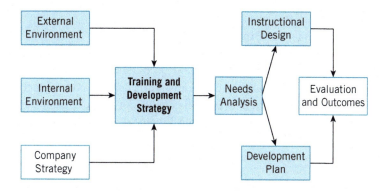

Learning Objectives

1. Develop a training program for international employees taking Hofstede's cultural dimensions into account.

2. Identify elements of organizational culture.

3. Critique onboarding programs to ensure they include recommended elements that span from recruitment through long-term mentoring programs.

4. Design orientation programs to meet corporate strategic objectives.

5. Summarize the different dimensions of diversity.

6. Discuss the importance of respecting differences in the workplace.

7. Recognize the stage of diversity awareness and consider those stages when designing a diversity training intervention.

8. Describe the ethical concerns associated with training, developing, and managing diverse others.

The Smithsonian Institution is known by most as a series of museums in Washington, DC. Of late, the Smithsonian has been lauded for its commitment to diversity. In fact, in 2018, *Forbes* magazine named the Smithsonian second on its list of America's Best Employers for Diversity (www.forbes.com/sites/jeffkauflin/2018/01/23/americas-best-employers-for-diversity/#62de3ff17164). The Smithsonian says the following on its website (www.si.edu/dashboard/people-operations#employees):

> The range of job types is immense—from scientific research to exhibition design to museum operations to security. The Smithsonian seeks to attract and maintain a creative workforce that is representative of America's diversity, including expanding employment opportunities for individuals with disabilities. Employees consistently rank the Smithsonian as one of the "Best Places to Work" among midsize federal agencies.

The Smithsonian's view of diversity, however, expands beyond demographic diversity and job types. The organization has employees in locations all over the world, including the United States and Panama, embracing global diversity and the value of cultural differences. The organization's mission has remained constant since its inception—*The Increase and Diffusion of Knowledge*. From this mission, the Smithsonian identifies the following as grand challenges to address:

- Magnifying the Transformative Power of Arts and Design
- Unlocking the Mysteries of the Universe
- Understanding and Sustaining a Biodiverse Planet
- Valuing World Cultures
- Understanding the American Experience

From this list, it is clear the Smithsonian values diversity in all forms, both within and outside of the United States. The organization celebrates world cultures and seeks to understand the experience of all Americans. Even the biodiversity of our planet and the universe are paramount to its mission. By broadly defining diversity and valuing the gifts that diverse perspectives and points of view bring, the Smithsonian lives and breathes its mission of increasing and diffusing knowledge.

As we noted in the introduction and in Chapter 1, important inputs into training and development strategy include the external and internal environments of the organization. The industry culture in which the company operates and the company culture work in synergy to influence company decisions. The permeable membrane that separates the organization from the environment within which it functions allows for an exchange of information such that the industry is influenced by the organization's practices, and the organization is influenced by the industry norms.

Because we exist in a global economy, organizations are not isolated from global events and thus must acknowledge and adapt to those events. National culture also plays an important role in how a company does business and how the employees within that company behave and develop expectations about their relationship with their employer. Yet we also know, even within a national culture, there are vast differences among individual employees, including their personality, their motivation, and their working and learning styles.

As the opening vignette states, understanding and recognizing differences is the gateway to knowledge about ourselves and others. These differences can pose challenges to organizational leaders, as well as their employees, but can also create great opportunities for learning and growth. While it is human nature to surround ourselves with people like us, we also know from research that homogeneity can be a problem for organizations that want to innovate and compete in a rapidly changing world.[1] Yet with both diversity and heterogeneity, organizations can also experience challenges with communication and increased conflict. How can an organization balance these challenges and find a solution to best meet its needs?

First, it is important to note the ways in which people and organizations may differ. Second, from this information, organizations can develop training strategies to help overcome the challenges of those differences while gaining the advantages that come with greater heterogeneity. By educating new and existing employees on company culture, individual differences, and even global differences in how work norms vary across different countries, the organization can begin to harness the value of diversity and better compete in the marketplace.

HOW PEOPLE, ORGANIZATIONS, AND THE GLOBAL CONTEXT DIFFER

As noted in the chapter framework, both the internal and external environment represent key ways that organizations and employees differ. This is also exemplified in our opening vignette about the Smithsonian Institution. At the macro level, countries differ along the lines of national culture. Geert Hofstede's dimensions of national culture represent how people from different nation-states vary on average on key dimensions. Referring back to the Smithsonian example, understanding and valuing world cultures is a key part of this organization's mission. At the next-highest level, companies have unique cultures that reflect their industry norms and the extent to which people in the organization share values, beliefs, and assumptions. At the most micro level, each individual, whether within a particular national culture or within a particular company, differ along many lines, including personality, demographics, and personal experiences. At the Smithsonian Institution, a focus on the transformative power of art and design aligns with our discussion about training for differences. Integrating art and design into training and development can transform how we think about learning in organizations. Later in this chapter (and in Chapter 12), for example, we discuss how improvisational theater training can help employees to work with diverse others. Overall, understanding the ways in which countries, organizations, and individuals may differ is important, and influences the training and development strategy a company chooses. Clearly, the Smithsonian Institution exemplifies valuing diversity at all levels.

Recognizing the ways in which an organization's employees may differ has an impact on discoveries during the needs analysis stage and subsequent training or development programs designed for its employees. For example, when training employees for global competency, whether for current jobs or for future job opportunities, understanding national culture and designing expatriate programs accordingly is key. As well, when you are hiring new employees and want them to understand your company culture, you can use a combination of training and development programs to best prepare them. Lastly, when addressing the ways people differ inside the company, training programs need to take individual differences into account, as well as help employees learn how to manage those differences to facilitate high performance among individuals and teams. Consistent with our discussion of practical skills as addressed in Chapter 12, improving

Exhibit 13-1 Levels of Training for Differences

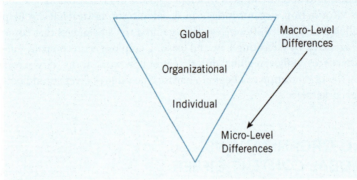

communication and conflict resolution skills should be central to traditional diversity training programs.

The sections that follow address diversity at different conceptual levels as they impact the organization. Taking these different levels of diversity into account, organizations can design training and development programs to meet diversity-related needs. We start with global-level differences, particularly how to handle preparing individuals for expatriate assignments. We follow this with a focus on organization-level differences, including company culture and how to get employees up to speed in the organization using orientation and socialization programs. Lastly, we address individual-level differences and the ways in which the company can better understand diversity and diversity management. Exhibit 13-1 illustrates the relationship between the levels of differences addressed in this chapter.

MACRO-LEVEL DIFFERENCES: NATIONAL CULTURE AND GLOBAL COMPETENCY

Global competency is essential for those businesses that are doing, or want to do, business internationally. While elements of global culture may be included in traditional diversity training programs, it is imperative that national culture be addressed when a company does business overseas. As well, if the company is sending expatriates abroad, specific training is needed to help prepare the expatriates and their families for the overseas assignment. Understanding the unique culture of the country within which they'll be living and working, as well as awareness of the psychological impact of living in a different culture, are the key goals of global competency training.

National Culture

Hofstede conducted extensive research looking at how countries differed on several dimensions: individualism, masculinity, uncertainty avoidance, and power distance,[2] later adding fifth and sixth dimensions—respectively, time perspective and indulgence.[3]

Exhibit 13-2 Hofstede's Six National Culture Dimensions

Individualistic/Collectivistic	How personal needs and goals are prioritized vs. the needs and goals of the group/clan
Masculine/Feminine	Different rules for work behavior for men and women vs. egalitarianism and equality between sexes
Uncertainty Avoidance	Comfort with uncertainty and changes in systems vs. systems with clear rules and norms
Power Distance	Acceptance of inequality in the distribution of power in society with unquestioning acceptance of authority vs. discomfort with status differences
Time Perspective	Long-term perspective plans for future vs. short-term perspective focused on near term for immediate gratification
Indulgence/Restraint	Allowing gratification of basic drives related to enjoying life and having fun vs. regulating basic drives through strict social norms

Source: Adapted from Geert Hofstede, Gert Jan Hofstede, and Michael Minkov, *Cultures and Organizations: Software of the Mind*, 3rd ed. (New York: McGraw-Hill, 2010).

Exhibit 13-2 defines the dimensions in some detail. While variance exists within each country with respect to individual behaviors around these dimensions, each country as a whole differs along these dimensions, landing somewhere on the continuum between the two poles of each dimension. For example, the United States is high in individualism, is slightly more masculine than feminine, is slightly more comfortable with uncertainty, is less comfortable with power distance, has a short-term time perspective, and is more likely to engage in indulgence. In comparison, Russia is much more collectivistic, is slightly more feminine, is very uncomfortable with uncertainty, is very comfortable with power distance, has a long-term perspective on time, and is more likely to engage in restraint than indulgence.

Global competence training should make employees aware of how employee behavior will differ given these dimensions. In the United States, people are more likely to question their bosses and offer ideas, but in Russia, employees rarely question the authority of their superiors and are more likely to follow orders without question. In the United States, individual achievement is expected and rewarded, but in Russia, the collective is more important than individual achievement. When working with companies or individuals from different national cultures, the approach to solving problems and general workplace norms will be different from one's own culture. Being aware of those differences, and having the tools to recognize and work with those differences, is important.

Training Employees for International Assignments

According to a study by Right Management, only 58% of overseas assignments are deemed successful.[4] Given the overall cost to a company for expatriate assignments, upwards of one million U.S. dollars according to the National Foreign Trade Council,[5] unsuccessful overseas assignments can be costly. Companies in Europe, the Middle East, and Asia Pacific are more likely to train their expatriates in cultural differences and language (33% of companies surveyed). In comparison, North American companies are far less likely to provide any training to their expatriate employees (18% of companies surveyed). Training on culture and languages, however, is not enough. Bram Lowsky, an executive vice president at Right Management, says, "The latest research suggests that the best companies utilize a comprehensive battery of assessments with the candidate to determine whether or not an expatriate assignment will actually work. Being aware of potential derailers that could stand in the way of success is critical to understanding and adjusting to an international role."

Before companies can think of training their expatriates, they must first select the right individuals, with the right temperament, for the assignment. Characteristics that increase the likelihood of success include tolerance for ambiguity, patience, observation skills, communication skills, emotional intelligence, resourcefulness, openness to learning, and adaptability.[6] If these skill areas sound familiar, remember the discussion in Chapter 12. Not only should trainers develop these skills, but they should consider ensuring their employees have developed skills in these areas as well.

After a rigorous selection process, training should be customized to the individual's needs. As previously noted, extensive instruction on the culture in which one will be working, as well as language training (if appropriate), is only the beginning. Culture training should include basic knowledge about the country culture and values, as well as the dos and don'ts for culturally appropriate behavior both in and out of the workplace, logistics on daily living in a foreign country, and instruction on common pitfalls one can expect. Whether or not expatriates' family members will be joining them, the family must also undergo training to prepare for the transition. Lastly, the expatriates and their families should be made aware of culture shock and how to best cope when they encounter symptoms.

Once individuals reach their assignment, training and development does not end there. Expatriates increase their likelihood for success when they have in-country coaches and/or mentors while on assignment.[7] Upon completion of their assignment, a repatriation-training program will help expatriates and their families begin the adjustment of leaving the host country and their assignment and reentering their home country. Finally, ongoing documentation, along with the debriefing process once expatriates are repatriated, provides the organization with information to understand the lessons learned from the assignment to share and use for future assignments. Therefore, a combination of job-specific training and career-specific development is imperative to ensure not only that expatriates succeed on the job, but that these experiences provide proper career development so that employees' careers advance, not stagnate, when they take on expatriate assignments.

ORGANIZATION-LEVEL DIFFERENCES: COMPANY CULTURE

Organizational culture can be defined in many ways, but researchers generally agree that culture is a system of shared assumptions, values, and beliefs that govern how people behave in organizations. Each company develops its own unique culture based on factors such as its history, products, market, technology, strategy, employees, management style, and national culture. Organizational culture manifests in three ways: artifacts, espoused values, and basic underlying assumptions.[8] Employees don't walk into an organization automatically knowing the company culture. If employees don't learn the rules of behavior for the organization, this inhibits their ability to perform to the best of their abilities. Organizations must share their cultural norms, formally and informally, explicitly and implicitly, with new and existing employees.

Artifacts

Cultural artifacts include things that can be seen, felt, or heard, such as office furniture and layout, slogans, logos, mission statements, dress code, and visible awards and recognition. From Apple Inc.'s "Think Different," to Lay's Potato Chips' "Betcha can't eat just one," to Southwest Airlines' "You are now free to move about the country," slogans should be easy for consumers to relate to, and represent how the company believes it differs from its competitors.

Organization leaders use artifacts to emphasize company values among their employees. Imagine walking into Apple on your first day of work and being told to "Think Different." This slogan informs new employees that Apple wants its employees to think outside of the box, and gives them license to innovate to increase company success. Understanding the company slogan has an important place in new employee training, discussed later in this chapter.

Espoused Values

Espoused values are the explicitly understood values of the organization and its employees. While the company mission statement may be considered an artifact, the company values statement represents the spoken, understood values shared by those in the organization. Build-A-Bear, headquartered in St. Louis, Missouri, states its core values as follows: Reach, Learn, Di-bear-sity, Colla-bear-ate, Give, Cele-bear-ate.[9] The company's values statement has a direct impact on training and development strategy. First, it encourages employees to continue to reach and learn, a value directly linked to training. The *Di-bear-sity* value means that diversity is important to the company, and will likely be reinforced in training programs. Lastly, the *Colla-bear-ate* value informs how the company trains groups and teams to work together to achieve a common goal. Values guide what companies share with new employees during orientation training, and also inform the different types of training programs the company may implement for current employees.

Basic Underlying Assumptions

The third and final component of organizational culture is the tacit assumptions made by employees that represent the unspoken rules about "how we do business." These assumptions are not always conscious or easily known. In fact, employees may spend years with a company before understanding those assumptions, if at all. Although training programs may not directly provide employees with information on these tacit assumptions, mentors may be able to unconsciously provide this information to their protégés over time as they help them navigate the organization's landscape. We discussed mentoring programs in Chapter 11, specifically highlighting the role of culture and tacit assumptions in designing mentoring programs.

ONBOARDING TO TRAIN FOR ORGANIZATIONAL CULTURE

Onboarding is the process by which new employees acquire the necessary knowledge, skills, and behaviors to become effective organizational members and insiders.[10] Because it is a process and not a discrete event, multiple factors and steps are involved in the onboarding process. Onboarding success is linked to three key antecedents: (1) new employee characteristics, (2) new employee behaviors, and (3) organizational efforts.[11]

Not all employees adapt well to onboarding programs. Certain types of personality characteristics and experiences increase the likelihood of successful onboarding outcomes. Being proactive, high in the Big 5 personality traits (openness, conscientiousness, extroversion/introversion, agreeableness, and neuroticism/emotional stability), and more experienced leads to better adjustment for new employees when participating in onboarding programs. Along with the characteristics of the new employees, the behaviors they engage in when newly hired will also impact onboarding success. New employees who proactively build relationships and seek information and feedback are more likely to succeed during the onboarding process.

Lastly, the onboarding activities the company uses also play an important role in successful outcomes. Onboarding actually begins during the recruitment process, proceeds through new employee orientation, and continues for months after a new employee is hired during the socialization process. In some instances, companies institute mentoring programs so new employees can become more socialized and effective on the job; thus, onboarding can reasonably continue through an employee's first year of employment by the company and beyond.

The outcomes one can expect from a good onboarding process are numerous. Employees experience greater adjustment when the previously noted antecedents are in place.[12] They are more likely to be clear in their role expectations, have higher levels of self-efficacy, experience greater acceptance from current organizational members, and obtain increased knowledge about the organizational culture. From there, one can expect to see greater employee satisfaction, higher levels of organizational commitment, higher job performance, and lower turnover. While many factors contribute to onboarding success, once it has identified and hired the right people, it is incumbent the company design an onboarding program that meets the needs of those employees. Exhibit 13-3 highlights the importance of proper onboarding programs, even for employees who are contract workers in the "gig economy."

Onboarding programs can be either informal or formal.[13] Informal plans involve employees learning about their new job without an explicit set of activities, whereas a

> **Exhibit 13-3 Onboarding for the Gig Economy**
>
> There was a time when workers who could not find a job would turn to contract or freelance work to make ends meet until they could secure a permanent position. While this may still be true for some workers, many are choosing freelancing work because it provides flexibility and new opportunities for their careers. Ridesharing with Uber or Lyft is an example of a gig job, but gig positions are not limited to driving people around on our downtime. People sell their crafts on Etsy, rent out a property on Airbnb, engage in ethical hacking for companies trying to secure their resources from cyber-attacks, or deliver items through Postmates. While gig workers are not technically employees in the legal sense of the word, if we want them to feel engaged with the company to which they are offering their services, it is important we provide customized onboarding experiences for them as well. Curtis Odom writes that "classic new-hire onboarding erodes trust with gig workers when they are not treated as welcomed individuals." Successful integration is critical to attract and retain gig workers over the long term. Activities such as providing them with a culture mentor helps gig workers to understand the existing company culture and how they fit into the organization's culture and mission. As well, providing them with social channels to network and discuss the unique issues and concerns of contract workers helps them feel connected to each other and to the organization. Socialization is important for many gig workers, so even something as simple as lunch with the company supervisor on occasion helps the gig workers to feel like they are a welcomed part of the company. Odom concludes his article: "Managing a gig workforce takes planning because of the complexity and diversity available to managers. Make a commitment to every employee and maintain a structure that keeps the gig workforce involved in the process." You should begin with the onboarding process and continue this throughout the employee's term with the company.
>
> *Source:* Adapted from Curtis L. Odom, "Onboarding in the Gig Economy," *TD Magazine*, September 2018.

formal plan is part of a coordinated set of policies and procedures to help employees adjust to their new job. The four distinct levels of onboarding, from lowest to highest, are compliance, clarification, culture, and connection.[14] Exhibit 13-4 highlights how these levels differ. The more levels an organization utilizes, the greater the likelihood it will have a successful onboarding program.[15] While compliance is the bare minimum organizations should strive for, research supports that onboarding needs to be broader than just the basic legal and policy-based issues the employee needs to know.[16] The previous section addressed the importance of understanding organizational culture; thus, the more cultural norms and relationships with others can be addressed in onboarding, the greater the likelihood the employee will experience success on the job.

Recruitment

Onboarding actually begins at the recruitment and selection stage of the employee–employer relationship.[17] Through realistic recruitment, employees get an honest view of the organization and its values. Job expectations, as well as explicit values and norms, can be shared up front during the recruitment process. Realistic recruitment

Exhibit 13-4	Onboarding Levels
Onboarding Level	**Description**
Compliance	Includes teaching employees basic legal and policy-related rules and regulations
Clarification	Refers to ensuring that employees understand their new jobs and all related expectations
Culture	Broad category that includes providing employees with a sense of organizational norms—both formal and informal
Connection	Vital interpersonal relationships and information networks that new employees must establish

practices result in greater employee retention because new employees know what to expect when they enter the organization. Along with greater knowledge about what to expect, how organizations treat prospective employees during the staffing process can also signal to the new recruits what the company culture is like and how they can expect to be treated upon hiring. A good first impression signals to the job candidate that the company is one in which they should work because they will be respected and treated well.

Orientation

The role of new employee orientation programs is to help new hires adjust to their new job and work environment, and instill a positive attitude and motivation from the very beginning of an employee's relationship with the organization.[18] A recent study by Accountemps, the world's first and largest staffing service for temporary accounting, finance, and bookkeeping professionals, found 34% of companies surveyed did not offer a formal orientation program for new hires.[19] Even when companies do have orientation

Exhibit 13-5 How Not to Make a Good First Impression

After a delayed start and the slowness of my decision-making during the benefits sign-up, the morning quickly became afternoon. When my supervisor was ready for me, personnel wasn't; when personnel was ready to deliver me, my supervisor was tied up in a meeting. So a departmental pinch hitter shuttled me off to the cafeteria for a Dutch-treat lunch. By the time I'd downed my dessert, I was feeling very unimportant. I wondered which of the two faces my new employer had shown me was true—the one when I was recruited or the one I'd just experienced.

Source: Excerpted from R. F. Federico, "Six Ways to Solve the Orientation Blues," *HR Magazine* 36, no. 5 (1991): 69.

programs, a 2000 study by the Association for Talent Development (formerly the American Society for Training and Development) found only 7% of training dollars allocated for new employee orientation. Given the importance of understanding the company's culture, as well as its policies and procedures, and sharing this information with new employees, this presents a problem for those companies that don't provide new employee orientation. If a company fails to make a good first impression with new employees, it is very difficult to undo that bad first impression. Exhibit 13-5 illustrates a typical scenario for many employees on their first day, underscoring the importance of making a good first impression.

Benefits of new employee orientation.

Impression management is the process by which individuals, and by extension the organizations in which they work, attempt to influence the perceptions of others about a person, object, or event. An orientation program is a key ingredient in a company's impression management program. After recruitment, organizations can best make a positive impression on new employees at the start of their employment. Orientation programs are instrumental in making employees more comfortable in the organization, increasing employee retention rates,[20] and improving employee productivity more rapidly than for companies that do not use orientation programs.[21] It is also important that the message communicated during recruitment is consistent with the message communicated during the orientation period. As Exhibit 13-5 illustrates, when the message communicated to new employees is inconsistent, this causes them to question their decision to join the organization.

Accountemps also asked human resource (HR) executives with orientation programs "What is the greatest benefit of your orientation program?"[22] Thirty-five percent responded that new employees would better understand company values, guidelines, and expectations. Another 20% stated new employees would make positive contributions more quickly (see Exhibit 13-6). Overall, orientation programs help new employees adjust to the organization's norms, while also helping the organization better understand the needs of new employees.

Exhibit 13-6 What is the greatest benefit of your orientation program?

New employees better understand company values, guidelines, and expectations.	35%
New employees make positive contributions more quickly.	20%
New employees feel a connection with the company more quickly.	19%
New employees are better prepared for long-term success with the company.	17%
The company better understands the needs of new employees.	9%

Source: Reprinted with permission from Robert Half.

Orientation program content.

While orientation programs are customized given the organizational context, according to an article in *Training & Development* magazine, three main components of orientation programs cross all organizations, and are essential for a successful orientation program.[23] First, the new employees need to feel welcomed. Second, they need to understand the organization in a broad sense. Third, they need to understand what the organization expects of them on the new job in terms of work and behaviors.

Welcoming employees.

Employees will feel good about their decision to join a particular organization if the organization is clearly happy to have them on board. As such, the consistent message during the orientation period should be that the employee is a welcome and important member of the organization. Along with a consistent message, who the organization brings to the orientation program to support the new employee is integral to communicating the welcome message. The new employee's supervisor, along with the HR manager and a peer advisor, are the minimum needed to provide a varied and consistent welcome.[24]

The HR manager, or a member of the HR staff, may conduct the orientation program, but involving the employee's supervisor is essential. In fact, the person with the biggest potential impact on making new employees feel welcome is their supervisor, because he or she is the most qualified to understand the unit within which the employee will work.[25] Providing peer advisors, or a "buddy," for new employees gives them a trusted confidante to whom they can direct questions about the organization. The peer advisor can be tasked with introducing the new employee to others in the department and the organization at large and helping the new employee navigate issues such as the location of key resources (e.g., lunchroom, bathroom, supplies).[26] The "buddy" can also be a great source of emotional support as the new person adjusts to the organizational culture.[27]

In smaller organizations, if the CEO is available, it is beneficial for him or her to take the time to make an appearance and communicate his or her own welcome message. When the CEO is not available, or if the organization is too large and geographically diffuse for a personal appearance, a video welcome from the CEO is important to include in the program.[28] If your organization uses a video, ensure it is updated regularly to reflect the changing nature of the organization's business.

Lastly, a nice gesture to make new employees feel welcome is to provide them with information about the area in which they are working—for example, restaurants, shopping, and recreational opportunities. In addition, having the buddy or supervisor take them out to lunch communicates how much the organization values its new employees. As illustrated in Exhibit 13-5, making new employees feel like an afterthought gives them mixed messages about the organizational culture, and may contribute to new employee turnover.

Understanding the organization.

The section on organizational culture makes clear why it is important for new employees to understand organizational artifacts and espoused values. In addition to the organizational culture, new employees need to know how the company functions, and why. Time should be set aside with both the HR department and the new employee's supervisor to go over cultural elements, as well as administrative issues essential to employee success. For example, learning organizational history and the company philosophy on work and standards of performance helps new employees understand company culture. Communicating information about the company strategy, products and services offered, and the customer base helps new employees understand the company's business orientation and how it differentiates itself in the market. Understanding the organizational structure, company policies, employee benefits, and general office procedures covers the administrative issues essential to help new employees navigate their workday.

Understanding the job.

Once a new employee has a clear vision of how the company functions and why, attention should turn to job-specific expectations. If the new employee has not already seen the job description, it should be introduced at this time. Along with the job description, specific performance expectations need to be established. The performance evaluation process should be communicated, including providing new employees with the performance appraisal instrument used to evaluate them annually, and the goal-setting process that guides employees through their first year on the job should be initiated. While expecting employees to be immediately fully functional on the job with this information is unreasonable, ensuring they have the information they need to succeed on the job is the first step toward bringing them up to speed as quickly as possible. This is consistent with the results from the Accountemps survey (see Exhibit 13-6) as orientation programs help new employees make positive contributions more quickly and be better prepared for long-term success with the company.

General Program Attributes

In addition to these three essential components are other programmatic considerations. All employees need to participate in orientations, not just certain job categories.[29] Depending on who is mandated to receive orientation, there may be a perceived sense of unfairness if job categories are left out, or if certain groups are considered "above" the need for an orientation program. All employees benefit from orientation programs, so a consistent policy is important.

Orientation programs should be provided immediately upon employee entry into the organization.[30] It is all too common, in the interest of saving money and manpower, for employers to perform orientation programs only when a critical mass of employees will attend. On the one hand, this may seem like a sound decision for budget considerations, but the longer an employee goes without a solid introduction into the organization and its culture, the more likely that employee will be to struggle and eventually leave, creating higher turnover costs. Thus, delaying orientation may seem cost-beneficial in the short run, but the long-run costs make delaying orientation an untenable option—a particularly salient point for small businesses to consider. Even if you are only orienting one or two new employees at a time, a high priority for the HR function should be to set aside the time needed to get these new employees functioning as quickly as possible.

Orientation programs are at their best when they are not a jam-packed, discrete, one-day event.[31] Just as onboarding is a process, so should be the orientation program, for several important reasons. First, despite all the excitement of starting a new job, some stress and apprehension also come with moving to a new organization, leaving behind the known and entering the unknown. That stress can make it difficult for employees to fully comprehend all the information provided to them on their first day. Second, regardless of the stress level, the scope of things essential for a new employee to be integrated into the organization is more extensive than can be communicated in one day. Information overload will make it challenging to absorb and comprehend everything employees have learned if it is compressed into a one-day event. Spreading the orientation process over a few days, or even weeks, to allow employees to fully digest all the information provided is beneficial.

Think back to our discussion in Chapter 4 on learning theories. Cognitive load theory argues we need to match the training delivery to maximize learning and manage cognitive load. This applies directly to orientation programs. If you only plan on one jam-packed day to orient your employees, this can add to stress and decrease the likelihood the information will be digested and learned at the level expected. Even if you are a small business, spreading the orientation program over the course of a few days will actually make it easier to dedicate the time needed to ensure all employees get what they need during orientation to be successful.

Given the increased importance of group process and the interdependence of jobs in a department or division, orientation needs to be an immersive experience so new employees can bond with their coworkers and fellow new employees as quickly as possible.[32] The quicker and more intensely new employees can bond with their colleagues, the greater their retention rate. TEKsystems, a leading provider of information technology staffing solutions and services, surveyed IT professionals about their opinions of onboarding programs.[33] Ninety percent of those surveyed said team building is essential to the onboarding process to make the employees feel like valued members of the team. Ninety-one percent said integrating employees into the team and encouraging relationship building is important. A team is only as strong as its weakest link, so bringing new members up to speed and helping them facilitate a bond with their new teammates will benefit the new employees and the team with whom they'll be working.

Use of an orientation program checklist can help companies ensure they have covered all the key elements needed for a successful onboarding experience.[34] New employees can carry the checklist throughout the orientation program, and when elements are completed, the person delivering the information checks off and initials the line item. This creates a paper trail as to what was communicated and by whom, and makes all participants accountable for providing an effective orientation program. The HR manager can then assess the effectiveness of the program at a later date. Exhibit 13-7 summarizes the major components to include in an orientation checklist.

> **Exhibit 13-7 Orientation Program Checklist**

1. **Employee and Position Summary**—employee name, start date, position, department, supervisor, peer advisor, orientation program leader
2. **Organizational Background**—history, philosophies, and goals
3. **Nature of Business and Facilities**—industry summary, customer profile, products and services offered, company financials
4. **Organizational Structure**—organizational and departmental charts, reporting relationships, and support staff
5. **General Performance Expectations**—expected productivity, professional and career development, organizational norms
6. **Policies**—performance appraisal procedures, compensation/incentive practices, benefits, safety and health policies/procedures
7. **Office Procedures, Equipment, and Supplies**—interoffice correspondence, supplies, requesting checks, expense reports, operate computer/telephone system, copy machine
8. **Specific Job Requirements**—job roles and responsibilities, work objectives and standards of performance, where job fits into the organization
9. **Orientation Follow-Up**—questions and answers, debrief orientation experience, needs assessment for additional training needs

Source: Adapted from Sabrina Hicks, "Successful Orientation Programs," *Training & Development* 54, no. 4 (2000): 59–60.

Delivery methods for orientation programs.

Organizations can deliver orientation programs in all types of formats, using a variety of materials to facilitate learning. With the growth of technology, many elements of the orientation program can be made available online through the company's intranet so the information is available 24/7 for employees to review. While online delivery is beneficial for many things, nothing can replace the interpersonal benefits received from a traditional face-to-face program delivery. Because making employees feel welcome in many circumstances requires a personal touch, when possible, face-to-face meetings are preferred. Further, rich communication media like face-to-face classroom instruction is essential for communicating company culture because of the ambiguity that may be inherent in understanding a company's unique culture. It isn't enough to read about a company culture. Oftentimes one must experience that culture firsthand to best understand how it is expressed in the company.

    A variety of materials can be made available for new employees to review, in digital and paper format, including employee handbooks, technical and procedural manuals, and benefits material. Videos, self-study modules, shadowing, and coaching/mentoring are also common ways to share company information and assist the new employee in learning essential information about the company. Just as there are a variety of ways to communicate training content, the same holds for orientation and onboarding programs.

Socialization.

Socialization is defined as the process by which new employees understand the company's policies, the internal culture, how the company hierarchy works, and the ways to function effectively in the organization. While the peer advisor, or "buddy," is tasked with assisting the new employee during the initial stages of the onboarding and orientation process, mentor programs are designed to assist new employees with adjusting to the organizational culture over the long term. Newcomers with mentors adjust to the company far quicker than do newcomers without mentors.[35] Some even argue that when a company socializes new employees consistently through the first year, the employees are more likely to be engaged, resulting in higher performance for the employees and greater benefits for the organization.[36] Further, when newcomers spend time with an assigned mentor and make the effort to get involved with company social events, they are more likely to internalize the key values of the organization's culture.[37] We discussed what makes a good mentor and how to set up a mentoring program in more detail in Chapter 11.

MICRO-LEVEL DIFFERENCES: INDIVIDUAL DIFFERENCES AND DIVERSITY TRAINING

Diversity initiatives are increasingly an important part of an organization's strategic plan. A cursory look at the website of any Fortune 500 company will reveal a commitment to diversity and inclusion. Even small businesses, despite their small size and propensity toward much more homogeneity than in larger businesses, recognize the value of diverse ideas and inclusion.[38] At this point in time, the value of diversity is not debated. What is in consideration is how companies address the challenges that come from having a diverse workforce. Diversity training is one way for organizations to help prepare their employees for a multicultural and diverse workforce. Before we address what to include in diversity training, it is important to discuss what constitutes diversity, as well as the advantages and disadvantages of having a diverse organization.

Types of Diversity

Diversity is as broad as the many ways people differ in personality, demographics, and experiences. While addressing issues of demographic diversity is an important consideration for organizations, diversity isn't limited to issues of race, sex, gender identity, or sexual orientation. Each category of diversity has its own unique challenges that diversity training must address in order for the company to work effectively. Exhibit 13-8 illustrates the 4 dimensions of diversity.

Exhibit 13-8 Diversity Dimensions

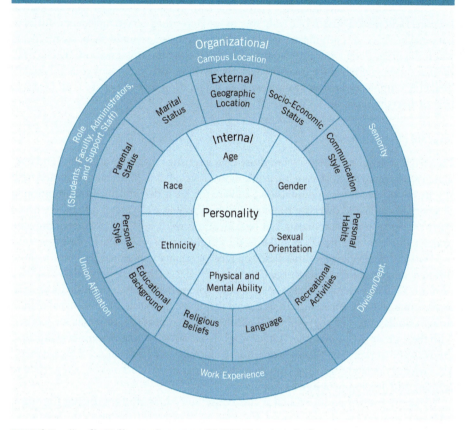

Source: https://syafika22.files.wordpress.com/2013/05/diversity_wheel_ppt.png.

Personality.

Personality, or deep-level diversity, is the individual difference in people associated with how they think, feel, or behave.[39] While many aspects of personality are biologically determined, researchers argue that the environment has a greater influence on personality than originally believed. Thus, a combination of nature and nurture affects how people think, feel, or behave in an organizational context.

Many aspects of personality influence how we do work and how we interact with others. The Big 5 traits, as noted in the section on macro-level differences, provide one explanation for people's differences that can affect how people function in an organization. Other aspects focus on how people make decisions, such as thinking versus feeling, or judging versus perceiving. No matter what personality dimension we consider, when people differ in basic personality traits, this creates a tension among the individuals working together.

Short of those determined to be psychotic and thus out of touch with reality, there isn't one right personality, or one right way to be. Depending on circumstances, different personalities have unique gifts to offer the organization. For example, there are moments when the gregarious nature of extroverts has value for the organization; by contrast, there are moments when the quiet thoughtfulness of the introvert yields greater benefits. Teaching employees how to grapple with so-called deep-level diversity is an essential part of diversity training.

Internal dimensions.

Internal dimensions of diversity are those characteristics that are immutable, and over which we have no control. Age, race, ethnicity, physical ability, sexual orientation, and sex are considered internal dimensions, and are the areas that get the most attention in diversity research and diversity training. Making employees aware of differences based on these categories is important, but organizations must take care in explaining why understanding these differences and how they impact employee behavior is important.

First, while people may differ based on race, or ethnicity, or sexual orientation, those differences are not linked to job-related characteristics, such as an individual's ability to perform a job or general intelligence. Someone who is Black is as capable of doing a job as someone who is Caucasian; a homosexual man is as capable as a heterosexual man in doing a similar job. The goal of diversity training is to combat the stereotypes associated with these groups—for example, "Older workers are not as willing to learn new things as are younger workers" or "Women are more emotional and less rational than are men." We covered the laws regarding managing differences in the workplace as they relate to training and development in Chapter 2.

Second, even if an individual is not consciously biased, the growing literature addresses the implicit biases or associations we make when encountering those who are different from us.[40] For example, while we may not consciously discriminate based on these immutable characteristics, the implicit biases we hold because of society's messages to us influence decisions we make. With respect to development opportunities, a male boss may be more likely to recommend male colleagues for development programs over females because of a similar-to-me bias, as well as because of implicit messages from society that men make better leaders than do women. As noted in Chapter 2 on legal issues, this need not be a conscious, purposeful decision to still have a detrimental impact on the career path of women. Making employees aware of such associations and implicit biases helps combat the unconscious influences and encourages employees to be aware when bias may enter their decisions.

A big part of unconscious biases is the concept of microaggressions. **Microaggression** involves the casual degradation of any socially marginalized group, typically through negligence, ignorance, or unconscious bias.[41] Comments such as "You don't sound like you are Black" or "I never knew you were gay—you *love* sports" are examples of casual comments that are not necessarily intended to hurt an individual's feelings but

Exhibit 13-9 Types of Microaggression

Microaggression	Definition	Example
Microassault	Explicit derogation, verbal or nonverbal, that includes name-calling, avoidant behavior, or purposeful discrimination	Anytime Roger, who is gay, walks up to the lunch table with his coworkers, Sam stands up and walks away, ignoring Roger.
Microinsult	Communication that conveys rudeness and insensitivity to a person's identity, unknown to the perpetrator but insulting to the recipient	Sarah met James for the first time and said to him, "All that time we spoke on the phone I had no idea you were Black. You are very well spoken."
Microinvalidation	Communication that excludes, negates, or nullifies the thoughts, feelings, or experiences of those in the marginalized group	Karen pointed out to her boss that every time she makes a suggestion, her boss minimizes it. But, when a male coworker makes the same suggestion, the boss is effusive in his praise of the idea. Karen's boss told her she was being oversensitive and to get over it.

Source: Adapted from Derald Wing Sue, Christina M. Capodilupo, Gina C. Torino, Jennifer M. Bucceri, Aisha M. B. Holder, Kevin L. Nadal, and Marta Esquilin, "Racial Microaggressions in Everyday Life: Implications for Clinical Practice," *American Psychologist* 62, no. 4 (2007): 271–286.

reflect a lack of sensitivity and understanding of the harm associated with stereotypes. Microaggressions can include a **microassault**, a **microinsult**, or a **microinvalidation**. Exhibit 13-9 defines these types of microaggressions and gives an example of each.

Microaggression typically leads to anger, frustration, or exhaustion for the recipient, and can ultimately result in lower self-confidence and self-image, as well as long-term depression, anxiety, and trauma.[42] Microaggression can interfere both directly and indirectly with an employee's development and career progression in the workplace. Addressing microaggressions and other conscious and unconscious biases is an important part of any diversity training plan.

Third, although minority groups are as qualified to do jobs as are majority groups, all things being equal, there are differences in the way minority groups experience the world that inform how they think about events and interactions with others. Here, the concept of privilege comes into play around the internal dimensions of diversity. Privilege is a special right or advantage available only to a particular person or group of people. It is not earned, but conferred on a person or group by society. Individuals may not be aware of their privilege because they take it for granted for no other reason than it is the only experience they know.

Having privilege doesn't mean the people who benefit from privilege have not worked hard to achieve their goals or asked for that particular privilege. But privilege means that they have not had to experience challenges or barriers to their success because of something they do not control, such as their sex or race. The concept of "driving while Black" is a well-known phenomenon, and one that Caucasian drivers do not understand or experience.[43] Being pulled over just because of the color of your skin is not something Caucasians have to worry about as they drive around neighborhoods or down the highway. Blacks are disproportionately pulled over for no other reason than they don't look like they belong in a certain neighborhood or because they "resemble" the description of someone reported to have committed a crime. They are also more likely to be pulled over for minor traffic violations and treated with unnecessary force, even when statistics show that Caucasians are as likely or more likely to have illegal drugs or firearms in their cars than are Blacks.[44] Just because a person has not experienced being pulled over like that doesn't mean, however, it is not a real phenomenon for Black drivers. Similarly, heterosexuals experience privilege simply by being able to keep photos of their family on their desk. It is an unquestioned taken-for-granted privilege; if gay and lesbian employees put photos on their desk, this may reveal their hidden sexual orientation and make them subject to potential discrimination in the workplace. Individuals with disabilities are also assumed to be incapable of doing a job because of their disability, but the capabilities of an able-bodied person are not questioned.

Each one of us can experience privilege given different aspects of our lives. Some of us might be privileged because we are White, but experience no privilege because we are gay, or grew up poor, or have family members who are incarcerated. The role of diversity training is to help inform those who have privilege, through no fault of their own, how those without privilege may experience the world. These experiences change the way individuals give meaning to the events and people they encounter. Understanding these differences and enabling people to walk in another's shoes is an important contribution of diversity training.

External dimension.

The third dimension of diversity is the external dimension, which includes different activities, beliefs, and experiences people hold over which they have some control. Religion, education, hobbies, military service, marital status, and parental status are just a few of the items that influence a person's interests, careers, and friendship networks. Religious or spiritual beliefs inform a person's core values. Someone who has served in the military has a different experience in the workplace than someone who is a civilian and has never served. If the veteran has experienced combat, she or he may interpret signs and events differently than does someone who has not experienced combat. These different experiences and beliefs are typically at the core of most workplace conflict, but they are also at the core of creativity and innovation. Diversity training benefits employees when they are taught how to constructively manage conflict and differences.

Organizational dimension.

The last dimension, the organizational dimension, includes factors such as whether or not you are in a collective bargaining unit, where your department resides geographically, how much seniority you have, and your job title. Intraorganizational conflict typically falls along job title and seniority lines. Companies regularly use cross-functional teams to work on assignments, and as such, the different workplace perspectives can create conflict for the team. An advantage of having cross-functional teams, however, is getting different perspectives from the group of employees depending on the position from which they view the assignment. From different, unique perspectives, the organization gains more creative and innovative solutions. Just as with the external dimensions, helping employees deal with conflict and differences of opinion is important in diversity training.

Challenges for diversity and diversity training.

Organizations must consider a number of issues when designing a diversity training program, beginning with the range of people's attitudes about diversity and inclusion.[45] Exhibit 13-10 highlights Milton Bennett's six stages of intercultural sensitivity: denial, defensive, minimizing differences, acceptance, adaptation, and integration. An individual in denial does not believe that differences are valid, but believes anyone different is considered not worth understanding, or even subhuman. White supremacist groups fall into this category. An individual who is defensive has negative impressions of cultural differences. The iconic Archie Bunker from the television show *All in the Family* is a great example of an individual in the defensive stage. He engaged in stereotypes to make sense of the world around him, even if those stereotypes were detrimental and derogatory. Individuals who engage in minimizing differences tend to embrace similarities (we are all human) but dismiss obvious cultural and sociological differences as irrelevant as compared to what is held in common. Although this view is to be commended at one level, it ignores the differences groups experience because of their race, sex, sexual orientation,

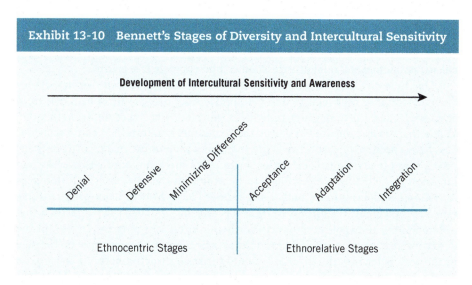

Exhibit 13-10   Bennett's Stages of Diversity and Intercultural Sensitivity

Source: Adapted from Milton J. Bennett, "Intercultural Communication: A Current Perspective," in *Basic Concepts of Intercultural Communication: Selected Readings*, ed. M. J. Bennett (Yarmouth, ME: Intercultural Press, 1998).

or national origin. These three groups are considered ethnocentric in focus because of the belief that differences don't matter.

In contrast, individuals in the acceptance stage recognize that people are different, and are tolerant of those differences even if others do not share their point of view. Those in the adaptation stage purposefully and willingly shift cultural perspectives to more deeply understand cultural differences. Lastly, those in the integration stage exhibit true multiculturalism and find it difficult to identify with any one culture. They take the viewpoint that those who identify with a culture socially construct it, and there isn't one right way to be. These three groups are considered ethnorelativistic because they view culture as relative to one's context and point of view, not an absolute.

While the company's goal might be to increase diversity awareness and intercultural competence, the trainer must be aware of the audience's comfort and stage of diversity awareness. The type of program organizations might design for employees who take an ethnocentric perspective is quite different from the type of program they might design for more ethnorelativistic employees. There isn't a one-size-fits-all approach to helping employees be more aware of diversity issues.

In considering the different benefits of addressing internal dimensions of diversity, addressing the problems with stereotyping may help those in the denial or defensive stages become aware that all employees are people with similar issues, hopes, and dreams. Addressing implicit biases may help those who are ethnorelativistic and comfortable with diversity and inclusion understand diversity in a deeper way. Lastly, helping employees understand privilege and why some groups experience events quite differently may help employees in the minimizing differences stage.

Another challenge, as noted, is the conflict inherent in diversity. Whether the dimensions are deep, involving personality, or more external, involving job titles or spiritual beliefs, differences in perspective, values, beliefs, or experiences create tensions when employees enter a discussion assuming their perspective is the right perspective to have with a problem. Communication and conflict resolution tactics should help people talk to one another and minimize the conflict inherent in diverse groups.

One final challenge should be noted. A 2006 study indicated that mandatory diversity training that focuses on avoiding lawsuits may result in backlash from employees, and those organizations may experience an increase in incidents.[46] While there is documented evidence that voluntary programs for cultural awareness have a positive impact on diversity and inclusion, how can mandatory programs be improved to avoid the backlash associated with them and improve diversity and inclusion as well? One suggestion is to focus less on the categories of differences in training, and focus more on helping trainees learn how to work with a diverse range of individuals.[47] Cultural awareness is fine, but the fear-laden approach that points fingers and scolds employees for being intolerant puts employees on the defensive and increases the likelihood they will ridicule the program and engage in the very behaviors the diversity training is trying to eliminate.[48] Focusing on communication and conflict management is a better approach[49] because it teaches people how to address the inherent conflict that comes with differences of opinion and perspective.

APPLYING PRACTICAL T&D SKILLS TO DIVERSITY TRAINING

In Chapter 12, we discussed a wide variety of important skills trainers and employees in organizations need for success. Not only do trainers benefit from developing these skills to best deliver training programs, but employees benefit from developing these skills to better do their jobs. As well, these skills can help us better navigate issues of differences. For example, earlier in this chapter, we discussed the importance of these skills to prepare employees for expatriate assignments.

Regardless of the level at which you are "training for differences," the practical skills discussed in Chapter 12 inform diversity training for employees at a deep level. Beyond the benefits for trainers, these skills are essential for employees to navigate working with diverse others. In fact, the trend in diversity training is moving more in the direction of conflict resolution and communication to address diversity-related issues and challenges.

A variety of exciting programs are available for trainers to use to help employees navigate the challenges that come with all levels of differences. Conflict resolution training highlighting "getting to yes"[50] and focusing on issues-based negotiating is important to include in diversity training programs. Beyond teaching people how to approach negotiations from a mutual gains perspective, some argue that a solid foundation has to exist before people can practice their negotiation and conflict resolution skills. Three factors erode one's ability to successfully negotiate through a challenging moment: distrust, bias in decision making, and displeasure or fear of conflict and negotiating.[51] Helping employees build trust, and training them to be aware of biases such as confirmation bias and emotionality, needs to precede negotiation training. Taking on the spirit of cooperation and helping others see the value of abandoning a zero-sum approach will make negotiating through a conflict more palatable and increase the likelihood of successful resolution with an increase in value for all.[52] The only way to do this is for organizations to work on building trust among their employees, and between employees and management, and teach them basic decision making and perceptual biases that can interfere with the ability to communicate and resolve problems.

Along with negotiation and conflict resolution skills, employees need to be engaged with activities that teach active listening and nonverbal communication. As noted in Chapter 12, most communication is nonverbal, including elements such as how close we are to someone's personal space (proxemics), tone of voice, and body language. Making sure words, tone, and body language are in alignment is essential to successful communication. Active listening skills are also important so that we don't just hear people talking but we are actually listening and engaging with them based on what they are communicating. Much of the conflict associated with differences may come down to differences in communication styles, or differences in experiences and assumptions. Helping people navigate better communication will not make conflict over differences go away, but it can help them work through those differences more readily.

Lastly, improvisational communication applies to diversity training as well. The origins of improvisation, as noted in the interview with Ed Reggi in Chapter 12 (see Exhibit 12-6, page 319), was to help people overcome differences to find common ground. Teaching people about "Yes, and . . ." will help them learn to stop and find ways to connect with someone else rather than say no and isolate themselves from others. Improvisation training can be a tremendous building block to help employees manage working with diverse others.

ETHICS AND TRAINING DIVERSE OTHERS

The Association for Talent Development's Code of Ethics states that training professionals should strive to recognize the rights and dignities of each individual.[53] Understanding how diverse others think, learn, and behave, and imparting this knowledge to trainees, is consistent with that section of the ethical code.

What ethical issues have an impact on working with and training diverse others? The intersection of ethics and the law illustrates how many ethical norms have been written into employment law to protect employees from all types of discrimination, as discussed in Chapter 2. The law, as we know, lags behind ethics in many areas, and as such, there are issues on which the law has not yet spoken. One example is the growing tension building around lesbian, gay, bisexual, and transgender (LGBT) employee civil rights. In areas where employment laws at the state and local level have not addressed LGBT rights, these employees may experience few opportunities for advancement, and may not have access to training and development opportunities. Even if these employees have advanced, if they are in a mentoring or coaching relationship with someone who does not accept LGBT workplace rights and there are no legal protections, will that hinder the efficacy of the mentoring and coaching relationship? While the law informs much of our workplace activities around discrimination, when the law is silent on these issues, we must turn to ethics to guide our decisions.

If we think about applying ethical theories to the challenges of how to work with diverse others in the workplace, across the board, ethics would argue that regardless of the law, it is ethical, or just, to ensure all employees are treated fairly. Whether we apply utilitarianism (greatest good for the greatest amount of people) or universalism (universal law to ensure intention to treat people fairly), or consider theories of justice and fairness, a society that does not treat all employees fairly despite their differences would not be ethical.

CHAPTER SUMMARY

Diversity impacts training and development in organizations in multiple ways. First, diversity is not only about the individual differences between employees, but it also reflects the differences in the company culture, as well as national culture. Each company culture differs on key values, and the means by which the company utilizes cultural artifacts to reinforce what it believes and how it wants employees to behave. Within each company culture, individual employees differ on everything from their personalities, to their demographic characteristics and experiences, to what they do in the organization itself. With all these issues in mind, organizations must take a multipronged approach to help employees adjust, and to promote the value of diversity and inclusion.

The onboarding process is the first and most important way that employees can learn about the company culture and about the different values the company holds. Expectations for behaviors and on-the-job performance are shared with the goal of getting employees up to speed as quickly as possible. Investing in a good onboarding program increases the likelihood of high company performance, and low employee turnover. Onboarding isn't limited to just new employee orientation programs, but is a part of a well-integrated and orchestrated program to recruit, train, and retain employees for the long term.

Second, the more important diversity is to the core mission and values of the company, the more important diversity training becomes for employees. Organizations must take care to train employees not only on the value of diversity, but also to help them deal with the challenges that arise when working in a diverse, heterogeneous organization. Reinforcing good communication skills, conflict resolution skills, and creative problem solving and decision making helps employees benefit from a diverse workforce. Voluntary programs with the goal of enlightening and helping employees become more aware of employee differences, and providing them with the tools they need for success, is the best approach.

Lastly, most companies today cannot afford to ignore global issues and how they impact their organization. Making employees aware of national culture differences is an important part of preparing them for work in the 21st century. Even more important is the need to ensure employees who will be working abroad have the skills they need for a successful expatriate assignment. Understanding culture, language, and the ins and outs of living in a foreign country are the minimum requirements for training expatriates and their families on the challenges of working abroad.

Learning how to work with diverse others—other businesses, other people, other cultures—is essential for success in today's competitive market. Training employees to work with others, improve communication, and navigate conflict will have a positive impact on the organization's bottom line. Diversity and inclusiveness can help organizations achieve and sustain a competitive advantage.

KEY TERMS

Microaggression. The casual degradation of any socially marginalized group, typically through negligence, ignorance, or unconscious bias.

Microassault. Explicit derogation, verbal or nonverbal, that includes name-calling, avoidant behavior, or purposeful discrimination.

Microinsult. Communication that conveys rudeness and insensitivity to a person's identity, unknown to the perpetrator but insulting to the recipient.

Microinvalidation. Communication that excludes, negates, or nullifies the thoughts, feelings, or experiences of those in the marginalized group.

Onboarding. The process by which new employees acquire the necessary knowledge, skills, and behaviors to become effective organizational members and insiders.

Organizational culture. A system of shared assumptions, values, and beliefs that govern how people behave in organizations.

Personality. The individual differences in people associated with how they think, feel, or behave.

Socialization. The process by which new employees understand the company's policies, the internal culture, how the company hierarchy works, and the ways to function effectively in the organization.

END-OF-CHAPTER QUESTIONS AND EXERCISES

Discussion Questions

1. What are the three levels of organizational culture? What impact does culture have on training and development? Why is it important to consider culture when developing a training and development strategy?

2. What are the three key antecedents for successful onboarding? How can the company use other HR functions, such as recruitment and selection, to ensure onboarding success?

3. What are the advantages and disadvantages of a formal versus informal onboarding program? Under what conditions might an informal plan be effective to help new employees learn about the job and the company?

4. What role does recruitment play in the onboarding process? How would you design a recruitment message so that it works in alignment with the onboarding plan for the company?

5. What are the three main areas an orientation program should address? What would happen if any of those areas were missing from orientation? What impact would that have on employee success?

6. Why utilize an orientation checklist? What benefit does this provide for the employee as well as the organization itself?

7. Diversity is complex and broader than someone's sex or race. What are the four dimensions of diversity, and how does understanding these four dimensions impact training and development decisions?

8. Describe the impact of microaggressions on training and development decisions. What can organizations do to improve implicit associations and remove unconscious bias when helping develop employees?

9. How do Bennett's stages of diversity sensitivity inform training and development strategy? Describe how a company should utilize the stages when designing diversity training programs. Also consider how the stages may impact training and development decisions (e.g., a manager makes decisions on who should get opportunities for promotion and development).

10. The textbook recommended several unique approaches to diversity training. Discuss in more detail how these programs could help organizations manage diversity training programs more effectively. Can you think of and describe other unique approaches to help employees become more sensitive to diversity and inclusion?

11. Discuss how national culture can have an impact on the employee receptiveness to training and development. How can/should training needs be adapted to manage differences in national culture?

12. What is the importance of training employees for international assignments? What are some essential elements that should be included in training, and why?

13. What impact do ethical standards for ATD have on training and managing diverse others? What considerations should trainers keep in mind when engaged in training and developing diverse employees?

Ethical Scenario: Development Opportunities for an Employee in Transition

Rachel is the HR director for a branch of an accounting firm of approximately 250 employees in the greater Cincinnati area. Although the firm headquarters is in Cincinnati, the branch in which Rachel works is located across the Ohio River in Kentucky. Recently, one of the firm's rising stars, who was on track to make partner, began transitioning from female to male. Rachel worked hard to understand and accommodate Adam (formerly Adele), but the firm partners seemed unclear on what to think of the whole issue. Adam had been with the firm 10 years and was well known for providing quality service to his clients. As Adele, Adam had passed the CPA Exam with flying colors and had handled many high-visibility clients—until recently. About eight months after Adam began transitioning, he walked into Rachel's office with a few concerns. Adam had a list of programs that he had consistently asked to attend to prepare himself for going up for partner the following year. When Adam was Adele, his managing partner was eager to send him to all sorts of conferences and development opportunities. Now, as Adam, every request he has made has been rejected, and others were sent to the events instead. Recently, one of his biggest clients had been handed over to another accountant to manage. Adam was frustrated and asked Rachel to help. Rachel agreed to investigate.

Rachel knew that there were no private employment protections for transgender employees in Kentucky, and there were inconsistencies across courts at the federal level, leaving Rachel unclear that the law would help her in this case. When Rachel approached Adam's managing partner, the partner simply stated that there was no discrimination because Adam was a man and it was important for the company to support female partners to demonstrate their commitment to diversity. "Besides, what would it look like for us to send Adam now? People know him by his former name, and I don't think anyone will take him seriously. This would embarrass the firm tremendously and create problems with our client base. While I'm all for keeping Adam on—he's a good hard worker—I just don't know if partner is the right thing for Adam," the partner stated unequivocally and firmly.

What are the firm's ethical obligations to Adam? What do you recommend Rachel do in the case of Adam?

13.1 The Hidden Brain

Review the following audio file on the NPR website Hidden Brain: Shankar Vedantam, "How Does Gender Affect One's Willingness to Compete?," *All Things Considered*, March 1, 2016. Available from www.npr.org/2016/03/01/468751715/how-does-gender-affect-ones-willingness-to-compete.

Shankar Vedantam summarized research that indicates women may not be drawn to compete, or perform well when they do compete. This can occur on tests, or in job situations. Specifically, in situations where men have a power edge (perhaps in male-dominated fields), women are less drawn to compete against men. However, when women are told men and women will be equally represented, they are much more likely to compete and succeed. This finding is consistent with the findings in the Glass Ceiling Report in 1993[54] that indicated in those industries that have best overcome the glass ceiling effect, companies are much more likely to make job opportunities available for all, regardless of race, sex, and so on. What implications do these findings have for training and development in organizations? How can companies guard against deterring women from competing for jobs and training and development opportunities? How can we make it safe for all to compete?

13.2 Onboarding at Bank of America

Bank of America has an excellent reputation for successfully onboarding and retaining executives in a highly competitive market. Critique the following elements of Bank of America's onboarding program. What recommendations would you make to address things the company may not have included in its program?

Onboarding Program	Description	Timeline
Orientation Program	Information on Bank of America including culture, values, business policies	First Day on the Job
Written Onboarding Plan	Plan organizes and prioritizes onboard process for the executive	First Week on the Job
Leadership Tools	Explains the leadership framework at Bank of America	First Week on the Job
Key Stakeholder Meetings	Meetings with important stakeholders to identify flow of information and expectations	Within the First Two Months
New Leader–Team Integration	Accelerates development of relationships between new executives and their team members	Occurs Between Two to Three Months on the Job
New Peer Integration	Accelerates development of relationships between new executives and other executive peers	Occurs Between Two to Three Months on the Job
Key Stakeholder Check-In Meetings	Helps diagnose potential problems, and receive developmental feedback	Occurs Between Three and Four Months on the Job
Executive Networking Forums	Helps new executives connect and network with other executives	Quarterly After Entry
360-Degree Feedback	Helps new executives gauge how they are performing based on key metrics as measured by those around them	Occurs After Six Months on the Job

Source: Adapted from Talya N. Bauer, *Onboarding New Employees: Maximizing Success* (SHRM Foundation's Effective Practice Guidelines Series, 2010).

13.3 Training and Development for Cultural Diversity: A Marks & Spencer Case Study

Source: Business Case Studies. Available from http://businesscasestudies.co.uk/marks-and-spencer/training-and-development-for-cultural-diversity/introduction.html#axzz473DHrgHR.

Marks and Spencer is a major retail organization, headquartered in London, England. The company has a reputation for selling high-quality products, and looks to hire and retain employees who exemplify that same high quality. Marks and Spencer's major concern with international expansion is finding and developing the same high-quality employees in locations where the Marks and Spencer reputation is relatively unknown. Read the following case and answer the questions that follow. There are links below to review. Use additional resources available on the internet as needed.

Case

Organisations that wish to be successful in the increasingly competitive markets of the 90s must consider how to provide rewarding roles which allow their employees to develop. In the UK, a career with Marks & Spencer is widely regarded as one of the most interesting opportunities for newly qualified university graduates.

There are always two sides to an employment relationship. Marks & Spencer wants the training and development of knowledge, skills and attitudes of its employees to fit corporate goals, while individuals will want their career to develop to meet their own personal expectations and aspirations. Throughout their working lives, an evaluation process takes place in which individuals constantly ask themselves:

- Where am I now?
- Where do I want to be?
- How will I get there?

The Marks & Spencer brand name evokes a strong, positive public image. Image is a combination of an individual's personal experience of a company or product, plus what they have read or heard from other sources such as family or friends. Many applications for graduate positions at Marks & Spencer are based upon what the applicants have heard from other people as well as their own experiences.

Image has helped Marks & Spencer attract high calibre people who reflect the organisation's core values of quality products and service. This is particularly important as creating the right opportunities for employees is about empowerment and trust.

The situation is quite different as Marks & Spencer expands into other countries. Many individuals have not heard of "Marks & Spencer" and do not associate it with the positive image which has been consolidated by over 100 years of trading in the UK. This case study therefore focuses upon a new experience for Marks & Spencer! As the growth of overseas business accelerates, Marks & Spencer faces two key issues:

1. how to recruit high-quality graduates from other countries
2. having appointed such graduates, how to then cater for the cultural differences in order to provide them with scope for progression which meets their personal requirements?

At the start of the process, other cultures were recognised and strategies were developed, taking into account, as appropriate, the culturally different requirements of both candidates and employees.

The Need to Build Momentum Across Europe

When organisations sell their goods in the UK, they are selling to a market of around 58 million consumers. As they extend their horizons further, the opportunities are greater. In today's rapidly changing markets, it is essential for ambitious organisations to develop their competitiveness on an international level. Organisations cannot sit behind geographical barriers, complacent in the belief that their product and market share is invincible. For organisations to compete successfully, they must learn to adapt and develop different methods of doing business which provide them with a cost advantage and the ability to differentiate their products from those of their rivals.

The European Union is a large economic region of almost 400 million consumers who have a relatively high annual expenditure on clothing, home furnishings, and food. Although Marks & Spencer may be a household name in the United Kingdom, this is not the case in many overseas markets. The "internationalisation" of Marks & Spencer has moved at a cautious pace so far, with developments in Belgium, France, Germany, Spain, Eire and the Netherlands. The new stores have been groomed for success by adapting to local markets, business practices, cultures, and consumer preferences.

One of Marks & Spencer's current objectives is to accelerate the growth of its international business in order to increase market opportunities. The key to this expansion is to offer outstanding value for money and good customer service. The organisation, which demands a lot from its staff, needs to offer plenty in return. It needs to take its responsibilities to the community seriously and value innovation. The objective of accelerated growth can only be met successfully if Marks & Spencer attracts and retains the best available staff.

The Problem

Marks & Spencer recruits around 250 university graduates in the UK each year. Marks & Spencer is well known and has a good relationship with graduate career advisors. Marks & Spencer also has a presence on campuses and a well-deserved reputation for training. A long-term presence in this labour market helps Marks & Spencer to find the high calibre graduates required for the opportunities it has to offer.

Given the aim of accelerated growth in Europe, Marks & Spencer recently set out to recruit a total of 100 graduates from the five European countries in which it operates. It soon became apparent that each of these countries had different higher education systems and widely different recruitment practices. For example, careers advisory services in Spain and the UK are not comparable and very few Spanish graduates have any work experience. In Germany, graduates leave university at the age of 27!

At Marks & Spencer, senior managers realised that there was no "European" way of doing things. Five different education systems, for example, meant that adaptation was inevitable in order to recognise cultural diversity and ensure equality of opportunity. So while Marks & Spencer wanted a coherent pan-European approach, slightly different strategies were implemented for each of the five countries.

The Process

Marks & Spencer began by highlighting the recruitment drive in the media of each country. This was particularly beneficial as it provided Marks & Spencer with high public awareness of store opening announcements and expansion plans, but at a lower cost than advertising. Although the objective was the same in each country, the approach was different. With few store announcements in the Netherlands, it was difficult to interest the press in Marks & Spencer activities. On the other hand, the trebling of the number of stores in Spain (to 12 by the year 2,000) and the employment opportunities this would create, was big news for the Spanish press.

Other problems arose. For example, 13.9% graduate unemployment in Spain meant that job advertisements could attract up to 10,000 applicants. The first stage in the graduate recruitment process is the completion of an application form. This form is then carefully checked to determine whether to invite the applicant for an interview. Before attending an interview, candidates must be prepared to answer probing questions. They may also be asked to carry out some research for discussion at the interview.

Marks & Spencer uses a structured behavioural interviewing format. This means that interviewers seek evidence of predetermined selection criteria. At the initial stage, these are:

1. leadership
2. planning and organising
3. assertiveness
4. analytical consideration
5. job motivation.

However, for continental Europe, assertiveness and analytical consideration were replaced by teamwork and adaptability as these were identified as particularly critical skills for success in a cross-cultural environment. Interviewers explore, in depth, candidates' experience in activities drawn from education, social life, or work (including placements) to determine the degree to which they possess these skills. Throughout the interview, interviewers will be looking for positive reasons to move the candidate on to the next stage of the selection process.

The next stage of the selection process is an assessment centre. This was a new concept for applicants from some countries. Having discussed what they have done in the past at interview, candidates are given the opportunity to actively demonstrate these qualities by performing a series of business related management exercises over a 24-hour period—in which both group and individual work is involved. Assessment centres measure candidates against all seven selection criteria—they have been proven to be the most effective method of predicting successful performance on the job.

After the assessment centre, successful candidates will be offered a job. Before they accept, they are invited to spend a day with Marks & Spencer to find out more about their role and to make a final check on whether they think a career with Marks & Spencer is suitable for them. The considerable evidence gathered at the assessment centre enables a "development needs profile" to be drawn up. This is fed back to the trainee on starting work and forms the basis of his or her individual development plan.

The Aim

In the past, Marks & Spencer used up to 34 different criteria when recruiting graduates in Europe. The danger was that in using widely different criteria and recruitment methods, both the quality and consistency of candidates might be affected. Marks & Spencer's goal was to recruit a truly European manager who could assimilate and work in different cultures, use different languages and be mobile—so that they could use their skills across national boundaries. For this reason, it helped if graduates had:

- been on an Erasmus programme
- undertaken part of their studies in another European country
- lived and worked abroad.

They also needed to understand Marks & Spencer and its operations. For this reason, successful candidates spend up to twelve months training in the UK.

Although it was clear that Marks & Spencer could not impose a single approach on candidates from different countries within Europe, Marks & Spencer wanted broadly similar selection processes, particularly as research within and outside the company had validated Marks & Spencer recruitment practices.

In the UK, Marks & Spencer ranks as one of the top five companies that graduates want to work for. A recent survey in Europe showed that Marks & Spencer did not rank even in the top 120. Thus a different type of problem began to emerge. Marks & Spencer could not simply lift what it did in the UK into Europe because of the different local factors. For example, Marks & Spencer wanted to recruit assertive people but there is no literal French translation for "assertiveness"!

Research and Consultation

It was important that the UK Head Office was not viewed as imposing its recruitment practices insensitively upon other regions and countries. Marks & Spencer managers therefore talked to Human Resources Managers from companies such as Barclays, United Distillers and Tesco, who had recruited graduates from around Europe. They also talked to recruitment consultancies and efforts were made to understand the comparative differences between educational systems and practices.

Marks & Spencer also consulted widely in continental Europe, using a series of focus groups to ask local managers what they would do if they wanted to recruit high quality graduates.

Developing Communication

The research helped to identify the appropriate attraction strategies for each country. This included:

- the design of the application forms
- how to publicise the company and the careers offered
- the nature of presentations to undergraduates on campus
- the development of materials for careers fairs
- the generation of interest in the media.

Information packs were sent to universities providing a basic understanding of Marks & Spencer. Presentations were then made on campus, often after liaison with Business Schools. Interviews were conducted with journalists which focused upon Marks & Spencer's expansion in Europe and the recruitment of European graduates. This was easier in some countries than others. The response from the media was better in Spain, France and Germany than it was in Belgium and the Netherlands.

Applications

Marks & Spencer received around 1700 application forms for the 100 posts required for five countries. Importantly, however, Marks & Spencer was attracting a low volume of applications from high calibre undergraduates, with 70% going through screening into the interview phase.

This contrasted directly with the high volume of applications in the UK (8500 forms are received for 200 posts) with a greater variation in graduates and only 35% going through to interviews. Research into targeting graduates in other countries provided experience that Marks & Spencer could transfer back to recruitment in the UK.

The assessment centres provided a fascinating insight into cultural diversity. Two experienced UK assessors were used for the assessment process along with two assessors from European management. Notable differences between groups of candidates were soon identified. Although it is difficult to draw generalisations about national characteristics, candidates from the Netherlands were more direct in their approach. In contrast, candidates from France were seen to be more analytical in style and were reluctant to make quick decisions. In fact, they felt that decisions were made too quickly in the UK. They wanted time to rationalise and explore detail before making decisions. The Spanish sessions were characterised by strong team-working skills.

Current research by Marks & Spencer focuses on the extent to which candidates from certain countries have had the opportunity, through their education system, to develop some of the skills necessary for success. So far, it has shown that good candidates from different cultures possess the skills, although they may display them differently. For example, assertiveness is displayed differently by individuals from different nationalities. Training assessors to recognise different cultural characteristics has therefore become a key feature of the assessment centres.

The degree to which successful candidates possess the different criteria is also important in identifying where development needs might lie. A critical criterion, however, is adaptability. Successful candidates, from early on in their career, have to learn to operate across borders and adapt the management style for the different cultures.

Conclusion

The recruitment of European graduates for Marks & Spencer has helped managers to appreciate cultural diversity. It has enabled them to step outside their own culture and develop an understanding and appreciation of multi-cultural perspectives in the working environment. It was a new experience for a business with an objective for rapid European growth. It was not known how difficult it would be and things did not always go right. However, Marks & Spencer has been able to recruit a pool of high quality graduates who learn and develop and also provide useful guidance upon developing strategies to create a platform for further growth.

Additional Sources

Marks & Spencer. Available from www.marksandspencer.com.

Marks & Spencer, "About Us." Available from http://corporate.marksandspencer.com/?intid+gft_company.

Questions

1. Describe the key challenge Marks & Spencer faced when deciding to expand internationally.

2. Why is cultural competence important in this context? Why not just manage employees in other locations as the company does in its home country?

3. Development activities are tightly linked with recruitment and selection processes in many companies, but especially within Marks & Spencer. Describe how the company uses recruitment and selection to help design appropriate development activities for its new employees. Could Marks & Spencer do the type

of employee development it wants to do if these activities were not linked? Why or why not?

4. What role do you think Hofstede's national culture dimensions played in the recruitment, selection, and development decisions Marks & Spencer made?

13.4 Congratulations! Your next assignment is . . . !

Your company is sending four employees on a two-year expatriate assignment overseas. You and your team in HR are responsible for designing the training programs needed for these four employees and their families. The families will not be traveling with them.

a. Pick a country you would like to research.

b. Identify Hofstede's dimensions for that country. Compare and contrast them to the United States' dimensions. What areas are most important for our new expatriates to consider because they are different from the U.S. dimensions?

c. Outline and describe what you would include in the expatriate training for the employees in a training plan. What would they need to know to live and work in that country? How would you deliver the training to the employees? Describe the training session from beginning to end.

d. Consider the employees' families. What, if anything, would you include in training for their families? What should be covered during the training for them? How would you deliver that training to them? Describe the training session in detail from beginning to end.

APPENDIX A
Semester-Long Project

PURPOSE AND DESCRIPTION

The purpose of this project is for you to practice what you have learned in this course in an integrated format. You will be responsible for all phases of the training and development process. You will start by conducting a needs analysis, then develop and implement the training, and finally evaluate it. This is meant to be a real-world project, and you should approach it like you would if you were assigned to conduct a training program at work. Once you have completed this project, you will be able to honestly report in an employment interview that you have successfully provided training and development.

Following some advice on becoming engaged in the project, each major component/deliverable will be explained.

BECOMING ENGAGED

Here is some advice on choosing and developing your training project (keep in mind that your instructor may include additional guidelines/requirements). First, pick a topic that you find interesting. This is a semester-long project, and you will be spending a lot of time working on it. Second, pick a topic with which you are already familiar. The less time you need to learn about the topic, the more time you will be able to focus on training others. Further, the more you know about the topic already, the more likely you are to find it interesting. Third, keep in mind resource limitations. You might have a great idea, but is it something that you can do in the time allocated? Similarly, ask yourself if you will have the time, ability, and/or money to produce the instructional aids you will need to do a good job. In the case that you feel your initial idea is too big to do, consider whether you can concentrate the training on a subset of the knowledge, skill, or competency.

So far, we have just made recommendations for ensuring you have an engaging and manageable training project for yourself, but remember that you will have trainees as well. Make sure you use what you are learning to make your training as engaging as possible. There are three reasons for this. First, training that is engaging should be more enjoyable. Once engaged, your classmates should learn more. Finally, making the training more engaging for others will likely mean that you are using more of the concepts and tools discussed in the textbook, which means that you will be learning more as well.

NEEDS ANALYSIS PROPOSAL

The first component/deliverable is the needs analysis proposal. As discussed in Chapter 3, conducting a needs analysis is important to create and deliver a successful training intervention.

Also as discussed in Chapter 3, a needs analysis can and should be conducted at three different levels (organizational, job, and personal). The best way to do this is to pick a real organization in which to base your training. This could be your current employer or the employer of a friend or family member. The important thing is that you have access to information about an organization's strategy and culture as well as a specific job.

As you put together this component/deliverable, keep in mind key material from the textbook.

Chapter 2 provides an explanation of marginal and essential job duties as well as other legal concerns.

Chapter 3 lists options for how to conduct the needs analysis and provides information to help you determine which would be most appropriate for this assignment.

The following is a checklist of what should be included in your needs analysis proposal. Be careful to note whether your instructor makes any additions or changes to the list.

1. Topic description
2. Needs analysis
    a. Organization analysis
        i. What is the organization's strategy?
        ii. Describe the organization's culture.
        iii. What type of policies and procedures are in place that may have an impact on the proposed training?
        iv. Perform an organizational SWOT analysis.
    b. Job-level analysis
        i. What needed tasks or competencies does the training address?
        ii. Does the training address marginal or essential job functions?
    c. Person-level analysis
        i. What is the trainees' level of motivation?
        ii. What is the trainees' level of readiness?
3. Assessment and implications
    a. Is there a good match/strong need for your training topic?
    b. Based on your answer in 3a, what are the implications for this level of match?

INSTRUCTIONAL DESIGN AND DEVELOPMENT PROPOSAL

The second component/deliverable is the instructional design and developmental proposal. After completing the needs analysis, you are ready to design the training and develop the materials needed for the training. In the design phase, you have to consider how people learn, the training objectives, and what you want the training session to look like. This includes the content, delivery format (e.g., lecture or role play), and general flow (schedule/timing).

As you put together this component/deliverable, keep in mind key material from the textbook.

Chapter 4 addresses a wide variety of learning theories. Which learning theory do you believe most closely maps to the training session you are designing? Is it basic operant conditioning, or are you focused more on experiential or action learning, as considered in andragogy? Decide on the learning theory(ies) that will guide your training session and ensure you have adequately considered what you want people to learn and how you want them to learn it.

Chapters 5 and 6 address evaluation. Whenever you develop training, you should consider how you are going to evaluate it. Also, because of time constraints of the semester, this is when you will need to submit your evaluation materials.

Chapter 7 addresses different options for delivering your training. These include methods/format (e.g., lecture or role play) as well as instructional aids (e.g., videos or handouts).

Chapter 8 addresses the layout of the classroom and related spatial and technological issues.

Appendix C provides additional information that will be useful for the creation of your instructional aids.

The following is a checklist of what should be included in your instructional design and developmental proposal. Be careful to note whether your instructor makes any additions or changes to the list.

1. Overview
    a. Short description of the topic
    b. List of learning goals/objectives
2. Training methods
    a. Identify and describe each method being used
    b. Provide a schedule
3. Instructional aids
    a. Provide samples, descriptions, and/or links
    b. Include trainer notes/script
4. Classroom issues
    a. Address layout and any potential constraints
5. Training evaluation
    a. Identify method and materials you will use to evaluate the training

Everything you use in the training must be either obtained or developed, including materials needed for the trainee, as well as guidelines/scripts/notes for the trainers. This is also inclusive of your evaluation materials. You should pilot test your procedure to ensure you have everything you need and have considered potential problems or hang-ups that might occur. It is also important to ensure you have a contingency plan in case something goes wrong. Do you have backup materials? Can you do the training without the internet or technology?

TRAINING DELIVERY

Before delivering your training, be sure to practice ahead of time. Also, refer to Appendix C for how to manage the training session. Additional information (e.g., time allotted for your training) will be provided by your instructor.

FINAL TRAINING EVALUATION REPORT

The final component/deliverable is the final training evaluation report. It is important to evaluate training both to document its success and to understand how to improve the delivery, both the training itself and yourself as the trainer.

As you put together this component/deliverable, keep in mind key material from the textbook.

Chapters 5 and 6 address evaluation. Although the evaluation materials have already been developed, these chapters provide useful information on administration and analysis.

The following is a checklist of what should be included in your final training evaluation report. Be careful to note whether your instructor makes any additions or changes to the list.

1. Present the results of your training evaluation
    a. Assess the success of the training
    b. Develop recommendations for how the training could be improved
2. Conduct a self-/group evaluation
    a. Reflect on the group's strengths and weaknesses in the process of completing this project, being sure to address:
        i. Needs analysis proposal
        ii. Instructional design and development proposal
        iii. Training delivery
        iv. Final training evaluation report
    b. Identify what you could do to become a better trainer
3. Discuss how the project helped you better understand the course

APPENDIX B
External Partnerships

Among employers' many options for providing their employees with training and development opportunities is to engage in partnership with an outside entity. Partnerships are more expansive than simply contracting with an outside provider to deliver training on-site or to send employees off-site for training. For one reason, partnerships are associated with a long-term ongoing relationship. As for the nature of the relationship, partnerships generally take one of two forms, or a combination of both. First, as the term *partnership* implies, both the organization and the other entity work together in the design and/or implementation of the program. Second, the other entity is a source of funding.

This appendix focuses on three specific types of partnerships. First, apprenticeships typically involve partnering with a labor union. Second, organizations can partner with community colleges in addition to taking advantage of the more general training and development programs or courses that they already provide. Partnering with community colleges can also make organizations available for additional governmental funds. Third, the government, at multiple levels (e.g., federal and state), can be a source of funding and other resources to support providing employees with training and development. In addition to these partnerships, organizations may enter into partnerships with nonprofits, small business development centers, and similar entities.

APPRENTICESHIPS

Apprenticeships represent one of the earliest methods of formalized instruction and occupational preparation.[1] The system of apprenticeships harkens back to the age of medieval guilds, which guarded the secrets of their crafts.[2] These guilds were organized around specific trades and controlled who was trained and allowed to do business. Examples of crafts include cordwainery (shoemaking), masonry, and all varieties of smith (e.g., black-, gold-, and silver-). While the system of apprenticeships may no longer be widespread for many of these traditional crafts, others have replaced them such as plumbing and electrical work. Apprenticeships continue to evolve. For example, Hilton Worldwide recently pledged to create the first tourism apprenticeship program. Individuals can also be apprenticed in high-tech fields like computer programming.[3]

Historical Overview of Apprenticeships

Within the guilds, three general classifications of individuals ranged from unskilled to highly skilled. The most skilled workers, as designated by the guild, were the masters. A master was allowed to do business in his own name and to take on apprentices to whom he would teach the secrets of the craft. If not a member of the master's family, an apprentice often had to pay for the right to be taught a skill. Further, during the period of apprenticeship, the apprentice would both work and live with the master. Someone could remain an apprentice for years before being accorded the status of journeyman. Becoming a journeyman meant that someone had achieved a specified level of competence and that he could seek wages and work under (i.e., journey to) any master.[4] Those journeymen who continued to develop their skills could eventually apply to their guilds for admittance to the ranks of master and continue the cycle.

With industrialization, this system changed. However, many of the guilds evolved and became the original trade unions. The strength of these unions, prior to the passage of pro-union legislation, rested in their ability to teach the next generation and thereby control the supply of labor. Not surprisingly, then, one of the goals of scientific management, besides improving worker efficiency, was to wrest knowledge from skilled workers so that employers would not be so dependent on unions.

Today, unions remain a major source for and partner in the creation of skilled workers—especially for unions that represent craft workers. You can usually identify a craft union because it has an occupation in its name (e.g., carpenters, masons, or plumbers) as opposed to an industry (e.g., autoworkers or communication workers). These programs are often in partnership with a local employer where the apprentice is employed.

One way of marking this modern era of apprenticeships is with the passage of the Fitzgerald Act. As a result of this legislation, the U.S. Department of Labor began registering apprenticeship programs in 1937. Today, there are over 21,000 registered programs that train over 500,000 apprentices.[5]

Contemporary Attributes of Apprenticeships

Given the historical overview of apprenticeships, it should come as no surprise that they are fundamentally different from, and considered to be of higher quality than, mere internships.[6] A key reason for this is that apprenticeship programs involve a combination of classroom and on-the-job training. The purpose of the classroom instruction is to provide foundational and/or theoretical knowledge. This is then integrated with an on-the-job training component provided by the apprentice's employer. Through the on-the-job training and supervised work tasks, the apprentice has the opportunity to engage in experiential learning and apply the more general information he or she has learned in the classroom.

Federally registered apprenticeship programs typically last four years but can vary between one and six years in duration. Program designers can choose a time-based, competency-based, or hybrid approach. The time-based approach, the most traditional design, involves apprentices spending 144 hours in a classroom for each year of their apprenticeship in addition to full-time employment and on-the-job training. Alternatively, a program can take a competency-based approach. These programs allow apprentices to progress at their own rate and replace hour requirements with tests. Finally, the hybrid approach represents a compromise of the first two.[7] As for content, the specifics of a program depend on the industry and occupation and should be determined through a needs analysis.

One important caveat for this discussion regarding apprenticeships is that it is based on the model that currently exists within the United States. While the overall concept of apprenticeships exists worldwide, the specific structure can vary by country.[8] Further, the components discussed (e.g., 144 hours of classroom instruction) may vary for an apprenticeship that is not federally registered. It should be noted, however, that there are several advantages to registering an apprenticeship program. First, it provides access to governmental resources, both technical and financial. Second, it provides credentialing, which demonstrates that the program meets specific quality standards.[9]

Pre-apprenticeship Programs

One of the most recent innovations in the system of apprenticeships in the United States is the emergence of pre-apprenticeship programs. The goal of these programs is to increase the diversity and success rate of apprentices. For example, BUD, a pre-apprenticeship program in Saint Louis, Missouri, is actually an acronym standing for building union diversity.[10]

Historically, the demographics of participants in a union apprenticeship program have mirrored its membership. In practical terms, this means that most apprentices have tended to be white males.[11] One simple reason for this, aside from any historical discrimination, is that many unions have relied heavily on word-of-mouth recruiting. Oftentimes, this resulted in the ranks of apprentices being filled by the children or relations of existing union members. Consequently, there is built-in inertia to expand racial diversity. Therefore, these programs purposefully engage in targeted recruiting to diversify the pool of potential apprentices.

While from a multicultural perspective this lack of diversity is a negative, there is an organizational advantage to it that represents the other goal of pre-apprenticeship programs. Specifically, apprentices who come from existing union households are likely to have an advantage over their peers in terms of acculturation and support. Pre-apprenticeship programs often provide these along with prerequisite knowledge skills. Together, they allow graduates to be more successful once they are accepted into an apprenticeship, which is now more likely because they have been in a pre-apprenticeship program.

COMMUNITY COLLEGES

Community colleges (also known as junior colleges) are an excellent, lower-cost option for taking college classes and achieving associate's degrees in a wide variety of areas. Lesser known is their work as a community resource for training and development partnerships. The mission of community colleges is to provide educational resources and support to their local community, hence the name. Under the Obama administration, the importance of community colleges was enhanced and became a focal point for providing extensive education in the area of workforce development (WFD).[12]

Degree Programs

WFD focuses on education for vocational and technical trades such as computer-aided drafting, manufacturing technology, welding, and auto mechanics, among many others. As noted in the previous section, apprenticeship programs can provide much of the technical skills needed for workers to perform these jobs successfully. WFD, however, is so much more than that because of the belief that our workers need to be able to reason, analyze, think critically, communicate, and work as team players, as well as be technically skilled to succeed.[13] The courses offered through a degree program in a community college can provide training in those additional, critical competency areas. Therefore, the WFD programs offered at community colleges play an important role in education and training above and beyond the skill-based technical training offered through apprenticeship programs. The strategic needs of the organization should dictate the type of program it pursues for its employees.

Training and Development Consulting Programs

Hand in hand with the WFD degree programs are the resources available at community colleges to develop training and development partnerships with local businesses. These services are typically non-degree-granting, but certificate or degree programs can be custom developed for clients as need be. According to Don Sosnowski, executive director of Invista Performance Solutions in Tacoma, Washington, the community college system plays an important role in the economic viability of any community.[14] Because community colleges exist to serve their geographic community, they can provide easy access to state resources to improve the skills of the local workforce and advance economic conditions in the area. Many state-funded grants and training opportunities can only be accessed through a partnership with the local community college. Among the many advantages of the community college is that it provides training resources at a lower cost than many independent consulting firms or service providers, and functions as a conduit to provide state-level workforce development grants and rebates for local businesses. Additional advantages of the community college over independent consultants are that community college consulting programs are able to access a wide variety of subject matter experts (SMEs), and that they can take advantage of the certificate and degree programs only offered through higher education institutions. Exhibit B-1 spotlights Don Sosnowski's work.

Exhibit B-1   Don Sosnowski: Profile of a Community College Trainer

Don Sosnowski is the executive director of Invista Performance Solutions (IPS), a collaboration of four community colleges and technical schools in the greater Tacoma area in Washington. Invista has upwards of $2.5 million in revenues annually, providing

(Continued)

> **Exhibit B-1 (Continued)**
>
> training and development programs to the local community. With clients such as Amazon, Goodwill, SEIU Healthcare, and the Washington State Department of Labor and Industries, IPS provides a wide variety of programs ranging from technical training such as welding, to a certificate in tribal gaming enterprise management, to soft-skill development such as communication, team building, and customer service. Don's road to training through the community college system didn't follow a typical career path in training and development.
>
> Upon graduation from college, Don ventured to Italy where he worked for two years teaching English as a second language. Upon his return, he eventually found himself starting his own business to provide language training for expatriate business employees. From there, his career in corporate training took off. The College of Lake County in Illinois initially hired Don to build a language training institute in the Chicago suburbs. After a few years, he became the director of the Workforce and Professional Development Institute and expanded his expertise from language training to embrace the field of corporate education. Now, as the executive director of IPS, he has a staff of seven, and access to a network of qualified trainers across the Sea-Tac area. As well, he is a Certified Professional in Learning and Performance, the highest certification offered by the Association for Talent Development.
>
> Don believes that the community college system is an ideal partner for businesses of all sizes to use for their training and development needs. With a focus on economic development for the Tacoma area, IPS offers a one-stop shop for a wide variety of training and development needs. IPS succeeds because of its commitment to provide high-quality training at a reasonable cost. Clients such as Amazon maintain a successful partnership with IPS by continually returning to the organization for its training needs.
>
> Don sees his job as central to the economic viability of the Tacoma area. IPS stands out as an excellent example of the important role community colleges play in the training and development industry. With their commitment to community investment and training excellence at a reasonable price, community colleges are a cost-effective way for businesses to enhance their training portfolio.

How to Choose a Training Vendor

Not all community colleges provide the same high-quality services, and the same can be said for external consulting companies and other training and development service providers. When researching the local community college as a potential resource, Don Sosnowski suggests doing your homework and asking a few important questions.[15] First and foremost, ask the community college about the process it uses to determine training and development needs. Providers that follow the ADDIE model (or some variation of it), described in the introduction to this textbook, are more likely to utilize a systematic and reliable process for determining training needs and delivering training. Consistently using a successful process will result in consistent delivery of high-quality training and development.

Second, ask the community college about its process for vetting trainers. Good training providers ensure that their trainers are qualified SMEs with credentials and experience in the field. The potential trainers should go through a detailed screening process including providing instructional demos, samples of instructional materials, references, and prior evaluations from past trainings. Once the trainer vetting process meets with your approval, the last step in securing the partner for training includes receiving references from satisfied (and perhaps dissatisfied) clients to get a sense of the type of work provided, and potential concerns to be aware of, when working with that vendor.

The community college system is a high-quality resource found in the organization's backyard. Its value to businesses, both large and small, cannot be underestimated. Because of their role in higher education, community college consultants have access to resources such as the college's learning management system (LMS), as discussed in Chapter 9. The cost of purchasing and utilizing an LMS can be prohibitive to small businesses, and therefore, this resource can be an asset to those organizations that may have avoided online training due to the associated startup costs. Overall, a good partnership with a community college can provide training advantages to smaller businesses by keeping prices down while not sacrificing quality of delivery. While any organization can benefit from a partnership of this type, small businesses can now compete with larger companies in terms of developing and retaining their employees when they work with their local community college.

GOVERNMENT

In Chapter 2, we covered how the government influences training from a compliance perspective. This view of government involvement in organizational training is to a degree negative and coercive. As discussed in Chapter 2, organizations provide training so that they comply with governmental regulations or else to protect themselves from legal liability. In addition to directing the content of training, the government influences the process of providing training and development, primarily in the areas of selection and accommodation to ensure equal opportunity.

Besides regulations and enforcement, governmental agencies can be a positive force in the provision of training and development. There is a long history of the federal government providing funds for employee training. Today, HR professionals should consider utilizing one of the numerous programs that promote employee training and development as part of their organization's overall training and development strategy.[16] For example, the federal government spent approximately $17 billion on training programs in fiscal year 2014,[17] not including any additional funds spent at the state level. As one might expect, the biggest provider of training programs is the U.S. Department of Labor,[18] but as shown in Exhibit B-2, it is not alone.

Given the scope, and changing nature, of federal programs and funding, this appendix is not able to provide a comprehensive list. However, this appendix does provide a general understanding of what resources, financial and otherwise, organizations can take advantage of when providing their employees with training and development opportunities. This discussion begins with a historical overview of major legislative initiatives and continues by identifying the ways that organizations can partner with and/or take advantage of government programs.

Exhibit B-2 Federal Spending on Job Training Programs

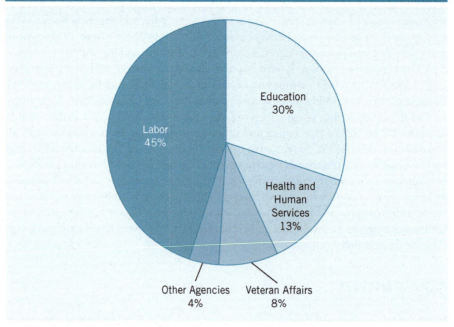

Source: Adapted (and rounded to nearest whole percent) from Kristen Fyfe-Mills, "Job Training Reboot Offers New Opportunities for Federal Agencies," *Public Manager* 43, no. 4 (2014): 17–19.

An Overview of Past Government Involvement

One of the main pieces of federal legislation that promotes workforce training today is the Workforce Innovation and Opportunity Act (WIOA). The WIOA was signed by President Obama in 2014 and replaced the Workforce Investment Act (WIA) of 1998. These acts were the latest in a series of federal efforts to promote workforce development going back to the 1960s. Exhibit B-3 provides an overview of the major training and development legislation that preceded the WIOA. In addition to the benefits of general workforce development efforts, employers were able to benefit from the on-the-job training and/or subsidized employment provided through these successive pieces of legislation.

The Manpower Development and Training Act (MDTA) of 1962 was originally marketed as an antipoverty program.[19] But its main purpose was to provide welfare recipients and disadvantaged youth with training and employment.[20] The MDTA was a very centralized program with the Bureau of Labor Statistics controlling funding. The training provided by the MDTA involved mostly classroom instruction (about two-thirds), with the remaining being on-the-job training (about one-third), and was overseen by 12 regional offices.[21]

Exhibit B-3 Major Federal Training and Development Legislation

Legislation	Year	Key Features/Innovations
Manpower Development and Training Act	1962	Centralized training programs that offered classroom and on-the-job options
Comprehensive Employment and Training Act	1973	Started process of decentralization and provided subsidized employment
Job Training Partnership Act	1982	Increased accountability and involvement of private sector employers
Workforce Investment Act	1998	One-stop career centers with a customer focused training model

When the Comprehensive Employment and Training Act (CETA) of 1973 replaced the MDTA, it instituted several important changes. One of the most important changes was decentralization with the creation of local advisory boards and a shift in control from the federal government to individual states.[22] Another key change was that CETA provided subsidized employment, both in the public agencies and with private employers, which served to supplement traditional training options.[23]

The Job Training Partnership Act (JTPA) of 1982 instituted its own set of adjustments to federally supported training. First, it continued the trend toward decentralization and increased involvement by the private sector on its advisory boards.[24] Another critical adjustment was increased accountability. Specifically, the JTPA required training programs to be evaluated.

A defining characteristic of the Workforce Investment Act of 1998 was its customer-focused approach as opposed to a one-size-fits-all model of training. Physically, the WIA created "one-stop career centers," which both improved access to services and reduced overlapping programs that proliferated under the JTPA. Training provided under the WIA fell into one of two general categories. First, there was on-the-job training, with firms being reimbursed for up to 50% of an employee's wage. Second, WIA provided occupational skills training, offered through a variety of sources (e.g., community college courses), and then trainees picked their preferred option for learning.[25]

An Overview of Current Government Involvement

In 2014, the Workforce Innovation and Opportunity Act was signed into law and superseded the WIA. An important emphasis of the WIOA is engagement with the business community to better align and spend federal training dollars. Through its workforce development boards, WIOA utilizes regional agencies that provide many services to area employers. While this section focuses on how organizations can partner and benefit in regard to employee training, it is useful to note the other services that these regional agencies provide. For employers, these agencies can provide assistance with recruitment and selection. Individuals can also benefit through a variety of job search assistance programs and services. In addition, government programs often provide supportive services (e.g., child care and transportation) for people engaged in training.[26]

WIOA and subsidies.

Among the main ways that employers can benefit from the WIOA is through various subsidy programs. Subsidies fall into two main categories. First, organizations can use subsidies for on-the-job training. Second, there are programs for subsidized public employment with training.[27]

While on-the-job training subsidies are directed toward traditional hires, subsidies for public employment with training tend to be provided for targeted populations. For example, during the summer, the federal government sponsors programs to promote youth employment. While the goal of these programs is to provide employment opportunities to at-risk youth to keep them off the streets, they also provide them with basic workplace competencies and skills, additional benefits for employers.

Another major category of beneficiaries comprises dislocated workers. The workers in these programs often already have skills, but unfortunately, these skills don't match those needed in the labor market, normally the result of a manufacturing plant closure. Companies identified as "at risk" of closure can also be the recipients of this type of funds with the goal of preventing the workers from becoming dislocated.[28]

Additional governmental support and incentives.

Governmental support and incentives for employee training and development are not limited to specialized federal legislation and programs that focus on workforce development. For example, both the Occupational Safety & Health Administration and the Equal Employment Opportunity Commission offer training resources for employers. As for financial incentives, the Fair Labor Standards Act allows employers to apply for a certificate that enables them to pay workers at a wage rate lower than the standard federal minimum.[29] In addition, the federal tax code encourages employers to provide employees with educational assistance benefits as part of their compensation package. Four tests or requirements must be met for a plan to qualify.[30] These tests/requirements are presented in Exhibit B-4.

Exhibit B-4 Tests/Requirements for a Qualified Educational Assistance Program

1. The program doesn't favor highly compensated employees.
2. Owners and shareholders do not receive more than 5% of the benefits.
3. Employees cannot receive cash or other benefits instead of educational assistance.
4. Employees receive reasonable notice of the program.

Source: Internal Revenue Service, "Employer's Tax Guide to Fringe Benefits: For Use in 2018" (Publication 15-B), February 22, 2018. Available from https://www.irs.gov/pub/irs-prior/p15b--2018.pdf.

Employers can also take advantage of state-level incentives in the form of either tax credits or direct subsidies.[31] For example, Georgia, Mississippi, and Rhode Island all provide a 50% tax credit for eligible training with amounts ranging from $1,250 to $5,000 per employee.[32] By comparison, the state of California uses a payroll tax to generate a pool of funds that it subsequently disperses to companies to assist with the provision of training.[33] It is important to note that this list is not exhaustive and that the number and nature of state training initiatives are likely to expand and change. Consequently, it is advantageous for human resource professionals to investigate exactly how their organizations can benefit from state initiatives.

APPENDIX C
Managing a Training Session

Whether you are the training specialist or an employee involved in peer training, you will need to effectively facilitate a training session to ensure the environment is conducive to learning success and desired training outcomes. This appendix focuses on integrating and presenting material addressed briefly in other chapters (e.g., learning methods, discussed in Chapter 7, and practical skills, discussed in Chapter 12), combined here in more depth for reference when preparing your training session materials. Many pointers are available on how to manage a training environment, and we offer here some best practices for how to facilitate learning in a training or development session.

A few fallacies exist out there about what makes a good facilitator.[1] The first fallacy is that all facilitators need to do is provide trainees with lots of information and read notes to them for them to learn. As we already discovered in Chapter 4, on learning theories, receiving too much information at one time can inhibit learning. It needs to be presented in a way that maximizes learning. The second fallacy assumes all facilitators need to be good trainers is to be good public speakers. While public speaking is necessary for a good trainer, it is not sufficient to facilitate a successful training session. The third fallacy assumes training is similar to college instruction simply because adults are receiving instruction in both situations. While some similarities may occur, by and large college instruction lasts over an entire semester and involves more than skill development. Training, on the other hand, is typically short term, and provides skills that employees can use on the job right away. Lastly, it is a poor assumption that a one-size-fits-all approach to learning is best for facilitating training. Again, each person learns differently, and when we take a multimodal approach to training facilitation, all trainees will benefit.

PRESENTATION SKILLS

Presentation skills are the primary way that trainers can deliver material to trainees. The following section highlights different aspects of the skills needed to present effectively.

Stay calm.

Even the most skilled performer, actor, trainer, or presenter experiences stage fright. Most conscientious trainers have "butterflies in their stomach" before an important session. The first trick of successful presentation skills is staying calm and remembering to breathe. Take a few minutes before the presentation to close your eyes, take some deep breaths, and center yourself. A lot of research supports the importance of simply breathing when we feel nervous or anxious.

Presentation materials.

Different tools are available to use for presentations. The most common is Microsoft PowerPoint, a staple in any Office Suite package. If you can't afford or access PowerPoint, open source tools are available. Apache Open Office allows you to create presentations with Impress, or produce drawings and illustrations with Draw. Adobe Spark is a free program to help you create visual stories, with options to upgrade to a subscription for more tools you can use in your presentation. Prezi is similar to Adobe Spark in that it offers free access with an option to upgrade to a subscription. Many online tutorials are available on how to use all of these presentation tools.

Regardless of the tools you use, there are rules of thumb to consider when designing your presentations. The most important rule is to keep it simple. PowerPoint presentations reinforce visual learning, but can be challenging to view if the slides are too busy or have too much information for learners to read and comprehend quickly. Use one message per slide, and limit the amount of text on each slide so trainees can read and understand what is being communicated.[2] While illustrations can help you communicate a message, be careful of graphics that can confuse and distract trainees from the important content.[3] Use a consistent slide design throughout, including color and font.[4] Exhibit C-1 offers guidelines for creating presentations.

Exhibit C-1 Guidelines for Creating Presentations

Slide Design

- Each slide should address a single concept.
- Slides should follow a logical progression, each building on the other. You may want to create your last slide first, so you are clear what you want the trainees to take away at the end of the presentation. You can then build the presentation with that last slide in mind.
- Use no more than six lines of text on any one slide.
- Use upper- and lowercase text, *not* all caps. Use no smaller than a 30-point font.
- Choose a color appropriate to the mood you want to convey (see below). Use a dark color for backgrounds and a lighter color for fonts.
- Avoid using too many colors (maximum of 5).
- Use photographs (with proper credit in a citation) to help the audience relate slide information to real-world situations.
- Use graphics that support your message, not distract the viewers.
- Avoid using distracting slide animations and noises. Keep the animations simple for transitions between slides, and for highlighting information on each slide. Don't use sound effects, and only use sounds if they are necessary to demonstrate a key point in the training (e.g., a sound trainees should hear if they make a mistake using a piece of equipment).

(Continued)

Exhibit C-1 (Continued)

Color

- **Dark blue** to project a stable, mature message—has a calming effect
- **Red** or **orange** to trigger excitement or an emotional response
- **Green** to make audience members comfortable
- **Yellow** to get audience attention quickly (more so than any other color)
- **Gray** to promote the idea of "quality"
- **White** to project honesty/sincerity
- **Black** is not appealing to most viewers

Source: Adapted from Dartmouth College Biomedical Libraries, "PowerPoint: Guides, Tips and Help." Available from https://www.dartmouth.edu/~library/biomed/guides/powerpoint.html.

Connecting with your audience.

Once you have created your presentation, as you begin your session you want to connect with the audience and engage trainees right from the start. Your opening should begin with a story, a question, or a shocking statistic to make an emotional connection with your trainees.[5] If you begin with a story, there are a few guidelines you should follow. First, make sure your story includes characters who are analogous to your training class.[6] For example, if you share a story about a workplace challenge, your example should be relatable to the audience and the lesson to be learned from the training session. As well, establish a relationship between the characters and the main point of the story.[7] Once you have introduced the story, challenge the trainees to think about what they would do differently in a similar scenario.[8]

Using humor and emotion is fine when you are trying to make a point. Be careful, however, not to cross a line and share something inappropriate or offensive to the trainees, if it is not directly relevant to the training session. For example, sharing a race-related joke or communicating about a racial stereotype is not acceptable except in the specific circumstance of demonstrating to trainees when engaged in diversity awareness training why telling race-related jokes or using stereotypes is not appropriate in the workplace. Even then, great care must be taken in how the material is delivered so it is not presumed that the facilitator shares those opinions or that those opinions are acceptable to the organization.

Presenting the material.

While we addressed communication style and nonverbal communication in Chapter 12, there are some communication points you should consider specific to presenting material to your trainees. First, don't read off the slides.[9] Trainees can read the slides themselves. Your job is to fill in the blanks between the bullet points to explain the points and provide examples. Second, monitor your tone and speak loudly so that people can hear you in the room.[10] Even if you are a soft-spoken person, a soft voice can often communicate lack of confidence to the audience. Practice changing the tone of your voice to emphasize points, and project your voice so all can hear you clearly.

Engage your trainees so they spend more time watching you than thinking about the ticking clock, and the work they could be doing if they were not in a training session. Ask them questions and encourage them to play devil's advocate. Even something as simple as pausing and asking if they have any questions keeps the trainees alert and reflective. As you transition between topics, go around the room and ask trainees to note one takeaway they learned they can use on the job right away. This forces them to refer to their notes and materials and think more deeply about how they can begin to apply the material learned on the job. You'll know you've accomplished high levels of engagement if the trainees remark at the end, "I don't know how the time flew by so fast, but boy, did I learn new things!"

There are several words to avoid while leading a training session.[11] First, avoid filler words such as *um* or *uh*. These words give the impression to the trainees you are unprepared or lack the proper knowledge to conduct the training session. As well, instead of saying "I hope you learn something," a statement that lacks confidence, focus on a more assertive statement such as "I am confident you will walk away with many important tools you can use on the job." Lastly, emphasize what you want trainees to do more affirmatively, and place less emphasis on what they shouldn't do (except in cases of workplace safety where the don'ts are as important as the dos). If you place primary emphasis on what people shouldn't do, then they are more likely to remember what not to do, and then do it anyway. As noted in the discussion on diversity training in Chapter 13, focusing on what not to do only reinforces the behavior you are trying to stop.

In terms of your body language, where and how you stand in the training session communicates a certain message.[12] Just as we'd arrange our tables in the room to facilitate learning, trainers position themselves in the room to create a relationship with the trainees. Consider standing somewhere between 2.5 and 7 feet from your trainees to create a personal and social relationship while conducting the training. Along with where you stand, consider making eye contact with one person at a time to build engagement and connection. Learn people's names and use them frequently to keep trainees engaged. Lastly, even if you have presentation butterflies, present yourself as confident to help the trainees connect with you as an expert on the content. Exhibit C-2 provides suggestions for how to appear confident, even if you are nervous.

> **Exhibit C-2 Tips for Appearing Confident**
>
> Tips for appearing confident while leading a presentation or training session:
>
> 1. Keep your shoulders back and stand tall.
> 2. Keep your arms at your side or held in front of your body when making gestures.
> 3. Keep your hands open or only slightly closed.
> 4. Smile slightly or keep your face neutral.
> 5. Take long, purposeful strides when you are walking into and around the room.
> 6. Make every movement purposeful and decided.
> 7. Treat props as though they are of value, and handle them with care.

Source: Adapted from Sarah Kessler, "How to Improve Your Presentation Skills," *Inc.* Available from http://www.inc.com/guides/how-to-improve-your-presentation-skills.html.

The best way to build confidence in your presentation skills is to practice in advance. You can practice in front of a mirror, or even videotape your presentation to diagnose challenges you may experience in presenting information. Look specifically for how you use your body and hands while presenting, as well as your tone of voice and volume, and listen for filler words that take away from the professionalism of your presentation. Don't memorize your presentation, but practice it enough that you know what to say, what to emphasize, and how to emphasize your points.

Questions are an important element in a training program. Few people understand something the first time they are told the information, so repetition is important, as is allowing for a vigorous question-and-answer session at the end of the training program. It is also important to allow for questions as you proceed through the material. Be careful, however, that questions don't sidetrack the flow of the training session. Keep the questions brief and don't allow them to derail the focus of the training session. If necessary, write the questions down on a flip chart or dry-erase board in what is euphemistically called "the parking lot," and come back to them at the end of the presentation. Alternatively, if the question is person specific, ask the person to speak with you during a break or after the session to address his or her questions. Never let a question go unanswered as it erodes confidence in the trainer's abilities.

TRAINING SESSION DISRUPTIONS

Even under the best of circumstances where we have prepared and practiced and are ready for our training session, things can happen that are out of our initial control and can disrupt our efforts to effectively lead the training. Two issues we need to address include technology and materials problems and disruptive trainees.

Exhibit C-3 Common Technology Problems

- The video can't be downloaded.
- There is no internet at the training location.
- The speakers or sound system are not working properly.
- The projector's light bulb shuts off in the middle of your presentation.
- The version of the software that you used to create your presentation is not compatible with the one on the computer or tablet that you are supposed to use.
- The wrong presentation is on the screen.
- The handouts and other materials arrived at the wrong venue, or the venue changed at the last minute.
- Someone forgot to rent the projector and the screen.
- The connecting cable is too short, and you can't see the next slide before it comes up.
- There is no adapter for your computer to connect to the projector.

Source: Adapted from Wanda Piña-Ramírez and Norma Dávila, "Become a Good Training Facilitator," *Association for Talent Development.* Available from https://www.td.org/newsletters/atd-links/become-a-good-training-facilitator.

Technology and materials.

Chapter 9 goes into great detail on how we can use technology to facilitate and enhance our training and development efforts. Even when we practice our delivery, problems can arise with the internet or equipment and supplies we are using in the room. Exhibit C-3 provides some examples of problems that may occur when using technology.

Having a backup plan is essential. Creating a checklist for the most common problems and solutions is helpful and should be a central part of your training design and implementation strategy. Arriving well in advance of your start time ensures you can troubleshoot and test technology for problems. Make sure handouts are printed in advance and/or you are carrying them with you. Download all materials onto the computer you are using in advance. Use your own computer where possible and ensure you have all the proper cables and adapters to project material (especially important for those who use Apple products). Save your work in multiple locations that are accessible in the moment, such as Google Drive, Dropbox, iCloud, or your email. Most smartphones can be tethered to a computer to function as an internet hotspot, so encourage your company to purchase that as an option with your company phone. In the end, if all else fails and major problems arise with the technology and materials, remember that it is you the trainees have come to hear, and be willing to improvise to ensure people can learn what they need to learn in the training session.

Trainee disruption.

Just because the company is enthusiastically offering a training session doesn't mean all trainees are equally enthusiastic to attend. Even the best employees with a great work ethic may feel like the training takes them away from doing their job, resulting in frustration and unintentional disruptive behaviors. Typical disruptions by trainees may include having side conversations, using their cell phones excessively, and dominating the discussion during the training session.[13] Some of these issues can be easily handled, for example, by asking trainees to leave their cell phones at the door, or to put their phones away unless they are expecting an important call from a client or family member. Other issues are more challenging but not impossible to address.

One way to avoid major issues is to ask the trainees at the beginning of the session to agree on "house rules." You will get greater compliance when the trainees have a voice in what the rules of engagement in the training room will be. All but the most disruptive situations may typically be managed with gentle, assertive interventions, and a reminder about expectations for session behaviors.[14] Exhibit C-4 lists and describes

Exhibit C-4 Description of Difficult Participants

Difficult Participant	Behavior Description
The Talker	Has opinions on every subject; states them in a very authoritative manner.
The Fighter	Quick to find fault with the material or instructor; picks apart statements in an inappropriate way. Often angry, but won't admit or explain anger.
The Quiet One	Nonparticipative and passive in the group; does not make an effort to become part of the discussion. Can be shy, depressed, afraid, or tired, or have a negative attitude toward the participants and process.
The Complainer	Complains about anything and everything, including the room, materials, topics, the instructor, the organization, the weather, refreshments, and so on. Focus is on what is wrong or bad rather than on what is right.
The Unconsciously Incompetent	Thinks that s/he already has the correct knowledge, skills, and abilities, when in truth s/he doesn't. Complains that attending the training session is a waste of time; doesn't feel the need to participate, since s/he is certain s/he knows everything.
The Distracter	Asks questions or raises issues that are not related to the topic being discussed. Talks on the side about unrelated things while the group is trying to work; jumps into discussion without raising a hand or using other courtesies for obtaining permission to speak.
The Rambler	Has difficulty making simple, concise statements; makes grandiose theories or complicates simple ideas with tangential ideas. Often confuses most or all of the rest of the group with these statements.

Source: Adapted from Laurel and Associates, "How to Handle Difficult Participants" (2010). Available from https://www.hse.ie/eng/about/who/qid/other-quality-improvement-programmes/opendisclosure/opendiscfiles/guidetomanagingdifficultparticipants.pdf.

the variety of difficult participants you can expect during a training session: the talker, the fighter, the quiet one, the complainer, the unconscious incompetent, the distractor, and the rambler.[15]

While participants may be difficult or disruptive for different reasons, there are some common solutions for how to address the issues. The first step when faced with a difficult participant is to ask yourself, "What is the root cause of the behavior?" Often, the simple answer is correct. The quiet one is likely an introvert, while the distracter is likely an extrovert. The complainer may have a legitimate concern, whereas the fighter may have been told at the last minute the training was mandatory, which completely disrupted the fighter's schedule. The unconsciously incompetent may simply not be aware his or her knowledge is incomplete.

Some issues can be handled in the group. Interruptions can easily be managed by passing a "talking stick" or Koosh ball from person to person, giving individuals permission to speak in the moment. Legitimate complaints should be acknowledged and investigated quickly to resolve the issues. Other issues may have to be addressed in private. For example, if a participant is directly hostile to the trainer, it may be beneficial to explore the source of such individuals' anger or simply ask them to leave since they are disruptive and not willing to stop. If the person is unconsciously incompetent, you may want to privately ask her or him to keep an open mind in case there is something new she or he can learn. Keeping control over the session is important, or the trainer loses respect in the eyes of the other participants. Staying calm, using humor, not taking the attacks personally, and not embarrassing or attacking a participant are good rules of thumb to manage any situation.

GLOSSARY

Acquired needs theory. The theory that states people are motivated by one of three needs (affiliation, achievement, or power).

Active learning theory. A constructivist theory by which learners have control over their learning, with learning occurring as an inductive process.

Active listening. The highest level of listening; occurs when the listener is fully engaged in the conversation (e.g., aware of context in addition to content).

ADDIE. An acronym that outlines the typical steps to instructional system design: analyze, design, develop, implement, and evaluate.

Adverse impact. A seemingly neutral policy that results in discrimination based on a protected class.

Adverse treatment. Discrimination directed at an individual based on a protected class.

Affective domain. How individuals relate emotionally to knowledge, such as how they gain feelings, values, and attitudes about a given topic; one of three main learning domains of Bloom's Taxonomy.

Affirmative defense. A legal argument where an organization provides evidence that it has taken actions to prevent discrimination or harassment to avoid being held liable.

Analyzer strategy. A company strategy that focuses on incremental innovation, in which the company is typically second or third to market with new products and balances its portfolio with both innovating, high-risk companies and stable cash generators.

Anderson Model for Learning Evaluation. Extends Kirkpatrick's model for evaluation by also assessing the impact of the company's learning evaluation program on strategic priorities.

Andragogy. The theory and practice of educating adults.

Assertive/supportive communication. A style denoted by honesty and tact that builds relationships and makes difficult conversations easier.

Assessment center. A process for identifying talent and developmental needs of employees as part of succession planning.

Assignments and enrichment opportunities. Development opportunities that are embedded in normal work activities and assignments, as well as special projects outside of the normal scope of work.

Association for Talent Development (ATD). The premier professional organization for those engaged in talent development, including training and development, activities in organizations. Offers certifications for talent development professionals.

Asynchronous. A typical characteristic of online instruction and communication where training/communication does not occur in real time.

Backwards design. A concept applied to curriculum design by Wiggins and McTighe that argues for understanding the outcomes you want to accomplish before designing the training curriculum, including the following steps: (1) identify the desired results from the training, (2) determine the acceptable evidence that the training goals were accomplished, and (3) design the learning experiences and instruction to achieve the desired results.

Balanced scorecard (BSC). A measure developed by Kaplan and Norton that provides organizations with a strategic focus and key metrics on which to focus for training evaluation; includes financial/production considerations, customer focus, internal systems, and learning/growth.

Behavior. Kirkpatrick level 3 evaluation that assesses knowledge transfer to the job and the organizational processes and systems in place to encourage the transfer of skills from the training session to the job.

Behaviorism. The theory that observable behaviors show evidence of learning.

Bloom's Taxonomy. A taxonomy of learning outcomes used in education and training and development; includes cognitive, affective, and psychomotor domains.

Boundaryless. A type of career where a person engages in a high level of mobility (physically boundaryless) and/or openness to opportunities (psychologically boundaryless).

Buy-in. The extent to which employees agree with the findings of an organizational decision, such as the results of a needs analysis.

Career anchor. A person's underlying motivation that drives career decisions.

Career plateau. Occurs when a person's career ceases to advance.

Career stage. A career theory with a temporal orientation that divides careers into four phases.

Chronemics. A category of nonverbal behavior involving the use of time.

Classical conditioning. Also known as Pavlovian or respondent conditioning, refers to a learning procedure in which a biologically potent stimulus (e.g., food) is paired with a previously neutral stimulus (e.g., a bell). It also refers to the learning process that results from this pairing, through which the neutral stimulus comes to elicit a response (e.g., salivation) that is usually similar to the one elicited by the potent stimulus.

Coaching. A development activity focused on helping employees achieve better daily performance to enhance their careers.

Cognitive domain. Knowledge and comprehension of facts and concepts; one of three main learning domains of Bloom's Taxonomy.

Cognitive load theory. An example of cognitivism concerned with the total amount of mental effort being used in working memory; when designing instructional programs, cognitive load must be reduced to maximize learning.

Cognitivism. A learning theory that views the learner as an information processor.

Competency-based job analysis. An approach to job-level needs analysis that focuses on the abilities and traits (e.g., creativity) employees need to be successful in their jobs.

Constructive feedback. Communication given to change a person's behavior that is done in an objective manner and provides information to help correct the behavior.

Constructivism. The theory that learning is an active, constructive process.

Control. The degree to which design and delivery of training are centralized within the organization.

Cost leadership strategy. A company strategy based on pricing, specifically setting prices low as compared to competitors.

Critical incidents analysis. A method for conducting a job-level needs analysis where the focus is on key events and interactions rather than all tasks that are performed.

Dashboard. The visual output of HRIS data.

Debrief. Discussion at the end of an experiential exercise to reinforce learning objectives.

Defender strategy. A company strategy that protects the company's market share, engages in little new product development, and focuses on improving the efficiency of the company's bottom line.

Depth chart. A method of identifying and organizing an organization's talent as part of succession planning.

Development. Learning or other types of activities that prepare a person for additional job responsibilities now and in the future and/or enable him or her to gain knowledge or skills.

Differentiation strategy. A company strategy that involves competition based on quality, product attributes, and customer service.

Distributive. An approach to conflict resolution where the outcome is perceived as zero-sum (i.e., winners and losers).

Dynamism. How static and one-directional information is provided online; the more static, the less dynamic.

Emotional intelligence. The ability to perceive, understand, regulate, and use emotions well in oneself and in others.

Equity theory. The theory that people are motivated by maintaining equilibrium between their contributions and organizational rewards.

ERG theory. The theory that people are motivated by one of three needs (existence, relatedness, or growth).

Expectancy theory. The theory that people are motivated by assessing the connection between their behavior and desired outcomes.

Experiential learning theory. The humanist theory that learning is a process done through experience and reflection on doing.

Experiential method. An umbrella term to describe instructional options (e.g., role play) that actively engage trainees.

External coach. Typically an independent consultant who contracts with the employee to provide career and performance advice. Expertise can range from spiritual and life coaching, to specialized executive coaching.

Far transfer. The training must generalize learned skills from the training session to different settings, people, or situations, and the learned skills must be maintained over time.

Fidelity. The degree to which the environment for training mirrors the environment where trainees will use what they learned.

Fixed costs. Costs that an organization must bear to provide training regardless of how many employees are trained.

Flow statistic. The primary type of data used to determine if a selection process results in adverse impact.

Gamification. Application of design principles from games applied to employee training.

General Duty Clause. An OSHA requirement that employers reasonably take actions to protect workers against potential hazards.

Haptics. A category of nonverbal behavior involving physical contact (e.g., pat on the back).

Heir model. An approach to succession planning that focuses on key individuals and positions.

Heutagogy. The study of self-determined learning whereby learners drive their own learning, rather than learning being conceptualized as teacher-centric.

Hook. A question at the start of training meant to generate interest in the topic.

Horseshoe. A classroom layout, where trainees are situated in a semicircle around the trainer, that promotes group discussion.

HR infrastructure. The horizontal integration of human resource functional areas, including job analysis, staffing, performance appraisal, compensation, training and development, and human resource information systems.

HRIS. Human resource information system; a software package that an organization can utilize to manage and monitor all aspects of employee training and development.

Human Resource Certification Institute (HRCI). An organization that provides resources, instruction, and certification for HR professionals.

Humanism. The theory that learning is a personal act that is instrumental in fulfilling one's potential.

Icebreaker. A short activity at the beginning of a training session to help get everyone engaged.

Improvisation. The concept of accepting what a person is given by a communication or negotiation partner with the goal of building upon it to create synergy and greater collaboration.

In-basket. A type of experiential exercise where trainees are given multiple short scenarios to which they need to respond.

Information processing theory. A theory of how learning is encoded in one's memory and then retrieved when needed.

Instructional aid. A device (e.g., computer) or supplement (e.g., handout) to facilitate and/or enhance learning.

Instructional systems design model. A framework that guides those involved in training and instruction through the steps needed to effectively design and implement learning opportunities.

Integrative. An approach to conflict resolution where there is a belief that a win-win outcome is possible.

Internal coach. Typically a supervisor or manager, in-house human resource professional, or dedicated internal coaching professional who provides career and performance advice to the employee.

International Coaching Federation (ICF). An organization that provides resources, instruction, and certifications for coaching professionals.

Job design development opportunities. Development opportunities that are embedded in the design of the jobs and work employees do, including job shadowing (following an experienced coworker around to learn the job) and job rotation (rotating through different job assignments to learn new skills).

Job incumbent. A person who is currently performing a specific job.

Job inflation. Occurs when job incumbents report that they engage in higher-level or additional tasks than they should be.

Job log. A method for conducting a job-level needs analysis where employees record each task that they perform as it is completed.

Job transition development opportunities. Development opportunities that include typical vertical promotions as well as horizontal lateral moves in job progression and career ladders.

Jurisdiction. Whether a law applies in a specific location or situation.

Kinesics. The most commonly thought of category of nonverbal behavior, which involves gestures and posture.

Knowledge transfer. The degree to which participants apply what they learned during training when they are back on the job.

Ladder. The most traditional career pattern where the career follows a predictable path of upward progression typically within a single organization.

Leadership development. A specialized type of employee development with the purpose of identifying and developing future leaders in the organization; works hand in hand with succession planning.

Leading indicators. Short-term observations and measurements suggesting that critical behaviors are on track to create a positive impact on desired results; includes customer satisfaction, employee engagement, sales volume, cost containment, quality, and market share.

Lean communication. Communication that lacks contextual information (e.g., tone and nonverbals), such as texting and email.

Learning. The acquisition of knowledge or skills through experience, study, or being taught.

Level 2 Learning. Kirkpatrick level 2 evaluation that assesses knowledge, skills, and abilities learned, and trainee attitudes, confidence, and commitment to use new skills learned in the training.

Learning agility. The mindset and corresponding collection of practices that allow leaders to continually develop, grow, and utilize new strategies that will equip them for the increasingly complex problems they face in their organizations.

Learning evaluation strategy. A guide for organizations to use to design and implement their learning evaluation that should naturally evolve from their corporate and training and development strategies, including five principles: (1) focus on high-priority learning areas, (2) address evaluation requirements of multiple stakeholders, (3) foster shared responsibility for performance improvement, (4) collect data and use resources efficiently, and (5) conduct action planning.

Learning modality. A sensory approach to learning (e.g., auditory or visual).

Learning objectives. The knowledge or skills that trainees will have to obtain and exhibit in the training session to achieve the training goals.

Learning styles. The way in which people learn; according to a range of theories, learners can be classified accordingly.

Lecture. A traditional method of providing training where the trainee passively receives information from a trainer.

LMS. Learning management system; a software package that an organization can use to manage the delivery of training.

Lobbed. A question that is asked of the entire group rather than a specific trainee.

Mentor. A senior employee who advises, counsels, coaches, and promotes the career development of a junior employee.

Mentoring. A development opportunity that involves an intense work relationship between senior and junior organizational members; and involves advising, counseling, career coaching, and promoting the career development of the junior employee.

Microaggression. The casual degradation of any socially marginalized group, typically through negligence, ignorance, or unconscious bias.

Microassault. Explicit derogation, verbal or nonverbal, that includes name-calling, avoidant behavior, or purposeful discrimination.

Microinsult. Communication that conveys rudeness and insensitivity to a person's identity, unknown to the perpetrator but insulting to the recipient.

Microinvalidation. Communication that excludes, negates, or nullifies the thoughts, feelings, or experiences of those in the marginalized group.

m-learning. Training that takes place via an app or mobile device.

MOBTS. The Management and Organizational Behavior Training Society provides lots of information on how to make instruction more engaging and effective.

MOOC. Massive online open course; a format of training that is often free and in which anyone can participate.

Near transfer. The job conditions to which the transfer is occurring are similar to the training conditions.

Negligent training. If harm results because an organization failed to provide an employee with training, the organization can be held liable for damages.

New World Kirkpatrick Model. The accepted standard for evaluating training at the reaction, learning, behavior, and results levels for the organization; based on Donald Kirkpatrick's doctoral dissertation, and adapted in 2010 to include 21st century considerations based on years of research.

Nine-box matrix. A tool for succession planning where employees are categorized based on both performance and potential.

Obsolescence. Occurs when a person's key knowledge, skills, and abilities have become obsolete.

OD Network. A professional organization for organizational development professionals. Provides resources and networking opportunities for those engaged in OD/change management activities.

OJT. On-the-job training; can be formal or informal and is provided in the trainee's work environment.

Onboarding. The process by which new employees acquire the necessary knowledge, skills, and behaviors to become effective organizational members and insiders.

One-shot case study. A nonexperimental design in which a group of employees are provided a training program and then tested to see if the training program was effective.

One-shot pretest–posttest design. A nonexperimental design similar to the one-shot case study, but that also includes a pretest as well as a posttest to assess learning effectiveness.

O*NET. A repository of basic information produced by the U.S. Department of Labor for all types of jobs.

Operant conditioning. Rewards and punishment are used as a way to reinforce the behaviors one wants an individual to learn.

Organization environment. The way a company is organized, through vertical and horizontal alignment, including policies and procedures.

Organizational culture. A system of shared assumptions, values, and beliefs that govern how people behave in organizations.

Organizational learning theory. A constructivist theory comprising two perspectives: (1) The organization learns as one big brain made up of its individual members, and (2) organization members construct their own knowledge through a community of practice in the organization.

Organizational processes and systems. Required drivers needed to reinforce, encourage, and reward performance of critical behaviors on the job.

Outcomes. The degree to which targeted outcomes occur as a result of the training and the support and accountability from leaders.

Pedagogy. The study of K–12 education and how to best teach.

People environment. The demographics of the workforce, including the knowledge, skills, abilities, experiences, education levels, and motivations of the employees.

Personality. The individual differences in people associated with how they think, feel, or behave.

Peter principle. The idea that successful people are promoted into positions of incompetence.

Pods. A classroom layout, where there is no central focus and trainees sit in groups, that facilitates group interactions.

Pool model. An approach to succession planning that looks to develop a robust workforce ready to assume leadership positions.

Posttest-only control group design. An experimental design similar to the static-group comparison nonexperimental design in which trainees are randomly assigned to training conditions, and pre- and posttest assessments are done to determine learning effectiveness.

Pretest–posttest control group design. An experimental design with two groups in which trainees are randomly assigned to training conditions, the experimental group gets the training, and pre- and posttest measures are compared to determine learning effectiveness.

Problem-based learning. A constructivist theory by which trainees are encouraged to apply knowledge to new situations; there are no right answers, problems/cases are context specific, trainees are self-directed and work in small groups, problem solving is done by consensus, and the trainer is a facilitator.

Prospector strategy. A company strategy that focuses on product innovation and market opportunity, along with a willingness to take risks.

Protean. A type of career that is self-directed and/or value-driven.

Protected class. The basis on which a person is covered by a piece of antidiscrimination legislation (e.g., race or sex).

Protégé. A junior employee who builds a relationship with a more senior employee for the purpose of career development.

Proxemics. A category of nonverbal behavior involving the use of space.

Psychomotor domain. The ability to physically utilize an object; one of three main learning domains of Bloom's Taxonomy.

Pyramid. The conceptualization that people are motivated by a hierarchy of five needs (basic physiological, safety, social, esteem, and self-actualization).

Reaction. Kirkpatrick level 1 evaluation that assesses trainee satisfaction, trainee engagement, and relevance of training to participants.

Reactor strategy. A nonstrategy in which the company reacts to environmental concerns rather than proactively develops a strategy for business success.

Reasonable accommodation. Action an organization takes to allow an employee to participate on the basis of a disability (e.g., providing closed-captioning for individuals who are hearing impaired) or religion (e.g., scheduling training so it doesn't conflict with a religious observance).

Reasoned action theory. A theory of motivation related to expectancy theory that adds the contribution of subjective norms to the equation.

Results. Kirkpatrick level 4 evaluation that assesses training outcomes and the leading indicators needed to create a positive impact on the desired training results.

Retaliation. Illegal actions that an organization takes to punish or discourage an employee for/from pursuing a claim of discrimination.

Return on investment (ROI). Expressed as a percentage, ROI assesses the benefits of training to the organization, as related to the cost of the training.

Reward value. The extent to which training is perceived as a reward provided by the organization.

RIASEC. A vocational interest model that breaks down the key factors that influence vocational interests and choices: realistic, investigative, artistic, social, enterprising, and conventional.

Rich communication. Communication that contains contextual information (e.g., tone and nonverbals); face-to-face communication is the richest type.

Role play. An experiential instructional method where trainees act out a scenario to better understand a concept or how to handle a situation.

Self-awareness. How well a person knows his or her motivations, preferences, and personality and understands how these influence personal judgments, decisions, and interactions.

Self-efficacy. Belief in one's ability to succeed in specific situations or to accomplish a task.

Social capital. The value of an individual's relationships.

Social environment. The social system within which employees work, including the ethical and organizational culture, leadership style, and company climate.

Social learning theory. The theory that people learn from each other via observation, imitation, and modeling.

Socialization. The process by which new employees understand the company's policies, the internal culture, how the company hierarchy works, and the ways to function effectively in the organization.

Society for Human Resource Management (SHRM). The umbrella professional organization for human resource professionals. Provides resources for all HR functions, including talent development. Offers certifications for HR professionals.

Solomon four-group design. An experimental design combining the pretest–posttest control group design and the posttest-only control group design in which trainees are randomly assigned to training conditions, and pre- and posttest measures are compared to determine learning effectiveness.

Standardization. The degree to which training is delivered in a consistent manner.

Static-group comparison. A nonexperimental design similar to the one-shot case study, but that involves two groups—one that receives the training and another that does not—and posttest measures are compared to assess learning effectiveness.

Succession planning. The process an organization engages in to make sure that it has the internal talent ready to become the next generation of leaders it needs.

SWOT analysis. A strategic planning method that is useful for conducting an organization-level needs analysis of strengths, weaknesses, opportunities, and threats.

Task-based job analysis. An approach to job-level needs analysis that focuses on the actions (e.g., writing a report) that employees perform in order to complete their jobs.

Task environment. What employees do, when they do it, and how often they repeat the tasks of their job.

Trainability. A measure of an employee's readiness to participate in training that encompasses both ability and motivation.

Training. A process that aims to improve knowledge, skills, attitudes, and/or behaviors in a person to accomplish a specific job, task, or goal.

Training and development function. A human resource management function concerned with developing and improving the performance of individuals and groups in an organizational setting.

Training and development strategy. The plan by which an organization ensures its employees have the knowledge, skills, and abilities to meet the organization's objectives.

Training manual. An instructional aid whose use is consistent with formal on-the-job training.

Variable costs. Costs of training that increase with the number of employees trained.

Webinar. A seminar that is presented in an online format.

NOTES

INTRODUCTION

1. Association for Talent Development, "About Us." Retrieved from https://www.td.org/about on August 24, 2018.
2. Maura Kennedy, "The ATD Framework: Evaluating Learning Impact," August 19, 2016. Retrieved from https://www.td.org/insights/the-atd-talent-development-framework-evaluating-learning-impact on August 24, 2018.
3. Vinesh, "The Role of Training and Development in Organizational Development," *International Journal of Management and International Business Studies* 4, no. 2 (2014): 213–220.
4. Karl Kapp and Robyn Defelice, "Time to Develop One Hour of Training." Retrieved from https://www.td.org/newsletters/learning-circuits/time-to-develop-one-hour-of-training-2009 on March 12, 2019.
5. Thomas N. Garavan, Pat Costine, and Noreen Heraty, *Training and Development in Ireland: Context, Policy and Practice* (Dublin: Oak Tree Press, in association with Irish Institute of Training and Development, 1995), p. 1.
6. Kapp and Defelice, "Time to Develop One Hour of Training."
7. Chuck Hodell, "All About ADDIE." Retrieved from https://www.td.org/newsletters/atd-links/all-about-addie on August 15, 2018.
8. Robert A. Reiser and John V. Dempsey, *Trends and Issues in Instructional Design and Technology*, 3rd ed. (Boston, MA: Pearson, 2012).
9. John L. Holland, *Making Vocational Choices: A Theory of Vocational Personalities and Work Environments* (Englewood Cliffs, NJ: Prentice-Hall, 1985).

CHAPTER 1

1. PepsiCo, "Talent." Retrieved from https://www.pepsico.com/sustainability/talent on March 15, 2019.
2. Masternak & Associates, "What Is Gainsharing? The Basics." Retrieved from http://www.masternak.com/gainsharing-what-is.asp on April 13, 2016.
3. Sumita Raghuram and Richard D. Arvey, "Business Strategy Links With Staffing and Training Practices," *Human Resource Planning* 17, no. 3 (1994): 35–73.
4. Herbert G. Heneman, Timothy A. Judge, and John Kammeyer-Mueller, *Staffing Organizations* (Middleton, WI: Mendota Press, 2014).
5. Peter Carbonara, "Hire for Attitude, Train for Skill," *Fast Company*, August/September 1996.
6. Julie Weber, "How Southwest Airlines Hires Such Dedicated People," *Harvard Business Review*, December 2, 2015. Retrieved from https://hbr.org/2015/12/how-southwest-airlines-hires-such-dedicated-people on 1/12/16.
7. Southwest Careers, "Benefits." Retrieved from https://careers.southwestair.com/benefits on March 15, 2019.
8. Laurence S. Fink and Clinton Oliver Longenecker, "Training as a Performance Appraisal Improvement Strategy," *Career*

    Development International 3, no. 6 (1998): 243–251.
9. Association for Talent Development, *Aligning for Success: Connecting Learning to Business Performance* (Alexandria, VA: Author, 2015).
10. Ibid.
11. Impact International, *White Paper: Aligning Training With Corporate Strategy* (2011). Retrieved from https://cdns3.trainingindustry.com/media/3674124/impact%20aligning%20training%20with%20corporate%20strategy.pdf on April 8, 2016.
12. Selva Staub, "Training and Development Programs as Support of Corporate Strategy Development," pp. 265–281 in *Selected Studies on Economics and Finance*, ed. Selim Başar, A. Alkan Çelik, and T. Bayramoğlu (Newcastle Upon Tyne: Cambridge Scholars, 2018).
13. Raghuram and Arvey, "Business Strategy Links With Staffing and Training Practices."
14. Michael E. Porter, *Competitive Strategy* (New York: Free Press, 1980).
15. Raymond E. Miles and Charles C. Snow, *Organizational Strategy, Structure and Process* (New York: McGraw-Hill, 1978).
16. Hai-Ming Chen and Shu-Tzu Hung, "Systematic Linking of Organizational Strategy, HR Strategy, and Training Strategy Across OLC," *International Journal of Business Strategy* 10, no. 1 (2010): 104–115.
17. Ibid.
18. Walmart, "Careers: The Business of Better." Retrieved from https://careers.walmart.com/values on March 15, 2019.
19. Chen and Hung, "Systematic Linking of Organizational Strategy, HR Strategy, and Training Strategy Across OLC," p. 5.
20. Procter & Gamble, "Careers." Retrieved from https://www.pgcareers.com/ on March 15, 2019.
21. U.S. Banking Act (1933). Pub. L. 73–66, 48 Stat. 162, enacted June 16, 1933.
22. Gramm–Leach–Bliley Act (1999). Pub. L. 106–102, 113 Stat. 1338, enacted November 12, 1999.
23. Association for Talent Development, "Vision, Mission, Code of Ethics." Retrieved from https://www.td.org/about/vision-mission-code-of-ethics on March 17, 2019.
24. Association for Talent Development, *Global Trends in Talent Development* (Alexandria, VA: Author, 2015).
25. The U.S. Congress passed the Sarbanes–Oxley Act of 2002 to help protect investors from fraudulent financial reporting by corporations. Also known as the Corporate Responsibility Act of 2002, it mandated strict reforms to existing securities regulations and imposed tough new penalties on lawbreakers. See www.investopedia.com/terms/s/sarbanesoxleyact.asp.

CHAPTER 2

1. *Hoffman v. Caterpillar Inc.*, 256 F. 3d 568 (Court of Appeals, 7th Circuit, 2001).
2. Julie Dabrowski, "The Exception That Doesn't Prove the Rule: Why Congress Should Narrow ENDA's Religious Exemption to Protect the Rights of LGBTQ Employees," *American University Law Review* 63, no. 6 (2014): 1957–1984.
3. Society for Human Resource Management, "Code of Ethics," November 16, 2007, as amended November 21, 2014. Retrieved from https://www.shrm.org/about-shrm/Pages/code-of-ethics.aspx on March 17, 2019.
4. United Farm Workers, "The Story of Cesar Chavez." Retrieved from https://ufw.org/research/history/story-cesar-chavez/ on March 17, 2019.
5. Daniel Reynolds, "Bill de Blasio Urges Boycott of Chick-fil-A," *Advocate*, May 8, 2016. Retrieved from http://www.advocate.com/

politicians/2016/5/08/bill-de-blasio-urges-boycott-chick-fil on March 17, 2019.

6. M. Alex Johnson, "Southern Baptists End 8-Year Disney Boycott," NBC News, June 22, 2005. Retrieved from http://www.nbcnews.com/id/8318263/ns/us_news/t/southern-baptists-end--year-disney-boycott/#.V408StIrLcs on March 17, 2019.

7. *McDonnell Douglas Corp. v. Green*, 411 U.S. 792, 802–805, 93 S. Ct. 1817, 36 L. Ed. 2d 668 (1973).

8. James E. Prieger and Wei-Min Hu, "The Broadband Digital Divide and the Nexus of Race, Competition, and Quality," *Information Economics and Policy* 20, no. 2 (2008): 150–167.

9. David M. Kaplan, "Can Diversity Training Discriminate? Backlash to Lesbian, Gay, & Bisexual Diversity Initiatives," *Employee Responsibilities & Rights Journal* 18, no. 1 (2006): 61–72.

10. Lainey Feingold, "Digital Accessibility and the Quest for Online Equality," *Journal of Internet Law* 21, no. 4 (2017): 3–12.

11. Kevin Gumienny, "E-learning FOR ALL," *Talent Development* 71, no. 8 (2017): 38–43.

12. Jennifer L. Thompson and Scott B. Morris, "What Factors Influence Judges' Rulings About the Legality of Affirmative Action Plans?" *Journal of Business Psychology* 28, no. 4 (2013): 411–424.

13. Michael Pires, "Independent Contractor or Employee? Are You Sure?" *Franchising World* 47, no. 5 (2015): 42–44.

CHAPTER 3

1. Judith Brown, "Training Needs Assessment: A Must for Developing an Effective Training Program," *Public Personnel Management* 31, no. 4 (2002): 569–574.

2. Sarah Cook, "Linking Learning Needs Analysis to Business Needs," *The Stairway Consultancy*. Retrieved from http://www.thestairway.co.uk/publications/learning-needs-analysis.html on March 18, 2019.

3. Marc J. Rosenberg, "The Four C's of Success: Culture, Champions, Communication, and Change," pp. 193–217 in *The ASTD E-learning Handbook*, ed. A. Rossett (New York: McGraw-Hill, 2002).

4. Yuka Fujimoto and Charmine E. J. Härtel, "Organizational Diversity Learning Framework: Going Beyond Diversity Training Programs," *Personnel Review* 46, no. 6 (2017): 1120–1141.

5. Cook, "Linking Learning Needs Analysis to Business Needs."

6. Erik B. Cline and Pennie S. Seibert, "Help for First-Time Needs Assessors," *Training & Development* 47, no. 5 (1993): 99–101.

7. Derek R. Avery, Patrick F. McKay, David C. Wilson, and Scott Tonidandel, "Unequal Attendance: The Relationships Between Race, Organizational Diversity Cues and Absenteeism," *Personnel Psychology* 60, no. 4 (2007): 875–902.

8. Society for Human Resource Management (SHRM), "How to Conduct a Training Needs Assessment." Available from https://www.shrm.org/resourcesandtools/tools-and-samples/how-to-guides/pages/conduct-training-needs-assessment.aspx?widget=mostpopular2.

9. Ronald L. Jacobs and Michael J. Jones, *Structured On-the-Job Training: Unleashing Employee Expertise in the Workplace* (San Francisco: Berrett-Koehler, 1995).

10. Roni Reiter-Palmon, Michael Brown, Darrel L. Sandall, Cara Beth Buboltz, and Thomas Nimps, "Development of an O*NET Web-Based Job Analysis and Its Implementation in the U.S. Navy: Lessons Learned," *Human Resource Management Review* 16, no. 3 (2006): 293–309.

11. SHRM, "How to Conduct a Training Needs Assessment."

12. Cook, "Linking Learning Needs Analysis to Business Needs."
13. Alison M. Dachner, Brian M. Saxton, Raymond A. Noe, and Kathryn E. Keeton, "To Infinity and Beyond: Using a Narrative Approach to Identify Training Needs for Unknown and Dynamic Situations," *Human Resource Development Quarterly* 24, no. 2 (2013): 239–267.
14. Cook, "Linking Learning Needs Analysis to Business Needs."
15. Ibid.
16. Ibid.
17. Jeffrey M. Cucina, Nicholas R. Martin, Nicholas L. Vasilopoulos, and Henry F. Thibodeaux, "Self-Serving Bias Effects on Job Analysis Ratings," *The Journal of Psychology* 146, no. 5 (2012): 511–531.
18. George C. Thornton III and Diana E. Krause, "Selection Versus Development Assessment Centers: An International Survey of Design, Execution, and Evaluation," *The International Journal of Human Resource Management* 20, no. 2 (2009): 478–498.
19. Ricky W. Griffin and Gregory Moorhead, *Organizational Behavior: Managing People and Organizations*, 10th ed. (Mason, OH: South-Western, 2008).
20. Abraham H. Maslow, *Motivation and Personality* (New York: Harper & Row, 1954).
21. Gregory J. Lee, "Training Match and Mismatch as a Driver of Key Employee Behaviours," *Human Resource Management Journal* 25, no. 4 (2015): 478–495.
22. Ibid.
23. Clayton P. Alderfer, *Existence, Relatedness, and Growth: Human Needs in Organizational Settings* (New York: Free Press, 1972).
24. David C. McClelland, *The Achievement Society* (New York: Van Nostrand Reinhold, 1961).
25. Victor H. Vroom, *Work and Motivation* (New York: Wiley, 1964).
26. Martin Fishbein and Icek Ajzen, *Belief, Attitude, Intention, and Behavior: An Introduction to Theory and Research* (Reading, MA: Addison-Wesley, 1975).
27. John Stacey Adams, "Injustice in Social Exchange," pp. 267–299 in *Advances in Experimental and Social Psychology*, Vol. 2, ed. L. Berkowitz (New York: Academic Press, 1965).
28. Lee, "Training Match and Mismatch as a Driver of Key Employee Behaviours."
29. Final Shipley and Pat Golden, "How to Analyze and Address Your Organization's Learning Needs," *T+D* 67, no. 3 (2013): 29–31.
30. Timothy McClernon, "Rivals to Systematic Training," *Advances in Developing Human Resources* 8, no. 4 (2006): 442–459.
31. Bill Stetar, "Training: It's Not Always the Answer," *Quality Progress* 38, no. 3 (2005): 43–49.
32. Shipley and Golden, "How to Analyze and Address Your Organization's Learning Needs."

CHAPTER 4

1. Kellye Whitney, "What's the Difference Between Learning and Training?" CLO Magazine, January 18, 2006. Retrieved from http://cedma-europe.org/newsletter%20articles/Clomedia/Whats%20the%20Difference%20between%20Learning%20and%20Training%20(Jan%202006).pdf on March 20, 2019.
2. Ibid.
3. Benjamin S. Bloom, ed., *Taxonomy of Educational Objectives: The Classification of Educational Goals*, Handbook I: Cognitive Domain (New York: Longman, 1956); Lorin W. Anderson and David R. Krathwohl, eds., *A Taxonomy for Learning, Teaching, and Assessing: A Revision of Bloom's Taxonomy of Educational Objectives* (Boston: Allyn and Bacon, 2001).

4. Yuly, "What Is Bloom's Taxonomy and Why Should It Be Used in Workplace Training?" *The Art of Instructional Design and E-Learning*, November 29, 2010. Retrieved from https://instructionaldesignblog.wordpress.com/2010/11/29/what-is-blooms-taxonomy-and-why-should-it-be-used-in-workplace-training/ on March 7, 2016.

5. "Ivan Pavlov: Biographical," *The Nobel Prize*. Retrieved from http://www.nobelprize.org/nobel_prizes/medicine/laureates/1904/pavlov-bio.html on March 21, 2019.

6. John B. Watson, *The Ways of Behaviorism* (New York: Harper & Brothers, 1928).

7. B. F. Skinner, "'Superstition' in the Pigeon," *Journal of Experimental Psychology* 38 (1948): 168–172.

8. Stephen Flora, *The Power of Reinforcement* (Albany: State University of New York Press, 2004).

9. Thomas Frazier, "Obey the Learning Laws," *TD* 72, no. 9 (September 2018): 26–31.

10. Albert Bandura, *Social Foundations of Thought and Action* (Englewood Cliffs, NJ: Prentice Hall, 1986).

11. Joan Grusec, "Social Learning Theory and Developmental Psychology: The Legacies of Robert Sears and Albert Bandura," *Developmental Psychology* 28, no. 5 (1992): 776–786.

12. Albert Bandura, "Self-Efficacy: Toward a Unifying Theory of Behavioral Change," *Psychological Review* 84, no. 2 (1977): 191–215.

13. Marilyn E. Gist and Terence R. Mitchell, "Self-Efficacy: A Theoretical Analysis of Its Determinants and Malleability," *Academy of Management Review* 17, no. 2 (1992): 183–221.

14. "Cognitivism," *Learning-Theories.com*. Retrieved from http://www.learning-theories.com/cognitivism.html on March 8, 2016.

15. John Sweller, "Cognitive Load During Problem Solving: Effects on Learning," *Cognitive Science* 12, no. 2 (1988): 257–285.

16. Richard C. Atkinson and Richard M. Shiffrin, "Human Memory: A Proposed System and Its Control Processes," pp. 89–195 in *The Psychology of Learning and Motivation*, vol. 2, ed. K. W. Spence and J. T. Spence (New York: Academic Press, 1968).

17. David E. Rumelhart, James L. McClelland, and PDP Research Group, *Parallel Distributed Processing: Explorations in the Microstructure of Cognition*, vols. 1–2 (Cambridge, MA: PDP Research Group, 1986).

18. "Problem-Based Learning (PBL)," *Learning-Theories.com*. Retrieved from http://www.learning-theories.com/problem-based-learning-pbl.html on March 8, 2016.

19. Bradford S. Bell and Steve W. J. Kozlowski, "Active Learning: Effects of Core Training Design Elements on Self-Regulatory Processes, Learning, and Adaptability," *Journal of Applied Psychology* 93, no. 2 (2008): 296–316.

20. Ibid.

21. Chris Argyris and Donald A. Schön, *Theory in Practice: Increasing Professional Effectiveness* (San Francisco: Jossey-Bass, 1974).

22. Jean Lave and Etienne Wenger, *Situated Learning: Legitimate Peripheral Participation* (Cambridge: Cambridge University Press, 1991).

23. David A. Kolb, *Experiential Learning: Experience as the Source of Learning and Development* (Englewood Cliffs, NJ: Prentice Hall, 1984).

24. Karsten Kenklies, "Educational Theory as Topological Rhetoric: The Concepts of Pedagogy of Johann Friedrich Herbart and Friedrich Schleiermacher," *Studies in Philosophy and Education* 31, no. 3 (2012): 265–273.

25. Malcolm Knowles, *The Adult Learner: A Neglected Species*, 3rd ed. (Houston, TX: Gulf, 1984).

26. Shirley J. Caruso, "Malcolm Knowles and the Six Assumptions Underlying Andragogy," *HRDevelopmentInfo*. Retrieved from https://hrdevelopmentinfo.com/malcolm-knowles-and-the-six-assumptions-underlying-andragogy/ on March 21, 2019.

27. Anne Hartree, "Malcolm Knowles' Theory of Andragogy: A Critique," *International Journal of Lifelong Education* 3, no. 3 (1984): 203–210.
28. Malcolm Knowles, *The Making of an Adult Educator: An Autobiographical Journey* (San Francisco: Jossey-Bass, 1989).
29. Sharan B. Merriam, Rosemary S. Caffarella, and Lisa M. Baumgartner, *Learning in Adulthood: A Comprehensive Guide*, 3rd ed. (San Francisco: Jossey-Bass, 2007).
30. Ann Hanson, "The Search for Separate Theories of Adult Learning: Does Anyone Really Need Andragogy?," pp. 99–108 in *Boundaries of Adult Learning: Adult Learners, Education and Training*, vol. 1, ed. R. Edwards, A. Hanson, and P. Raggatt (London: Routledge, 1996).
31. Stephen Brookfield, *Understanding and Facilitating Adult Learning: A Comprehensive Analysis of Principles and Effective Practice* (Milton Keynes: Open University Press, 1986).
32. Barry Chametzky, The Interconnectedness of Learning: How Andragogy Can Improve the Online Learning Experience," *American Journal of Educational Science* 4, no. 4 (2018): 93–99.
33. Stewart Hase and Chris Kenyon, "From Andragogy to Heutagogy," *Ultibase*, December 2000.
34. Ibid.
35. Alan Clardy, "Learning on Their Own: Vocationally Oriented Self-Directed Learning Projects," *Human Resource Development Quarterly* 11, no. 2 (2000): 105–125.
36. Alexis Carr, K. Balasubramian, Rosemary Atieno, and James Onyango, "Lifelong Learning to Empowerment: Beyond Formal Education," *Distance Education* 39, no. 1 (2018): 69–86.
37. Frank Coffield, David Moseley, Elaine Hall, and Kathryn Ecclestone, *Learning Styles and Pedagogy in Post-16 Learning: A Systematic and Critical Review* (London: Learning and Skills Research Centre, 2004).
38. Christopher W. Allinson and John Hayes, "The Cognitive Style Index," *Journal of Management Studies* 33 (1996): 119–135.
39. Richard M. Felder, "Are Learning Styles Invalid? (Hint: NO!)," *On-Course Newsletter*, September 27, 2010.
40. Ibid.
41. Doug Rohrer and Harold Pashler, "Learning Styles: Where's the Evidence?" *Medical Education* 46 (2012): 34–35.
42. Michael Urick, "Adapting Training to Meet the Preferred Learning Styles of Different Generations," *International Journal of Training and Development*, 21 no. 1 (2016): 53–59.
43. Thomas C. Reeves and Eunjung Oh, "Generational Differences," *Handbook of Research on Educational Communications and Technology* 3 (2008): 295–303.
44. Janice Ware, Rosemary Craft, and Steve Kerschenbaum, "Training Tomorrow's Workforce," *Training and Development* 61, no. 4 (2007): 58.
45. Ibid.

CHAPTER 5

1. Keith H. Hammonds, "Why We Hate HR," *Fast Company*, August 2005.
2. Grant Wiggins and Jay McTighe, *Understanding by Design* (Upper Saddle River, NJ: Merrill Prentice Hall, 1998).
3. Ibid.
4. Richard Griffin, "A Practitioner Friendly and Scientifically Robust Training Evaluation Approach," *Journal of Workplace Learning* 24, no. 6 (2012): 393–402.
5. Marjorie Derven, "Building a Strategic Approach to Learning Evaluation," *TD*, November 2012. Retrieved from https://www.td.org/magazines/td-magazine/building-a-strategic-approach-to-learning-evaluation on March 22, 2019.

6. Ibid.
7. Ibid.
8. Deborah Spring Laurel, "Jump Start Your Learning Objectives," *InfoLine* 25, no. 0804 (April 2008).
9. Michael R. Lewis et al., "How to Write Training Objectives," *wikiHow*. Retrieved from www.wikihow.com/Write-Training-Objectives on January 31, 2017.
10. Donald L. Kirkpatrick, *Evaluating Human Relations Programs for Industrial Foremen and Supervisors* (Unpublished Dissertation, 1954).
11. ATD Staff, "ASTD: A New Study Shows Training Evaluation Efforts Need Help," *Association for Talent Development*, November 17, 2009. Retrieved from https://www.td.org/Publications/Blogs/ATD-Blog/2009/11/ASTD-New-Study-Shows-Training-Evaluation-Efforts-Need-Help on October 4, 2016.
12. Kirkpatrick Partners, "The Kirkpatrick Model Is 50 Years New." Retrieved from https://www.kirkpatrickpartners.com/Products/Dr-Donald-L-Kirkpatrick-Dissertation on March 22, 2019.
13. Jim Kirkpatrick and Wendy Kirkpatrick, "The Four Levels of Evaluation: An Update," *TD at Work* (February 2015): 5.
14. Ajay Pangarkar and Teresa Kirkwood, "Flipping the Levels of Evaluation," *ATD Links*, 2015. Retrieved from https://www.td.org/newsletters/atd-links/flipping-the-levels-of-evaluation on March 22, 2019.
15. Stephanie Beadell, "Surveys 101: A Simple Guide to Asking Effective Questions." Retrieved from https://zapier.com/learn/forms-surveys/writing-effective-survey/ on March 22, 2019.
16. Ibid.
17. Ibid.
18. Ibid.
19. Ibid.
20. ATD Staff, "ASTD."
21. Ibid.
22. Kirkpatrick and Kirkpatrick, "Four Levels of Evaluation," 4.
23. Ibid., 8.
24. Terence R. Mitchell, "Motivation: New Directions for Theory, Research, and Practice," *Academy of Management Review* 7, no. 1 (1982): 80–88.
25. Kirkpatrick and Kirkpatrick, "Four Levels of Evaluation," 4.
26. Ibid.
27. Albert Bandura, "Self-Efficacy: Toward a Unifying Theory of Behavioral Change," *Psychological Review* 84, no. 2 (1977): 191–215.
28. Albert Bandura, *Self-Efficacy: The Exercise of Control* (New York: Worth, 1997).

CHAPTER 6

1. Donald Kirkpatrick and James D. Kirkpatrick, *Transferring Learning to Behavior: Using the Four Levels to Improve Performance*, digital book location 94 (San Francisco: Berrett-Koehler, 2005).
2. Ibid.
3. Ibid.
4. Andrew Downes, *Learning Evaluation Theory: Anderson's Value of Learning Model*. Retrieved from https://www.watershedlrs.com/hubfs/CO/Anderson_White_Paper/Learning_Evaluation_Anderson.pdf on March 23, 2019.
5. James M. Kouzes and Barry Z. Posner, *The Leadership Challenge* (San Francisco: Jossey-Bass, 2012).
6. Ibid.
7. Kirkpatrick and Kirkpatrick, *Transferring Learning to Behavior*, digital book location 382.
8. Ibid., digital book location 638.
9. Albert Bandura, *Social Foundations of Thought and Action* (Englewood Cliffs, NJ: Prentice Hall, 1986).

10 Chris Argyris and Donald A. Schön, *Theory in Practice: Increasing Professional Effectiveness* (San Francisco: Jossey-Bass, 1974).

11 David Kolb, *Experiential Learning: Experience as the Source of Learning and Development* (Englewood Cliffs, NJ: Prentice Hall, 1984).

12 Ann Latham, "Why Training Fails," *ATD Management Blog*, October 2, 2013.

13 Ibid.

14 Alan Clardy, *Transfer of Training Literature Review* (Towson University Working Paper 2006), 7.

15 James Kirkpatrick and Wendy Kirkpatrick, "The Four Levels of Evaluation: An Update," *TD at Work* (February 2015): 3.

16 Robert O. Brinkerhoff, *Telling Training's Story: Evaluation Made Simple, Credible, and Effective* (San Francisco: Berrett-Koehler, 2006).

17 Dan Ariely, Uri Gneezy, George Loewenstein, and Nina Mazar, *Large Stakes and Big Mistakes* (Working paper series: Federal Reserve Bank of Boston, No. 05-11, 2005).

18 Daniel H. Pink, *Drive: The Surprising Truth About What Motivates Us* (New York: Riverhead Books, 2009).

19 Kirkpatrick and Kirkpatrick, "Four Levels of Evaluation," 2.

20 Ibid., 7.

21 ATD Staff, "The Value of Evaluation: Usage and Value of Kirkpatrick/Phillips Model," *Association for Talent Development*, October 29, 2009. Retrieved from https://www.td.org/insights/the-value-of-evaluation-usage-and-value-of-kirkpatrick-phillips-model on March 24, 2019.

22 Ibid.

23 Kirkpatrick and Kirkpatrick, *Transferring Learning to Behavior*, digital book location 117.

24 Robert S. Kaplan and David P. Norton, "The Balanced Scorecard: Measures That Drive Performance," *Harvard Business Review* (January–February, 1992).

25 "Training Evaluation Metrics." Retrieved from https://training-evaluation-metrics.com on January 9, 2017.

26 Bryant Nielson, "Top 10 Training Metrics," *Your Training Edge*, May 9, 2018. Retrieved from http://www.yourtrainingedge.com/top-10-training-metrics/ on March 24, 2019.

27 Kirkpatrick and Kirkpatrick, "Four Levels of Evaluation," 2.

28 Clardy, *Transfer of Training Literature Review*, 2.

29 Dennis R. Laker, "Dual Dimensionality of Training Transfer," *Human Resources Development Quarterly* 1, no. 3 (1990): 209–235.

30 J. Kevin Ford and Daniel A. Weissbein, "Transfer of Training: An Updated Review and Analysis," *Performance Improvement Quarterly* 10, no. 2 (1997): 22–41.

31 Otto Jelsma and Jeroen J. G. van Merriënboer, "The ADAPT Design Model: Towards Instructional Control of Transfer," *Instructional Science* 19, no. 2 (1990): 89–120.

32 Clardy, *Transfer of Training Literature Review*, 4.

33 E. L. Thorndike and R. S. Woodworth, "The Influence of Movement in One Mental Function Upon the Efficiency of Other Functions," *Psychological Review* 8 (1901): 247–261.

34 Timothy T. Baldwin and J. Kevin Ford, "Transfer of Training: A Review and Directions for Future Research," *Personnel Psychology* 41 (1988): 63–105.

35 Clardy, *Transfer of Training Literature Review*, 14.

36 Elwood F. Holton III, Reid A. Bates, and Wendy E. A. Ruona, "Development of a Generalized Learning Transfer System Inventory," *Human Resource Development Quarterly* 11, no. 4 (2000): 333–360.

37 Ibid.

38 Sharon S. Naquin and Elwood F. Holton III, "The Effects of Personality, Affectivity, and Work Commitment on Motivation to Improve Work Through Learning," *Human Resources Development Quarterly* 13, no. 4 (2002): 357–376.

39 David M. Herold, Walter Davis, Donald B. Fedor, and Charles K. Parsons, "Dispositional

Influences on Transfer of Learning in Multistage Training Programs," *Personnel Psychology* 55, no. 4 (2002): 851–870.

40. Michela Vignoli and Marco Depolo, "Transfer of Training Process: When Proactive Personality Matters? A Three-Wave Investigation of Proactive Personality as a Trigger of the Transfer of Training Process." *Personality and Individual Differences* 141 (2019): 62–67.

41. Raymond A. Noe, "Trainees' Attributes and Attitudes: Neglected Influences on Training Effectiveness," *Academy of Management Review* 11, no. 4 (1986): 736–749.

42. Scott I. Tannenbaum and Gary Yukl, "Training and Development," *Annual Review of Psychology* 43 (1992): 399–442; Marilyn E. Gist, Cynthia K. Stevens, and Anna G. Bavetta, "Effects of Self-Efficacy and Post-Training Intervention on the Acquisition and Maintenance of Complex Interpersonal Skills," *Personnel Psychology* 44, no. 4 (1991): 837–861.

43. Maria Simosi, "The Moderating Role of Self-Efficacy in the Organizational Culture-Training Transfer Relationship," *International Journal of Training and Development* 16, no. 2 (2012): 92–106.

44. Clardy, *Transfer of Training Literature Review*, 24.

45. Ibid., 25.

46. Elwood F. Holton III, Reid A. Bates, Dian L. Seyler, and Manuel B. Carvalho, "Toward Construct Validation of a Transfer Climate Instrument," *Human Resources Development Quarterly* 8, no. 2 (1997): 95–114.

47. Ibid.

48. Clardy, *Transfer of Training Literature Review*, 36.

49. Zuowei Wang, Renlai Zhou, and Priti Shah, "Spaced Cognitive Training Promotes Raining Transfer," *Frontiers in Human Neuroscience* 8 (2014): 1–8.

50. Clardy, *Transfer of Training Literature Review*, 38.

51. Kirkpatrick and Kirkpatrick, "Four Levels of Evaluation," 9.

52. Ibid., 11.

CHAPTER 7

1. Vincent Bruni-Bossio and Chelsea Willness, "The 'Kobayashi Maru' Meeting: High-Fidelity Experiential Learning," *Journal of Management Education* 40, no. 5 (2016): 619–647.

2. Robert Sallin (Producer) and Nicholas Meyer (Director), *Star Trek II: The Wrath of Khan* [Motion picture]. United States: Paramount Pictures, 1982.

3. J. J. Abrams (Producer & Director), *Star Trek* [Motion picture]. United States: Paramount Pictures, 2009.

4. Bruni-Bossio and Willness, "'Kobayashi Maru' Meeting."

5. Judith Scully Callahan, D. Scott Kiker, and Tom Cross, "Does Method Matter? A Meta-analysis of the Effects of Training Method on Older Learner Training Performance," *Journal of Management* 29, no. 5 (2003): 663–680.

6. Ibid.

7. Cody Brent Cox, Laura G. Barron, William Davis, and Bernardo de la Garza, "Using Situational Judgment Tests (SJTs) in Training," *Personnel Review* 46, no. 1 (2017): 36–45.

8. Pam A. Mueller and Daniel M. Oppenheimer, "The Pen Is Mightier Than the Keyboard: Advantages of Longhand Over Laptop Note Taking," *Psychological Science* 25, no. 6 (2014): 1159–1168.

9. Callahan et al., "Does Method Matter?"

10. David A. Kolb, *Experiential Learning: Experience as the Source of Learning and Development* (Englewood Cliffs, NJ: Prentice Hall, 1984).

11. Ronald R. Sims, "Debriefing Experiential Learning Exercises in Ethics Education," *Teaching Business Ethics* 6, no. 2 (2002): 179–197.
12. Ibid.
13. Robert F. Dennehy, Ronald R. Sims, and Heather E. Collins, "Debriefing Experiential Learning Exercises: A Theoretical and Practical Guide for Success," *Journal of Management Education* 22, no. 1 (1998): 9–25.
14. Paul Donovan and John Townsend, "The Disaster Approach: Countering Learner Apprehension in Role-Play," *Management Teaching Review* 3, no. 2 (2018): 172–180.
15. Cox et al., "Using Situational Judgment Tests (SJTs) in Training."
16. Mark A. Clark, Donna Blancero, Carol Luce, and George Marron, "Teaching Work Group–Task Congruence: The Fit for Performance Exercise," *Journal of Management Education* 25, no. 5 (2001): 531.
17. Bradford S. Bell, Adam M. Kanar, and Steve W. J. Kozlowski, "Current Issues and Future Directions in Simulation-Based Training in North America," *The International Journal of Human Resource Management* 19, no. 8 (2008): 1416–1434.
18. Robert E. Wood, Jens F. Beckmann, and Damian P. Birney, "Simulations, Learning and Real World Capabilities," *Education & Training* 51, no. 5 (2009): 491–510.
19. William A. Drago and Richard J. Wagner, "Vark Preferred Learning Styles and Online Education," *Management Research News* 27, no. 7 (2004): 1–13.
20. Jeanne Liedtka, "The Promise and Peril of Video Cases: Reflections on Their Creation and Use," *Journal of Management Education* 25, no. 4 (2001): 409–424.
21. Tara Olivia Loughrey, Geneviève K. Marshall, Alana Bellizzi, and David A. Wilder, "The Use of Video Modeling, Prompting, and Feedback to Increase Credit Card Promotion in a Retail Setting," *Journal of Organizational Behavior Management* 33, no. 3 (2013): 200–208.
22. David R. Bowes, "Using Television Commercials as Video Illustrations: Examples From a Money and Banking Economics Class," *American Journal of Business Education (Online)* 7, no. 4 (2014): 333–338.
23. Anthony Fee and Amanda E. K. Budde-Sung, "Using Video Effectively in Diverse Classes: What Students Want," *Journal of Management Education* 38, no. 6 (2014): 843–874.
24. Zane L. Berge and Lin Muilenburg, "Designing Discussion Questions for Online, Adult Learning," pp. 183–189 in *The ASTD e-Learning Handbook*, ed. A. Rossett (New York: McGraw-Hill, 2002).

CHAPTER 8

1. McDonald's, "Hamburger University: Our Curriculum." Retrieved from https://corporate.mcdonalds.com/mcd/corporate_careers2/training_and_development/hamburger_university/our_curriculum.html on March 26, 2019.
2. Jessica Wohl, "Hamburger University Grills Students on McDonald's Operations," *Chicago Tribune*, April 18, 2015. Retrieved from http://www.chicagotribune.com/business/ct-mcdonalds-hamburger-university-0419-biz-20150407-story.html on March 26, 2019.
3. Natalie Walters, "McDonald's Hamburger University Can Be Harder to Get Into Than Harvard and Is Even Cooler Than You'd Imagine," *Business Insider*, October 24, 2015. Retrieved from http://www.businessinsider.com/mcdonalds-hamburger-university-2333/#ray-kroc-the-illinois-native-who-bought-mcdonalds-in-1961-for-27-million-and-built-it-into-the-most-profitable-fast-food-chain-

in-the-world-is-known-for-implementing-the-three-legged-stool-business-model-at-mcdonalds-the-model-represents-the-triangular-relationship-between-owner operators-suppliers-and-company-employees-and-is-still-taught-at-hamburger-university-today-11 on March 26, 2019.

4   Timothy D. Butler, Craig Armstrong, Alex Ellinger, and George Franke, "Employer Trustworthiness, Worker Pride, and Camaraderie as a Source of Competitive Advantage," *Journal of Strategy and Management* 9, no. 3 (2016): 322–343.

5   Vincent Bruni-Bossio and Chelsea Willness, "The 'Kobayashi Maru' Meeting: High-Fidelity Experiential Learning," *Journal of Management Education* 40, no. 5 (2016): 619–647.

6   Malcolm Knowles, *The Adult Learner: A Neglected Species*, 3rd ed. (Houston, TX: Gulf, 1984).

7   Paul W. Thayer and Mark Teachout, *A Climate for Transfer Model*, AL/HR-TP-1995-0035 (Texas: Brooks Air Force Base, 1995).

8   Peter Cappelli, "Why Do Employers Retrain At-Risk Workers? The Role of Social Capital," *Industrial Relations* 43, no. 2 (2004): 421–447.

9   Jenepher Lennox Terrion, "The Impact of a Management Training Program for University Administrators," *The Journal of Management Development* 25, no. 2 (2006): 183–194.

10 Odd Nordhaug, "Reward Functions of Personnel Training," *Human Relations* 42, no. 5 (1989): 373.

11 Victor H. Vroom, *Work and Motivation* (New York: Wiley, 1964).

12 Sajjad Nazir, Amina Shafi, Wang Qun, Nadia Nazir, and Quang Dung Tran, "Influence of Organizational Rewards on Organizational Commitment and Turnover Intentions," *Employee Relations* 38, no. 4 (2016): 596–619.

13 Abraham H. Maslow, *Motivation and Personality* (New York: Harper & Row, 1954).

14 William J. Rothwell and H. C. Kazanas, "Planned OJT Is Productive OJT," *Training and Development Journal* 44, no. 10 (1990): 53–56.

15 Gary R. Sisson, *Hands-On Training: A Simple and Effective Method for On-the-Job Training* (San Francisco: Berrett-Koehler, 2001).

16 Michael J. Jones and Ronald L. Jacobs, *Structured On-the-Job Training: Unleashing Employee Expertise in the Workplace* (San Francisco: Berrett-Koehler, 1995).

17 Marcel van der Klink and Jan Streumer, "Effectiveness of On-the-Job Training," *Journal of European Industrial Training* 26, no. 2–4 (2002): 196–199.

18 Ibid.

19 Jones and Jacobs, *Structured On-the-Job Training*.

20 Ibid.

21 Ibid.

22 Thomas McNulty and Jacqueline Schmidt, "Designing an Effective Training Room," *Training & Management Development Methods* 19, no. 3 (2005): 331–334.

23 Ibid.

24 Mark D. Allen, "Introduction: What Is a Corporate University, and Why Should an Organization Have One?" pp. 1–14 in *The Corporate University Handbook*, ed. M. Allen (New York: AMACOM American Management Association, 2002).

25 Jeanne C. Meister, *Corporate Universities: Lessons in Building a World-Class Work Force* (New York: McGraw-Hill, 1998).

CHAPTER 9

1   Matt Richtel, "Technology Changing How Students Learn, Teachers Say," *New York Times*, November 1, 2012. Retrieved from http://nyti.ms/W8Zv7M on March 15, 2016.

2   Ibid.

3   Karla Gutierrez, "Four Ways Technology Is Changing How People Learn," *SHIFT eLearning*, February 20, 2014. Retrieved from

https://www.shiftelearning.com/blog/bid/336775/Four-Ways-Technology-Is-Changing-How-People-Learn-Infographic on March 15, 2016.

4. Richard L. Daft and Robert H. Lengel, "Organizational Information Requirements, Media Richness and Structural Design," *Management Science* 32, no. 5 (1986): 554–571.

5. Jo Cook, "A Group You Cannot See," *Training Journal* (January 1, 2015): 5–8.

6. Robyn A. Berkley, Roxanne Beard, and David M. Kaplan, "Leveraging Diversity in a Virtual Context: Global Diversity and Cyber-Aggression," pp. 504–522 in *Handbook of Research on Workforce Diversity in a Global Society: Technologies and Concepts*, ed. C. L. Scott and M. Y. Byrd (Hershey, PA: IGI Global, 2012).

7. Pnina Shachaf, "Bridging Cultural Diversity Through E-mail," *Journal of Global Information Technology Management* 8, no. 2 (2005): 46–60.

8. Phil Gorman, Teresa Nelson, and Alan Glassman, "The Millennial Generation: A Strategic Opportunity," *Organizational Analysis* 12, no. 3 (2004): 255–270.

9. Dian L. Seyler, Elwood F. Holton III, Reid A. Bates, Michael F. Burnett, and Manuel A. Carvalho, "Factors Affecting Motivation to Transfer Training," *International Journal of Training and Development* 2, no. 1 (1998): 2–16.

10. Alice F. Stuhlmacher, Maryalice Citera, and Toni Willis, "Gender Differences in Virtual Negotiation: Theory and Research," *Sex Roles* 57, no. 5–6 (2007): 329–339.

11. Helene Tenzer and Markus Pudelko, "Media Choice in Multilingual Virtual Teams," *Journal of International Business Studies* 47, no. 4 (2016): 427–452.

12. Michael J. Kavanagh, Hal G. Gueutal, and Scott I. Tannenbaum, *Human Resource Information Systems: Development and Application* (Boston: PWS-Kent, 1990).

13. Ibid.

14. Howard Hills, "Learning Management Systems: Why Buy One?," *Training Journal* (January 2003): 12–14.

15. Gorman et al., "The Millennial Generation."

16. Julie Willems, "Equity in Distance Education," pp. 17–35 in *Global Challenges and Perspectives in Blended and Distance Learning*, ed. J. Willems, B. Tynan, and R. James (Hershey, PA: Information Science Reference, 2013).

17. William Horton, *Designing Web-Based Training: How to Teach Anyone Anything Anywhere Anytime* (New York: Wiley, 2000).

18. Philip N. Howard, Laura Busch, and Penelope Sheets, "Comparing Digital Divides: Internet Access and Social Inequality in Canada and the United States," *Canadian Journal of Communication* 35, no. 1 (2010): 109–128.

19. Lainey Feingold, "Digital Accessibility and the Quest for Online Equality," *Journal of Internet Law* 21, no. 4 (2017): 3–12.

20. Kevin Gumienny, "E-learning FOR ALL," *Talent Development* 71, no. 8 (2017): 38–43.

21. Shonn R. Colbrunn and Darlene M. Van Tiem, "From Binders to Browsers: Converting Classroom Training to the Web," pp. 85–95 in *The ASTD e-Learning Handbook*, ed. A. Rossett (New York: McGraw-Hill, 2002).

22. Charissa Tan, "e-Learning and Development," pp. 214–231 in *e-HRM: Digital Approaches, Directions & Applications*, ed. M. Thite (New York: Routledge, 2019).

23. Brandon Hall, "Six Steps to Developing a Successful e-Learning Initiative: Excerpts From the e-Learning Guidebook," pp. 234–250 in *The ASTD e-Learning Handbook*, ed. A. Rossett (New York: McGraw-Hill, 2002).

24. Horton, *Designing Web-Based Training*.

25. Tan, "e-Learning and Development."

26. Shachaf, "Bridging Cultural Diversity Through E-mail."

27. Jim Moshinskie, "How to Keep e-Learners from e-scaping," pp. 218–233 in *The ASTD e-Learning Handbook*, ed. A. Rossett (New York: McGraw-Hill, 2002).

28. Kirstie Donnelly, "Learning on the Move: How m-Learning Could Transform Training and Development," *Development and Learning in Organizations* 23, no. 4 (2009): 8–11.

29. Naomi Norman, "Mobile Learning Made Easy," *T+D* 65, no. 12 (2011): 52–55.
30. Ibid.
31. *Oxford English Dictionary*, "Gamification." Retrieved from https://en.oxforddictionaries.com/definition/us/gamification on December 29, 2018.
32. Wendy H.-Y. Huan and Dilip Soman, *A Practitioner's Guide to Gamification of Education*, Research Report Series: Behavioural Economics in Action (Toronto: Rotman School of Management, 2013).
33. Ibid.
34. Cook, "A Group You Cannot See."
35. Ibid.
36. Tan, "e-Learning and Development."
37. Cook, "A Group You Cannot See."
38. Tan, "e-Learning and Development."
39. David M. Savino, "The Impact of MOOCs on Human Resource Training and Development," *Journal of Higher Education Theory and Practice* 14, no. 3 (2014): 59–64.
40. Christopher Pappas, "7 Tips for Using MOOCs in Corporate e-Learning," *eLearning Industry*, October 13, 2016. Retrieved from https://elearningindustry.com/tips-using-moocs-corporate-elearning on March 28, 2019.
41. Savino, "Impact of MOOCs on Human Resource Training and Development."
42. Melissa Richardson, "Mentoring for a Dispersed Workforce," *Training & Development* (October 2015): 18–19.
43. Jenny Headlam-Wells, Julian Gosland, and Jane Craig, "'There's Magic in the Web': e-Mentoring for Women's Career Development," *Career Development International* 10, no. 6/7 (2005): 444–459.
44. Richardson, "Mentoring for a Dispersed Workforce," p. 19.

CHAPTER 10

1. Carol Hymowitz, "Xerox's Ursula Burns on Her Career Path and Changing Company Strategy," *Bloomberg*, August 8, 2013. Retrieved from http://www.bloomberg.com/news/articles/2013-08-08/xeroxs-ursula-burns-on-her-career-path-and-changing-company-strategy on March 29, 2019.
2. MAKERS Team, "How Ursula Burns Worked Her Way Up to CEO of a Fortune 500 Company," *MAKERS Motivation*, January 6, 2015. Retrieved from http://www.makers.com/blog/how-ursula-burns-worked-her-way-ceo-fortune-500-company on March 29, 2019.
3. Adam Bryant, "Xerox's New Chief Tries to Redefine Its Culture," *New York Times*, February 20, 2010. http://www.nytimes.com/2010/02/21/business/21xerox.html?pagewanted=all&_r=0
4. Rita J. S.-V. Fossen and Donald J. Vredenburgh, "Exploring Differences in Work's Meaning: An Investigation of Individual Attributes Associated With Work Orientations," *Journal of Behavioral and Applied Management* 15, no. 2 (2014): 101–120.
5. Ibid.
6. Donald E. Super, *The Psychology of Careers* (New York: Harper, 1957).
7. Douglas T. Hall and Associates, *The Career Is Dead—Long Live the Career* (San Francisco: Jossey-Bass, 1996).
8. Michael B. Arthur, "The Boundaryless Career: A New Perspective for Organizational Inquiry," *Journal of Organizational Behavior* 15 (1994): 295–306.
9. Jon P. Briscoe and Douglas T. Hall, "The Interplay of Boundaryless and Protean Careers: Combinations and Implications," *Journal of Vocational Behavior* 69 (2006): 4–18.
10. Edgar H. Schein, "Career Anchors Revisited: Implications for Career Development in the 21st Century," *Academy of Management Executive* 10, no. 4 (1996): 80–88.

11. Sherry E. Sullivan, David F. Martin, William A. Carden, and Lisa A. Mainiero, "The Road Less Traveled: How to Manage the Recycling Career Stage," *Journal of Leadership & Organizational Studies* 10, no. 2 (2003): 34–42.
12. Kay Maddox-Daines, "Mid-career as a Process of Discovery," *Career Development International* 21, no. 1 (2016): 45–59.
13. Denise Rotondo, "Individual-Difference Variables and Career-Related Coping," *The Journal of Social Psychology* 139, no. 4 (1999): 458–471.
14. Corinne Post, Joy A. Schneer, Frieda Reitman, and dt ogilvie, "Pathways to Retirement: A Career Stage Analysis of Retirement Age Expectations," *Human Relations* 66, no. 1 (2013): 87–112.
15. Sullivan et al., "Road Less Traveled."
16. Ibid.
17. Herbert G. Heneman III, Timothy A. Judge, and John D. Kammeyer-Mueller, *Staffing Organizations*, 7th ed. (New York: McGraw-Hill Irwin, 2012).
18. Sean T. Lyons, Linda Schweitzer, and Eddy S. W. Ng, "How Have Careers Changed? An Investigation of Changing Career Patterns Across Four Generations," *Journal of Managerial Psychology* 30, no. 1 (2015): 8–21.
19. Ibid.
20. Briscoe and Hall, "Interplay of Boundaryless and Protean Careers."
21. David M. Kaplan, "Career Anchors and Paths: The Case of Gay, Lesbian, & Bisexual Workers," *Human Resource Management Review* 24, no. 2 (2014): 119–130.
22. Briscoe and Hall, "Interplay of Boundaryless and Protean Careers."
23. Schein, "Career Anchors Revisited."
24. Laura Wils, Thierry Wils, and Michel Tremblay, "Toward a Career Anchor Structure: An Empirical Investigation of Engineers," *Relations Industrielles* 65, no. 2 (2010): 236–256.
25. Daniel C. Feldman and Mark C. Bolino, "Careers Within Careers: Reconceptualizing the Nature of Career Anchors and Their Consequences," *Human Resources Management Review* 6, no. 2 (1996): 89–92.
26. "Lucien Alziari (CHRO, Maersk) Discusses Strategic Challenges in HR," Darla Moore School of Business, January 17, 2017. Retrieved from https://www.youtube.com/watch?v=7Fngi6jIT6c&index=8&list=PLUElH5PMd16kn9p29AbXCJLvTiVUJRjLu on March 29, 2019.
27. Laurence J. Peter and Raymond Hull, *The Peter Principle: Why Things Always Go Wrong* (New York: William Morrow, 1969).
28. William J. Rothwell, "Replacement Planning: A Starting Point for Succession Planning and Talent Management," *International Journal of Training & Development* 15, no. 1 (2011): 87–99.
29. Michael H. Morris, Roy W. Williams, and Deon Nel, "Factors Influencing Family Business Succession," *International Journal of Entrepreneurial Behaviour & Research* 2, no. 3 (1996): 68–81.
30. Rothwell, "Replacement Planning."
31. Sheri-Lynne Leskiw and Parbudyal Singh, "Leadership Development: Learning From Best Practices," *Leadership & Organization Development Journal* 28, no. 5 (2007): 444–464.
32. Stephen L. Guinn, "Succession Planning Without Job Titles," *Career Development International* 5, no. 7 (2000): 390–393.
33. Robert M. Guion and Scott Highhouse, *Essentials of Personnel Assessment and Selection* (Mahwah, NJ: Erlbaum, 2006).
34. International Taskforce on Assessment Center Guidelines, "Guidelines and Ethical Considerations for Assessment Center Operations," *Journal of Management* 41, no. 4 (2015): 1244–1273.
35. Ibid.
36. Ibid.
37. James A. Breaugh, "Modeling the Managerial Promotion Process," *Journal of Managerial Psychology* 26, no. 4 (2011): 264–277.

38. Stephen Swailes and Michelle Blackburn, "Employee Reactions to Talent Pool Membership," *Employee Relations* 38, no. 1 (2016): 112–128.
39. Robert M. Fulmer, Stephen A. Stumpf, and Jared Bleak, "The Strategic Development of High Potential Leaders," *Strategy & Leadership* 37, no. 3 (2009): 17–22.
40. David G. Collings and Kamel Mellahi, "Strategic Talent Management: A Review and Research Agenda," *Human Resource Management Review* 19, no. 4 (2009): 304–313.
41. Noko Seopa, Albert Wöcke, and Camilla Leeds, "The Impact on the Psychological Contract of Differentiating Employees Into Talent Pools," *Career Development International* 20, no. 7 (2015): 717–732.
42. Swailes & Blackburn, "Employee Reactions to Talent Pool Membership."
43. Jon P. Briscoe, Douglas T. Hall, and Rachel L. Frautschy DeMuth, "Protean and Boundaryless Careers: An Empirical Exploration," *Journal of Vocational Behavior* 69, no. 1 (2006): 30–47.

CHAPTER 11

1. Keith Ferrazzi, "7 Ways to Improve Employee Development Programs," *Harvard Business Review*, July 31, 2015.
2. Adam Mitchinson and Robert Morris, *Learning About Learning Agility* (Brussels, Belgium: Center for Creative Leadership, 2014).
3. Ibid.
4. Jerome Ternynck, "7 High-Impact Approaches for Employee Development," *Inc.*, February 2, 2015. Retrieved from http://www.inc.com/jerome-ternynck/7-high-impact-approaches-for-employee-development.html on March 30, 2019.
5. J. Richard Hackman and Greg R. Oldham, *Work Redesign* (Reading, MA: Addison-Wesley, 1980).
6. Georgia T. Chao, "Mentoring Phases and Outcomes," *Journal of Vocational Behavior* 51, no. 1 (1997): 15–28.
7. Kathy Kram, *Mentoring at Work: Developmental Relationships in Organizational Life* (Glenview, IL: Foresman, 1985).
8. Society for Human Resource Management, "Basics of a Mentoring Program" (2016). Retrieved from www.shrm.org on February 1, 2017.
9. Earnest Friday and Shawnta S. Friday, "Formal Mentoring: Is There a Strategic Fit?," *Management Decisions* 40, no. 1/2 (2002): 152–157.
10. Society for Human Resource Management, "Basics of a Mentoring Program."
11. Kram, *Mentoring at Work*.
12. Rajashi Ghosh, "Antecedents of Mentoring Support: A Meta-analysis of Individual, Relational, and Structural or Organizational Factors," *Journal of Vocational Behavior* 84, no. 3 (2014): 367–384.
13. Cherie Rusnak, "The Power of Coaching," *The Public Manager*, October 2010. Retrieved from https://www.td.org/magazines/the-public-manager/the-power-of-coaching on December 11, 2017.
14. International Coach Federation, *2016 ICF Global Coaching Study*, 7–8. Retrieved from https://coachfederation.org/app/uploads/2017/12/2016ICFGlobalCoachingStudy_Executive Summary-2.pdf on December 11, 2017.
15. Ibid., 9.
16. Ibid.,12.
17. International Coach Federation, "ICF Credential." Retrieved from https://coachfederation.org/icf-credential/ on December 11, 2017.
18. Society for Industrial and Organizational Psychology, "When to Use Internal Versus External Coaches." Retrieved from http://www.siop.org/workplace/coaching/internal_versus_exte.aspx on February 4, 2018.

19. Anna Blackman, Gianna Moscardo, and David E. Gray, "Challenges for the Theory and Practice of Business Coaching: A Systematic Review of Empirical Evidence," *Human Resource Development Review* 15, no. 4 (2016): 459–486.
20. Merrill C. Anderson, "Executive Coaching: What ROI Can You Expect?," *Leadership Excellence* 22, no. 5 (2005): 10.
21. Steve Gladis and Kimberly Gladis, "Coaching Through Questions," *Talent Development* 69, no. 3 (2015): 32–36.
22. Ibid.
23. Skills You Need, "Coaching Skills." Retrieved from https://www.skillsyouneed.com/learn/coaching-skills.html on February 4, 2018.
24. Ibid.
25. Ibid.
26. Phil Donnison, "Executive Coaching Across Cultural Boundaries: An Interesting Challenge Facing Coaches Today," *Development and Learning in Organizations* 22, no. 4 (2008): 17–19.
27. Claudio Fernández-Aráoz, Andrew Roscoe, and Kentaro Aramaki, "Turning Potential Into Success," *Harvard Business Review*, November–December 2017.

CHAPTER 12

1. Larry David (Writer) and Alec Berg (Director), "Vow of Silence" (Television series episode), in L. David (Producer), *Curb Your Enthusiasm* (New York: HBO, 2011).
2. "Peter Drucker Quotes," available from https://www.azquotes.com/author/4147-Peter_Drucker.
3. Shilpee A. Dasgupta, Damodar Suar, and Seema Singh, "Impact of Managerial Communication Styles on Employees' Attitudes and Behaviours," *Employee Relations* 35, no. 2 (2013): 173–199.
4. Ibid.
5. Graham L. Bradley and Amanda C. Campbell, "Managing Difficult Workplace Conversations," *International Journal of Business Communication* 53, no. 4 (2016): 443–464.
6. Suzanne de Janasz, Karen O. Dowd, and Beth Schneider, *Interpersonal Skills in Organizations*, 5th ed. (New York: McGraw-Hill, 2015).
7. Ibid.
8. Gayle Cotton, "Gestures to Avoid in Cross-Cultural Business: In Other Words, 'Keep Your Fingers to Yourself.'" *Huffington Post*, August 8, 2013. Retrieved from https://www.huffingtonpost.com/gayle-cotton/cross-cultural-gestures_b_3437653.html on April 5, 2019.
9. Kenneth A. Hunt and William Hodkin, "The Criticality of Cultural Awareness in Global Marketing: Some Case Examples," *Journal of Business Case Studies (Online)* 8, no. 1 (2012): 1.
10. Jennifer Mayhan, "Make an Impact With Development Plans," *Nursing Management* 48, no. 7 (2017): 11–13.
11. Michael Burns, Livia Armstrong, and Kat Koppet, "Listen Up!" *Career Development* 34 (2017): 1–15.
12. Tanya Drollinger, Lucette B. Comer, and Patricia T. Warrington, "Development and Validation of the Active Empathetic Listening Scale," *Psychology & Marketing* 23, no. 2 (2006): 161–180.
13. Ibid.
14. Stephen P. Robbins and Phillip L. Hunsaker, *Training in Interpersonal Skills: Tips for Managing People at Work*, 3rd ed. (Upper Saddle River, NJ: Prentice Hall, 2003).
15. Hunt and Hodkin, "Criticality of Cultural Awareness in Global Marketing."
16. Jack Zenger and Joseph Folkman, "Why Do So Many Managers Avoid Giving Praise?" *Harvard Business Review*, May 2, 2017. Retrieved from https://hbr.org/2017/05/why-do-so-many-managers-avoid-giving-praise on April 5, 2019.

17. Susie S. Cox, Laura E. Marler, Marcia J. Simmering, and Jeff W. Totten, "Giving Feedback: Development of Scales for the Mum Effect, Discomfort Giving Feedback, and Feedback Medium Preference," *Performance Improvement Quarterly* 23, no. 4 (2011): 49–69.
18. Robbins and Hunsaker, *Training in Interpersonal Skills*.
19. Herman Aguinis, *Performance Management*, 2nd ed. (Upper Saddle River, NJ: Pearson Prentice Hall, 2009).
20. Shawn Clark and Abbey S. Duggins, *Using Quality Feedback to Guide Professional Learning: A Framework for Instructional Leaders* (Thousand Oaks, CA: Corwin, 2016).
21. Ibid.
22. Robbins and Hunsaker, *Training in Interpersonal Skills*.
23. Clark and Duggins, *Using Quality Feedback to Guide Professional Learning*.
24. Aguinis, *Performance Management*.
25. Andy Molinsky, Thomas H. Davenport, Bala Iyer, and Cathy N. Davidson, "Three Skills Every 21st-Century Manager Needs," *Harvard Business Review* 90 (January 2012).
26. Morten Emil Berg and Jan Terje Karlsen, "An Evaluation of Management Training and Coaching," *Journal of Workplace Learning* 24, no. 3 (2012): 177–199.
27. Kenneth W. Thomas, "Conflict and Conflict Management," in *The Handbook of Industrial and Organizational Psychology*, ed. M. Dunnette (Chicago: Rand McNally, 1976).
28. Athanasios Laios and George Tzetzis, "Styles of Managing Team Conflict in Professional Sports: The Case of Greece," *Management Research News* 28, no. 6 (2005): 36–41.
29. Ibid.
30. Beverly DeMarr and Suzanne C. DeJanasz, *Negotiation and Dispute Resolution*, 2nd ed. (Chicago: Chicago Business Press, 2019).
31. De Janasz et al., *Interpersonal Skills in Organizations*.
32. John D. Mayer and Peter Salovey, "What Is Emotional Intelligence?," pp. 3–31 in *Emotional Development and Emotional Intelligence: Educational Applications*, ed. P. Salovey and D. Schluyter (New York: Basic Books, 1997).
33. Daniel Goleman, *Emotional Intelligence* (New York: Bantam Books, 1996).
34. Reuven Bar-On, *The Emotional Intelligence Inventory (EQ-i): Technical Manual* (Toronto, ON: Multi-Health Systems, 1997).
35. Richard E. Boyatzis, Daniel Goleman, and Kenneth Rhee, "Clustering Competence in Emotional Intelligence: Insights From the Emotional Competence Inventory (ECI)," pp. 343–362 in *The Handbook of Emotional Intelligence*, ed. R. Bar-On and J. D. A. Parker (San Francisco: Jossey-Bass, 2000).
36. Nicola S. Schutte, John M. Malouff, Lena E. Hall, Donald J. Haggerty, Joan T. Cooper, Charles J. Golden, and Liane Dornheim, "Development and Validation of a Measure of Emotional Intelligence," *Personality and Individual Differences* 25 (1998): 167–277.
37. K. V. Petrides and Adrian Furnham, "Trait Emotional Intelligence: Behavioural Validation in Two Studies of Emotion Recognition and Reactivity to Mood Induction," *European Journal of Personality* 17 (2003): 39–57.
38. John D. Mayer, Peter Salovey, David R. Caruso, and Gill Sitarenios, "Modeling and Measuring Emotional Intelligence With the MSCEIT V2.0," *Emotion* 3 (2003): 97–105.
39. Drollinger et al., "Development and Validation of the Active Empathetic Listening Scale."

CHAPTER 13

1. Karen A. Bantel and Susan E. Jackson, "Top Management and Innovations in Banking: Does the Demography of the Top Team Make a Difference?" *Strategic Management Journal* 10 (1989): 107–124.
2. Geert Hofstede, *Culture's Consequences: International Differences in Work-Related Values*, 2nd ed. (Beverly Hills CA: SAGE, 1984).
3. Geert Hofstede, Gert Jan Hofstede, and Michael Minkov, *Cultures and Organizations: Software of the Mind*, 3rd ed. (New York: McGraw-Hill, 2010).
4. Roy Maurer, *Survey: Companies Fail to Train Managers for Overseas Assignments* (Society for Human Resource Management, 2013). Retrieved from http://www.shrm.org/hrdisciplines/global/articles/pages/fail-train-managers-overseas-assignments.aspx on February 24, 2016.
5. Richter International Consulting, "Facts and Figures." Retrieved from http://www.richterintl.com/?page_id=12 on April 7, 2019.
6. Ibid.
7. Neal Goodman, "Helping Trainees Succeed Overseas," *Training*. Retrieved from https://trainingmag.com/trgmag-article/helping-trainees-succeed-overseas on February 24, 2016.
8. Edgar Schein, *Organizational Culture and Leadership: A Dynamic View* (San Francisco, CA: Jossey-Bass, 1992).
9. Holly Lebowitz Rossi, "7 Core Values Statements That Inspire," *Fortune*, March 13, 2015. Retrieved from http://fortune.com/2015/03/13/company-slogans/ on February 10, 2016.
10. Talya N. Bauer and Berrin Erdogan, "Organizational Socialization: The Effective Onboarding of New Employees," pp. 51–64 in *APA Handbook of Industrial and Organizational Psychology*, Vol. 3: Maintaining, Expanding, and Contracting the Organization, ed. S. Zedeck (Washington, DC: American Psychological Association, 2011).
11. Talya N. Bauer, Todd Bodner, Berrin Erdogan, Donald M. Truxillo, and Jennifer S. Tucker, "Newcomer Adjustment During Organizational Socialization: A Meta-analytic Review of Antecedents, Outcomes and Methods," *Journal of Applied Psychology* 92 (2007): 707–721.
12. Ibid.
13. Talya N. Bauer, *Onboarding New Employees: Maximizing Success* (Arlington, VA: SHRM Foundation, 2010).
14. Ibid.
15. Amanda M. Meyer and Lynn K. Bartels, "The Impact of Onboarding Levels on Perceived Utility, Organizational Commitment, Organizational Support, and Job Satisfaction," *Journal of Organizational Psychology* 17, no. 5 (2017): 10–27.
16. Bauer et al., "Newcomer Adjustment During Organizational Socialization."
17. Howard J. Klein, Jinyan Fan, and Kristopher J. Preacher, "The Effects of Early Socialization Experiences on Content Mastery and Outcomes: A Mediational Approach," *Journal of Vocational Behavior* 68 (2006): 96–115.
18. Judith Brown, "Employee Orientation: Keeping New Employees On Board," October 20, 2015. Retrieved from https://www.ipma-hr.org/docs/default-source/public-docs/importdocuments/pdf/hrcenter/employee-orientation/cpr-eo-overview on April 7, 2019.
19. "Accountemps Survey: One in Three Employers Lacks Orientation Program for New Hires," *PR Newswire*, March 20, 2012.

20. Max Messmer, "Orientation Programs Can Be Key to Employee Retention," *Strategic Finance* 81, no. 8 (2000): 12–14.
21. Sabrina Hicks, "Successful Orientation Programs," *Training & Development* 54, no. 4 (2000): 59–60.
22. "Accountemps Survey," p. 1.
23. Hicks, "Successful Orientation Programs," p. 59.
24. Ibid.
25. David K. Lindo, "New Employee Orientation Is Your Job!" *SuperVision* 71, no. 9 (2010): 11–15.
26. R. F. Federico, "Six Ways to Solve the Orientation Blues," *HR Magazine* 36, no. 5 (1991): 69.
27. Christopher Orpen, "The Effects of Mentoring on Employees' Career Success," The Journal of Social Psychology 135, no. 5 (1995): 667.
28. Federico, "Six Ways to Solve the Orientation Blues," p. 69.
29. Rebecca Ganzel, "Elements of a Great Orientation," *Training* 35, no. 3 (1998): 56.
30. Ibid.
31. Ibid.
32. Ibid.
33. "Onboarding Programs Need More Focus on Job Expectations and Team Building, Finds TEKsystems," *TEKsystems*, August 8, 2012. Retrieved from https://www.teksystems.com/en/insights/press/2012/teksystems-onboarding-programs-need-more-focus-on-job-expectations-and-team-building on April 7, 2019.
34. Hicks, "Successful Orientation Programs," p. 60.
35. Cheri Ostroff and Steve W. J. Kozlowski, "The Role of Mentoring in the Information Gathering Processes of Newcomers During Early Organizational Socialization," *Journal of Vocational Behavior* 42 (1993): 170–183.
36. Alan M. Saks and Jamie A. Gruman, "Socialization Resources Theory and Newcomers' Work Engagement: A New Pathway to Newcomer Socialization," *Career Development International* 23, no. 1 (2018): 12–32.
37. Jennifer A. Chatman, "Matching People and Organizations: Selection and Socialization in Public Accounting Firms," *Administrative Science Quarterly* 36, no. 3 (1991): 459–484.
38. Linda S. Hartenian and Don E. Gudmundson, "Cultural Diversity in Small Business: Implications for Firm Performance, *Journal of Developmental Entrepreneurship* 5, no. 3 (2000): 209–219.
39. American Psychological Association, "Personality." Retrieved from http://www.apa.org/topics/personality/ on March 23, 2016.
40. Project Implicit, "Education: Overview." Retrieved from https://implicit.harvard.edu/implicit/education.html on May 3, 2016.
41. Michele Paludi, *Victims of Sexual Assault and Abuse: Resources and Responses for Individuals and Families* (Women's Psychology) (Westport, CT: Praeger, 2010).
42. E. J. R. David, *Internalized Oppression: The Psychology of Marginalized Groups* (New York: Springer, 2013).
43. David A. Harris, "The Stories, the Statistics, and the Law: Why 'Driving While Black' Matters," *Minnesota Law Review* 84, no. 2 (1999): 265–326.
44. Sharon LaFraniere and Andrew W. Lehren, "The Disproportionate Risks of Driving While Black," *New York Times*, October 24, 2015. Retrieved from http://www.nytimes.com/2015/10/25/us/racial-disparity-traffic-stops-driving-black.html?_r=0 on February 23, 2016.
45. Milton J. Bennett, "Intercultural Communication: A Current Perspective," in *Basic Concepts of Intercultural Communication: Selected Readings*, ed. M. J. Bennett (Yarmouth, ME: Intercultural Press, 1998).
46. Frank Dobbin, Alexandra Kalev, and Erin Kelly, "Best Practices or Best Guesses? Diversity Management and the Remediation of Inequality," *American Sociological Review* 71 (2006): 589–617.

47. Peter Bregman, "Diversity Training Doesn't Work," *Harvard Business Review*, March 12, 2012. Retrieved from https://hbr.org/2012/03/diversity-training-doesnt-work on February 23, 2016.
48. Dobbin et al., "Best Practices or Best Guesses?"
49. Bregman, "Diversity Training Doesn't Work."
50. Roger Fisher and William Ury, *Getting to Yes: Negotiating Agreement Without Giving In* (New York, Houghton Mifflin, 1981). Available from http://www.williamury.com/books/getting-to-yes/.
51. Keld Jensen, "Why Negotiators Still Aren't 'Getting to Yes,'" *Forbes*, February 5, 2013. Retrieved from http://www.forbes.com/sites/keldjensen/2013/02/05/why-negotiators-still-arent-getting-to-yes/#398372276453 on February 23, 2016.
52. Ibid.
53. Association for Talent Development, "About Us." Retrieved from https://www.td.org/About/Mission-and-Vision on February 24, 2016.
54. Bob Adams, "The Glass Ceiling: Are Women and Minorities Blocked From the Executive Suite?," *CQ Researcher* 3, no. 40 (1993). Retrieved from https://library.cqpress.com/cqresearcher/document.php?id=cqresrre1993102900 on April 7, 2019.

APPENDIX B

1. Stephen Billett, "Apprenticeship as a Mode of Learning and Model of Education," *Education & Training* 58, no. 6 (2016): 613–628.
2. Ruben Schalk, "From Orphan to Artisan: Apprenticeship Careers and Contract Enforcement in the Netherlands Before and After the Guild Abolition," *The Economic History Review* 70, no. 3 (2017): 730–757.
3. Kathy Gurchiek, "Apprenticeships: One Way to Create a Work-Ready Talent Pool," *HRNews*, October 24, 2016. Retrieved from https://www.shrm.org/resourcesandtools/hr-topics/organizational-and-employee-development/pages/apprenticeships-one-way-to-create-a-work-ready-talent-pool.aspx on April 2, 2019.
4. Ibid.
5. U.S. Department of Labor, "Apprenticeship Data and Statistics." Retrieved from https://www.doleta.gov/OA/data_statistics.cfm on April 2, 2019.
6. Stephanie Overman, "Apprenticeships Provide Skills Needed for Hard-to-Fill Health Jobs," *HRNews*, February 8, 2017. Retrieved from https://www.shrm.org/resourcesandtools/hr-topics/talent-acquisition/pages/apprenticeships-skills-needed-healthcare-jobs.aspx on April 2, 2019.
7. U.S. Department of Labor, "About Apprenticeship." Retrieved from https://www.doleta.gov/OA/employer.cfm#programlength on April 2, 2019.
8. Billett, "Apprenticeship as a Mode of Learning and Model of Education."
9. U.S. Department of Labor, *A Quick-Start Toolkit: Building Registered Apprenticeship Programs*. Retrieved from https://www.doleta.gov/oa/employers/apprenticeship_toolkit.pdf on April 2, 2019.
10. John S. Gaal, "Recruiting Young: Three Vignettes, Three Approaches," *Benefits Magazine* 55, no. 3 (2018): 30. Retrieved from https://www.ifebp.org/inforequest/ifebp/0200896.pdf on April 2, 2019.
11. Jennifer E. Germaine, "New Requirements Aim to Increase Apprenticeship Diversity," *Benefits Magazine* 54, no. 4 (2017): 24–29.
12. George Lorenzo, *The State of Workforce Development Initiatives at America's Community Colleges* (Williamsville, NY: Lorenzo Associates, 2013). Retrieved from http://hdl.voced.edu.au/10707/250116 on April 2, 2019.

13. Ibid.
14. Robyn Berkley, personal interview with Don Sosnowski, January 2, 2019.
15. Ibid.
16. Society for Human Resource Management, *Using Government and Other Resources for Employment and Training Programs* (Alexandria, VA: Author, 2015).
17. *Ready to Work: Job-Driven Training and American Opportunity* (White House report, July 2014). Retrieved from https://obamawhitehouse.archives.gov/sites/default/files/docs/skills_report.pdf on April 2, 2019.
18. Kristen Fyfe-Mills, "Job Training Reboot Offers New Opportunities for Federal Agencies," *Public Manager* 43, no. 4 (2014): 17–19.
19. Christopher J. O'Leary, Robert A. Straits, and Stephen A. Wandner, "U.S. Job Training: Types, Participants and History," pp. 1–20 in *Job Training Policy in the United States*, ed. C. J. O'Leary, R. A. Straits, and S. A. Wandner (Kalamazoo, MI: W. E. Upjohn Institute for Employment Research, 2004).
20. Robert J. LaLonde, "The Promise of Public Sector-Sponsored Training Programs," *Journal of Economic Perspectives* 9, no. 2 (1995): 149–169.
21. M. Jared McEntaffer, *The Promise of Worker Training: New Insights Into the Effects of Government Funded Training Programs* (Doctoral dissertation, 2015). Available from ProQuest Dissertations and Theses Database (UMI No. 3712676).
22. LaLonde, "Promise of Public Sector-Sponsored Training Programs."
23. McEntaffer, *Promise of Worker Training*.
24. Ibid.
25. Ibid.
26. O'Leary et al., "U.S. Job Training."
27. U.S. Department of Labor, What Works in Job Training: A Synthesis of the Evidence (July 22, 2014). Retrieved from https://www.dol.gov/asp/evaluation/jdt/jdt.pdf on April 2, 2019.
28. Ibid.
29. Fair Labor Standards Act of 1938, 29 U.S.C. § 203.
30. Internal Revenue Service, "Employers Guide to Fringe Benefits: For Use in 2018" (Publication 15-B), February 22, 2018.
31. Carl E. Van Horn and Aaron R. Fichtner, "An Evaluation of State-Subsidized, Firm-Based Training: The Workforce Development Partnership Program," *International Journal of Manpower* 24, no. 1 (2003): 97–110.
32. Alastair Fitzpayne and Ethan Pollack, *Worker Training Tax Credit: Promoting Employer Investments in the Workforce* (Washington, DC: The Aspen Institute, 2017).
33. Employment Training Panel, "Welcome." Available from ETP.ca.gov.

APPENDIX C

1. Wanda Piña-Ramírez and Norma Dávila, "Become a Good Training Facilitator," *Association for Talent Development*. Retrieved from https://www.td.org/newsletters/atd-links/become-a-good-training-facilitator on September 2, 2018.
2. Dartmouth College Biomedical Libraries, "PowerPoint: Guides, Tips, and Help." Retrieved from https://www.dartmouth.edu/~library/biomed/guides/powerpoint.html on September 2, 2018.
3. Ibid.
4. Ibid.
5. Sarah Kessler, "How to Improve Your Presentation Skills," *Inc*. Retrieved from http://www.inc.com/guides/how-to-improve-your-presentation-skills.html on March 27, 2017.
6. Dartmouth Library, "PowerPoint."
7. Ibid.
8. Ibid.

9. Piña-Ramírez and Dávila, "Become a Good Training Facilitator."
10. Ibid.
11. Ibid.
12. Ibid.
13. James Summers, "How to Deal With Participants Who Deliberately Disrupt or Sabotage Training," *Langevin Learning Services*, January 22, 2018. Retrieved from http://blog.langevin.com/how-to-deal-with-participants-who-deliberately-disrupt-or-sabotage-training on September 3, 2018.
14. Ibid.
15. Laurel and Associates, "How to Handle Difficult Participants" (2010). Retrieved from https://www.hse.ie/eng/about/who/qid/other-quality-improvement-programmes/opendisclosure/opendiscfiles/guidetomanagingdifficultparticipants.pdf on April 2, 2019.

INDEX

Absorb LMS, 232 (exhibit)
Abstract conceptualization, 106–107
Accessibility to technology, 57–58, 229, 236–237
Accredited Coach Training Program (ACTP), 13
Acquired needs theory, 83–84
Active experimentation, 106–107
Active learning theory, 104–105
Active listening, 321 (exhibit), 322–323
ADDIE model. *See* Instructional systems design model (ADDIE model)
Adobe Captivate, 232
Adobe Connect, 242
Adobe Spark, 381
Adverse impact, 51, 52–54
Adverse treatment, 51–52
Affective domain, 96 (exhibit), 97
Affirmative action, 58–59
Affirmative defense, 60
Age Discrimination in Employment Act (1967/1978), 50 (exhibit), 58
Aldi, 40–44
Alternate/parallel forms reliability, 134 (exhibit)
Amazon WorldWide Research and Development Center, 121–122
Americans with Disabilities Act (1990/2008), 45–46, 50 (exhibit), 56–59
Analyzer strategy, 28
Anderson Model for Learning Evaluation, 160
Andragogy, 107–109, 209
Apache Open Office, 381
APHR certification, 12
Apple Inc., 23, 26–27, 206
Apple University, 27 (exhibit)
Apple Watch, 240
Applied Improvisation Network, 319, 320
Apprenticeship programs:
    attributes of, 371–372
    historical perspective, 370–371
    pre-apprenticeship programs, 372
    unions, 372

Archival records, 73–74
Assertive/supportive communication, 315–317
Assessment centers, 79 (exhibit), 80, 264–266
Assignments and enrichment opportunities, 282–284
Associate Certified Coach, 13
Associate Professional in Talent Development (APTD), 11
Association for Talent Development (ATD):
    Aligning for Success, 16–17, 24, 32–33
    Associate Professional in Talent Development (APTD), 11
    ATD Competency Model, 11, 12 (exhibit)
    certifications, 11
    Certified Professional in Learning and Performance (CPLP), 11
    Code of Ethics, 31 (exhibit), 356
    defined, 1
    employee orientation, 342–343
    global context, 32–33
    internet resources, 11
    learning objectives, 126
    mission, 1
    specialist skills, 1
    training and development strategy, 16–17, 24, 31–33
    training defined, 2
Associationist school, 170
Asynchronous instruction, 236 (exhibit), 238–239
Attentional learning, 100
Attentive listening, 321–322
Audio presentations, 195 (exhibit), 197
Australian Women in Resources Alliance (AWRA), 244

Baby Boomers, 113–114
Backwards design, 124, 159
Balanced scorecard (BSC), 161, 168
Bandura, Albert, 100
Bank of America, 359, 360 (exhibit)
Behavior from training, 162–166, 169–174
Behaviorism, 97, 98–102
Bench strength, 268, 269

Berkley, Robyn, 316 (exhibit), 328 (exhibit)
Bersin by Deloitte, 17, 93–94
Blackberry, 26
Blackboard (Higher Ed), 232 (exhibit)
Blackboards, 195 (exhibit), 196
Bloom, Benjamin, 96
Bloom's Taxonomy:
  for evaluation of reaction and learning, 127 (exhibit)
  for evaluation of transfer and results, 170, 174
  learning theories, 96–97, 101, 102, 103, 105, 106
Boundaryless careers, 250, 251, 258–259, 260, 270
Bridge, 232 (exhibit)
Budget for training:
  ADDIE model, 4–5
  evaluation of transfer and results, 176–177
  face-to-face training, 208 (exhibit), 209–210
  fixed costs, 210, 238
  variable costs, 210, 238
BUD pre-apprenticeship program, 372
Build-A-Bear, 339
Burns, Ursula, 248–249, 260
Buy-in problem, 78–79

California, 379
Canvas, 232 (exhibit)
Capto, 242
Career anchor theory, 250–251, 252, 261–262
Career plateau, 255
Careers:
  boundaryless careers, 250, 251, 258–259, 260
  career anchor theory, 250–251, 252, 261–262
  career paths, 256–258
  career plateau, 255
  career stage theory, 250, 251, 252–256
  disengagement stage, 255
  establishment stage, 253
  exploration stage, 252–253
  fork pattern, 256, 257 (exhibit), 258, 259, 286
  job distinction, 249–250
  knowledge, skills, abilities (KSAs), 253, 254, 257, 258
  ladder pattern, 256, 257 (exhibit), 258, 259
  lattice pattern, 257–258, 259, 286
  maintenance stage, 254
  mobility patterns, 256–258
  obsolescence stage, 254–255
  organizational diversity, 248–249
  organizational guidelines, 251–252
  protean careers, 250, 251, 258–259, 260–261
  recycling stage, 255–256
  ridge pattern, 257–258, 259, 286
  study guide, 271–275
  theoretical perspectives, 250–252, 258–262
  traditional careers, 258–260
  See also Succession planning; Training and development careers
Career stage theory, 250, 251, 252–256
Case, 189, 194 (exhibit)
Case role play, 190–191
Caterpillar Inc., 45–46
Center for Creative Leadership, 281
Certifications:
  Accredited Coach Training Program (ACTP), 13
  aPHR certification, 12
  Associate Certified Coach, 13
  Associate Professional in Talent Development (APTD), 11
  Association for Talent Development (ATD), 11
  Certified Professional in Learning and Performance (CPLP), 11
  Human Resource Certification Institute (HRCI), 12–13
  International Coaching Federation (ICF), 13
  Master Certified Coach, 13
  PHR certification, 12–13
  Professional Certified Coach, 13
  SPHR certification, 12–13
Certified Professional in Learning and Performance (CPLP), 11
Change management, 160–161
Chavez, Cesar, 49
Chick-fil-A, 49
Chief learning officer (CLO), 93–94
Chronemics, 318 (exhibit), 319
Civil Rights Act (1964/1991), 47, 49–56
Classical conditioning, 98
Classroom setting:
  constraints, 219
  features, 218–220
  layout, 219–220
Closed-ended questions, 100
Coaching programs:
  defined, 282 (exhibit), 298–299
  e-coaching, 245
  employee benefits, 301–302 (exhibit)
  for employee development, 276–277, 282 (exhibit), 287, 298–306
  example of, 276–277

external coaching, 299–301
guidelines for, 303 (exhibit)
internal coaching, 299–301
mentoring distinction, 287
organizational benefits, 301–302 (exhibit)
phases of, 302–304
success qualities, 304–306
See also Mentoring programs
Coach University, 277
Cognitive domain, 96–97
Cognitive load theory, 102–103
Cognitive Style Index (CSI), 111
Cognitivism, 97, 102–103
Collings, Laura, 227
Common Sense Media, 228
Communication:
 assertive/supportive communication, 315–317
 for diversity training, 355–356
 improvisational, 319–320
 lean communication, 230
 nonverbal, 317–319
 rich communication, 230
 for training and development, 314, 315–320
 for training session management, 383
 virtual communication, 229–230
Community college programs:
 subject matter expert (SME), 373–374 (exhibit)
 training and development consultant programs, 373–374
 training vendors, 374–375
 for workforce development (WFD), 372–373
Community of practice, 105–106
Compensation, 22 (exhibit), 23
Competency-based job analysis, 73
Comprehensive Employment and Training Act (1973), 377
Computer-based training (CBT), 24, 236 (exhibit), 237–238
Computer presentations, 195 (exhibit), 196
Concentration statistics, 53
Concrete experience, 106–107
Concurrent validity, 135 (exhibit)
Conferences, 218, 221
Confirmation questions, 198, 199
Conflict resolution:
 for diversity training, 355
 example of, 313–314, 325–326
 training and development skills, 313–314, 315 (exhibit), 325–326, 325–327

Connectionist model, 103
Constructive feedback, 323
Constructivism, 97, 103–106
Construct validity, 135 (exhibit)
Content validity, 135 (exhibit)
Control of training, 208
Corporate universities, 205–206, 207, 208 (exhibit), 209, 210, 211, 212, 218, 221–222
Cost leadership strategy, 27–28
Courses, 218, 221
Criterion validity, 135 (exhibit)
Critical incidents analysis, 74–75
Crossword puzzles, 192 (exhibit)
Curb Your Enthusiasm, 313–314, 325–326

David, Larry, 313–314, 325–326
DB Schenker, 157–158
Debriefs, 187–188
Defender strategy, 27–28
Depth charts, 268–269
Developmental role play, 191
Development programs:
 assignments and enrichment opportunities, 282–284
 coaching, 276–277, 282 (exhibit), 287, 298–306
 construction industry, 287–288 (exhibit)
 defined, 2–3
 extra-role enrichment activities, 282 (exhibit), 284
 guidelines for, 279 (exhibit)
 job characteristics theory, 283–284
 job design opportunities, 284–286
 job enrichment activities, 282 (exhibit), 283–284
 job promotions, 282 (exhibit), 286–287
 job rotation, 282 (exhibit), 285–286
 job shadowing, 282 (exhibit), 284–285
 job transition opportunities, 286–287
 knowledge, skills, abilities (KSAs), 277–278, 279, 280, 282, 283, 284, 285
 lateral job moves, 282 (exhibit), 286
 leadership competencies, 307 (exhibit)
 leadership development, 306–308
 learning agility, 281
 mentoring, 282 (exhibit), 286–298
 performance evaluation, 281–282
 social learning theory, 280
 special assignments, 282 (exhibit), 283
 strategic value, 278–280
 strategies for, 281–287
 stretch assignments, 282 (exhibit), 283

study guide, 308–312
telecommuting employees, 280
Dictionary of Occupational Titles (U.S. Department of Labor), 74
Differentiation strategy, 26–27
Discriminatory practices. *See* Legal environment
Discussions, 187, 194 (exhibit)
Dislocated workers, 378
Disney Corporation, 49, 206
Disparate impact, 51
Disparate treatment, 51
Distributive mindset, 327
Diversity Awareness Partnership, 10
Diversity training:
    challenges, 353–354
    communication skills, 355–356
    conflict resolution, 355
    ethical principles, 356
    external dimension, 352
    gig economy, 341 (exhibit)
    impression management, 342 (exhibit), 343
    individual differences, 335–336, 348–354
    intercultural sensitivity continuum, 353–354 (exhibit)
    internal dimensions, 350–352
    international assignments, 337–338
    LGBTQ community, 356
    macro level, 336–338
    microaggression, 350–352
    microassault, 351 (exhibit)
    microinvalidation, 351 (exhibit)
    national culture, 335, 336–337
    negotiation skills, 355
    onboarding process, 340–348
    organizational artifacts, 339
    organizational assumptions, 339–340
    organizational culture, 335, 338–348
    organizational dimension, 352–353
    organizational example, 333–334
    organizational values, 339
    orientation programs, 342–348
    personality diversity, 349–350
    recruitment process, 341–342
    skills development, 355–356
    study guide, 356–365
Double-loop learning, 105, 109
Drama therapy, 319–320 (exhibit)
Drucker, Peter, 314
Dynamism of technology, 242–243

E-coaching, 245
Economic environment, 29, 30 (exhibit)
Edmodo, 232
Educational assistance benefits, 378
E-mentoring, 244–245
Emotional Competence Inventory, 328–329
Emotional intelligence, 328–329
Emotional Quotient Inventory, 328–329
Employee development. *See* Development programs
Employee-level needs analysis, 67 (exhibit), 79–86, 88–89
Engagement questions, 198–199
Equal employment opportunity, 49–59
Equal Employment Opportunity Commission, 378
Equity theory, 86
ERG theory, 83
Ethical principles:
    in diversity training, 356
    legal environment, 48–49
    training and development strategy, 30–32
Evaluation of reaction and learning:
    alternate/parallel forms reliability, 134 (exhibit)
    backwards design, 124
    Bloom's Taxonomy for, 127 (exhibit)
    concurrent validity, 135 (exhibit)
    construct validity, 135 (exhibit)
    content validity, 135 (exhibit)
    criterion validity, 135 (exhibit)
    evaluation summary, 133–134
    experimental designs, 130 (exhibit), 132–133
    internal consistency reliability, 134 (exhibit)
    interrater reliability, 134 (exhibit)
    knowledge, skills, abilities (KSAs), 121–122
    learning evaluation strategy, 124–125
    learning from training, 136 (exhibit), 137 (exhibit), 143–145
    learning objectives, 125–129
    New World Kirkpatrick Model, 135–145
    nonexperimental designs, 129 (exhibit), 130–132
    one-shot case study, 131
    one-shot pretest-posttest design, 131–132
    performance evaluation, 143
    posttest-only control group design, 133
    predictive validity, 135 (exhibit)
    pretest-posttest control group design, 133
    random assignment design, 132–133
    reaction to training, 136 (exhibit), 137 (exhibit), 140–143
    reliable measures, 134

sample learning objective, 128 (exhibit)
SMART goals for, 128
Solomon four-group design, 133
static-group comparison, 132
study guide, 146–156
test-retest reliability, 134 (exhibit)
training design for, 129–134
training strategy for, 123–125
valid measures, 134–135
Evaluation of transfer and results:
   Anderson Model for Learning Evaluation, 160
   backwards design, 159
   balanced scorecard (BSC), 161, 168
   behavior from training, 162–166, 169–174
   Bloom's Taxonomy, 170, 174
   change management, 160–161
   far transfer, 170
   knowledge, skills, abilities (KSAs), 159, 166
   knowledge transfer, 159–162, 164
   leadership, 160
   learning from training, 161, 162 (exhibit), 163 (exhibit)
   Learning Transfer System Inventory (LTSI), 171–173
   measurement system, 161
   mentoring programs, 157–158
   military knowledge transfer, 170, 171 (exhibit)
   near transfer, 170
   New World Kirkpatrick Model, 162–169
   organizational climate, 174
   post-training experiences, 174
   pre-training experiences, 173
   program design/delivery, 174
   reaction to training, 161, 163 (exhibit)
   results from training, 163 (exhibit), 166–169
   strategic focus, 159–160
   study guide, 177–182
   trainee personality, 173
   trainee self-efficacy, 173
   trainee trainability, 173
   training budget, 176–177
   training evaluation analysis, 175–176
   training transfer, 169–174
   training transfer influences, 171–174
Expectancy theory, 84–85, 144
Experiential learning methods, 187–193
Experiential learning theory, 106–107
Experimental designs, 130 (exhibit), 132–133

External coaching, 299–301
External organizational environment, 29–31
External partnerships:
   apprenticeship programs, 370–372
   community college programs, 372–375
   government training programs, 375–379
Extraneous cognitive load, 102–103
Extra-role enrichment activities, 282 (exhibit), 284

Face-to-face training:
   andragogy impact, 209
   classroom constraints, 219
   classroom features, 218–220
   classroom layout, 219–220
   conferences, 218, 221
   control of training, 208
   corporate universities, 205–206, 207, 208 (exhibit), 209, 210, 211, 212, 218, 221–222
   costs of training, 208 (exhibit), 209–210
   courses, 218, 221
   employee motivation impact, 209, 211–212
   fidelity of training, 208–209
   fixed training costs, 210
   human capital value, 201
   instructional site, 206–207
   instructional site selection, 207–212
   knowledge, skills, abilities (KSAs), 210, 221
   off-site training, 207, 208 (exhibit), 209, 210, 211, 212, 218
   on-site training, 206–207, 208 (exhibit), 209, 210, 211, 212
   on-the-job (OJT) training, 208, 209, 212–218
   reward value, 208 (exhibit), 211–212, 215–216
   social capital value, 208 (exhibit), 210–211
   speakers, 218, 221
   standardization of training, 208
   study guide, 222–225
   unspecified training sites, 207, 208 (exhibit)
   variable training costs, 210
   workshops, 218
Fair Labor Standards Act, 378
Far transfer, 170
Fast Company, 122, 141
Feedback skills, 314, 315 (exhibit), 323–324
Fidelity:
   face-to-face training, 208–209
   technology-mediated training, 237–238
Finamore, Joe, 227

Fitbit, 240
Fitzgerald Act (1937), 371
Fixed training costs, 210, 238
Flipcharts, 195 (exhibit), 196
Flow statistics, 53–54
Focus groups, 74 (exhibit), 75
Fork career-pattern, 256, 257 (exhibit), 258, 259, 286
4/5ths rule of discrimination, 53

Gainsharing system, 21
Games, 191–193, 194 (exhibit)
Gamification, 241–242
General Duty Clause (OSHA), 60
General Electric (GE), 93–94
Generational learning:
    Baby Boomers, 113–114
    Generation X, 113–114
    Millennials, 113–114
    technology-mediated training, 229–230, 235
Generation X, 113–114
Georgia, 379
Germane cognitive load, 102–203
Gestalt school, 170
Gestures, 317, 318 (exhibit)
Gig economy, 341 (exhibit)
Goleman, Daniel, 328
Google Hangouts, 242
Government training programs:
    dislocated workers, 378
    educational assistance benefits, 378
    federal expenditures for, 375, 376 (exhibit)
    federal legislation for, 376–378
    historical perspective, 376–377
    incentives for, 378–379
    subsidy programs, 378
    tax credits, 379
Gramm-Leach-Bliley Act (1999), 30
Gray, Myron, 227

Hamburger University, 205–206
Hammonds, Keith, 122
Handouts, 195 (exhibit), 196
Haptics, 318
Harassment, 60
Hazard Communication Standard, 60
Heir model, 263
Heutagogy, 109–111
Hicks, Wayland, 249

Hierarchy of needs, 82 (exhibit), 83
Hilton Worldwide, 370
Hire Heroes Act (2011), 171 (exhibit)
History effect, 131–132
Hoffman, Shirley, 45–46
Hook questions, 199
Horseshoe classroom arrangement, 220
Hostile environment, 60
HR infrastructure, 18, 20–24
HRIS. *See* Human resource information system (HRIS)
HTC Vice, 226
Human capital management system (HCM), 230
Human capital value, 201
Humanism, 97, 106–107
Human Resource Certification Institute (HRCI):
    aPHR certification, 12
    certifications, 12–13
    internet resources, 12
    PHR certification, 12–13
    SPHR certification, 12–13
Human resource generalist, 9
Human resource information system (HRIS), 24, 81, 230–235
Human resource management system (HRMS), 230
Human resource specialist, 9–10

Icebreakers, 192
Illinois, 47–48
Impact International, 24–25
Impression management, 342 (exhibit), 343
Improvisational communication, 319–320
In-basket activities, 191, 194 (exhibit)
Independent contractors, 61
Information processing theory, 103
Information technology (IT), 24
Institute for Corporate Productivity, 141
Instructional aids, 194–198
Instructional systems design model (ADDIE model):
    analysis phase, 4
    budget approval, 4–5
    defined, 3
    design phase, 4–5
    development phase, 5
    evaluation phase, 5–6
    implementation phase, 5
    research application, 6–8
    training delivery considerations, 5

Integrative mindset, 327
Interactivity of technology, 242–243
Internal coaching, 299–301
Internal consistency reliability, 134 (exhibit)
Internal organizational environment, 18–24
International Coaching Federation (ICF):
    Accredited Coach Training Program (ACTP), 13
    Associate Certified Coach, 13
    certifications, 13
    founding of, 277
    internet resources, 13
    Master Certified Coach, 13
    Professional Certified Coach, 13
Internet resources:
    Absorb LMS, 232 (exhibit)
    Association for Talent Development (ATD), 11
    Blackboard, 232 (exhibit)
    Bridge, 232 (exhibit)
    Canvas, 232 (exhibit)
    certifications, 11, 12, 13
    Diversity Awareness Partnership, 10
    Human Resource Certification Institute (HRCI), 12
    International Coaching Federation (ICF), 13
    military knowledge transfer, 170
    Moodle, 232 (exhibit)
    OD Network, 13
    O*NET, 74
    organizational diversity, 333
    Safety Training Resources, 10
    Smarter U LMS, 232 (exhibit)
    Society for Human Resource Management (SHRM), 11
    Women on Fire, 277
Interrater reliability, 134 (exhibit)
Interviews, 74 (exhibit), 75–76
Intrinsic cognitive load, 102
Invista Performance Solutions (IPS), 121–122, 373–374 (exhibit)
Involving questions, 199

Jobs:
    career distinction, 249–250
    job analysis, 22
    job characteristics theory, 283–284
    job descriptions, 72–73
    job design, 284–286
    job enrichment, 282 (exhibit), 283–284
    job incumbents, 78
    job inflation, 78
    job-level needs analysis, 67 (exhibit), 72–79, 88
    job logs, 74 (exhibit), 76
    job promotions, 282 (exhibit), 286–287
    job rotation, 282 (exhibit), 285–286
    job shadowing, 282 (exhibit), 284–285
    job transition, 286–287
    lateral job moves, 282 (exhibit), 286
    See also Careers
Job Training Partnership Act (1982), 377
Join.Me, 242
Jurisdiction, 47–48, 50 (exhibit)

Kerr, Steve, 93
Kinesics, 318
Kirkpatrick, Donald, 122–123, 135, 159
Kirkpatrick, James, 159
Knowledge, skills, abilities (KSAs):
    in careers, 253, 254, 257, 258
    in development programs, 277–278, 279, 280, 282, 283, 284, 285
    evaluation of reaction and learning, 121–122
    evaluation of transfer and results, 159, 166
    face-to-face training, 210, 221
    in learning theories, 95, 99, 101, 102
    in legal environment, 50–51, 54
    needs analysis, 69, 80
    technology-mediated training, 232, 238
    for training and development, 2–3
    training and development skills, 314
    training and development strategy, 22, 23, 24
Knowledge transfer, 159–162, 164
Kouzes, James, 160

Ladder career-pattern, 256, 257 (exhibit), 258, 259
Lateral job moves, 282 (exhibit), 286
Lattice career-pattern, 257–258, 259, 286
Leadership, 160
Leadership Challenge, The (Kouzes & Posner), 160
Leadership development:
    defined, 306
    essential competencies, 306, 307 (exhibit)
    organizational benefits, 308
    stages of, 306–307
Leading indicators, 169
Lean communication, 230
Learning, 94–95
Learning agility, 281

Learning evaluation strategy, 124–125
Learning from training, 136 (exhibit), 137 (exhibit), 143–145, 161, 162 (exhibit), 163 (exhibit)
Learning management system (LMS), 230, 231–233, 234 (exhibit)
Learning methods:
   audio presentations, 195 (exhibit), 197
   blackboards, 195 (exhibit), 196
   case role play, 190–191
   cases, 189, 194 (exhibit)
   closed-ended questions, 100
   computer presentations, 195 (exhibit), 196
   confirmation questions, 198, 199
   crossword puzzles, 192 (exhibit)
   debriefs, 187–188
   developmental role play, 191
   discussions, 187, 194 (exhibit)
   engagement questions, 198–199
   experiential learning methods, 187–193
   flipcharts, 195 (exhibit), 196
   games, 191–193, 194 (exhibit)
   handouts, 195 (exhibit), 196
   hook questions, 199
   icebreakers, 192
   in-basket activities, 191, 194 (exhibit)
   instructional aids, 194–198
   involving questions, 199
   learning modality, 195
   lectures, 185–187, 194 (exhibit)
   lobbed questions, 199
   Management and Organizational Behavior Teaching Society (MOBTS), 193
   open-ended questions, 100
   overheads, 195 (exhibit), 196
   provoking questions, 199
   questionning methods, 198–199
   quizzing questions, 199
   role play, 189–191, 194 (exhibit)
   selection guidelines, 193–194
   study guide, 200–204
   targeted questions, 199
   traditional methods, 185–187
   video presentations, 195 (exhibit), 197–198
   whiteboards, 195 (exhibit), 196
Learning modality, 195
Learning objectives:
   defined, 125
   guidelines for, 128–129 (exhibit)
   planning, 126
   quantifying, 128
   writing, 126–128
Learning style:
   for technology-mediated training, 228–229
   theoretical perspective, 111–113
Learning Style Inventory (LSI), 111
Learning theories:
   abstract conceptualization, 106–107
   active experimentation, 106–107
   active learning theory, 104–105
   affective domain, 96 (exhibit), 97
   andragogy, 107–109
   attentional factors, 100
   behaviorism, 97, 98–102
   Bloom's Taxonomy, 96–97, 101, 102, 103, 105, 106
   chief learning officer (CLO), 93–94
   classical conditioning, 98
   cognitive domain, 96–97
   cognitive load theory, 102–103
   cognitivism, 97, 102–103
   community of practice, 105–106
   concrete experience, 106–107
   connectionist model, 103
   constructivism, 97, 103–106
   double-loop learning, 105, 109
   experiential learning theory, 106–107
   extraneous cognitive load, 102–103
   generational learning, 113–114
   germane cognitive load, 102–203
   heutagogy, 109–111
   humanism, 97, 106–107
   information processing theory, 103
   intrinsic cognitive load, 102
   knowledge, skills, abilities (KSAs), 95, 99, 101, 102
   learning, 94–95
   learning style, 111–113
   memory capacity, 103
   motivational factors, 100
   negative punishment, 99
   negative reinforcement, 99
   operant conditioning, 98–100
   organizational cognition, 105
   organizational learning theory, 105–106
   pedagogy, 107–109
   personality assessment training, 100
   positive punishment, 99

positive reinforcement, 99
problem-based learning, 104
psychomotor domain, 96 (exhibit), 97
reciprocal determinism, 101
reflective observation, 106–107
reproductive factors, 100
retentional factors, 100
self-determined learning, 104–105, 110
self-directed learning, 110–111 (exhibit)
self-efficacy, 101–102
single-loop learning, 105
social learning theory, 100–102
stage theory, 103
study guide, 115–120
for technology-mediated training, 228
Learning Transfer System Inventory (LTSI), 171–173
Lectures, 185–187, 194 (exhibit)
Legal environment:
 adverse impact, 51, 52–54
 adverse treatment, 51–52
 affirmative action, 58–59
 affirmative defense, 60
 Age Discrimination in Employment Act (1967/1978), 50 (exhibit), 58
 Americans with Disabilities Act (1990/2008), 45–46, 50 (exhibit), 56–59
 Civil Rights Act (1964/1991), 47, 49–56
 concentration statistics, 53
 discriminatory practices, 45–46, 47–59
 disparate impact, 51
 disparate treatment, 51
 equal employment opportunity, 49–59
 ethical principles, 48–49
 evaluation of training, 54
 federal legislation, 45–46, 47, 49–59
 flow statistics, 53–54
 4/5ths rule of discrimination, 53
 General Duty Clause (OSHA), 60
 geographical jurisdiction, 47–48
 harassment, 60
 hostile environment, 60
 independent contractors, 61
 jurisdiction, 47–48, 50 (exhibit)
 knowledge, skills, abilities (KSAs), 50–51, 54
 LGBTQ community, 47–48, 49, 55
 liability, 59–61
 negligent training, 60
 organizational jurisdiction, 47
 people with disabilities, 45–46, 50 (exhibit), 56–59
 protected classes, 49–50, 51–54
 quid pro quo harassment, 60
 reasonable accommodation, 45–46, 55–57, 58
 religious beliefs, 55–56
 retaliation of organization, 54–55
 safety and health training, 59–60
 Section 8, Rehabilitation Act, 57–58, 237
 stock statistics, 53–54
 study guide, 61–64
 training and development strategy, 30
 training participant selection, 45–46, 51–54
 training program delivery, 54
 training technology accessibility, 57–58
 training transfer, 54
Leonard, Thomas, 277
LGBTQ community:
 boycotts, 49
 discrimination, 47–48, 49
 diversity training, 356
 protections by state, 48 (exhibit)
 reasonable accommodation impact, 55
Liability of organization, 59–61
Listening skills, 314, 315 (exhibit), 320–323
Lobbed questions, 199
Lyft, 341 (exhibit)

Management and Organizational Behavior Teaching Society (MOBTS), 193
Manpower Development and Training Act (1962), 376, 377 (exhibit)
Maslow, Abraham, 82–83
Massive online open courses (MOOCs), 243, 244 (exhibit)
Master Certified Coach, 13
Maturation effect, 131–132
Mayer-Salovey-Caruso Emotional Intelligence Test, 328–329
McCarthy Building Companies, 287–288 (exhibit)
McCarthy Partnership for Women, 288 (exhibit)
McDonald's Corporation, 23, 205–206
Memory capacity, 103
Mentoring programs:
 for career development, 288–289, 293–295
 coaching distinction, 287
 construction industry, 287–288 (exhibit)
 cultivation stage, 291
 defined, 282 (exhibit), 288–289

e-mentoring, 244–245
for employee development, 282 (exhibit), 286–298
for employee orientation, 348
evaluation of transfer and results, 157–158
formal mentoring, 296–297
informal mentoring, 296–297
initiation stage, 291
organizational benefits, 289–290
participant training, 295–296
protégé, 288–289
for psychosocial support, 288–289, 293–295
redefinition stage, 293
relationship stages, 291, 293
relationship threats, 297–298
sample contract, 292 (exhibit)
separation stage, 293
success qualities, 290–291
support antecedents, 293–295
See also Coaching programs
MetrixGlobal, 302, 304
Microaggression, 350–352
Microassault, 351 (exhibit)
Microinvalidation, 351 (exhibit)
Military knowledge transfer, 170, 171 (exhibit)
Millennials, 113–114
Mississippi, 379
Missouri, 47–48
M-learning, 240–241
Mobile instruction, 240–241
MOBTS. *See* Management and Organizational Behavior Teaching Society (MOBTS)
MOOCs. *See* Massive online open courses (MOOCs)
Moodle, 232 (exhibit)
Morgan, Maryann, 157–158
Motivation factors:
　extrinsic motivation, 211–212
　intrinsic motivation, 212
　learning theories of, 100
　in needs analysis, 81–86
　in performance evaluation, 143
　reward value of, 211–212, 215–216
　trainee rewards, 209, 211–212
　trainer rewards, 215–216
Motorola Corporation, 221
Motorola University, 221
Mulcahy, Anne, 248
Myers-Briggs Type Indicator (MBTI), 111

Narayan, Vinay, 226–227
Near transfer, 170
Needs analysis:
　acquired needs theory, 83–84
　archival records, 73–74
　assessment centers, 79 (exhibit), 80
　buy-in problem, 78–79
　checklist, 67 (exhibit)
　competency-based job analysis, 73
　critical incidents analysis, 74–75
　employee data collection, 79–81
　employee level, 67 (exhibit), 79–86, 88–89
　employee motivation theories, 81–86
　equity theory, 86
　ERG theory, 83
　expectancy theory, 84–85
　focus-group data, 74 (exhibit), 75
　hierarchy of needs, 82 (exhibit), 83
　inappropriate training programs, 87–89
　interview data, 74 (exhibit), 75–76
　job data collection, 73–77
　job data sources, 77–79
　job descriptions, 72–73
　job incumbents, 78
　job inflation, 78
　job level, 67 (exhibit), 72–79, 88
　job logs, 74 (exhibit), 76
　knowledge, skills, abilities (KSAs), 69, 80
　learning objectives, 87
　observation data, 74 (exhibit), 76–77
　O*NET, 74
　organizational alignment, 68–70
　organizational culture, 68–69
　organizational level, 67–72, 87–88
　organizational mission, 68
　organizational procedures/policies, 69
　organizational resources, 70
　organizational strategic orientation, 68
　outcomes, 86–89
　performance evaluation, 79 (exhibit), 80–81
　placement tests, 79 (exhibit), 80
　pyramid model, 82–83
　questionnaire data, 74 (exhibit), 77
　reasoned action theory, 85
　skills inventory, 79 (exhibit), 81
　study guide, 89–92
　SWOT analysis, 70–72
　task-based job analysis, 73

technology-mediated training for, 231
trainability, 79
Negative feedback, 323
Negative punishment, 99
Negative reinforcement, 99
Negligent training, 60
New World Kirkpatrick Model:
   administration guidelines, 137–140
   attitude, 144
   balanced scorecard (BSC), 168
   behavior from training, 136 (exhibit), 138 (exhibit), 162–166
   commitment, 145
   confidence, 144–145
   customer satisfaction, 142
   dimensions of, 135–136
   engagement, 142
   evaluation of reaction and learning, 135–145
   evaluation of transfer and results, 162–169
   knowledge, skills, abilities (KSAs), 143, 144
   knowledge transfer, 164
   leading indicators, 169
   learner-focused questions, 141 (exhibit)
   learning from training, 136 (exhibit), 137 (exhibit), 143–145, 161, 162 (exhibit), 163 (exhibit)
   model overview, 136 (exhibit), 163 (exhibit)
   observations, 138
   online surveys, 137–138
   organizational processes and systems, 164–165
   paper-and-pencil surveys, 138
   reaction to training, 136 (exhibit), 137 (exhibit), 140–143, 161, 163 (exhibit)
   relevance, 142–143
   results from training, 163 (exhibit), 166–169
   results of training, 136 (exhibit), 138 (exhibit)
   return on investment (ROI), 167–168
   survey questions, 139–140
   surveys, 137–138, 139–140
   trainee encouragement, 165
   trainee monitoring, 165
   trainee reinforcement, 165
   trainee rewards, 166
   training metrics, 168 (exhibit)
Nine-box matrix, 267–268, 270
Nonexperimental designs, 129 (exhibit), 130–132
Nonverbal communication, 317–319

Observation, 74 (exhibit), 76–77
Obsolescence stage, 254–255
Occupational Safety and Health Act (1970), 50 (exhibit)
Occupational Safety and Health Administration (OSHA), 59–60, 378
OD Network, 13
Off-site training, 207, 208 (exhibit), 209, 210, 211, 212, 218
Onboarding process, 340–348
One-shot case study, 131
One-shot pretest-posttest design, 131–132
One-stop career centers, 377
O*NET, 74
Online instruction. *See* Technology-mediated training
On-site training, 206–207, 208 (exhibit), 209, 210, 211, 212
On-the-job (OJT) training:
   benefits of, 208, 209, 212–213
   control of training, 208
   as formal training, 212–213, 214
   as informal training, 212–214
   standardization of training, 208
   time provision, 215
   trainer checklist, 216
   trainer rewards, 215–216
   trainer selection, 213–214
   trainer skills, 215
   trainer support, 213 (exhibit), 214–216
   training design, 213 (exhibit), 216–218
   training evaluation, 217–218
   training manuals, 217
   training objectives, 216–217
   transferability of training, 209
Open-ended questions, 100
Operant conditioning, 98–100
Organizational climate, 174
Organizational cognition, 105
Organizational culture, 68–69
Organizational development (OD), 13, 20
Organizational learning theory, 105–106
Organizational-level needs analysis, 67–72, 87–88
Organizational processes and systems, 164–165
Organization environment, 19–20
Orientation programs:
   attributes, 345–348
   benefits, 343
   checklist, 347 (exhibit)
   content, 344

delivery methods, 347–348
impression management, 342 (exhibit), 343
for job expectations, 344–345
mentors, 348
objectives, 342–343
for organizational expectations, 344–345
peer advisors, 344, 348
socialization process, 348
welcoming process, 344
Overheads, 195 (exhibit), 196

Passive listening, 321
Pedagogy, 107–109
Peer advisors, 344, 348
People environment, 18–19
PeopleSoft, 230
People with disabilities, 45–46, 50 (exhibit), 56–59, 237
PepsiCo, 19
Perez, Juan, 227
Performance evaluation:
   for development programs, 281–282
   needs analysis, 79 (exhibit), 80–81
   supportive context, 143
   trainee ability, 143
   trainee motivation, 143
   training and development strategy, 22 (exhibit), 23
Personality, 349–350
Personality assessment training, 100
Peter principle, 263
Phillips, Debbie, 276–277
PHR certification, 12–13
Placement tests, 79 (exhibit), 80
Pods arrangement, 220
Political environment, 30
Pool model, 263–264
Positive feedback, 323
Positive punishment, 99
Positive reinforcement, 99
Posner, Barry, 160
Posttest-only control group design, 133
Post-training experiences, 174
PowerPoint, 232, 381
Predictive validity, 135 (exhibit)
Pregnancy Discrimination Act (1978), 50 (exhibit)
Pretest-posttest control group design, 133
Pre-training experiences, 173
Prezi, 232, 381

Problem-based learning, 104
Proctor & Gamble, 28, 157–158
Professional Certified Coach, 13
Promotability ratings, 266–268
Prospector strategy, 26–27
Protean careers, 250, 251, 258–259, 260–261, 270
Protected classes, 49–50, 51–54
Provoking questions, 199
Proxemics, 318–319
Psychomotor domain, 96 (exhibit), 97
Pyramid model, 82–83

Questionnaires, 74 (exhibit), 77
Questionning methods, 198–199
Quid pro quo harassment, 60
Quizzing questions, 199

Random assignment design, 132–133
Reaction to training, 136 (exhibit), 137 (exhibit), 140–143, 161, 163 (exhibit)
Reactor strategy, 29
Reasonable accommodation, 45–46, 55–57, 58
Reasoned action theory, 85
Reciprocal determinism, 101
Reflective observation, 106–107
Reggi, Ed, 319–320 (exhibit)
Regression to the mean, 132
Reliable measures, 134
Religious beliefs, 55–56
Reproductive learning factors, 100
Results from training, 163 (exhibit), 166–169
Retaliation of organization, 54–55
Retentional learning factors, 100
Return on investment (ROI), 167–168
Reward value, 208 (exhibit), 211–212, 215–216
Rhode Island, 379
RIASEC model, 9
Rich communication, 230
Ridge career-pattern, 257–258, 259, 286
Role play, 189–191, 194 (exhibit)

Safety and health training, 59–60
Safety Training Resources, 10
Schutte Self-Report Inventory, 328–329
SCORM (Sharable Content Object Reference Model), 232
Screen-O-Matic, 242
Section 8, Rehabilitation Act, 57–58, 237

Selection effect, 131
Self-awareness, 315, 327–329
Self-determined learning, 104–105, 110
Self-directed learning, 110–111 (exhibit)
Self-efficacy, 101–102
SHIFT eLearning, 228
Siemens, 36–40
Single-loop learning, 105
Skinner, B.F., 98
Skype for Business, 242
Smarter U LMS, 232 (exhibit)
SMART goals, 128
Smithsonian Institution, 333–334
Social capital value, 208 (exhibit), 210–211
Social environment, 19
Socialization process, 348
Social learning theory, 100–102, 280
Society for Human Resource
    Management (SHRM):
  Code of Ethics, 48
  examinations, 11
  internet resources, 11
  SHRM-CP exam, 11, 12–13
  SHRM-SCP exam, 11
Society for Industrial and Organizational
    Psychology, 300
Sociocultural environment, 30–31
Solomon four-group design, 133
Sosnowski, Don, 373–374 (exhibit)
Southwest Airlines, 23, 206
Southwest Airlines University, 23
Speakers, 218, 221
Special assignments, 282 (exhibit), 283
SPHR certification, 12–13
Spolin, Viola, 319–320 (exhibit)
Staffing strategy, 22–23
Stage theory, 103
Standardization of training, 208
Star Trek, 184
Static-group comparison, 132
Stock statistics, 53–54
Strack, Rainer, 36
Stretch assignments, 282 (exhibit), 283
Subject matter expert (SME), 373–374 (exhibit)
Subsidy programs, 378
Succession planning:
  approaches to, 263–264
  assessment centers, 264–266
  bench strength, 268, 269
  boundaryless careers, 270
  defined, 262–263
  depth charts, 268–269
  heir model, 263
  methods and tools, 264–269
  nine-box matrix, 267–268, 270
  Peter principle, 263
  pool model, 263–264
  promotability ratings, 266–268
  protean careers, 270
  study guide, 271–275
  technology-mediated training for, 231
  traditional careers, 270
SWOT analysis:
  defined, 70
  organizational opportunities, 72
  organizational strengths, 72
  organizational threats, 72
  organizational weaknesses, 70–71

Targeted questions, 199
Task-based job analysis, 73
Task environment, 18
Tax credits, 379
TD magazine, 124
Technology-mediated training:
  accessibility issues, 57–58, 229, 236–237
  advantages, 236 (exhibit)
  asynchronous instruction, 236 (exhibit),
    238–239
  coaching programs, 245
  computer-based training (CBT), 24, 236 (exhibit),
    237–238
  concerns with, 229–230
  cost factors, 236 (exhibit), 238
  dashboard interface, 232, 233 (exhibit),
    234 (exhibit)
  disadvantages, 236 (exhibit)
  dynamism of, 242–243
  e-coaching, 245
  e-mentoring, 244–245
  fidelity of training, 237–238
  gamification, 241–242
  generational learning, 229–230, 235
  human resource information system (HRIS), 24, 81,
    230–235
  information technology (IT), 24

interactivity of, 242–243
knowledge, skills, abilities (KSAs), 232, 238
lean communication, 230
learning facilitation, 228–229
learning management system (LMS), 230, 231–233, 234 (exhibit)
learning style for, 228–229
learning theories for, 228
massive online open courses (MOOCs), 243, 244 (exhibit)
mentoring programs, 244–245
m-learning, 240–241
mobile instruction, 240–241
for needs analysis, 231
online instruction, 235–245
opportunities for, 230
people with disabilities, 237
rich communication, 230
self-paced instruction, 236 (exhibit), 239
study guide, 245–247
for succession planning, 231
training and development strategy, 24, 30
for training evaluation, 234–235
training session problems, 385
virtual communication, 229–230
virtual reality, 226–227, 238
webinar, 242–243
Telecommuting employees, 280
Testing effect, 132
Test-retest reliability, 134 (exhibit)
Trainability, 79
Training, 2–3
Training and development:
development, 2–3
instructional systems design model (ADDIE model), 3–8
knowledge, skills, abilities (KSAs), 2–3
professional organizations for, 1, 2, 10–13
study guide, 13–15
training, 2–3
training and development function, 2
See also Development programs
Training and development careers:
Association for Talent Development (ATD), 1, 2, 11, 12f
certifications, 11, 12–13
educational opportunities, 10
external organizations, 10, 370–379
Human Resource Certification Institute (HRCI), 12–13
human resource generalist, 9
human resource specialist, 9–10
interest assessment, 9
International Coaching Federation (ICF), 13
internet resources, 11, 12, 13
OD Network, 13
opportunities for, 9–10
organizational development (OD), 13, 20
preparation for, 8
professional organizations for, 1, 2, 10–13
RIASEC model, 9
Society for Human Resource Management (SHRM), 11, 12–13
Training and development function, 2
Training and development skills:
active listening, 321 (exhibit), 322–323
assertive/supportive communication, 315–317
attentive listening, 321–322
chronemics, 318 (exhibit), 319
communication guidelines, 317 (exhibit)
communication styles, 314, 315–320
conflict resolution, 313–314, 315 (exhibit), 325–326, 325–327
constructive feedback, 323
content of feedback, 324
currency of feedback, 324
delivery of feedback, 324
distributive mindset, 327
drama therapy, 319–320 (exhibit)
emotional intelligence, 328–329
feedback guidelines, 324 (exhibit)
feedback skills, 314, 315 (exhibit), 323–324
gestures, 317, 318 (exhibit)
haptics, 318
improvisational communication, 319–320
integrative mindset, 327
kinesics, 318
knowledge, skills, abilities (KSAs), 314
listening skills, 314, 315 (exhibit), 320–323
negative feedback, 323
nonverbal communication, 317–319
passive listening, 321
positive feedback, 323
proxemics, 318–319

self-awareness, 315, 327–329
self-awareness guidelines, 328 (exhibit)
study guide, 329–332
Training and development strategy:
  analyzer strategy, 28
  Association for Talent Development (ATD), 16–17, 24, 31–33
  compensation, 22 (exhibit), 23
  computer-based training (CBT), 24
  corporate strategy, 24–29
  corporate theory, 26–29
  cost leadership strategy, 27–28
  defender strategy, 27–28
  defined, 6–7
  differentiation strategy, 26–27
  economic environment, 29, 30 (exhibit)
  ethical principles, 30–32
  external environment, 29–31
  framework for, 7 (exhibit)
  gainsharing system, 21
  global context, 32–33
  HR infrastructure, 18, 20–24
  human resource information system (HRIS), 24
  information technology (IT), 24
  internal environment, 18–24
  internal environment interdependence, 20, 21 (exhibit)
  job analysis, 22
  knowledge, skills, abilities (KSAs), 22, 23, 24
  organization environment, 19–20
  people environment, 18–19
  performance appraisal, 22 (exhibit), 23
  political-legal environment, 30
  prospector strategy, 26–27
  reactor strategy, 29
  social environment, 19
  sociocultural environment, 30–31
  staffing strategy, 22–23
  study guide, 33–44
  task environment, 18
  technology environment, 24, 30
  unionization impact, 21
Training & Development, 344
Training manuals, 217
Training project:
  delivery practice, 369
  description of, 366
  engagement process, 366
  final training evaluation report, 369
  instructional design/development proposal, 366–369
  needs analysis proposal, 366–367
  purpose of, 366
  resource limitations, 366
  topic selection, 366
Training session management:
  audience connection, 382
  body language, 383
  communication skills, 383
  difficult participants, 386–387
  disruptions, 384–387
  practice session, 384
  presentation guidelines, 381–382 (exhibit)
  presentation materials, 381–382
  presentation process, 383–384
  presentation skills, 380–384
  question-and-answer segment, 384
  technology problems, 385
  trainer demeanor, 380, 384
Trait Emotional Intelligence Questionnaire, 328–329
Transfer of training. *See* Evaluation of transfer and results
Transferring Learning to Behavior (Kirkpatrick & Kirkpatrick), 159
Transition Assistance Program (U.S. Department of Labor), 170, 171 (exhibit)

Uber, 341 (exhibit)
Uniformed Services Employment and Reemployment Rights Act (1994), 50 (exhibit)
Unionization:
  apprenticeship programs, 372
  training and development strategy, 21
United Farm Workers, 49
UPS, 226–227
UPS (Finamore), 227
U.S. Banking Act (1933), 30
U.S. Department of Labor, 74, 170, 171 (exhibit)

Valid measures, 134–135
Variable training costs, 210, 238
Vertex Solutions, 114
Veterans Employment and Training Service (VETS), 171 (exhibit)

Veterans Opportunity to Work (VOW), 171 (exhibit)
Video presentations, 195 (exhibit), 197–198
Virtual communication, 229–230
Virtual reality, 226–227, 238

Walmart, 28
Web Content Accessibility Guidelines (WCAG), 58, 237
Webinar, 242–243
Whiteboards, 195 (exhibit), 196

Women in Construction Operations, 288 (exhibit)
Women on Fire, 277
Workforce Innovation and Opportunity Act (2014), 376, 377–378
Workforce Investment Act (1998), 376, 377
Workshops, 218

Xerox Corporation, 248–249, 260

Zoom, 242